BAYONETS IN THE WILDERNESS

CAMPAIGNS AND COMMANDERS

CAMPAIGNS AND COMMANDERS

GENERAL EDITOR

Gregory J. W. Urwin, *Temple University, Philadelphia, Pennsylvania*

ADVISORY BOARD

Lawrence E. Babits, *East Carolina University, Greenville*

James C. Bradford, *Texas A & M University, College Station*

Victor Davis Hanson, *California State University, Fresno*

Robert M. Epstein, *U.S. Army School of Advanced Military Studies, Fort Leavenworth, Kansas*

David M. Glantz, *Carlisle, Pennsylvania*

Jerome A. Greene, *National Park Service*

Herman Hattaway, *University of Missouri, Kansas City*

Eugenia C. Kiesling, *U.S. Military Academy, West Point, New York*

Timothy K. Nenninger, *National Archives, Washington, D.C.*

Bruce Vandervort, *Virginia Military Institute, Lexington*

Bayonets in the Wilderness

Anthony Wayne's Legion in the Old Northwest

ALAN D. GAFF

UNIVERSITY OF OKLAHOMA PRESS : NORMAN

ALSO BY ALAN D. GAFF

(ed.) *The Second Wisconsin Infantry* (Dayton, Ohio, 1984)

Brave Men's Tears (Dayton, Ohio, 1988)

If This Is War (Dayton, Ohio, 1991)

(ed., with Maureen Gaff) *Adventures on the Western Frontier* (Bloomington, Ind., 1994)

(with Maureen Gaff) *Our Boys: A Civil War Photograph Album* (Madison, Wisc., 1996)

On Many a Bloody Field (Bloomington, Ind., 1996)

Library of Congress Cataloging-in-Publication Data

Gaff, Alan D.
Bayonets in the wilderness : Anthony Wayne's legion in the Old Northwest / Alan D. Gaff.
p. cm. — (Campaigns and commanders; 4)
Includes bibliographical references (p.) and index.
ISBN 0-8061-3585-9 (alk. paper)
1. Indians of North America—Wars—1790–1794. 2. Wayne, Anthony, 1745–1796.
3. Wayne's Campaign, 1794. 4. Northwest, Old—History—1755–1865. 5. Indians of North
America—Northwest, Old—Wars. I. Title. II. Series.

E83.79.G34   2004
973.4'1—dc22
2003063413

Bayonets in the Wilderness: Anthony Wayne's Legion in the Old Northwest
is Volume 4 in the Campaigns and Commanders series.

The paper in this book meets the guidelines for permanence and durability of the
Committee on Production Guidelines for Book Longevity of the Council on Library Resources, Inc.∞

1   2   3   4   5   6   7   8   9   10

My country calls me to those fields of death,
    The standard waves, the clarion sounds th' alarm;
Expiring heroes, bleeding on the heath,
    Call loud for justice's avenging arm!

Farewell, ye flow'ry fields, ye sylvan shades,
    And all the fond delights of rural life!
I go to wander through the desert glades,
    I march to mingle with the sons of strife.

Sgt. James Elliot, August 1793

To my sons, Don and Jeff,
who share the family bond of history, cemeteries, and cooler water.

CONTENTS

ILLUSTRATIONS

Figures

Maps

PREFACE

It is impossible to live in Fort Wayne, Indiana, without bumping into constant reminders of the city's namesake, Maj. Gen. Anthony Wayne, hero of the Revolution and conqueror of the Northwest Territory. There are streets named after him—Anthony Boulevard, Wayne Street, South Wayne Avenue, and Wayne Trace, the latter running over the old military road cut by Wayne's Legion of the United States as it advanced to the junction of the Saint Joseph and Saint Marys Rivers, whose commingled waters from there flow to Lake Erie in the Maumee River. Dozens of businesses still sport his name and likeness as part of their corporate logos, civic organizations honor his memory, and there is even a Wayne High School, its sports teams competing under the rather obvious nickname "Generals." An equestrian statue of the general watches over city residents as they gather in Freiman Square, a popular downtown park. As a child I grew up playing along the banks of Spy Run Creek, so called for Capt. William Wells, commander of Wayne's elite company of mounted spies. Two blocks west of the creek is Wells Street, while four blocks to the east runs Spy Run Avenue, both major north-south arteries honoring the old frontier scout. Needless to say, Fort Wayne is a city that still honors its namesake.

Before starting research for this project, I had only a passing interest in Wayne and his campaign. But as my investigation continued, I became more fascinated with the general's military operations in a hostile wilderness, especially his use of tactics and logistics. It soon became obvious that previously published material, those "standard references" found in all the bibliographies, were of little help. In fact, a great deal of material was confusing, ill-constructed, and often just plain false, some mistakes being repeated so often that they bordered on mythology. Just as an example, virtually every author has parroted John McDonald's thrilling tale of the capture of Christopher Miller, even though all important details of his story were wrong. The only way to get to the heart of Wayne's campaign was to start at the beginning, examining the voluminous Anthony Wayne manuscripts at The Historical Society of Pennsylvania and the William L. Clements Library. I then obtained virtually everything written by members of Wayne's legion, supplemented by many books and articles written by civilian contemporaries. As I had expected from experience on previous projects, the largest source of "new" information came from the many newspapers published during the 1790s, which often printed letters from legion officers and, occasionally, enlisted men. Although most scholars had consulted a few newspapers, they generally confined their search to those published in Philadelphia or New York or to Cincinnati's *Centinel of the North-Western Territory*, missing some of the best material available on the campaign.

It is regrettable that the Native American story of Wayne's advance into the Northwest Territory cannot be told more fully. An inability to permanently record events often meant the only account of an Indian attack or raid would be penned by an American, surely no objective reporter by any definition. On some occasions the Indian side would be supplied by either British officers or white captives. Those few surviving Indian accounts by warriors who opposed Wayne have been filtered through the American writers who ultimately recorded them. This lack of a written language has hamstrung any attempt to relate the Indian version of events. It is an immeasurable loss to history.

The Northwest Territory was America's first western frontier, and in 1792 it was a dangerous place to live. When Anthony Wayne assumed command of the U.S. Army, soon to be renamed the Legion of the United States, white settlements in the territory were tiny, isolated, and barely self-sufficient. Indians owned the night. Frightened soldiers and settlers huddled inside their military posts and fortified hamlets from sundown to dawn, then ventured out to till, plant, and patrol, always keeping a musket within reach. By 1794, Wayne had raised his new army, merging new troops with frontier veterans; trained it to move and fight in the wilderness; and soundly beaten a determined Indian confederation that had inflicted embarrassing defeats on two other armies. Given the many obstacles in Wayne's path, it was one of the most stupendous undertakings in U.S. history. Because of television and movies, Americans now consider "The West" to be the Great Plains, the Yellowstone country, the Rockies, the Desert Southwest, and California. No narrative from these regions is more fascinating or more replete with memorable characters than the story of Gen. Anthony Wayne and his legion in the Northwest Territory, back when "The West" meant Ohio and Indiana.

ACKNOWLEDGMENTS

Research for this narrative began, logically enough, in Fort Wayne, Indiana, at the Allen County Public Library (ACPL). An aggressive acquisition policy over the decades has made the ACPL collection a virtual gold mine for historians. This growth continues today under the guidance of Jeff Krull, its current director. Although the ACPL's name belies its importance, famous research libraries would be jealous of its collection. I am blessed to have such a world-class library just a few miles from home.

ACPL's commitment to excellence is best typified by the Historical Genealogy Department, managed by Curt B. Witcher, which is recognized as the second-largest genealogy collection in the country. Where others see genealogy, I see history. The overwhelming majority of publications cited for this publication are available in the genealogy department's collection of over 300,000 books and periodicals, complemented by 300,000 items of microform material. One unique and indispensable research tool compiled by ACPL is the Periodical Source Index (PERSI), which allows historians to search nearly ten thousand historical and genealogical publications in a matter of seconds. Historians researching American history prior to 1900 should, without exception, make Curt Witcher's department their first stop.

Of course, no library can house everything, so I must thank a number of professionals for their assistance in procuring those hard-to-find publications that often have the best information. At the Helmke Library, Indiana University–Purdue University, Fort Wayne, Cheryl Truesdell, manager of Document Delivery Services, was instrumental in convincing libraries at the Bloomington campus to share their resources. Christine Smith successfully sought out and requested more microfilmed eighteenth-century newspapers than she even knew existed before meeting me. Virginia Willig and Blaine Thompson kept the copying machines maintained and stocked with paper, no small task considering the amount of time spent there.

While the Helmke Library concentrated on newspapers, the Fort Wayne office of the Indiana Cooperative Library Services Authority (INCOLSA) searched for other resources. Under the direction of Laura Eme, who was always willing to interrupt her hectic schedule to answer questions, Margie Holderman, Christine Ade, and Anne Smith located and processed everything from long-forgotten books to microform copies of manuscript collections. For the truly obscure research questions, Tammy Dahling always seemed to find the correct answer. This book would not have been possible without the assistance provided by the courteous and professional staff of the ACPL, Helmke Library, and INCOLSA. I thank them all.

Many individuals at other institutions offered assistance. Among them were Brian L. Dunnigan and John C. Harriman at the William L. Clements Library, David L. Poremba at the Burton Historical Collection, Barbara J. Meiring at the Fort Recovery State Museum, and Walter Font at the Allen County and Fort Wayne Historical

Society. Others who proved helpful were Thomas Knoles of the American Antiquarian Society, John Becker of the Champlain Society, Maggie Yax of the Cincinnati Museum Center, Thomas A. Mason of the Indiana Historical Society, Nicholas Graham of the Massachusetts Historical Society, and Jordan Rockford of The Historical Society of Pennsylvania.

As this project became a manuscript, my son Jeff provided important technical support for a father who had learned keyboarding skills on a manual typewriter. My son Don also assisted his technophobic father by drawing the maps that illustrate the text. Both of them read the manuscript and offered suggestions. Once the manuscript had been completed, Mickey Choate of Lescher and Lescher undertook the task of finding a publisher willing to accept a work on this little-known period of American history. Happily for all concerned, Chuck Rankin of the University of Oklahoma Press saw the potential for such a book and oversaw its editing and preparation. I am indebted to them all.

But I am particularly indebted to Maureen Gaff for her patience, support, and scholarship. She is the only person I trust completely to help me research a project, and her suggestions have been implemented throughout the writing process as well. In addition to being my professional partner, Maureen is also my beloved wife of thirty-four years. Who could ask for more?

INTRODUCTION

The American Revolution did not end with the Treaty of Paris in 1783. British authorities refused to relinquish their military posts on U.S. soil, using them as bases to supply the Indian nations that inhabited the Northwest Territory. Emboldened by British provisions, arms, ammunition, and encouragement, these Indians waged a bitter war against American settlers on the Ohio River frontier. In 1790 Pres. George Washington sent an army under Brig. Gen. Josiah Harmar against this loose confederacy, but his force was defeated on two separate occasions and forced to retreat. The following year, Washington sent a larger army, this one commanded by Maj. Gen. Arthur St. Clair, to chastise the Indians who had beaten Harmar. Handicapped by a lack of provisions and equipment, St. Clair's force was ambushed on November 4, 1791, and suffered the most humiliating defeat ever inflicted upon an American army, losing one-half of its numbers in about three hours before running from its wilderness battlefield. These two victories gave the Indian confederacy large quantities of arms and supplies, as well as the confidence to boldly reject peace proposals from the United States.

To regain the honor of his young country, President Washington formed a third army, styled the Legion of the United States, and selected Maj. Gen. Anthony Wayne to lead it. A Revolutionary War commander of note, Wayne was given plenary powers by the administration. With his decisions subject only to review by President Washington and Secretary of War Henry Knox, the general would conduct his Indian campaign as he saw fit. He would organize the army, decide when and where it would be deployed, and fight it wherever and whenever he chose. If he found that circumstances warranted the action, Wayne was given authority to fire upon British troops stationed on American soil, even if that action provoked a second war with Great Britain. He came perilously close in 1794 to starting such a conflict at Fort Miamis along the Maumee River, a post that British forces had constructed by order of the governor of Canada in clear violation of international law. This was not the only time soldiers from Wayne's legion encountered foreign troops. British officers and artillerymen had accompanied the Indian army in its attack on Fort Recovery on June 30, 1794, and a company of British-Canadian militia actually fought against Wayne at the Battle of Fallen Timbers on August 20 of that year. The Revolution had supposedly ended in 1783, but there was still a shooting war between Britain and the United States in the Northwest Territory.

Although British troops did play a role against Wayne in his campaign, subjugation of the Indians and bringing peace to the frontier were his primary goals. These tasks seemed overwhelming. Every piece of equipment required by the legion—paper, weapons, uniforms, sheet iron, shoes, buttons, needles—had to be purchased in the Atlantic states, carted overland to Pittsburgh, then shipped down the Ohio River to Fort Washington at Cincinnati. From there it had to be hauled overland, generally by packhorses, to the advanced forts. Construction projects were often delayed until soldiers could craft the tools they needed. The firm of Elliott and Williams had contracted to provide rations for the legion but found itself with an overextended supply line and unable to meet its obligations. A schism developed within the officer corps, some aligning themselves with Wayne and others with his second in command, Brig. Gen. James Wilkinson, a suave and charismatic officer who was also notoriously corrupt and a traitor. Wayne's force was always understrength, and many of his soldiers were of poor quality, resulting in a constant stream of deserters. There were no reliable maps of the territory, and even basic information regarding the rivers and streams was nonexistent. The list of problems confronting Wayne was almost endless.

In his typical fashion, the general methodically overcame each of these obstacles. Supplies were hauled forward by convoys of hundreds of pack animals, protected from Indian attack by large escorts of troops. When Elliott and Williams failed to meet its contractual obligations, Wayne ordered his quartermaster to take over operations and bring forward what he needed. The general encouraged his favorite officers and shifted troublemakers to out-of-the-way posts. He countered desertion by instilling discipline, tempered with patience and mercy, and encouraging his soldiers to believe in themselves and the power of the legion. To counter the lack of knowledge about the wilderness in which he must maneuver, General Wayne employed scouts and spies familiar with the region, including men such as William Wells and Christopher Miller, who had formerly been Indian captives. Despite every obstacle in his path, Wayne, who proved to be as adept at organization and supply as he was at battlefield command, remained focused on his mission to defeat the Indians and establish peace.

Wayne's unique organization of his command allowed him the flexibility to operate successfully in any situation. In addition to the standard branches of service—infantry, cavalry, and artillery—he employed riflemen, light infantry (armed with muskets of his own design), and mounted volunteers from Kentucky, who added mobility and firepower to the main body. This arrangement allowed Wayne to locate the enemy, absorb his attacks, and respond with overwhelming force at the critical point. His army was screened by parties of scouts on foot, while other scouts, called spies, ranged far afield on horseback, even penetrating into Indian camps in search of intelligence. Standard tactics were adapted to the wilderness environment. In the field, Wayne had his men on the move by dawn and marched them rapidly until early afternoon, when he invariably halted and fortified a camp against surprise attack.

Although generally successful in raids against convoys of wagons and packhorses that supplied American forts, the Indian confederacy failed miserably in an ill-advised attack upon Fort Recovery, which had been built directly on top of General St. Clair's battlefield. An ambush on the morning of June 30, 1794, succeeded in destroying a supply convoy, inflicting heavy casualties among both soldiers and horses. But the Indian army, estimated to number as many as two thousand warriors, could not seize the fort, whose garrison, augmented by survivors of the convoy escort, numbered less than two hundred. This successful defense of Fort Recovery was the key episode in Wayne's campaign, and the Indians lost their best chance to defeat a significant detachment of the American force.

When Wayne's legion finally met the Indians in battle upstream from Fort Miamis, its success was assured. With a loss that would hardly merit a mention in later wars, General Wayne defeated the Indian army at Fallen Timbers and, more importantly, crushed the Indian spirit. With an understanding of the psychology of warfare, Wayne constructed forts upon the battlefields of both Harmar and St. Clair as permanent reminders of U.S. superiority. When Indian nations sued for peace, Wayne convened a grand treaty negotiation at Fort Greeneville that would set the standard for future treaty talks. But more importantly, the nation had seen that a standing army, no matter how much it smacked of British rule over its colonies, was a necessary evil for enforcing the peace and assuring freedom and prosperity on the United States' first frontier. America would hereafter bargain with the Indians from a position of strength.

Anthony Wayne had an influence that lasted long after his defeat of the Indians. His army was a training ground for officers who would win fame by their own exploits. William Henry Harrison, one of Wayne's aides, would eventually be elected president of the United States. John Adair, Charles Scott, and John Posey would be elected governors. William Clark would team up with Meriwether Lewis, a late addition to the legion, for their historic journey to the Pacific Ocean. Zebulon Montgomery Pike would explore the trans-Mississippi frontier. William Eaton would lead a small band of U.S. Marines across hundreds of miles of desert "to the shores of Tripoli." Some officers who stayed in the army would become generals in the War of 1812. All owed a debt of gratitude to Anthony Wayne and his military leadership. Unfortunately, this period of American history has become a history based upon myth and legend, making a careful examination of Wayne's significant contributions long overdue. Far from the popular impression that he was somewhat crazy (or "mad"), Wayne was in fact a thoughtful, resolute, prudent, and diplomatic officer whose successful campaign brought an end to forty years of border war and a final conclusion to the Revolutionary War. According to no less an authority than Theodore Roosevelt, "It was one of the most striking and weighty feats in the winning of the West."

BAYONETS IN THE WILDERNESS

The Destruction of St. Clair's Army

As soldiers of Maj. Gen. Arthur St. Clair's army slept during the early hours of November 4, 1791, a large force of Indians moved into position for an early morning ambush. A native of Scotland and a well-respected commander during the Revolution, St. Clair had been sent into the trackless wilderness of the Northwest Territory to defeat an Indian confederacy that threatened to snuff out fledgling American settlements along the Ohio River. Pres. George Washington had repeatedly cautioned his army commander to guard against surprise as he advanced toward his goal, a collection of native villages where the Saint Joseph and Saint Marys Rivers join to form the Maumee in what is now northeastern Indiana. But St. Clair was lost. He had camped on a small branch of the Wabash River but mistook that stream for a tributary of the Saint Marys, so his mixed force of regulars, short-term levies, and Kentucky militia was much farther from the junction of Three Rivers than he assumed. St. Clair had also failed to heed Washington's warning. His force of 1,669 officers and men, in addition to many hundreds of teamsters, packhorse drivers, wives, children, and other civilians, had not fortified its camp in a small, open meadow. The Kentucky militia, "a great part of which had never been in the woods in their lives, and many never fired a gun," had crossed the stream and bivouacked in the forest about a quarter mile in advance and out of sight of the main body. Disaster loomed in the morning mists.[1]

At daybreak, two Kentucky officers strolled out to investigate some firing by outposts during the night. Captain Lemon was instantly killed, but Lieutenant Briggs, though mortally wounded, managed to stumble back into camp while crying out that Indians were coming. As Briggs emerged from the forest, Robert Branshaw stood talking with a fellow Kentuckian next to a cook fire. He recalled what happened: "Suddenly I saw twenty or thirty painted savages dodging around among the trees in front of us, as if they planned to attack by surprise. Supposing the ones I saw to be the entire party, and thinking it a good chance to bring down one of them and at the same time to alarm the camp,

I instantly raised my rifle to my eye, took a quick aim, and dropped the nearest Indian. The smoke had not cleared away from my rifle when a terrific volley was poured in upon us. It was accompanied by appalling yells from a thousand throats. At the same instant I saw Indians springing from behind their covers and rushing down upon us in overwhelming numbers." Branshaw turned to run but tripped over the body of his friend, who had just been shot through the head. Lt. Col. William Oldham's militia fired a sort of ragged volley at the screaming attackers, then fled toward St. Clair's main camp. Stace McDonough noticed that some Kentuckians "were so panic stricken, that they rushed about from one side of the camp to the other, like a herd of cattle, without the least attempt to fight, or defend themselves. They were butchered, like so many bullocks in a pen."[2]

Frightened militiamen ran from their bivouac to the imagined security offered across the stream, dissolving many of St. Clair's outposts before them. Robert Branshaw had eluded several warriors in his dash for safety, his only injury being a chunk of ear clipped off by a rifle ball. As he gained the main campground, Branshaw saw as many as three hundred women and children huddled together behind the soldiers. He remembered, "Some were running to and fro, wringing their hands and shrieking out the terrors; some were standing speechless, like statues of horror, with their hands clasped and their eyes fixed upon the not very distant scene of strife; some were kneeling and calling on Heaven for protection; some were sobbing and groaning in each other's arms; and several who had swooned from fright lay as if dead upon the ground." Although Branshaw had lost his rifle, he turned from this melancholy sight, snatched up another laying upon the ground, took cover behind a tree, and began firing.[3]

St. Clair had posted his troops in a rough rectangle, the front (facing west) and rear lines approximately four hundred yards long on a piece of ground that his adjutant general, Winthrop Sargent, said "did not exceed six or seven acres." Oldham's "pannack Struck Meletia" crashed completely through the main camp, being joined by a few men from Maj. Henry Gaither's battalion of levies, but were thrown back by Indians concealed on the opposite side. Sargent complained that "their conduct was cowardly in the most shameful degree," while another officer dismissed the militia as "cowardly rascals." A few rounds from the artillery and fire from the camp guards checked the Indian attack momentarily, but warriors simply filed off to the right and left and within minutes had encircled St. Clair's battalions "like a swarm of bees round the whole camp."[4]

Hidden sharpshooters targeted the gunners and officers, "distinguished by their dress," who manned the artillery on the western front. Maj. William Ferguson and Capt. James Bradford soon fell dead, and Capt. Mahlon Ford was wounded, leaving Lt. Edward Spear as the only artillery officer still unhurt. After over one-half of the gunners had been shot down, Lts. Cornelius Sedam and Bartholomew Schaumburgh rounded up about thirty artificers to man the guns. Capt. Nicholas Hannah of the Virginia levies came running forward with another small party, which dragged away the dead and wounded, and within minutes these officers "set the artillery again a roaring." Spear fell wounded, but Captain Hannah defended his adopted cannon until the last moment, spiking one gun himself with a bayonet. Although it was impossible to identify individual targets, artillerymen continued to fire "a large quantity of cannister and some round shot" into the forest. One officer saw that warriors "would frequently advance very close under the smoke of our cannon, and as soon as it began to clear away, their fire became very fatal."[5]

Benjamin Van Cleve, a packhorse driver, had taken a rifle from a wounded soldier and joined the fight. While passing these guns, he spotted "about 30 of our men & officers laying scalped around the pieces of Artillery; it appeared the Indians had not been in a hurry for their hair was all skinned off." Lt. Col. William Darke ordered a bayonet charge to drive off the screaming foe. Maj. Jonathan Heart stepped forward and led the Second Regiment some four hundred yards into the woods, but it was driven back, rallied, and charged again. Heart was shot dead, being succeeded by Capt. Patrick Phelon, who ordered a third charge, then he too fell. Every time the Americans would advance, Indians would work around their flanks and kill the wounded. When soldiers fled in terror from these encroachments, some women "drove out the skulking militia and fugitives from other corps from under wagons and hiding places by firebrands and the usual weapons of the sex."[6]

Despite pleas and threats from their officers, soldiers "huddled together in crowded parties in various parts of the encampment where every shot from the enemy took effect." Lieutenant Colonel Darke saw that men "would not form in any order in this Confution" and said disgustedly that "the whole Army ran toGether Like a Mob at a fair." Robert Branshaw watched the army dissolve in "a wild, horrible dream, in which whites and savages, friends and foes, were all mixed in mad confusion. They melted away in smoke, fire, and blood, amid groans, shouts, shrieks, yells, clashing steel, and exploding firearms." When an enemy ball fractured his wrist, Branshaw bound up his wound and sought shelter, but he was appalled at the scene that greeted him: "On my way to the center of the camp, I met pale, frightened men running in all directions. Numerous dead bodies, some of them scalped and presenting ghastly spectacles, proved that many of the Indians had been there before me. Wounded soldiers called to me and begged for help and water. But I could do nothing for them, and I hurried on. When I came within sight of the spot where the women and children had been collected, I beheld a large body of Indians busy at their work of slaughter."[7]

One officer remembered: "At length our men got into confusion, and almost every other man, who were yet able to keep together, was bleeding with wounds. The Indians in the meantime were contracting their circle and keeping up a constant fire both with rifles and smooth-bored muskets. A number of arrows were also thrown into our encampment in the course of the action, but they did no great execution." St. Clair's command structure had vanished, and men followed their instincts, each reacting differently under the stress of combat. Lieutenant Colonel Darke noted that Capt. Jonathan Snowden was "not Calculated for the army," while Ens. John Sullivan Jr., son of a Revolutionary War general, appeared to be "as Grate a polt[r]oon as I ever saw in the world." Darke was more impressed with a couple of civilians. Daniel Bissell was singled out for

praise because "he made the freest use of the Ba[y]onet of any Man I noticed in the Car-
cases of the Savages." John Hamilton, a packhorse master, gathered up muskets from
fallen soldiers and fired them until the Indians broke into the camp, when he switched
weapons and "took up an ax and [went] at them with it." Darke may have been incapable
of judging the military abilities of others. Winthrop Sargent admitted that Darke was
"most passionately intent upon Indian-killing himself, but inadequate to performing it
by battalion, or even platoons." Basic maneuvers that could be handled by ensigns were
simply "beyond his capacity."[8]

After three hours of fighting, General St. Clair realized that the situation was hopeless. According to Adjutant General Sargent, "The men must either retreat, or be sacrificed without resistance, as the enemy were shooting them down at pleasure from behind
trees and the most secure covers, whilst they could scarcely be led to discharge a single
gun with effect." Ebenezer Denny agreed, saying: "The only hope left was, that perhaps
the savages would be so taken up with the camp as not to follow. Delay was death; no
preparation could be made; numbers of brave men must be left a sacrifice—there was no
alternative." A few officers stepped forward and raised the cry, "Charge the road and go
home!" Benjamin Van Cleve recalled, "I saw an officer (who I took to be Lieut Morgan
an aid to Genl Butler) with six or eight men start on a run a little to the left of where I
was. I immediately ran & fell in with them—in a short distance we were so suddenly
among the Indians who were not apprised of our object that they opened to us & ran to
the right & left without firing." Soldiers "broke through the Indians like a torrent" from
the northeast corner of the camp. Once freed from the circle of fire that had raked their
ranks, men abandoned all discipline and took to their heels in a retreat characterized as
"in a most supreme degree disgraceful." Arms and equipment were discarded whenever
they retarded flight. Attempts by the few remaining officers to form a rear guard failed
miserably.[9]

Back among the tents and wagons, soldiers immobilized by wounds met their doom
with "determined resolution." Sargent sadly mentioned their fate, telling how they
"charged their pieces with a coolness and deliberation that reflects the highest honor
upon their memory." Death was certain for those left behind, but they sold their lives
dearly to buy time for the remnants of the army to escape. Sargent explained, "the firing
of musketry in camp after we quitted it, leaves us very little room for doubt that their latest efforts were professionally brave and that where they could pull a trigger they avenged
themselves." Among those abandoned to their fate was Maj. Gen. Richard Butler, St.
Clair's second in command, who had been "shot from his horse about half an hour before
the action was over, and, from the nature of his wound, must have expired within a few
minutes of the troops quitting the field."[10]

As survivors fled for the safety of Fort Jefferson, the weak and wounded soon lagged
behind, along with most of the remaining women and children, "who could not keep
pace with the fugitives" and became fodder for the tomahawk and scalping knife. Benjamin Van Cleve's legs began to cramp from the exertion of running, and the Indians,
despite stopping to kill stragglers, began to gain on him. Throwing away his shoes, Van

Cleve managed to pass about six other people, whose slower gait improved his own chance of escape by offering more tempting targets to the pursuers. After about four or five miles, the Indians lost interest in chasing the Americans and turned back to loot the abandoned camp. Overjoyed to be alive, Van Cleve explained how he continued the trek south to safety: "I fell in with Lieutenant Schaumburgh (who if my recollection serves me was the only officer of artillery that got away unhurt) with Corporal Mott & a woman who was called red-headed Nance—the latter two were both crying Mott was lamenting the loss of his wife & Nance of an infant child Schaumburgh was nearly exhausted & hung on Motts arm I carried his fusee & accoutrements & led Nance." Van Cleve concluded his account of the retreat with the simple statement, "In this sociable way we came together & arrived at Jefferson a little after sunset."[11]

Stephen Littell crouched noiselessly in a pile of old underbrush until the sounds of fighting receded in the distance, then cautiously crept out to view the blood-soaked battlefield. The sight was staggering. Hundreds upon hundreds of Americans soldiers and army followers lay in contorted silence or wallowed helplessly in their own gore. The frosty air on that fatal Friday was filled with the stench of gunpowder and the smell of blood, wisps of steam escaping from ghastly wounds and scalped heads. Groans and heartrending cries of distress echoed across that horrible wilderness meadow. As he emerged from his hiding place, wounded men begged Littell to carry them to a place of safety to avoid the torture, mutilation, and death that would soon be their fate. Others beseeched him to end their suffering, but he refused to do so. Stephen began to carry off injured soldiers, one by one, concealing them in places of imagined safety, hiding them behind trees and under bushes. Soon he spotted an officer lying silently upon his face, who from a distance bore a keen resemblance to his own father, Lt. Eliakim Littell of Pike's company from the New Jersey battalion of levies.

Just as Stephen bent down to confirm the officer's identity, hideous shouts from the warriors, returning to celebrate their devastating victory over the Americans, sent shivers of fear shooting through his body. He ran to a nearby fallen tree and dived in among the branches and dead leaves, covering himself from casual observation just as the Indians came screaming onto the battlefield after their pursuit of the fragments of St. Clair's army. Hidden from view yet fully able to see events as they unfolded, the nineteen year old could only keep silent and watch the unspeakable carnage that unfolded. Whooping with laughter, grinning warriors swiftly scalped those corpses that had thus far escaped this ritual mutilation. They then stripped the bodies and commenced a macabre masquerade, dressing up in Continental uniforms and firing captured weapons into the air. A few captives, men lucky enough to have survived unhurt or having but slight wounds, won reprieves and were hustled away to a life of slavery.

Those men who still lived, suffering from crippling wounds and a despair that their own unspeakable torture would soon follow, became silent spectators to a bloody spectacle that swept through the meadow and surrounding woods. As warriors moved from one fallen soldier to the next, hideous screams filled the air as they tore off legs and arms and thrust them into the faces of still-living victims. Other soldiers were skewered with

their own bayonets while they begged for mercy. Women who had followed their husbands into this grim wilderness died amid ghastly shrieks when wooden stakes were
driven through their bodies or their breasts were cut off. Some warriors propped bleeding men up against trees and stumps and used them as targets for their tomahawks and
knives, throwing first at the extremities, then working their way toward the vital organs.

Suddenly, young Littell thought he had been discovered. One tomahawk missed its
mark and landed just a few feet from his hiding place among the branches and leaves.
The weapon was so close that he could have touched it, but its Indian owner was so
intent upon his game that he did not notice the terrified young man, who had closed his
eyes in anticipation of receiving his own death stroke. Instead, the warrior retrieved his
tomahawk and buried it in the head of a victim, then moved away to commit still more
butchery. Littell breathed easier after that and even considered giving himself up to a
white man who seemed to exercise some authority over the bloodthirsty Indians, until
the he realized that this white stranger acted even more cruelly than his comrades. This
man was probably William Wells, who had been adopted into the Miami Nation after
being captured at the age of fourteen in Kentucky. Now known as Apekonit, or Wild
Carrot, because of his flaming red hair, he had been particularly adept at luring unsuspecting white settlers to their deaths along the Ohio River. Wells would later boast that
on November 4, 1791, "he tomahawked and scalped the wounded, dying and dead, until
he was unable to raise his arm." After all the victims had been slaughtered and their
butchers had finally left the field, Stephen Littell arose from the fallen tree and started
walking south. He was the last person to leave St. Clair's battlefield alive.[12]

CHAPTER 1

The Frontier in Flames

GENERAL ST. CLAIR CONVENED a council of war at Fort Jefferson and decided to leave his wounded with a strong detachment under Capt. Joseph Shaylor, taking the remainder of his army back to Fort Washington. Adj. Gen. Winthrop Sargent carefully tabulated the casualties. Of 1,669 effectives in action, sixty-four officers and 807 enlisted men had been killed or wounded, almost 50 percent of the American force. Casualties among packhorse drivers, artificers, the sick, and civilians (including many women and children) pushed St. Clair's total loss to well over one thousand. The general himself had escaped on an old horse, but all his senior commanders had been shot down: Major General Butler, dead; Major Heart, Second Regiment, dead; Lieutenant Colonel Darke, First Levies, wounded; Lt. Col. George Gibson, Second Levies, mortally wounded; Major Ferguson, artillery commandant, dead; Capt. Alexander Trueman, commander of the cavalry, wounded; and Lieutenant Colonel Oldham of the Kentucky militia, dead.[1]

As for the army's equipment, Capt. John Buell said it best when he wrote, "they left their artillery, tents, baggage, their beef, their flour, their every thing." Among the ordnance lost were eight pieces of artillery (three brass 6-pounders, three brass 3-pounders, and two iron carronades), fifteen fusees, 1,193 muskets, 1,237 bayonets, twenty-five swords, and twenty-four pistols. Other material was simply too numerous to list, although Sargent placed the total monetary loss at $32,810, an enormous sum for a nation with little money. That was certainly enough plunder to overwhelm the native economy, for warriors under the leadership of Eel River Miami chief Little Turtle had numbered, according to William Wells, only eleven hundred men. Wells explained that among the various nations were "Miamies, Potawatomies, Ottoways, Chippeways, Wyandots, Delawares, Shawanees, and a few Mingoes and Cherokees. Each nation was commanded by its own Chief, and the Chiefs appeared to be all governed by Little Turtle, who made the arrangements for the action, and commenced the attack with the Miamies under his immediate command." He estimated that the Indian army lost only thirty killed and some fifty wounded.[2]

Frontier settlers were terrified. One of them explained that St. Clair's defeat had removed all restraint from the Indians in their wilderness coverts, and the Americans now feared for their lives every hour of every day—"We never go to our fields but we are seized with an involuntary fear, which lessens our strength, and weakens our labour." Even their homes offered no protection: "We never sit down either to dinner or supper, but the least noise immediately spreads a general alarm and prevents us from enjoying the comfort of our meals," family members eating "just enough to keep us alive." And the dead of night gave no peace of mind, especially when the dogs began to bark: "We leap out of bed and run to arms; my poor wife with panting bosom and silent tears takes leave of me, as if we were to see each other no more; she snatches the youngest children from their beds, who, suddenly awakened, increase by their innocent questions the horror of the dreadful moment. She tries to hide them in the cellar, as if our cellar was inaccessible to the fire. I place all my servants at the windows, and myself at the door, where I am determined to perish." The master of this house claimed that it was "a dreadful situation" that was "a thousand times worse than that of a soldier engaged in the midst of the most severe conflict." Not even the children were exempt from the Indian terror, parents telling them to be good little boys and girls or "the Shawnees will catch you!"[3]

When Pennsylvanians cried for help, Secretary of War Henry Knox authorized Gov. Thomas Mifflin to call out one company of militia for each of the frontier counties. But riflemen did not respond to this call for militia, fearing that their families would be exposed to Indians "going Round our Garrisons and Comeing on the Weomen and children and Murdering them." Fortunately, a severe winter kept warriors from pressing their advantage. Despite these several months of inactivity, the militia was not ready for action when it came. Detachments seldom left their posts or failed to complete their assigned scouting duties. Residents complained about the scarcity of arms, many of them having "sold their guns to people going down the River." But when arms were provided, they were often neglected by their owners. Maj. George McCully reported that in the spring he found about two dozen nearly worthless muskets in the blockhouse at Reed's Station, "the Barralls only required care, for they had Scarce left a lock, Rammer or Bayonet on any of them, many of the Stocks Broken." The disgusted major added, "Yet they will make noise to Government about Arms."[4]

An affair at Reed's Station in Westmoreland County best illustrates how ill-suited the militia was to defend settlements. On May 22, a party of forty Indians suddenly appeared outside the blockhouse at Reed's Station, which was garrisoned by a squad under Lt. William Cooper. That officer was a drunk and had not sent out a single scout. The militia "had been frolicking and were Surprized" and had little ammunition when the Indians attacked, killing one and wounding another. The raiders passed by this strongpoint "without any exertions being made by the Rangers" to stop them and murdered a family within three hundred yards of the blockhouse, then continued on into the settled portion of the county, proclaiming their arrival by burning houses as they advanced. After dividing into small parties of five to seven warriors, one resident noted that an "ardent desire to get Horses seems to divert their attention from shedding Blood." Naturally, inhabitants began "to fly before them with the greatest rapidity," and the Indians wandered at will for almost a week, killing, wounding, or capturing eleven people, taking at least thirty horses, and torching many homes. In reporting this catastrophe, one observer wrote, "You will perceive by the Map that Westmoreland is now Desolate to near the Center, and the rest much disturbed."[5]

On the Virginia frontier, residents felt that St. Clair's recent expedition had "only served to agrivate the savages against us." Capt. William McMahon had been authorized to raise a company of rangers, but delays resulted when some of the best frontiersmen in Ohio County crossed over the state line and offered their services to Pennsylvania, which offered higher pay for the same duty. One band of Indians boldly stole eight horses within five miles of McMahon's home, an insult to the whites that irritated the captain to no end. Noting that his neighbors "neither look for nor expect any mercy from these Savage Enemys," McMahon prophesied that these latest raids "are only drops of the shower." Every man who owned a weapon, of necessity, became a soldier, oftentimes being the only person available to defend his homestead against raiders who might appear at any moment. This was important since some of the scouts hired to protect settlers proved to be undependable braggarts. One man came in with six bullet holes in his shirt and two through his hat, boasting he had escaped after discovering a party of twenty Indians. When threatened with a whipping, the loudmouth confessed that he had "shot the holes though his clothes himself." When another scout claimed to have found an Indian campsite, a detachment of militia sent to find it quickly learned that the man had lied. At least one attack credited to the Indians was thought to have been perpetrated by white hunters masquerading as warriors.[6]

There was very little news from the U.S. Army during the first few months of 1792. Five daring soldiers had followed the buzzards to St. Clair's battlefield and arrived there on January 5, counting 538 bodies during their brief stay. A few days later, the enigmatic James Wilkinson was appointed lieutenant colonel of the Second Regiment and assumed command of the army in the West, St. Clair having gone to Philadelphia to salvage his reputation. Wilkinson had been a general in the Revolution and later moved to Kentucky, where he became a businessman, speculator, militia officer, and paid informant on the payroll of the Spanish crown. Now he appealed to the militia of the settlements north of the Ohio River to join an expedition to St. Clair's battlefield, where he planned to retrieve the lost cannons and bury the dead. The lieutenant colonel started on January 24 with 150 regular troops escorting supplies destined for Fort Jefferson, 130 mounted militia following the next day. Trudging through heavy snow, Wilkinson's militia party reached the desolate field on February 1, one volunteer having counted seventy-eight bodies along the route.[7]

An officer described what they saw upon reaching that fatal field: "Upwards of six hundred bodies, horribly mangled with tomahawks and scalping knives, and by wild beasts, lay on the ground, and presented a spectacle too horrible for description." Corpses were collected for burial, but the task was simply too overwhelming, with limited man-power and but a few spades. Pits were dug, and those bodies "that were exposed to view, or could be conveniently found" were buried. John Matson was on this burial detail and recounted the gruesome details: "The men had been all scalped, and so far as their cloth-ing was of much value, all stripped. Hardly one could be identified, the bodies being blackened by frost and exposure, although there did not appear any signs of decay, the winter having set in early, and proving very severe." While the burials continued, other parties swept the field for anything that could be salvaged. They found one gun, an iron carronade, still on its carriage, but the other cannons had vanished, either buried under the deep snow or thrown into the stream, which was now covered with thick ice. Before leaving the field, Winthrop Sargent thoroughly inspected the area and noticed that "Every Tree and shrub along the Lines bears the mark of the Enemy's Fire." After a severe march, Wilkinson's detachment reached Fort Washington on February 5, when the volunteers were dismissed with his thanks.[8]

Joseph Shaylor, a Connecticut veteran of the Revolution, commanded Fort Jeffer-son, one of the most miserable assignments imaginable. About three hundred sick and wounded soldiers had been left there after the battle, making the fort more of a crowded hospital than a military post deep inside enemy territory. No one was safe outside its walls. On February 11, Captain Shaylor left the post with a small hunting party, includ-ing Lt. Russell Bissell, Ephraim Kibbey from Columbia, and Shaylor's own son Joseph. Indians suddenly ambushed the men, and four Shawnee warriors came after Shaylor and his son, the captain detailing what happened to them: "They first discharged their pieces and then rushed on us in the most savage manner imaginable. He endeavoring to defend me lost his life. I endeavoring to defend him got myself in such a situation that I despaired of living another moment, for both of us had discharged our pieces, and with-out much effect; we had both rifles without bayonets. The savages rush on us with tom-ahawk and arrows which prevented us from loading a second time. I was therefore finally obliged to attack one with my fist, while another with his tomahawk was within a breath of taking my life. I, however, escaped with having an arrow shot into my side about half through my body." After burying his son with military honors, Shaylor was relieved of his command and tried by a court-martial for leaving the garrison. He was found guilty of "hazarding the immediate safety of the Garrison" and making an "uncandid report" of the affair to Wilkinson. Capt. Joseph Montford of the First Regiment succeeded Shaylor at Fort Jefferson and then, in a bizarre turn of events, was himself killed on April 27, when Indians lured him outside the post by calling like turkeys.[9]

Mindful that convoys moving from Fort Hamilton to Fort Jefferson would take two days to cover that distance, Lieutenant Colonel Wilkinson decided to build a new post halfway between those two garrisons. He described this new post as "a four sided poly-gon, with small but regular Bastions, on a square of 120 foot." The palisade was con-structed of large logs, with a ditch and embankment all around the perimeter. "A fine spring gushing out of the Earth" about sixty paces from the palisade ensured a constant supply of fresh water for the garrison. Wilkinson christened this new post Fort St. Clair.

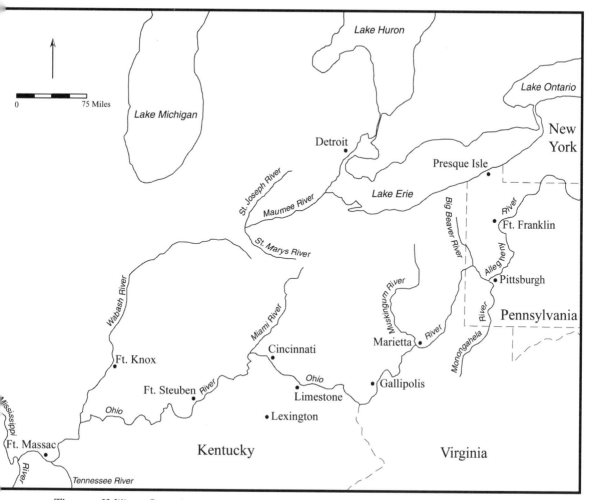

Theater of Military Operations, 1792–94

Several months after the fort's construction, Wilkinson reported the strength of garrisons at the western posts under his command, which serves to illustrate the miniscule number of troops available to protect settlers in the Northwest Territory:

	Officers	Enlisted Men
Fort Washington (Cincinnati)	9	277
Fort Hamilton	2	105
Fort St. Clair	5	129
Fort Jefferson	6	143
Fort Steuben (Louisville)	2	59
Fort Knox (Vincennes)	4	87

These totals included all soldiers present, including the sick and officers' servants who, in Wilkinson's opinion, "will probably never perform soldiers duty."[10]

There were several controversies involving Wilkinson's soldiers and civilian authorities, the first of which started on February 12, 1792, with a quarrel between Capt. Thomas Pasteur, assigned to the garrison at Fort Washington, and a storekeeper named John Bartle. Pasteur lured Bartle to the fort on a pretext of conducting some business, then "falling on him there in the presence of his myrmidons, beat him very severely." Bartle immediately sought out an attorney, John Blanchard, who filed suit against the captain. Pasteur became so enraged at how Blanchard characterized him in court that he sent Sgt. David Nesbit and about thirty privates "to inflict personal chastisement on the lawyer and all who might be disposed to defend him or his cause." A riotous "affray" ensued when Nesbit's party encountered a posse of civilians, led by Judge William McMillan, on Main Street. This affair could have gotten out of hand and, in Wilkinson's opinion, "might have proved fatal to 40 or 50 Persons, but for the seasonable interposition of Capt. Haskell, who was an Accidental Spectator of the commotion."

Wilkinson reported the affair to Secretary Knox, saying this "most lawless outrage" had threatened "to destroy that harmony & mutual confidence between the Citizens & Soldiers of the United States." "To avert such consequences in future, and to restrain the licentious habits of the soldiery," Wilkinson decreed that henceforth all duties beyond the confines of Fort Washington, even such routine tasks as going for water, wood, or provisions, would be done only by regular detachments under noncommissioned officers, who would be held responsible for any misconduct. No private would be allowed outside the garrison without written permission from an officer. Nesbit was reduced to private, then turned over to the territorial judge, who tried him in civil court for "riotously and unlawfully assaulting William McMillan Esquire." He was found guilty, fined three dollars, ordered to post a bond to guarantee his good behavior for six months, and sentenced to receive fifteen lashes (which was remitted). The following year Captain Pasteur was found guilty of instigating the assault and also fined three dollars.[11]

The next serious confrontation with civilian authority resulted from a garrison order issued by Lieutenant Colonel Wilkinson on May 11. Apparently, he had relaxed the strictures imposed after the Pasteur incident, but the result was "a drunken Garrison and a Guard house full of prisoners." Frustrated by the continual "scandalous and ungentlemanly abuse of this indulgence" and having found that neither orders nor admonitions were effective at curbing the evil, Wilkinson took a drastic step. His new policy was simple yet effective: "Any private therefore, who may hence forward be discovered drunk beyond the walls of the Garrison, shall receive fifty Lashes on the spot where he may be detected, and for the Execution of this order, a Commissioned officer with a patrole will daily visit the Village, and its environs at irregular Hours." Within two days, Ens. William Henry Harrison discovered an artificer drunk outside the post and immediately inflicted the prescribed punishment on him, then gave ten lashes to another artificer "for an insolent and seditious interference." Both men complained to the chief artificer, who lodged a complaint with Wilkinson, his argument being that men in his department were civilian employees of the army and not soldiers, thereby being exempt from such summary punishment. Wilkinson quickly amended his garrison order on May

14, explaining, "The order of the 11 Inst does not apply to the Corps of artificers; These necessary Servants of the public, whilst connected with the army, are Subject to the Law Martial, but are entitled in all Cases to a fair trial, and are on no pretence to be mal-treated or punished but under the Sentence of a Court martial."[12]

Both artificers filed suit against Ensign Harrison. Wilkinson refused to allow the sheriff inside the gates to serve his writ, then wrote a letter of explanation to Winthrop Sargent, acting as governor of the Northwest Territory during Arthur St. Clair's absence. He admitted that Harrison's action had been "contrary to the Spirit & interest" of his May 11 order, which had waived the court-martial process in favor of speedy punishment for offenders. But this lawsuit had infected the artificers, as well as the soldiers, with a sort of "licentious freedom, incompatible with their respective Stations, tending to the subversion of discipline, destructive to those principles of subordination with out which an army cannot exist, and of consequence pregnant with anarchy & disorder." Acting Governor Sargent sympathized with Wilkinson's fight against "that destructive Vice of Drunkenness so prevalent in your Army" but confessed that the great number of unreg-ulated "tippling Houses" must "continue the Soldiery and some of the Inhabitants in a most shameful State of Debauchery." He pledged to stop "vexatious Interference of the Civil Power and groundless Prosecution" as well as to convince civilians that harmony with the military was in their best interest. But Sargent emphatically reminded the com-manding officer that "there is no Sanctuary from the sovereign Authority of Civil Law" and that any person interfering with the serving of a writ (such as Wilkinson had done) could be prosecuted as an accessory to a felony. After reviewing the entire case, Sargent wrote to Judge John C. Symmes and explained that the artificers had been "regularly engaged as Retainers or Followers of the Army and consequently as subject to the mar-tial Law as any Soldiers in Service." The bottom line was that the two men punished by Ensign Harrison had "voluntarily subjected themselves" to military discipline, and that officer's misinterpretation of Wilkinson's order could not be prosecuted in a civilian court.[13]

While Wilkinson haggled with civilians, President Washington decided to send messengers of peace to the hostile Indian nations. Secretary Knox selected Maj. Alexan-der Trueman, a veteran of the Revolution who had been wounded in St. Clair's defeat, to carry a speech and a belt of wampum to the Indian confederacy. Trueman's instruc-tions read in part: "As the confederacy of Indians is supposed to be extensive, it will require time to bring your negotiations to a favorable issue. Your patience, your forti-tude, and your knowledge of the human character, will all be tested by the objects of your mission." The Washington administration did not make Trueman's task any easier by including in its message an ill-advised, arrogant, and insulting paragraph that read:

> BROTHERS: The President of the United States entertains the opinion, that the war which exists is founded in error and mistake on your parts. That you believe the United States want to deprive you of your lands and drive you out of the country. Be assured this is not so; on the contrary, that we should be greatly

gratified with the opportunity of imparting to you all the blessings of civilized life, of teaching you to cultivate the earth, and raise corn; to raise oxen, sheep, and other domestic animals; to build comfortable homes, and to educate your children, so as ever to dwell upon the land.

After receiving his instructions from Secretary Knox, Major Trueman descended the Ohio River and reported to Wilkinson at Fort Washington. Wilkinson had decided to lighten Trueman's burden by sending a duplicate message with John Hardin, a colonel in the Kentucky militia who had fought with General Harmar at the Miami villages in 1790. Although not explicitly stated by Knox, verbal orders must surely have confirmed instructions given to earlier messengers of peace, which stated: "We cannot ask the Indians to make peace with us, considering them as the aggressors; but they must ask a peace of us. To persuade them to this effect is the object of your mission." National integrity had to be preserved at all costs.

Trueman had been promised "personal reputation and honor" if he should succeed in bringing about a peace conference, as well as having all his expenses paid and being "liberally rewarded in a pecuniary manner." Wilkinson promised Hardin "a guinea a day" while on his hazardous assignment and told the colonel that, if he should not return, his wife would receive "not less than two hundred dollars" every year for the rest of her life. Hardin told his spouse that he expected no trouble since his speech and belt of wampum had been sent by President Washington. Wilkinson used a bit of common sense in sending the Kentuckian to the Sandusky towns along Lake Erie and Trueman to the Miami villages along the headwaters of the Maumee River. The two officers were to eventually meet at Roche de Bout, near the mouth of the Maumee, where they hoped to hold a preliminary conference with chiefs from the Indian confederacy. On May 19, shortly before his departure, Colonel Hardin wrote a letter to his wife, Jane, and confessed, "But oh, my dear love, as I meditate on myself to think I have left a peaceable home and so dear a family, and throw my life into the hands of a cruel and savage enemy, I cannot prevent the tears flowing from my eyes at present; and I do my love, implore your prayers daily at the throne of Grace for my protection from both spiritual and temporal enemies." A few days later, Major Trueman and Col. John Hardin, accompanied by their servants and interpreters, started north into the trackless wilderness to deliver their message of peace. The two officers were never again seen alive.[14]

On the afternoon of July 7, 1792, ten-year-old Oliver Spencer joined some men and a woman in a canoe bound for Columbia, but one of the men proved to be drunk. Oliver asked to be put on shore, where he was walking along barefooted, "now listening to the merry conversation of my companions, and now amusing myself by skimming small flat stones over the surface of the water," when two gunshots suddenly rang out. One man tumbled into the river mortally wounded, another fell out wounded, and the lady pitched into the water as the canoe overturned. Spencer saw an Indian grab the nearest man, "striking his tomahawk into the head of the unfortunate stranger, seizing him by the hair, passing his knife quickly around the scalp, and tearing it violently off, he held it up for a moment with fiendish exultation." Young Spencer turned to run but was captured by a second Indian. Satisfied with their success and ever mindful of pursuit, the two warriors immediately set off into the woods with their prisoner. Spencer glanced back "to see Mr. Light, who, although wounded in the left arm, was with his right swimming out into the river, about a hundred yards from shore; the dead body of the stranger lying just in the edge of the water; Mrs. Coleman about two rods out in the river, her clothes spread over the water, and with her head near its surface, apparently floating, and the desolate canoe slowly descending with the current."

Word of the ambush reached Cincinnati when Mrs. Coleman was pulled from the Ohio by people who heard her cries for help, but Mr. Light had reached Fort Washington a few minutes earlier with the shocking news. A party of soldiers set out in pursuit and tracked the Indians and their captive about fifteen miles but could not catch up. Winthrop Sargent asked Secretary of War Knox for help in ransoming the boy, and Knox assured him that he would "take all the steps which individually I may do upon the subject." Through the intercession of highly placed men in Philadelphia and Detroit, Spencer was eventually released in the spring of 1793. This sad tale points out the most important lesson to be learned about life on the frontier—no one was ever safe from Indian raiding parties. In the words of Theodore Roosevelt, "the whole forest was to the whites one vast ambush."[15]

That fact should have been readily apparent following the attack on a party of soldiers near Fort Jefferson, a favorite target of Indian raiders. On June 25, Maj. David Strong sent a sergeant, a corporal, and ten privates to collect hay. Some militia rangers and a small dragoon detachment acted as guards. About nine o'clock, after the haying party had been at work about an hour, a band of about seventy Indians, some of them mounted, attacked and drove off the guards. A detachment of the cavalry rode to assist, but they blundered into an ambush formed by another group of warriors. A close reconnaissance of the field that evening discovered four bodies "on whome was marks [of] the greatest emity & cruelty practised." Sixteen soldiers were missing, and most of the hay had been burned. The Indians left behind a war club "with a very extroordinary Spike in the head of it" and a bit of a mystery. Survivors of the attack swore that most of the Indians had worn white shirts, an odd circumstance since they generally did not wear any shirts while seeking the enemy. Brig. Gen. Rufus Putnam reported the affair to Secretary Knox and speculated that the Indians "had ben very lately & very generally furnished with new Shirts by the British Superintendent." He also believed that "my self was the oreginal object of that exppidition" since he had sent a speech from Pittsburgh telling the Indians that he would arrive at Fort Jefferson on that date.[16]

Additional information about this encounter came from an unlikely source on July 8, when two soldiers escaped from their captors and arrived at Fort Jefferson. Pvt. Henry Schaffer, a native of Hagerstown, Maryland, had been taken on October 19, 1790, during Harmar's attack on the Miami villages. William Dever had served in Buchanan's company before being wounded and captured at St. Clair's defeat. On July 5, the two men had been sent to hoe corn some two miles from the Potawatomi village where they resided and took advantage of this opportunity to escape. They soon discovered Harmar's trace and followed it a few miles before turning off on a path that led them to St. Clair's battlefield, where they saw several of the abandoned cannons.

Schaffer had learned the Potawatomi language and provided much valuable information when interviewed by Winthrop Sargent. He had been marched off to a series of Potawatomi camps, where he was "treated with great cruelty, . . . frequently Beat, half starved, kept almost naked, and exposed to every species of severe labor." Two days before his escape, Schaffer talked with some Chippewas who had participated in the attack on the Fort Jefferson mowing party. Indians told him that their whole group, composed of Chippewa, Shawnee, and Delaware warriors, numbered about one hundred. They had disposed of prisoners from the mowing and guard detachments in different ways. The Chippewas retained their captives and took them home to work as laborers, but the Shawnees burnt theirs to death. The most important information he imparted was that Captain Trueman and Colonel Hardin had been killed before they could deliver their messages of peace. When this intelligence reached Philadelphia, Josiah Harmar curtly observed, "Murdering of flags does not seem to indicate a speedy peace with the savages."[17]

The settlement at Gallipolis was a favorite target of Indian raiders. On August 13, one man was taken prisoner and another, Adam Miller of Hughes's company, was shot through the body and left arm and scalped, although he was able to stagger back to the garrison. Five days later, Indians attacked four men as they worked in the fields. The laborers raised an alarm, and a militia lieutenant shot one of the warriors through the body, although he evaded capture. The following day another hostile party was sighted near the creek about a quarter mile from the fort but disappeared after the blockhouses were manned and the garrison made a show of force. Lt. Richard S. Howe assured General Wilkinson that both he and Lt. George Demlar had done everything possible to defend the place. Howe explained: "We are pen'd up within half a mile circumference and should the Enemy continue around us any time, the inhabitants will be in a starving condition. . . . It is very sickly at this place, the ague and fever prevails very much, and the troops almost destitute of Cloathing."[18]

Although nothing could be done about the fear that confined settlers to the immediate area around their fort, the diseases had been brought on by poor sanitation. When Ens. John Lowry relieved Lieutenant Howe at Gallipolis, he was shocked to find the interior of the fort filled with sheds for cattle and horses and pens for hogs, the surface being simply "one Bed of Mud." The new commander immediately banished all animals to pens outside the garrison, despite objections from owners who claimed their property would be more vulnerable to the Indians. Lowry ordered a fatigue party to tear down the original sheds and to haul away the accumulated manure, some sixty-five cartloads by the time it had finished. The stockade itself had been so badly fitted that an enemy could fire between the upright logs, or in Lowry's words, "the geese may pick the ducks through between the piquets." Routine maintenance had been ignored to such an extent that one night nine of the upright logs were simply blown down by the wind.[19]

While isolated garrisons did their best to protect settlers from hostile raids, hatred against all Indians ran deep on the frontier. This was evident in Cincinnati when one of the Eel River Miami chiefs died there while visiting family members captured in the Wabash raids of 1791. When the chief was buried on July 17, 1792, Generals Wilkinson and Putnam insisted upon the corpse receiving military honors. A large procession, composed of military officers, gentlemen from the town, and a number of Indians, followed the remains to the town's cemetery. After the chief's burial, three volleys were fired and a large pole bearing a white flag was planted at the head of the grave. That night "malicious people" tore down the flag and threw it into a mudhole. They then dug up the body, dragged it into town, and stood it up for everyone to see. The generals were outraged by this ungodly conduct, had the Indian reburied, and erected a new flag. Winthrop Sargent, acting governor of the territory, offered a one-hundred-dollar reward for the names of the perpetrators of this foul deed. The next night, the flag and proclamation were torn down, although the grave was not disturbed. Another flag was set up and a guard posted over the grave, which put a stop to nighttime desecration.[20]

Amid such a hostile environment, Rufus Putnam had been instructed to negotiate a treaty of peace with as many Indian nations as possible but particularly with the Wea and Eel River Nations, which had been anxious to reach an accommodation with the Americans ever since their villages had been scourged by mounted Kentuckians in 1791. The Wea chiefs preferred to negotiate at Fort Knox, and Putnam agreed to meet them there. Referring to the deaths of Trueman and Hardin, the general confessed, "it Certainly is very mortifying to Make overtures of peace to the Indians while the ground is yet Reeking with the blood of our Messengers." His most pressing need was for a reliable interpreter, a vacancy that was filled by hiring William Wells at the wage of one dollar a day. This new interpreter, after nearly nine years of living in captivity with the Indians, had recently been reunited with his family in Kentucky. Comparing and contrasting the lifestyles of the two cultures, Wells had chosen the comfort and stability of the Americans. According to him, Indians "live almost wholly to the present, they give little or no remembrance to the past, and hope nothing for the future." Given the unique circumstances of Indian life, warriors had "no claims to liberty or happiness." Heightening his personal interest for serving Putnam was the fact that both his wife and adoptive Indian mother were among a group of prisoners at Fort Washington.[21]

Wells arrived at Fort Washington on July 12 and "shed many tears" in a reunion with his Indian family. He then met with Putnam and his assistant, John Heckewelder, both of whom seemed impressed with their new employee. The general wrote that Wells appeared to be "a young man of good natural abilities and of an agreable disposition." Heckewelder noted that Wells had fought with the Indian army against St. Clair and gave "good, thorough and reliable accounts" of his actions as well as important information about "where the cannons of the Indians lie buried." On August 16, Wells, sixty soldiers, and the Indian prisoners boarded boats bound downriver for Fort Knox, followed two days later by Putnam and Heckewelder. Arriving on September

13, Putnam immediately released the captives and convened a council. Although Wells had confided that the Wea and Eel River warriors were "great liers," the general concluded a peace treaty with seven nations on September 27 and celebrated this first wedge driven into the vaunted Indian confederacy.[22]

Accepting an invitation to visit President Washington at Philadelphia, sixteen chiefs from the Wabash and Illinois Nations began the long journey eastward after affixing their marks to Putnam's treaty. This delegation was escorted by Capt. Abner Prior, who had studied medicine and served as a surgeon's mate during the Revolution. Some of the prominent Indian diplomats were Duquoin (Little Bearskin), Como (Drowning Man), Oeoseto (Whirlwind), Amequah (Little Beaver), Swekaniah (Three Legs), and Chemaukin (The Soldier). Acting Governor Sargent had warned residents north of the Ohio that "a few Chiefs of the friendly Tribes of Indians" were expected to arrive soon and were to be "received and treated as the Friends of the United States."[23]

Prior's delegation reached Fort Washington on October 25, but the whites and Indians got along almost too well, Sargent complaining that he had witnessed "a number of Indians mixing with the Inhabitants of the Town in a State but little removed from Intoxication and I am apprehensive that disagreeable Consequences may ensue." He assured Prior that he could restrain his "frontier people" as long as they were sober, but to do so when intoxicated would prove "a too arduous Task." Sargent then warned the sheriff of Hamilton County about the potentially explosive mixture of frontiersmen, Indians, and whiskey. James Wilkinson arrived at Fort Washington on October 27 and hosted a large banquet for the distinguished visitors and about thirty officers and government officials. Ever a proper host, the general arranged his seating so that the Indians were scattered among the other guests. Wilkinson pointed out why he had done so in his welcoming speech: "My copper-colored Brethren from the Wabash, see how we are seated at this large table, there is no difference between us and you! You have lately made peace with us and today already you sit among us and eat with us from one dish." John Heckewelder observed that "the cordiality during the dinner was very great on both sides."[24]

The Indian delegation headed upstream on the evening of November 1. Wilkinson took advantage of their departure to send along a keg of "*Ohio Water* Fish" to Secretary Knox. The first few days of their journey passed quietly, and the Indians received a friendly reception from both shores of the Ohio. But as the vessels approached Limestone, Kentucky, the mood onshore turned ugly. Heckewelder remembered: "It seemed in truth as if the Indians, and perhaps we, their companions, would also here find our graves. Several hundred men had assembled on the riverbank, of whome one-third were on horseback and uttered many threats. Just at this juncture 16 Kentucky boats passed. They had 400 soldiers on board, who cursed us vehemently." Prior kept his soldiers poling and paddling until late that night, then stopped and made camp on the north shore. Pickets were stationed to warn of the approach of any Kentuckians who might try to carry out their threats, but no one in camp got much sleep that night.[25]

Prior's party finally reached Pittsburgh early in December. Residents there had no use for these "savages," and word spread that only two of the party were really natives. *The Pittsburgh Gazette* explained that there were, in fact, three "real Indians" and "the rest were the next thing to it, mulattoes, and Canadian bastards, that had inter-married in royal families." After learning that several of the chiefs had later died in Philadelphia, the editor wondered, "would it not be a good scheme, to send out interpreters, and make a trade of bringing in savages, under pretence of chiefs, and having them killed up at the seat of government? It would be less expence than supporting an army. It cost but 1900 dollars to bring the late party as far as Pittsburgh."[26]

CHAPTER 2

A New Commander, a New Army

A NEW, VIABLE ARMY had to be created out of the remnants of St. Clair's shattered command, but the first task at hand for the Washington administration was to appoint a general to oversee its formation. On March 9, 1792, after discussing a variety of military topics, President Washington and his cabinet considered a list of generals from the Revolution who were available and not compromised either by advanced age, extreme ill health, disinclination for command, or some other peculiar circumstance. Only three major generals received consideration. Benjamin Lincoln was dismissed as being "past the vigor of life." Baron Frederick William Augustus de Steuben, who had brought military order and discipline to the American army, was deemed "impetuous in his temper; ambitious, and a foreigner." William Moultrie was somewhat of a mystery, for he had served exclusively in South Carolina and Washington had little information on which to judge his ability. The politicians then talked about those officers who had been brevetted to the rank of major general during the war. Lachlan McIntosh was pronounced unable to "obtain much confidence, or command much respect." Washington thought Anthony Wayne to be "more active and enterprising than Judicious and cautious," while Secretary of State Thomas Jefferson noted him to be "Brave and nothing else," saying that he "Deserves credit for Stony Point but on another occasion [had] run his head against a wall where success was both impossible and useless." George Weedon was not considered "to be an Officer of much resource" and "rather addicted to ease and pleasure." Edward Hand had unquestioned integrity but seemed too inactive. Charles Scott was reported to be "an officer of inadequate abilities for extensive command; and, by report, is addicted to drinking." Jedediah Huntington had "never discover'd much enterprise."

Moving down the seniority list, Washington and his advisors then discussed those who had served as brigadier generals during the Revolution. The president thought James Wilkinson had exhibited no history of achievement "as he was but a short time in Service," but Jefferson noted that he was "Brave, enterprising to excess, but [had] many unapprovable points in his character." Mordecai Gist had little to recommend him, and his attention to duty was questioned. William Irvine had nothing in his background to mark him "as a decidedly good, or indifferent Officer," although Secretary of the Treasury Alexander Hamilton noted, "All that he did during [the] war was to avoid any censure of any kind." Daniel Morgan had a widespread reputation as a heavy drinker and was bothered by "a palpitation" that occasionally incapacitated him. Jefferson opined: "No head. Health gone. Speculator." Morgan was also illiterate. Otho Holland Williams had always acted in a subordinate role, with no chance to show any talents as an independent commander, but the biggest objection to choosing him was his "delicate health." Rufus Putnam had exhibited "nothing conspicuous in his character" that would indicate an ability to command the army. Charles Pinckney, a brigadier general by brevet, was virtually unknown outside South Carolina, appeared to be "immersed in business," and had refused previous appointments. Although not general officers, three other men came up for consideration. Henry "Light Horse Harry" Lee, a lieutenant colonel of dragoons and presently governor of Virginia, seemed to have "A better head and more resource than any of them." Secretary of War Henry Knox said that Thomas Sumter, a general in the South Carolina militia, was "Incapable of subordination" and must be "commander in chief or nothing." Another South Carolina militia general, Andrew Pickens, appeared "Sensible, modest, enterprising, and judicious," yet he was "untried" and believed incapable of commanding the army.[1]

Washington and Knox hoped to appoint a major general from this list of Revolutionary War notables and planned to select four brigadier generals to serve under him. Not only was there no clear-cut candidate for the top spot based upon character and war record, but the selection process also had one overriding difficulty. Everyone understood that vanity would not allow any of these men to serve under an officer of lesser rank. That was the major disadvantage of Governor Lee, Jefferson admitting that "being a junior officer, we should lose benefit of good seniors who would not serve under him." No matter what the outcome, some of these famous patriots were bound to be offended. The president's final decision would have to be based upon important political and military considerations. He must appoint someone who would be acceptable to Congress, whose military fame would stimulate recruiting, and who could, once and for all, put an end to the Indian war north of the Ohio River. Washington and his advisors must have agonized over this momentous choice.[2]

After weighing all of his options and narrowing the field of candidates to Wayne, Morgan, and Wilkinson, Washington instructed Knox to begin a confidential correspondence with Anthony Wayne, inquiring whether he would be willing to accept command of the U.S. Army. Wayne responded on April 1 with a sincere yet blunt letter. After thanking both men for their confidence in him, the "Hero of Stony Point" got right to the heart of the matter. Wayne told Knox that he would serve "if subject only, to the Orders and advice of the President and yourself." He continued, "I can not therefore think of committing my Military character (which is dearer to me than life) to the fortuitous events of War—which I can not direct—and shou'd it be crowned with success—

the Glory & honor will belong to another—whilst on the contrary—shou'd it be unfortunate, I must share in the disgrace, after giving up peace and ease—and relinquishing certain pleasing prospects in the *civil* line to which I am invited by my fellow citizens." There was his answer in no uncertain terms. If he were appointed to command the army, it would be *his* army and he would run it the way *he* saw fit, his actions subject only to review by Secretary of War Knox and, ultimately, President Washington.[3]

Expecting some resistance to this choice, Washington urged Jefferson to test the political waters in the Senate by contacting James Monroe. The secretary of state informed his friend that Washington was considering Wayne as the army commander but "would not appoint one to whom he could foresee any material opposition." Senator Monroe responded that some resistance might be expected, although it appeared that a rejection of Wayne would not necessarily produce "a more suitable person." Encouraged by Monroe's assessment of the situation, Washington, "by and with the advice and consent of the Senate," appointed Anthony Wayne to the rank of major general "and of course commanding Officer of the troops in the service of the United States," his commission being effective from March 5, 1792. Wayne accepted this honor on April 13 with the following statement: "I clearly foresee that it is a command which must inevitably be attended with the most anxious care, fatigue and difficulty, and from which more may be expected than will be in my power to perform. Yet I shou'd be wanting both in point of duty and gratitude to the President were I to decline an appointment (however Arduous) to which he thought proper to nominate me." Horatio N. Moore, an early biographer of Wayne, thus describes the weighty responsibility thrust onto the general's shoulders: "The honor of the federal government, public confidence in his wisdom, . . . the respect of foreign nations—all combined, with the security of the frontier, so long the scene of ambush, conflagration, and slaughter, to demand victory at his hands."[4]

It could be argued that his family upbringing had propelled Anthony Wayne toward the appointment coveted by so many distinguished American officers. The major general's grandfather, also named Anthony Wayne, had been born in Yorkshire, England, in 1666, but in 1681, during the reign of Charles II, he left his native country and settled in County Wicklow, Ireland. Wayne became a gentleman farmer but joined the Protestant army of William of Orange in his fight against the Catholic forces of James II, commanding a squadron of dragoons at the Battle of the Boyne on July 1, 1690, and participating in the siege of Limerick. Wayne remained in Ireland until 1722, when he emigrated with his family to Pennsylvania and purchased a substantial farm in Chester County. After Anthony Wayne's death in 1739, his property passed to a son, Isaac, who became an influential member of Chester County society and a militia captain during the French and Indian War. Isaac improved the farm by building, and later expanding, a large brownstone mansion that he called Waynesborough. He represented Chester County in the legislature, built a tannery, and lived the life of a country squire on his estate, which was located just two miles from Paoli and four miles from Valley Forge. Isaac's marriage to Elizabeth Iddings produced three children, two girls, Hannah and Ann, and one son, Anthony, who was born on New Year's Day, 1745.[5]

Anthony was described as a "pretty wild boy" who had inherited his father's interest in military affairs. Little is known of his childhood beyond a letter written by Gilbert Wayne, who had undertaken to teach his teenaged nephew. Anthony apparently "had no taste for dead Latin and Greek" but was enthralled by all things military. The frustrated schoolmaster wrote to Isaac, "What he may be best qualified for, I know not—one thing I am certain of, he will never make a scholar, he may perhaps make a soldier, he has already distracted the brains of two-thirds of the boys under my charge, by rehearsals of battles, sieges &c." After Gilbert Wayne's other students began to sport black eyes and bandaged heads, evidence that the spirit of war had invaded his school, he candidly told Isaac that if young Anthony did not shape up, he would be dismissed. Father and son had a heart-to-heart talk, in which Isaac promised "to withdraw him from his classes and place him upon the farm at hard work, if failing to conduct himself differently in the future, and give over his sham battling, erection of redoubts, military rehearsals, and building of mud forts." Anthony promised to behave and returned to school determined to learn all that he could from his uncle. After about eighteen months of diligent study, Gilbert recommended that his pupil be sent to the Philadelphia Academy. Isaac Wayne concurred, and so at the age of sixteen, Anthony went to study in the colonial capital, remaining there for two years before returning home to begin work as a surveyor.[6]

Social and professional contacts brought Anthony Wayne in touch with a group of prominent Pennsylvanians, including Benjamin Franklin, who had formed a company to speculate in lands in Nova Scotia. Although then but twenty-one years of age, Wayne was chosen as an agent of the company and sent to that region to find the best land for establishing colonies of settlers. He spent two years in the Canadian wilderness, a life "full of dangers, hardships and trials, of thrilling adventures with wild beasts and wily savages—a school for discipline, resourcefulness, caution, courage, industry, energy and achievement." After almost two years of this "semi-military training school," Wayne returned to Pennsylvania, his efforts in Nova Scotia being rewarded with a one-thousand-acre tract of land in that province. On March 25, 1766, after a short romance, he joined in marriage with Mary Penrose, daughter of Bartholomew Penrose Jr., a prominent and prosperous Philadelphia merchant. The newlyweds moved into the family home at Waynesborough, where Anthony slowly began to take over operations from his father. The couple became the proud parents of two children, Margaretta, born in 1768, and Isaac, born in 1770. Wayne gradually became a leader among his neighbors in criticizing Great Britain's handling of her American colonies, winning several political offices, including a seat in the Pennsylvania assembly, and lobbying for a larger and better supplied militia. Although Anthony had raised a regiment of minutemen in Chester County for service in the war that started in April 1775, such opportunities for a long-delayed military career were tempered by the death of Isaac Wayne that December.[7]

Upon appointment as colonel of the Fourth Battalion of the Pennsylvania Line on January 3, 1776, Anthony Wayne promptly resigned all of his civilian offices and threw himself wholeheartedly into raising and training the best unit in the Continental Army. One historian has characterized the colonel as "an anachronism in the eighteenth century" who truly believed himself to be a "knight errant riding forth to do great and noble deeds," with "a romanticism found back in the days of chivalry." Wayne was, indeed, one of those officers who discovered the key to future success on the battlefield often could be found in the actions of great commanders of the past. His favorite texts were Julius Caesar's *Commentaries* and Maurice de Saxe's *My Reveries upon the Art of War,* although he was certainly exposed to other classic military works, such as *The Instruction of Frederick the Great for His Generals* and Vegetius's *Military Institutions of the Romans.* It seemed that Wayne's preference was for the writings of Saxe, and his letters occasionally referred to that author. The new Pennsylvania colonel certainly took to heart the maxim of Chevalier Follard, quoted by Saxe, who said, "War is a trade for the ignorant and a science for the expert." Wayne was a military scientist who combined his book learning with "that rare faculty which the French call the *coup d'oeil,* which consists in detecting, by a glance at the battle-field, the purpose of an enemy, or any fault in his arrangements of which advantage may be taken."[8]

Wayne quickly raised and organized the Fourth Pennsylvania Battalion, which was ordered to reinforce those troops that had undertaken the invasion of Canada. He saw his first action on June 9, 1776, at Trois Rivieres along the St. Lawrence River, where a badly bungled attack on British forces commanded by Gen. John Burgoyne resulted in an American defeat. Wayne performed well during his first chance to lead troops in combat and received a wound in his right leg before taking command of the rear guard as the invaders began their long withdrawal from Canada. Troops from this ill-fated adventure eventually ended up at Fort Ticonderoga in northern New York, which soon turned into a quiet backwater as most of the attention shifted to the Continental Army under Gen. George Washington. That winter Colonel Wayne declared his thoughts on recent American reverses in a letter to a friend: "I condole with you on the Distresses of our Common Country . . . ; but let not this in the least Intimidate us—our Growing Country can meet with Considerable losses and Survive them; whilst our Defeat will forever Ruin the *English Rebel Army*—they may for a while Embarrass us much—we shall soon learn to meet them in the Open field—let them Conquer our Maritime towns—they can't Subjugate the free Sons of America, who very shortly will produce a Conviction to the World that they deserve to be free." Victory would not come unless the Americans could overcome adversity, some of which Wayne encountered during his frontier assignment, especially the depletion of his command as the best troops were either sent home after their enlistments expired or dispatched to reinforce Washington's main army. Mulling over his own fate should he happen to be captured by the enemy, Wayne expected to be ridiculed with "insult and contempt" at the "motley appearance" of his garrison, which he described as "one-third negroes, mullattoes and Indians, one-third children, and little boys wretchedly clothed and more wretchedly armed and disciplined—but the other third will entitle me to some respect."[9]

Col. Anthony Wayne was appointed to the rank of brigadier general in the Continental Army on February 21, 1777, and joined Washington's command that spring, thereafter participating in most of the well-known battles of the Revolution. He led a division in three engagements during the space of just over three weeks in the fall of that year—at Brandywine, Paoli, and Germantown. Paoli was a personal embarrassment for Wayne, his camp being overrun in a British night attack just a couple of miles from Waynesborough. In fact, British soldiers pursuing fugitives from that fight came to Wayne's home, where they expected to find the rebel general, and actually ran their swords and bayonets into bushes where they thought he might be hiding. Wayne was wounded for the second time at Germantown on October 4, being slightly injured by a musket ball that grazed his left hand and a solid shot that "a little bruised" his left foot.

When the British occupied Philadelphia, Washington's army went into winter camp at Valley Forge. There Wayne concentrated on filling the depleted ranks of the Pennsylvania Line, finding enough for the men to eat, and keeping them clothed against the harsh winter weather. In the spring of 1778, Wayne wrote to Pennsylvania authorities and urged them "to order Recruits to be clothed & appointed before they leave Lancaster as they can't be supplied here." He confided, "there are near one third of my men that have no kind of Shirt under Heaven," leaving them "in a worse Condition than any troops on the ground, nay worse than Falstaff's Recruits; they had a shirt and a half to a Company." Wayne also confessed to being "heartily tired of this way of life," then explained why: "I am not fond of Danger—but I would most Cheerfully agree to Enter into Action once every week in place of visiting each *hutt* in my Encampment—where Objects perpetually strike my eye & ear whose wretched condition cannot well be worsted—the Ball or Bayonet can only hurt the body—but such Objects effects the mind & gives the keenest wound to every feeling of Humanity." An epidemic of measles swept through the Pennsylvania camps, resulting in "some hundreds" being deposited "some six feet under Ground." Wayne continued to plead for clothing to relieve "our poor worthy fellows from the vermin which are now devouring them." He assured his friend Richard Peters, "I would Rather Risque my life, Honor & the fate of America on our present force—properly uniformed—than on Double their number Covered with rags & Crawling with vermin."[10]

General Wayne took advantage of the lull in activity at Valley Forge to study Saxe and put his precepts into practice with the Pennsylvania Line. According to Saxe, "It is a false idea that discipline, subordination, and slavish obedience debase courage. It has always been noted that it is with those armies in which the severest discipline is enforced that the greatest deeds are performed." In the spring of 1778, even though his men were half-naked, Wayne had his officers drilling them at least twice a day "in their march and wheelings," practicing Saxe's belief that "The foundation of training depends on the legs and not the arms." Finding that too many soldiers failed to appear for drill, he had the following order placed on the doorway of every hut in camp: "No soldier in future is to be absent on the hours allotted for exercise, either for water, provisions or any other pretext, what soever, except on duty on pain of being severely punished." Another of Saxe's maxims was that an officer could be "exact and just, and be loved at the same time as feared." To win the respect of his men, Wayne set limits on the hours they could perform guard duty. In order to keep his men healthy, the general told them to keep the parade ground and camps clean and set aside Friday afternoons for bathing (no man in the water for more than ten minutes) and washing their clothes. He also ordered that each hut contain at least two windows for proper ventilation and, when one regiment became too sickly, moved soldiers from that command into tents.[11]

Wayne's service during the next two years attracted much attention. At Monmouth Court House, New Jersey, on September 28, 1778, while leading about one thousand troops under the overall command of Maj. Gen. Charles Lee, Wayne led an attack on the British army as it retreated from Philadelphia to New York. Not properly supported, Wayne fell back until General Washington, who had become irate at Lee's conduct of the battle, arrived on the scene and took control of the troops himself. Washington ordered Wayne to form a line and hold back the British while he rallied the remainder of his army behind the Pennsylvanians. Falling back under increasing pressure, Wayne joined Washington's defensive line, helped repel the British advance, then advanced and began to drive the enemy from the field. This action was little more than an annoyance to Sir Henry Clinton and his redcoats, but Washington praised General Wayne to Congress, specifically mentioning his "good conduct and bravery thro' the whole action." By the spring of 1779, losses in the Pennsylvania Line had been so heavy that a reorganization had become necessary. For three years, Anthony Wayne had led these proud troops, but this new plan would demote him from division to brigade command, Maj. Gen. Arthur St. Clair replacing him—it should be noted that this new arrangement had been carried out by the Pennsylvania legislature and not General Washington. Unwilling to accept a demotion, Wayne wrote to Washington and asked to lead an independent "Light Corps" that the commander had considered implementing. Rather than allow one of his best fighting generals to resign, Washington agreed and sent Wayne on leave while the necessary arrangements were worked out. When Washington ordered him to return on June 21, 1779, Wayne responded, "Now for the field of Mars," leaving the comfort of Philadelphia and Chester County society to assume command of the best officers and enlisted men in the army.[12]

Wayne joined with Washington in planning an assault on Stony Point, a British fortification along the Hudson River. The attack was to take place at midnight on July 16, 1779, two separate bodies of troops advancing with unloaded muskets and fixed bayonets. Small parties were sent ahead to distract the British and to clear away obstructions from the line of advance, succeeding in their assignments despite high casualties. Two columns, the southernmost commanded by Wayne, dashed forward over entrenchments and into the fort without firing a shot, bayoneting enemy soldiers who failed to surrender. The British commander capitulated in a matter of minutes after losing 133 soldiers killed and wounded. The Americans found themselves with almost 450 prisoners, fifteen cannon, and large quantities of stores, at a cost of only 100 casualties. Among those struck down was General Wayne, hit in the head by a musket ball while leading his column, although his third wound did not prove serious. It was said that when Wayne fell he cried out, "March on, carry me into the fort; for should the wound be mortal, I will die at the head of the column." The wounded general announced his success to Washington with the following laconic note:

> Stony Point, 16TH July, 2 O'clock, A.M.
> Dear General:—The fort and garrison with Col. Johnson are ours. Our officers and men behaved like men who are determined to be free.
> Yours most sincerely
> An'y Wayne

Although Stony Point was soon after abandoned and reoccupied by the British, Wayne found himself treated as a bona fide hero throughout America for his bold and audacious attack. Washington praised him to Congress, which responded by unanimously passing a resolution of thanks for his "brave prudent and soldierly con[duct] in the spirited and well-conducted attack on Stony Point" and voting him a gold medal to commemorate the victory. In a surprisingly beneficent mood, Congress also voted to distribute the value of the captured British stores, over $158,000 worth, to the men of Wayne's command.[13]

Befitting his reputation as a hard-fighting general, stories began to circulate about Anthony Wayne. It was rumored that when summoned to attend a council of war, he would always arrive carrying a book, usually a popular novel of the time, and go off into a corner of the room and begin to read. While other high-ranking generals debated the course that Washington and his army should pursue, Wayne would ignore their conversation and continue reading. When all the officers had given their opinions, Washington would invariably turn to Wayne and inquire, "Well, general, what do you propose to do?" He would look up from his book and say, "Fight, sir," then return to his novel. That story was undoubtedly apocryphal, but the Pennsylvania general had acquired a nickname, "Mad Anthony," that proved immensely popular with his troops. As the story goes, an Irish soldier of the Pennsylvania Line named Jemmy the Rover, who occasionally served as one of Wayne's spies, was apparently subject to fits of insanity, becoming "noisy and troublesome." On one occasion when he seemed particularly bothersome in camp, General Wayne peremptorily ordered a sergeant to place Jemmy under arrest until his fit passed. Upon being released from the guardhouse a few hours later, the Irishman asked the sergeant if "Anthony," as he always referred to the general, had locked him up because he was mad or whether he did it in fun. The sergeant replied that Wayne had been quite upset by his outburst and any repetition of it would result in Jemmy being whipped. Vowing loudly to behave himself, Jemmy thereafter referred to himself as "mad Anthony's friend." Thus the name Mad Anthony, "dropped casually from the lips of a simpleton, obtained some sort of circulation, and became used in a jocular way among the rank and file of Wayne's command, but never in a sense intending disparagement or disrespect."

The nickname in no way implied that Wayne was crazy. Joseph J. Lewis of West Chester inquired into the matter and reported, "It was deemed to have a meaning in no wise derogatory to him personally, but rather as a compliment—rugged and coarse, indeed, but still a compliment—to those qualities which the common soldier most highly appreciates and most truly admires." Lewis decided that the supposition that Wayne was rash and impetuous "originates with writers of books and of magazine articles of a subsequent period, whose opinions on military matters must be taken with many grains of allowance." Lewis concluded his inquiry into Mad Anthony with the simple statement, "It has no rightful place in history, for it represents an idea which is false."[14]

General Wayne and the Pennsylvania Line were dispatched to assist the Marquis de Lafayette in Virginia, leaving their staging area at York, Pennsylvania, on May 26, 1781. An examination of Wayne's itinerary indicates that he preferred to have his men up at daybreak and in motion by sunrise, covering between eleven to eighteen miles per day, except when marching was curtailed by inclement weather. He joined with Lafayette's force, and on July 6, the two generals advanced upon what they thought to be the rear guard of Lord Cornwallis's army at Green Spring Farm near Jamestown, Virginia. Cornwallis deployed his troops so as to lure Wayne's men into a trap, concealing his main force behind screens of cavalry and infantry pickets. When the American discovered the danger, instead of ordering an immediate withdrawal as most other generals would have done, he boldly advanced his line as if to attack, then quickly withdrew. This unusual and unexpected maneuver confused Cornwallis, who allowed Lafayette's force to escape. Wayne's Pennsylvanians continued to maneuver around the Virginia countryside until the arrival of the Count de Grasse with a fleet of twenty-eight French ships of the line and Gen. Marquis de St. Simon with seven thousand French troops to reinforce Lafayette's command. High spirits over their arrival were tempered by events on the night of September 2, when Wayne and some staff officers rode to Lafayette's headquarters. A nervous American sentry fired upon the mounted party, and one ball struck Wayne in the thigh, inflicting his fourth wound, a nasty injury that never fully healed until the projectile was extracted in February 1786. That trauma also brought on an attack of gout, a disease that had not manifested itself up to this time but that would periodically reappear and eventually kill the general. Wayne would take little active part in the operations against Cornwallis's army at Yorktown, but he would recover sufficiently to attend the surrender ceremonies on horseback.[15]

Following the capitulation of Cornwallis, Wayne and his troops were ordered to join Maj. Gen. Nathaniel Greene in South Carolina. Shortly thereafter, Wayne learned that he had been given an independent assignment, "To reinstate, as far as might be possible, the authority of the Union within the limits of Georgia." On January 12, 1782, the "Hero of Stony Point," accompanied by one hundred dragoons, crossed into Georgia and began the task of bottling up the British garrison at Savannah. The British commander, learning of the approach of Wayne's mixed force of Continentals and militia, commanded his officers to collect all the provisions from the countryside, burn everything that could not be moved, and retire behind the city's entrenchments. In a letter to General Greene, Wayne explained the problems he had encountered in the desolate countryside: "The duty we have done in Georgia was more difficult than that imposed upon the children of Israel. They had only to make bricks without straw, but we have had provision, forage, and almost every other apparatus of war to procure without money: boats, bridges, &c. to build without materials except those taken from the stump: and, what was more difficult than all, to make *Whigs* out of *Tories*." Before being bottled up inside Savannah, British officers had carried on a brisk trade with the Creek and Cherokee Nations. Kind treatment and lavish presents from the Americans had kept most of these Indians peaceful at this stage of the war, though with one important exception.[16]

Guristersigo, a Creek chief, gathered together three hundred warriors and a few whites in response to a plea from the British garrison and traversed almost the entire width of Georgia to attack the Americans. Believing the only force that could threaten him lay in Savannah, the rear of Wayne's camp was guarded only by a single sentinel, who was quickly killed by the Creeks as they emerged from their hiding place in the swamps. Expecting to find only a small detachment, Guristersigo raised a cry, and his entire force swarmed into the American camp in the middle of the night on June 24, overrunning the gunners and capturing their cannons. After a few moments of confusion, Wayne's light troops retreated to headquarters, where they quickly formed into line and, charging with bayonets, drove the attackers back to the guns. Wayne's horse was killed under him, but he struggled free and led his men forward. The Indians were trying to turn the captured cannons toward the Americans when the Creeks discovered that "the rifle and the tomahawk are unavailing when confronted by the bayonet in close quarters." Guristersigo and seventeen of his warriors were killed before the Creeks fled in a precipitate retreat. Lt. Col. Thomas Posey led a party in pursuit and captured a dozen Creeks, who were brought back to camp and put to death by Wayne's order.[17]

The British shortly afterward found Savannah to be untenable and evacuated the city on the morning of July 11, 1782. Wayne's forces marched in and took possession that same afternoon, his troops having been ordered to make themselves "as respectable as possible" for the occasion.. To show their appreciation to the general who had driven out the British, Georgia legislators bestowed upon him the title to an 847-acre rice plantation, Richmond, formerly owned by a son of the loyalist governor, although it would be several years before he actually received a clear deed for the property. On August 9, Wayne left Savannah and marched to join Greene in South Carolina, where he lobbied without success for another independent command. Shortly after his arrival, the general was stricken by one of the fevers, this one probably malarial, that were endemic in the swamplands along the Atlantic seaboard of the southern states. This "Caitiff & Dangerous fever" prostrated Wayne for almost four weeks before he began to slowly recover his health, but the disorder would recur as long as he lived. After regaining enough strength to take the field, Wayne occupied Charleston, South Carolina, on December 14 after the British garrison marched aboard transports and sailed away. He spent the remainder of the war at routine duty in South Carolina and Georgia and, after demobilizing Greene's army, finally sailed home on July 27, 1783. For Brig. Gen. Anthony Wayne, the war was finally over, although he would continue with administrative assignments and receive a brevet to the rank of major general on September 30, 1783, several years after he should have been given the full rank.[18]

Lionized as one of America's most successful generals during the Revolution, Anthony Wayne did not adapt well to civilian life. He aspired to a political career, served a term in the Pennsylvania assembly, and, as a Federalist, attended the Pennsylvania convention that ratified the U.S. Constitution. Wayne spent several years trying to make his rice plantation a success but accomplished little more than plunging himself deeper and deeper into debt and temporarily lost the title to Waynesborough. Throughout his personal difficulties, Wayne continued to look fondly upon his military experiences and condemn those civilians and politicians who refused to acknowledge or reward the sacrifices of their soldiers. He summed up his attitude in a letter written to William Irvine, an old comrade in the Pennsylvania Line, on May 18, 1784:

> The revolution of America is an event, that will fill the brightest page of history to the end of time; & the conduct of her Officers & Soldiers will be handed down to the latest ages as a model of Virtue, perseverance & bravery;—the smallness of their numbers, & the unparalleled hardships & excess of difficulties & dangers that they have encountered, in the defence of this Country, from her *coldest* to her *hotest Sun:* places them in a point of view, hurtful to the eyes of the leaders of *faction & party,* who possessed neither the virtue or fortitude to meet the Enemy in the field, & seeing the involuntary deference *yet* paid by the bulk of the people to their protectors & Deliverers,—envy that green eyed mo[n]ster, will stimulate them to seize with avidity every pretext, to depreciate the merits of those who have filled the breach & bled at every pore;—nor is this Caitiff principle the growth of any particular Country or Climate.

Wayne concluded his discourse with the personal observation, "I believe that there are too many of our Citizens that would not hesitate, to *wipe* off the large debt due to the army, with a Sponge."[19]

As his dreams of becoming a rice planter evaporated in clouds of debt, Anthony Wayne turned to politics in Georgia, announcing himself as a candidate for the congressional seat in the First District and running against the incumbent, an old comrade named James Jackson. His 1790 campaign was described as "successful but flawed," being marked "by horrendous corruption," although Wayne was not personally involved in the frauds, which in at least one case resulted in "reporting more votes for Wayne in one precinct than there were eligible voters." Aided by enthusiastic, if unprincipled, supporters, Wayne won election to the Second U.S. Congress, although his victory was contested by Jackson. Ultimately, Jackson's appeal was upheld, and Wayne's seat was declared vacant on March 21, 1792. Richard C. Knopf captured the discouraging situation in which this former hero of the Revolution found himself upon being removed from office: "His return, however, to his ancestral Waynesborough, had been cut off because of disagreements between him and his wife, Polly. His reputation as a philanderer was well known—he really did not try to hide it—and, thus, in 1792, he found himself homeless, divorced from his family, and nearly penniless in Philadelphia." Within ten days of being booted out of office, Secretary of War Henry Knox stepped forward and offered Anthony Wayne command of the U.S. Army.[20]

Maj. Gen. Anthony Wayne. From *The National Portrait Gallery of Distinguished Americans*, 1834.

After Wayne accepted command of the army, he quickly discovered that there was as yet no army to command. The War Department had prematurely released a list of four men who had been appointed to the rank of brigadier general, but Daniel Morgan, John Brooks, and Marinus Willet quickly declined; only James Wilkinson accepted his appointment. Willet's response was particularly mortifying. In a letter to President

Washington, he confided: "It has been uniformly my opinion that the United States ought to avoid an Indian war. I have generally conceived this to be our wisest policy." This public relations disaster was compounded by yet another ill-timed release to the press, in which Otho H. Williams was appointed to replace Morgan and Rufus Putnam in place of Willet. Although Henry Knox had explained that his appointment "would be highly gratifying to the President," Williams quickly wrote back that he was in "precarious" health and asked to be excused. In fact, he wrote, "I could not, at this time, accept a command in the army, even if the President were to think me worthy of commanding in chief." Putnam accepted his commission, but a behind-the-scenes attempt to persuade William Hull to replace Brooks failed. Hull wrote that he would have accepted if the commission had been offered immediately, but he had to support his family of six children, the eldest aged nine, and his father-in-law was on his deathbed with many legal entanglements unresolved. The end result of this confusion was that instead of four subordinate generals, only two accepted their appointments, and both had been rivals for Anthony Wayne's job.[21]

During the deliberations over who should command the army, both Washington and Knox had taken into account which officers were heavy drinkers. Although they had been unable to determine whether Wayne was "a little addicted to the bottle," both men knew firsthand that drinking and its consequent dissipation pervaded all ranks. In fact, "the appellation of old soldier was always associated with the idea of a hard drinking man." Washington confided his feelings on that subject in a letter to Knox, saying, "so long as the vice of drunkenness exists in the Army so long I hope, Ejections of those officers who are found guilty of it will continue." Knox expressed his own opinion in letters to his two ranking generals. To General Wilkinson he wrote, "I hope in God that a spirit will arise among the officers in such a degree that every officer who is a drunkard shall be expelled [from] the Army." The secretary emphasized this same thought in a message to Wayne, exclaiming, "The crime of drunkenness is so undignified and so unsuitable to the character of an Officer that it is much to be desired that it should be expelled the army entirely." A second letter on this subject offered the hope that Wayne "will be able to purge your Army of drunken and unsuitable characters whether commissioned, non commissioned or privates."[22]

Whiskey was considered "indispensible" during this period of American history, and it was widely remarked that "a man could not be born, married, or buried without it." Drunkenness, accompanied by the consequent evils of idleness and gambling, was certainly widespread among officers stationed in the frontier posts. Judge Jacob Burnet recalled, "This may be attributed to the fact, that they had been several years in the wilderness, cut off from all society but their own, with but few comforts or conveniences at hand, and no amusements but such as their own ingenuity could invent." To combat an overwhelming sense of boredom and isolation, Burnet remembered that "the bottle, the dice-box, and the card-table, were among the expedients resorted to, because they were the nearest at hand, and the most easily procured." He also claimed that settlers in and around Cincinnati picked up these same intemperate habits from contact with the soldiers, a rather ludicrous assertion.[23]

The army desperately needed competent and sober officers to command the recruits that would flow in from the various recruiting stations, and completing the officer corps was a top priority. After Wilkinson's promotion to brigadier general, the offices of lieutenant colonel in both the First and Second Regiments were vacant. There were three majors in the First Regiment. The senior major, John F. Hamtramck, was considered "an excellent disciplinarian," but his actions while holding independent command "did not appear to have such a result as to mark the commandant with any eclat, or as possessing uncommon talents." There was some question as to whether Hamtramck was the "proper person" to command the regiment. Maj. David Ziegler ranked behind Hamtramck and, although his fitness at that rank was unquestioned, there seemed to be reservations about whether he "has talents sufficient to command a regiment of the magnitude proposed." The third major, Richard Call, was presumed unpromotable due to unspecified "imputations" against him. Ziegler's resignation, effective March 5, 1792, exacerbated the problem by creating yet another vacancy.[24]

There were no majors in the Second Regiment. Jonathan Heart had been killed in St. Clair's battle. Lemuel Trescott and John Burnham had both resigned after Wilkinson, originally a civilian, had been promoted lieutenant colonel over them. In his letter of resignation, Burnham admitted, "it is not in my power to do justice to the public and to myself in the office which I sustain," and his departure would mean that "others will be brought forward better able to serve." There was no public criticism of Burnham, but the resignation of Trescott was said to be "universally approved by all military characters." Following these resignations, the old First and Second Regiments desperately needed two lieutenant colonels and four majors. In Wilkinson's personal opinion, the officer pool had few men worthy of their commissions, the best men preferring to make their fortunes in civilian life, leaving only "the Beasts & Blockheads" to staff the army. He claimed to know of majors and captains who could just barely read or write.[25]

Assessing the abilities of the four senior captains, Secretary of War Knox considered them plain, brave men who had no claims of distinction, although all had served honorably during the Revolution. Knox believed that promotion above the grade of captain should not be based on talent, the judging of which "would require, in practice, more impartiality and more accurate judgments than commonly belong to human nature." In his opinion, "seniority is the surest rule to be adopted generally for promotion, always however retaining to the Government the right of extraordinary promotion." Deferring to this system, Capt. Erkuries Beatty thus became a major in the First Regiment and Capts. David Strong, John Smith, and Joseph Asheton filled the vacant majorities in the Second Regiment. Although Congress had approved three new regiments, the War Department had decided to organize only two of them, naturally designated the Third and Fourth Regiments. These regiments needed two lieutenant colonels and six majors, and Knox called on men with experience in Indian campaigning to fill the positions of major. Thomas Butler, Henry Gaither, John Clark, and Henry Bedinger had all commanded battalions of levies during St. Clair's campaign. Captain Trueman had led a company of St. Clair's cavalry on November 4, 1791, and William McMahon was one of the most intrepid and experienced Indian scouts on the frontier. While these selections filled all vacant majorities, the positions of lieutenant colonel in all four regiments remained unfilled as the War Department waited to see which of the majors should prove worthy of promotion.[26]

Vacancies at the company level in the First and Second Regiments were filled by advancing lieutenants to captains and ensigns to lieutenants.. The artillery battalion, crippled by normal attrition and heavy losses on November 4, 1791, was similarly reorganized under command of Maj. Henry Burbeck. The captains of his four artillery companies were Mahlon Ford, John Peirce, Moses Porter, and Daniel McLane. The War Department commissioned eighteen new ensigns to complete these infantry and artillery organizations.[27]

St. Clair's failure had emphasized the need for cavalry in Indian campaigns, so the War Department created a squadron of light dragoons under the command of Maj. Michael Rudolph, formerly a captain in the First Regiment. His captains were John Watts, John Craig, Lawrence Manning, and John Stake, all veterans of the Revolution. The first three of these officers refused to accept their commissions, perhaps declining to serve under a former infantry officer. The real reason may have been pride. One friend of Secretary Knox advised him that, at least in Massachusetts, "you will find but few of the Old Officers from this State that are desireous of engaging in the Service unless they are promoted one grade at least above that they held in the late Army." This embarrassing situation, reminiscent of the War Department's problem with its appointments to brigadier, was ended by the creation of another list of captains, so Watts was succeeded by William O. Winston, Craig by Jedediah Rogers, and Manning by Henry Bowyer.[28]

President Washington signed commissions for twelve new captains to command companies in the newly authorized Third and Fourth Regiments. Their names and the home states where they were ordered to recruit their companies were: William Eaton, Vermont; Isaac Guion, New York; Zebulon Pike, New Jersey; Jacob Slough, Pennsylvania; James Wells, Delaware; Henry Carbery, William Buchanan, and William Lewis, Maryland; Nicholas Hannah, Joseph Brock, and John Heth, Virginia; and Joseph Kerr, North Carolina. The latter company was selected for service south of the Ohio River, while all of the others were destined for duty against the Indian confederation north of that river. These infantry units would be complemented by twelve new companies of riflemen. Captains of the six rifle companies to be raised in Pennsylvania were Edward Butler, John Guthrie, Richard Sparks, William Faulkner, Uriah Springer, and John Cooke. The six Virginia rifle companies would be commanded by Benjamin Biggs, John Crawford, Thomas Lewis, William Lewis, Hugh Caperton, and James Stephenson. As with the dragoon appointments, several of these captains also declined to serve. John Guthrie was succeeded by William Powers, who was himself succeeded by John Cummins. Benjamin Biggs declined and was replaced by William Lowther, who was replaced by William Preston. William Lewis was superseded by Alexander Gibson, and Hugh Caperton by Howell Lewis.[29]

CHAPTER 3

Filling the Ranks

OFFICERS FROM THE TWO OLD regiments and the two newly constituted regiments spread out across the country to begin the arduous task of filling the ranks of their companies. Each of them carried along his detailed instructions for the recruiting service, which stressed that officers must conduct themselves "with candor, integrity, and industry." Noting that recruits often became "unwarily and unworthily entangled, contrary to their intentions," the War Department realized that such men either deserted or set bad examples for others. Recruiters were cautioned not to abuse the system in an effort to fill their companies. In order to avoid mistakes by officers who had no experience in recruiting soldiers, the War Department sent each of them a form containing general rules for their conduct. Soldiers were to be enlisted for a term of three years, unless sooner discharged, and each was to receive a bounty of eight dollars to be paid only after swearing to the following oath before a magistrate: "I, ———, do solemnly swear (or affirm, as the case may be) to bear true allegiance to the United States of America, and to serve them honestly and faithfully against all their enemies or opposers whomsoever, and to observe and obey the orders of the President of the United States of America, and the orders of the officers appointed over me according to the articles of war." Prior to taking this oath, prospective soldiers were read the regulations regarding mutiny and desertion, pay, rations, clothing, and compensation in case of disability incurred during their service. Officers were to receive two dollars "for the trouble and expence of inlisting each recruit," although this payment would be withheld if the recruit deserted before leaving the rendezvous.

Each new soldier, with the exception of musicians, had to be between the ages of eighteen and forty-five; at least five feet, five inches tall, "without shoes"; and "healthy, robust, and sound in his limbs and body." He should not be intoxicated at enlistment, nor could he swear to the oath until after a waiting period of at least twenty-four hours. Officers were forbidden to enlist Negroes, mulattos, Indians, or vagrants. If possible, recruits were to be "natives of fair conduct, or foreigners of good character for sobriety and fidelity, and who have been some years in the country." According to these instructions, quality was stressed over quantity. Yet officers were encouraged to exert themselves in raising their companies, for "any remarkable deficiency" in filling a company would be reported directly to the president, who could revoke their commissions. While the War Department assumed that quality soldiers would be forthcoming, in actuality, captains and lieutenants generally took anyone who could be had.[1]

To facilitate signing up new soldiers, recruiting rendezvous were established throughout the New England and Mid-Atlantic states. These were located at Bennington, Vermont; Springfield, Massachusetts; Albany, New York; Christiana, Delaware; Middletown, Connecticut; Elizabethtown, Brunswick, and Trenton, New Jersey; and Baltimore, Chestertown, Fredericktown, and Hagerstown, Maryland. Hoping to obtain more response from the threatened frontiers, the army also sent recruiters to six points in Pennsylvania and seven in Virginia. The Pennsylvania stations were Philadelphia, Lancaster, Reading, Northumberland, Union Town, and Washington, while the Old Dominion rendezvous points were Richmond, Alexandria, Fredericksburg, Fincastle, Staunton, Winchester, and Shepherdstown.[2]

As soon as recruits began to assemble at a rendezvous, they were to be taught "by gentle methods" how to conduct themselves as soldiers. They spent at least four hours every day learning the principles of discipline and drill, supplemented by instruction in sanitation and proper nutrition. John Robert Shaw, who acted as drill sergeant during this period, recalled how he handled the recruits in his company. He first divided his men into those who had some military experience and those who had not. The former became the "grand squad," and the latter went into an "awkward squad." As the awkward newcomers progressed, they moved into the grand squad. Drill was conducted according to Baron Frederick von Steuben's *Regulations for the Order and Discipline of the Troops of the United States*. Shaw remembered that he took "particular care to give them an erect and soldierly appearance, both in attitude, look, and walk." After teaching the men to look like soldiers, the drill sergeant then "taught them to wheel and form in every position, from right to left, and from left to right, and from the centre, until I had them sufficiently versed in all the evolutions." Only then did the recruits receive their muskets, old French Charleville models left over from the Revolution.[3]

Most officers recruited in their hometowns, where they were generally well known and had a network of friends and acquaintances, then sent their new enlistees on to the established rendezvous for their region. Capt. John Pratt had been born in Hartford, Connecticut, on October 12, 1753, and joined the Fourth Regiment, Pennsylvania Line, as an ensign in July 1779. He was promoted lieutenant the following May and ended his Revolutionary service as regimental quartermaster of the Third Pennsylvania. Pratt joined the U.S. Army as a lieutenant on July 15, 1785, and was promoted captain in the First Regiment on March 4, 1791. Sent east to recruit in the spring of 1792, the captain opened his office in the city coffeehouse in Middletown, Connecticut, and quickly placed an advertisement in the *Middlesex (Conn.) Gazette, The Connecticut Courant,* and *The*

American Mercury. Pratt's announcement, promising "a bounty of eight silver dollars," "elegant cloathing," "fine accomodations," and "the best provision furnished in abundance," read in part: "He takes this opportunity to urge all those young gentlemen who are possessed of enterprise, and have a wish to render their country very important services, to repair without loss of time to his recruiting rendezvous in the city of Middletown, where they can be freed from the anxiety of providing a support by hard and constant labour; he has a sample of his young soldiers there, who are daily entertaining themselves in amusements honorable, beneficial, and perfectly satisfactory." Captain Pratt was ably assisted by Ens. Daniel Bissell, another Hartford native, who at the age of twelve had served in the militia for two months during the Revolution. He had joined the First Regiment in 1788 at the age of eighteen and served with distinction for three years before being discharged as a sergeant on May 19, 1791. Joining in St. Clair's campaign as an unpaid volunteer, Bissell fought in the terrible battle of November 4. The young ensign later recalled that he "purchased my first Commission by the efforts of my bayonet on that fatal and memorable day, *by bayoneting two of the enemy in front of the line in presence of Colo Dark & other Officers,* receiving a Slight wound, my hat perforated with balls, Cartridge box shot from my Side & musket shattered in my hands."[4]

Other officers competed with Captain Pratt in the race to fill their companies. Capt. John Hutchinson Buell used his own home as a recruiting station and, like Pratt, advertised in the state's newspapers. His notice in *The Connecticut Courant* stated, "any young Gentlemen that have thoughts of ingaging, and will call at my house in Hebron, shall have a fair stating of the business, after which they will be at liberty to act their pleasure." Buell was another veteran of the Revolution, his service having commenced in April 1775, when he marched with his neighbors to the relief of the minutemen of Lexington and Concord. Buell's recruiting efforts were compromised by the lingering illness and ultimate death of his wife, Phoebe, from consumption on October 20, 1792. Thereafter, he was forced to tend not only to his official business but also to his three young, motherless children. Ens. Samuel Drake also tried to entice the young men of Connecticut into joining up. Operating from "the sign of the BULL'S HEAD in the Main Street" of Hartford, this young officer promised that military service would be "easy, pleasing and profitable." Drake urged all men to "take the road that leads to honor," with himself as "an experienced Guide, who has trod the path with singular satisfaction."[5]

At least three officers canvassed the state of Massachusetts for volunteers. Lt. Richard H. Greaton arrived in Boston in mid-February 1792. He had served in the Third Massachusetts from 1781 to 1783, then joined St. Clair's army and was wounded on November 4, 1791. Ens. Edward D. Turner, a native of Boston, had preceded Greaton to that city, where both men began recruiting for the Second Regiment. Lt. Cornelius Lyman, who had served over two years in the Second and Tenth Massachusetts and was also a veteran of St. Clair's campaign, began recruiting in Springfield. By the end of July, Lyman would be promoted captain and Turner lieutenant, but Greaton's promotion to captain would be delayed for nearly a year. One of the first duties performed by these three officers was to serve as a court-martial for a sergeant and five privates of the Second Regiment. Charged with desertion, the soldiers claimed that they were driven to leave by "the approbious insults and sneers respecting their pay, &c. which they were continually receiving from the vulgar part of the community." Five of the soldiers were found guilty and sentenced to corporal punishment. The sergeant received one hundred lashes, while four of the five privates received seventy lashes each. One private was pardoned "on account of his sometimes being insane!"[6]

There was good reason for plebeians to ridicule the pay of a soldier. Better pay was available in a number of occupations, but perhaps the best comparison would be with the wages of common laborers during this period. While privates received only three dollars per month, hands engaged in cutting a road from the Delaware River to Cayuga Lake in west central New York were paid eight dollars per month. The Western Inland Lock-Navigation Company sought to hire two hundred "able bodied labourers" at a half dollar per day under the following conditions:

> to begin work on each day at sunrise, to be allowed one hour for breakfast, and one hour for dinner, until the 15th of June—from thence, until the 15th of August, two hours for dinner, and thence forward one hour, and then to work until sunset. To be allowed no provisions nor liquor at the expense of the company; but as it may be inconvenient for them to provide their own provisions and liquor, good salted pork, salted beef, and fresh meat when it can be procured, flour, pease, Indian meal, and rum, will be provided, and sold to them at the first cost, with only the expence of transportation added thereto.
>
> Each company will be allowed four shillings per day to hire a cook to dress their victuals; kettles for cooking and wooden bowls will be furnished them at the expence of the Navigation Company; but they must find their own bedding and tools.

To ensure that the company received a good return for its investment, the contract stipulated, "No wages will be allowed them when they are sick and do not work, nor on Sunday." It is readily apparent that while higher-paying employment was available, men digging canals and cutting roads worked much harder than did soldiers, who might spend a few hours a day in drill and guard duty.[7]

Like their counterparts in Connecticut, officers in Boston posted their own advertisements in the city press, hoping to lure prospective soldiers to their office at 28 State Street. The notice dated April 18, 1792, read: "To the sons of Ambition—Those noble fellows whose courage and superiority of soul dictate to them to enter the list of FAME, have now a fair and advantageous opportunity—Her field is now open, and filled with every inducement for a Soldier: every necessary of life, and every chance for fortune: It will be your fault if she does not stamp on your names HERO; to be caught by every ear, and lisped by every mouth to the latest posterity. Who is there that is not fired by the prospect, and would not wish to possess it?" To any man longing for adventure, the publication of a small pamphlet in Stockbridge, Massachusetts, must have been a stirring call to action. This pamphlet, titled *The Remarkable Adventures of Jackson Johonnet*, virtually cried out to all willing to undertake a hazardous enterprise in the western wilderness. Johonnet had served under both Harmar and St. Clair, and his story contained "an account of his captivity, sufferings and escape from the Kickapoo Indians."[8]

Capts. William Kersey and Cornelius Sedam set up their offices in the old barracks at New Brunswick, New Jersey. Kersey announced his arrival in the press and expressed his intention "to recruit one hundred good and able bodied YOUNG MEN, of a fair character." Kersey continued, "They are to serve to the westward, where there will be an opportunity of exploring a delightful country, where they may if so inclined, after discharged, settle to great advantage." But Kersey was an old soldier himself, rising from private to brevet captain in New Jersey regiments during the Revolution and joining the First Regiment in 1784 as an ensign. He showed his understanding of enlisted men by simultaneously publishing a public notice to the citizens of New Brunswick, advising them "not to trust any of the soldiers or recruits belonging to the 1st U.S. Regiment as the subscriber will not settle any accounts that he is not consulted on."[9]

Captain Sedam was also a veteran of the Revolution, joining the New Jersey militia at the age of sixteen and rising to the rank of ensign, as well as the campaigns of Harmar and St. Clair. Like Captain Kersey, Sedam posted a recruiting advertisement in *The Brunswick (N.J.) Gazette*, but his was a work of art compared with other such notices. His fulsome and eloquent appeal read:

> The advantages to be derived from an expedition in the western territory, must be obvious to all; the many who have already amassed considerable landed fortunes in that country, I should suppose a sufficient inducement for all those who are not possessed of real property.—Likewise all worthy fellows that are unfortunately connected with women who come under the denomination of termagants [scolding or abusive women], now is their time to get clear of the greatest earthly curse possible;—also young men whose parents have through age become morose and parsimonious will here be tenderly treated and furnished with a sufficiency of money. All these circumstances taken into consideration, what life can be equal to that of a Soldier! If disabled in service they are amply provided for while living, and after death their memories will be handed down to posterity as the saviours and protectors of their country.

Who, indeed, would not want to be a soldier after reading such a notice![10]

There were a few tragedies associated with the recruiting business, but the most serious involved Capt. James Wells. A lieutenant in a Delaware regiment during the Revolution, Wells had established his headquarters at Christiana and began to raise his company. But recruits were apparently hard to come by, and Wells quickly exceeded his financial allowance, going into debt by some two hundred dollars. When ordered to report at Pittsburgh with his recruits, this embarrassing situation caused him to remain in Delaware. An urgent appeal for relief to the War Department was summarily refused. On June 9, Captain Wells seated himself at a table in his office; wrote a letter explaining what he was about to do; sealed it; addressed it to his lieutenant, William Diven; and stepped into an adjoining room. As Diven opened the mysterious letter, a pistol shot suddenly rang out from behind the closed door. Rushing in, the lieutenant found Captain Wells dead of a self-inflicted gunshot wound.[11]

Misfortune also visited some of the newly recruited enlisted men. When the first detachment of Stakes's company marched from Elizabethtown, New Jersey, to Trenton, one of his troopers dozed off, fell from his horse, and broke his neck. In late July, Sergeant Keech was instructing Hannah's company in the manual of arms at its camp in Alexandria. One of the corporals had mistakenly taken up a loaded musket and, when Keech commanded him to "Present!" and "Fire!" he fired a ball into the sergeant's body and "put a period to his existence." Keech was described as "a young man of great military promise," and his military funeral was attended by a crowd of civilians as well as his fellow soldiers. They interred him in the burying ground of the Episcopal church, and a minister delivered a discourse based upon the Biblical text "Wherefore let him that thinketh he standeth, take heed, lest he fall."[12]

Another incident in Richmond nearly resulted in fatal consequences. About the first of August, four soldiers left their encampment near that city and went to a neighboring farm in search of something to augment their sumptuous and tasty rations. As a precaution against a less-than-patriotic farmer, the men took along their muskets. They soon spied a melon patch and began to pick the succulent fruit. An overseer came running up, ordered them off, and waved a shotgun for emphasis. Three soldiers took heed, but one man refused to be intimidated and continued to pick melons. The overseer promptly fired a load of birdshot into the soldier's belly, whereupon another soldier fired his musket at the overseer, hitting him in the arm and shoulder. A friend of the overseer then charged the soldiers with his cane and disarmed one of them before driving the others away, leaving their wounded comrade behind.[13]

While these various misfortunes were of interest to local authorities, Capt. William Preston found his actions being questioned by Congress. Born at Greenfield, the family home in Botetourt County, Virginia, on September 5, 1770, Preston was too young to serve during the Revolution. As a youth, he had an interest in military affairs and received a commission as cornet in the Montgomery County militia at the age of eighteen. After the defeat of St. Clair, he served as an ensign in the militia company of Capt. John Preston, assigned to defend the counties of Wythe, Russell, and Montgomery from incursions by Indians. Although commissioned captain in the Second Regiment on March 5, 1792, William continued to fill the office of county surveyor until June 5, 1793, when the county courts ruled him ineligible to hold that office while serving in the army. Preston was a physically imposing man, standing six feet, five inches, and weighing at one time near four hundred pounds, with strength to match his size. One man remembered the captain as "a man of wit, daring and genial temper."

Captain Preston's trouble came about when his brother Francis ran for Congress against Abraham Trigg. William's company of some sixty to seventy men was quartered near the county courthouse. On election day, he marched his troops around the courthouse several times, then paraded them near the front door. Showing their support for candidate Preston, some soldiers threatened to thrash anyone who voted for Trigg. At one point, three soldiers blocked the entrance when an outspoken Trigg supporter attempted to vote. Another soldier knocked down a magistrate overseeing the election. Eventually, the unarmed soldiers were driven back to camp by a crowd of civilians, who promptly retreated after the fighting men retrieved their muskets and fired a few warning shots. Trigg contested the election of Francis Preston, but the Committee on Elections of the House of Representatives, after hearing all of the evidence, ended the affair by voting to seat Preston.[14]

Other Virginia officers made preparations for their departures by completing last-minute legal details. Capt. Howell Lewis of the Third Regiment, "being desirous of doing every justice to his creditors," hired two attorneys, John Peyton and Elias Langham, "to make use of his estate, both real and personal, as far as may be necessary, to satisfy his creditors." Peyton and Langham urged claimants "to bring them forward to us as speedily as possible" so that their claims could be settled. Capt. William O. Winston, lately sheriff of Hanover County, could not leave Virginia before the settlement of a series of lawsuits involving "one hundred and twenty-four Negroes, forty-five horses, two hundred and eight cattle, and twenty-two hogs."[15]

Captain Winston's personal business resulted in a prolonged delay in Richmond, which in turn prompted a long and animated correspondence with Secretary of War Knox. When Knox criticized him for not regularly filing reports, the captain responded on August 3 that "the neglect has been in my Subalterns in my absence." Although ordered to march his men to Pittsburgh after they had received their clothing, he begged to be excused. When Knox failed to reply, Winston wrote again on August 22 and blamed the secretary for his continued stay in Richmond, complaining, "had I of got your answer and approbation my Business would of been complete."

Knox responded on September 6 with a mild rebuke: "It is an unfortunate event that you have not been successful in raising your troop and it is equally so that at the time when all your exertions are wanted to recruit your number you should apply for permission to attend to your private concerns." Noting that Winston had only raised thirty-one of the required eighty enlisted men, Knox urged him to put forth "the highest exertions" to fill his troop before departing from Richmond on October 1, "with out fail." After receiving Knox's letter, the captain assured his superior that he intended to visit "a part of the Country where in all probability I may meet with some Recruits." By this time, Major Rudolph had been so disappointed with Winston's performance that he personally began to recruit for the Virginian's deficient unit. Winston then criticized Rudolph by telling Knox that the major "has only twenty men" when he had claimed to have "nearly as many as would complete my Troop!!"

Assuming that Winston had by now settled his private affairs, Knox sent marching orders on October 5 (four days after his previous deadline had passed). The captain was commanded to march his recruits "yourself with your Cornet, and let your Lieut. remain to complete your Troop, as your presence is much wanted at Head Quarters." Despite these specific orders from Knox, Winston still refused to join the army at Pittsburgh.

The secretary wrote again on March 22, 1793: "I am surprised to hear that you are yet at Richmond. It is my positive Orders, that you immediately repair to the Head Quarters of Major General Wayne.... The pressing demand for Officers on the Frontiers requires that you should go forward without further delay."

Winston wrote back on April 4, stating, "necessity has compel'd me to be detain'd." After returning from a trip to western North Carolina, the captain found himself without money enough for a journey to Pittsburgh. He explained: "What moneys I have rec'd of the public is exausted in equiping myself.—As soon as I can raise money to carry me on to Head Quarters [I] shall commence my Jurney." Apparently, Winston made little effort to raise the necessary cash, for an obviously frustrated Knox wrote to him again on July 29. This latest message began, "In case this Letter should find you at Richmond or any other place in Virginia, it is my positive orders that you will immediately repair to the Head Quarters of Major Genl Wayne, at Fort Washington on the western frontier."

This was no longer a message that could be ignored. Major Rudolph had resigned on July 17, so by virtue of his seniority, Captain Winston was now commanding officer of the dragoon squadron. He had reached this important office despite spending over a year in completing his personal business and virtually ignoring the company he had been authorized to raise. Knox was serious now and wanted an answer as to whether or not Winston would join the army, warning that he would "be under the disagreeable necessity of reporting you to the President of the United States." As if to emphasize his point, Knox closed, "No further excuse will be admitted." Winston replied on August 12 and assured the secretary that he would join his command "without farther delay." Then in typical fashion, he closed his letter with the remark, "I hope to leave this in a few days."[16]

Fortunately for the country, not all Virginia officers were as dilatory as Winston. Capt. James Stephenson, born on March 20, 1764, had served as a lieutenant during St. Clair's battle and was one of the more conscientious officers appointed in the spring of 1792. The residents of Berkeley County always remembered Stephenson for a duel that he was to have fought with Col. William Darke. Both men were of proven courage, and they had agreed to fight their duel with swords. Stephenson, of small and slight build, came armed with a rapier. Darke, a giant of a man, arrived carrying "a broad sword, as large as an ordinary mowing scythe." When the seconds began to move the combatants into position, the disparity of men and weapons proved just too ridiculous, and they burst out in uproarious laughter. Stephenson and Darke, until then intent upon killing one another, quickly realized how silly they looked, and the duel was averted.[17]

In late July, Captain Stephenson and his company put on a mock battle for the residents of Shepherdstown, Virginia. The unit was divided into two groups, each beginning at the opposite side of a grove of trees. The first group, under Stephenson, wore their uniforms, while the second group, led by Lt. James Glenn, were "dressed and painted in the Indian mode." Stephenson and Glenn sent spies forward, followed closely by their main bodies. Soon the fighting began in earnest. The "Indians" skulked behind trees and fired at the soldiers, who maneuvered to surround them. Finally, the soldiers charged and harassed the enemy as they fled from the field. There was praise for all the participants. One observer noted that it "would not be possible more exactly to copy the attire, paint, sculk or whoop of the aborigines" and praised "the most masterful evolutions and firings" of the soldiers. Stephenson's exhibition was summed up in this fashion: "The day was favorable, the scene so judiciously and seasonably changed, as both to surprise and delight; while the good conduct of both officers and soldiers, was strikingly conspicuous." While this military exercise gave the Virginians a chance to practice their tactics, the good will built up with the citizens was probably of a more lasting benefit.[18]

Later that fall, Stephenson marched the last of his recruits to Hagerstown, where he formed a junction with soldiers from the three new Maryland companies. This combined force left that city on November 8 under the command of Captain Stephenson and Ens. Campbell Smith to join the main army at Pittsburgh. It was one of the most arduous marches imaginable. On November 11, the detachment reached Old Town, Pennsylvania, where it was forced to stay two days after running out of provisions. Rain began to fall on November 13, and the soldiers slogged through mud and rain for five straight days. On the eighteenth, the weather became so bad that, as the captain recalled, "we relinquished our Tents and the men slept in the barn." Next day the rain turned to snow, and Stephenson's party halted on November 20 and remained at Beesontown four days until the weather cleared. The detachment reached Red Stone on November 25 and, after procuring a boat the following morning, Stephenson embarked his men, set off down the Monongahela, and arrived in Pittsburgh at midnight.[19]

Capt. Bezaleel Howe was the recruiting officer stationed at West Point, New York. Born on November 28, 1750, he was a descendant of John Howe, the first white settler of Marlborough, Massachusetts. His military career began only six days after the Battle of Lexington. A company had been raised to join the colonial army at Boston, and the young Howe recalled: "On the morning when the soldiers were to march, I stood looking on. One of the recruits, an old man, was surrounded by his wife and daughters who hung about his neck and wept bitterly. The scene affected my heart and I dashed up to him and said, 'Give me your gun and I will go for you and if the Government ever gets able to give me a gun I'll send the old thing back to you.'" The new recruit marched to Boston, where he saw limited action, although he remembered, "I loaded and fired several times but the old gun kicked so it almost dislocated my shoulder." After fighting as an enlisted man at Long Island and White Plains, Howe was promoted lieutenant in the First New Hampshire. He was detached from that regiment and assigned to General Washington's Life Guards on September 5, 1782. Serving in that capacity until the war ended, Howe was selected to command the escort that returned the general's personal baggage and important papers to Mount Vernon.

Howe's distinguished wartime record guaranteed him a commission when the Second Regiment of Infantry was organized in 1791 for service in St. Clair's army, although he missed the disaster of November 4. Captain Howe was ordered to assume recruiting duties at West Point in April 1792 and began funneling recruits off to Wayne's army almost immediately. Life was easy at this established military post. Howe's wife and daughter came to stay with him, the household chores being done by a black slave. The captain was paid forty dollars a month, plus all his expenses, in addition to two dollars for each recruit he enlisted, a total income much higher than that for officers of similar rank serving in the field. He befriended a number of recruits and took a personal interest in their careers as a way of repaying anonymous benefactors who had befriended him during his own formative years. Although a kindly guardian angel to some recruits, Howe had no patience with those who chafed under his military discipline, and some soldiers joined Wayne's army with marks from the whip on their backs.[20]

Cornet Solomon Van Rensselaer was the complete antithesis of Bezaleel Howe. While Howe was a self-made man and seasoned veteran of the Revolution, Van Rensselaer was a mere youth descended from the most prominent of the old Dutch patroon families. Born on August 6, 1774, Solomon was the fourth child of Maj. Gen. Henry R. Van Rensselaer, whose estate, Greenbush, lay along the Hudson River opposite Albany. Following the defeat of St. Clair, the young man announced to his father "that he *must go* if only as a private soldier to join the army." General Van Rensselaer humored his son by pulling a few strings and arranging for him to be commissioned a cornet in the dragoons on March 14, 1792, although he was not yet eighteen years of age. Some of the family, at least, thought that Solomon had made a serious mistake in choosing a military career. His uncle, Peter Van Rensselaer, wrote that "he left his *Studies* too soon—and entered in the Army with a full Determination of grafting the Soldier on the Citizen, and sacrafice a Good prospect with an unalterable determination of devoting his life to his Country, and to the Profession of Arms." Admitting that "no further prosecution of the Sciences can be made but what he obtains in the Army," his uncle requested that General Wayne take Solomon under his "patronage and Care."[21]

Cornet Van Rensselaer accepted his appointment, "with joy" according to his daughter, and was assigned to Capt. Jedediah Rogers's dragoon troop, which was headquartered in Albany, although the young officer did his recruiting among the farmers and villagers of Rensselaer County. The two officers met with only moderate success in their search for volunteers before being ordered by the War Department to march to New Brunswick, New Jersey, with their recruits. This dragoon detachment was supposed to be supplemented by men raised at Hagerstown, Maryland, by Lt. William Davidson. But Davidson's conduct, both as an officer and as a recruiter, was reprehensible. The lieutenant enlisted Morris Clark in Philadelphia on April 12, appointed him a sergeant, and ordered him to commence gathering men at Hagerstown, concentrating his efforts on "the Yeomanry of the Country of good Character and Morals." Clark arrived at the rendezvous on April 27 and waited anxiously for Davidson to either forward funds or come in person and direct the recruiting, but neither occurred. After waiting several days, the earnest sergeant borrowed "several small sums of money" from local residents, promising that they would be repaid before the troops left town. Morris then set to work searching for volunteers, not an easy task given that Capt. William Lewis was already recruiting an infantry company there.

In the absence of any commissioned officer, Sergeant Clark bore the entire responsibility of the dragoon rendezvous. He canvassed the area for volunteers, arranged for their care and lodging, pursued those who deserted, and generally kept order and discipline. Although Lieutenant Davidson did stop by on two occasions, he brought no money and did not stay, leaving Clark to go deeper into debt as he struggled to raise his quota of dragoons. By August, the sergeant had enlisted a dozen men, paying their bounties with still more borrowed money.

Responding to an order from the War Department, Davidson appeared in Hagerstown to march Clark's recruits to Pittsburgh. Clark immediately appealed to his commander for funds to pay off the debts he had incurred in the public interest. Aside from reimbursing one individual, the sergeant found that he "could not prevail upon him to pay any of these sums." Naturally, when Davidson and the dragoon detachment left town on the morning of August 10, Clark's creditors filed suit against him. As the dragoons marched away, Sheriff John Shryock marched Morris Clark to the Hagerstown jail. That evening, Captain Lewis and a number of Clark's creditors posted bail for the luckless sergeant so that he might plead his case to the War Department. A petition to Secretary of War Knox was endorsed by a number of Hagerstown gentlemen, who certified that "said Sergeant Morris Clark, since his arrival here, has been attentive and diligent in his duty, orderly and circumspect in his behaviour, and had added much to the respectability of the Troop."

Davidson did not long survive his shabby treatment of Clark. On September 18, he submitted a letter of resignation, claiming that he found himself "unhappy in my present situation and beg Leave to Depart from the Army and Return Home." Wayne accepted this resignation the same day, stating in his general orders that "he never wishes to Continue any Officer in the Legion, Contrary to his own inclination." In a letter to Secretary Knox, the general confided two other reasons that led him to accept Davidson's resignation so quickly. In the first place, Major Rudolph had advised him that the lieutenant's most prominent character traits were "a fondness for Ardent spirits—& frequent inebriation." Wayne also wanted to send a message and "to produce a conviction to *some other Officers* that if their resignations were offered they wou'd be accepted."[22]

In addition to this detachment of dragoons from Hagerstown, Maryland also furnished recruits enough to fill three infantry companies. Henry Gaither had led a battalion of levies in 1791, but his promotion to major in the Second Regiment kept him from commanding the new Maryland companies. That must have been perfectly fine with some of his subordinates, for he was once described as "an ignorant, debauched, unprincipled old batchelor, [who] appears willing to sacrifice the purest character to gratify the spleen of his soul." Benjamin Price had been killed in St. Clair's fight, but the other three Maryland captains of Gaither's battalion raised new companies to serve under Anthony Wayne.[23]

Capt. William Lewis, a popular veteran of the Revolution, had raised his company of levies for St. Clair's army in the Hagerstown region, advertising for "able bodied young men" who wished to serve their country and "see a new country, free of expense." Lewis returned to Hagerstown by January 1792 "in tolerable health," but it was April before he advised the public that he was ready to settle the pay accounts of his soldiers, including widows and heirs of the slain. By that time, *The Washington Spy* had announced, "The recruiting service is again commenced in this town, under the direction of that gallant officer and soldier's friend, Captain Lewis, who is ready to engage all able-bodied and *honest* fellows." Although the terrible experience of St. Clair's campaign could never be forgotten, William Lewis was more than willing to hazard another attempt to break the Indian alliance.[24]

Henry Carbery recruited a company in Frederick County, with his rendezvous in Fredericktown. While other captains had to improvise accommodations for their men, Carbery had the luxury of quartering his recruits in stone barracks that had been erected during the Revolution. Used primarily as a prison for important captives taken at Saratoga, Trenton, and Yorktown, the site was at this time a state arsenal. A captain in the Revolution, Carbery was wounded in 1779 and retired from the army in 1781, although he again served as a captain of levies in 1791. His lieutenant was Benjamin Price, who had been wounded on November 4, 1791, while also serving as a lieutenant in his uncle's company. Carbery's ensign was a well-connected youth named Campbell Smith, whom he described as "a Young Gentleman of birth and Education." While bringing Ensign Smith to the notice of General Wayne, the captain wrote, "a little of the attention with which Young Men of Genius are some times honored, may be useful to him." All three officers used local contacts to collect recruits, but Captain Carbery's activities were not exclusively devoted to military affairs; he also had time to woo and wed Miss Sybila Schnertzell.[25]

Obeying orders to march his recruits to Pittsburgh, on July 3 Carbery gave Price instructions for the movement, which would take him by way of Hagerstown, where he would be joined by the recruits of William Lewis's company. The editor of *The Washington Spy* thought Carbery's written orders so "intrinsically excellent" that he published them so "that they may be of use to other officers, let their rank be what it may":

> I recommend to you the most kind and gentle treatment to your men, and the most unexceptionable conduct towards the inhabitants of the country, through which you may pass—the first, are your brother soldiers, with whom, in all probability, you will have to encounter savages, and, perhaps, to bleed again in defence of the helpless—the others, peaceful citizens, who will treat you with civility, if they are not afraid of your company—I have experienced hospitality from them, in like situations—and I wish it to you. My utmost exertions have been used to accommodate the men, under your command, to military order and discipline—and to impress them, by every means in my power, with a proper sense of their important duty, and a ready and willing obedience to the dictates of their officers. I believe you will have the satisfaction to march into Pittsburg, recruits that will not be excelled (at least in those respects) by any that have not been inlisted a longer period—and I acknowledge, with pleasure, your industry and assistance.

He concluded his message with the remark, "Should I see you no more, I wish you a happy and successful campaign."[26]

Captain Carbery's instructions to Price also appeared in *The Baltimore Daily Repository*, where they were undoubtedly read by Ens. William Pitt Gassaway, who marched Capt. William Buchanan's recruits from the Baltimore rendezvous to the general rendezvous at Hagerstown. One editor commented on the party's departure, "Much may be expected from the martial appearance, order and discipline of these gallant heroes of the blade, if ever they should come within view of the scalping knife and tomahawk of their ferocious adversaries; but if we may be allowed to hazard a conjecture, this is an event not very likely to happen." Apparently, Samuel Lewis, a twenty-nine-year-old cooper, did not wish to view any scalping knife or tomahawk. He dressed himself rather ostentatiously in "a striped red and white pea-jacket, a cocked hat, ruffled shirt, a white under-jacket, black breeches, white stockings, and a pair of good shoes" and deserted.[27]

Although no companies were raised in Carlisle, Pennsylvania, most of the eastern troops passed through that town on their march to join the army at Pittsburgh. Designated as a general rendezvous for St. Clair's campaign, the post, commonly called Carlisle Barracks, opened there on May 9, 1791, and was operated by the Ordnance Department. Eventually, the garrison boasted a staff of 150 that was responsible for processing recruits as well as working in the various ordnance buildings.[28]

Maj. Thomas Butler commanded Carlisle Barracks in 1792. Born May 28, 1748, in Cumberland County, Pennsylvania, he was the son of Sir Richard Butler of Ballentemple, County Carlow, Ireland. The elder Butler had once held a commission in the British army but resigned and came to America when a junior officer was promoted over him. Thomas had studied law under James Wilson, one of the signers of the Declaration of Independence, but gave up that profession to join the Pennsylvania Line during the Revolution. He served in almost every major engagement in the Mid-Atlantic states and won praise from General Wayne for defending an important defile at the Battle of Monmouth.

Thomas and his younger brother Edward, a captain, fought under their elder brother Richard Butler in St. Clair's fight. Richard and Thomas both carried swords with identical inscriptions. On one side was the motto "NO ME SACQUE SIN RAZON (Draw me not without just cause)," and on the other was engraved "NO ME EMBAINES SIN HONOR (Sheathe me not without honor)." After General Butler was mortally wounded, Edward carried him back to his tent, then returned to the fight only to discover that Thomas had been shot through both legs. When he carried Thomas back to Richard's tent, the general, who appeared to be mortally wounded, ordered his younger brothers to escape. Edward caught an artillery horse, lifted Thomas onto its back, and led him to safety with the disorganized remnants of the army. On November 11, Edward sent word of the family's loss to his brother Percival: "Yesterday I arrived here [Fort Washington] with our worthy brother, Major Thomas Butler, who is illy wounded, he having one leg broken, and shot thro' the other. I hope, however, he will do well. He has borne the hard fortune of that day with the soldierly fortitude you might have expected from so brave a man. We left the worthiest of brothers, Gen. Richard Butler, in the hands of the savages, but so nearly dead that, I hope, he was not sensible of any cruelty they might willingly wreak upon him." Major Butler's wounds would keep him from any field command during Wayne's campaign, but Edward Butler raised a company of riflemen to avenge his brother's death.[29]

In addition to overseeing the post of Carlisle Barracks, Major Butler had the additional responsibility during 1792 and 1793 of receiving detachments of recruits and supplying them with food, shelter, equipment, and supplies for the next portion of their journey. The first group to arrive comprised 150 infantry, 65 artillerymen, and 25 riflemen under the command of Maj. Joseph Asheton. Their departure was followed closely by the arrival of Capt. John Stake's troop of dragoons from New Jersey. The dragoons, described as "well mounted and perfectly equipped," marched off on the Fourth of July, receiving a salute from the local militia units assembled in the public square. A few days later, Capt. John Cooke marched his rifle company from Northumberland, Pennsylvania, into the barracks. Although individual companies and small parties arrived almost constantly, the next large detachment came during the first week of August, when Capt. John Mills brought almost three hundred New Englanders to the post. Troops continued to march westward via Carlisle Barracks through the fall of 1792, then the movement stopped for the winter before starting again in the spring of 1793.[30]

Uriah Springer had reached the rank of captain in 1778, and his company from Monongalia County, Virginia, served at Fort Pitt during the last years of the Revolution. Perhaps no other captain had more trouble recruiting his company in 1792 than did Springer. He first established a rendezvous at Bedford, Pennsylvania, but had little luck in that quarter. Part of the reason for his lack of success could be blamed on his lieutenant, William C. Smith, who exhibited a distinct lack of ability as a recruiter and was unable to complete his quota of riflemen. Wayne considered him either "very negligent or unfortunate in recruiting" and admitted that "he can be of no service here without men to command." Worst of all, Smith had squandered all of his recruiting money.

Undismayed by his bad luck, Captain Springer received permission to shift his efforts to Union Town in Fayette County. By this time, his accumulated recruits had been sent off to Pittsburgh along with some of his valuable noncommissioned officers. Springer wrote a plaintive appeal to General Wayne asking for assistance: "If Sergt Newgent can have permission to Return to this place to join my Recruiting party I think it wou'd be of Infinite Service to me in that business." Springer was still struggling to fill his ranks in December and described some of his difficulties to the commanding general. To begin with, he had "lost five men by Indentures being produced on them." Then two others were detained because they owed substantial sums of money to their fellow citizens. Finally, he had kept four men as a recruiting party, although two of them were off chasing a deserter. Perhaps the greatest difficulty encountered by Captain Springer and others operating in western Pennsylvania was that the region was vulnerable to Indian attack, thus men were unwilling to enlist and leave their families defenseless.[31]

Having examined some of the personalities and problems involved in recruiting a new army, perhaps it would be informative to follow a single company from its organization until its arrival at Pittsburgh. Under the plan for raising new regiments, Capt.

William Eaton, Lt. James Underhill, and Ens. Charles Hyde received commissions and were ordered to raise a company in Vermont. Bennington, in the southwest corner of the state, was selected as the rendezvous. Ever mindful of the Green Mountain State's military history during the Revolution, the *Vermont Gazette* announced on May 4, 1792, that Ensign Hyde "had commenced the business of recruiting in this town" and expressed hope that Vermont "will speedily furnish her quota of active young recruits—whose valor in the field will add fresh lustre to the established reputation of the state." Operating from Dewey's Tavern, Hyde met with great success and within two weeks had enlisted nearly one-fourth of the company. These volunteers were described in glowing terms as "young, likely, active men, who, while they display all the fire of military spirit in their general deportment, behave orderly and civilly to citizens of every description, and seem to bid fair to render their country important services." In addition to men raised at Dewey's, the recruiters also had success in Windsor. In mid-June, Sergeant Perkins marched a squad of ten men from there to the rendezvous with the promise of more to come.[32]

Captain Eaton arrived in Bennington on May 17, and his presence gave the recruiting business "additional spirit." The *Gazette*'s editor observed that "the prospect appears flattering that the complement of men will speedily be obtained, and the NEW will not disgrace the OLD GREEN MOUNTAIN CORPS." Born in Woodstock, Connecticut, on February 23, 1764, William Eaton was the second son of Nathan and Sarah Eaton. The father supported his wife and thirteen children as a farmer in the growing season and as a schoolteacher during the winter months. At the age of sixteen, Eaton ran off and enlisted in the American army, reaching the rank of sergeant before being discharged on April 1, 1783. After farming, teaching school, and studying under a local minister, the young veteran was admitted to Dartmouth College in May 1787 and received a bachelor of arts degree in 1790. He was chosen clerk of Vermont's House of Delegates in October 1791. Inflamed by the defeat of St. Clair the following month, he sought a commission in the army and obtained his captaincy through the influence of Sen. Stephen Bradley. This appointment was the fulfillment of a boyhood ambition inspired by reading Plutarch's *Lives* and dreaming of military glory. Eaton retained an intense interest in history, geography, and tactics, and "military parade and the sound of the drum and the fife gratified and animated him to the last."[33]

Soon after Eaton's arrival, two young men came to the rendezvous and stated their intention to enlist. Peter Davis, standing five feet, four inches, slim, and rather effeminate, was accepted and given the first portion of his bounty money. The other youth, Jack Tarbox, was rejected as being too small and too young for the service. Davis pleaded that the recruiting officer reconsider his decision, asserting that "tho' his companion was small he was dam'd hardy, and could bear a devilish deal of fatigue." When the officer still refused, Davis confided that the two were the closest of friends and could not bear to be separated. Moved by Davis's emotional appeal, the recruiter allowed his new volunteer to return his bounty money. He then gave the two friends a few coins to drink to his health and sent them on their way. They left town immediately, and a "good authority" afterward declared that "they were a couple of young girls belonging to Shaftsbury, who had undertaken this matter in consequence of a wager laid between them and some of their male friends a few evenings before." The story quickly found its way into the local paper, but the editor discreetly omitted the name of the officer who had been fooled into enlisting a woman as a soldier.[34]

Another disruption in military routine occurred on June 30. A vagrant from Canada made friends with some of the recruits and tried to induce them to desert, promising grants of land from the beneficent King George III to anyone who did so. An "honest corporal" discovered the scheme and informed Captain Eaton. By this time, the Canadian had made his escape, but Eaton sent a squad of his "warhounds" after the scoundrel; they returned with him about two hours later. Eaton questioned him closely, but his explanation was deemed false, and the soldiers prepared to drum him out of camp. A sympathetic justice of the peace came to the Canadian's rescue and made a public scene. He shouted that martial law was trampling on the rights of ordinary citizens, raised a mob of civilians, and took the accused under his protection. Eaton demanded his return and swore to hang the man for treason. The captain, the justice, and the Canadian started off to see the sheriff, but soldiers and the civilian mob "went to loggerheads." Eaton started back "to quell the fracas," and the Canadian took advantage of this disruption and fled, never to be seen again.[35]

Peculiar events continued to affect the Vermont company. Eaton's noncommissioned officers had apprehended four deserters lurking in the region, and the four were confined under the watchful eyes of two sentinels. One of these sentinels was under strict orders to challenge anyone on the parade ground after tattoo and demand either the countersign or an accounting of the person's presence. This order was necessary because some of the soldiers were in the habit of leaving their barracks after dark and practicing "abuse upon the citizens." At 1:00 A.M. on August 6, the sentinel challenged a man staggering across the parade ground. He proved to be a private named Walsh, an Irishman about forty-five years old and "very subject to intoxication." Walsh was drunk that night and refused to give the countersign. Expecting him to physically resist, the guard began to cock his musket, hoping that would scare some sense into him. But his thumb slipped from the hammer, and the musket discharged a ball through the heart of Walsh, who "died without a gasp!" An inquest was held, and the verdict was that Walsh had died as the result of an accident. Eaton agreed that Walsh's death was "a very unfortunate accident," and the local editor declared that the incident was "a solemn warning to his surviving comrades not to trespass on decorum, or submit to a derangement of their senses by indulging appetite at the expense of reason."[36]

Captain Eaton, Ensign Hyde, and about seventy of the Green Mountain boys marched out of Bennington on August 31 and started off to join the army at Pittsburgh. The *Vermont Gazette* reported that knowledgeable observers declared the company to be "by far the best that have marched from any rendezvous whatever." Its editor also wrote, "They left the ground in good spirits and with that military ambition that becomes a soldier." As one of his last official acts before departing, Eaton posted a notice offering sixty dollars for the return of six deserters from his company. The fugitives were all in their early twenties, but only one of them had lived in Bennington. Of the others, one came from Vermont, one from New York, one from Connecticut, and two from New Hampshire. This would indicate that either the recruiters went far afield in search of volunteers or that the men they signed up were drifting in and out of the region in search of work. Lieutenant Underhill stayed behind at the rendezvous with a squad of soldiers to coax additional men into the ranks by any means possible. One of Underhill's first official acts was to offer leniency to any runaway who would rejoin the ranks: "All deserters from the recruiting rendezvous at Bennington, who will return to their duty within two months from this day, shall be ensured a pardon and exemption from punishment; but those who neglect this opportunity, and are taken and tried as deserters, inevitably suffer death; agreeable to an order of the commander in chief of the United States troops." This "carrot and stick" approach seemed to have no effect whatsoever.[37]

The first stop on the company's journey was in Albany, where Captain Eaton noticed the loss of his vellum pocketbook containing about $220, a sizeable sum that undoubtedly included money to be used on the march. His men passed through New York City on September 6, and one editor opined that "an army composed entirely of such men, would strike terror in the hearts of the most bloodthirsty of the aborigines of America." The Green Mountain men reached New Brunswick on September 9, where they were described as "a company of brave and hardy looking men." Eaton's company was augmented by thirty recruits from New Brunswick and Trenton and an artillery company commanded by Capt. John Peirce, and the expanded column reached Philadelphia on September 16. Completely outfitted by now, the company resumed its westward march on September 21, "making a very handsome and martial appearance." Writing from Lancaster on September 30, Eaton bragged that "not a single man has attempted to escape me since I left Bennington, and I have the reputation of marching the best company of recruits that have passed through this country."[38]

On October 22, after a march of fifty-three days, the company reached Pittsburgh, located at the confluence of the Allegheny and Monongahela Rivers where they unite to form the Ohio River. At that time, Pittsburgh contained "about 200 houses, stores and shops," and Ensign Hyde thought the region was "the finest part of America—the very Eden of it—Heaven itself is alone more pleasant." He was less pleased with the soldiers and civilians he found there, remarking that "billiards lead many officers and citizens astray, and cards are too often introduced." Hyde had harsh words for some of his brother officers, declaring, "Our army at present contains a number of *Jack-Asses*; short will be their lives; God speed their flight." Despite a dislike for fellow officers, the ensign confessed that duty was fairly easy and consisted of "now and then a duel for variety—then a ball—then on fatigue—then tea with the ladies." General Wayne was unimpressed with the much publicized Green Mountain boys. He confided to Henry Knox that "Captain Eaton of whom we have heard so much in all the papers has brought forward 44 Non Commissioned Officers & privates."[39]

While Captain Eaton and Ensign Hyde danced and drilled in Pittsburgh, Lieutenant Underhill continued to man the Bennington recruiting station. He issued a public notice that asked, "Is there still remaining in Vermont, or its vicinity, any of the hardy
sons of Mars who wish to flourish in the world of fame?" If there were any men willing
to risk their lives to save defenseless women and children "from the merciless tomahawk
and scalping knife," he urged them "to repair to the Federal Standard, on Mars Hill."
There, according to the lieutenant, "they may depend on receiving a generous bounty, a
good supply of clothing, and rations of provisions, and to meet with a number of agreeable companions in red and blue; and the most cordial reception, and tenderest treatment from their fellow soldier." Underhill had turned into a proficient recruiter, and he
knew exactly how to reach young men, starting with an appeal to their patriotism, then
an appeal to their manhood, and finally a promise to make them one of a large family,
with every physical want supplied by a kindly father figure.[40]

Apparently, most able-bodied men on the eastern seaboard were able to resist such
temptations, leaving officers but little selection and forcing them to accept all too many
members from the lower classes of society. Out of one detachment of nine soldiers, only
one could sign his own name. A recruiting officer captured the situation best:

> Where I am, the recruiting business goes on heavily, none but the refuse of the
> creation to be picked up—gallows looking fellows (like Sir John Falstaff's regi-
> ment) who only enlist with a design to desert—and when collected will, I fear,
> be pronounced
>
>> So worn, so wasted, so despis'd a crew,
>> As e'en the Indians might with pity view.

It is doubtful that the Indians would have shown much compassion for these new soldiers, but the inhabitants of western Virginia certainly felt sorry for them. Thomas
Underwood, an artillery recruit from Richmond, remembered, "as we passed through
the upper part of Virginia the people would often say what a pitty such a likely parcel
of young men were Going to be slaughtered by the indians as Gen'l St. Clairs army
was." As if this attitude was not enough, many detachments "passed through the battle Ground where Gen'l Braddock was defeated by the French & indians" in 1755, a
sobering sight indeed.[41]

In Philadelphia, government leaders wondered why recruiters were having such trouble filling their quotas. The War Department had selected well-qualified officers and sent
them detailed instructions, then waited for a flood of men to swell the army's ranks. When
that expected deluge proved instead to be a halting trickle, President Washington and
Secretary Knox fretted and fumed about the delay in raising an army to avenge St. Clair's
defeat. Knox had high hopes when the process first started and confided to Winthrop
Sargent: "I know not yet what impulse the recruiting service has received. I hope for the
best. The troops will, I am persuaded, be better and more numerous than the last campaign." That initial optimism soon faded as irregular reports began to reach Philadelphia.

On June 20, Secretary Knox ordered the officers to bring forward all of their recruits, with the exception of small parties that would remain at each of the rendezvous.[42]

Nine days later Knox wrote to General Wayne, observing: "The recruiting service languishes in the western district of this State. If you can devise anything to push it, I pray you to do so." But there was little the general could do since the recruiting officers reported directly to the War Department and would not be under Wayne's actual command until they joined the main army. On July 7, the secretary repeated his assessment that "the recruiting service seems to languish." A few days later Knox confessed, "the success is by no means equal to my expectation and almost precludes the hope of an active campaign this year even if the Conduct of the Indians will require it." He was under ever increasing pressure from Washington, who viewed the whole situation as "painful" and urged, "Endeavor to rouse the officers who are engaged in this business, to fresh exertions." Knox wrote to Wayne again on August 17 and (using his favorite verb) stated, "the recruiting service still languishes," although there were high hopes that "better things" would occur "after the hurry of farming is over." Five days later, Washington advised Knox that "some stimulus" was needed to motivate recruiters, who needed to be "*absolutely* restrained from enlisting improper men." The president had been informed that "*boys in many instances,* and the *worst miscreants* in others are received," all contrary to the instructions given them. While their leaders complained about the quality and quantity of recruits from their desks in Philadelphia, out in the countryside, officers accepted whatever men they could get.[43]

CHAPTER 4

The Legion of the United States

WHILE SECRETARY OF WAR KNOX prodded, pleaded, and begged his officers to stimulate the recruiting business, Anthony Wayne left the friendly confines of Philadelphia society on May 25, 1792, bound for Pittsburgh. Escorted by six dragoons, the general reached Carlisle on June 6, when he was forced to stop for a few days "to refresh the Cavalry and men." In a letter to his friend Sharp Delany, Wayne confessed, "it will be some time before there will be anything like an Army collected at that point." As if to emphasize the assertion, he pointed out that his total force at Pittsburgh would consist of the local garrison of about seventy infantry plus the six dragoons of his personal escort, "rather an awkward situation for a Commander in chief to be placed in, on a frontier and in the vicinity of a savage Enemy!" He reiterated his awkwardness in a candid observation to Knox, writing that "a General without Troops is something Similar to a fish out of Water."[1]

Wayne had planned to arrive in Pittsburgh on June 17, but his hard-riding party reached its destination three days early. There he found Capt. Thomas Hughes and his company of the Second Regiment occupying the newly constructed Fort Fayette, located about a quarter mile up the Allegheny from the ramshackle old Fort Pitt. American officers and distinguished residents from Pittsburgh had spent the afternoon of May 12 mingling and gossiping over a light lunch and glass of wine. At two o'clock, the American flag of fourteen stars and fourteen stripes was raised to the top of the fort's flagpole that towered ninety-two feet above the parade ground. Following a toast, cannons were discharged, and Fort Fayette was officially given its name. Two cannons used during the ceremony, "old double fortified twelve pounders," had a unique history. Originally brought to the forks of the Ohio by the French for use in Fort Duquesne, they later passed into British hands and were used in Fort Pitt before being moved into Fort Fayette by the Americans.[2]

Although Secretary Knox had promised that one thousand recruits would soon be arriving at Pittsburgh, the only evidence of the new army was Captain Butler, his lieutenant, ensign, and forty enlisted men, who had arrived from the Cumberland valley on May 17. Butler did not remain long. Shortly after General Wayne's arrival, a captive soldier escaped and brought startling news that General Butler might still be alive. The captain quickly obtained a leave of absence to investigate this claim and journeyed to Detroit, where he had an interview with the post commander. That British officer assured Butler that this rumor about his brother being alive and a prisoner of the Indians was "without foundation." He then proceeded to relate the "melancholy particulars" of Richard Butler's death. The general had been found by Simon Girty, one of the frontier's most notorious renegades, who recognized him. Mortally wounded, Butler begged his fellow white man to put an end to his suffering. Girty declined to do so, but he turned to an Indian onlooker and whispered that the wounded officer had commanded the American army. The Indian sprang forward and sank his tomahawk into the general's head, killing him instantly. Other Indians crowded forward, scalped the still-warm corpse, and "opened his body, took out his heart, cut it in as many pieces as there were tribes in the action, and divided it among them." Convinced that his brother was indeed dead, Captain Butler returned to Pennsylvania with the shocking details.[3]

During his first days at Pittsburgh, General Wayne conferred with three individuals who would be vital to his future campaign. The first of these men was Maj. Isaac Craig, who had been born in 1742 in County Down, Ireland, and had emigrated to America in 1765. His service as an artillery captain during the Revolution included the Battles of Princeton, Trenton, Brandywine (where he was wounded), and Germantown. In 1778, Captain Craig was assigned to Carlisle, Pennsylvania, where he learned to manufacture munitions, or "the art of the laboratory," as it was then called. In 1780, after a campaign against hostile Indians in the Genesee valley, he was ordered to Fort Pitt and remained in that area for the remainder of his life. Craig had "a very respectable knowledge of Mathematics, was an excellent carpenter, and was fond of mechanic art generally, and philosophical experiments," all of which, no doubt, led to his selection as a member of the American Philosophical Society in 1787. When Henry Knox became secretary of war in 1791, he immediately sought out Craig and appointed him deputy quartermaster general, to be stationed at Pittsburgh with the responsibility for supplying all troops on the western frontier.[4]

With Major Craig safely entrusted with assembling troops and supplies for the new army at Pittsburgh, Knox appointed Maj. John Belli as a deputy quartermaster general to operate on the frontier at the western end of the tenuous Ohio River supply line. Born in Liverpool, England, in 1760, and the son of a French father and Dutch mother, Belli became the master of three languages and received the benefits of schooling from an English military academy. Bearing a letter of introduction from John Jay that described him as "a young man worthy of trust," he emigrated to the United States in 1783 and settled in Alexandria, Virginia. There he rose from a mere clerk to a prosperous merchant who became a friend and neighbor to George Washington. Belli left on a confidential mission to Kentucky Territory and the Northwest Territory in the fall of 1791 and returned in the spring of the following year, receiving his commission on April 11, 1792.

His administration of Treasury funds was beyond reproach, and the major successfully performed his dual tasks of buying rations, forage, and animals in Kentucky and forwarding those stores, as well as those coming down from Pittsburgh, to the army in the field. Belli adapted well to dealing with the roughhewn frontier settlers, but he could never bring himself to dress in homespun hunting shirts and leggings, as was the general custom, preferring to clothe himself as befitted a continental gentleman.[5]

With both ends of the supply line in capable hands, Knox appointed James O'Hara to be quartermaster general of the army. The descendant of the O'Hara family of County Mayo in western Ireland, he came to America about 1772 and resided for a time in Philadelphia. The immigrant soon moved westward and spent the years before the Revolution as an Indian trader and government agent to tribes in western Pennsylvania and Virginia. O'Hara had spent three years as an ensign in the Coldstream Guards of the British army, so he was commissioned a captain in the Virginia forces when the war began. His company operated around the mouth of the Kanawha River until 1779, when his men and supplies were transferred to Fort Pitt. O'Hara was later appointed commissary in the hospital department and stationed at Carlisle. This military service, combined with his success in business after the war, persuaded Secretary Knox that O'Hara would be the best man to oversee the army's supplies and logistics.[6]

Quartermasters earned every cent of their pay. Major Craig found that duty at Pittsburgh was one headache compounded by another. His first problem was that no one knew how to manufacture musket cartridges. Then he received a shipment of fifty rifles from Lancaster, Pennsylvania, that seemed in good order, although there were no markings to denote that the weapons belonged to the United States; without markings stamped on the barrel and lock, unscrupulous soldiers could easily steal and sell the rifles to unsuspecting civilians. No powder horns or shot pouches accompanied the shipment of rifles, so Craig had to borrow those items from Maj. George McCully's Pennsylvania militia. Solid shot was discovered to be "very badly executed," being "neither round nor smooth," and totally unsuitable for brass cannon.

On April 6, Craig informed Knox that "there is very little camp equipage and stationery on hand at this post and not one camp-kettle, nor sheet-iron to make them of." The secretary immediately arranged for a large shipment of sheet iron for the fabrication of camp kettles. Major Craig responded on May 4 with the cutting remark, "There is only one man at this place that understands making camp-kettles. I am, therefore, apprehensive that three tons of sheet-iron cannot be manufactured into kettles as soon as they may be wanted." The sheet iron still had not arrived by May 13, and Craig suspected that it, along with six cannons, had been left along the road by wagon drivers who had "halted at their homes, perhaps to plant their corn, and thereby have neglected the public business." His suspicions were well-founded. On June 22, the major reported, "the 6 dismounted cannon left by John Gisch, a wagoner, on the road, arrived at this place; also several other wagons loaded with military stores." But the howitzers were clearly defective, and the trunnions of two pieces were damaged during test firing. A third howitzer lost a piece of its muzzle during similar testing.

The list of deficiencies and problems continued to mount. Rifle powder was tested and found to be inferior to that sold by Pittsburgh merchants, so Craig reported to Philadelphia that "it don't please the officers." There was no oil for the armorer. Cartridge paper was in short supply, as was flannel for artillery cartridges. Stocks of sulfur, saltpeter, slowmatch, and other artillery chemical compounds were exhausted. When Capt. Jonathan Cass wrote and requested a flag to fly over Fort Franklin, Major Craig admitted, "there is nothing suitable for that purpose to be got here," and dispatched a request to the government for red, white, and blue bunting.[7]

One of General Wayne's first acts upon reaching Pittsburgh was to compose a friendly letter to James Wilkinson, who had been a rival for the army command, as perhaps a first step in mending fences with his second in command. After congratulating him on his promotion to brigadier general, Wayne confessed that he "felt a singular pleasure in having with me, a Gentleman who I have always esteemed as a friend, and who I know to be a brave, and an experienced Officer." He then offered Wilkinson "my warmest wishes for your prosperity, success & honor." After requesting a complete report on the troops and posts in the western territory, Wayne as much as lied to his subordinate when he wrote that "the recruiting service has been attended with better success than we had reason to expect" and the army would be completely organized that summer. Wayne closed his interesting message with an admonition for Wilkinson to keep headquarters informed of any hostile incursion on the frontier. This letter started a correspondence between the two generals that began on a superficially friendly tone but soon became cold and testy.[8]

The first sizeable detachment of recruits arrived in mid-July under Major Asheton. Unfortunately, some of Asheton's men had contracted smallpox. Surgeon John Francis Carmichael was directed to lay out grounds for a hospital that would accommodate those already infected and those who needed to be inoculated. O'Hara supplied the necessary tents. Vaults, or latrines, were dug and shades erected to shield patients from the summer sun. Then Dr. Carmichael discovered that a number of Asheton's party also suffered from a virulent venereal disease; these men were also isolated to prevent spreading this affliction to the civilian population. Carmichael, the only army surgeon at Pittsburgh, found himself greatly overworked and laboring without sufficient medicines or medical stores. Wayne wrote to Knox for more doctors, saying, "do be so good as to order on a *Dozen* of them."[9]

In addition to its infectious diseases, Major Asheton's detachment also brought along an alleged mutineer. On the night of June 27, Henry Hamilton offered armed resistance to a lawful order by Ens. William Diven by "sticking him in the breast with a bayonet." Hamilton was brought along under guard to Pittsburgh, where he was tried for mutiny, found guilty, and sentenced to death. General Wayne approved the sentence and set the hours between 11:00 A.M. and noon on Saturday, August 4, as the time of execution. He ordered that the prisoner be informed of the decision "to the end that he may be prepared for that awfull change." Wayne also issued a warrant to hang the soldier "as an Awfull example of the fatal consequences attending a crime of so deep a die, a Soldier who lifts his arm against his Officer ought not to be permitted to live." Asheton read the death warrant, and Hamilton, appearing "manly, firm and penitent," exhorted his fellow soldiers to avoid the grievous mistake that he had made. A noose was placed around his neck, and Hamilton waited stoically "to be launched into eternity." As the assembled troops held their breath, an officer stepped forward with a reprieve. After hearing an "earnest Solicitation" from Ensign Diven and "mature deliberation and much difficulty in his own mind," Wayne had decided to extend mercy to the accused, the first soldier sentenced to death in his army. Henry Hamilton was pardoned and ordered back to duty, while "Pleasure was pictured in the countenance of every one."[10]

As various detachments arrived at Pittsburgh, the general was faced with the daunting task of turning raw recruits into dependable soldiers. Blank cartridges had been issued for a Fourth of July celebration, as well as for training maneuvers, and many disorderly soldiers fired off muskets, rifles, and pistols in camp using leftover powder. Wayne forbade that practice but quickly instituted a regular system of target practice for both riflemen and infantry, admonishing them to keep their arms "in the most perfect and soldierly order, and ready for action at a moment's warning." Major Craig sought volunteers for laboratory duty and began the manufacture of thousands of musket cartridges. Powder of the lowest proof went into rounds for practice firing, while the best was made into cartridges for actual service. These live rounds consisted of either one ball with three buckshot or nine buckshot without a ball.[11]

Wayne and his officers also experimented with an improvement to the old Charleville muskets, surplus weapons from the Revolution. They suggested that the old perpendicular touch holes be filled in and new, larger ones be drilled in an oblique direction. By using a finer grade of powder in the cartridges, the act of ramming a ball would automatically prime the muskets, and "the eye of the soldier will therefore be constantly upon his Enemy, and he can *pursue* & load in full *trot*." Wayne reckoned that under this new system, the rate of fire while standing could be improved by one-half and doubled while running. He sent a sample of the powder to Secretary Knox, with the hope a large quantity would be sent "with all possible dispatch." Knox passed Wayne's letter on to President Washington, who urged that the requested powder be sent, not because he necessarily approved but so "there may be no room for complaint here after on that score." As for the proposition to alter the muskets, Washington opposed that plan. He explained his concerns to Knox, writing, "I am no friend to his proposal with respect to enlarging the touch holes; for part of the force of the powder must be expended that way, and when the musket gets a little foul, it may not communicate with the pan." The president found no problem with the old system, which employed "a little more time in loading, where every shot ought to be well and deliberately aimed." For the time being, the administration would not allow any alteration to the standard-issue muskets.[12]

By the end of July, Wayne could report that "discipline begins to make its appearance," and two small redoubts, one on Grant's Hill and one on Eyer's Hill, had been constructed to provide additional security. Riflemen fired at targets nailed to trees so they could recover and reuse the lead, a practice that must have been gratifying to penny-pinching politicians in Philadelphia. The infantrymen to this point had been dry firing with wooden snappers on their locks but would soon switch to gunpowder "to inure the *Cavalry* to noise & fireing in their front" and to give the troops a chance to load and fire while advancing. Wayne had been promised sixteen small howitzers, and his artillerymen had stockpiled "plenty of round pebbles" for use as projectiles in place of expensive iron shot. The gunners desperately needed something to do, and Wayne confessed that they "have everything yet to learn."[13]

A report reached headquarters on August 8 that a large body of Indians had crossed the Allegheny River and was threatening the American camp. Wayne ordered his troops formed for action, then sent word to sentries in the redoubts to maintain their ground "at every expence of blood" until he could unleash his dragoons upon the enemy. But instead of holding their ground, fully one-third of those in the outposts fled in fright. Referring to an "excess of Cowardice" and "Pusillanimity in a few individuals," the commander was afraid that such defects would spread unless instantly checked, and he vowed to "make a severe example of part of those who deserted from their posts in the hour of Danger." Wayne offered a ten-dollar reward for each deserter and sent Cornet James Taylor with a detachment of dragoons toward Greensburg. His orders were explicit: "Should your party fall in with them they will be entitled to the reward, upon delivering them at this post—should they attempt to resist you—you will put them to instantaneous death."

The commander was incensed at those men (he thought them unworthy of being called soldiers) who had deserted their posts, "by which treacherous, base and cowardly conduct, the lives and Safety of their brave Companions, and worthy citizens, were committed to Savage fury." The following day, Wayne issued a general order confirming his intention to stop this evil "by the most exemplary punishment, as well as by liberal rewards." The ten-dollar reward for any deserter apprehended was extended to civilians too. Country folk caught two fugitives that same day and continued to bring in every suspicious soldier found lurking about the region. The whole affair was a huge embarrassment. And the large body of Indians threatening Pittsburgh "turned out to be a party of about *Six*—who finding themselves discovered went off without doing any Damage."[14]

As for the "exemplary punishment," General Wayne had a cruel and barbaric remedy for desertion. He had "in contemplation a Brand with the word *Coward*, to stamp upon the forehead of one or two of the greatest Caitiffs." To his credit, the general did try other corrective measures before implementing this drastic measure. As courts-martial began to hand down increasingly stiffer sentences, Wayne began to approve punishments of from fifty to one hundred lashes for deserters, although mitigating circumstances and the opinion of company officers were always given due consideration. To make a point, the commander approved a death sentence for Pvt. Hugh Laughlin, who was hanged before the troops on August 13. Laughlin's execution was a complement to the parole and countersign of the preceding night, which were "Desertion" and "Death," respectively.[15]

General Wayne had written Secretary of War Knox about his idea for branding deserters, but he did not wait for a response before forging ahead with the new policy.

Pvt. George Russell, described as "an old offender," was tried and sentenced "to have his head and eye brows shaved, to be branded in the forehead with the Letter D, to receive one hundred lashes," and to be dismissed from the service. His punishment was meted out on the evening of September 1. This ceremony was duplicated by another nine days later when John Fisher, alias James Robinson, alias John Young, endured a similar fate, although he suffered the further ignominy of being led around camp "with a Halter about his Neck." Meanwhile, Knox had passed Wayne's idea on to President Washington, who doubted both its legality and wisdom, writing that "the bad impression it may make in the country, may considerably out-weigh the good effects it may produce in the army." Philadelphia authorities feared that if word of the branding became common knowledge, potential volunteers might be scared away. Knox wrote to Wayne on September 14, "The Branding . . . is a punishment upon which some doubts may be entertained as to its legality." He pointed out that such punishments "not sanctioned by Law should be admitted with caution." The general took the hint, and branding was never again employed in his army.[16]

The same court that had sentenced George Russell to be branded also condemned Jacob Hollom, Charles Jordan, John Elias (alias Ebbert), and Samuel Rivers (alias Reid) to be shot on the morning of September 2 for repeated desertions. Despite feelings of "inexpressable Anxiety, paine & regret," Wayne confirmed their sentences. The doomed men were visited in their prison by Rev. Benedict Joseph Flaget, a French priest whose journey to Kentucky had been postponed by low water in the Ohio River. When he visited the condemned prisoners, Flaget found that two of them were Catholics, one was a Protestant, and the fourth an infidel of French birth. Although he could speak but little English, the priest accepted the Protestant into his church and, after administering the Sacraments to all three, "mingled his tears of joy with theirs of repentance." Although they shared a common nationality, John Elias refused to talk with Flaget. The French priest pleaded for their lives with General Wayne, who remained adamant in his determination to carry out their executions. Flaget accompanied the prisoners to the parade ground, where they were to be shot, but walked away before the fatal moment. Overwhelmed by grief, he fainted, and it was several hours later before he learned that Wayne, at the last possible moment, had pardoned John Elias because the priest had claimed he was unprepared to meet his maker.[17]

The branding and executions seemed to have had an effect, and on September 7 Wayne could tell Knox that "no desertions have taken place from this post, for two weeks past." Now he could concentrate on improving morale and instilling pride in his soldiers. Pride was essential to a successful campaign, and the commander considered it "a substitu[t]e for almost every other Virtue." To that end, he asked Knox to send along a large quantity of blue cloth, with needles and thread, so that men could patch their uniform coats and keep their clothing "decent & comfortable." To promote a friendly rivalry among the troops, the officer of the day was ordered to have his guards fire their weapons at marks placed "*waist band* high." One gill of whiskey was awarded to the best marksman and one-half gill to the second best for both the infantry and riflemen. If by chance the infantry scored better, the riflemen forfeited their whiskey. Troops quickly learned to become proficient marksmen, the rifles and muskets being about evenly matched, which produced "a happy competition." Wayne boasted that "the very men who four or five weeks since, scarcely knew how to load, or, draw a tricker—begin now to place a ball in a deadly direction." Most of the early arrivals in camp could "hit within one or two inches of the center, and sometimes to drive it, off Arm, at fifty five yards distance."[18]

Soldiers fought sham battles under the watchful eye of their commander. The first encounter occurred in mid-August, with riflemen acting as Indians to oppose the infantry and dragoons. The army held its ground with "skill & fortitude," driving off the enemy after dragoons forded the Allegheny to outflank the foe. Wayne reported that "this little representation of an Action has had a good effect, by inspiring the respective Corps with a spirit of Emulation." But the soldiers were perhaps a bit too enthusiastic, their general confessing, "I had no idea that the mind cou'd be so diffusively inflamed by imagination only." There were real casualties. A few men had their faces burned by powder, and several others were slightly hurt by wadding, though thankfully "in a manner that caused more anger than hurt." One civilian gave a breathless account of one such engagement: "The army was detached in two divisions, one in their uniform, and the other painted in the Indian mode; and both parties having their spies out, and their Aid-de-Camps riding to and from the General with despatches, when . . . an advance immediately commencing on both sides, the conflict began, when the most masterly evolutions and firing were displayed;—while the Indian party skulked from tree to tree, in their native covert the woods, the other continued the charge, surrounding and harrassing them." Spectators could find no fault with the "attire, paint, sculk or whoop" of the Indians, and the whole scene made for a striking and, apparently, realistic battle in which new soldiers could get used to "the noise of their own muskets."[19]

These pretend battles were important teaching tools for the new army, and Wayne's instructions began to stress some basic military maxims. First of all, he insisted that "the flankers and Van Guard must sustain the force of the Enemies fire untill called in" after the main body had formed. When the vanguard was recalled, they were to fall back, firing as they came and inclining to the right and left of the main line, which could then deliver its fire. One field day was devoted to a simulated attack upon the army column as it marched through the woods, flankers and the vanguard holding off the enemy while other troops built a breastwork. These guards for the moving column were thus enjoined to buy critical time for the army should it be attacked while on the march. Officers were to ensure that "the men form in open order and level well." Wayne was preparing his men to wage an Indian war, not a European war, so he planned to retain the traditional military formations with an important modification. His soldiers would form and fight in open order, not shoulder to shoulder according to Steuben's manual, thus allowing much greater freedom of movement on a wilderness battlefield. As for leveling, the infantrymen, who constituted the bulk of the army, were not to take aim per se but simply point their muskets toward the enemy, relying upon their numbers to send a storm of balls toward the Indian main body. Riflemen and light infantry would concentrate on individual targets.[20]

The difficulty of training was compounded by a lack of drill manuals, especially needed by those officers "new to Manoeuvre—& Discipline." An embarrassed Secretary Knox responded to Wayne's request for more copies by stating that Steuben's book was currently out of print, although he promised to reissue it "with all expedition." Despite their "conceited and refractory" attitude, Wayne asserted that even old officers of the Revolution were "rather *rusty*" and complained of the harsh duty schedule after years of easy living. He assured Knox, "I have *comforted* them by an Assurance that it will not be lessen'd but rathar increased." As if to emphasize that fact, one officer complained on September 6, "since my arrival I have been five days and nights out of eight on piquet-guard." Wayne also ordered that every foot officer be issued an espontoon, a short pike, for use on parade, although he planned to arm them with fusees or light muskets for field duty.[21]

On September 4, Secretary of War Knox implemented the long-awaited restructuring of the U.S. Army, which was thereafter styled the Legion of the United States. Wayne's command would consist of four sub-legions, each of which would contain an artillery company, a dragoon troop, eight companies of infantry, and four companies of riflemen. This organization was modeled on the old Roman legion, with each sub-legion capable of campaigning and fighting independently of the others. Wayne ordered distinctive markings for the caps of enlisted men in the different sub-legions: First—white binding, white plumes, black hair; Second—red biding, red plumes, white hair; Third—yellow binding, yellow plumes, black hair; Fourth—Green binding, green plumes, white hair. Officers were to wear plain cocked hats with the plumes of their sub-legion, but during actual field service, they would wear caps identical to those of their enlisted men.[22]

Flags were needed to designate the various sub-legions during parade and maneuver, and Wayne requested some from the War Department. Secretary Knox replied that four "excellent large standards" had been sent to Fort Washington to be used by the regiments of St. Clair's army. He thought that the addition of the various sub-legionary colors would make them acceptable for use, but the real reason may have been that "they are of silk and were expensive." Wayne directed Quartermaster O'Hara to furnish sixteen camp flags, two feet square with eight foot poles, each painted with the sub-legion number and corresponding color. Knox had urged the adoption of a distinctive headquarters flag bearing "the representation of a bald Eagle as large as life formed of Silver," although approval had not yet been given for such a standard.[23]

There were some problems with the legion organization. Wayne did not have enough officers in proportion to his noncommissioned officers and privates, so he suggested a system of brevet promotions that would increase the officer ranks. He thought this would give him "a choice of fine young fellows of education, while the recruiting Officers are completing their respective Corps." Ever sensitive to the problem of rank, Wayne also pointed out that the majors should all receive brevets to lieutenant colonel "so as not to be Commanded by Militia Lieut Colonels" in joint operations. But beyond a doubt, the worst problem with the officer corps was the drain of experienced talent. Within three months of the legion's initial formation, four majors and several captains, along with a number of lesser officers, had either died or left the service. Of the majors, Alexander Trueman was dead. Maj. Richard Call was the next to go, dying on September 29 in the fort at Rock Landing, Georgia, where he commanded the regular troops in that state. Joseph Asheton, who had marched the first sizeable body of new recruits to Pittsburgh, resigned on November 27 after "lingering" at Philadelphia "in an uncandid manner." By coincidence, Maj. Erkuries Beatty resigned on the same day after a long career as army paymaster.[24]

A situation involving Capt. Ballard Smith was rather notorious. During the first week of October, Smith had exhibited "behavior unlike a Gentleman and Officer and repugnant to the dignity of the army" by keeping the wife of one Sergeant Sprague in his own tent. According to charges preferred by Maj. George Bedinger, this tended to produce "discontent to the Sergeant" and was "destructive to discipline," both doubtless understatements of actual conditions. Things came to a head when the woman in question got into a row with a Sergeant Thorpe of Smith's company. This noisy and sometimes physical confrontation ended in the captain's tent, where the woman took refuge and threatened to kill Thorpe with her lover's pistols. The sergeant of the guard came running up, but Smith refused to acknowledge his authority without written orders. After these were produced, the captain ignored them. Major Bedinger ordered his adjutant to arrest Captain Smith, but he refused to be placed in confinement. For his part in this sordid episode, but especially for "laboring under the Character of a Drunkard in General—but in particular for being drunk on the Day and Night of the 3d instant and submitting to the Noise, Riot and fighting which took place in his own tent," Smith was found guilty by a court-martial. He was sentenced to be suspended from command, with loss of all pay and emoluments, for six months, a sentence that General Wayne approved, although he considered it "mild" given the base nature of the charges.[25]

While older officers of higher rank were leaving the legion for one reason or another, its commander was attempting to fill the lowest ranks with young men of talent and ability. On September 7, he recommended three young men—Abraham Jones, George Dunn, and Richard Butler—for commissions, calling them "fine young fellows." The former two were soldiers, but Secretary Knox had to ask "who Richard Butler is" before proceeding with any referrals for commissions. Wayne replied, "he is the eldest son of Colo Wm Butler about the age of Ninteen years, Athletick, modest, sober, & fond of a Military life, he acts as a Volunteer in Capt Edwd Butlers Company, & has enlisted ten or twelve good fine men—he is a genteel young fellow, but has had the misfortune to loose the sight of One eye by the small pox—notwithstanding this Accident, he is one of the best shot[s] upon the ground." Both Jones and Dunn quickly received commissions as cornets in the dragoons, but Butler's application was shelved temporarily. President Washington objected to appointing anyone under the age of twenty-one to the rank of either ensign or cornet. Knox explained his reasoning to Wayne: "The nature of the service requires that the Officers should be possessed of mature powers of mind & body. The lives of Men are of too much importance to be confided to the inexperience of a raw Youth." Washington must have had a short memory. He himself was but twenty-two when, as a lieutenant colonel in the Virginia militia, he precipitated the French and Indian War at Great Meadows in May 1754.[26]

The president's age requirement was subject to modification, especially if the applicant involved had connections with men who had been prominent in the Revolution. Such was the case with William Henry Harrison, the son of Benjamin Harrison, one of the signers of the Declaration of Independence. In April 1791, young Harrison went off to Philadelphia to study medicine under Dr. Benjamin Rush, but his father's death left him under the care of Robert Morris, another signer of the Declaration and a senator from Pennsylvania. His social connections were described as "respectable," Harrison being related to Martha Washington, wife of the president, and Attorney General Edmund Randolph. After declining a job offer from Randolph, Harrison chanced to meet Gov. Henry Lee, who was then visiting the city. Lee suggested joining the army, and the young man agreed. Lee personally took his application to the War Department, and within a few hours, young Harrison had received his commission as an ensign in the First U.S. Infantry. At least in the case of William Henry Harrison, President Washington apparently saw no problem with committing men's lives "to the inexperience of a raw Youth," especially when the eighteen year old in question was so well connected politically.[27]

Anthony Wayne needed competent officers, whether young or old, to keep his soldiers in line. Fear of harsh punishment was not enough to retain some men in the ranks, and desertion continued to be a problem for the legion. One officer just off a stint on a court-martial referred to deserters as "restless, treacherous, cowardly villains, sacrificing the good of their country, and with it all principle." Yet he was quick to point out that "the vigilance of the firm soldier, and well disposed inhabitant, in the pursuit and detection of those miscreants, is striking, and worthy of the highest commendation." Nearly all of those apprehended had either "lost, sold, or defaced" uniforms in their flight, leaving the prisoners "actually naked, except a tattered shirt & overalls p[er] man." Wayne proposed to issue them condemned clothing and deduct money from their wages to pay for it, meaning the government would no longer have to warehouse worthless clothes and could recoup some of the expense for its manufacture.[28]

One of the most flagrant desertions occurred on the night of September 20, when James Nugent (alias McMullen), a dragoon from Rogers's troop, stole the sorrel horse ridden by Capt. John Stake. He also made off with Stake's silver-mounted bridle and saddle, his brace of pistols, and all of the captain's accouterments. Next morning, Sgt. Abraham Jones and two privates were sent after the deserter by Major Rudolph, who gave them verbal orders to track down the fugitive no matter how long it took. Due to the outrageous nature of the case, Jones was also authorized to offer a reward of forty dollars. By three o'clock that afternoon, the dragoons had reached Greensburg. Captain Cummins, who had a recruiting office in that town, advised Sergeant Jones that Nugent had passed through some four hours earlier. His horse had appeared to be overheated and worn out, so Jones and his men continued the pursuit. Despite diligent inquiry at nearly every house, there was no further trace of Nugent. Jones figured that they could catch

Lt. William Henry Harrison. From Robert R. Jones, *Fort Washington at Cincinnati*, 1902.

up with the deserter near Bedford, but when Nugent failed to appear there, the dragoons set out on the Cumberland Road with an intention of following the fugitive all the way to Baltimore or Alexandria if necessary.

Passing through Hancocktown, the dragoons finally reached Hagerstown, where the sergeant commissioned a local printer to furnish one hundred handbills with a description of Nugent. Jones arranged accommodations for him and his men, but they did not have time to enjoy their stay in town. Capt. William Lewis, recruiting there for his infantry company, became suspicious of the three newcomers. He went to interrogate the sergeant, taking along a party of armed soldiers from his company. When Jones could provide no written orders to justify his presence, Lewis concluded that the three horsemen were deserters themselves who had concocted the Nugent story to cover their escape. He disarmed the dragoons and marched his prisoners to what Jones called "the most loathsome criminal Room I have ever seen." There they were confined with "one Highwayman, and a Negro," without food for thirty-six hours and without blankets. To add insult to their degrading situation, Captain Lewis allowed their horses to be run in local races.

On October 1, Sergeant Jones was permitted to write a letter directly to General Wayne, and he carefully explained why he had been unable to capture Nugent, including his arrest by the "haughty and imperious" Captain Lewis. For his part, Lewis wrote to Wayne and clarified his handling of the suspicious dragoon party. When these letters reached Pittsburgh, the general was livid at Lewis's interference. This unique situation was exacerbated by the fact that, since his departure, Abraham Jones had been promoted to the rank of cornet, meaning Lewis had unwittingly imprisoned an officer commissioned by the president. Major Rudolph ordered the immediate release of Cornet Jones and his men, telling Lewis, "whatever may be his objects you have no business with him, and I am warranted to inform you, from his Excellency Major Genl Wayne, that your conduct on this occasion may turn out a very disagreeable business." The captain released the dragoons on October 22 but took umbrage at Rudolph's "ungentlemanly domineering production" and requested General Wayne to convene a court of inquiry. But he was seeking redress in the wrong place, for the offensive language had been dictated by Wayne himself. In typical military fashion, there was great irony in this whole affair. James Nugent had been captured by another party, found guilty of desertion by the unanimous decision of a court-martial, and hanged on September 30 while Jones was still in jail.[29]

CHAPTER 5

Winter Camp at Legionville

SOMETHING HAD TO BE DONE with the army that had been created at Pittsburgh. Almost a thousand troops of the old First and Second Regiments remained at various western posts, but as of November 6, 1792, some nineteen hundred new soldiers had assembled around Fort Fayette. Enough recruits to fill two additional companies were on the march to that place, while about three hundred officers and men stayed behind at the various recruiting rendezvous. Despite this sizeable addition to the nation's fighting force, the Legion of the United States was still almost fifteen hundred men short of its authorized strength. With his force incomplete and winter coming on, Anthony Wayne had to decide where to encamp his growing command.[1]

Everyone agreed that no sizeable military action could be taken against the Indians that year, so President Washington advised Secretary of War Knox of his own views on disposing the troops for winter. He preferred to keep the army together in one large encampment "for the purpose of disciplining, and training the men to such kinds of manoeuvres and firings as are proper for Indian Warfare." While this idea would facilitate training and thus increase the legion's chance of ultimate success, two unacceptable choices must surely result: the frontier must either be left exposed to Indian incursions or be protected by a large force of militia that would be too expensive to maintain. Neither option was acceptable, so the president offered his own plan, proposing to station one sub-legion, under Brig. Gen. James Wilkinson, in the western forts; one sub-legion at Marietta (in present-day Ohio) under Brigadier General Putnam; and the remaining two sub-legions, under Wayne, in the Pittsburgh area. Washington's plan would accomplish a number of things. First, the army could defend the Ohio River settlements without having recourse to a militia force. Second, by keeping the bulk of the legion at Marietta and Pittsburgh, stores of rations, forage, and supplies could be built up at the advanced posts by keeping consumption there to a minimum. Third, by remaining at Pittsburgh,

General Wayne could keep in close touch with the War Department in Philadelphia, and his orders could be conveyed downstream to Fort Washington in about a week's time.

When it came to the western frontier, President Washington suggested an aggressive defense. He had little faith in established posts such as Forts Hamilton, St. Clair, and Jefferson, thinking them fit only to store supplies and to provide security for convoys. Otherwise, "they are of no use but to protect the people within them," who must be "always cooped up" within the stockades. Indians could quickly discover the strength of isolated wilderness garrisons, which could then be "insulted or avoided at the option of the enemy." The only way these forts might offer any effective defense was if they served as bases for scouts who were to range the frontier in search of enemy war parties. When Indian trails were discovered by these scouts, they would report on the size and direction of the warriors so that a military intervention could occur.[2]

General Wayne shared some observations with Secretary Knox prior to forming a detailed plan of operations. He thought the Indians to be "confident haughty & insolent" following their success against Harmar and St. Clair and rightly so. Additionally, Wayne pointed out that there was a silent conspirator at work in the current Indian war. King George III had agreed by Article VII of the Treaty of Peace of 1783 to "withdraw all his armies, garrisons and fleets from the said United States, and from every post, place and harbour within the same." Yet after nine years, the British still maintained military posts at Detroit, Michilimackinac, and Niagara, all three within those boundaries acknowledged by the king when he signed the treaty. Wayne had no doubts that this British presence emboldened the Indians, "for altho' they may not *directly*—I am convinced that they do *indirectly* stimulate the savages to continue the War." Calling British assistance to the Indians a "daring violation of neutrality," William Henry Harrison would later declare unequivocally Wayne's belief that "the war of the Revolution continued in the western country until the peace of Greenville, in 1795."[3]

The legion commander favored a "combined Operation" of one force advancing overland from Fort Washington and another operating on Lake Erie from a base at Presque Isle, Pennsylvania. But this plan was not practicable as long as the British maintained their posts in U.S. territory. Any military operation on Lake Erie ran the risk of provoking the British, who, at least in Wayne's opinion, "wou'd with avidity avail themselves of that pretext to assist the savages openly." At the urging of President Washington, Wayne shelved his preferred plan as "being out of the question at present." Instead, he advocated an advance similar to that undertaken by St. Clair, with Fort Washington as the supply base and Fort Jefferson as the point of departure for the legion's campaign.

Wayne was quick to point out that his march would differ substantially from that of his predecessor. He intended to establish "small intermediate Forts" on the route between Fort Jefferson and the Miami villages at Kekionga, where the government had decided to erect a substantial fortification. Taking his cue from Roman commanders of old, this new legion commander declared, "I wou'd make it an invariable rule to hault early each day & to secure my camp before evening with small temporary breast works & Abbatis such as to cover the troops—so as [to] enable them to repel every kind of attack of the Savages." Wayne also assured Knox that he would not repeat the mistakes made by St. Clair, for "Our *Indians* guides, scouts, spies & Cavalry, *who shall always patrole & hover widely round me* will not suffer the savages to advance undiscovered, nor will I wait their attack."

The general also contemplated two diversionary attacks, or "desultory parties of Operation" as he called them, by mounted volunteers instead of militia. The first of these forces, composed of men from western Pennsylvania and Virginia, would march against the Sandusky towns from around Big Beaver River. Another expedition, this one composed of Kentucky volunteers, would advance from Fort Washington to Fort Jefferson, thence strike off toward the Indian towns on the Saint Joseph River of the Lake. In the general's opinion, "these Movements wou'd probably be crowned with briliant success, but shou'd they have no other Effect—would distract the savage Councils—& create a Jealousy for the safety of their Women & Children." But the seasoned commander had yet another surprise in mind for his Indian foes. He was already formulating a plan to establish a new post "*upon Genl. St. Clair's field of Battle,*" thereby reclaiming the very ground upon which the Indian confederacy had been most successful.[4]

These proposals could not be implemented for many months, so the immediate problem faced by General Wayne was to protect the frontier until his legion could begin active operations in the field. The enemy's proximity to Pittsburgh had been impressed upon Wayne on June 29, when Major McCully presented him with a fresh Indian scalp that had been taken just the day before. Fortunately for the United States, the Six Nations, or Iroquois League, remained friendly despite the defeat of St. Clair. The Seneca Nation was particularly attached to the American army, following the lead of Cornplanter, its most influential chief. Lt. John Jeffers considered the chief "to be as friendly as any one of our own people" and recounted how he ordered two minor chiefs and ten warriors to act as scouts and "let me know if the bad Indians should either advance against me or any of the frontiers of the United States." Broken Twig and John Deckard, two other Seneca chiefs, swore in Jeffers's presence that they would each take two scalps to avenge the death of their friend Richard Butler. On another occasion, a Delaware aroused concern by his strange actions at Fort Franklin. A group of Senecas held an inquiry, found the Delaware to be a spy, and tomahawked him on the spot.[5]

While Cornplanter represented the pro-American faction of the Six Nations, Joseph Brant, chief of the Mohawk Nation, operated in a more suspicious manner. Born in 1742 on the banks of the Ohio River, Brant had been educated in Lebanon, Connecticut, and fought for the British in the French and Indian War. During the Revolution, he received a captain's commission in the British army and led a series of devastating raids against American settlers in the Mohawk valley. An implacable foe of the Americans during the war, the chief seemed to accept defeat gracefully. Respected by the British, the U.S. government, and Indians of nearly every nation, he participated in major peace negotiations and other efforts to pacify the frontier. Yet the biographer of this apparent peacemaker states positively that Brant had been with the Mohawk detachment that had fought against St. Clair. There could be no greater example of the government's naiveté in Indian relations than in June 1792, when Brant was welcomed with open arms by Philadelphia politicians, Washington included, less than six months after he helped destroy the American army.[6]

Fort Franklin, along with the friendly Six Nations, protected the western Pennsylvania frontier from hostile incursions. Located on the south bank of French Creek near its confluence with the Allegheny River, this American fort had been built near the old British Fort Venango in 1787. Fort Franklin consisted of a three-story blockhouse, centered inside a one-hundred-foot-square earthwork that boasted four bastions containing small artillery pieces, the whole surrounded by a palisade sixteen feet in height. For a few months after Wayne's arrival at Pittsburgh, Lieutenant Jeffers used Franklin as the base for his company of forty rangers. A number of Cornplanter's warriors had attached themselves to this ranger company, which began to style itself the "Hell Hounds." Despite performing valuable service during a critical period, Wayne soon sent the Senecas home and disbanded Jeffers's rangers because they "were much averse to that kind of service—which had caused many desertions."[7]

Capt. Jonathan Cass commanded the garrison at Fort Franklin until he left to recruit a new company in Connecticut, being replaced by Captain Hughes, whose command was to number ninety-five. Of that total, he was to send a sergeant, a corporal, and twelve men to garrison Mead's Station, halfway between Fort Franklin and Presque Isle, where the squad could protect both settlers and a sawmill that could furnish much-needed lumber for the legion. Ens. John Steele commanded a small detachment of riflemen stationed in the blockhouse at Big Beaver River, where he had been cautioned "to guard against a surprise from the Indians, who are an artful and insidious enemy, who generally strike before they are seen." If Indian signs were discovered and a party sent in pursuit, the blockhouse would always be held by at least one sergeant and ten men. In November, additional detachments of riflemen were sent to Coe's Station and Green's Station, with each commander enjoined "to protect the inhabitants from insult or injury, as well from his own party as from the indians." Wayne's intent was for each of these scattered outposts to act as a base from which constant patrols would cross and recross the northern frontier in search of Indian war parties. When the enemy was discovered, officers were ordered to "punish them in an exemplary manner for daring to venture so far within our chain of patroles & posts."[8]

Wayne had been making great progress in turning a gaggle of volunteers into a well-trained military machine. While drill and discipline were essential parts of a soldier's training, the general did not forget that "the health and comfort of the Soldiers are objects of the first consideration." To assist the overworked Dr. Carmichael, he sought out "two industrious humane and honest" matrons who would assist with nursing and cooking for the pay of eight dollars per month, two dollars more than sergeants earned. Surgeon's Mate Charles Brown arrived in late September and took over the day-to-day ministering to the sick, allowing Carmichael to spend more time on administrative duties. On October 2, the temporary smallpox hospital was broken up, and the most seriously ill soldiers were carried into the barracks at Fort Fayette, while convalescents were sent back to their companies. In a move designed to cut down on malingering, anyone on the sick list would henceforth forfeit his whiskey ration so that it could be "bartered or exchanged for roots and vegetables."[9]

Among the popular pharmacology of this era, a cure for the putrid sore throat consisted of three tablespoons of cayenne pepper and two teaspoons of salt added to a half pint of boiling water. After the water cooled, this liquid was added to a half pint of strong vinegar. Dysentery could apparently be eased by a number of medicines. One called for two teaspoons of hot hickory or oak ashes to be mixed with two ounces of whiskey, spirits, or milk. Another combination consisted of three-quarters of an ounce of the rind from an old cheese scraped into a pint of new milk and thickened with flour to the consistency of mush. A third cure was tea made from the bark of a white-oak sapling and sweetened with "double refined leaf sugar."[10]

Rabies could supposedly be cured by a mixture of six ounces of rue (a bitter herb), four ounces of garlic, four ounces of treacle or mithridate (a remedy against poison), and four ounces of pewter scrapings. These ingredients were boiled in two quarts of ale until half of the liquid had evaporated. Stored in an airtight bottle, nine spoonfuls of this medicine were given on seven successive days to human patients and six spoonfuls for nine days to animals bitten by infected dogs. This particular recipe came from Cathrop Church in Lincolnshire, England, where it had been reported with all seriousness that "the whole town almost being bitten, and not one person who took this medicine but what was cured!" Regarding another grave disease, a simple sentence summed up the latest medical advance: "Repeated applications of leeches to Cancers have been attended with great success."[11]

When homemade remedies such as the these failed to produce a desired effect, professional druggists were consulted. One widely touted preparation was called the Universal Tincture or, more commonly, Red Bottle. Advertisements claimed it to be "a medicine of great use and efficacy for complaints in the stomach and bowels, such as the cholic, gripings, wind, sickness, and weakness thereof." Red Bottle was also effective against all types of rheumatism and joint stiffness in addition to "strains and bruises, burns and scalds, wounds and cuts, old ulcers, sores, scorbutic complaints, and a sure and safe cure for the tooth ache and scurvy of the gums."[12]

Given the wondrous nature of the Universal Tincture, one might question if other medicines were even necessary. Yet patent medicines abounded in a number of forms. Tinctures were solutions of alcohol and medicinal plants. Cordials were invigorating stimulants, usually taking a liqueur form. Elixirs were sweetened solutions of alcohol, water, and medication. Carminatives caused the expulsion of gas from the stomach and intestines. These types of remedies were supplemented by a wide variety of powders, pills, drops, oils, and essences.

Any patient stopping in to see his local druggist would be confronted by a bewildering array of bottles, all of which boasted "proven" remedies. Among them would be, in no particular order (and without the author's endorsement), Daffy's Elixir; Essence of Real Gorgona Anchovies; Essence of Spruce, "infallible" for toothache; Oriental

Vegetable Cordial, "the most efficacious remedy for all disorders of the stomach and bowels"; John Earl's "infallible remedy for the hooping cough"; Maridant's Antiscorbutic Drops; Darby's "wonderful" Carminatives; Dr. James's Analeptic Pills; Dr. James's Fever Powder; and Ward's Efficacious White Drops for scurvy. The list would also include Dr. Kenyon McHans's Asthmatic Drops; Golden Spirits of Scurvy Grass; Rymer's Codiac and Nervous Tincture, "for histerical affections, nervous head-ach, spasms, &c."; Dr. Lockyer's Famous Pills; Tincture of Gold; Baker's Celebrated Tincture, "for the tooth-ach and swelling in the face"; and Pike's Ointment "for the itch." The above list contains only a very few of the wondrous patent medicines available to suffering patients during the early 1790s.[13]

One of the most amazing remedies was French Creek Seneca Oil. This oil, now known as petroleum, seeped from springs along French Creek, a tributary of the Allegheny, some one hundred miles north of Pittsburgh in land occupied by the Seneca Nation. Oil emerged mixed with water but soon separated and rose to the top, where it could be gathered on feathers swept across the surface. A rare and expensive medicine because of the location and method of collection, French Creek Seneca Oil was praised for its "penetrating and healing Virtues." A teaspoon taken internally every morning was an excellent remedy for consumption when taken in conjunction with a sensible diet. According to one source, an occasional dose "strengthens the stomach and Breast, causes an easy Respiration, and strengthens, in general, the whole Body and preserves Health, causing a good appetite to eat." Applied externally, this celebrated oil was a surefire remedy for rheumatism, pain in the limbs, sprains, dislocations, ringworm, the itch, ulcers, running sores, and venereal diseases. Druggists advertised that "the Use of this excellent oil will in a short Time be of more Benefit than any other Medicine or remedy."[14]

On October 22, General Wayne and a suitable escort set off for Indian country, though not toward the fabled petroleum springs on French Creek. Instead, he marched down the Ohio River in search of a spot to build a cantonment for the winter. After a four-day tour of territory west of the Allegheny River, the legion commander found a suitable location on the banks of the Ohio River some twenty-two miles from Pittsburgh and seven and one-half miles above the mouth of Big Beaver River. The place chosen was near the site of Logstown, a Shawnee village that at one time had been the principal settlement in that territory and the scene of important Indian conferences before the Revolution. The only disadvantage was the area's inaccessibility by land and a consequent complete dependence upon the Ohio River as a supply line. This new training camp would be christened "Legionville."[15]

On November 8, Wayne assembled a force to begin preparing the Legionville site. Captain Faulkner was placed in command of all the artificers to be found in the various sub-legions, a detachment that numbered 62 noncommissioned officers and privates. Captain Eaton would lead a covering party of 102 enlisted men. That evening both groups marched aboard boats provided by Quartermaster General O'Hara, the soldiers taking with them their tents, baggage, and twenty-four rounds of ammunition per man. Contractors loaded enough rations to last a month, and O'Hara issued the tools necessary to build huts, ovens, and stables. The two captains received specific instructions from their commander to be diligent "in guarding against surprise from the Enemy, & providing ample & sufficient Quantities of boards & Clab boards—for the purpose of covering the whole of the troops, & for the inside work of the Huts." As the winter season was fast approaching, Wayne considered their mission "of the first consequence to the comfort and security of the troops." As they set off on the morning of November 9, the challenges facing Faulkner and Eaton were immense. In addition to the typical problems of constructing a fortified camp in the wilderness, low water in the Ohio created still more burdens. For three months, every mill in western Pennsylvania had been idle. Wayne explained to Knox that "the greater part of the flower we now use is ground by *Horse Mills*" and every single board had to be cut with whip saws, the latter adding immensely to the labor at the site. Overriding the entire operation was a concern in Philadelphia about the expense being incurred, with Washington urging only "what is *indispensably* necessary to cover and service the Officers and Soldiers from the weather, avoiding *all decorations*, and as *much as possible all conveniences*."[16]

While Faulkner and Eaton were off constructing the Legionville cantonment, some men from their own companies got into serious trouble back at Pittsburgh. Sgt. John Trotter of Faulkner's company formulated a plan to desert, and "thro his persuasion and influence" convinced two other men, Cpl. William McHenry and Pvt. George Donaldson, to join him. The three men left camp on the night of Saturday, November 10, but were quickly captured the following morning. Trotter was tried before a court-martial convened at 1:00 P.M. on Sunday. He was found guilty of desertion and sentenced to death for the heinous nature of his crime. After reviewing the facts of the case, General Wayne declared that "when an Officer of such high trust and Confidence, as a Sergant of the Legion of the United States, shews so horrid, so dangerous, and so pernicious an example, the principles requires the most exemplary and prompt punishment in order to produce a Conviction to the Minds of every individual of the Army that a Crime of so great a Magnitude, as that of wich Sergant Trotter was found guilty, can never pass with impunity." Wayne approved the court's sentence, and Sergeant Trotter, in a conspicuous example of the commander's belief in expedited justice, was shot to death on the parade ground that evening, less than twenty-four hours after the commission of his offense. Believing that McHenry and Donaldson had been "deluded away" and "prevailed upon" by their shifty sergeant, Wayne remitted their corporal punishment and returned the pair to duty, although the former was reduced to the ranks.[17]

Several of Captain Eaton's men had also deserted and, after being apprehended, were awaiting trial. From the "youth, inexperience and general good conduct of the criminals," Eaton felt compelled to plead that some degree of mercy might produce better results than a severe sentence. He explained to Wayne that some of them were "from respectable families in Vermont, totally unacquainted with service and, till the present instance, since they enlisted have been uniformly sober and faithful." Eaton quickly pointed out that "the most finished villain among them" had masterminded the plot to desert, although he had managed to evade his pursuers. The captain's plea must have been well received, for there is no evidence that any of the Vermonters forfeited their lives as a result of deserting their comrades.[18]

Sometimes deserters had influential friends who sought clemency from the legion commander. One youth by the name of Richardson, described as "being sort of an ideot," foolishly enlisted in Buchanan's Maryland company. When Richardson deserted, his "respectable" parents contacted Gov. Thomas Lee, who wrote directly to President Washington about the boy. Washington obliged the governor by instructing Knox to discuss the matter with Wayne. Knox suggested that "if he should be apprehended and you can embrace any favorable means to satisfy the laws without condemning him to die it will prevent the misery of his worthy parents." Not all men chose to desert when they tired of military life, and some requested discharges through proper channels. Edward Bratten, one of Captain Springer's riflemen, asked to be released from service, claiming, "I have received many bruises internally & am troubled, perplex'd & discruciated by pains in several other instances too numerous to intimate." He also added that his various pains were compounded by "superannuation," or old age. Michael Powers had been kept in irons for some five months before being acquitted by a court-martial. The day after his release, Powers petitioned General Wayne for relief, expressing his wish "to go home to his Wife & Children which he left behind at Carlisle." Unfortunately, incomplete records leave no evidence of the disposition of these cases.[19]

Early in the morning of November 28, all of the artillery, infantry, and riflemen, along with their baggage, descended the Ohio to Legionville, except for a small garrison left at Fort Fayette. Dragoons crossed the Allegheny simultaneously and began an overland march, with the expectation of reaching winter quarters at the same time as the boats. After his troops had departed, General Wayne boarded his personal barge and set off downstream amid an artillery salute fired by the Pittsburgh militia. Arriving at their destination that same evening, soldiers disembarked and inspected the new camp. At this point, the Ohio River ran due north, and Legionville had been built on the second terrace of the eastern bank. The site was bounded on north and south by small creeks, while rows of huts extended eastward in the following order: artillery and cavalry enlisted men, artillery and cavalry officers, infantry officers, and infantrymen. A wide parade ground separated the camp from woods that surrounded the site. Legionville had been laid out as a camp, not a regular fortification, so there was no stockade or blockhouses for protection. But four small redoubts had been thrown up at the corners of the camp. Wayne was pleased with the "example & unremitting industry of the Officers, who nobly & generously submitted to every inconvenience & inclemency" while living in "cold linen tents." A suitable headquarters building was quickly built in the southwest corner of the camp behind Redoubt No. 1. By December 6, Wayne could assure Knox that the soldiers were "nearly under cover," and in a few days more, everyone would be "warm and secure."[20]

When the legion left its Pittsburgh camp, many merchants and dealers sought to follow this large market for their various wares. Some did so in an approved fashion. Among them was the Achison and Hennon firm of Washington. The two partners, according to Presley Nevill, were "deserving young men" who would "pay a punctilious

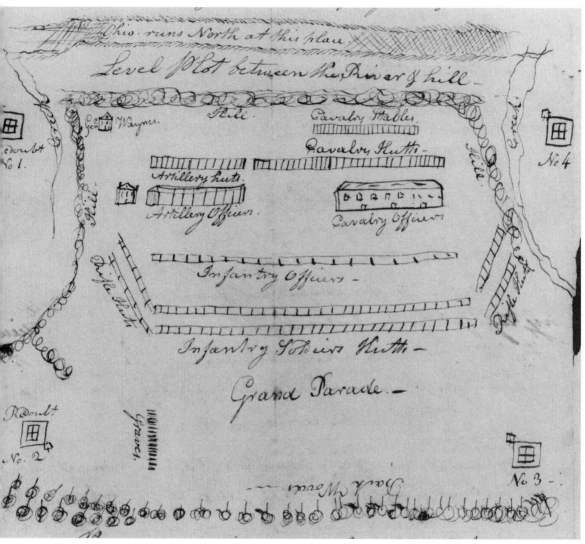

Sketch of Legionville by Surgeon's Mate Joseph Strong. The view is looking due west, with the Ohio River running north toward the right. Courtesy Beinecke Rare Book and Manuscript Library, Yale University.

attention to all orders for the Camp Regulation." Other businessmen did not adhere to Wayne's strict guidelines. Jonathan Hill built a distillery on Crow's Island, within sight of Legionville, and began to sell his whiskey, an "obnoxious fluid," to soldiers who sneaked away from camp against orders. General Wayne had no objection to whiskey but wanted consumption confined to the regular army ration. When he discovered this threat to army discipline, the general ordered a cannonball fired through a large sycamore tree that stood beside the clandestine distillery. This warning worked to perfection, and Hill immediately ceased selling liquor to the troops.[21]

In addition to the detachment that had remained at Fort Fayette, three soldiers had been left behind in the Pittsburgh jail: William Smith had been indicted for stealing a silver locket; John O'Brian had been jailed for theft of a pocket pistol and silver shoe buckle; and James Robison had been caught taking twenty bushels of potatoes. Three justices wrote to Wayne regarding the disposition of their cases: "Removing soldiers from the eye of their officers and shutting them up in jail disuses them to discipline and deprives their country of their service—and ought never to be done without necessity. . . . The time of a soldier belongs not to himself nor his labour and punishing him there punishes the Government not him." Under Pennsylvania law, criminals found guilty of stealing were to restore the goods (or their value) to the owners, pay fines equal to the stolen items to the Commonwealth, and be confined at hard labor. The justices suggested that "the men should be given up to you on assurance that the value of the property be restored to the owners and the costs paid out of the pay of the soldiers." Under this suggestion, the army would get back its soldiers, who would be punished by sentence of a court-martial and make restitution; owners would be reimbursed for their stolen property; and the citizens of Pittsburgh would be rid of three undesirable prisoners. Wayne could hardly refuse the offer.[22]

In addition to troublemakers among the enlisted men, the legion commander experienced problems with some of his officers as well. Ens. William T. Payne of the Third Sub-Legion had been tried before a court-martial and convicted of breaching military decorum. Upon the recommendation of members of the court, Payne was allowed to resign on November 17. Captain Hughes, commander at Fort Franklin, presented another problem. Ens. Lewis Bond, in charge of a small detachment at Mead's Station, where the food supply had dropped to a critical stage, wrote to Wayne on December 16 complaining about his treatment by Hughes. Bond advised the general that he would "be able with Difficulty from my present supply to hold out until the begining of Jany," even though "the troops at Fort Franklin have plenty." The men at Mead's Station were on half rations, but Hughes adamantly refused to send them food. Bond complained that "he Damns me & Says I do not belong to his Company & Shall not be Supplyed from there." Wayne firmly explained to Captain Hughes that he must share his stockpile of foodstuffs with others.[23]

Lt. Nathaniel Huston wrote to his commander on the day after Christmas to complain of how he had been treated by other officers. Huston had been in trouble back in September, being convicted of "disobedience of orders and unOfficerlike Conduct" for failure to obey the commands of a superior officer. Wayne had shown mercy and returned him to duty with a stern warning. Whether it was this incident or the fact that he had been a weaver before joining St. Clair's army, many of his peers insinuated that Huston, an Irishman, was "not a proper person to be in the Service or an Officer." The lieutenant stated, "I have been told Sir, by Lieutenant [Daniel St. Thomas] Jenifer that I was no Gentleman & such was the Sentiments of a number of other officers." Feeling himself "grossly injured," Huston asked for a court of inquiry, a request that Wayne wisely ignored.[24]

These three situations were far overshadowed by a petition signed by a number of subordinate officers and sent to Philadelphia in hopes of increasing their daily ration (or the equivalent in currency). Its arrival coincided with the introduction of a bill in the House of Representatives that called for reduction of the legion, an obvious embarrassment to the Washington administration. The president huddled with Secretary of War Knox, who quickly shot off a harshly worded message to General Wayne. Stating that there had been few complaints over the ration for the past fifteen years, Knox characterized the memorial as "an extremely improper measure, and tending to produce insubordination and every military evil consequent thereon." In the interest of political expediency, this insolent document would be concealed from the public, although the administration promised that it would be "duly considered, and such measures taken thereon, as shall be thought proper." The proposal found its way into a bureaucratic pigeonhole, and Wayne was left to fume over the unauthorized actions of his officers.[25]

Although exasperated with many of his quibbling subordinates, the general did have one who had already become a reliable Indian hunter. Maj. William McMahon had spent most of the year commanding various detachments of Virginia levies and a few companies of legion riflemen assigned to protect the frontier. McMahon was always ready to personally lead a scout, or a "tower in the woods" as he styled it. His last tour began on November 8, when he left Old Mingo Town in command of sixty-four rangers, each man carrying enough flour and salt to last twenty days, fresh meat to be supplied by hunting. Five days later, he reached the Muskingum River, where he left an ensign and the bulk of his command, continuing on with his lieutenant and sixteen men. Heading due west for four days, McMahon's group finally discovered the trail of a small party of Indians with some stolen horses. Pursuing them closely that day and into the night, the rangers finally came up to the Indian camp.

McMahon personally crept up to within fifteen yards of their fire and found four Indians "Singing and under No Apprehension of danger." The major returned to the waiting rangers and told them his plan. Since General Wayne always wanted to interrogate prisoners, they would creep back to the campsite, kill three of the Indians while they slept, and capture the fourth. The rangers waited for daylight in a heavy rain, but their plan was disrupted when one of the Indians unexpectedly walked out and discovered the ambush. McMahon's men began firing into the camp, killing two and severely wounding a third. Although they did not capture a prisoner, the major reported, "we got all their Guns, Tomahawks, and knives with all their Cloths, and three horses." The two Indians who managed to escape "Ran away Naked as they were Born except their Breech Clouts." An examination of their booty revealed some old army clothing and several pairs of leggings made by cutting off soldiers' overalls. The rangers started home on November 19, and after a week en route, Major McMahon and his party returned to Charles Town "with every Man Safe." The intrepid commander wrote a report of his scout and sent it off the General Wayne, thoughtfully accompanied by one of the Indian scalps.[26]

Such news must have raised Wayne's spirits, although his physical ailments troubled him through the holiday season. His first serious health problem had occurred during late September, when he confessed to having been "seared with a chilly fit & vomiting." This episode passed, but by Christmas the general was seriously ill. He told a friend in Philadelphia: "my monster still continues to vent & caution me, in fact I have had a most serious & alarming attack of the most violent lax [loose bowels] & bilious vomiting that I ever experienced, nor has it been in the power of the Physicians to check it or relieve it. three days since I threw up a green seated jelley from my Stummach." Laudanum and other prescribed medicines had no effect, so Wayne took a dose of tarter emetic, against the advice of the doctors, and it seemed to alleviate the pain in his chest. The general then took quinine, which seemed to soothe his stomach and bowels, but on Christmas Day, he admitted to being "very weak, & my spirits rather low."

Despite his debility, every fair day he would mount his horse and ride around the camp and redoubts for a few hours. Wayne was content with the state of his legion and the Legionville camp, and he could boast "that were all the Indians in the Wilderness to assemble for the Occasion, it wou'd not be in their power to dislodge us." Although peace reigned through the United States, there was "war serious war in the Western Country," and it would not end "until those Indians experience our superiority in the field." Although General Wayne had accomplished a great deal in the months since assuming command of the army, much more remained to be done in the new year as he continued to teach his troops "the dreadful trade of death."[27]

Ens. Hugh Brady was one man who needed some instruction from the older officers. He had been born on July 29, 1768, into one of the most notable families on the Pennsylvania frontier. Hugh's father, Capt. John Brady, and a brother named James had been killed by Indians during the Revolution, while another brother, Samuel, became one of America's most celebrated scouts and frontiersmen. Hugh had participated in a number of scouting parties, but his only confrontation with the Indians had occurred on May 22, 1791. In describing that affair, Brady said honestly: "I had a fair shot at the bare back of one of them. I do not know whether I hit him or not. He did not fall, and I think I was somewhat excited." Ensign Brady's first duty after reaching Legionville was to command a picket guard. Maj. John Mills was officer of the day and noticed that Hugh, according to his own admission, was "very green." Mills made a point of visiting Brady's guard at midnight and "took much pains" giving him some basic instructions, inspiring the young officer so that he could "perform any duty in a suitable manner." After the coaching, the ensign admitted, "I had Baron Steuben's Tactics, and a good old sergeant, and was pretty well prepared to receive the rounds when they approached." So he was, but Hugh Brady and his fellow officers would soon learn that routine guard duty was just one small step in preparing for service in the impenetrable wilderness of the Northwest Territory.[28]

By now, Wayne had learned of the fate of Major Trueman and Colonel Hardin. The news came from a totally unexpected source. James Wilkinson, who never did anything above board if a devious option presented itself, had sent several spies into the Indian country that spring. The first to return was William May, a private in Armstrong's company who had set out from Fort Hamilton on April 13. Described by Wilkinson as "one of the most sublime scoundrels in the Army" but "of desperate courage," May had been

instructed to follow the trail of Major Trueman. On the seventh day, he discovered Trueman and his servant "dead, scalped and stripped" on Harmar's trace. After being captured
by a party of Chippewas, the spy discovered that St. Clair's cannons remained on the
battlefield, either buried under fallen trees or dumped into the creek.

William May had been born in Delaware and was familiar with the operation of
small boats, so Capt. Matthew Elliott soon purchased him to work on a schooner that
carried cargo between Detroit and Roche de Bout. During the latter part of June 1792,
an Indian came aboard with the scalps from Trueman and his waiter. On a later trip, he
saw another scalp that was said to belong to Colonel Hardin. Casual conversation disclosed that all papers found on the bodies of these peace messengers had been sent to the
British at Detroit. May also reported that a delegation of ten Indians accompanied three
Creeks, veterans of the St. Clair fight, to their southern homeland. This embassy took
along seven horses loaded with presents for the Creek Nation, hoping that great numbers of them could be persuaded to come north and fight the Americans.[29]

Shortly after May appeared, Sgt. Reuben Reynolds of Buell's Connecticut company
came in from the wilderness with another interesting story. Sent by Wilkinson in the
guise of a deserter, Reynolds left Fort St. Clair on May 12 and was captured by a Miami
hunting party over a week later. After various wanderings, the sergeant found himself at
Fort Michilimackinac, where he worked as a kitchen servant. This British fort was garrisoned by a company of soldiers from the Twenty-Fourth Regiment of Foot under command of Capt. William Doyle. Although never allowed inside the circular stone fortress,
he often saw Indians emerging with arms, ammunition, scalping knives, and provisions.
After staying at Michilimackinac for about three weeks, Reynolds received a pass to visit
Montreal and came from there through Vermont to Pennsylvania, where he made his
report. Sergeant Reynolds had met several prisoners taken from St. Clair's army but
could get no information from them since they did not understand the Indian language.
From his conversations with various Englishmen, Reynolds concluded that the Indians
would be able to assemble an army of between three thousand and five thousand warriors to oppose Wayne's legion.[30]

There were no secrets in the army, and General Wilkinson quickly heard rumors
that one of his operatives had reached Pittsburgh. Concerned that this news might be
made public, he wrote, "If this be true, it is unfortunate because it not only destroys the
agent's future utility in the same line, but will bar the door against our Emmisaries from
every quarter." Advising Wayne that men named May and Reynolds had acted as confidential agents, he urged that "if the person in question answers to either of the above
names, he should be retained in service, and sent to this post as a Guide for future occasions," adding that his information would prove "more valuable than Gold or precious
stones." When he learned that it was May's story that had been released, Wilkinson
lamented that "it will not only shut up this avenue of Intelligence, but will endanger the
Lives of some valuable Men, whom I have insinuated into the Belligerent Tribes, and
who, at this time, reside among them." But when May returned to the frontier, he
bragged openly about being a spy, a practice not usually employed by clandestine agents.

Wayne gave him two hundred dollars and a promotion to sergeant of dragoons. Wilkinson soon after inquired whether the commander in chief could help procure a pardon from the governor of Delaware, for May had escaped from prison there while under sentence of death. Shortly thereafter, two deserters from the legion eagerly told British officers about the American spy who had been to Detroit and deceived both the British and the Indians. Those who had been duped by William May swore to get even.[31]

CHAPTER 6

Wilkinson Defends the Frontier

CONDITIONS ON THE FRONTIER were harsh. One officer described the situation at his post: "To give you an idea of this place, read some Fairy Tale—a cruel giant's castle—in the midst of an almost impenetrable forest—surrounded by moats, swamps, &c. secluded from all the rest of mankind—and you have the picture complete. As for music, we have at night the most enchanting concert of wolves, bears, panthers, &c. imaginable. At this instant there is one of the latter (or some devil of an Indian who can imitate them all) howling round the garrison, a note sufficient to strike terror to the heart of man. There are very few nights that we are not under arms, being alarmed by our sentinels firing on the enemy, who, we know, have two or three spies constantly about us. We dare not go beyond the gates."[1]

Weighed down by the pressure of commanding the garrison at Fort St. Clair and long a habitual drunkard, Maj. John Smith finally began to lose his reason. In late October 1792, Smith imagined that Lt. Daniel Tilton, Ens. Jacob Kreemer, and Surgeon's Mate Samuel Boyd had joined in a conspiracy to kill him. The problem began when Smith admitted to "being in a bad State of health" and asked Boyd for relief. The surgeon's prescription produced total constipation, which was only relieved by the use of opium. This combination kept Smith from sleeping, which produced "a total debility" that threatened his life. While in this state of exhaustion, he imagined being menaced by Kreemer, "who frequently threatened to blow my Brains out provided I should not die of the operations of the Drugs" administered by Boyd. When Smith ordered a guard posted to protect himself from his young subordinates, Capt. Daniel Bradley removed the guard, disarmed the major, and assumed command of the garrison.[2]

James Wilkinson was stunned to receive a letter from Captain Bradley with the news that Major Smith had been removed from command because of "indisposition." Bradley advised his commander: "He has been so deranged for this four days past, as to be incapable of any Command, he entertains strange Notions that Messrs Tilton, Kreemer, and

Doctor Boyd are in a plot to murder him, his Conduct has been such (towards those Gentlemen) that I thought it my duty to secure his arms, which I did on the 20th Inst, and took Command of the Garrison." Admitting that "our situation is peculiarly disagreeable," Bradley explained that Smith continued to demand that the conspirators be thrown in irons and he be given back his command. Wilkinson received Bradley's letter on the evening of October 24 and replied to express "my mortification and my sorrow for the occasion." After promising a thorough and impartial investigation since "the precedent is of so alarming a nature," Wilkinson cautioned Bradley that "you stand highly responsible for the safety of the post, now under your Command, and therefore must act with redoubled vigilance and Caution." The troubled Smith was discreetly sent back to Fort Washington.[3]

Although distracted by problems with his subordinates, Wilkinson prophetically advised Secretary of War Knox that, unless he received reinforcements, "the Enemy will give us a Stroke before the expiration of the present Month." A few minutes before 11:00 A.M. on November 6, a Kentucky riflemen and three packhorse drivers arrived breathlessly at the gates of Fort Hamilton. They gasped out that Maj. John Adair's escort and a convoy of packhorses had reached Fort St. Clair the previous evening and camped within two hundred yards of its walls. Indians had attacked the camp that very morning and routed his entire force. Wilkinson was shocked and complained to Knox that Adair must have been overconfident, stating emphatically, "I have not in the Course of eight years experience seen five [men], who could maintain that incessant vigilance, necessary at all times, places & seasons to guards against the stratagem of a wily Enemy."[4]

Born in Chester County, South Carolina, in 1759, John Adair had abandoned his schooling to take an active part in the American Revolution, although he was soon captured. When British officers threatened to execute a group of prisoners if they refused to enlist in the redcoat army, Adair defiantly declared, "Lead us to the gallows." After a brief escape, the prisoner was shackled to the floor and remained for three months in a "gloomy, foul, and miserable dungeon." He gained his freedom only after his brother captured two British officers and offered them in exchange. In 1786, Adair moved to Mercer County, Kentucky, where his biographer describes how he won the trust of his neighbors: "Whenever Indian murders or depredations were committed, every eye was turned on him with that ready and implicit confidence which a master spirit inspires in extreme danger. Sagacious in council, prompt and daring in execution, he vindicated their choice by his success, and became almost equally an object of terror to the savages and of affection to his countrymen."[5]

Despite his well-earned reputation as an Indian fighter, Major Adair had the misfortune this time to be matched against the Eel River chief Little Turtle, certainly one of America's greatest military leaders. Born in 1752 on a tributary of the Eel River, he was the son of a chief and a Mohican woman and so was considered a Mohican in the matrilineal practice of Indian nations. His first experience as a war chief of the Eel Rivers came in 1780, when a ragtag band of frontiersmen under the command of Augustus de la Balme marched northward from Vincennes and overran the settlement at the Miami villages. After plundering Indian homes and French trading houses, Balme marched westward to Aboite Creek, where he encamped and awaited reinforcements for an attack on Detroit. Little Turtle gathered together the scattered warriors and attacked Balme's camp, killing every man but one, who was taken prisoner and sent to Canada.[6]

For the next decade, Little Turtle's reputation grew as he led raids against Kentucky settlements and boats on the Ohio River. On one occasion, he agreed to allow a white captive to accompany a war party into Kentucky. This man had been a prisoner for many years and had won the complete confidence of the Indians. The warriors located a cabin surrounded by cleared ground and began to stealthily advance toward it about dawn, the white man being among those foremost in the attack. As they crept noiselessly along, following Little Turtle's hand gestures, suddenly the captive jumped up and ran toward the cabin, crying, "Indians! Indians!!" Little Turtle supposedly said of the affair, "From that day I would never trust a white man to accompany me again in war." During Harmar's campaign in 1790, he commanded a force of Miamis and Eel Rivers numbering three hundred. At St. Clair's defeat the following year, Little Turtle exercised command over the entire Indian army, composed of warriors from the Miami, Eel River, Potawatomi, Ottawa, Chippewa, Wyandotte, Delaware, Shawnee, Mingo, and Cherokee Nations. His victories over Generals Harmar and St. Clair had won him well-deserved fame and influence far beyond that which an ordinary chief of the small Eel River Nation might normally have enjoyed.[7]

Interrogation of three soldiers captured at Fort Hamilton on November 3 had disclosed the schedule of Major Adair's convoy. An attempted ambush on the main road was thwarted when Adair decided to rest his men and horses an extra day at Fort Jefferson. But when his party camped within sight of Fort St. Clair on the evening of November 5, Indian scouts carried news back to Little Turtle. The chief assembled three hundred Eel River, Delaware, Shawnee, Miami, and Potawatomi warriors and moved them into attack position. Before the sun came up, Little Turtle's men suddenly charged out of the darkness, firing their rifles and screaming their "hideous yells." Rushing from three sides, the Indians quickly entered Adair's camp, where hand-to-hand fighting began. Terrified horses ripped loose from their picket ropes and raced to and fro through the light from the campfires. The major immediately ordered a retreat beyond the "*shine of the fires*" and rallied his men at the garrison's stock pens, where he divided his force into three groups. Adair sent Lt. George Madison with one party to the left with orders to turn the Indians' right flank. He intended to send another detachment to the right under Lt. Job Hale, but that officer had already fallen. Instead, he gathered together about two dozen men and led them forward himself, sword and tomahawk in either hand, to take some pressure off of Madison's flanking party. By then there was enough light to distinguish friend from foe, and Joel Collins remembered that "there ensued some pretty sharp fighting, so close in some instances as to bring in use the war-club and tomahawk." Adair reported that Ens. James Buchanan, "after firing his gun, knocked an Indian down with the barrel."

The Indians had rapidly plundered the baggage and driven off what horses had not been killed in the initial fighting. Little Turtle sent part of his force to keep Adair's men at bay while the remainder made off with their booty. Lieutenant Madison was wounded before his small force had made any impression, and they all fell back to the fort. Adair's detachment pushed forward some six hundred yards, but the Indian resistance stiffened, and the major ordered a retreat, "which they did with deliberation, heartily cursing the Indians." The Kentuckians retreated to their camp, where they, in turn, made a stand. As the Indians started to withdraw, Adair ordered his men inside the garrison to draw ammunition since theirs was almost expended.

The major then sallied forth with his riflemen and began what was termed "a kind of running fight" until after sunrise. Joel Collins said that the campsite "presented rather a discouraging appearance." Only about six or eight horses remained, all the others having been driven off or killed. Everything of value had been taken. Out of an escort numbering about 120 riflemen, Adair reported a loss of 6 killed and 5 wounded. One other unwounded man, John James, had been scalped. Of the latter, Collins recalled, "in the heat of the action he received a blow on the side of his head with a war-club, which stunned so as to barely knock him down, when two or three Indians fell to skinning his head, and in a very short time took from him an unusually large scalp, and in the hurry of the operation a piece of one of his ears." James and the other wounded were carried into the garrison, where they were tended by Dr. Boyd.[8]

In a report of the action, Major Adair commended his officers and about fifty of his men as having "fought with a bravery equal to any men in the world." He then added, "had not the garrison been so nigh, as a place of safety for the bashful, I think many more would have fought well." After the fight, Adair was quite vocal in his criticism of Captain Bradley, who had done nothing to assist the Kentuckians other than to resupply their ammunition. The captain's aloofness was not shared by a lieutenant of the legion, who told Adair, "I went on my knees, and begged him to let me take fifty men to your assistance; but he refused, and said it would be sending them to be murdered." But General Wilkinson would steadfastly defend the apparent inaction of Bradley, for he was following specific instructions issued after the Shaylor incident earlier that year. On February 13, 1792, Wilkinson had published an order that "positively prohibits the Commanding Officers of Garrisons, leaving the walls of their respective fortresses, beyond musket shot, on any pretence." The general insisted that his garrisons had been posted "for defence, and not offence."[9]

In a communication to Secretary of War Knox, Wilkinson asserted that "the check which the enemy have experienced in this little affair, will produce good effects, and the event reflects honor upon the Major and the yeomanry of Kentucky." This was pure fantasy, and Wilkinson knew it. The result of Little Turtle's attack was a complete inability of the army to carry provisions to its advanced forts since the packhorses had been killed or captured and the escort dismounted. It was a masterful stroke and well executed, from the taking of prisoners to gain information, to laying the ambush, to a battle plan that disrupted the army supply line, and it resulted in a great quantity of captured horses, all at the cost of two warriors killed. In addition to public embarrassment, the army's loss in stock and supplies was estimated to be about fifteen thousand dollars. Writing from

Fort Washington, one man observed: "If these Indians had writers among them, what honorable testimony and eulogy might they not give of the noble spirit and heroic bravery of the native American character, unimproved by European science. I cannot but think these warlike nations worthy of our admiration and of our alliance."[10]

By sunset on November 6, the survivors of Little Turtle's attack had constructed "some kind of rough coffins" for their departed friends, who were interred in a single grave about fifty paces west of Fort St. Clair. Reminiscing about the affair over fifty years later, Joel Collins still carried some emotional scars: "Dejection and even sorrow hung on the countenances of every member of the escort as we stood around or assisted in the interment of these, our fellow-comrades. . . . It was dusk in the evening before we completed the performance of this melancholy duty. What a change! The evening before nothing within the encampment was to be seen or heard but life and animation. Of those not on duty, some were measuring their strength and dexterity at athletic exercises; some nursing, rubbing and feeding their horses; others cooking, etc. But look at us now, and behold the ways, chances and uncertainties of war. I saw and felt the contrast then, and feel it still, but am unable further to describe it here!"[11]

Major Rudolph with a detachment of three troops of dragoons and three companies of riflemen arrived at Fort Washington on November 7, 1792, the first sizeable body of reinforcements to reach the western theater since St. Clair's disaster. That officer scouted around and selected a campground less than a mile below Cincinnati, christening his temporary stopping point Park Abbey. Writing a chatty letter that began "Well, my friend, how goes it?" Rudolph announced his arrival "in the neighborhood of our savage acquaintances" to Major Bedinger. The riflemen in his detachment had been assigned to various posts, but the dragoons remained at Park Abbey, where they quickly got into the habit of "getting up soon & looking out" for Indians. After making some inquiries into the current state of affairs, Rudolph gave General Wilkinson great credit for keeping the forward posts supplied and communication open between the various forts. He also praised the usefulness of Major Adair's Kentucky riflemen, for the "poor creatures" of the legion were so dispirited that they, at least in their own minds, "must be beat on all occasions" and were fit only for garrison duty. He had little use for the officer corps, which he noted "swig cheerfully," some half dozen of whom he found "in arrest for a variety of crimes, and some the most unpardonable." All in all, Rudolph summed up the situation with a depressing assessment, "We cannot stand on our present foundation." Having been ordered to Fort Hamilton once his dragoons were mounted, he declared, "I want to give the Indians one trial." He then assured his friend Bedinger, "you may count on one of two things—that I give them a damned flogging, or that you and I do not meet again until in the Elysian fields."[12]

While he waited for Rudolph's dragoons, Wilkinson inspected the newly arrived rifle companies. He found these Virginians "equal to any I have ever beheld in Service, they shoot pretty well, & may soon be made good marks-men, but their arms are somewhat defective." Two captains of these rifle companies from Augusta County, Virginia, would soon rise to prominence in the legion. Alexander Gibson had raised his men in the

Staunton area, where he owned a large farm on which he raised horses and cattle. Gibson had also served as captain of a light company in the First Regiment of Virginia militia. Thomas Lewis, a young veteran of the Revolution, came from a strict Presbyterian family. One Sunday morning, when Thomas was home after serving in Wayne's army, he chanced to see some wild ducks on Sweet Spring Creek. He grabbed a fowling piece and crawled along a fence until the birds were in range. Just as he raised up to fire, a sharp pain in his back caused him to turn around. There was his father with a birch rod in his hand, exclaiming, "I'll teach you not to profane the Sabbath here!"[13]

On January 14, 1793, Major Rudolph reported to General Wayne that since his squadron had left Pennsylvania, he had lost twenty-five "of our likeliest fellows chiefly Virginians & Yorkers" to desertion. Rudolph called this situation "a scene of disgrace vexation & perplexity," and it did not abate until capital punishment was employed. Rudolph personally presided over the court-martial of seven deserters at Fort Hamilton four days later and found all of them guilty. Two men received a sentence of imprisonment in irons, two others were forced to run the gauntlet sixteen times, and the remaining three received death sentences. Those soldiers sentenced to be hanged on a gallows erected below the fort were James Monahon, a Virginia rifleman, and John Brown and Seth Blinn, two dragoons from the New York troop. General Wilkinson approved the sentences of death.[14]

The condemned prisoners were described as "young men of spirit and handsome appearance, in the opening bloom of life, with their long hair floating over their shoulders." Nothing further is known of Monahon, but John Brown was whispered to have belonged to a family of "very respectable connections" in Albany, New York. The young man had fallen in love with a lady beneath his social station, although his parents strictly forbade him to continue the relationship. Heartbroken at this turn of events and unwilling to court the lady selected for him, Brown left home and joined Rogers's dragoon troop. Brown ran afoul of Major Rudolph's harsh discipline on several occasions. When asked by his executioner why the sentence should not be imposed, Brown pointed to Rudolph and responded "that he had rather die nine hundred deaths than be subject to the command of such a man." He died "without a murmur." Blinn was said to be the only son of a widowed mother in New York and the last to carry the family name. The executioner did not properly adjust the rope, and Blinn struggled for some time before he died.[15]

By now, Deputy Quartermaster Belli had already canvassed northern and central Kentucky in search of horses for both dragoon and transport service. He had begun on June 2, 1792, announcing his intention to purchase horses for the dragoon squadron, each "to be about 15 hands high, generally dark coloured, are to be well broke to trot and gallop, high spirited and handsome, to be from 5 to 8 years old, warranted perfectly sound and sighted, and free of all distempers." Belli reported that these Kentucky horses were "generally strong, active sizeable and young, the last I thought a great object, for an old horse is difficult to fatten, whilst a younger one recruits rapidly." Major Rudolph reported "great satisfaction" with his Kentucky mounts and praised Belli for procuring better horses than had heretofore been obtained. In keeping with cavalry tradition, the dragoon horses for each troop were all of one color. Those of the First Troop were grays, the Second Troop were blacks and browns, the Third Troop were bays (reddish brown), and the Fourth Troop were sorrells (light brown).[16]

When fully mounted and equipped, Rudolph marched his dragoons to their new station at Fort Hamilton. Fearful that three troops of dragoons might not be numerous enough to counter the Indian threat, Wilkinson scrounged enough horses to mount about three dozen infantry under Ens. Stephen Trigg of Kentucky. According to Wilkinson, "These Corps compose my Escorts, Scouts & Patroles, & constitute my chief Security against the Petit Guerre of the Enemy." But the general understood that, in reality, the security of his communication and supply line between Fort Washington and Fort Jefferson was simply smoke and mirrors. He privately advised Wayne that, with the exception of the former post, "we are vulnerable to the Enemy at every point, the moment we step beyond the walls of our little fortresses, and the Enemy if he knew our real situation, would greatly embarrass, if not cut off, all communication from Post to Post." Wilkinson repeated that gloomy prediction to Secretary of War Knox, telling his superior, "should they act with vigor, there will be no security for any escort."[17]

By November 13, General Wilkinson had become fed up with orders from Wayne's headquarters that obviously failed to take into consideration the problems of transporting forage north from Fort Washington. He tactfully observed, "I do conceive you must be illy advised of the Nature of our Soil & Climate, and the consequent dificulty of our Roads, and the (almost) impracticability of the transport service, at the present & impending season." Wilkinson then shared some observations:

> A single Trip from this post to Fort Jefferson & back again, for loaded pack Horses, will employ ten Days.
> Each Horse to load four Bushells & to feed eight Quarts per Day, will leave a deposite of one & one half Bushells per Horse.
> The Horses especially employed in this Service, thus fed & thus driven, cannot make more than six trips, & in general will fail on the fifth.

Given these indisputable facts, Wilkinson stated that the best he could do with three hundred horses and six wagons would be to deposit enough forage for use by the dragoons, plus a few thousand extra bushels.[18]

The supply line from Fort Washington to Fort Jefferson was no more tenuous than that from Pittsburgh to Fort Washington, where the transport of reinforcements and supplies depended completely upon the Ohio River. Two examples will reveal some of the hardships encountered by these heavily laden craft. Ens. Robert Hunter, an experienced Ohio River navigator, was selected to command a boat convoy that left Pittsburgh in early August 1792. The water was so low that he had not gone ten miles before his boats began to run aground, which they continued to do every day until Hunter's party reached Wheeling. Up to this point, the soldiers had been compelled to tie their boats to the riverbank every night when they stopped. Concerned for the security of his cargo and men, Ensign Hunter went ashore at Wheeling on August 11 to procure anchors so that they "could Lay in the Stream at night, in some measure secure from the depredations of the Savages." One of his boats had grounded on a sandbar more than a mile above Wheeling, and the crew could not get it afloat by strenuous rowing or pushing. A squad from another boat went to help while Hunter arranged for the anchors, but four men took advantage of this confusion and deserted. Battles with low water continued, and the ensign was forced to draw additional rations at Marietta and Gallipolis in order to finish his journey. This particular trip, undertaken during low water in the summer, took almost exactly one month, while the journey could have been accomplished in less than a week had the water been at a normal stage.[19]

Capt. Isaac Guion encountered another type of obstacle in his descent of the Ohio River. He departed from Legionville on December 12 in command of a fleet of ten large boats, and his detachment made rapid progress until some thirty-five miles past Marietta, when large cakes of ice forced the captain's boat aground on a bar in the middle of the river. Another boat beached on an island, but the remainder of the convoy got safely to shore. Guion and his crew struggled unsuccessfully in waist-deep water to get their craft afloat. Ice continued to press against the boat until after midnight, when all at once the stern and part of one side gave way, plunging most of the soldiers into four feet of freezing water and ice. What could be saved of the personal baggage and government stores was thrown into a few pirogues and the vessel and its cargo abandoned. Guion ordered that the grounded boat on the island should be unloaded and a canvas cover used to protect the corn.

Now minus two of his craft, the captain set off with what remained of his corn fleet. He had not gone five miles when he reached a point where the Ohio turned south at a right angle and was completely jammed with ice. Three boats reached shore, but two others became caught in the middle of the river. They waited ten hours in hopes that the ice ahead would break up, but instead pressure from ice that continued to pile up behind the trapped boats crushed them. Soldiers saved themselves by scrambling across the ice jam to shore, where they built cribs and unloaded corn from the surviving craft. Captain Guion celebrated New Year's Day, 1793, by writing an account of his disastrous journey for General Wayne. His adventures and those of Ensign Hunter proved that timing was critical when dispatching boats down the Ohio supply line.[20]

Even when the river allowed the easy transport of army supplies to Fort Washington, they often arrived in a jumbled confusion. Packages were directed to officers no longer there, rifle clothing was sent to infantry companies and vice versa, uniforms were dispatched for full companies though they did not muster sixty men, and musket balls were labeled horseshoes and vice versa. Many stores seemed to be shipped "without Order regularity of Invoice marks or numbers." At one point, Wilkinson wrote to Wayne in exasperation, "I have received 1410 Square tin Boxes, but am at a loss in what manner to apply them." Wilkinson had expected two hundred rifles, but only half that number had arrived and were inferior to what could be purchased privately for the same price. There was only enough rifle powder to last a month and "not a Rifle Flint to be found."

Musket powder was of good quality, but three thousand pounds more were needed. Four tons of musket balls and close to a ton of cannon powder came to hand, "neither of which articles were needed." In addition to these supply problems, Wilkinson complained that "the nation is now twelve months in arrears to the Body of the Troops on this Station," and "many men of the old Corps, have not received a farthing of pay since January 1791!"[21]

There was no doubt that stores sent down the Ohio, especially clothing, were desperately needed. When Captain Bradley's two companies from Fort St. Clair rotated back to Fort Washington, a Kentucky civilian was appalled by their appearance. Editor John Bradford gave readers of *The Kentucky Gazette* a glimpse at the troops who were defending the northwestern frontier: "He observes that these troops cut a shocking figure, and look more like a band of beggars than Federal soldiers posted for the defence of our frontiers.—God help us if we had no other defence, than such a set of poor neglected taterdemalions.—Falstaff's company were princely clad when compared to these wretched broken spirited creatures.—For they were not only bare of shirts, and bare headed, but were without a single pair of shoes, and a majority of them were obliged to conceal their posteriors with ragged blankets." Claiming that these observations had not been exaggerated, Bradford then urged Congress to examine "why an army is kept drinking, gaming, fooling, and frolicking at Pittsburgh, whilst a handful of men are constantly obliged to pad the hoof from Fort Washington to Fort Jefferson." A defender of the army stepped forward and pointed out that Bradley's command had been sent back to Fort Washington to receive its annual allowance of clothing. Now if the Kentuckian would revisit the post, he could discover that the "taterdemalions" were "as well clothed as any Kentucky Beau."[22]

At one point during the summer of 1792, Capt. Jonathan Haskell had sent in returns of his ordnance and quartermaster stores at Fort Harmar but "omitted an inspection return of Clothing as the troops are almost naked; they have not any that can be returned." Several of his men had lost most of their clothing in St. Clair's fight, while others had been issued inferior uniforms when mustered in a year previously, and "service on the river, and scouting in the woods has rendered them unfit for further use." A veteran of the Revolution, Haskell ruled the Marietta community with strict military discipline. Joseph Barker, one of the first settlers there, remembered, "The Gates were Closed at sundown & sentrys sat on the adjacent Blockhouses, which prevented any passing until sunrise next morning; this produced some confliction between the Military & the Citizens." Some civilians chafed at Captain Haskell's restrictions and refused to live inside the stockade, braving the Indian threat so they could stay in their homes. Despite the isolation, military duty at Fort Harmar was not particularly onerous. One private described his feelings while stationed there: "We are now very well off, and receive the best of provisions, cloathing and money every three months—besides that, the pleasure of hunting and sporting upon the beautiful banks of the pleasant Ohio." He boasted, "I never lived better and more at my ease since I was born, than I do now."[23]

When General Wilkinson distributed his troops for the winter, he was careful to send at least one of his new rifle companies to each of the advanced posts. Troops followed a basic schedule that began at reveille. Riflemen and infantry were drilled in the "common evolutions of marching and wheeling" one hour in the morning and one hour in the afternoon according to Steuben's *Blue Book*. Riflemen drilled according to an abbreviated version of Steuben, their commands being simply "Advance, Poise, Trail, Order or Ground Arms." They also practiced firing at marks at the discretion of their captains between ten o'clock and noon. Horsemen and their mounts drilled daily at ten in the morning. These regular drill sessions were often interrupted by guard details, fatigue duty, scouting parties, and convoy escorts.[24]

Wilkinson issued a series of orders to promote pride, health, and cleanliness among his troops. Soldiers assigned to guard were to appear with their arms "in prime order" and dressed in their best uniform. They were to be shaved and have their hair powdered. Dragoons were to be "in perfect uniform" with their hair tied. Latrines were dug two hundred yards from camp and a "necessary for the night" prepared closer to quarters. Soldiers caught relieving themselves within two hundred yards of the forts were to be confined and punished. Sentinels were posted to prevent "wood, water, or any kind of filth" from being thrown upon the parade ground. When work parties put in long hours during inclement weather, their rations were increased by one-half. Extra whiskey was issued on Christmas, but the sale of whiskey to soldiers was strictly forbidden, "except under the recommendation of a Surgeon, in Cases of Indisposition." Since card playing had produced "discordance" among the troops, Wilkinson prohibited the use of playing cards, "either for Sport or amusement," by any of the soldiers under his command. The general added his own personal observation: "A Gambler considered in whatever view, is an unsuitable associate for a man of Honor, and the Brig General fondly hopes, no such Character will ever be found even in the lowest orders of military men."[25]

The western garrisons were already woefully short of officers, their number being reduced again on January 23, 1793, with the death of Capt. Richard S. Howe. According to Wilkinson, Howe "cut his own throat, and expired a few hours after, obstinately opposing every aid offered for his relief." The shocking tragedy was recounted by another correspondent, who wrote that Howe, "in order to save the Indians the trouble, has put an end to his own existence, by cutting his throat." Those officers remaining on duty varied in ability. Captain Pasteur, an old infantry officer who had been reassigned to command a rifle company, was "unfit for it as a Babe." Wilkinson praised Captain Ford, who had put the troops at Fort Jefferson "in a high state of discipline & under admirable police." But Captain Shaylor, commanding Fort St. Clair, was a different sort. The general described him as "a Man of mechanical invention, & is a thorough going subject in his own way, but has no Idea of military pride, precision, neatness, & punctuality." Wilkinson's senior officers were a disgrace, and he complained to Wayne "that out of three Majors, one, is so extremely illiterate as scarcely to write his *own* name; another (Majr. Smith) charged with insanity—and the other a confirmed sot." Passing on this blunt assessment to Secretary Knox, Wayne admitted, "nor will it be bettered by the promotion of one or two next in rank."[26]

With Wilkinson able to do little more than maintain the status quo because of problems with personnel, munitions, and supplies, defense of the frontier settlements in 1792 rested squarely on the shoulders of the various county rangers. There were two types of white settlers. First, there were those men "who went forward with families, and erected blockhouses, and forts, and remained stationary to defend them, and to cultivate the earth." These were the most efficient settlers, but "the ground on which every cabin was raised, and every field which was prepared for corn, had to be fought for." This duty fell to a second category of settlers, the rangers, a unique blend of "expert woodsmen, and intrepid soldiers." An old frontiersman wrote of them, "The lives of whole settlements depended on the fidelity, firmness, and activity of these rangers." The border war between whites and Indians was simply a war of extermination. No quarter was asked for and none was given. Ranger John McDonald recalled: "Sometimes pursuing. sometimes pursued by our red neighbors. Sometimes we lost a comrade. sometimes we took the life of an enemy. Disasters of this kind were so common, that they produced but little sensation or inquery if a comrade was killed, he was a friendly clever fellow. good by to him. it will probably be our lot next." He explained further: "When they had killed their enemies, they thought no more about it than a butcher would after killing a bullock. It was their trade."[27]

Rangers employed in Mason County, Kentucky, were fairly typical. John McDonald described the system used by the mounted rangers: "On Monday morning, two of them would leave Limestone, and reach Sandy by Wednesday evening. On Thursday morning, the other two would leave Limestone for the mouth of Sandy. Thus, they would meet or pass each other about opposite the mouth of Scioto river; and by this constant vigilance, the two sets of spies would pass the mouth of Scioto, in going and returning, four times in each week." Sometimes the rangers varied their usual mode of overland travel by using canoes. Then, according to McDonald, "one of them would push the canoe, and the other would go on foot, through the woods, keeping about a mile in advance of the canoe, the footman keeping a sharp look out for ambuscade, or other Indian sign." Whenever fresh evidence of an Indian raid was discovered, rangers rode off to warn the nearest settlement.[28]

Among the Mason County rangers were two famous frontiersmen, Cornelius Washburn and Samuel Davis. Washburn "was more than six feet in height, with broad shoulders and a very symmetrical body, although his hands and feet were small." Despite being "active and powerful," he was soft spoken, had "remarkably acute" hearing, and had a step "as light and as stealthy as a cat's." McDonald remembered that boys, "as soon as they were able to hold up a rifle at off hand, take a gun lock apart, oil it, and put it together, thought themselves men, and ranked with them as hunters and soldiers." Washburn was no exception, and he killed and scalped his first Indian at the age of sixteen. Before he had reached the age of eighteen, Washburn gained widespread fame among his peers by suddenly attacking a camp of five warriors and killing four of them. He had one close call in 1792 when he was ambushed about a mile from the Big Sandy. Concealed warriors fired at him and killed his horse, then sprang forward to capture the ranger. Washburn ran back and swam the river, killed one of his pursuers, and eluded the remainder in the woods. His success as a ranger was ascribed to the fact that "he was a thorough master of every species of Indian tactic."[29]

Samuel Davis was a native of New England and first came to the Ohio country as a private in the army. He was described as "about six feet high, well set, and strongly made; keen gray eyes—a sallow complexion—hard rough features; and when things went well with him, he was very cheerful—full of fun and laughter; but, generally, his habits were taciturn and sulky, leaning towards melancholy." Following the 1792 ranger season, Davis and a friend went on a winter hunt up the Big Sandy. After several weeks of successfully trapping beaver and killing deer, the two woodsmen were captured by a band of Indians led by the Shawnee chief Captain Charles Wilky. As the captives were being taken toward Sandusky, Davis, who realized that his fate might end in torture and death, escaped from his captors. After three days and two nights without food or fire in December storms, he finally reached the Ohio and was taken aboard one of the last boats to descend the river that year. John McDonald told Davis's story and summed it up by saying that his "escape from captivity, was effected in the most bold and fearless manner, and shows that resolute men can effect what common men would quail at."[30]

John McDonald, who spent his later years at Poplar Ridge, Ross County, Ohio, chronicled the lives of many of these early frontiersmen. He remembered that they had a unique outlook on life: "There were but very few of our frontiersmen who took any interest in learning, as school masters and books were scarce, scarcely any of them could either read or write. When some one would come from the east side of the mountains and settle among them, and begin discourses about arts and sciences, our frontier men would call them fools for talking about such giberish and nonsense as they considered no arts of any value except prepairing amunition, fighting, hunting, fishing, raising cabins and a little corn." Born on January 28, 1775, in Northumberland County, Pennsylvania, McDonald was descended from Scottish Highlanders and asserted that "a wild highlander of that day wanted but little training to convert them into genuine frontiersmen." In 1789, the McDonald family moved to Washington in Mason County, where young John quickly became acquainted with the famous Kentucky scout Simon Kenton, "who first learned me to be a hunter and a woodsman."

McDonald went on his first Indian scout in 1790 after three men had been ambushed about ten miles from Washington. Two were killed outright, but the third managed to reach Kenton's Station. Simon Kenton mounted a horse and rallied the neighbors until nearly twenty men had assembled. John begged for permission to go along, but his father told the fifteen year old that he was too young. After Kenton's party rode off, John took a rifle and his father's horse and set out to join the avengers. The Kentuckians reached the hunter's camp before sunrise but found the Indians had fled. Young McDonald never forgot the scene: "One of the hunters had fallen in the fire he was scalped and tomahawked, and much of his body consumed burned to a crisp in the fire. The other hunter was scalped, Tomahawked and striped of his clothing. The stench of the rosted man, was the most loathing smell that ever entered my nostrils. Every time I would think of the camp for a considerable time after imagination would renew the stench from the roasted man fresh to my olfactories, and allmost cause me to vomit." Upon his return home, John's father said nothing about his son's disobedience and never again tried to stop him from scouting and ranging. Yet the experience had made a lasting impression on the young man, and "the mangled corps of the hunters, the half burned body of one of them, produced such a lothing, that I was almost cured of wishing to be a soldier."[31]

CHAPTER 7

A Winter of Discord

ANTHONY WAYNE GAINED MORE valuable information about affairs on the western frontier when yet another of James Wilkinson's secret operatives came out of the wilderness. This time it was Joseph Collins, a twenty-eight-year-old native of Bordentown, New Jersey, who had been hired to journey through the backcountry by way of the Illinois River. His instructions were "to penetrate the Indian Country in order to sound & find out the real intentions of the leading men or Indian Chiefs as to peace & War, the situation of the Country, and water courses,—and to discover the part in which they would be most Vulnerable and easiest of success, as well as to examine the most proper places for garrisons or posts on the Illinois river & likewise to endeavor to discover the best & easiest route to the site of the Miami Villages." Collins was free to return "by any route he thought safe & proper" but was to complete his tour within six months and report to American military authorities. He was to be paid fifty dollars per month.

Collins left Fort Washington and descended the Ohio with Gen. Rufus Putnam's negotiating party in July 1792. He went ashore at Fort Steuben and traveled overland to Fort Knox, leaving there for the Illinois settlements, while Putnam conducted his peace talks. Collins journeyed to Cahokia before following the Illinois River to Lake Michigan. Posing as a British trader, the spy gathered information all along his route, either from white men due to his own fluency in the French and Spanish languages or from Indians through his interpreter. After passing the portage between the Des Plaines and Chicago Rivers, he floated down the latter stream to its mouth, where he found what appeared to be an excellent harbor and "a beautiful site for a town." Continuing his masquerade, Collins left the Chicago River on November 16 and moved overland to the Saint Joseph River. At old Fort Saint Joseph, he encountered over two hundred Potawatomi warriors, many of whom had fought against St. Clair and who still wore army clothing taken in that battle. The Indians also had about thirty white prisoners who had been captured at various times on the frontiers of Kentucky and Virginia.

Here Wilkinson's agent learned of a secret plot that had been designed to disrupt General Putnam's peace negotiations at Vincennes. Some of the Eel River Nation, friends and relatives of the prisoners taken by Wilkinson and released by Putnam, planned to blow up the blockhouse at Fort Knox. After receiving their customary gifts from Putnam, among which was a large quantity of powder for use in hunting, the Indians arranged to dig a trench from the riverbank up to and under the fort's blockhouse. After depositing their newly acquired powder, they would conceal themselves nearby until after dark. At a given signal, the blockhouse would be blown up and, while everything was in confusion, warriors would rush in and massacre the garrison. An Indian of the Kaskaskia Nation friendly to the whites learned of this plot, and it was abandoned. To protect the conspirators, this potential informer was stabbed to death in a "Drunken frolick" staged that same night. Collins said that "this Intelligence may be depended upon as a fact" since the information came from Indians who were at the treaty signing. As if thumbing their noses at the Americans and their precious piece of paper, about twenty Indians who had met with Putnam set off on November 18 to steal horses in Kentucky. The prospects for peace did not seem auspicious.

On December 1, Collins set off for the headwaters of the Saint Joseph. The spy chanced to stop at the house of a French trader, who told him that his Indian guide was "a great raskal" and planned to murder him and steal his rifle. The situation became even more tense when a Miami chief named White Pigeon accused Collins of being an American and threatened to kill him. The Frenchman advised the spy to make his escape, gave him a horse and guide, and sent him off toward Detroit, for the Indians "wou'd certainly kill him if he staid any longer." Upon reaching Detroit, he could no longer claim to be British, so Collins passed himself off as a trader from Kentucky who wanted a contract to furnish supplies for the Indian trade. The commandant sent him off to Niagara, but by this time Collins had learned that the Indians were "Unanimously determined for War, unless every American withdrew to the South side of the Ohio." While at Detroit, he had also seen a number of Indians who fought against Major Adair's men at Fort St. Clair. They had no respect for the Kentucky riflemen and said their attack "was like fighting a parcel of turkies."

At Niagara, Collins was interrogated by Lt. Gov. John Graves Simcoe on several occasions. Simcoe encouraged him to bring supplies northward from Kentucky and, in fact, gave the spy an official license to deal in "Tobacco, Cheese, Hams, Butter, Pork Salted, Cotton, Hogs Lard, and Peach Brandy." In exchange for his support of the trading venture, Simcoe wanted information. He specifically inquired "about the Strength, situation & number of our posts & Garrisons on the North side of the Ohio, with the number of Inhabitants." All of Collins's answers were carefully written down and notations made upon a map of the western frontier. Simcoe then gave the erstwhile Kentucky trader a pass, dated January 19, 1793, to return to the United States. He came by way of Captain Joseph Brant's territory and found the Mohawks still professing their neutrality, although one of them covertly showed him a scalp that he had taken during the fight with Adair's escort. Collins traveled on to Cornplanter's settlement, thence on to Fort

Franklin and Legionville, where he imparted his valuable information directly to General Wayne.[1]

Although he would not personally see the western country until spring, Wayne had already made great progress in getting the Legion of the United States ready for its upcoming campaign. Legionville had been turned into a first-rate winter camp, described by one visitor as "a town with streets at right angles." Huts for officers had been so tastefully built and decorated that one man thought it a shame that they must soon be abandoned. The preeminent feature of this camp was the general's "elegant" house, nestled on a high bank in the corner formed by the Ohio River and a deep ravine. All of the buildings had been fabricated with wooden pegs and pins instead of nails, thereby keeping construction costs down and the Washington administration happy.[2]

Legionnaires appeared to be happy, healthy, and well dressed, with "silence, industry, and discipline" evident throughout the encampment. Dragoons astonished visitors at their ability "to leap over obstacles, and ascend and descend heights at a gallop." Infantrymen, generally despised as marksmen by civilians, had made such great progress with their musketry that one man could claim, "I have been at shooting matches in the country, and have never seen better shots by rifles." Detachments were posted in the four redoubts, while smaller squads served as guards for the provost, at the boat landing, and in the infantry camp. One observer noted that "the general seems to have set his heart, on having the army in good state," and the bulk of the army took its cue from Wayne. Captain Eaton wrote: "We are commanded by a man industrious, vigilant, brave—He would rather fight than leave it alone—I like his arrangements and so does every subordinate officer."[3]

The tedium of winter camp was broken on February 22 with the celebration of President Washington's birthday. At precisely ten o'clock, the legion, arranged on its parade ground in two columns, began a series of maneuvers and firings that were "highly pleasing to every spectator." Then a number of infantrymen and riflemen marched off and took up position as a mock enemy force. Wayne marched his soldiers toward the unseen enemy in two columns, with his artillery and baggage wagons in the center and riflemen acting as flank guards. A sham engagement then began, the main body forming a hollow square to protect the baggage, while artillery and riflemen responded to the enemy's fire. After about twenty minutes, a troop of dragoons emerged from the square and, accompanied by the riflemen, charged and dispersed the enemy. The legion was reformed and marched back to its parade ground, where soldiers fired three volleys "with their usual regularity." Howitzers then fired three federal salutes of fifteen shots each, the shells exploding high in the air. Following an intermission for the midday meal, the legion reassembled at three o'clock for a review by General Wayne. The troops were then dismissed and all officers invited to a dinner hosted by their commander. Following an obligatory series of patriotic toasts, the day ended "with the utmost hilarity and good order throughout the whole army." A fireworks display staged by the artillerymen capped off the day's events.[4]

Despite this outward appearance of conviviality among the officers, some deep-seated resentments lurked among them. Shortly after the birthday celebration, Dr. Joseph

Strong, who had only recently arrived at Legionville, observed: "There is in general a friendship subsisting between the officers; but some bitter enmities. The Cavalry & Artillery agree much better than Infantry & Artillery." On March 4, Lts. William Diven and Daniel St. Thomas Jenifer had a rancorous argument that ended in one challenging the other to a duel. In this case, the shedding of blood was averted, but Strong noted his disdain for those who stooped to that level: "Duelling is in my opinion a wretched resort for the protection of military honor, yet many consider it the only palladium for a broken character."[5]

On March 17, during a general review at Legionville, Captain Eaton disobeyed a direct order from Captain Butler, acting adjutant general of the legion, while trying to maneuver his column according to a previous order. In the presence of General Wayne, the two officers had words. Butler threatened that he would make Eaton repent; Eaton dared him to do so. Butler became enraged and advanced on horseback with his sword upraised; Eaton stepped forward with his espontoon. At this point, General Wayne "emphatically observed that this was no place to altercate, and ordered the march to continue." After the troops had been dismissed, Eaton wrote the following challenge:

> Legionville, 17th March, 5 o'clock, P.M.
>
> Sir,
> I am to understand—and am to be understood by Capt. Butler.
> Eaton
> The Acting Adj. Gen.

Capt. Jacob Slough, a friend of Eaton, delivered the note to Butler, who responded the next morning:

> 18th March, 1793.
>
> Sir,
> I received your note by Capt. Slough, and had wrote last evening in answer (if it be possible to answer one so equivocal:) however, ere I had quite finished, company came in and prevented me. On a review of the contents this morning, least any ill natured person should put wrong constructions, I will first make you this proposal, that as I feel myself exceedingly aggrieved in your conduct of yesterday, we will take the opportunity of a general explanation in the presence of the gentlemen who commanded in your column, and who must generally understand what passed, and the cause—
>
> Should this explanation not prove satisfactory, you shall be apprized of my further intentions—You can name the place if you please; and let me know.
> Yours, &c.
> E. Butler
> Capt. Wm. Eaton.

Butler's suggestion that the two men present their versions of events to the officers present during the review offered an honorable way to defuse the tense situation.

Eaton took advantage of the olive branch extended by the adjutant general and replied:

Monday Evening, 18th March.

Sir,
With pleasure I wait on you in company with the gentlemen of my column—
Please, Sir, name the time and place.

Eaton

Capt. Butler, Acting Adj. Gen.

The adjutant general answered:

18th March, 1793.

Sir,
Having received your note of acquiescence, I have appointed Capt. Price's
hut as the place of meeting. I shall endeavor to attend there in one hour.

Monday, half past 6 o'clock, P.M.

E. Butler
Capt. Eaton.

Both captains met at the time and place stated, presented their cases to the assembled officers, then left the hut while the gentlemen deliberated the merits of their presentations. Butler and Eaton were soon summoned back inside, and Capt. Benjamin Price read the following opinion: "The referees, to determine the difference between Captains Butler and Eaton, are of opinion that however wrong Capt. Eaton was, in the first instance, Capt. Butler was equally if not more so in the second; and as they were both unfortunate in being culpable, so it is incumbent on both to come forward and bury the matter in oblivion, by again renewing their former friendship." Each man accepted this ruling and they shook hands, thereby ending a nasty situation involving two of General Wayne's favorite officers.[6]

One day following the Butler and Eaton reconciliation, another confrontation, this one ultimately fatal, developed when General Wayne ordered officers of the Fourth Sub-Legion to select a new paymaster to replace Benjamin Price, who had just been promoted to captain. Lieutenant Jenifer offered himself as a candidate, while some other officers put forward the name of Ens. Campbell Smith. While soliciting votes, Jenifer stopped at the hut of Ensign Gassaway, who was confined to his quarters by ill health. Gassaway promised the lieutenant his support, but after the election was held, it was discovered that both candidates had received the same number of votes. Wayne ordered a new election to be held on March 21. Gassaway told Jenifer that he intended to vote for Smith this time, as he would have done so in the first election had he known that Smith was a candidate. Jenifer responded by calling Gassaway "a trifling puppy and no gentleman," whereupon the ensign challenged him to a duel. The two officers met on March 23. Their seconds, Lts. Piercy Pope and Henry Towles, measured off the ground on which the fight would take place. They agreed that the two would stand with their backs to each other at a distance of eight yards. At a predetermined signal, they would turn and advance toward one another and "fire when they pleased." At the signal, Gassaway advanced three paces and fired but missed Jenifer. The lieutenant walked up to within one yard of the now defenseless ensign, raised his pistol, and shot him in the breast. Captain Slough wrote that "the ball entered his right side and lodged in his backbone; he was immediately brought home and every possible assistance given him, notwithstanding which, he died that night at 12 o'clock." In a letter to Gassaway's brother, Slough continued: "He retained his senses till the last moment, and though he must have suffered the most excruciating pain, he bore it all like a soldier, without complaining. His remains were handsomely interred; since then, a neat fence has been put round his grave." The captain closed by assuring Gassaway's family that the ensign's death was "universally lamented by all officers."[7]

Since dueling was illegal in Pennsylvania, those involved in Gassaway's killing had much to fear from the civil authorities. Pope and Towles, seconds in the "unfortunate contest" as they termed it, fled to the blockhouse at Big Beaver to avoid prosecution. Considering "Self Preservation as one of the first lessons of Nature," the officers explained why they had left Legionville and appealed to General Wayne for advice. They were soon allowed to return without fear of punishment, but Jenifer presented another problem. He was undoubtedly a murderer and could be tried on that capital charge if the civil courts could take him into custody. Wayne's solution was to send him off to General Wilkinson's command. On March 28, he ordered Jenifer "immediately to descend the Ohio to Fort Washington" in charge of a convoy of forage boats. The lieutenant's flight with the fleet was troublesome from the beginning, for the two- and three-man crews could not keep their heavily laden boats in the current during high winds. One of the vessels soon ran aground on an island, and three of his men fell sick after spending most of the day in icy water trying to free her. Jenifer approached Major McMahon at Wheeling and asked for more men, but the major said his command was too small already and refused. Despite the lack of manpower, Jenifer finally got the remainder of his boats safely to Fort Washington and himself a safe distance from the Pennsylvania courts.[8]

Understandably, Gassaway's family wanted justice. They learned of William's death third hand, although the original account came from Lieutenant Glenn, who said that "Jenifer was much sensured for his conduct." John Gassaway, a brother of the deceased, wrote directly to Secretary of War Knox and requested that the affair be thoroughly investigated. Calling Jenifer "a murderer and assasin" and "a man wanting the principles of honour and humanity," he declared, "was my Situation in life different from what it is, without a Wife and three Children, I should not rest til I reap'd that Satisfaction which is due to an injured family." Noting that he and two other brothers had served as officers during the Revolution, John Gassaway said they had hoped that young William would have "returned again to us crown'd with the honours of a soldier." Now this would never happen, and the Gassaways demanded justice. Secretary Knox asked for an explanation from General Wayne, who tardily replied that "this business has been exaggerated & wrong represented." He then glossed over the "unfortunate misunderstanding," giving no satisfaction whatsoever to the grieving family in Maryland, who found themselves without further recourse since the legion would not, and the Pennsylvania courts could not, punish the killer.[9]

Judicial officials, however, had no intention of releasing those legionnaires still incarcerated in Pittsburgh's jail. Judge Alexander Addison's reasoning was rather straightforward—we have them and will not release them until justice has been served. General Wayne sent Lt. Samuel Andrews with a request that seven prisoners be released into that officer's custody, along with charges and sworn testimony. The general's request was diplomatically presented so as "to prevent any improper or necessary interference between the Civil & Military jurisdiction—& to preserve that harmony that ever ought to subsist between the Citizens & Soldiers of America." Addison refused to release the offenders, explaining that "when a soldier commits an offence against the usual laws of the land, he may and in many cases ought to be tried by the Courts of Common law. Though a soldier is he not a citizen?" In addition to keeping the soldiers in jail, the judge refused to furnish testimony for a court-martial. He asserted, "we will not as a Court be the handmaids of a Court martial," and "if we are to take testimony to convict or acquit we will pass sentence also." Wayne must have looked forward to the day when he could take his army to the frontier and thereby escape meddling civilians challenging the legion's way of doing business.[10]

A major obstacle to completing the legion came from Congress, where legislation had been introduced in the House of Representatives that would have reduced the number of troops in service. After much debate, the bill finally failed to pass, although its uncertain outcome resulted in the War Department delaying a large number of promotions. This policy had "a very visible and injurious effect upon the minds of the Officers," many of whom had already resigned or signified their intention to do so. Wayne saw that some of those who remained "feel neither interest or pride in the discipline or appearance of their men" and held their commissions "upon the Whim or Caprice of a restless juncto." Denouncing those who "perplex & impede every measure of Government," the general expressed his hope that "the good sence of the friends to order & the Constitution will prevail." In a confidential letter to Secretary Knox, Wayne railed against "the mistaken, idle and groveling economical ideas of the Senate" that would force him to commit "the lives of good men, the Interest of my Country, & my own honor & Character, into the hands of men devoid of Military abilities & who are novices in the profession of Arms."[11]

There clearly were not enough officers at Legionville. Six companies were commanded by sergeants; several others had only one officer present. To correct this deficiency, on January 24, 1793, General Wayne had sent to Philadelphia a list of men whom he wished to have commissioned ensigns. The War Department ignored these recommendations until March 5, when Knox authorized them to be called "into immediate service." Wayne promptly ordered his appointees to begin serving as ensigns. Four days later, Knox dispatched another letter that read, "the provisional Ensigns are not to be called into service until further orders," which would come only after their nomination and confirmation by the Senate. The legion commander was outraged at these contradictory messages and told Knox that "most of those Officers wou'd not chose to descend the river, under so *precarious a tenor of commission*," especially those "of the most sense." In his opinion, the troops would actually be better off under old sergeants.[12]

Despite the pressing need for junior officers, some applicants were unsuccessful despite what appeared to be glowing recommendations. Thomas Taylor Underwood had enlisted in the artillery and had risen to the rank of sergeant major by the spring of 1793. Edward Carrington, along with a number of officials from Goochland County, Virginia, recommended him to the secretary of war as deserving promotion. Although Lt. Gov. James Wood did not know Underwood personally, he also recommended the young man as "a youth of an Unblemished reputation; sober, active, sensible, and Brave." Charles Dabney wrote and described Underwood as "a young Man of good character, and respectable family." On March 18, his commanding officers—Major Burbeck, Captain Peirce, and Capt. Moses Porter—endorsed Sergeant Major Underwood as "a person whose activity Sobriety fedelity & genl good character & abilities well qualifys him to act in the capacity of a Subaltern officer in the Army of the United States." In spite of these impressive credentials, Underwood would not be commissioned (as a lieutenant) for another two years.[13]

While some deserving applicants were undoubtedly overlooked, nepotism flourished. Lt Col. David Strong's son, Elijah, joined the legion as an ensign in February 1793. Captain Slough's brother, Matthias Slough Jr., became a cornet in the dragoons in July of that year. Lt. Campbell Smith's brother William, although exhibiting "no character but that of a Buck," received a commission as an ensign in May 1794. Zebulon Montgomery Pike, son of Capt. Zebulon Pike, was appointed a cadet in his father's company at the age of fifteen in 1794. Undoubtedly, there were more relatives who served together in the legion, but they cannot now be ascertained.[14]

In addition to a dearth of junior officers, General Wayne was also burdened by unfit older officers who had been promoted strictly according to Secretary Knox's seniority system rather than for demonstrating ability. The problem with the drunken John Smith, now elevated to command the Third Sub-Legion at the rank of lieutenant colonel, needs no further comment. As for Lt. Col. John Clark, commanding the Fourth Sub-Legion, Wayne had nothing but contempt for him as an officer. The general confessed to Knox that Clark "may possibly possess a degree of personal bravery—but no other earthly qualification, for the Command of even twelve men. I do not say this out of any disrespect for him as a man,—on the Contrary, I consider him as a good natured, *quiet* inoffensive *thing*, that means no harm—& who would make a kind & obliging neighbour; but as an Officer—he really does not possess two Military ideas." To his credit, Clark admitted his own deficiencies in tactics, saying that "he knew nothing about *those kind of things*." But Clark did proclaim, "Give me *twenty* good rifle men, that understand fighting Indians—(and all as good *shoots* as myself) [and] I wou'd not be afraid to fight with an equal number of Savages." Wayne observed that the command of twenty riflemen would be his *neplus ultra*, the summit of his achievement. In order to keep Lieutenant Colonel Clark safely out of the way, Wayne proposed giving him overall command of the posts on the frontiers of Pennsylvania and Virginia, together with overseeing the scouts, all of them similarly good "shoots" and "better adapted to his genius than any other Command."[15]

On March 30, 1793, the various garrisons on the upper Ohio reported their strength:

Post	Officers	Enlisted Men
Mead's Station	1	21
Fort Franklin	2	74
Kittanning River		14
Reed's Station		14
Fort Fayette	3	46
Big Beaver	1	21
Mingo Bottom	1	21
Wheeling	1	21

In addition to these, the Ohio River was also protected by two officers and sixty men at Marietta and one officer and forty-three men at Gallipolis. Rangers, paid by the U.S. government, operated in the following counties: Ohio, Randolph, Harrison, and Kanawha in Virginia; Westmoreland, Allegheny, and Washington in Pennsylvania; and Mason, Bourbon, Nelson, and Jefferson in Kentucky. Each county was authorized eight rangers, except for Westmoreland and Washington, which were allowed twelve.[16]

Duty at the outlying posts was dull and onerous. When Lt. Samuel Tinsley heard that he had been ordered to relieve Maj. Thomas Hughes and take command of Fort Franklin, he confessed to being "mortified." He immediately wrote to General Wayne and urged him to send another officer, explaining that "there is no danger I would not rather Encounter than remain in active while I feel myself able to be other wise." Wayne refused to send another officer, so Tinsley had to go. His march to Fort Franklin was a nightmare. While fording the treacherous and aptly named Slippery Rock Creek, one soldier lost his footing and nearly drowned. Of sixty privates in Tinsley's detachment, nine were so sick they had to ride on packhorses. One of the men arrived just in time to be buried, while two others seemed so far gone as to soon "undergo the same ceremony." There was no aid for the ailing troops since the fort's medicine chest was empty and the surgeon had departed with Hughes's detachment. As for the fort itself, Tinsley reported, "the repairs necessary for this Post would require as a fatigue more than my Detachment" because timber would have to be dragged almost a half mile by hand in the absence of horses and oxen. As if to underscore that fort's dilapidated condition, Tinsley confided that the bastions "cannot stand three months."[17]

Although plans for the legion's descent of the Ohio had already begun, the Washington administration was willing to give peace negotiations one more try. The prospects did not look good. After his own successful negotiations at Vincennes the previous fall, General Putnam had sent his interpreter, William Wells, with a few Eel River chiefs, to make an overture of peace to Indians at the Miami villages and the Auglaize. Wells was to be paid handsomely for this dangerous journey, three hundred dollars for the mission and two hundred more if he could induce any chiefs to meet with Putnam at Marietta. Setting out on October 7, Wells seemed to vanish soon afterward. Nothing more was heard from him, and Putnam feared that he had shared the fate of Trueman and Hardin. His only hope was that the interpreter had somehow made his way back to Vincennes or "ben detained by the way." Whether Wells was alive or dead, Putnam was convinced that "the tribes to whome he was Sent have not listened to the v[o]ice of peace, nor do I beleve they ever will untill they get a good whiping."[18]

This time, instead of sending individual messengers through the wilderness to the hostile nations, the United States would send an official delegation of prestigious individuals to Sandusky. By taking a route through Canada, the peace commissioners would be assured of British protection for most, if not all, of their journey. These men were scheduled to depart from Philadelphia about the first of May, with the talks to begin about one month later. The federal government appropriated $100,000 for the endeavor, a huge sum by contemporary standards but well worth the price if the frontier war could be concluded. Since the commissioners would not be accompanied by a military escort, their safety depended upon restraint by the legion as well as settlers. If any raids against the Indians were conducted during the peace talks, Secretary Knox was fearful that the commissioners "would be sacrificed." As for himself, General Wayne would have preferred to cross Lake Erie to meet the Indians at Sandusky with "Twenty five Hundred Commissioners properly appointed," while General Wilkinson advanced northward with another large party of "commissioners." Wayne advised Knox that he did "not wish to have a single Quaker" in his negotiations.[19]

Still snug in its winter quarters, the legion's main problem continued to be desertion. One particular case stood out. On January 3, 1793, Paul Reardon, a private in Butler's company, crept into Capt. Henry DeButts's tent after midnight and made off with "a new beaux suit of Clothing." Reardon also stole a small purse of money. That same night, his wife, Mary, snatched a number of articles from the hut of Captain Butler, where she worked as a servant. Worst of all, by the light of a fire in DeButts's tent, Reardon had discovered a small, newly tapped keg of Madeira, a white wine from the Portuguese islands, which he and his wife took along as they escaped. Wayne expressed a personal interest in the wine theft and complained, "we have not more of that article on hand than will last one week." After nearly depleting headquarters of one of its most popular drinks, the Reardons left Legionville for parts unknown. Butler offered a ten-dollar reward for both of them, advising that the husband might be found at an ironworks since he had experience in that industry. Paul was described as ruddy faced and "rather handsome, somewhat given to drink," while Mary was portrayed as "a small hussy, with black hair, talks with the *brogue,* loves strong drink." The loving couple was never seen again.[20]

As winter weather turned to spring, desertion became more prevalent. On March 7, four men of Guion's company "engaged in a plot for desertion to the British Lines with their Arms and Accoutrements." Worse yet, they persuaded others to join them. All four were quickly captured; two received one hundred lashes, one received fifty lashes, and the fourth man was acquitted. Three soldiers from Mills's company also schemed to quit the army but abandoned the plan before it could be implemented. All three were found not guilty and returned to duty. On March 11, two men from Eaton's Vermont company deserted while on guard after trying to talk others into joining them. They too were soon caught and sentenced to one hundred lashes each. Peter Freeman, a private in Guion's company, apparently joined with the two Green Mountain boys, but he, as a habitual offender, received the death penalty. Killing soldiers for desertion had slowed that evil habit the previous year, so General Wayne approved Freeman's sentence. He now announced that desertion must result from one of only two causes, either "excess of Cowardice" or "a base *depravity of heart*." No longer could discontent with military life be an excuse, "for no Soldier in the Universe have less Just Ground of complaint than those of the present Legion of the United States of America." At least that was Wayne's opinion. He also warned his soldiers that thenceforward, he would not pardon any man found guilty of desertion. To remove the hope of reaching safety at British posts, he informed them that the commissioners had been instructed to demand the return of all American deserters who had heretofore managed to reach those garrisons. As for Private Freeman, he was shot to death on the morning of April 16, becoming yet another example of Wayne's absolute control over his command.[21]

Yet a few men refused to be bound by the general's iron rule. Pvt. Daniel Murphy of Slough's company was determined to get out of the army one way or the other. First, he shot himself through the left wrist and was sent to Fort Fayette for medical treatment. When this wound did not produce a discharge, he simply deserted from Surgeon John F. Carmichael's hospital. Some days later, Surgeon's Mate John C. Wallace was called upon to determine the mental condition of a Sergeant Miller. While commanding the garrison guard at Fort Fayette, Miller became insolent when Wallace ordered him to pass out a soldier from the hospital, saying he would only obey the order of Lieutenant Andrews. When that officer questioned Miller, he continued his insolence until Andrews asked him "if he was drunk, whether he was crazy, & what could induce him to behave so." When Miller put on his hat in the officer's presence and refused to remove it, Andrews struck him, relieved him from duty, whipped him, and sent him to the guardhouse. That night the sergeant vowed to draw as much blood from the lieutenant as he had shed. When Andrews entered the guardhouse next morning, Miller jumped forward and struck him in the face. Andrews then "drew my dirk & plung'd it at him, but fortunately his hand only received the point." Wallace was summoned to tend the wound and examine the patient's state of mental health. As to the claim that Miller was deranged, the doctor reported, "we have discovered no other Symptoms than his late mutinous conduct." The lieutenant sent his insolent sergeant to General Wayne for punishment.[22]

Typically, physicians treated physical ailments rather than mental disturbances. Hospital stores were classified into one of two categories. First were the physical implements necessary for treatment of wounds, such as scalpels, amputation devices, and trepanning instruments. Second were the drugs and supplies used to treat various diseases and restore the health of convalescent soldiers. The prescribed use of medical supplies often varied from doctor to doctor. It was Surgeon Carmichael's opinion that coffee was too difficult to prepare and "but seldom necessary," while common spirits was in many cases "absolutely necessary in a Hospital." Bohea and Souchong, both black teas from China, were standard fare, along with chocolate, in legion hospitals. Port and sherry wines were often prescribed. Among the spices, the most frequently used were sugar, cloves, nutmeg, and mustard. Army surgeons were kept busy. Dr. James O'Fallon served as a sort of contract surgeon for the garrison at Fort Steuben at the Falls of the Ohio. Over the course of one forty-two-day period, O'Fallon made twelve trips across the Ohio from Louisville to visit patients at the fort. During that time, he attended forty-one soldiers and their dependents, performed seventy-three cases of surgery (generally minor), and gave out 246 prescriptions. The doctor reported that this medical treatment was in addition to "extensive Pharmacentic, Culinary and nursing *written* directions accommodated to those Prescriptions, which from the incapacity of the Soldier who acted as a kind of Mate I was constrained to write."[23]

Medical news from Waynesborough was not good. Mary, the general's wife, and Elizabeth, his mother, were both in failing health. Long estranged from both women and also distant from his children, Wayne found himself, at least for the most part, liberated by Mary's death on April 19 and Elizabeth's on May 5. He still kept in touch with daughter Margaretta, though often smarting from her criticism, and son Isaac, who resented his father meddling in what he considered his own adult life. The general confessed to Secretary Knox that his mind had been "in such a state of torture for the recent loss of my long loved & very esteemed *Maria*" that he could not attend to a recent request. But that was no doubt just a public face. If anything, these two deaths allowed Wayne to pursue his infatuation with Mary Vining, the daughter of Congressman John Vining of Delaware. But whatever his inclination in that direction, nothing could now distract him from getting the legion ready to descend the Ohio.[24]

As the day for embarkation drew near, the general in chief was proud of the fighting force that he had created and was eager to lead his men into battle should the proposed peace negotiations fail. His tactics had been decided upon and practiced to perfection. He would rely upon "a light Operating Corps," or light infantry using his improved style of musket (a design finally approved by the War Department) that would self-prime with cartridges of fine powder and buckshot without ball. They would rouse the Indians from their hiding places and keep up a running fire. The regular infantry would then follow, using the standard Charleville musket with a cartridge of one ball and three buckshot. All the while his "*flying* Howitzers," designed for use in a trackless and wooded wilderness, would throw shells into the enemy forces. Finally, Wayne would administer the *coup de grâce* by throwing forward his dragoons with their flashing sabers.[25]

Before the legion left its winter camp, Secretary Knox reiterated the administration's policy as first set down on May 25, 1792. The goal for the upcoming campaign remained the same—establish a strong fort with a large garrison at the Miami villages, with smaller posts constructed to the east along the Maumee River toward Lake Erie and down the Wabash River to the west. "Posts of communication" were to be built along the line of march about every sixteen to twenty miles, but work on these by the main force was to be limited to one day so as not to retard the advance, garrisons left in them being responsible for their completion. Wayne was urged to gather intelligence about the location and numbers of the Indians opposed to him, in which pursuit "no trouble or reasonable expence should be spared." He was also authorized to call out Kentucky volunteers to augment the legion. Knox then advised his general, "the execution of the objects entrusted to you are considered as intimately blended with the welfare and reputation of the Government and that a successful issue to this War will enhance your reputation and that of the Troops under your command." Finally, the secretary passed along some words of warning from President Washington, alerting Wayne to "observe the highest degree of caution in your modes of marching and encamping and keeping out incessant patroles so as to preclude a possibility of being compelled to engage in a disagreeable situation." George Washington's message was clear. Gen. Anthony Wayne was not, under any circumstances, to repeat the blunders of Gen. Arthur St. Clair. The country simply could not afford yet another defeat at the hands of the Indian confederacy.[26]

CHAPTER 8

Downstream to Hobson's Choice

GENERAL WAYNE HAD STRIPPED HIS Pennsylvania garrisons of men so he could send as many troops to the frontier as possible. Local residents were told evasively that "some other troops will be sent to take possession of the Posts" in a few days. Sergeant Major Toomy was to take over the post at Fort Franklin with a detachment of only twenty men, less than one-third of its normal garrison, with orders to "defend to the last extremity." When David Mead, founder of Mead's Station, learned that the garrison there would be withdrawn, he knew the settlement must be abandoned too. All Mead could do was write to Pennsylvania authorities and ask for "a surgeant's command of State troops" to replace the legionnaires who had already left. As the various detachments assembled at Legionville, preparations for a descent of the Ohio River continued, those noncommissioned officers and privates eligible for discharges were paid off and sent home, and everyone destined for frontier service was paid up through January 1, 1793. The quartermaster reissued tents that had not been used since the army moved from Pittsburgh along with material to repair those damaged by hard use and storage. The quartermaster and adjutant compared notes and assigned troops to the proper number of boats. For several weeks, all was hustle and bustle at Legionville, where the troops were "in good spirits" and anxious to start.[1]

There were still a few last minute details. General Wayne made a hurried trip to Pittsburgh, where he received a testimonial from that town's inhabitants. They wished "to express their respect" for Wayne personally and his "just attention to the rights of the citizens while your army lay at this place, and from your observations of your unremitted exertions to preserve, improve, and prepare the troops." The general responded that their expressions "have made an indelible impression of esteem and gratitude in my breast, that can only end with life." Wayne then told them that if the commissioners could not attain a peace without sacrificing national honor, he hoped "the citizens of the United States of America, will have but one mind, as to the *vigor* with which the war shall be pursued." Someone also dropped by to visit the forlorn grave of Ensign Gassaway, enclosed within a small picket fence. Musing over his tragic and unnecessary death, the visitor noted that according to the code duello, Lieutenant Jenifer had every right to kill him, "but by the laws of humanity he had not." He bitterly noted that honest, brave men often became "the dupes of fools" when they were drawn into fighting duels, and "every man who approves of duelling is answerable for a drop of the blood of Gassaway." Sadly, officers in the legion learned nothing from the death of the young ensign.[2]

As April drew to a close, preparations for the descent of the Ohio intensified. Quartermaster James O'Hara had already furnished General Wayne with an estimate of the number of vessels that would be required to transport the legion to Fort Washington. His calculations indicated a need for thirty boats to transport two thousand men and their baggage; eight for horses and oxen; six for the artillery, forges, and military stores; eight for quartermaster stores; one for the hospital; and ten to carry forage. On February 5, there were only a dozen boats on hand fit for use, so O'Hara signed contracts for the remainder, these craft to be delivered by April 15, the original target date for starting downriver. There were no large boatyards, so Wayne's fleet was constructed by a number of small contractors. Those furnishing the most boats were William Plumer and John Perry on the Youghiogheny River and Neal Gillespie at West Brownsville on the Monongahela River. The only setback in delivery resulted from the accidental burning of John Perry's sawmill. Wayne's departure was first postponed until April 20, then put off for another nine days, then delayed another day when it was discovered that a large number of boats leaked after being loaded. The legion finally shoved its boats out into the current at eleven o'clock on the morning of April 30 and began its long-awaited voyage.[3]

A pilot boat took the lead, followed at a distance of two hundred yards by the remainder of the fleet in single file, each boat one hundred yards behind the one ahead and following "exactly in the wake of its van," or leading boat. A group of "guard boats" followed the rear of the column at a distance of three hundred yards, their crews having specific orders to not pass any other boats under any circumstances, to dislodge those that might run aground, and to bring along all crippled craft. General Wayne would be aboard his own boat, named *Federalist*. The fleet was arranged in the following order, with the leading boat in each section displaying a flag in its stern by day and a lantern by night:

> Rifle corps of the right wing
> Dragoons of the right wing
> Artillery of the right wing, one howitzer and one 3-pounder under Capt. John Peirce
> Infantry of the right wing, under Maj. John Mills, composed of the First and Fourth
>   Sub-Legions
> Quartermaster stores and forage
> Military and ordnance stores
> General Staff
> Hospital and hospital stores

Infantry of the left wing, under Maj. John Buell, composed of the Second and Third
    Sub-Legions
Artillery of the left wing, one howitzer and one 3-pounder under Capt. Moses Porter
Dragoons of the left wing
Rifle corps of the left wing

Drum calls would alert crews as to whether to speed up or slow down. If the fleet continued downstream after dark, boats would float with the current, the men using their oars only to steer or maintain the proper distance. Whenever the legion was to land, the pilot boat would tie up to the northern bank of the river, and each boat would land downstream in succession. Upon reaching shore, the riflemen were to immediately disembark and advance a half mile, forming a chain to cover the landing "at every expence of Blood." Temporary breastworks would be constructed before the troops came ashore.[4]

Captain Eaton served as commander of the guard boats on the final half of the journey, and he recorded the wondrous sights of this new western country:

> Never was my eye so much delighted with the rude uncultured grandeur of nature. A description of the banks of the Ohio mocks, or can but ape reality. Geography has never yet done justice to the subject. For more than two hundred miles I saw not a hill incapable of culture. All so far as the eye can ken is a fertile bottom variegated with gentle rises. The rank and rapid growth of vegetation, and the prodigious weight of timber, demonstrate the natural luxuriance of the soil. The sycamore, the elm, the beach, the aspin, the hicory, the walnut, and the maple, or sugar tree, are large beyond credibility. The trees even at this early season were in full foliage. The herbiage which covered the surface of the bottom, was nearly two feet high.

Occasionally, Eaton would stop and walk along the northern bank with two soldiers from his guard detachment, often straying two or three miles from the river in this amazing wonderland. Fortunately, they did not encounter any Indians, but the soldiers saw plenty of tracks of deer, bear, and buffalo that had been frightened off by the legion's noisy passage. As for the Ohio itself, the captain described it as "the most capricious stream I ever saw," rising as much as ten to fifteen feet in a single day during heavy rains. He added: "Its current is rapid, at the rate of five miles an hour in time of the freshes; consequently the unwieldy boats which float down, never ascend. Keel bottom boats and canoes are rowed against the current, but with considerable labor."[5]

Troops passed a number of important sites on their way westward, the wilderness between being broken only by a few settlers' huts. First was the Big Beaver River, with its small blockhouse and tiny garrison. Then came the settlement of Georgetown, a few cabins at Mingo Bottom, with another small garrison, and the town of Wheeling in Virginia. The walls of Fort Harmar at the mouth of the Muskingum announced the presence of more settlers, these from New England, followed by settlements at Belpre on the north side and Bellville on the south side of the Ohio. Next came the French settlement at Gallipolis; the Sandy River, which was the boundary between Virginia and

Capt. William Eaton. From Meade Minnigerode, *Lives and Times*, 1925.

Kentucky; the Scioto River; and the town of Limestone on the Ohio's south bank. The latter had been described by one officer as a place where the streets "were abominably filthy and dirty, owing to their hogsties being contiguous to them, and from laziness, or some other reason incomprehensible to me, their suffering the filth and excrements to run into the streets." Huts and cabins became more frequent as the boats approached the town of Columbia, at the mouth of the Little Miami, and even more so toward the village of Cincinnati, situated directly across the Ohio from the mouth of the Licking River, with Fort Washington sitting atop the highest river terrace to its rear. The distance from Legionville to Fort Washington was calculated at just over 495 miles, and Wayne's army reached its destination on May 6 after a fairly rapid descent.[6]

The only event of note occurred shortly after the fleet had passed the Pennsylvania border. A sudden, ragged volley of shots from near the mouth of Yellow Creek on the north shore put everyone on alert. But this was not an Indian attack; it was merely a group of rangers who had been on a scout firing their rifles to salute the passing fleet. Wayne ordered the *Federalist* to shore, where he heard a fascinating tale of their encounter with and lucky escape from a group of about twenty Indians a few days before. After learning they were scouts in government employ, the general ordered a boat filled with his riflemen to land and engage them in a shooting match. The rangers proved to be the better marksmen. Wayne complimented them as "damned fine shots," passed around a bottle of brandy, and resumed the passage.[7]

The high water that allowed such a fast trip had been calamitous for the residents in Cincinnati. Unaware of the flooding capability of the river, many new arrivals had built their cabins, planted crops, and constructed fences on low ground. When the river began to rise during the spring rains, it did not stop until all of the low-lying portions of Cincinnati had been swept away, some of the houses actually floating downstream in the floodwaters. Luckily, the river rose gradually so that most personal property had been saved. It was in the midst of this crisis that the legion made its appearance. General Wayne was not impressed by what he found and must have agreed with Lt. William Harrison's opinion when he first set eyes on Cincinnati in 1791, describing the town as "a hamlet of logs and mud." Nothing had changed in the past eighteen months, except that now there was more mud. Many years later, Solomon Van Rensselaer remembered that the village consisted of but "a few rudely constructed log cabins along the bank of your river, and the challenge of the sentinels on the parapet of old Fort Washington, alone interrupted the universal silence." After inspecting the countryside, Wayne decided to bivouac in beech woods on high ground near the mouth of Mill Creek, a short distance beyond the fort. Constrained by floodwaters and instructions from Secretary of War Knox that he must encamp where the price of rations would be the cheapest (that is, along the banks of the Ohio), Wayne had no other choice but to stop where he did. Recalling the old story of Tobias Hobson at Cambridge, who gave his customers but one choice, either take it or go away, the general dryly called his new cantonment Hobson's Choice.[8]

Ezra Ferris, although only ten years of age at the time, recalled that the legion's arrival "was hailed with joy, and the people now felt as though they were secure." Everyone wanted to go see the soldiers. After the legion had been in camp for a few weeks, Ferris got permission to accompany a neighbor, who filled a small canoe with vegetables to sell to the soldiers, and they set out from Columbia. After passing Cincinnati and while drawing near to Wayne's camp, as it was commonly known, a sentinel hailed the canoe and ordered it to land. After a sergeant examined their cargo for contraband whiskey, the two were allowed to walk about to satisfy their curiosity. Hobson's Choice had been laid out with the white tents, "in rows as straight as a line," parallel to and extending down the river close to a half mile, with a large swamp to the north, or front, side. Boats had been dismantled and the timber used to construct stables. In the second row of tents from the rear, with an open space between it and the river, stood Wayne's headquarters marquee. Tents of the junior officers were interspersed among those of their troops. Many of the beech trees remained standing, their uniform size making a natural awning over much of the camp, but those on the parade ground had been cut down and the stumps removed so officers would have a place to drill their men. After the undergrowth had been removed, the entire camp seemed in "perfect order," especially to a youth like Ferris, who for years had seen nothing but inferior log cabins and a few rude, unpainted frame houses. Forty years later, Hugh Brackenridge, then but a youngster of seven, could still remember "the beating of drums, the clangour of trumpets, and the movements of horse and foot."[9]

Hobson's Choice was only the latest addition to the many wonders that could be seen in the Cincinnati area. Perhaps the most fascinating of all were the large earthen mounds that abounded in the Ohio valley. Generally of circular or elliptical form, the largest of those at Cincinnati measured about six hundred feet in diameter. The plain surrounding that village was literally covered with what appeared to be low embankments, and according to Lieutenant Harrison, "the number and variety of figures in which these lines were drawn was almost endless." Many had eroded over the centuries, and some sections had entirely disappeared, but so many still remained that he and General Wayne spent almost one whole day examining them. The tallest of the mounds, although not of great surface area, stood almost forty feet high. Wayne had some eight feet removed from the top of this one and put up a sentry box, where a sentinel could overlook both Cincinnati and Hobson's Choice. (All that remains of these spectacular monuments in the twenty-first century is embodied in the name Mound Street.)[10]

It was generally conceded that there might be friction between officers and men of the First and Second Sub-Legions, mostly older troops, and those of the Third and Fourth Sub-Legions, who had joined in 1792. But the arrival of Wayne's men from Legionville brought something more sinister than protection for the frontier and much-needed currency for the western economy. A revolution had been raging in France, and it culminated on January 21, 1793, with the death of King Louis XVI. That stunning news reached Pittsburgh two months later and was disseminated to the various forts, but the "seeds of disorganization" had been sown already in some of the officers. These men became sympathetic to the abstract "principles of liberty and equality" that drove the French Revolution, although those doctrines had no place in a military organization that stressed obedience and subordination. One man observed that "certain officers, tinctured with the prevailing mania, were little disposed to yield that entire obedience which was deemed essential to the safety of the army." Although President Washington successfully kept supporters of the French Revolution from embroiling the United States in European affairs, some of its advocates in the legion would prove very troublesome in the future.[11]

Although Hobson's Choice had many disadvantages, the major one was its proximity to Cincinnati, which lay directly on the camp's right flank. Wayne had only been there three days before he began to complain to Secretary Knox about the village, which was "filled with ardent *poison* & Caitiff wretches to dispose of it." The consumption of alcohol by his troops increased dramatically at Hobson's Choice, and the first instance of related trouble occurred on May 8, when Pvt. James Davis was discovered drunk and asleep while on guard. This case was followed shortly thereafter by charges against James Douglass (alias James Spencer) of Sedam's company for "repeated Drunkenness, being absent from Roll Call and Mutinous Conduct in repeated Instances." Perhaps the most egregious violation of orders came on the night of May 20, when Cpl. John Ferriss gave one of the guard money to buy whiskey and sent him off to do so. The consequence was that four of the guards were arrested after being found drunk and asleep. Ferriss was sentenced to receive fifty lashes, and one of the guards was acquitted, but a court-martial sentenced the other three, all from Hannah's Virginia company, to be shot to death. Wayne remitted their sentences but warned all future offenders that since "the lives and Safety of the Legion and of the Country [depend] upon the Vigilance of the Centinels," no further mercy would be shown.[12]

When Wayne visited Cincinnati and discovered the "Intoxicated and Beastly situation" of "a great Number of the Soldiery belonging to almost every Corps," he banned all passes except for those signed by the field officer of the day, and then not more than one per company, each applicant being recommended by a company officer. Any soldier caught without a pass or carrying a forged one was to immediately receive twenty lashes without the formality of trial. Any sentinel improperly allowing an enlisted man to leave without a pass would receive fifty lashes. Confining the troops to camp cut down on alcohol consumption, but it did nothing to improve sanitation. Following an inspection that "found so much filth" among the tents, the camp itself was ordered to be cleaned. Two men from each detachment, supervised by a corporal, cleaned their company area each morning. Soldiers were threatened with punishment if they continued to throw waste water and animal bones into the drainage ditches or onto the parade ground. Offal from the slaughterhouse, an adjoining storehouse, and the cattle pens—all upstream from Hobson's Choice and overrun with filth, rats, and insects—had caused "a Putricity in the Water along Shore." Not surprisingly, water from the Ohio River was judged "unfit for use and injurious to the Troops, as well as intollerable offensive to the Encampment." These operations were immediately moved three hundred yards *downstream*, the old site cleaned up, and all waste buried. Water quality began to improve, and an epidemic may have been averted.[13]

Although his detailed report on the western posts would not be offered until May 15, General Wilkinson made sure that he was on hand to greet the legion commander and welcome him to the frontier. General Wayne began a frank discussion by disclosing the objectives of the projected campaign. Wilkinson briefed Wayne on the current situation—one soldier wounded at Fort Jefferson and a rifleman taken prisoner near Fort Hamilton by marauders—and suggested that some of the new troops be sent forward to the advanced garrisons, thus allowing the commanders there to keep out larger patrols. Wilkinson then discussed the status of the road he had built from Fort Washington to

Fort Hamilton, varying from forty to sixty feet in width and suitable for wagon traffic, which still needed additional bridges and causeways over the streams but could be completed in ten days. The trace from Fort Hamilton to Fort Jefferson was unsuitable for wagons, although "a convenient waggon way" could be constructed by five hundred men within the space of three weeks. Wilkinson then proposed that the "Veteran Companies" at Fort Steuben and Fort Knox be relieved by detachments of sick and invalid soldiers from the advanced posts. Wayne approved both the plan to complete and extend the wagon road as well as the replacement of the Ohio River garrisons.[14]

He selected Lieutenant Colonel Strong to complete the wagon road to Fort Jefferson, cautioning him to keep guards out upon his front, flanks, and rear, while the main portion of his command cut the road. Strong was told to fell large trees on each side of the road and parallel to it so they could be used as breastworks if the road builders were attacked. Toward evening, the workers were to make a small, rectangular fort by felling more trees to the front and rear across the roadway. This temporary breastwork would protect Strong's detachment "against insult & numbers be they what they will" at the cost of perhaps an extra hour of labor each day. If it proved expedient, he was also given the option of going forward and constructing his fortification first, then cutting the road forward and backward from his defensive position. Wayne wanted this road to be completed as quickly as possible since the quartermaster was bringing forward additional horses and oxen to be used to stockpile forage and supplies at the head of the line. There were no attacks on Strong's road party, although several of the men became lost at various times and claimed to have been chased by Indians, but their stories were dismissed as fiction.[15]

Capt. Thomas Cushing inspected the advanced garrisons, where he found 103 enlisted men "unfit for Field Duty." Except for those too sick to travel, these soldiers were brought back to Fort Washington and formed into two detachments for use in the garrisons of Forts Knox and Steuben. Captain Pasteur was dispatched with one detachment to Fort Knox, where he relieved Lt. Col. John Hamtramck and the old garrison except for Lt. Ross Bird, who remained behind as the new second in command. Lt. Robert Hunter took the other group of invalids to Fort Steuben, where he relieved Maj. Thomas Doyle and his old company of the First Sub-Legion. Both Pasteur and Hunter received the same warning from General Wayne: "You are to use every possible precaution to guard against surprise—& you are never to permit more than two or three Indians to enter the walls of your Command at any one time." Although the peace commissioners had proclaimed a temporary truce with the Indian nations, the general warned, "whilst you treat them with kindness & hospitality—you must be guarded against every insidious attempt." Pasteur was unimpressed with his new assignment. He found the fort needing several repairs and had no carpenter among the soldiers of his command. But worst of all were the men, and Pasteur confessed, "I would rather have half my own Company than one hundred of such as composes the Detachment."[16]

Lt. William Clark and a small group of riflemen occupied a blockhouse at the mouth of the Kentucky River, and it had originally been Wayne's intention to relieve that command as well. But an order from Knox to transport five hundred muskets, twenty rifles, two thousand pounds of powder, five thousand flints, four thousand pounds of lead, fifteen hundred bushels of corn, one hundred bushels of salt, and one thousand gallons of whiskey to the Chickasaw Nation changed his mind. After the keelboats reached Hobson's Choice with the troops from Forts Knox and Steuben, they were loaded with these supplies and sent back downstream. Clark and his men climbed aboard, finding them "slender and leaky," and acted as convoy guards for the journey to a rendezvous on the Mississippi with the friendly Chickasaws. Wayne thought the supply boats might run into trouble at a Spanish fort about eighty miles below the mouth of the Ohio River, so he advised Clark "to drop down by that post in the Night time, to prevent any difficulty or disagreeable consequence."[17]

Detachments continued to flow down the Ohio River to Hobson's Choice to join the legion. First to arrive was the cantankerous Major Hughes and the old garrisons from Fort Franklin and Mead's Station. These companies reached Pittsburgh on May 7, their arrival being delayed by men "eating some wild greens in the woods" and then becoming "Extremely sick." The major carried a letter from Lieutenant Colonel Clark with information that the Indians had boldly stolen some contractor's horses within a short distance of Pittsburgh and had made an appearance in force near Mingo Bottom. Washington County rangers followed the latter enemy track and traded rifle fire, but they retreated across the Ohio River when the Indians appeared to be in greater strength. Ensign Brady, with thirty-five men, was sent to pursue them. Clark informed Wayne that, following this latest incursion, "the frontiers of Washington is very much alarmed."[18]

Writing to Wayne in mid-May, General Wilkinson pointed out that he had "not enjoyed ten Days respite from active & laborious Duty" in over sixteen months and asked for permission to pay his attention "to a long absent & beloved Wife." Unbeknownst to the general, Ann Wilkinson was actually on her way to join him. She and her son embarked on May 28 aboard "a Kentucky boat particularly fitted up for their accommodation." The Wilkinsons shared their vessel with Brig. Gen. Thomas Posey and his staff, Cornet John Posey and Ens. William A. Daingerfield, the former a son and the latter a son-in-law. Lieutenant Harrison, returning from a furlough in Virginia, acted as an escort for Mrs. Wilkinson, and Capt. Samuel Andrews, recently replaced as commandant at Fort Fayette, completed the distinguished party. A second Kentucky boat went along to carry horses and baggage, although low water in the river forced the horses to be taken overland to Wheeling.[19]

General Posey, who had been appointed to replace the recently resigned Rufus Putnam, would be a welcome addition to Wayne's command. Born in Virginia along the banks of the Potomac on July 9, 1750, Thomas Posey was from a "respectable, but not wealthy" farm family. Educated in country schools, he first took up arms in Dunmore's War and fought at Point Pleasant in 1774. At the commencement of the Revolution, he raised a company of Virginians that was eventually assigned to Col. Daniel Morgan's regiment of picked riflemen. Posey's war service included the Battles of Saratoga, Monmouth, Stony Point, and Yorktown. He served with Wayne in Georgia, and in the battle with Guristersigo's Creek warriors near Savannah on June 24, 1781, he killed several Indians by his own hand. Posey settled in Spotsylvania County after the war, where he served as a militia colonel and county lieutenant. Wayne was overjoyed to be joined by an old comrade, "with whom I have participated in almost every vicissitude of fortune, from the frozen lakes of Canada to the burning sands of Florida." Secretary Knox took advantage of Posey's departure to send a private letter to Wilkinson in which he thanked the general heartily "for the various, extensive and important information you have communicated from time to time, all of which was duly communicated to the President of the United States." He also expressed his wish that this conduct would continue and that Wilkinson would "unite cordially with General Wayne and promote a spirit of harmony throughout the Several Corps."[20]

More troops had also been ordered to join the legion at Hobson's Choice. John Pratt marched his new company of the First Sub-Legion from his rendezvous at Middletown, Connecticut, on June 14. He would soon be joined en route by detachments forwarded from Maj. Jonathan Cass in New Hampshire, Capt. Cornelius Lyman in Massachusetts, Captain Sedam in New Jersey, Captain Kersey in Philadelphia, and Lieutenant Underhill in Vermont. Captain Pratt appointed Lent Munson, one of those old sergeants upon whom officers so frequently depend, to act as his orderly sergeant for the long journey to the frontier. Munson had been born on March 3, 1768. in Harwinton, Connecticut, and joined the Continental Army as a musician at the age of ten. He joined the First Regiment in 1788 and served at Fort Harmar and Fort Washington before volunteering for recruiting duty in 1790. Munson was assigned to the Middletown rendezvous, where Pratt found him to be "honest, prudent, charitable, and just in all his dealings." These qualities, combined with his "amiable disposition," won him many friends among soldiers and civilians alike.[21]

After inspecting and mustering the various detachments at Trenton, New Jersey, Pratt prepared his troops for the long march to Pittsburgh. This movement would be governed by a lengthy set of regulations that offer a intimate glimpse into military life in the legion:

> The Revallee to beat at day breaking, upon which the Rolls are to be called, every man turn out and prepare for a March. The General 15 minutes after, at which the Tents are to be struck, carefully packed up, the polls, pins, Camp Kettles, Axes &c. collected and with the other baggage put into the Waggons under the direction of Sergeant Armstrong, who will attend particularly to this duty the whole March and is to be accountable for all the Camp Equipage. The Long Roll, 20 minutes after the General at which the Men are to parade in one Rank the talest on the right. The even numbers at the word "to the right double," are to fall in the rear of their right hand Man. The whole incline to the right and close the files, forming two ranks, then told off into sections of eight, each section given in charge to a Sergeant who will be accountable for the same. This position places all the talest Men on the right and shortest on the left, who are alternately to March in front.

The Camp Guard is to follow the Waggons and serve as a rear Guard for the purpose of bringing forward all stragglers and assist in getting on the Baggage &c.

The troops being thus formed are to move on slowly by direction of the Commanding Officer who will cause frequent halts at convenient places for the refreshment of the Men. At the word *Halt* the sections are to move up into their places and order their pieces. The Water call will then beat, at which one Man from each section is to take all the Canteens of the same and parade in front, forming a Water Party, which when compleat is to be conducted to the Watering place by two Non Commissioned Officers, and when supplied returned to the Detachment dismissed and Join their sections. At beating the long Roll, the Men are to fall in, the Roll to be called and reported to the Commanding Officer, who will direct accordingly.

Any Non Comd Officer or Soldier who shall be found stragling from the Detachment for the purpose of falling into Houses, Gardens, Orchards, Corn-fields, or any other enclosures, and taking therefrom any of the property of the Inhabitants, shall be severely punished on the spot.

The Taptoo is to beat at 9 o'clock, the Rolls are then to be called by the Sergeants Commanding squads and reported to the Commanding Officer. The Sergeants are also to see that their Men turn in to rest.

By the time they reached Pittsburgh, after marching over a month under these directives, the new recruits had learned the principles of military subordination.[22]

Captain Pratt left Lt. Peter Grayson and fifty-two enlisted men at Pittsburgh, with orders to erect a blockhouse at Wheeling, then set off down the river, followed shortly by a detachment of thirty soldiers under Lieutenant Tinsley. These two parties joined together at Wheeling, where Pratt, "to guard against the difficulties and dangers," issued a set of orders that would govern the descent of their fleet to Hobson's Choice. The boats would descend in the following order:

Keelboat carrying ammunition, acting as the pilot with a red flag in the stern
Commanding officer's boat
Large covered boat with quartermaster stores
Colonel Thompson's boat, a civilian craft
Boat with contractor's stores
Boat carrying the wagons and a guard detachment
Lieutenant Tinsley's boat acting as rear guard

The boats would keep a distance of almost four hundred yards, and if any vessel should run aground, assistance would be sent in canoes. Should the convoy be attacked, the other boats would align on that of the commander, they would all be lashed together, and the fleet's two howitzers manned. No enlisted men were permitted to land without permission, and the firing of weapons was strictly forbidden. If it became necessary for the troops to go ashore, guards would advance and form a line of pickets one hundred yards beyond the landing site. Each soldier was to have six rounds of ammunition and one flint, with every weapon "fit for Action." Captain Pratt's attention to details resulted in a relatively uneventful trip from New Jersey to Hobson's Choice.[23]

As detachment after detachment descended the Ohio River, it seemed to the American public that these servicemen had simply dropped off the face of the earth. One editor complained, "While we have daily accounts of the operations of foreign armies, we cannot, on the most critical enquiry, obtain the least information respecting our western army, if any exists." Perhaps, he opined, they were "concealed in some desolate woods, while their savage enemy are openly committing the most cruel murders and depredations on the defenceless inhabitants of our frontier." But news moved slowly in the western country. When Ebenezer Denny carried the news of St. Clair's defeat to President Washington, it was not delivered until December 19—forty-five days after the battle. This intelligence was undoubtedly, due to its national importance, delivered at the utmost speed possible, including the use of a fourteen-oar barge for travel up the Ohio. Floods or low water slowed travel on the river, while searing heat and wintry conditions added days to overland journeys. It is safe to say that it was just as fast for eastern editors to obtain news from Europe as it was for them to receive it from the advanced forts in the Northwest Territory. Just by way of illustration, the brig *Mary*, out of Boston under command of one Captain Tripe, made the passage from Liverpool, England, to Portsmouth, New Hampshire, in fifty-six days. Other ships made the journey faster, others slower, but this seems to be about the average length of time at sea on the run from Europe.[24]

While General Wayne understood the capabilities of the troops he had brought from Legionville, he wanted to learn the status of those who had been serving under Wilkinson. That officer pointed out to his superior that his soldiers were "in general well Clad; they enjoy good health, & have made great proficieny in Marks-Manship; my officers are in the Habits of vigilance & industry, they are in general, tolerably versed in the fundamentals of their profession, and no pains have been spared to inculcate a just sense of subordination, & to impress accurate ideas of discipline, upon their Minds." He added that his enlisted men "have been tried in the Field, are men of vigorous constitutions, & capable of energetic exertion." But there were some problems. Many enlistments would soon expire, so Wilkinson urged Wayne to take steps "to reengage those men." Out of necessity, so many soldiers had been sent hither and yon on various assignments that companies were hopelessly jumbled. Wilkinson suggested that the men be returned to their own companies and officers as soon as circumstances would permit. Many of the muskets in service recoiled so violently that they produced "a considerable degree of apprehension" while being aimed. The old troops still wore cross belts and a cartridge box, while the new arrivals had pouches held with straps around the waist and over the shoulder. Wilkinson wanted his men to use the new-style pouch too, though he suggested several modifications to increase comfort and accessibility in action. Headgear had not been modified to the new standard for lack of material. Axes and entrenching tools were in short supply. Despite the shortcomings, Wayne assured Secretary Knox that Wilkinson's conduct "merits my highest approbation."[25]

Wilkinson did give Wayne some additional information about the two most unusual characters in his command. He had retained both Henry Schaffer, the escaped prisoner with a command of the Potawatomi language, and William May, the spy who had been to Detroit while in the general's employ. He had given the two men rations and pay, employing them "occasionally as scouts and expresses," but they had no regular military duties to perform. Wilkinson kept them around simply because he felt they might be useful as scouts when the legion moved northward into Indian territory—Schaffer because of his knowledge of the Potawatomi Nation and May because he was "a Fellow of great activity & resource, of dauntless spirit & violent Passions," although a notorious villain. Both men had been apprehended in Cincinnati on January 6 while engaging in "riotous disorderly Conduct" by firing their rifles, screaming savage yells, and generally "creating false Alarms to the Terror of the People." Schaffer and May must have thought their actions to be riotously funny, but residents of the town did not share the hilarity. Nevertheless, Wayne endorsed Wilkinson's decision regarding these two special cases, and they would both perform valuable services in future campaigns.[26]

CHAPTER 9

Preparations for an Advance

ONE OF THE FIRST THINGS new troops learned at Hobson's Choice was that the specter of St. Clair's defeat still hung over the land. Veterans told stories about the fighting. Officers argued over what they had done during the campaign. Mutilated bodies still lay on the battlefield. Captives were being ill treated by their Indian masters. There was even a casualty from that battle still receiving treatment in the hospital at Fort Washington. Joseph Moorhead, an ensign in Maj. Jonathan Clark's battalion of levies, was severely wounded in the left arm and had been treated by the surgeons for almost eighteen months by the time General Wayne reached the frontier. The ensign had not received any regular pay after the levies were discharged, although the paymaster had advanced him "several small supplies of money." When the legion fleet arrived, Moorhead sought out Paymaster Caleb Swan, told him that he was fit for service, and asked for help in obtaining a new commission. Swan obliged by sending a letter to the general, but the doctors would not approve his application. When Surgeons Richard Allison, Nathan Hayward, and John Elliot examined Moorhead on August 19, 1793, they found him unable to use his arm and totally disabled.[1]

News of those taken prisoner continued to filter out of the Indian country, and occasionally a captive or two would escape and reach American settlements. Margaret Pendrick had been captured on that bloody field, along with her small child, who was "tomahawked on the spot." Her captors took her to Grand Glaize, a concentration of Indian villages at the confluence of the Auglaize and Maumee Rivers, where she remained until October 2, 1792, at which time she escaped with another woman. The two traveled over three weeks through the woods until they reached Detroit. After being well treated by the British, Pendrick finally reached safety in June 1793, along with two men who had been captured along the Little Miami, one in 1791 and the other in January 1793. Shortly after the return of Margaret Pendrick, a settler who had been taken at Marietta returned with information about some New England men from St. Clair's army. He remembered seeing Pvt. Edward Hinmon and a Sergeant Hall from Shaylor's company, a couple of men named Ames and Monatt from Massachusetts, and Peter Larkins and someone named Atkins, both from Connecticut. Such information, no matter how meager, was published by local newspapers and disseminated through the national press.[2]

Within hours of reaching the Cincinnati area, General Wayne had to confront one of St. Clair's old officers, the dissolute Lt. Col. John Smith. He had been sentenced to dismissal for reprehensible conduct at Fort St. Clair by a court-martial, but he advised the general, "My fate rests with you, Sir," and requested an immediate interview. Wayne sent his regrets regarding the embarrassing affair, urging Smith to resign and cite "long indisposition" as the reason. The general promised to accept this excuse "in a manner that will not be displeasing either to you or your friends" and "prevent this unfortunate affair from appearing to the World." Smith declined to resign "under the imputation of Censure," so Wayne sent him a copy of the charges and sentence of the court as a gentle prod to reconsider his decision. Citing irregularities that may have prejudiced the court, Smith again asked for a personal meeting to discuss his unpleasant situation.[3]

The lieutenant colonel must have been persuasive in his arguments, for on May 25 General Wayne made a startling reversal of the court's sentence. Following "a full and Deliberate Examination and Digest of the Evidence on record," he concluded that Smith's intemperance and strange behavior resulted from "the Unhappy mallady with which he was then afflicted." The mistaken belief that Lieutenant Tilton, Ensign Kreemer, and Dr. Samuel Boyd had conspired to take his life issued from a "Disturbed Imagination" and was, therefore, considered rather "a Misfortune than a Crime." Yet Major Adair's testimony left no doubt that Smith had been "disordered" and "much Deranged in his reason." Wayne then took the unusual step of freeing Smith from arrest, approving the conduct of Captain Bradley in relieving his post commander, and exonerating Tilton, Kreemer, and Boyd of the conspiracy claim. Lieutenant Colonel Smith was elated at this turn of events and requested a three-month leave of absence to arrange his military accounts in Philadelphia, citing the fact that he was "inadequate in the present moment to taking the Field." Wayne had intended to advance northward on the first of July, a target date later pushed back to the middle of that month, and he wanted to know whether Smith would be "sufficiently recover'd to take the field." If not, the general wanted his immediate resignation. Despite Wayne's insistence that "an explicit answer is requested," Smith did not respond until July 2, when he agreed to take command of the Third Sub-Legion despite being "impaired from former & late indisposition."[4]

The commander of the First Sub-Legion, Lieutenant Colonel Hamtramck, was then on his way up the Ohio from Fort Knox. Stopping at Fort Steuben on July 7, he wrote to his friend Gen. Josiah Harmar: "I am now on my way to Head Quarters, I shall go & look at them, & if I find that the army is not sufficient to do what is Expected of them, I shall quit the service. Indeed, if I had not been promoted I should have resigned this spring." Confessing that the legion arrangement was "a new affair" to someone who had been away from civilization for so long, Hamtramck asked his friend for an opinion on its organization. Then the lieutenant colonel passed along news that a rift had developed between Wayne and Wilkinson. According to rumors that came down the river, the two generals, "after being for some time very great, have declared war." Hamtramck assured Harmar, "I shall find out all about it when I get up, & will tell you the affair as it is." He must have had grave misgivings about continued service in the legion. First, President Washington had shown no confidence in Hamtramck's ability to negotiate a treaty at Fort Knox, and now he was the third-highest-ranking officer in an organization that he did not understand. To make matters even worse, his two superiors were apparently at odds with one another.[5]

With turmoil among the most senior officers of the legion becoming more pronounced, Wayne still kept his watchful eye open for minor transgressions of discipline. The general's wrath first burst forth on Uriah Springer, whose company, despite "pointed and Repeated orders," had arrived at Hobson's Choice wearing the old style of headgear. Wayne put the entire company on fatigue duty for ten days until the hats had been cut down into caps according to previous instructions. Springer took offense at the general's characterization that he was wanting "Soldierly Genious," asking for a court of inquiry that never came. Shortly thereafter, all officers were ordered to have the men repair their torn and worn-out clothing since low water in the Ohio would stop shipments, and the impending advance would take the legion farther and farther from its base of supplies.[6]

While most officers tried to avoid the commander in chief's ire, the same old troublemakers seemed to always attract attention. Shortly after reaching Hobson's Choice, Maj. John Buell had a disagreement with Lieutenant Diven, so the latter challenged the former to a duel. Buell refused Diven's challenge and had the hothead arrested, although he was released by a court-martial. Wayne expressed his hope that officers would find other ways of settling their differences rather than clogging the military courts with frivolous charges. Soon after, Diven appeared in front of another court-martial, this time pressing charges against Lieutenant Jenifer, the killer of Ensign Gassaway. In commenting on Jenifer's acquittal, General Wayne said the accusations appeared "to be only the counterpart of those exhibited by Mr. Junifer against Mr. Divin" the previous December. These new charges appeared to be based on "malice, and personal Resentment" rather than on "the Honour or Dignity of the Legion." Again, Wayne said that there were other ways of settling personal quarrels, and in the future, he hoped that there would be no more trials "that tend only to disgrace the Orderly Books of the U. States of America."[7]

On June 20, Major Buell preferred charges against Captain Guion for unmilitary behavior and disobedience of orders, but the New Yorker was acquitted. Three days later, Captain DeButts, Wayne's aide-de-camp, hauled Lt. John Sullivan before another court for disobeying orders and for "an instant, open, and contemptuous Violation" in resisting these lawful orders. Wayne called Sullivan's actions either "Stupid Ignorance, or Criminal Impertinence" and made it clear to everyone that an order coming through his aide would be the same as if it came from the general himself. Two weeks later, Guion charged Ensign Drake with neglect and abuse of duty for his conduct while in command of the camp guards. Although guilty of neglecting a portion of his responsibilities, Drake was

returned to duty. Despite Wayne's plea for an end to retaliatory prosecution, this practice continued as officers sought to publicly humiliate their rivals and enemies.[8]

Courts-martial certainly had enough of their time taken up with meting out justice
to enlisted men who came before them on a litany of serious charges. It seemed that
infractions of discipline increased significantly after leaving Legionville, and the orderly
books list dozens of offenders and their sentences. The most common violations were
disobedience of orders, striking a superior, desertion, desertion and enlistment in another
company, sleeping on post, and using insolent language. Despite warnings about imposing the death sentence for the most serious violations, courts-martial generally used one
hundred lashes as the most extreme punishment. Leniency was occasionally shown for
past good conduct or being sick when the infraction occurred. Sometimes the number
of lashes would be reduced, sometimes the lashes would be inflicted over a specified
period of time rather than all at once, and at least once the guilty parties were simply
made to wear their uniform coats inside out. Every soldier, without exception, was
required to conform to regulations. Even Sergeant Reynolds, one of Wilkinson's secret
operatives now serving in the dragoons, violated the established rules. He was charged
with "Riotous behaviour," disobeying orders, neglect of duty, and absence without leave.
Reynolds was found guilty, sentenced to be suspended from the rank and pay of sergeant, and directed to serve as a private for two months. Wayne, citing his former service, reduced the sentence to a mere two weeks.[9]

Many enlisted men ran afoul of regulations because of whiskey, even though General Wayne had essentially banned its use. On the cash-strapped frontier, where a man's
labor and produce were often the medium of exchange, merchants eagerly sold whiskey
for cash. There was little specie, or hard currency, in circulation, so most goods purchased
prior to Wayne's arrival had been done so with government drafts that were often passed
among businessmen as currency. The new arrivals brought real paper money issued by
the Bank of the United States. Most of these bills were of the three-dollar denomina-
tion, that being the monthly pay of private soldiers, commonly called oblongs. The firm
of Smith and Findlay, anxious to receive as many oblongs as possible, built its own distillery and sold whiskey for one dollar per gallon. Perhaps the largest merchant in Cincinnati was the firm of Abijah Hunt and Company. Hunt was a close friend of Paymaster
Swan, who would tip off the merchant whenever large payments to the troops would be
expected. Then Hunt and his brothers would make sure their store was fully stocked
when the payments began, their markup from wholesale to retail being close to 100 percent. Other merchants marked up their wares as much as 200 percent. While that seems
excessive, the large increase compensated merchants for many goods that were damaged
in shipment, either overland from eastern cities to Pittsburgh or on the Ohio River leg
of the shipment. Much of the commercial business, including that done by the Hunt
firm, was conducted in pounds, shillings, and pence rather than in dollars and cents. The
official exchange rate was $4.44 for one pound sterling, but the actual exchange on the
frontier was closer to $2.66. The Hunt brothers also furnished whiskey to the army,
Abijah at one time commenting that its consumption was "Monstrous."[10]

There was much money to be made by supplying the legion in the Northwest Territory. John Johnston was sixteen years of age and working as a clerk for Judge John Creigh in Carlisle, Pennsylvania, when he heard stories of the rivers, lakes, prairies, and trackless forests from survivors of St. Clair's expedition then stationed at the barracks there. Determined to see the western frontier, Johnston and Judge Creigh's son Samuel set out for Pittsburgh with "a mercantile establishment" in early January 1793. Creigh rode ahead to make arrangements for river transportation, while Johnston traveled on foot with the wagons through the Pennsylvania winter. Reaching Pittsburgh with their goods safely intact, the two young men took along a passenger for the river portion of their trip. This new addition was a French lady who had come from Paris to join her husband, one of the immigrants who had settled at Gallipolis. The trip to that settlement was uneventful, although the two merchants discovered that the Frenchmen had built a fort and formed their own militia company, outfitted in blue uniforms with white trimmings. Upon arriving at Cincinnati, Johnston and his partner found that every type of merchandise was in demand, consequently it commanded a high price at Fort Washington and Hobson's Choice. The two youths rented an empty building and set up shop.[11]

Construction of Fort Washington and Wayne's decision to encamp at Hobson's Choice gave the village of Cincinnati its preeminent standing as *the* business center of the Northwest Territory. One historian explained the army's influence by stating that Fort Washington "was larger and more important than the village." The military road recently completed to Fort Jefferson created smaller markets at the advanced posts, but when the legion advanced, it would become a thoroughfare funneling food and supplies northward into the heretofore untenable Indian country. For the present, the supply of those forts offered jobs and a source of income much more predictable than the often unreliable occupations of farming and hunting. Of course, the legion offered a number of employment opportunities, and Quartermaster James O'Hara hired men to serve as artificers for a term of two years, preferring those who had experience as carpenters, wheelwrights, tinners, saddlers, blacksmiths, and farriers.[12]

The firm of Elliott and Williams had contracted to furnish provisions and forage to the legion and became the largest civilian employer in the territory. Although Robert Elliott, one of the partners, was often at headquarters, the most important representative of that firm was Robert Benham, who was styled the "Pack Horse Master General." Benham had the responsibility for delivering rations and forage to the advanced posts from the Elliott and Williams distribution center at Fort Washington. A descendant of John Benham who arrived in the Massachusetts colony in 1630, Robert had been born in Pennsylvania in 1750. In a fight with Indians along the Ohio River in 1779, he had the misfortune to have both thighs broken by a rifle ball. He eventually recovered from these debilitating wounds and became one of the first settlers at Cincinnati, where he was credited with building the first hewn-log house. Benham worked for the contractors who supplied the armies of Harmar and St. Clair, being wounded in the latter campaign by a ball that entered his wrist and lodged near the elbow. While recuperating from this latest wound, he established the first regular ferry across the Ohio River at Cincinnati before signing on with Elliott and Williams.[13]

Benham was assisted by subordinate captains, called packhorse masters, who were each responsible for the care and performance of a brigade of forty horses, along with enough men to load and unload them, drive them in convoy, and care for them while not on the march. Each horse had a saddle to which the load, usually weighing about two hundred pounds maximum, was lashed with ropes. Two men could control a string of ten to fifteen horses, all tied together single file, one walking alongside the leading horse and choosing the route, while the other brought up the rear and kept an eye on the freight. Brigades of packhorses were often consolidated into large convoys that would be protected by military escorts. Under General Wayne's order of June 17, 1793, such escorts would consist of one captain, two subalterns, eight noncommissioned officers, and sixty privates of infantry, supplemented by one subaltern, two noncommissioned officers, and eighteen privates of the dragoons. Escorts would shuttle back and forth between Forts Hamilton and Jefferson, with all soldiers serving "in due rotation, so that each Corps may participate in the fatigue, as also in the Glory, should they be fortunate enough to fall in with the Enemy."[14]

Packhorse masters were men such as John Sutherland, William McClellan, and Elias Wallen. The first mentioned was a native of Scotland who had immigrated to the United States in 1788 at the age of seventeen. Sutherland worked with the pack trains for a few years, then accepted an appointment in the Commissary Department. He soon after began trading with the Indians, which proved to be the beginning of a business that made him one of the wealthiest men in the region. Among the packhorse drivers, none was more famous than Robert McClellan, who occasionally worked with his brother William. The two had grown up in Cumberland County, Pennsylvania, where they learned the packhorse trade and worked at it for a number of years after the Revolution. Robert moved west in 1790 and began service as a ranger around the Hocking River. He reunited with William in 1792, and the two began hauling provisions and stores for the army. By this time, Robert had become famous for his athletic feats. He enjoyed showing off by jumping over horses "without apparent exertion" and on one occasion leaped over a yoke of oxen that stood in his way. Eyewitnesses even claimed to have seen him jump over a wagon with a canvas top that stood eight and a half feet high. There was no doubt that Robert McClellan possessed "extraordinary strength and agility" and was a valuable addition to the packhorse service.[15]

Wages could be earned by performing other jobs for Elliott and Williams. Matthew Hueston, a native of Cumberland County, Pennsylvania, was twenty-two years of age when he began to work for the contractors. After receiving a common-school education, Hueston worked first as an apprentice and then as a journeyman in the tanning business. He saved his earnings and, in the spring of 1793, descended the Ohio with a stock of leather goods. After selling some of his stock and being cheated out of the rest, Hueston ended up working with the McClellan brothers as a packhorse driver. Subsequent to completing a trip to Fort Jefferson, he signed on to accompany a drove of cattle to that same post, receiving fifteen dollars a month in wages. He was also to oversee the butchering and dressing of the beef, but upon his arrival, Hueston found that there was no salt in the garrison. The only thing that could be done was to dry the meat on racks in the open air until a shipment of salt could be arranged.[16]

Most of the preservative used by the legion came from salt licks in Kentucky, much of it shipped up the Ohio River from Louisville. Benjamin Van Cleve and Stace McDonough hired on to bring salt and corn to the legion at the rate of six shillings and six pence for each barrel of freight. Elliott and Williams furnished the men with a boat, which they loaded with flour and piloted downstream from Fort Washington. At Louisville, they unloaded the flour, arranged for a load of either salt or corn, and hired a crew for their return journey, each man being paid five dollars for the trip upstream. After three trips, Van Cleve and McDonough had each made a profit of seventy-five dollars, a tidy sum when paying jobs were extremely scarce.[17]

The money to be made in transporting supplies occasionally lured men to their deaths. A teamster named Scott Traverse used oxen to haul his wagon, filled with goods, to the advanced posts. As an individual entrepreneur, he prided himself on safely passing back and forth between the forts whenever he desired, even though he always traveled alone and snubbed his nose at a military escort. His friends urged caution and called him foolhardy, but Traverse continued to operate his solitary wagon and boasted of his good luck in avoiding the Indians. Then the inevitable happened one day near Fort Hamilton when Indians ambushed and killed Traverse and his oxen, burnt the wagon, and destroyed or carried off his goods.[18]

While civilians toiled to supply the outposts and soldiers waited impatiently in obedience to President Washington's order to suspend active operations, Indians continued desultory raids against the advanced forts. On May 24, a quartermaster employee named Maupin was mortally wounded by a small party as he traveled along the road from Fort Hamilton to Lieutenant Colonel Strong's road-cutting detachment. Indians had been seen "skulking about" near the fort, and Maupin's death was attributed to them. A few weeks later, six canoes were found drawn up on shore about a half mile above Fort Hamilton. Sergeant Morral, "a trusty fellow," was sent out to examine the site, and he discovered three large trails heading southward and paralleling the road by about a mile. Morral estimated the Indians as numbering close to one hundred. As for their target, Captain Bradley advised Wayne that only "God noes," although a strike at a convoy seemed likely. Another group of warriors struck at Fort Hamilton on the night of August 1, stealing some contractor's horses. Lt. James Taylor was sent out with a mounted party to follow their trail. After some twenty-five miles, Taylor and his men came suddenly upon a dozen Indians and frightened them off. Dragoons stopped to hastily examine the Indian packs, which contained only jerked venison, tobacco, blankets, tomahawks, and scalping knives, then they mounted up and continued the pursuit. The Indians ran in a body for another three miles, then quickly scattered as the horsemen drew near.[19]

To strengthen defenses along the road north, Wayne decided to send Major McMahon, his most trusted and experienced Indian fighter, to Fort Jefferson with over one hundred of the best riflemen available. McMahon was to scout from that post to the Miami River, thence down that stream to Fort Hamilton. If the major and his woodsmen were to find any of "the red Gentry," he was to "chastise them for stealing our Horses." This plan was part of Wayne's overall strategy to bulk up the garrison at Fort Jefferson, a scheme definitely not endorsed by either President Washington or Secretary of War Knox. But the post needed reinforcements since the sick list there was longer than anywhere else, brought on by tainted salt beef and exposure to inclement weather while making hay. Illness also struck at Fort Hamilton, where Maj. Thomas Hunt and Captain Bradley, along with many of their men, fell sick with tertian fever, a form of malaria. General Wilkinson complained that the medicine chest there had "not a single grain of the Bark of the Jesuits," a form of quinine.[20]

At Fort St. Clair, its garrison was often depleted to a single company as the remainder of the troops marched north and south as convoy escorts. Captain Shaylor reported that it was "impossible" to furnish escorts as well as perform ordinary duty and keep the blockhouse manned. Capt. Alexander Gibson relieved that officer in August and, after an inspection, found the post in a shambles. He reported to Wilkinson that "Captain Shaylor gave the Soldiers under his Command free priviledge from the receipt of his marching orders." Gibson found everything in a "very indifferent order." Many of the bunks had been destroyed, and much of the glass in the windows broken. Most of the rooms needed to be repaired and cleaned. The blacksmith shop and tools were "in very bad order." Large portions of the stable roofs had even been torn off for firewood by dragoons in the escorts.[21]

Capt. Howell Lewis complained to Wayne that the burden of providing escorts had fallen disproportionately upon his Virginia riflemen, following their arrival at Fort Hamilton. He stated bluntly that "nine tenths of the escorts & scouting parties that were furnished from Hamilton whilst I remained there was from my Company." His men had each drawn six pairs of shoes since reaching that post, but by July most of them were either barefoot or wearing moccasins. Their coats were "generally useless." Lewis begged for "a frock for each soldier with one pair of shoes also" so they might be reasonably clothed for a few months. Recognizing the need, General Wilkinson sent Howell Lewis's and Thomas Lewis's rifle companies back to Hobson's Choice for refitting on August 16. He entrusted them with the flags of the old First and Second Regiments, which were to be given directly to General Wayne, commanding Lewis "to perish with his whole detachment, or deliver them in safety to your Excellencys Hands."[22]

Preparations for an advance by the legion had alarmed the Indian nations assembled at Sandusky to treat with the U.S. commissioners, who passed along their concerns to Secretary Knox. Determined not to jeopardize this peace mission, Knox reminded Wayne that his previous orders "would not authorize any movements which could be construed as a breach of the truce which is understood to exist on our parts until the treaty is finished." No violation of the status quo would be tolerated. Knox gave Wayne explicit orders on July 20: "I now Sir desire you in the name of the President of the United States that if any troops should have been advanced to Forts Hamilton St. Clair or Jefferson exceeding the usual Garrisons of those posts that you instantly withdraw them upon the receipt of this letter which I have directed to be forwarded by an express Boat from Pittsburg. This order will also comprehend the withdrawing of any parties or the demolition of any other posts toward the head of your line than those before mentioned." Although the peremptory order would, of course, be obeyed and some detachments would actually be withdrawn to Hobson's Choice, the administration's course of action was not popular in the West. James Wilkinson wrote that "the Policy of our Masters" was simply "unexplicable." He told Wayne, "The Savages know their Country to be defenceless, during the inclemency of Winter—to accomplish their security during the passing season & to gain time to extend & to consolidate their Confederacy & to increase their Population on the Tawa River, they have averted offensive operations on our part, by a Peace overture which they full well know we can never accept."[23]

The general in chief was annoyed by Knox's criticism of his "*preparatory arrangements*" and assured him that "no road has been opened Beyond Fort Jefferson, nor in any other direction but towards it, except to avoid impracticable ground." As for Indian assertions that a large number of troops had been seen with packhorses and oxen outside that post, Wayne explained that it was merely a typical guard for the livestock and for the men making hay in the prairie. As for the "tremendous additional force" that the Indian scouts claimed they had seen, Wayne protested it was merely Lieutenant Colonel Strong's road cutters who had finally reached the head of the line, where they remained to cut grass. Wayne grumbled about "the idle & fallicious reports of *Hostile Savages*" and the "credulity upon the part of our Commissioners." Then he complained, "I had presumed that as Commander in Chief of the Legion of the United States, some *confidence* ought to have been placed in my *honor* as well as *Conduct*." He closed his letter by saying he had ordered Strong's party to return, together with all the accumulated quartermaster and contractor teams. The general's parting shot for the whole episode was a request that Knox tell the commissioners "that I have never yet forfeited either my *word* or *honor*, to living man."[24]

From his position as commander of the Legion of the United States, Wayne had little respect for the peace commissioners and their Quaker entourage. The general was also losing patience with his army's only chaplain, Rev. John Hurt. Although he had been unwell and unable to perform his duties as chaplain, Hurt set out from Philadelphia on April 23 to join the legion. Instead of recovering, he developed a bad cough and chest pains and advised Wayne that he could not join the army because of his "indisposition & broken constitution." Rumors circulated that Hurt would soon resign or be sacked because he "ought to have ben with the army," so Rufus Putnam suggested Rev. Daniel Storry of Marietta as a replacement. The retired general described his friend as "a gentleman of Learning, good morals, polite maners, Liberal Sentiment, and popular tallants as a preacher." Putnam confessed that, at present, the community at Marietta could not support the minister, so it was willing to loan him to the legion until the Indian war ended. Ignoring Putnam's offer, Wayne ordered his current chaplain to descend the Ohio no later than August 15 because an active campaign loomed, telling Hurt that he was needed so "the troops may benefit by your precepts example and advice preparatory to that awful change, which many will Naturally experience at our next interview with the Savages." Wayne waited in vain for his chaplain, and his troops faced an uncertain future with only their personal religious beliefs for comfort. In the words of one artillery sergeant, "We have little to fear, accept our God and fear him in love."[25]

If Wayne could not continue to cut roads and advance provisions to Fort Jefferson, he could at least perfect the legion organization. He began to do so on August 22 by invoking the power vested in him by President Washington and announcing a series of promotions, some of which officially confirmed men to ranks they already held. In the dragoon squadron, Michael Rudolph had resigned, so Capt. William Winston was advanced to major and made commandant of the horse soldiers. Despite prodding by Secretary Knox, Winston was still attending to personal business in Virginia and now found himself commanding the squadron despite never having left home. Turnover among the dragoon officers had been so dramatic that Lt. Solomon Van Rensselaer now found himself a captain at the age of nineteen and commanding Winston's former troop. Among those who left the service was Capt. Henry Bowyer, who apparently found the arms of his young wife too inviting and abandoned dragoon life for the comforts of home. He was succeeded by Tarleton Fleming of Virginia. Another Virginian, William K. Blue, received a commission as cornet after having been recommended by all of the dragoon officers then at Hobson's Choice. Blue's appointment completed the officer corps of Wayne's mounted arm.[26]

Among the other eighteen men in the legion who received promotions was Maj. Richard Brooke Roberts of South Carolina. He had married Everada Catherine Sophia Van Braam at Charleston in 1786, and the couple had a son whom they named after the famous Roman Lucius Quintius Cincinnatus. Roberts's most prized possession was the sword of his father, who had been killed in the Battle of Stono Ferry, South Carolina, on June 20, 1779. The son, an artillery captain, was in the same battle and accepted the blade from his dying father, who told him "never to sheath it until he saw his country free."[27]

The list also contained a few names that would prove to be embarrassments in the not too distant future. John Smith had seemingly dried out after escaping dismissal for his bizarre behavior at Fort St. Clair and was now officially a lieutenant colonel commanding the Third Sub-Legion, a title that heretofore had been used in a strictly honorary fashion. Ballard Smith had behaved himself after returning from his six-month suspension for drunkenness and was now rewarded with an advancement to major. Thomas H. Cushing, an officer who would prove to be an adamant foe of General Wayne, was also promoted major. Born in Hingham, Massachusetts, on March 21, 1747, Cushing was described as "rather short, but very muscular and stout-limbed; eyes black, and of the keenest luster, piercing and intelligent; face well formed, with an expression of firmness and dignity seldom seen; very courteous and affable in his intercourse with mankind, whether rich or poor." Cushing had come a long way since enlisting in the Continental Army as a sergeant in 1776, but in the past two years, he had become devoted to General Wilkinson, a connection that would strain the major's relationship with General Wayne.[28]

In addition to filling vacancies through promotions, the commander also changed the organization of his legion. The various companies in each sub-legion were to be "leveled," or adjusted in strength so that each unit was comparable in size. Enough men were then to be drafted from these companies to form a new "light company" of infantry, to be armed with the improved muskets. Each sub-legion would thus be composed of a dragoon troop, an artillery company, a light company, two infantry battalions, and one rifle battalion, all battalions containing three companies. Believing that rifles were "only useful in the hands of *real Riflemen*," Wayne ordered surplus riflemen in the Third and Fourth Sub-Legions to exchange their rifles for "Muskets & bayonets, as the more formidable weapon." These changes were implemented over the next few weeks, the companies of Henry DeButts and Howell Lewis moving from the rifles to the infantry. Reaction among the officers was mixed. Captain Slough offered to command one of the light companies for the simple reason that he was "quite as well qualified for active service" as any other officer. But Capt. Jacob Kingsbury found his transfer from the infantry to a rifle company to be "very disagreeable," for he was "entirely unacquainted with any part of that duty." Carping by some of the officers involved in these changes caused Wayne to caution them against criticizing "the Necessary and Essential Business." When some protested that officers from their companies were still seeking recruits, the general quickly pointed out that they "were supposed to be Recruiting for the respective Sub Legions, and not for any particular Company."[29]

CHAPTER 10

Personalities and Problems Abound

EVERY WHITE PERSON WEST OF THE Allegheny Mountains waited anxiously for the outcome of the treaty negotiations, while those residents in the eastern states, safe from the Indian menace, showed a more apathetic attitude. Many frontiersmen were hopeful that an agreement would bring an end to the protracted hostilities, but more pragmatic settlers were resigned to a negative outcome. One gentleman from western Pennsylvania wrote to explain the true state of affairs to his eastern friends. This anonymous correspondent confided that he and his neighbors put no stock in any treaty, "unless it is founded on fear and terror on the side of the Indians." They also doubted the sincerity of any British officials who sought to mediate the negotiations. The Pennsylvanian then noted the result of previous agreements: "Partial treaties with vagabond tribes of perfidious savage robbers, and negotiated too by men of but little influence, and still less honesty, have always proved no better than adding fuel to fire, in proportion to the presents they receive." Unfortunately, innocent frontier settlers bore the brunt of ill-advised political and military miscues. This writer advised his eastern associates that there was scarcely a family on the borders of Pennsylvania and Virginia that did not bewail the loss of at least one member butchered or carried away by the enemy. As for himself, he had witnessed the results of one such attack, where "a father, his son and several daughters, were strewed about the door all dead and almost immersed in blood, his wife taken off, and an infant, half murdered, poor thing, crying and calling for its mother." The irate settler testified that others had witnessed "the opening of a womb, to take from it the hidden fetus for the pleasure of dashing out its brains, thrusting stakes into the bodies of both sexes, with burning of prisoners, &c."

   In the opinion of this frontiersman, a solution to the Indian problem was quite simple and did not include any negotiations. He suggested establishing on the frontier a series of posts wherein would be collected the "expert hunters and woodsmen of our frontier, from lake Erie to Illinois country." These hunters would be turned loose upon the Indian nations in a war of retaliation. No Indian would be safe, "their hunting grounds, their trapping waters, their trails, even their towns and villages, would every where be infested by an enemy more vigilant and more subtle than themselves." Liberal bounties would be given for Indian scalps and ears, "without regard to age or sex." There would be no other compensation beyond the posted rewards, thus stimulating production in the genocide. Border residents were in complete agreement that the Indians "ought to be exterminated like savage beasts," a just penalty for those "who live by murder and rapine." The frontier people would "rejoice" at such a policy, and the writer confessed that, despite his seemingly outrageous suggestion, "I have no difficulty upon my mind about the matter."[1]

Such opinions were bolstered by news reports of atrocities throughout the West. One such account told how six traders bound for the Illinois country with a load of merchandise were ambushed near the mouth of the Ohio. All of the men were killed, and "their heads and hands cut off, and their bodies ript open," an especially inflammatory story given the restrictions placed on Anthony Wayne's legion by Washington's administration. In addition to accounts like these, intelligence from the commissioners by way of Detroit did not sound promising. Reports circulated that two thousand warriors had assembled at a council, but they refused to meet with the commissioners because of rumors that General Wayne was marching northward with a huge army. These Indians selected a delegation to confront the government representatives and inquire whether they had authority to give up all claims to land north of the Ohio and west of the Allegheny. If the commissioners did not have sufficient power to do so or operated under instructions to ignore such a demand, there would be no negotiations.[2]

At Hobson's Choice, officers had heard rumors that Indian demands were too extravagant, and "the probability is a peace will not take place." Rumor said that the legion would advance within twenty-four hours of hearing that negotiations had broken down, but in the meantime, routine duty had to be performed. Maneuvers were practiced every day until noon, often in pouring rain. To pass the time, many officers studied tactics and brushed up on their dueling. The latter practice took on even more urgency following the trial of Lieutenant Diven on charges preferred by Lt. Andrew Marschalk, who claimed to have been falsely accused of lying, cheating, and defrauding men under his command. A court-martial, presided over by General Posey, found Diven guilty of lying about an incriminating piece of paper and sentenced him to be reprimanded in general orders. After General Wayne reviewed the findings, he lashed out at the young troublemaker: "This is the third instance in the Course of Eight Months in which Lieut. Divin has unfortunately been either Plaintiff or Defendant, upon Charges found on Personal Malice, and Resentment, and without any Regard to the Benefit of the Service or to the Honor of the Legion, which upon Investigation have generally prov'd Idle and Disgraceful to the Practice." Wayne then expressed his hope "that Gentlemen would have adopted some other mode of settling their private disputes (and which are only Personal) than by that of Court Martials."[3]

The same court-martial that censured Lieutenant Diven also sentenced Lieutenant Jenifer, the killer of Ensign Gassaway, to be dismissed from the service. Although there was no doubt that Jenifer had killed Gassaway in cold blood, his dismissal was not related to the murder. Instead, he had been accused of calling Lieutenant Glenn, his superior, "a Damn'd Rascal and a Coward" in front of four sergeants of the rifle corps and speaking "Disrespectfully" of Captain DeButts and other higher-ranking officers. To compound these public assertions, Jenifer denied in writing that he had done so, which was "contrary to the Principles of Truth and Honour." Wayne approved the sentence, commenting that "Military Discipline is the Soul of all Armies," and without it, soldiers would be "no better than so many Contemptible Rabble." Taking aim at the principles espoused by the French Revolution, the general continued, "it is a false Notion that Subordination and Prompt Obedience to Superiors is any debasement of a Mans courage or a Reflection upon his Honour or Understanding." Jenifer's dismissal became effective on September 10, 1793.[4]

Three days later, Wayne received a letter requesting clemency for the "unfortunate young man." Motivated by a "sensibility of Friendship," this message was signed by eight captains and twenty-one subalterns, all of them from the Third and Fourth Sub-Legions or the dragoon squadron. Not one old officer endorsed the petition. This memorial expressed regret that "a young man of ability in the flower of age and vigor of usefulness, should to expiate the folly of indiscretion, be doomed to undergo a punishment which at once looses him the confidence of his Country, shuts the door of society against him, and bars him from the pursuit of every honorable and desirable acquisition." Friends of Jenifer hoped that "the sensibility of his feelings and consequent sufferings of his mind" should be punishment enough for a "misdemeanor." They claimed that the hotheaded lieutenant's "contrition of heart and determined resolution to correct the caprices of his passions" should induce the commander to restore him to his former rank. If his conviction could not be overturned, Jenifer expressed a desire to accompany the legion as a volunteer so that he could sacrifice his life, "a life which is no longer desirable," for his country. After several days of suspense in waiting for a response, Jenifer wrote to Wayne and offered to serve as the most lowly ensign if he could be retained in the service. All this was to no avail. The general remained unmoved, and one more troublemaker was purged from the legion.[5]

With so many courts being convened to dispense justice to both officers and enlisted men, General Wayne decided to select a judge advocate general instead of temporarily detailing officers to fill that position. Two strong candidates presented themselves for his consideration. The first was Lt. Campbell Smith, an aide to General Posey and politically well connected in Maryland. His friends had sent a petition to headquarters bearing the names of nearly every officer off duty at Hobson's Choice when it was circulated for signatures, a few having declined "from delicate motives." Smith then followed up with a letter to Wayne, confessing that he had "always borne a wishful eye" toward that post, which the lieutenant had always considered "one of the most dignified confidential and honorable appointments in the Staff Department." The aspiring officer then reminded Wayne that he had served as judge advocate on several courts, for which duty he had heard "no complaint."[6]

Campbell Smith's rival for the appointment was Ensign Hyde, then assigned to Jeffers's company of light infantry in the First Sub-Legion. Hearing of the petition favoring Smith, Hyde immediately wrote to General Wayne and explained why he desired the office. When he first offered his name for a commission, the senators and representatives of Vermont generally assured him that he would receive the captaincy reserved for the Green Mountain State. When that appointment went instead to William Eaton, Hyde accepted a commission as ensign, "with the strongest assurances from the Secretary of War, of having the Permanent Appointment of Judge Advocate of the Legion." Secretary Knox told Hyde that, after consulting with President Washington, he had written to Wayne and urged his nomination. Excited by this turn of events, the young ensign prematurely released news of his appointment, which proved to be another embarrassment for an administration that had undergone a string of public-relations disasters by that time. After reaching Pittsburgh, Hyde "waited with patience" for an office that never came, although many officers assumed it was a foregone conclusion. Afraid that the petition might tip the scales in favor of Smith, Hyde suggested that he be announced in general orders as judge advocate general. He would then resign that rank, along with his commission as ensign in the line, and serve through the upcoming campaign as a volunteer with his honor and dignity intact. The legion commander postponed his final decision, appointing Charles Hyde to the post of "Judge Advocate pro tem," although Smith eventually received the permanent assignment.[7]

Hyde's primary task was to prosecute officers and enlisted men who transgressed army regulations, an overwhelming percentage of those crimes linked to the abuse of whiskey. Often, whiskey offered the only solace for a soldier in some isolated frontier post. The standing army was decidedly unpopular in the eastern states, where it was looked upon as "dangerous to liberty," and Congress passed appropriation bills with reluctance. James Hall, an early historian of this period, observes that "the army was left to sustain itself—miserably paid, wretchedly clad, badly supplied, and carelessly governed; its honor was supported alone by the patriotism and gallantry of those who composed it." Unfortunately, the history of enlisted men in Wayne's legion offers a striking parallel to that of their Indian adversaries. Most soldiers were illiterate and could not record their own experiences, like their Indian foes who had no written language, so historians have been forced to focus on accounts by the officers. Often, the only mention of enlisted men by name is in court-martial records so that the worst individuals receive the most attention. This situation is regrettable given that most soldiers behaved themselves, served honorably, and left the legion with a commendable military record. Detailed references to the common soldiers are rare, yet a brief glance at a few of them will serve to illustrate the type of men who served in the Legion of the United States.[8]

One of the oldest soldiers in the ranks was John Lusk, of Dutch extraction, who had been born at Staten Island on November 5, 1734. He began his military career during the French and Indian War, being in the memorable fight on the Plains of Abraham when the British wrested control of Canada from the French. Lusk participated in the conquest of Acadia and aided in the displacement of the Acadians to other American colonies. His next service came during the Revolution, joining the army that followed Gen. Benedict Arnold to Quebec. Lusk was wounded at Fort Edward and fought in the Battles of Saratoga and Yorktown. The veteran then returned to civilian society but became restless in his life of "inglorious ease," and at the age of about sixty he joined Wayne's legion. Lusk remained in the service and finally, "worn down with age and infirmities," accepted a discharge when approaching the age of eighty, having devoted nearly his entire adult life to military service.[9]

Another old veteran, and perhaps the oldest soldier in Wayne's army, was Andrew Wallace, who had been born in Inverness, Scotland, on March 14, 1730. Wallace fought with the Highlanders at the Battle of Culloden in 1746 but left his homeland and emigrated to America in 1752, settling in Chester, Pennsylvania. Two years later, Wallace served in General Braddock's army, although he fortunately missed the disaster that befell that force near the headwaters of the Ohio. During the Revolution, the Scotsman enlisted in Col. Anthony Wayne's Fourth Pennsylvania Battalion and served through the war as a sergeant in a number of other commands, fighting at the Battles of Brandywine, Germantown, Monmouth, Stony Point, Cowpens, Eutaw Springs, Camden, and Yorktown. Although unwounded during the war, Wallace just managed to escape the massacre at Paoli, where a brother was killed, by hiding in a thicket. He enlisted for several Indian campaigns, finally joining the company raised in 1791 by Capt. Thomas Doyle, and was wounded in the right arm by a ball in St. Clair's fight. Although never able to straighten his arm after it healed, he remained in the army and served as a sergeant under General Wayne. Like Lusk, Sergeant Wallace spent his declining years in the army, finally being discharged in 1811 for "debility" resulting from a stroke. The old veteran collected a pension until his death on January 22, 1835, at the age of 104.[10]

Old men such as Lusk and Wallace gave stability to the ranks, their long and varied service being a source of tradition in the new American legion. Other soldiers, much younger than these old timers, had begun their military careers during the Revolution. Among these men were veterans such as Cornelius Sullivan, who had been born in Philadelphia County, Pennsylvania, on December 30, 1755. Sullivan was living at Bordentown, New Jersey, when the war started and he enlisted in the first militia company raised in that city. This was the first of a series of enlistments in that state's militia units, the longest term being for six months. Sullivan witnessed Washington's defeat on Long Island, at one point being under fire at such short range that he could actually see the buckles of the British soldiers shooting at him. He also participated in the attack on Trenton, where he saw the surprised Hessian troops fighting "with nothing but their shirts on." Sullivan relocated in Burlington County, New Jersey, after the war and began working as a weaver. At the age of thirty-seven, this gray-haired veteran enlisted in Melcher's company, which was raised in Philadelphia in 1793, and headed west to fight Indians.[11]

Younger men made up the bulk of Wayne's legion. Joseph Fitzgerald had been born on July 30, 1772, near Staunton, Virginia, and was working as a hostler in that town when he joined Gibson's company of riflemen on July 13, 1792. Fitzgerald was joined on August 20 by the Neely brothers, Samuel and David, who signed on with Gibson at New

Glasgow. Reuben Thacker, a native of Fluvanna County, Virginia, worked as a black-smith in Albemarle County until he joined Capt. Howell Lewis's riflemen. William Christy was a carpenter in Mifflin County, Pennsylvania, before trading his tools for a rifle and joining his brother James in the company of Edward Butler. Some of the married men arranged for their wives to accompany them to the frontier garrisons, and occasionally the laughter and cries of their young children could be heard inside the palisades.[12]

For soldiers unwilling to serve their full three-year enlistment, furnishing a substitute to complete that term was always an option. John Cope appears to have enlisted to escape the everyday pressures of married life. He left Richmond with Smith's company, leaving behind his wife and two small children. Embarrassed by "the unhappy situation to which he has reduc'd himself," his father had one of Cope's brothers obtain a conditional discharge from Secretary Knox, who agreed so long as a substitute would be furnished to complete the original enlistment. When Cope did not return home even after the substitute reached the legion, his father wrote to General Wayne and, expressing "the most poignant grief," inquired into his son's whereabouts.[13]

Captain Eaton had solicited a discharge for Anthony Smith of his Vermont company at Legionville, but that request had been denied. Another inquiry to headquarters regarding the possibility of obtaining a substitute was ignored, although Major Mills, then commanding the infantry, saw no problem with an exchange. Smith hired a man named Montgomery for twenty-five dollars to serve in his place, and the substitute promptly joined the legion and began to do duty in Eaton's company. But Smith could not be released from service without approval from headquarters, and Montgomery could not draw pay or rations or clothing since he would not be borne on the company rolls as long as Smith remained. Eaton considered the newcomer as a better soldier, for he was "young, hardy, ambitious and well pleased with his situation," whereas Smith was "disabled, disheartened and discontented." Chagrined by the situation he had allowed to develop, the captain confessed to Wayne that he was "sorry and ashamed" by the whole affair and asked that Smith be immediately released to put things right.[14]

Some enlisted men set their sights on becoming officers, and a lucky few, often due to family connections, attained commissions. Joseph Campbell was the son of Lt. Col. Richard Campbell, who had fallen at Eutaw Springs in the Revolution. He entered the service as a volunteer and served "with the greatest propriety" as an acting sergeant major for many months under Captain Shaylor. When forced out of service because there was no provision by law for volunteers, the officers with whom he had served recommended that he be made an ensign. Campbell's petition was eventually granted, but the application of Sgt. Eli Edmondson was disapproved, despite being recommended by three times as many officers as Campbell. His conduct in St. Clair's battle had "evinced the intrepidity of his mind," and Edmondson's superior officers considered him officer material "from his personal and acquired abilities, from his attention to duty, and from his general good character." A few men chose to serve as volunteers at headquarters, hoping that their conduct would win them a commission. Richard Chandler tried for an appointment in the rifle corps but had been told there were no vacancies despite recommendations from

Thomas Jefferson and Beverley Randolph. He enlisted a few men in Virginia, then attached himself to Thomas Lewis's company at Greenbrier Court House and came west. Chandler did not receive a commission until almost two years after his original application.[15]

Wayne had once confided to Knox that "it requires three years—for a soldier to learn to live upon his ration & to take proper care of his Arms and Clothing." His new companies had advanced faster than anticipated, and the general was looking forward to using his full legion in the field, yet the enlistments of many of the older soldiers in the First Sub-Legion had started to expire. Nearly four hundred of them could claim their discharges by year's end, a loss that Wayne considered "a very serious disaster." Steps were taken to reenlist those so inclined, but discharged veterans who had experienced civilian life were seldom interested in returning. More success came by reenlisting troops still in service, their new three-year terms (and bounty money) commencing immediately rather than after the expiration of their original enlistments. There was simple logic to Wayne's program, for he now was convinced that "even two years service of a Veteran soldier, in the full powers of health, is better than three years of a raw recruit."[16]

In addition to losing men to civilian life, many soldiers had become lost in the legion's tangle of red tape. Before the new sub-legions left Legionville, thirty-seven men were discharged for disability and a large number of others were detached for duty at the various western Pennsylvania forts. Paymaster Caleb Swan reported that all of these soldiers were still borne on the rolls as present, "without any remark against them to elucidate where they are." This problem was duplicated in May, when two dozen more men were discharged and two companies of valetudinarians were detached to serve at Forts Steuben and Knox. When musters were taken at Forts Jefferson and St. Clair, Swan discovered that both those discharged and those sent downriver were all listed as serving at Fort Washington. Some men present with one company were listed on the muster rolls of another. Paymaster Swan then offered the most glaring example of a soldier trapped in the paperwork maze: "There is also one other man who has been for near a twelve month past shifted from one Company to another so that he has been mustered in three Companies of the 1st Sub Legion for the same time, and is at last lost, by being transferred to the 3rd Sub Legion while on furlough to Philadelphia." The ultimate result was that, by being borne as present on several company rolls, an unscrupulous soldier could theoretically be paid multiple times. In a similar fashion, discharged soldiers could return and accept payment for service they had not performed. Swan urged General Wayne to correct the problem by ordering an immediate and complete muster of the entire legion, supplemented by frequent and regular future musters. Captain Butler, the legion's acting inspector general, admitted "some small risque to the Public in the possibility of double payments" but urged the general to postpone such a muster until after all the companies had been leveled, the riflemen and light infantry selected, and the legion organization perfected. Wayne agreed, and the confusion continued unabated.[17]

Even though the legion could not keep track of all the soldiers in the ranks, recruiters continued to funnel new men westward. Lieutenant Glenn had been sent back to Shepherdstown, Virginia, in January 1793, with orders to send forward as many men as possible before rejoining the legion in mid-April. Glenn took with him Sgt. Henry Hunsell and his servant, although he was not furnished with any funds to pay expenses and bounties. A month later, Glenn was still without money but had lined up a few good men whom he wished to appoint as sergeants to assist his recruiting efforts. He finally received three hundred dollars from Philadelphia, but the tardiness in sending cash, combined with a fit of sickness, resulted in Glenn being able to recruit only twenty-eight men for the legion as a whole and three more specifically for Crawford's company.[18]

Captain Lyman returned to Springfield, Massachusetts, to recruit a new company. He announced his arrival in the local press, using many of the old tried-and-true blandishments to enlist "ambitious, honest, and steady young men." At his "agreeable rendezvous," he promised they would receive a "handsome uniform, immediate pay, fine quarters, receive wholesome food, kind treatment, a generous bounty, and every thing necessary for the welfare of good soldiers." While there, Lyman won praise from the citizens of Springfield for his assistance in detecting the perpetrators of a theft from the store of William Smith. Goods to the amount of sixty pounds sterling had been stolen, and soldiers were suspected. Lyman began an investigation and, by "spirited exertions, and ample use of the Cat," obtained a confession from one of the criminals, who incriminated three others and gave directions to the hidden stash of stolen property. The four thieves were confined to jail and their captain hailed as a "meritorious *Citizen-Soldier*."[19]

Lyman established a satellite recruiting station in Guilford, Vermont, which Sgt. James Elliot used as a base for recruiting in northern Hampshire County, Massachusetts, and southern Windham County, Vermont. Born August 18, 1775, to "poor, but honest and religious" parents, Elliot underwent a series of misfortunes as a child. Following the death of his father, a seaman based in Gloucester, his mother supported herself and three children by sewing. At the age of seven, young James began working for a farmer and merchant named Sanderson as "a plough and go to mill boy." His mother had previously taught him to read, although his only texts had consisted of "the Bible, Dilworth's Spelling Book, Pilgrim's Progress, and the Catechism." Sanderson taught Elliot a little grammar, but the youngster was fascinated by two volumes in the household, a book on the early Jewish wars by Josephus and Charles Rollin's *Ancient History*. Elliot remembered, "From the moment when I first perused Rollin, I had felt an ardent ambition to become a soldier." A passion for athletic sports and the continued study of history helped confirm his decision. His soldierly preparations became complete after he "became a gamester at cards, and on occasion could swear with a good grace," although he never developed a fondness for whiskey. Leaving Sanderson's employ after seven years, Elliot labored as a farmhand and store clerk, working in the latter capacity while the Indian war raged on the frontier. He saw this conflict as an opportunity "not only of indulging my inclination for a military life, but of gratifying my desire of travelling, and particularly of viewing the western regions." The young man followed the campaigns of Harmar and St. Clair in the press and confessed, "I almost regretted that I had not been an actor in the horrid catastrophe of the 4th of November, 1791." He had put off joining the army to spare his mother's feelings, but on July 12, 1793, James Elliot stepped forward at the Springfield rendezvous to become the first noncommissioned officer in Captain Lyman's new company.[20]

Recruiting officers faced a variety of problems while conducting their business. Weekly reports had to be sent off to the War Department, yet expense money was often in arrears. Many of the available men inclined for service had already enlisted, making the job even more difficult. Ensign Bissell discovered this latter fact at the Middletown, Connecticut, rendezvous, where he commanded a party consisting of one sergeant and eight privates. During the week ending September 28, 1793, he only managed to sign up one man. Ens. Levi McLean was based at York, Pennsylvania, but was subject to the orders of Major Butler at Carlisle. McLean complained that as soon as he enlisted four or five men, Butler ordered them sent forward. Without sufficient soldiers to guard his newest arrivals, the ensign reported that one-third of his enlistees had deserted. Despite pleas from Philadelphia, officers continued to enlist lawbreakers. One of the most flagrant was Lemuel Washburn, a private in Heth's Virginia company who had been held in the Henrico County jail after two businesses sued him for damages. Unwilling to await judgment, Washburn assaulted one of the jailors and forcibly made his escape. John Bullitt was already a horse thief and jail breaker when he enlisted in Fauquier County, Virginia, and, not surprisingly, he deserted soon afterward. Upon being apprehended, authorities from Augusta learned of Bullitt's arrest, took him into custody, tried him for stealing a horse, found him guilty, and hanged him.[21]

In addition to the typical troubles experienced by every recruiter, Major Cass had the misfortune to run afoul of the formidable Dr. Amos Mead in Horseneck, Connecticut. Having left New Hampshire to join the legion, Cass and his family of seven stopped in that village on Saturday, October 21, 1793. The following morning, the major stood watching as house servants loaded the family baggage into his carriage. There he was accosted by Dr. Mead, who proclaimed that Cass must not travel on Sunday as it was a criminal offense to do so on the Lord's day. The major protested that he was not actually traveling, and besides, he was an officer following orders to join the legion and did not realize that traveling on Sunday was a criminal offense in Horseneck. Words were passed "with warmth on both sides" until Mead placed Cass under the watchful eyes of a constable and four men. He remained under guard until a local attorney vouched for his appearance the following morning, when Cass appeared before Mead, who also happened to be a justice of the peace. Mead found him guilty of violating the Sabbath and fined the officer ten shillings, plus twenty shillings and eight pence for costs. Incensed by the affair, a bitter Major Cass wrote out his version of events for the press and urged the public to consider "whether they have not put too much confidence in the aforesaid Amos Mead, by enabling him to make a person prisoner in his own quarters, on suspicion that he had the appearance of intending to travel on Sunday."[22]

Not all civilians were as antagonistic toward legion officers as Dr. Mead, and many appreciated the discipline that kept troops in line after their enlistment. When Captain Hannah marched his last detachment from Alexandria, one newspaper reported that "the conduct of these soldiers, during their encampment in the suburbs of that town, has been uncommonly correct, and reflects great honor on their commanding officer." Capt. William Lewis received similar praise for the men he had raised at Elizabethtown, Maryland: "As a tribute justly due to captain Lewis, we cannot at present forbear mentioning the great good order and regularity which he maintained among the troops, during his command here. For though free citizens will never with impunity, submit with insults from the soldiery, yet during this gentleman's command, none were offered; the whole behaving not as mercenaries, but like true citizen-soldiers." When he left Hagerstown with his detachment, Lt. John Whistler was lauded for "his indefatigable assiduity in disciplining his men, and rendering them orderly and inoffensive to the inhabitants." The local editor concluded his notice of Whistler's departure by writing, "We wish them an agreeable march, and a successful campaign."[23]

In addition to the new recruits sent down the Ohio to Hobson's Choice, Secretary Knox ordered Lieutenant Colonel Clark to forward "all the continental troops above Fort Washington, save 120 non commission officers & Privates." Following the departure of these men, defense of the Pennsylvania and Virginia frontier fell primarily upon companies of militia raised for six months' service, although Clark did oversee the construction of a small fort at Wheeling. The bungled administration of Clark's small command on the Upper Ohio infuriated Wayne, who termed his conduct to be "highly criminal, being a Neglect of duty & disobedience of Orders." Apparently, that officer had all but ignored the posts at Gallipolis and Marietta, both of which could have used some guidance. By the end of August 1793, the small garrison at Gallipolis, commanded by Captain Cummins, had been ravaged by intermittent fever. Cummins, the only officer present, reported that he had been suffering from that malady for ten days and that two dozen of his forty-two men were sick. While Cummins battled disease, Captain Haskell primarily contended with "unfavorable ideas towards the soldiery" at Marietta. Some Virginia state troops stationed there were "under no discipline or subordination" and spent their time insulting the regular troops. Traders in the village stirred up trouble when Haskell refused to pay the debts of his men, even though he had warned merchants not to trust the soldiers. Haskell's "delicate" situation was compounded even further by his inability to convene a court-martial to punish incorrigibles in his company. When these two companies joined the legion shortly afterward, twenty of Cummins's troops were still "sick debilitated & unfit for duty," and fourteen of Haskell's men had contracted smallpox.[24]

As various officers floated down the Ohio with their detachments to Hobson's Choice, Lieutenant Clark returned from his journey to deliver goods to the Chickasaw Nation. His convoy had left the mouth of the Kentucky River on June 23 and proceeded to the Falls of the Ohio, where the boats were delayed three days. At the mouth of the Tennessee River, three Frenchmen invited the soldiers to land, but Clark wisely declined and learned later that thirty Cherokee warriors had planned to ambush them when they came ashore. On July 3, Clark's boats reached the Mississippi, and the following day he stopped on an island some nine miles above the Spanish post at Lance la Grace. He intended to follow General Wayne's instructions to pass that garrison at night so as to avoid a potential confrontation. Clark was therefore stunned when a pirogue came by and friendly traders told the Americans that they had been expected for several days. The secret nature of his mission having become public knowledge, Clark boldly approached the fort at noon on July 5 and announced his intention to pass. Instead of meeting with insolence and hostility, the Spanish commander invited the lieutenant to have supper. Clark accepted and reported, "I was treated with the respect due to an American officer."

On July 9, Clark and his convoy reached Chickasaw Bluffs near the mouth of Wolf River, the place where he was to deliver his stores. A band of about 150 Chickasaws were there, subsisting themselves on blackberries, acorns, and roots while they waited for the delivery of the desperately needed supplies. The Americans were invited to one of the main Chickasaw towns, some eighty miles distant, where they found the natives "rejoicing and much pleased" with their arms and rations. After procuring packhorses and provisions, the lieutenant and his men set out overland for Nashville, about 250 miles to the east. From there the soldiers, accompanied by the chief Captain Underwood and a group of eight warriors, headed north to Fort Steuben, where they arrived on August 21. Leaving their packhorses at that post, Clark's party ascended the Ohio River to Hobson's Choice without incident. His mission had been a complete success, and the delivery of the supplies would allow the friendly Chickasaws to counterbalance a hostile Cherokee and Creek threat in Georgia and Tennessee. General Wayne reported that Lieutenant Clark had acted with "a promptitude & address that does him honor & which merits my highest approbation!" The mission had cemented a friendship between the United States and the Chickasaw Nation that would result in the latter providing many warriors to serve as scouts for the legion. The great Chickasaw chief Piomingo, or Green Mountain Leader, who had served under St. Clair, was already headed for Philadelphia to confer with President Washington on the matter. Wayne enthusiastically embraced Piomingo's offer of men, and the general's policy of employing Indians to hunt Indians would be common practice with U.S. troops for the next century.[25]

CHAPTER 11

Last-Minute Dispositions

WHILE THE LEGION WAITED IMPATIENTLY at Hobson's Choice, its commander fretted as the summer campaigning season slipped away. Yet with his hands tied by the Washington administration, Anthony Wayne could do little more than practice his troops at fighting Indians. While relying on Steuben's drill manual for basic maneuvers, the general repeatedly emphasized the importance of every movement being made in "open order," with at least two paces between men in the ranks. When moving in the old European fashion, troops always tended to string out while advancing and to bunch up when called upon to halt. This resulted in the loss of valuable time while properly re-forming the line and a consequent confusion if done so under fire. Wayne felt that marching in open order was the "Essential Tactic" for fighting Indians in their wilderness homeland, where maneuverability was of more importance than massed firepower. Detailed instructions for the legion field days mention this over and over as the general continued to hammer home his point that all maneuvers should be made with "the utmost Velocity" and in open order.[1]

Every movement by the legion would be screened by the rifle companies, which would form the front, flank, and rear guards. If the column should be attacked on a march, riflemen were to hold their ground while other rifle companies advanced and sought to turn the enemy's flank. For example, if an attack came against the right side of the column, the riflemen forming the right-flank guard would "sustain the force of the fire" as riflemen from the front and rear guards would advance toward the attackers. The legion's main body would immediately begin to form its line of battle behind this screen. To ensure that the riflemen did their duty, Wayne announced the "fatal consequence" that would befall them if they retreated without orders—the dragoons would charge and "put them to the Sword." Should the horsemen "shamefully give way," the light infantry had orders to shoot them from their saddles. Likewise, if the light infantry lost its nerve and retired, the main column would direct musketry and artillery fire upon them. The message was clear: Each man was to do his duty or be shot down by other elements of the legion. After announcing such an extraordinary policy, Wayne then declared a hope that he would "never be reduced to the painful Necessity of putting these Orders into Execution." Expecting to hear that the treaty negotiations had failed, Wayne stepped up training because "every hour is now precious."[2]

Field days held at Mill Creek repeatedly emphasized the importance of riflemen and light infantry absorbing the first shock of battle as the entire legion formed behind them. At the end of each exercise, Wayne would set loose his dragoons, generally on the flanks, to deliver the *coup de grâce* while the foe ran in terror. As with other branches of service, the "invariable rule" was that dragoons would also advance in open order. The horsemen were "to move easy until they gain their proper position in front of the Light Infantry & then to advance with Velocity—every man charging twenty Indians." Wayne felt them "fully equal" to such a bold movement once the infantry had driven the enemy from cover and exposed them to the slashes and thrusts of dragoon swords. Their maneuvers must be flexible and suited to the terrain, with no thought given to European texts "by Bland, Dalrymple & others, for charging Squadrons of Dragoons or Battalions of Infantry on the plains of Germany." While relying on established authorities for basic training, legion tactics would depend upon flexibility and adaptability for success in the American wilderness.[3]

Quartermaster General O'Hara had purchased enough packhorses to carry the ordnance and ordnance stores on the impending campaign. This pack train would be of an imposing size. According to an estimate prepared by Major Burbeck, each horse could carry 144 dozen cartridges. With one hundred rounds allowed for each soldier, in addition to what he carried in his cartridge box, the estimated field force of three thousand men would require 174 packhorses. One horse could carry a 2.75-pounder howitzer and its carriage, and 3 horses could carry enough ammunition for two howitzers. Plans called for advancing with twenty howitzers, which would then add another 50 packhorses to the train. If Wayne decided to take along four 3-pounder guns, it would necessitate yet another 20 horses, three for each gun and carriage and two more to carry ammunition for each piece. There is no surviving estimate for the number of horses required for hauling baggage.[4]

The rush to stockpile forage and rations at the forward posts had resulted in much of it being unusable. A board of survey appointed by General Wilkinson examined the forage at Fort Hamilton and discovered that close to one-half of the corn was "extremely dirty" and "considerably damaged," the latter condition "from being put up damp, and impregnated with the Sweat of Horses, or Dampness Received in the Boats in which it was transported." The remainder was either slightly damaged or in need of cleaning. A similar board examined the salted beef in stock at Fort Jefferson and found that of 152 barrels, but "one only is fit to issue, and that in case of great necessity." These officers recommended that the beef "ought to be removed as a nuisance which if continued would endanger the health of the garrison." A month later, there was no beef left that could be issued "on any pretence whatever." A supply convoy had brought forward twenty-five oxen, but Lieutenant Colonel Strong reported them "so poor, that it was with the utmost difficulty I could prevail on the troops to receive it." Although his men were involved in heavy fatigues during these hot summer days, Strong admitted that there was "not an ounce of soap" in the fort.[5]

Given the condition of rations at these advanced garrisons, it was little wonder that soldiers at Fort Hamilton supplemented their rations with food from the surrounding countryside. On August 31, the men started building a fish dam across the Miami River about a mile above the fort. Although the dam had not yet been completed, on the first night of operation, Captain Bradley said the soldiers drove about 800 pounds of fish into the waiting net. On September 2, the men caught 1,750 pounds of catfish, perch, buffalo, eels, and other edible species. Bradley gleefully wrote in his journal, "We have more fish than the whole garrison can make use of." Enjoying the fun furnished by their dam, soldiers continued to drive fish downstream into the waiting net and caught another 5,000 pounds on September 3 and 4. There were so many fish at Fort Hamilton that Wilkinson sent some back to Hobson's Choice for the enjoyment of Generals Wayne and Posey. When they tired of fishing, soldiers carefully wandered about in search of fruit. Among the most popular discoveries were pawpaws "as large as a common apple and very luscious," with "the taste of a pine apple." May apples were plentiful as were hawthorns, grapes, cherries, and plums, the latter twice as large as the damson variety grown back east.[6]

General Wilkinson presided over this western paradise from his comfortable private quarters at Fort Hamilton, but his relations with Wayne had started to worsen. The first sign of his dissatisfaction had surfaced when the legion commander insisted upon retaining final approval of sentences passed by courts-martial appointed by his subordinate. An irritated Wilkinson wrote that, according to his construction of military law, "the Power of appointing the Courts & deciding on the sentences, are coexistent and coextensive," except when they involved the dismissal or death of a commissioned officer. Wayne's insistence upon approving sentences meant unwarranted delays in removing criminals from the legion. Wilkinson inquired whether "Law or Policy" influenced Wayne to restrict his power and claimed that he asked "no more than my legal due."[7]

Captain Guion quickly allied himself with the friends of General Wilkinson when he requested General Posey to order the arrest of Captain Butler, then serving as deputy adjutant general and inspector general of the legion. Citing Butler's status, Posey refused, since such an arrest should properly be approved by General Wayne. Guion then referred the matter to Wayne, charging Butler with "a partial, unjust, and unmilitary discharge of his duty as Deputy Adjutant General to the manifest and great *prejudice* of both Officers and private soldiers of a part of the Legion, and of the service of the United States." Wayne immediately replied that this was "a business of a very serious nature" that must not be entered into "but upon some very extraordinary occasion." He demanded that Guion "specify and particularize" the grounds for such an arrest. After considering his delicate situation, the captain backed down and waived his previous request. Noting that "too little harmony, and too much discontent obtains in the army,"

Guion agreed for the present to sacrifice his own feelings in the matter so as "to restore content and Union" in the legion. By audaciously threatening Butler, one of Wayne's most loyal and trusted officers, Guion quickly became the darling of what would soon develop into a Wilkinson faction among the officer corps.[8]

Supporters of both Wayne and Wilkinson served on the general court-martial that finally disposed of the case of Ens. John Morgan, even though detaching so many officers became a hardship for the legion as it prepared for the field. Morgan had acted as brigade major of the right wing of St. Clair's army, which was commanded by the late Gen. Richard Butler. When a portion of St. Clair's official report cast aspersions upon the military character of Butler, Morgan stepped forward to defend that dead officer's honor. He wrote directly to Henry Knox on February 9, 1792, and informed him that St. Clair had maligned the reputation of Butler by trying to shift to him some of the blame for losing the battle. One week later, Morgan sent a copy of this message to Mary Butler, the general's widow, with a cover letter that ended, "You are at liberty to make such use of it as you think proper." She promptly sent Morgan's correspondence to the *Carlisle Gazette* for publication.[9]

Incensed by the insolence of this young ensign who styled himself the guardian of Butler's honor, General St. Clair had him summarily arrested for mutiny on March 5. Morgan struck back in the press by publishing a letter in which he claimed that the general's report had been written "with *intentional error and meditated malice.*" Not content with a simple attack in the press, Morgan delivered his personal narrative of St. Clair's campaign to the congressional committee investigating the disaster. That narrative made a litany of allegations against St. Clair, including "want of military abilities," "deficient and bad arrangements," "miserable management," "supercilious insolence and disrespect" to high ranking officers, and "ignorance and torpidity during the battle."[10]

Ensign Morgan's repeated requests to be brought before a court-martial in Philadelphia were ignored, and he was ordered to Fort Washington. By the time Morgan actually went before a court, General St. Clair had added another charge to that of mutiny: "falsehood, unbecoming the character of an officer and a gentleman." Officers who attended the trial thought that things were going Morgan's way, much of the testimony exonerating him of the falsehood charge. After the prosecution had concluded its case, the court inquired how much time Morgan would need for his defense. The ensign boldly replied, "Gentlemen, I do not wish to say a word in my defence, but to submit the matter to you on evidence before you, well assured of a honourable acquittal." After the proceedings had closed but before a verdict had been reached, St. Clair, who was "indefatigable" in his prosecution, asked the court to delay its deliberations so that he might present additional testimony. It seems that St. Clair had failed to prove that Morgan had either written or caused to be published the letter to Secretary of War Knox that had precipitated his arrest. To avoid further delay, Morgan foolishly confessed that he had, indeed, written the letter in question. This admission appeared to swing the judges against him. The panel of officers found Morgan guilty of mutiny, and Wayne quickly sent him off to Philadelphia along with a transcript of the court-martial. After his case had been reviewed, John

Morgan was cashiered and dismissed from the legion on December 31, 1793, much to the delight of St. Clair and the relief of Knox.[11]

While his officers occasionally gave him fits, General Wayne's greatest distractions at Hobson's Choice surely came from the various civilians who contacted him to settle personal and legal problems. Having no one on his staff skilled in public relations, he had to handle these matters personally at a time when the legion demanded his constant attention. An attorney attempted to collect a debt of 158 pounds in Virginia currency from Joseph Cracraft of Springer's company. Cracraft had indicated his willingness to pay his debt if he could only return to Pennsylvania and sell off his property there. Wayne refused Freeman's request, stating that "to attempt to withdraw a single man from the Defense of his Country at this crisis is very improper." Abel Hennon also contacted the general in an attempt to collect monies owed him for goods furnished from his store at Legionville. In the course of doing business there, Hennon had sold merchandise on credit to soldiers of Stephenson's company, some of them going into debt for two, three, and even four months' pay, all with the verbal approval of Ens. Patrick Sharkey. The ensign, then senior officer with the company, agreed that Hennon would receive his money once the soldiers were paid. Before the merchant could be reimbursed, Stephenson resigned, and Henry DeButts assumed command of the company. DeButts refused to authorize repayment of these debts, claiming that the men required their money for more-pressing needs. Some of the soldiers, "perhaps not Strictly Honest" in Hennon's opinion, had persuaded others not to honor their obligations because no officer had approved the credit in writing. Both Stephenson and Sharkey had resigned, the legion had relocated to Hobson's Choice, and many of the men had been scattered by transfers to different companies. Hennon had no desire to "extort" the entire sum and was willing to accept installment payments. Since Wayne had given a license to Hennon and his partner Acheson to operate the store where the indebtedness occurred, they appealed to him for justice. Written on September 10, Hennon's petition was ignored by Wayne at a time when more urgent business demanded his attention.[12]

On September 11, an express boat arrived from Fort Fayette with the following letter from the peace commissioners:

> Fort Erie, August 23d 1793
>
> Sir,
>
> We are on our return home from the mouth of Detroit River, where we lay four weeks, waiting for the Indians to close their private councils at the Rapids of the Miamis, that we might all remove to Sandusky & open the Treaty. But after sending repeated deputations to obtain answers to particular questions they finally determined not to treat at all. This final answer we recd on the 16th inst when we immediately began to embark, to re-cross Lake Erie.
>
> Although we did not effect a peace, yet we hope that good may hereafter arise from the Mission.
>
> The tranquillity of the Country, North West of the Ohio, during the (supposed) continuance of the Treaty, evinced your care of our safety; and we could not

leave this quarter without returning you our unfeigned thanks.

    We are, Sir, with due respect,

        Your most obedient

            hum Servants

        B. Lincoln   Commissioners

        Beverley Randolph   of the

        Timothy Pickering   United States

After verifying the authenticity of this letter through a prearranged code in the text and confirming the signatures against autographs sent earlier, Wayne saw that the Washington administration had been duped by the Indian confederacy. His legion had been held in check all summer by the president's hope for a successful treaty, when, in fact, there had been no negotiations at all. Now unfettered by political restraint, Maj. Gen. Anthony Wayne was ready for war.[13]

By a strange twist of fate, William Wells, who had returned from General Putnam's earlier mission only to be sent to this latest Indian council by Lieutenant Colonel Hamtramck, stumbled into Fort Jefferson on the afternoon of September 11, too fatigued to go any farther. Hamtramck sent an express rider galloping off to Fort Hamilton to inform General Wilkinson that the negotiations had failed. After resting overnight, Wells set off for Hobson's Choice, bearing a letter from Hamtramck to Wayne. To lay to rest any lingering doubt about Wells being a possible double agent, Hamtramck wrote that he had given "a very Convincing proof of his Attachment to his Country." He then urged that the frontiersman be given an officer's commission since "there is not an inch of ground in this Country, but he is well Acquainted with, he knows every trail, knows where the Indians could be found if they did not chose to show themselves." Acknowledging his influence with the Wabash nations, Hamtramck added that Wells might convince some of those warriors to serve as spies for the legion.[14]

Wells reached Hobson's Choice on September 14, and Wayne interrogated him "very minutely" that day, followed by additional questioning. The general was convinced that Wells told the truth since his answers "did not deviate from the first to last." The scout told a fascinating story. He had arrived at the rapids of the Maumee on July 10 and found fourteen hundred Indians already assembled there. Six days later, that number had increased to twenty-four hundred, of whom eighteen hundred were warriors. A grand council representing the various nations met every day, and the majority at several times had decided to meet with the American commissioners to seriously negotiate a peace. Only the Shawnees, Delawares, and Wyandottes remained adamantly opposed to any discussion. Delegations sent to the commissioners at Detroit insisted upon the Ohio River as a boundary between the United States and the Indian confederacy, but privately the chiefs groused that "they ought to be paid for all the Lands in the State of Kentucky."

Each time the council seemed to favor peace, Col. Alexander McKee, British Indian agent, offered extravagant promises and convinced the Indians to remain firm in their demands. Wells reported, "Colo McKee always promised, that the King their father would protect them & offerd them every thing they wanted in case they went to war such as arms ammunition & provision." To ensure that the British position remained perfectly clear, the notorious Simon Girty sat as a member of the council, while the Indian agent and three other officers occupied McKee's home, some fifty yards from the council house. Every night, chiefs of the war faction held private talks with these British officials. This portion of Wells's narrative was soon confirmed by a Seneca warrior, a nephew of the respected chief Cornplanter, who reached Fort Franklin shortly after the Indian council had broken up. He assured American authorities that McKee's interference had prevented a treaty and the British officer "told them, if they would make a peace, they would be ruined for ever, and that he would supply them with any thing they should stand in need of, as he was authorized to furnish them with anything they wanted, but men."

After the U.S. commissioners sent their coded message of failure to Wayne and started home, Colonel McKee followed through on his promise and "furnished the whole of the Indians with arms ammunition scalping knives & tomahawks . . . & promised them Clothing when they wanted it." Chiefs received pistols and swords, while their warriors got either light muskets or rifles, the latter firing an ounce ball and having adjustable sights "in proportion to the distance at which they fire." Wells estimated that over fifteen hundred Indians could take the field immediately but that a tardy advance by the legion would allow an additional five hundred to join the Native American force. He reported that the Indians would first attack the exposed convoys as they shuttled rations and forage forward to Fort Jefferson. They would then keep the Americans constantly on the alert by nighttime feints, wearing the men down with a lack of sleep. Whenever the legion seemed vulnerable after passing St. Clair's battlefield, "they will immediately attack." Should the column penetrate as far as the rapids of the Maumee, Wells was convinced that British regulars, supported by Canadian militia, would contest any further advance. Following their rebuff of the U.S. commissioners, all the warriors started a huge war dance, being joined by British officers, one of whom appeared "painted as an Indn." The nations departed the rapids on August 28 under an agreement to meet twenty-five days later at the Grand Glaize, where they would await Wayne's advance and seek "a favorable moment to strike." Scouts would keep an eye on the legion, any important intelligence being conveyed by runners who could cover over sixty miles "between daylight & dark."[15]

Thankful for such detailed information, Wayne wrote to Secretary of War Knox and complained about the commissioners being taken in by "artful designing" British officials, who only appeared to act as sincere facilitators between the United States and the Indians. These gullible commissioners had foolishly wasted many weeks of valuable campaigning weather as they vainly waited for a phantom peace proposal. Now instead of a full-scale movement into Indian territory, Wayne advised Knox that he would advance to the large prairie some six miles beyond Fort Jefferson. There he would encamp and neutralize the enemy by threatening their families and homes "until some favorable circumstance or Opportunity may present to strike with effect!" But an outbreak of influenza swept through the legion, depleting the ranks before an advance could begin.

Even after garrisoning Forts Hamilton, St. Clair, and Jefferson with valetudinarians, the legion would only be able to muster twenty-six hundred effectives, officers included. To augment this force, Wayne called upon Charles Scott, an old friend from the Revolution, to bring forward a force of mounted volunteers from Kentucky. While he waited for reinforcements, Wayne advised Knox, "I will not commit the Legion Unnecessarily" and "will content myself by taking a strong position advanced of Jefferson," where his forces could protect the frontiers until the advent of spring in 1794.[16]

The Indians seemed intent on mischief that fall. On the morning of September 17, 1793, a party of about thirty warriors waylaid a private at Fort Jefferson. The soldier knocked down two Indians but was then killed and scalped within sight of the garrison. Shots were fired at the attackers, though without any apparent effect. Hamtramck sent a detachment out in pursuit, but "the murderous Dogs instantly dispersed & fled." A party sent from Fort Jefferson to reinforce a convoy discovered where a group of about ten mounted Indians had watched the road between that post and Fort St. Clair before disappearing. Wilkinson reported that "many light parties" lurked about the advanced posts, waiting patiently to gain intelligence and take prisoners. It was not a time for soldiers to be about in the woods, yet two men deserted from Fort St. Clair on the night of September 16. They had apparently taken coals from the kiln outside the fort. When it grew dark, sentinels noticed a strange glow, and the two conspirators volunteered to investigate. Both being expert woodsmen, they slipped into the darkness and vanished. Ensign Trigg took a party to search for them but found no trace of either soldiers or Indians. Aware of his lonely, exposed position at Fort St. Clair, Captain Gibson complained that he had but few men, and those "not of the better kind." The captain reported to Wilkinson that he did as his predecessor had done: "Shut the big Gate, and keep a good look out."[17]

Surgeons began examining the sick and invalids at Hobson's Choice on September 23, assigning each man to one of four categories: first, those who could march all the way to Fort Jefferson; second, those who could only march as far as Fort St. Clair; third, those who could only reach Fort Hamilton; and fourth, those who were too sick to leave Hobson's Choice. The healthy companies at these three advanced posts would be withdrawn and replaced with detachments of invalids who were unfit for field duty but still capable of performing service in garrisons. The first invalids to reach Fort Hamilton, a detachment commanded by Ens. John Bradshaw, were "in miserable plight," thoroughly exhausted by the march, some without arms, and all without cooking utensils; they would have been no match for a zealous and confident enemy. One invalid did not join those sent on garrison duty. Lieutenant Colonel Smith, besotted for many years, had finally admitted he would be unable to command troops in the field. On September 25, Smith told Wayne that his "truly alarming state of health" had forced him to offer his resignation, and he would leave for home as soon as he could travel "without torment." The general had shielded Smith from being cashiered by a court-martial, but he was undoubtedly glad to see this high-ranking officer, who had done no duty for months, leave his army.[18]

Shortly after the legion's arrival at Hobson's Choice, Secretary Knox had authorized Wayne to call upon auxiliary forces from Kentucky should conditions on the frontier warrant such an act. But Knox quickly pointed out the difference between the two types of troops that could be raised: "The Kentucky People dislike greatly to serve as mere Militia. Were you to call for that sort of Militia you would probably receive substitutes only—On the other hand the Citizens of that State delight to serve on Horseback and it is alledged in that case the bravest and best Men of that State may be brought into the field as Volunteers.—Although the expence of mounted Volunteers is great, yet considering their quality and estimated efficacy, it may ultimately be the cheapest to employ them in preference to drafted men and substitutes." Heretofore, the administration had made suggestions. Now General Wayne was given "plenary powers" to conduct his operations, Knox leaving all arrangements, including the use of Kentucky manpower, to his discretion. Writing from Philadelphia, Knox confessed, "Your nearer view of the business will enable you to discover advantages or disadvantages which cannot be perceived at this distance." In essence, Anthony Wayne had been given complete and total authority to direct the Indian war.[19]

This unparalleled delegation of authority to a general officer proved to be an almost divine inspiration, for by now most of the residents of Philadelphia had fled to escape a yellow-fever epidemic. One government official who had remained in the city described how "the scene has surpassed everything that I have before seen—the dying groans has filled our Ears all night, and the dead has rushed on our Eyes with the returning day—whole families have been swept away." Newspapers ceased publication, and nearly half of the citizens had abandoned the nation's capital. President Washington left for Mount Vernon, the secretary of the Treasury had gone to New York, the secretary of state headed for Virginia, and Secretary Knox decamped for Boston. All business was at a standstill, and Major Craig noted there was "no communication with, nor dispatches from the War Office."[20]

Although he had received permission to call out the Kentucky troops whenever he deemed it necessary, Wayne had serious doubts about how well they would perform on a campaign. He had no wish to commit the legion to combat while the Kentuckians were "stealing a March very wide from the Army—in order to burn a few Wigwams & to capture a few women & Children." But with his command still short of its authorized strength, Wayne had no choice but to heed Knox's advice and issue a call for mounted volunteers from the Bluegrass State. A letter to Gov. Isaac Shelby had prompted that official to convene a council of general officers of the Kentucky militia on June 24, 1793. Maj. Gens. Charles Scott and Benjamin Logan attended, as did Brig. Gens. Thomas Kennedy and Robert Todd. The council agreed unanimously on several points. First, all officers called into federal service should be appointed by General Wayne. Second, no officer should be appointed more than one grade lower than the commission he presently held from the State of Kentucky. Third, the officers agreed that volunteers "should be engaged against the Enemy separate from the Regular Troops so far as may be consistent with the general Interest of the army." Governor Shelby endorsed this last proposal and informed Wayne that it was the wish of the council that General Scott should lead the Kentucky volunteers. Scott carried this news to Hobson's Choice, where he presented his views on the "comparative military Talents" of the various militia officers.[21]

Charles Scott was one of the most unique characters on the frontier. Born in 1739 in Virginia, he was apprenticed to a carpenter in 1755 following the death of his father, who had been a member of the House of Burgesses. As the youngest in the shop, Scott did the family marketing in Charlottesville. One day while returning home with a quarter of a beef, he heard martial music as a recruiting sergeant appealed for recruits. As a mere youth, Scott was "perfectly charmed" by the uniforms and the beautiful tunes, though especially by the bounty money exhibited by the sergeant. He promptly laid down his beef on a stump and signed on to fight in the French and Indian War. After service at various frontier posts, where he won a reputation as an expert woodsman, Scott returned to Virginia, married, and raised a family on a large plantation along the James River. Organizing a company early in the Revolution, he was promoted to lieutenant colonel and colonel in 1776, participating in most of the important campaigns in the early years of that conflict, and was advanced to brigadier general in 1777. After serving with Wayne at Stony Point, he served as Washington's chief of intelligence for a time before being sent to posts in Virginia and South Carolina. Captured at Charleston in 1780, Scott was not exchanged for two years and saw no further field service.[22]

Impressed by the prospects in Kentucky, the veteran sold his Virginia property and settled along the Kentucky River in Woodford County in 1787. He planned to establish a town called Petersburg, which he hoped would grow and be recognized as the state capital. In June of that year, his son Samuel and a friend were going to fish across the river from the family farm but were shot by Indians while in their canoe. The warriors then swam out and scalped Samuel while he was still alive. Charles Scott and others heard the shots, ran to the riverbank, and witnessed Samuel's death, though he could only watch the murder in shock and horror. Scott lost a second son to the Indians in 1790. While he was serving in the House of Delegates at Richmond, his son Merritt served as a captain with the Kentucky militia that accompanied General Harmar's advance to the Miami villages. Seriously wounded while standing his ground as others fled from the field, Merritt's body was never recovered, and Charles Scott held out hope that he had been taken prisoner by the Indians. The general was always ready to avenge the death of his sons in any way that presented itself, whether on an independent raid or in conjunction with the Legion of the United States. Although men were slow to respond to Wayne's call, Scott was a popular choice to lead the Kentucky contingent. Herman Bowmar described the six-foot-tall general as "Genteel, handsome, dark skin, regular neat figure, dark hair and beard, neat in his person always." Fond of telling tales and stories, he also liked to drink and swear, two more attributes that endeared him to his Kentucky comrades. Bowmar once gave him the perfect frontier compliment, saying, "I never heard any man that could swear pretty, except *Genl Scott*."[23]

Acting on the Kentuckian's advice, Wayne appointed all general and field officers for the mounted corps to be called into federal service should the treaty negotiations fail. He then urged a majority of these officers to meet with Governor Shelby to recommend

Maj. Gen. Charles Scott. From B. O. Gaines, *History of Scott County, Kentucky*, 1905.

men to fill the ranks of captain, lieutenant, and cornet in eighteen separate companies. By July 17, four of the twelve majors had refused to serve and had to be replaced. Three days later, Lt. Col. John Adair gave Wayne an assessment of the officer situation. He confided that he did "not think the *best* men, that might have been, were nominated," and "those who were fit & who had it in their power to arm themselves are not willing to serve." Wayne originally wanted the Kentuckians equipped as dragoons, but that proved unrealistic since swords and pistols were too scarce. The volunteers would have to serve as mounted riflemen. As for himself, Adair admitted, "I am anxious to command men who do not wish to fight from behind trees, but will face Death in any form."[24]

By the end of July, Scott could report, "the prospects of Completing the Volunteers is flattering but they are giting a little flattened for want of a Certinty of being calld into service." General Wayne could do nothing to aid Scott until he heard from the commissioners, but afterward the long-awaited call came swiftly. Wayne wrote to Scott on

September 12, warning that "our movements must be Certain & rapid & we must strike with effect" and ordering him and his fifteen hundred Kentuckians to join the legion at Fort Jefferson on October 1. To assist Scott in his efforts to assemble his volunteers, Wayne wrote an inspiring letter on September 18, a copy of which soon appeared in *The Kentucky Gazette:*

> I received an express the night before last from the Secretary of War, dated the 3d instant, with positive orders from the President of the United States, to make those audacious Savages feel our superiority in arms, and to prevent the murder of helpless women and children. He is confident that I shall be well and powerfully supported in this arduous task, by the brave and virtuous mounted Volunteers of Kentucky. Advance then my dear sir—participate in the glory—and produce a conviction both to him and the world—that that confidence has been well founded.
>
> Present my best and kindest wishes to our brothers in arms, and assure them that there shall be ample justice done to their bravery and conduct in my communications to the President of the United States.

Here was a wonderful opportunity for the men of Kentucky. A few weeks on active duty would save the lives of countless innocent women and children while having that altruistic service reported directly to President Washington. Friends would shower the mounted corps with rewards and praise, while the haughty Indians and their British allies would slink away from the brave Kentucky volunteers.[25]

Apparently, most of the volunteers were less than enthusiastic when Wayne's call finally came. On September 26, the legion commander confessed to being "truly astonished at the reluctance discovered by too many of the mounted volunteers to meet the common enemy, in order to save the effusion of much innocent blood." He explained that this was not "a little predatory war, made by a few tribes of Indians" but rather "a confederated war forming a chain of circumvalation round the frontiers of America, from Canada to east Florida." Wayne warned that Indian warriors would spread death and desolation on every part of the frontier from Lake Erie to Georgia. He therefore called upon Governor Shelby for a requisition of militia to make up the projected shortfall of mounted volunteers. General Scott was ordered to march by October 1, leaving behind enough officers to muster and bring forward these militia levies. To stimulate the militia, Wayne announced that those who immediately came forward mounted and properly equipped would be treated and paid as if they were mounted volunteers. All this would take valuable time, so he ordered the militia to rendezvous with the legion and Scott's mounted corps on October 15, a delay of two weeks from the original target date for starting the campaign. The draft seemed to have spurred enlistments, and even after the companies had left, enough men continued to come forward "by twos & threes" so that Scott hoped that the legion and their Kentucky allies could still "give them Fellows a Disissive Stroke."[26]

At Hobson's Choice, legionnaires waited impatiently for the arrival of the Kentuckians so the campaign could begin. Captain Eaton wrote that they were ready for action: "We are well disciplined and well reconciled to the expedition, and whatever may be our success, I will venture to assure you, that we shall not fly. Our business will be serious and decisive provided we are engaged, of which I have not a doubt." Another observer stated that the legion was "in good health, good spirits, and in a high state of discipline." In the opinion of a third officer, "General Wayne deserves the greatest credit for the good discipline of the army," having spent five or six hours each day on horseback while teaching his troops the maneuvers "suitable for Indian war." After noting the imminent arrival of the Kentucky volunteers, he then asserted, "this I think will do the business for those yellow fellows who made that hideous shrieking noise on the 4th of November 1791."[27]

The best assessment of conditions at Hobson's Choice on the eve of the march to Fort Jefferson was given by Surgeon John M. Scott of the Second Sub-Legion. Born in Pennsylvania, Scott studied medicine under an uncle in New Jersey. He was appointed surgeon's mate in the old First Infantry in 1789 and became devoted to Josiah Harmar. A close friend of William Henry Harrison, one of that officer's biographers described Surgeon Scott in this fashion: "His uncommon wit, vivacity, and humour made him every where sought for by the young and lively, while his good sense, his professional skill, and his incorruptible honor and integrity procured him the esteem of the wise and good." Scott wrote to Harmar on October 6, the day before the legion left Hobson's Choice. He told his former commander, "the most sanguine expectations are formed from the known war-like abilities of the Comdg Genl—the unequalled military discipline of the army— the promptitude & alertness of the Heads of departments under his direction, in making regular & systematic arrangements—superadded to all this, the invincible bravery of the troops." But there was danger lurking, and Scott wrote, "I fear our General has not the entire confidence of his army." He then told Harmar what he meant: "In my department, having the different complaints & disorders to manage & cure, I meet with one that is pretty general & which will yield to no remedies which I can apply, Viz—*general discontent*. I believe the cause may be traced to the *head* of our Chief. I don't know how it is, but I think that there are many that would give more general satisfaction."[28]

CHAPTER 12

The Legion Marches North

THE LEGION MARCHED ON OCTOBER 7, 1793. When drums beat the "General" instead of "Reveille" that morning, Hobson's Choice became a flurry of activity. Soldiers struck their tents and packed them away in baggage wagons. They stored personal gear in their knapsacks. Those troops detailed as pioneers, six men from each battalion, reported to the quartermaster, who issued them axes and spades for use in "opening making & repairing the roads & bridges." Husbands said goodbye to their wives, some legally married and others in common law, and children, all of whom would remain behind in Cincinnati. Wives who were "industrious" and willing to perform washing and nursing duties at Fort Washington would be allowed rations, though no pay, for their labor. Capt. John Peirce was appointed commandant of that post, with Captain Cummins, the contentious Lieutenant Diven, and Ens. John Wallington being assigned to duty there too. When all was ready, "Assembly" sounded, and the pickets and quartermaster guards rejoined their companies. A single cannon was fired from the artillery park, and lead elements of the legion started to march northward along Mill Creek in the manner prescribed by general orders issued on August 25 and 29. Superbly trained, officered, and equipped, Wayne's command bore little resemblance to the armies of Harmar and St. Clair that had preceded it into the wilderness.[1]

The column was led by Capt. James Flinn's Company of Spies and Guides. Flinn had arrived in the territory with his father and two brothers in 1781, and the clan settled at the tiny village of Columbia. All the brothers became noted woodsmen, James being the most prominent. The territorial governor appointed him captain of the first militia company organized there, and he held that position of trust for many years. His greatest adventure occurred in 1789, when a party of Shawnees stole some horses at Columbia and the militia set out in pursuit. Flinn, while scouting in advance, was captured and taken to the Indian camp. Suspecting that he was about to be beaten, the scout sprang up, eluded his captors, and rejoined his friends, who soon after captured some of the

Indian horses. Several days later, these same warriors boldly came back to Columbia and traded Flinn's rifle for their captured horses, swearing that another party of "bad" Indians had stolen the Columbia stock. Flinn learned firsthand about the skill of Indian warriors in battle during the winter of 1792, when his company participated in General Wilkinson's trip to St. Clair's battlefield, where they solemnly surveyed the mute evidence of incredible slaughter. Now, he had been commissioned a captain in the federal service, with authority to recruit a company of forty men who would receive one dollar per day plus rations for a period of six months. Flinn's men would act as scouts for the legion during its advance. They included a variety of frontier types, including the troublemaking William May and Henry Schaffer, the former packhorse driver Robert McClellan, and George Shrim, who would soon organize his own elite company of spies and guides.[2]

Protected on all sides by a screen of riflemen, the legion noisily moved northward, a cacophony of clatter in the silent wilderness. Like all armies on the march, there was a myriad of human voices, animal sounds, creaking of wheels, metal striking metal, the chopping of trees by pioneers, the tramp of feet, creaking leather harness and accouterments, the rustle of underbrush, and a thousand other sounds of a multitude in motion. Practice at Legionville and Hobson's Choice had not prepared these soldiers for the tedious overland marching of their first campaign, but Wayne's force made about ten miles before halting that afternoon. This was not a bad first day since, according to Surgeon Scott, "the army had not got properly in their geers." The legion reached Fort Hamilton on October 8, everyone "extremely fatigued" after a second day of hard marching. Captain Bradley watched the arrival of the long-awaited legion and thought that the campaign would end by mid-November. He confided in his journal, "Whether we can beat the Indians, or not,—I leave it to fate I pray we may be successful."[3]

Sgt. George Will Jr. described the procedure used by the legion in erecting daily camps while it was on a campaign:

> On a march, we generally halted early in the afternoon; say, two or three o'clock; the quarter-masters of the several sub-legions, with the quarter-master-general, surveyor, and engineer, went ahead with the front guard, selected the ground, laid off the encampment, and marked the bounds of each sub-legion, so that when the army arrived, the troops proceeded to pitch their tents. After this was done each company had to commence fortifying twenty feet in front of the company. This was done by cutting down timber, trimming off the limbs, and putting up [a breastwork] from two to four logs high, according to the timber; so that in one hour from the commencement a complete breast-work was formed around the whole encampment. There were no gates—a few light logs were put up something in the form of bars.

Simultaneously with this construction, the picket guards threw up small redoubts three hundred yards from each corner of the camp. Two-thirds of the pickets cut timber for the redoubts, while the remaining third were stationed one hundred yards apart, well in advance of the works and surrounding the entire camp, thus providing "a complete chain of sentinels" to protect against Indian attack. Riflemen and light infantrymen then constructed similar redoubts three hundred yards from each side of the main camp and equidistant from the corners.[4]

Much has been made by historians of parallels between the campaigns of Anthony Wayne and Gaius Julius Caesar, but the similarities have been overstated. As a typical scholar of his day, young Wayne had learned to read and write Latin so that he undoubtedly had translated at least portions of Caesar's classic works on his conquest of Gaul and the civil war against Pompey the Great. English translations of these works were readily available, and Wayne surely had copies in his personal library. But as with the tactics he had adapted for the legion's use, Wayne also changed Roman guidelines to suit the needs of his forces in a primitive wilderness. The daily camps offer a good example of Wayne's modification. The Roman field camp, *castra aestiva*, was generally located on the slope of a slight hill near water and wood, although not too close to forests that could conceal a hidden enemy. Wayne generally camped near water whenever possible, but a wood supply was never a problem, for in most cases the only cleared ground was the road that his pioneers had slashed through the forest. Romans built a right-angled, quadrilateral camp with rounded corners that would "afford more room for defence." Camp gates were left open and defended by semicircular traverses of banked earth. Wayne's camp was also quadrilateral but had bastions on each corner for artillery, and its gates were a few logs that could be raised or lowered like on a farm fence. Each of Caesar's camps were surrounded by a deep and wide ditch, the dirt from which was thrown inside and formed into an earthen wall. Roman legionnaires fought from atop the wall, while the ditch kept any enemy at a respectable distance. Wayne's camp was simply a large breastwork of timber, augmented by earth in the few rare instances when suitable timber was scarce or too distant. Roman camps could be constructed in from four to five hours, while Wayne's men could build one in an hour. This time savings allowed the Americans to cover more miles on a march each day than their Roman predecessors and did not wear down manpower with excessive fatigue work.

These comparisons between camps of the American and Roman legions indicate how Wayne modified a reliable system from ancient history to suit his own pressing demands. Wayne and the Roman commanders realized that the square corners of a camp were weak points. Romans rounded theirs to cram more men into that space, while Wayne made them into strong points by building bastions for his artillery. The American campaigned in a wooded backcountry, where a constant supply of building material allowed him greater mobility and kept his soldiers fresher. But this same wilderness offered cover and concealment to an advancing foe, so Wayne developed his defense in depth, with eight redoubts equally spaced around the exterior of his camp and a line of pickets advanced even farther into the forest. While neither type of camp was permanent, Wayne's temporary forts lasted long enough to provide places of refuge for convoys and troops as they passed back and forth on the road from Fort Washington into the heart of the Indian country.[5]

While encamped near Fort Hamilton, General Wayne issued some new orders to govern the remainder of the march. James Wilkinson would henceforth command the right wing of the legion, composed of the First and Fourth Sub-Legions, and Thomas Posey would lead the left wing, composed of the Second and Third Sub-Legions, both officers receiving an equal share of new and old troops. In the future, if any accident should befall a wagon, it was to be pulled aside, bypassed, and repaired before the rear guard arrived. There would be no break in the column and no partial halt "on any pretence whatever." Soldiers were ordered to fix their bayonets and throw away their scabbards and frogs. Any man losing a bayonet would be fined one month's pay. With these new orders in effect, the legion left Fort Hamilton at 10:00 A.M. on October 9 and stopped for the night at the Five Mile Spring (the distance in the name being measured from the Miami River at Hamilton).[6]

Here Wayne received a letter from Major McMahon, who informed him of the fate of a convoy under the command of Capt. Jacob Melcher. That officer had reached Fort St. Clair on the night of October 6 and reported that his entire convoy had arrived except for a rear guard, which was some two miles behind with a few packhorses that had problems with their loads. The truth was that only Melcher and four of his men had arrived, the remainder of the convoy being dispersed for almost ten miles along the road to Fort Hamilton. Enlisted men of the escort, who had been left behind by the captain, broke into the stores and stole whiskey, flour, and salt to the value of one hundred pounds sterling. McMahon reported with disgust that most of Melcher's command were so drunk and disorganized that "ten Indians could have Massacred the Detachment." McMahon arrested Melcher and sent Captain Preston with a detachment of sixty trusted men to collect the drunken soldiers and all public stores concealed in the weeds along the roadway. Melcher offered some lame excuses for his conduct, saying the packhorse men were drunk and did not follow his orders, the night was dark, the contractors exaggerated their losses, it was impossible to keep the convoy together, and such. But his most amazing claim was that Wilkinson had given him positive orders to reach Fort St. Clair that night, so he abandoned his command in order to personally obey those instructions. The captain remained under arrest for two months awaiting trial, then concluded that he could offer no defense for his conduct in this "mortifying and unhappy Situation" and asked if he could resign. After depositing a sum equal to the loss of the contractors, Melcher was allowed to leave in disgrace.[7]

On October 10, the legion traveled twelve miles, but now the men were beginning to break down. Dr. Scott remembered, "our line of march extended for near five miles, owing to the rapidity of the marching, and the badness of the roads for our transportation, superadding the straggling soldiers, worn down with fatigue and sickness, brought up by the rear guard whom they retarded considerably." The legion made twelve miles on October 11 and ten more miles the following day, which was marred by a number of wagons breaking down on account of rough spots in the road. As the column neared Fort Jefferson on October 13, firing was suddenly heard ahead, and everyone thought that Indians had attacked the advance guard or some flanking party. Guns were loaded, the pace quickened, and comments such as "Let them come" or "We are ready for them" were uttered. Major Buell commanded the rear guard. When he had gotten to within six miles of the fort, a dragoon came riding up and reported that he had heard heavy firing ahead. Soon after, Capt. William Lee rode back to Buell and gave his opinion that the forepart of the column was under attack. Both officers strained to identify the noise but could not decide whether it was the rumbling of wagons or the sound of musketry. After marching a short distance, Buell distinctly heard heavy firing, so he ordered his rear guard forward "as fast as possible expecting every moment to be attacked." But there had been no enemy foray. Lieutenant Colonel Hamtramck had taken a portion of Fort Jefferson's garrison out for a sham battle, the sounds of which were misconstrued by the column. Many had been frightened by the firing, but all put on a brave face before camping about a mile south of the post.[8]

Next day, the legion marched past Fort Jefferson, and Surgeon Scott noted that, because of Hamtramck's little sport, many soldiers ignored the post, "indeed some of us turned our heads the other way with disdain." The column halted and established a camp six miles beyond Fort Jefferson on a slight hill near the edge of a "large, extensive, verdant *prairie*, or natural meadow, covered with grass and innumerable flowers." To the south, this prairie extended for miles, with only isolated groves here and there, resembling islands in a sea of grass. To the west, north, and east, the unbounded forest contained beech, maple, magnolia, ash, oak, hickory, walnut, and sycamore trees. These latter grew to tremendous size, one specimen boasting a circumference of nearly fifty feet. The southwest branch of the Big Miami River flowed placidly along the western margin of this prairie. One soldier characterized the spot as a "terrestrial paradise" and offered a glowing description, "Murmuring rills, and gentle cascades; an exuberant variety of herbs, plants, and flowers, fragrant and beautiful beyond description; the wild plumb, and many other trees, blooming in all the pride of nature; the melodious notes of innumerable feathered songsters." Added to the usual assortment of nuts, fruits, and berries was a species of wild onion that made "as palatable sallads as were ever tasted." The location was indeed a paradise on earth.[9]

General Wayne was pleased with the manner in which the march from Hobson's Choice had been conducted and expressed his satisfaction in a general order on October 14, praising the officers for their attention to duty during this rapid advance, certainly "a pleasing presage of future success." Wayne did, however, note "with concern & regret the apparent want of Harmony & due subordination in a few *a very few* Gentlemen of the Legion, at a Crisis when they ought to unite as a band of Brothers." No names were mentioned, but the general expressed a hope that harmony would prevail in future operations. Maj. Ballard Smith would not be a part of that harmonious band of brother officers. He was arrested on October 15 "for Intoxication when on duty on the 13th instant; and for disobedience of orders & neglect of Duty as Field Officer of the day in posting the Guards & Sentries on the said 13th instant to the imminent danger of the Legion." Specifically, he had been charged by Maj. Thomas Cushing with failing to issue the parole and countersign to the guards before they were posted that evening. Given the fact that Smith had already served a six-month suspension for intoxication, his career as a field officer was over, and he was ordered back to Fort Washington to await a general court-martial.[10]

Smith's dereliction of duty became especially heinous given the events that transpired over the next few days. Major Buell was officer of the day on October 16. While riding along the stream bank and looking for a way to cross between posts numbers four and five, Captain Price yelled that several Indians had been seen there just a few moments before. Buell turned his horse and rode off to headquarters to report that information. A short time earlier, Cornet William Blue had taken a couple of dozen dragoons from Captain Lee's troop out into the large prairie to graze their horses. After they had spent a few minutes allowing their mounts to feed, Blue saw a slight movement in the grass and naively thought it was some wild turkeys. He quickly discovered that it was actually two Indians who had been watching the dragoons. Drawing his sword, Blue shouted for his men to charge. He spurred his horse forward, followed only by two sergeants and a private. The dragoons chased these Indians over one hundred yards toward the trees along the Miami, when suddenly four more warriors rose up from behind a log and fired, killing both sergeants. Blue wheeled about to encourage his remaining men but saw only a single private, the remainder of his detachment having fled as soon as the Indians had been flushed from their hiding spot. Cornet Blue and the brave private turned and made their escape as the warriors ran away into the forest.[11]

General Wayne was outraged at this conduct by his vaunted dragoons. He immediately ordered every one of the cowardly runaways placed under arrest and convened a court-martial to deal with the rascals. Pvt. Daniel Davis, who had led the mass desertion, was singled out for prompt punishment. He was charged with misbehavior before the enemy, abandoning his post, and beating a hasty retreat when ordered to charge the Indians. Captain Slough presided over the court as it listened to testimony, but justice promised to be swift and certain, so a grave was dug before a sentence had been reached. Shortly after the dead sergeants had been recovered and buried, Davis was found guilty on all charges and sentenced to be shot to death. Wayne confirmed the death sentence, but an appeal from several of the officers convinced him to pardon Davis and his frightened comrades. He now reiterated his previous order that any soldier seen retreating before the enemy without authority was instantly to be shot down. There would no longer be any acceptable excuses. To emphasize that fact, two soldiers, Edward O'Brien and Matthew Gill, who had been found asleep at their posts the next night, were sentenced to be shot. Wayne confirmed the court's findings, saying he was "at last compelled to produce an Awfull conviction on the Minds of the Soldiery that the Dangerous Crimes of a Centineal sleeping on his Post, in the Heart of an Enemies Country can no longer pass with impunity."[12]

Just as the legion began to recover from this disgraceful incident, the Indians struck. Lt. John Lowry and Ens. Samuel Boyd commanded an escort of about ninety soldiers from the companies of Captains Shaylor and Prior who guarded a convoy of twenty quartermaster wagons bound for headquarters. Lowry's convoy had stopped on October 16 about four miles beyond Fort St. Clair at Twenty-Nine Mile Creek, and his sentinels fired a number of times during the night at Indians probing the camp's perimeter. Next morning, between daybreak and sunrise, the Ottawa chief Little Otter sprang an ambush as the convoy began to get under way, rushing forward "with savage fury and yells which panic struck the whole party." Frightened teamsters fled for their lives. Daniel Voorhis and his son cut the horses loose from their wagon, mounted, and galloped off. Matthias Ross, although nearly sixty years of age, dashed into the woods and escaped. A few soldiers followed the teamsters, but Lowry and Boyd organized most of them and began to return the Indian fire. According to one account, Lowry was heard to shout, "My brave boys, all you that can fight, now display your activity and let your balls fly!" When the lieutenant was killed, his men lost heart and began to give way. Boyd tried unsuccessfully to rally the stragglers, then, choosing to die rather than flee, charged the enemy by himself and was shot through the breast. The survivors fled, but Sgt. Lent Munson saw no hope in flight and resolved to sell his life dearly. He was too exhausted to put up much of a fight and was soon overpowered and disarmed by the Indians, who immediately stripped him of his clothing, except for shoes, stockings, and overalls.[13]

Sergeants Thomas Underwood and Reasinover, the former slightly wounded, carried news of Lowry's defeat to Fort Jefferson. Lieutenant Colonel Hamtramck forwarded word of "the Bad fortune of the Day" to General Wayne, then dispatched Captain Kingsbury with 120 infantry to the battleground. This force was augmented by one hundred Kentucky Volunteers under Lieutenant Colonel Adair, who had been similarly defeated the previous year near Fort St. Clair. Kingsbury's rescuers found that Little Otter's party had already disappeared, taking about seventy horses but leaving the stores, primarily corn, untouched in the wagons. A few horses had been killed in the attack, but the ox teams were unscathed. One wagon belonging to Abijah Hunt had been plundered at a considerable loss to that merchant. Besides this, the only loss was a quantity of whiskey, some of which had been taken and the remainder poured onto the ground. Lowry, Boyd, and eleven enlisted men had been killed, while another eleven men were missing and presumed captured. Some of the wagon drivers and soldiers joined Kingsbury from hiding places in the woods, but most straggled back to Fort St. Clair "by twos and threes." Kingsbury secured the battlefield and protected the wagons and their loads until replacement horses could be procured. Adair followed Little Otter's trail with a portion of his men for nearly forty miles, but the Kentuckians could not catch up to the Indians and returned since they lacked provisions for a prolonged chase.[14]

Captain Kingsbury brought the wagons and their loads into Fort Jefferson on the afternoon of October 19. Wayne sent Captain Springer back with two troops of dragoons, one company of light infantry, and one company of riflemen to escort the ill-fated convoy on to headquarters. The dead were recovered and returned to Fort St. Clair for burial. There was sincere regret over the death of Ensign Boyd, who was described by Wayne as "that Gallant young Gentleman Mr. Boyd, who bid fair to be an ornament to his profession." One young officer wrote of his deceased comrade, "I lost the dearest connection I had in the army, a young man of the most amiable manners and improved understanding—who added to the best qualities of the heart, the distinguished sentiments of a soldier." Previously, a physician who had studied under Maj. Gen. Edward Hand in Lancaster, Pennsylvania, Boyd "preferred the use of the espontoon to the lancet" and obtained a commission in the line, falling in his first action. His friend assured the public that, "so long as social worth and military ardor is admired, the name of BOYD will be remembered in the army."[15]

The eleven American captives were driven along by their mounted captors for almost a week, but one man who could not keep up that exhausting pace was killed and scalped. Their misery was compounded by a lack of food since, to elude pursuit, Little Otter had fled before his prisoners received any provisions. The captives were bound every night, each man sleeping between two warriors, so there was no chance for escape. Sergeant Munson had been given an old shirt and coat, and on the third day, probably because of his courage, the Indians painted his face as a token of life. Little Otter's party finally reached their village, where Munson's hair was cut and a jewel placed in his nose, though his determined refusal won a respite from having his ears pierced. There he lived for about eight months, subsisting almost entirely upon corn since he could not force himself to eat the putrefied meat served with Indian meals. Two prisoners, John Connor and Henry Davids, the latter of whom had served under General Burgoyne in the Revolution, were turned over to the British. About a month later, another prisoner, a Frenchman, shot his captor, tomahawked his wife, and escaped. Trophies from Lowry's detachment, including an American officer's sword, were taken to Colonel McKee for inspection, then the scalps were sent on to the various Great Lakes nations to encourage them to join forces against the Americans.[16]

Following Lowry's defeat, there was speculation in the legion that this loss of valuable livestock would be "a great detriment" to a continued advance. When word of the affair reached Cincinnati, Governor St. Clair regretted the misfortune, "not that the thing is of much consequence of itself," but that as news spread throughout the country, "it will be magnified into a capital loss of both Stores and Troops." St. Clair offered the obvious advice that it appeared the Indian confederacy may have decided against a pitched battle in favor of intercepting the vulnerable convoys that carried the legion's provisions. General Wayne had already arrived at the same conclusion. In a letter to Sen. John Edwards of Kentucky on October 22, he wrote, "It would appear that the savages mean to bend their force against our convoys." Wayne then confessed that the legion found itself "arrested on this spot for want of provision & the means of transport on the part of the Contractors." The general was more blunt in a letter to Secretary of War Knox, blaming Elliott and Williams for deceiving him about the quantity of stores at Fort Jefferson and their "incapacity to comply with the requisition for the daily Issues & deposits." He further accused them of "much evasion & equivocation" in explaining their inability to live up to the contract they had signed. Speaking for the contractors, Robert Elliott confided to Otho Williams, brother of his partner, that Wayne, "som times about the full of the Moon gits out of all bounds," and it was getting harder and harder to "deal with a fool." To ease the supply crunch, Quartermaster O'Hara had been ordered to suspend transporting government supplies and assist in shipping corn and flour for the contractors. In fact, Lowry and Boyd had been killed protecting one of O'Hara's convoys.[17]

Three days after Lowry's defeat, Indians attacked a small settlement just nine miles north of Cincinnati. White's Station was located on Mill Creek about half way between Cincinnati and Fort Hamilton, the settlement being protected by seven men and a ten-year-old boy. There was no palisade, two rows of cabins being encircled by a simple rail fence, while three other cabins stood isolated across the creek. About five o'clock in the evening on October 19, dogs at White's Station began barking loudly on one of the neighboring hillsides. Andrew Goble assumed the dogs had treed a raccoon and said he would go out after it. Capt. Jacob White, thinking there might be Indians out there instead of raccoons, forbade him to leave the station. Goble stubbornly set out anyway and had walked only a few hundred yards before being killed by a party of about forty Indians concealed in the woods. The warriors emerged from hiding and ran toward the station, yelling and screaming as they came. On the north side of Mill Creek, the only residents were Elizabeth Pryor and her three children. Indians spotted Pryor's daughter, then about four years old, playing along the north bank and shot her dead. The attackers then turned their attention to the small blockhouse and traded rifle fire with its defenders for about thirty minutes after retiring to cover in the trees. Women of the station loaded surplus rifles for their men so they could keep up a rapid rate of fire. Suddenly, the Indians charged down the hillside and began to climb the rail fence outside the blockhouse. But their leader was killed, forcing a retreat to the wooded hillside, where the Indians fired away at the citadel for another hour before silently disappearing.[18]

After killing the Pryor child, several Indians left the main party to plunder cabins on the north bank. Elizabeth Pryor saw them coming, grabbed her two-year-old son, and ran for the blockhouse, splashing across the creek to safety amid the gunfire. The Indians searched the three cabins, filling bed ticks with anything of value, took Pryor's baby from its cradle, and "dashed out its brains against a stump near the cabin door." These Indians also slipped away into the wilderness. Shortly after the attack began, Andrew Pryor, brother-in-law of Elizabeth, started out to get assistance from the garrison at Fort Washington and the town of Cincinnati. He arrived there about midnight and related news of the attack to Governor St. Clair, who immediately sent a party of twenty militiamen to White's Station. Soldiers pursued the war party for a short distance but failed to catch any of the marauders. Back at the station, Goble and the two Pryor children were given Christian burial, but the Indian who had fallen at the fence was dragged into the woods and left there to rot. As a further insult, on the same day White's Station was attacked, another party of Indians broke apart the fish dam near Fort Hamilton and set fire to a small blockhouse at the ford there.[19]

When he first heard of the attack on White's Station, Governor St. Clair wrote to Captain Peirce at Fort Washington and asked that a sergeant and a dozen men be sent there to perform guard duty while the residents belatedly cut pickets and erected a stockade around their settlement. The governor portrayed White's Station as "an important link in the chain of Communication with Fort Hamilton," besides having a valuable deposit of nearly fourteen hundred bushels of corn. Peirce declared that the station was outside his authority, but to appease the governor, he sent forward a corporal and six men with the understanding that St. Clair would write and explain the situation to Wayne. Residents at White's Station were "in hourly apprehension of another Visit," but people in Cincinnati were also afraid that another war party might circumvent the legion and attack more of the virtually defenseless towns and stations. To protect Cincinnati, St. Clair ordered the militia commander of Hamilton County to mount a guard every night from sunset to sunrise, with patrols "to be kept out constantly." He also instructed those same precautions to be undertaken at Columbia and North Bend.[20]

While things were going to hell in the rear, Maj. Gen. Charles Scott's Kentucky volunteers finally reached Fort Jefferson, but lateness of the season and a shortage of provisions left them with nothing to do. Scott's volunteers, over one thousand men superbly mounted, had reached Fort Hamilton on October 11 and camped on the west side of the Miami River at One Mile Creek. Here they learned that a few men from an advance party of volunteers had lost their horses near Fort St. Clair on the night of October 8. The main body continued its march next morning, while those unlucky men searched for their strays. One man found his quickly and hurried on to catch up, while the others took more time to locate their horses. As this last group came forward, they found their lone comrade lying dead in the road, shot and tomahawked, his horse and equipment missing.[21]

On October 12, the Kentucky campground was shifted about three-fourths of a mile up the creek to better grazing ground, and Colonel Adair took one hundred men toward Fort Jefferson as an escort to a convoy of contractor's stores. Next morning, there was an alarm when three hunters were chased back to camp by Indians. Capt. John Hall took forty men and scouted the area but returned about noon without discovering any lurking enemy. There was another alarm on October 16 after a sentinel fired on an Indian scout. When nothing transpired from this latest incident, the general and field officers met and perfected their organization. A military board arranged each of the officers according to seniority, then passed the roll on to General Wayne for his final approval. Although he did change the original designation of "cornet" to "ensign" since the volunteers had not been organized as dragoons, Wayne approved the entire list and appointed the officers to their respective ranks "to be respected & obeyed accordingly."[22]

These Kentucky men were a hardy lot. Gen. Robert Todd, one of Scott's brigade commanders, was a native of Pennsylvania but came to Kentucky in the spring of 1776 and was wounded in an Indian attack on McClellan's Station in December of that year, thus having "a practical experience in Indian warfare from the beginning." While convalescing from his wound, Todd had an unlucky encounter with a buffalo bull, which "pierced his lungs with a horn, broke his shoulder blade, and for a period he was regarded as mortally wounded." Following his recovery, he married a cousin, Nancy Todd, in 1781 and became the public surveyor of Fayette County. (A descendant of his brother Levi eventually became Mrs. Abraham Lincoln.) His first encounter with Indians did not deter future campaigning, and he was a captain under George Rogers Clark during the

Illinois campaign. Todd served under Clark on numerous other campaigns against the Indians, and it was said of him, "He was one of the bravest soldiers and esteemed as one of the most rigidly honest men in Kentucky."[23]

The other brigade commander, Gen. Thomas Barbee, had been born in Culpeper County, Virginia, in 1753, the eldest of six brothers who all served during the Revolution. The first notice of Thomas came when he was yet a teenager. He had an argument with his stepmother, who said his father would whip him when he returned home. Thomas prudently set up a ladder under the window to his room and, when his father returned and called for his cowhide, the youngster used it to escape punishment. Barbee served with distinction in the army and was a captain commanding a company at the Battle of Eutaw Springs in September 1781. After "draging a wounded soldier by the belt strap out of danger," Captain Barbee was captured and paroled. At that time, he was considered "one of the bravest of men of great bodily strength & very determined in purpose." Following the war, the Barbee brothers moved to Danville, Kentucky. Although married twice, both of Thomas's wives died childless. While in Danville, he captured a notorious, large-framed, extremely muscular killer whom the sheriff claimed he could not take into custody with fifty men. Volunteering to apprehend the man, the no-nonsense Barbee walked over to where the accused felon stood waiting. He pulled a stake from a fence and, "without saying one word to the murderer raised the stake & knocked the man on the head which brought him down when the sheriff was able to secure him."[24]

Many of the men who followed these intrepid leaders were veterans of several Indian expeditions, in fact it seemed as though some Kentuckians would volunteer whenever a new campaign seemed necessary. Among those were Zachariah Holliday of William Lewis's company who had settled in Kentucky in 1783. He had been out in Clark's 1786 Wabash campaign, had followed Scott and Wilkinson on their mounted raids, had fought under Adair at Fort St. Clair, and was now back on his fifth outing against the Indians. Born in County Carlow, Ireland, on Christmas Eve, 1770, Garret Burns was a descendant of the poet Robert Burns. He came to America in 1784 and eventually settled in Bourbon County, where he worked as a hatter. Burns went as a substitute in Harmar's army and fought in both battles at the Miami villages, in the latter of which he assisted two neighbors from the field after they had been wounded. He fought again under St. Clair and went along on Scott's campaign against the Eel River towns in 1792. Now he was out again, earning one dollar per day as a mounted volunteer in Rawlings's company.[25]

Some men had interesting tales to tell of their experiences with Indians, perhaps none more so than John Stilley. His father, John Stilley Sr., had settled along Raccoon Creek, about sixty miles north of Wheeling, in 1773 and was killed four years later by the accidental discharge of a rifle while on an Indian scout. In 1781, a party of Wyandottes came into that settlement and captured five members of the Kennedy and Stilley families, including John, who was then about eight years of age. The youngster was taken to Upper Sandusky, where he was adopted by an old Wyandotte couple. They taught him their language as well as how to hunt, trap, and fish in the Indian fashion. He enjoyed the sports of wrestling, foot races, and playing ball, seemingly at home with his adopted family. At the close of the Revolution, the Wyandottes considered young John as a member of their own nation and did not turn him over with the other white captives. At that time, Stilley appeared to be a typical Indian youth: "He was then dressed in the Wyandot manner, his hair all plucked out save a small scalp-lock, which was ornamented with gay colored feathers. They had pierced his ears and the cartilage of his nose, and inserted rings and a brooch therein. When painted he resembled the true Indian. He was then something over twelve years of age, full of life and adventure." John Stilley, like William Wells and numerous other children before him, had truly become "more an Indian than a white boy." It was only after great difficulty and much persuasion that he was convinced to return home. He remained with his mother for five years, then in 1789 descended the Ohio to Limestone and eventually settled along the Elkhorn River, where he became associated with frontiersmen such as Simon Kenton and Cornelius Washburn. Stilley finally decided he would try soldiering and joined Garret Burns in the company commanded by Capt. Nathaniel Rawlings.[26]

CHAPTER 13

Construction of Fort Greeneville

GENERAL SCOTT STARTED NORTH FROM Fort Hamilton early in the morning of October 17, escorted by Capt. Robert Floyd and twenty-five men. General Todd followed four hours later with the main body of volunteers. While en route, the Kentuckians met an express rider who told them of the defeat of Lieutenant Lowry's escort near Fort St. Clair, and that night one of the sentinels saw an Indian scouting their camp. Although the men were eager to be off next morning, Todd's column waited until about noon for the arrival of Mrs. Wilkinson, who was on her way north in a carriage accompanied by Major Beatty and a sizeable escort of volunteers. The lady's vehicle broke down well short of Fort St. Clair, and she proceeded the rest of the way on horseback, her party reaching Fort Jefferson a day ahead of the main column. Todd and the Kentuckians arrived at that post on October 20 and encamped for the night two miles north alongside Wayne's road. They remained here until October 24, when General O'Hara established a new bivouac within sight of the legion's camp. Francis Jones, aide to Scott, described the place as "an isleand surrounded by Prieries and the South west Branch of the Miami on the West." He found "the Soil good and timbred with large oak," surrounded by "beautifull waving ground and delightfull extensive views up & Down the Prieries." Given its distinctive location, this new campground was named Island Camp.[1]

Officers visited back and forth between Island Camp and the Grand Camp of the legion, although the dinner fare for invited guests was almost identical if one were not sitting at a general's table. Resourceful Kentuckians discovered natural orchards of plum and crabapple trees and used fruit from the latter to make "some excellent apple Toddy." Conviviality and overconfidence in their numbers caused a lapse in discipline. Major Price, officer of the day in Island Camp, discovered Benjamin Vanventer of William Lewis's company and Elias Farmer of Bartlett's company asleep at their posts. Worse still were the desertions of Pvts. John Ensworth and Andrew Ware from the legion camp "when on centry." Despite the possibility of being killed or captured by Indians and the certainty of severe and possibly lethal punishment if retaken by the military, a few men continued to desert. Foremost among them was Patrick O'Hara of DeButts's company, who was described as "about five feet nine inches high, rather fair complexion, short black curled hair, black eyes, a mason by trade, a thief and a drunkard." Of O'Hara it was said, "if vilany could be called an accomplishment, he is accomplished in a high degree." As if to prove that claim, the rogue ran off into the woods on October 25 "from under guard, with hand-cuffs on."[2]

Soldiers and volunteers alike chafed at the inactivity, but none more so than the most experienced Indian fighters, Major McMahon and Capt. Simon Kenton. Both officers, frustrated by the slow pace of the campaign, declared bitterly that they would rather kill Indians than build forts. Informed of their discontent, on October 26 General Wayne ordered McMahon and Kenton on a scout toward the Auglaize River with a force of eighty-four riflemen and sixty-three mounted volunteers. Thus, the most famous Indian fighters from Kentucky and Virginia set out to appease their lust for blood. This combined force struck the Auglaize River and followed that stream almost to its juncture with the Maumee. As the column advanced, scouts reported numerous trails made by large bodies of Indians, all seemingly bound for the Grand Glaize villages. Both officers were equally brave, but McMahon was more impetuous and bold, while Kenton was more cautious and wary. The captain did not like the looks of the situation and suggested that they abandon their hunt and withdraw. McMahon would not think of a retreat without fighting. Kenton again said that it was "imprudent" to go farther, but if the major ordered an advance, his volunteers would follow, and "all should be done that men could do." He did, however, gently remind McMahon that the Kentuckians were mounted and thus "would have some advantage in a rapid retreat." No decision was reached that night, but early next morning, McMahon agreed that Kenton's suggestion to retreat was probably the best plan. The officers brought the command safely back to camp, where General Wayne approved of their decision and praised them for having "some conduct with their courage."[3]

While at Island Camp, William Shannon, adjutant general of the mounted volunteers, fell sick of a fever, which quickly required his removal to Fort Jefferson for treatment. Herman Bowmar, an ensign in Bartlett's company, took over Shannon's duties for the remainder of the campaign. Bowmar had served on General Scott's Wabash campaign and credited his appointment to that officer's good will. The ensign had previously served as adjutant of Lt. Col. Horatio Hall's regiment for several months. Bowmar admitted that he was "raw material," but Hall, "a full master disciplinarian, of great military pride, of the highest order of valour," and a veteran of several campaigns, taught the young man how to be a good officer. When General Scott first assembled his entire volunteer force, "their officers could form only a crooked line." After Bowmar took charge, rectifying the line and posting the officers properly, Adjutant General Shannon saw that he had the assistance of "one Adjutant, and no more." Shannon appointed Bowmar to the post of brigade major, then, after falling ill, recommended him to be adjutant general pro tempore.[4]

A number of events kept the Kentucky Volunteers on the alert. There were almost nightly alarms by guards, both in Island Camp and Grand Camp, who fired at shadows or shadowy Indians. One man out searching for a stray horse was fired upon by an Indian, hid in the grass until after dark, then returned to camp, where he was shot at by three jumpy sentinels. Cold weather, with snow and high winds, swept Island Camp on the night of October 26. When General Todd awoke next morning, he discovered "a snake [had] crawled into his bosom & coiled up to keep warm!" About noon, the prairie caught fire as a result of careless guards trying to keep warm on their posts, and by the next day, it had developed into "a very great fire" that threatened the outposts, if not the main camp. A heavy frost finally extinguished the last embers, then a wet snow fell, followed three days later by several hours of rain. When Captain Butler appeared and began the laborious process of mustering the volunteers, the Kentuckians became even more dispirited.[5]

On October 31, General Wayne convened a council of war consisting of Generals Wilkinson, Posey, Scott, Todd, and Barbee. He began by reading the various instructions he had received from Secretary of War Knox since his original letter of May 25, 1792. Wayne supplemented this with intelligence regarding Indian activity and estimated numbers, a complete field return of both the legion and the volunteers, and the number of rations that Elliott and Williams had stockpiled. The commander in chief then asked his subordinates for their opinions on three questions:

1. Under the present existing circumstances will the safety & protection of the Western frontiers, the reputation of the Arms of the United States, & the honor dignity & interest of the Nation be enhanced by a forward move of this Army?
2. Will our present force, state of provision & means of transport, justify the advance of the Legion to a position at or near the field of action of the 4th of November 1791?
3. In what mode, manner, or enterprise shall the mounted volunteers be employed?

He then mentioned that Governor Shelby and many other Kentucky leaders had pressured him to send the mounted volunteers "in a desultory expedition against the Indian villages of Au Glaize."

In a joint letter, Generals Wilkinson and Posey responded "no" to the first two questions. As to the third question, they claimed to be "at a loss for a Reply, because of our Ignorance of the State of the Horses of the Kentucky Volunteers & the temper of the Men." In a supplemental letter, Posey gave the reasons for his negative response to the two questions. First, he said that the forage and provisions were insufficient to sustain such an advance. He also pointed out the "great Deficiency of Officers" and the fact that many men were in dire need of new uniforms for the winter. Perhaps most importantly, Posey asserted that "should the Legion take a Position at or near the Field of Action of the 4th of Novr 1791, and be afterwards reduced to the necessity of relinquishing it and retreating, it may be considered as little better than a Defeat and will consequently reflect great Discredit on the Arms of the United States." He recommended unequivocally that "a *Stand* should be made at this place."

The Kentucky generals did not feel qualified to answer the first two of Wayne's questions and advised that, in their collective opinion, any movement against the Auglaize villages would be "too hazardous" an undertaking. General Scott explained why. After leaving behind the sick and those men who had lost their horses, the volunteers could not muster more than nine hundred men. Given that most of their horses had received no forage since leaving home, fully one-third of them would be unable to complete such an expedition, especially since frost had killed the grass. The entire Indian confederacy, supposed to be gathered at the Grand Glaize waiting and watching the American army, could be brought to bear against the Kentuckians. If there should be a battle, any wounded men would necessarily retard the column and make it an easy target for an active enemy. Finally, Scott had no confidence that the necessary guides could be procured. General Barbee agreed, saying that "to attempt the Au Glaze at this time would be Attended with very considerable Risque," especially "in consequence of the imbicellity of our horses."[6]

General Wayne glumly reported the results of this council of war to Secretary Knox, explaining that he now had no choice but to "halt & Hut at this place for the present." Now positioned six miles north of Fort Jefferson, Wayne had not wavered from his previous assertion and still felt that he could protect the frontier and his convoys "from the depredations & insults of the Savages" by remaining within striking distance of the Auglaize villages. Whether the Indians gave battle or fled from there, Wayne assured Knox that "a post will be established at that place *at an early period*." This fort planned for the junction of the Auglaize and Maumee Rivers would be the fourth Wayne expected to construct beyond Fort Jefferson, the others being at the Miami villages (by order of Secretary Knox), on St. Clair's battlefield, and along the southwest branch of the Miami, where the legion would go into winter quarters. These proposed forts and their locales would greatly influence the campaign Wayne expected to mount in the spring of 1794.[7]

On November 3, 1793, General Scott took his command back to Fort Jefferson, where they were to receive rations and corn for their horses in anticipation of a raid against Indian villages along the White River on the return march to Kentucky. Francis Jones noticed that the men were "in disorder and very mutinous." Next day, a portion of the mutineers rode back to the legion camp to express their dissatisfaction, then headed home immediately "in a Cowardly Dastardly manner." Others had started before them, and officers could not stop the exodus. Those who remained were described as "noisy and troublesom." This mutiny depleted Scott's volunteer force by half, falling from a strength of 989 officers and men on November 4 to only 488 the following day. General Todd managed to retain 292 men in his brigade, but General Barbee could muster only 196. General Wayne sent William Wells to the Kentuckians to act as a guide for their raid, though he admittedly knew little about that part of the frontier. Based on Hamtramck's recommendation and his performance as an agent at Indian councils, Wells had been offered a position as sort of an official jack-of-all-trades, subject only to Wayne's demands. He was to receive the same pay and emoluments as a legion captain for one year, in exchange for which he agreed to "obey & execute such orders & instructions" as he might receive from the general "from time to time." "Captain" Wells, due to the vague nature of his assignment, could not swear the standard oath but did agree to follow any orders "as far as practicable" and to the best of his "power knowledge & abilities."[8]

Shortly before nine o'clock on the morning of November 5, General Scott ordered his men to mount, and what remained of the Kentucky Volunteers rode off behind their guide in search of some Indians to fight. Among that number was Garret Burns, who remembered, "Being well mounted, and feeling myself capable of going through as much as any other man in the campaign, I volunteered to make one of the party." Scott's column headed south-southwest, crossing creeks, traversing prairies, pushing through brush-choked woods, wading swamps, and enduring rain and wet snow that soaked them to the skin. On the second day, advance scouts fired at two Indians who seemed to be spying on the Kentuckians. Their only captures were a few old blankets and one horse loaded with some skins and branded "EW," the property of Elliott and Williams. Short of provisions, the volunteers had to resort to hunting, and the constant firing at game alerted any Indians of their approach. Garret Burns admitted that, "instead of our pursuing Indians, they were following us." Stealthy warriors shadowed Scott's command, looking for an opportunity to steal horses, but they were thwarted because, as Burns recalled, "we tied our horses up every night within the camp." Turning their mounts southeast, the column reached Fort Hamilton on the afternoon of November 9 after a march of about one hundred miles. Scott reported to Wayne that he had "don nothing more than breaking up one Small Indian Camp of five men," all of whom escaped. Burns was more succinct, admitting, "we scoured the whole country and finally returned without accomplishing anything." Chagrined by failure, the Kentuckians went home. Lieutenant Smith said it best when he wrote that they had done nothing more than consume valuable provisions.[9]

With the legion now on its own, General Wayne began to erect a strong fortress at General Camp. On November 3, Generals Wilkinson and Posey allotted sections of timber in the woods to the various companies for use in both fortifying and building huts. Soldiers began to cut pickets ten feet in length for construction of a stockade. Three days later, Quartermaster O'Hara had laid out the ground, marking where enlisted men from each unit were to construct their huts, which were to be fourteen feet wide and number six to a company. Huts were built first, then soldiers erected cabins for the officers and a headquarters building for General Wayne. These were followed by eight blockhouses for the guards as well as buildings for a magazine, a laboratory, bake houses, quartermaster stores, artificer shops, an office for Elliott and Williams, and storage facilities and stables for the contractors, all in addition to bridges over creeks and ravines. For defensive purposes, loopholes about seven feet above ground level were cut in the main stockade and the pickets surrounding each blockhouse, "high enough to prevent the Enemy from benefiting from them, should they have the Temerity to press forward." Banquettes about two feet in height were constructed of earth so that soldiers could stand upon them and shoot through these elevated loopholes while denying Indians an

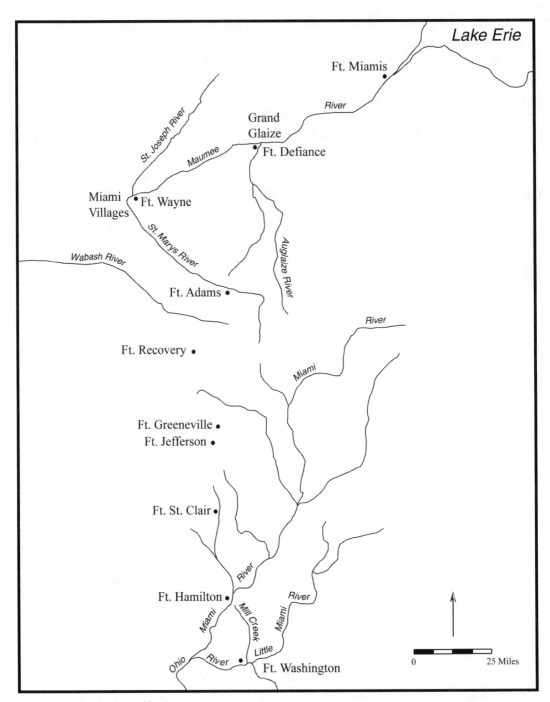

Lake Erie

Ft. Miamis

River

Grand
Glaize

Ft. Defiance

St. Joseph River

Maumee

Miami
Villages

Ft. Wayne

St. Marys River

Wabash River

Auglaize River

Ft. Adams

River

Ft. Recovery

Miami

Ft. Greeneville

Ft. Jefferson

Ft. St. Clair

River

River

Ft. Hamilton

Miami

Mill Creek

Miami

Little

Ohio

River

Ft. Washington

0   25 Miles

Forts of the Northwest Territory

opportunity to return the fire. According to general orders, "The Banquets round the Stockade of the Encampment must be rais'd so high that the shortest man may fire with effect, so as to take an Enemy in the Centre, at twenty Yards Distance." In its final appearance, Captain Bradley described this new fort as forming "an oblong square about six hundred yards long & three broad." The stockade stood about 50 yards beyond the soldiers' huts, and the eight blockhouses were about 250 yards beyond the palisade. After most of the heavy construction had been finished, brick chimneys were dismantled at Fort Jefferson and sent on to be reassembled at the new post. Soldiers moved into their huts, many of them still without doors or bunks, on November 20. Next day, General Wayne announced to the legion, "This encampment shall in future be known & distinguished by the Name of Greeneville," in honor of his old friend from the Revolution, Gen. Nathaniel Greene, who had died in 1786.[10]

Construction at Fort Greeneville did not include stables and huts for the dragoons because Wayne had decided to send them to winter quarters in Kentucky; O'Hara urged that the dragoon squadron be quartered near Lexington, that being the largest settlement in the state. Due to the continued absence of Maj. William Winston, Capt. Robert MisCampbell would assume command of the squadron. Wayne ordered him "to establish the most exact discipline" by cracking down on the dual vices of drunkenness and gambling. MisCampbell was also to keep the men hale and hearty by having his camp well policed and conforming to the standing order that "cleanliness is ever conducive to Health." After the huts and stables had been erected, the men were to devote their energy to improving and repairing equipment for both horses and riders. Since the squadron had to be ready to move "at the shortest notice," no furloughs or leaves were granted. Wayne concluded his instructions with the reminder that "the most exact Economy be observed, upon all occasions."[11]

The dragoons reached their winter encampment, about six miles southwest of Lexington, on November 30. The spot was located close to wood and water, the men were in good spirits, and work commenced immediately on stables. All horses were under cover by December 10, and the soldiers moved into their huts one week later. An experienced officer who was familiar with the deceptive ways of enlisted men, Captain MisCampbell took the precaution of publishing a warning in *The Kentucky Gazette:* "The commanding Officer of the Dragoons takes this early opportunity to caution the good citizens in the neighborhood of the cantonment, against any dealings with the soldiery of the squadron, without a written permission from a commissioned Officer, which will be always granted in proper cases. He hopes this friendly notice will not give offence, as it is only intended to preserve the public property inviolate, and prevent any misunderstanding between the troops of the United States and the people of Kentucky." To further protect the citizens, the captain published the names of all officers then with the squadron, lest any dishonest soldier try to swindle or cheat the neighbors with forged documents. As he expected, soldiers soon made "nocturnal visits to the Inhabitants," a situation made even more dangerous since the dragoons had been exposed to smallpox. MisCampbell christened his dragoon encampment Bellipherontia, a classical reference to Bellerophontes, the ancient Greek warrior who had ridden Pegasus, the mythical flying horse.[12]

Wayne was baffled by the lull in Indian activity as construction continued on Fort Greeneville. He advised Secretary Knox: "I am at a loss to determine what the Savages are about & where they are. I have searched in almost every direction for them & without effect." To gain some sense of the enemy's whereabouts, Wayne sent Captain Flinn with his spies and guides north on several scouts toward the Auglaize, with orders to keep the general informed of any discoveries by sending back runners. He told the captain, "I want intelligence & scalps," reminding him there was a reward for each. Flinn scouted to and beyond St. Clair's battlefield without finding any trace of hostiles. Wayne felt that the Indian disappearance "portends some premeditated stroke," perhaps at the convoy then en route under command of General Wilkinson. He warned that officer the Indians might have thrown a strong party between Forts Hamilton and Greeneville and recommended that detachments be kept out on all sides of the convoy. Wayne especially warned that the area of fallen timber between Forts Hamilton and St. Clair be thoroughly examined before the column should be allowed to enter.[13]

Wilkinson had taken a "super convoy" back to Fort Washington, leaving Fort Greeneville on November 13. This column was part of a new system instituted after Lowry's defeat. No longer would supply trains be guarded by detachments of only 150 men, for now escorts consisted of about a dozen companies and numbered about 500 men. The first of these convoys set out on November 2 under Lieutenant Colonel Strong, bound for Fort Hamilton. Strong's instructions clearly specified that he would conduct his march as if he commanded a mini-legion. There would be front and rear guards as well as flankers, with small patrols surrounding the whole. When not at a regular fort, the convoy would halt at one of the legion's fortified camps, either Twenty-Eight Mile Tree or Five Mile Spring. Packhorses would be corralled inside the existing breastworks, while soldiers of the escort would occupy one of the bastions, turning it into a "stronghold" by adding a new wall on the inside. Remembering the cowardly conduct of those dragoons who had been with Cornet Blue, General Wayne also reminded Strong, "should any soldier be so base as to turn from his enemy or discover in action any fear or reluctance at obeying orders & discharging his duty like a gallant soldier that the Espontoon or bayonet put an immediate period to his existence."[14]

The escort for General Wilkinson's super convoy, which left Fort Greeneville on November 13, consisted of Major McMahon, Major Mills, and the companies of William Kersey, Thomas Pasteur, Asa Hartshorne, Samuel Andrews, Daniel Bradley, Zebulon Pike, Isaac Guion, Thomas Lewis, Jacob Slough, John Cooke, and William Preston. When the column reached Fort Jefferson, Lieutenant Colonel Strong, who had just been granted a brief furlough, and Capt. John Tillinghast, who had resigned, decided to hurry ahead and took the old road accompanied only by ten dragoons. When within four miles of Fort St. Clair, Indians fired upon the two riders in advance, killing one and shooting the other "through his clothes." Strong ordered the remaining dragoons to draw their sabers in preparation for a charge, but when over a dozen howling Indians ran toward the soldiers, he shouted for them to retreat. Tillinghast was mounted on a slow pack-horse, and the Indians were "almost at his heels" when his hat fell off. He reined in to retrieve it, but one glance convinced him that was a bad idea. One dragoon had stopped the dead rider's horse, so Tillinghast quickly switched mounts and raced off, leaving his hat and other baggage for the Indians. In a letter to Major Buell, the captain complained that "the rascals were ungenerous to push him so hard when he had just relinquished all hostile intentions against them." Strong's party reached Fort Jefferson safely that night, the officers now much more inclined to stick with the security of a slow-moving convoy rather than striking out on their own.[15]

Upon reaching Fort Washington, officers of Wilkinson's overland convoy discovered that Lieutenant Colonel Clark had arrived there on November 12 with a convoy of eight Kentucky boats from Fort Fayette. His command consisted of Capt. Tarleton Fleming of the dragoons, Lt. John Reed, and sixty-one enlisted men. The newcomers had several exciting stories to tell. On the night of November 8, when Clark's fleet was near the mouth of the Scioto, about a dozen Indians were discovered crossing over to the Virginia shore between two of the legion boats. Three days later, close to Twelve Mile Creek, a "considerable number" of Indians were spotted on the north bank. Soldiers let fly a volley of small arms and discharged one round from a howitzer at the party, which immediately disappeared into the forest without firing a shot. A smaller detachment of forty-six noncommissioned officers and privates under command of Lt. Hastings Marks reached Fort Washington on November 14 without incident.[16]

Wilkinson's super convoy left Fort Washington on November 24 with 365 packhorses loaded with 1,209 bushels of corn. Of that total, 59 bushels were left at Fort St. Clair and 298 were stowed in storage sheds at Fort Greeneville on December 2, a net deposit of 357 bushels, the remainder being consumed en route. But the convoy had also been issued 411 bushels of corn from the stockpiles at Forts Jefferson and Hamilton, so in fact Wilkinson's contractor and quartermaster horses had eaten more corn going and coming than they were able to carry, a net loss of 54 bushels. This was not the way convoys were supposed to operate. Major Belli pointed out this folly to Wayne and urged him to stop sending packhorses and slow-moving wagons in the same convoy. Wheeled vehicles retarded the convoys, kept them on the march longer, and consequently resulted in faster consumption of precious forage. In addition, Belli found the packhorses "by these slow movements & tying up of nights for so long a time reduced to a very small number fit for service." In his opinion, there was only one option, "I think it would be best to send all the Packhorses to Kentucky to be recruited until spring when the transportation is more easy as well as more advantageous; besides it will be the means of reducing the Wages of Packhorse drivers which is & has been extravagantly high since the voluntiers were called from Kenty." He had tried to implement the shipment of corn by water up the Miami to Fort Hamilton but had been frustrated by low water and a lack of coopers to fabricate casks and barrels. The resourceful quartermaster did, however, arrange for the construction of sixteen sleighs to be used for hauling critical supplies during the winter months.[17]

One day after the convoy reached Fort Greeneville, the packhorses were sent south again with an escort commanded by Lieutenant Colonel Hamtramck. That officer had requested a leave of absence to arrange his financial affairs at Vincennes, including the purchase of land and the letting of contracts entered into before his last promotion. Hamtramck claimed that if he could not attend to these financial matters, he would "inevitably be ruined, or at least lose the greatest part of my property," which should make him "a very poor man for all the Days of my life." Wayne indulged his senior field officer with a leave of absence until March 31, when he was to report to wherever headquarters might be located. Although Hamtramck had command of the escort, Gen. Thomas Posey accompanied the column to Fort Washington. He too had been granted a leave through the end of March and now had another duty to perform, one of a more political nature. Wayne begged him "to make a point of impressing every member of Congress with whom you may converse with the absolute necessity of the immediate completion of the Legion, and that you also pay a visit to the seat of government, and wait personally upon the President and Secretary of War, and give them every information, *viva voce,* that they may wish to receive relative to the situation of the Legion, together with the motives and circumstances which influenced an advance and halt at this place." Ever the loyal friend, Posey agreed to do so and promised to "contradict misrepresentations, and exaggerated accounts, which may be mentioned either before me, or in circulation."[18]

Hamtramck's escort for his super convoy consisted of the companies of John Pratt, Jacob Kingsbury, Cornelius Sedam, Jonathan Haskell, Bezaleel Howe, Richard Greaton, Uriah Springer, Richard Sparks, Nicolas Hannah, Edward Butler, Joseph Brock, and Maxwell Bines, with Major Buell, Lt. Edward Turner, and Surgeon Nathan Hayward also assigned to the column. The command left Fort Greeneville on December 3 and arrived at Fort Washington in the cold and snow six days later. This would be the last convoy before winter set in, so the contractors and quartermaster made every effort to get supplies up to the advanced posts. Captain Brock set out on December 12, his company acting as the escort for eight hundred head of cattle and their drivers. Lieutenant Colonel Strong succeeded Hamtramck and started north on December 15 with eight hundred packhorses loaded with "clothing, salt, flour, corn, &c., &c." Strong's column safely reached headquarters after seven days on the road without seeing a single Indian. While General Wayne was pleased to receive this last large shipment of stores, his men were overjoyed to see that the paymasters had come along with some long overdue wages.[19]

Conditions at the posts farther down the Ohio River were even harsher than those in the line of forts stretching north from Cincinnati. Lieutenant Hunter had sent five men from Fort Steuben to Fort Knox, one of whom was so sick that he remained at the latter post. The other four started back through the woods but lost their way. Three of them fell sick, and the remaining man left them behind and came on to Fort Steuben. Two of the sick men, minus their arms, accouterments, and outer clothing, stumbled back to Hunter's post twenty days later, "being fourteen days without Subsistence farther than what they pick'd up in the woods." The other man was missing and "in all probability" dead. Fort Steuben's stock of provisions failed, and Hunter's utmost exertion could do nothing more than keep one or two days ahead of starvation. Even the whiskey was gone. As the weather grew colder, it became more and more difficult to obtain firewood for daily consumption. The forest had been cut down to a considerable extent around the post so that all firewood had to be carried on the shoulders of convalescent soldiers, "which renders it very fatagueing to many of them who is lame and weak." As if it were a metaphor of the sorry state at Fort Steuben, Hunter reported that the "Flag Staff makes a naked appearance for want of its usual uniform, which is some time since worn out."[20]

One major drawback to duty at these detached, lonely garrisons was that commanders had to remain there until relieved. Officers with the main body could at least hope to receive furloughs or leaves of absence. Once it became apparent that the legion would not advance any farther, many sought to receive the same indulgence granted to Posey and Hamtramck. Their letters ran the gamut of possible excuses. Captain Lee had only recently arrived but asked to return to Virginia "to bring to the Army some Recruits that left me on the March." Captain Faulkner, the most illiterate of Wayne's company commanders, wished "a ferlow from yower Exulencie To go home for sum short time" to conduct "Bisness." Captain Ford requested leave to stay at Fort Washington over the winter since there were two lieutenants "equal to the task" of caring for his company. Portraying himself as "an old servant of the Publicks," Ford pointed out that he had "spent my health and property in their Service." When his first appeal was ignored, a second letter pointed out that he was recovering from an injury, had received but one furlough since 1784, and had a new wife who was anxious for his return. Major Doyle also asked to spend the winter at Cincinnati, citing the situation of his family and the "bad State" of his health. Specifically, Doyle confessed that his vitality was being sapped by "the inveteracy of my wound which is becoming more painful and which from the want of proper accomodation here cannot be treated with the necessary indulgence." Having lost a leg in the Revolution, the major suggested that he might be assigned to garrison duty in place of a more active officer capable of enduring field service. Although the numerous applications for leave had become "very unpleasant & troublesome business," Wayne did approve Doyle's request due to the unique disability involved.[21]

Two officers requested furloughs to go home to New England to settle personal and public business. Prior to receiving his commission, Russell Bissell had been a constable and collector of state taxes in Connecticut. Although only part of his collecting had been finished, Bissell threw himself into recruiting a company with the intention of completing the tax business before leaving his rendezvous. This plan was foiled when the War Department ordered him to march the first group of Connecticut recruits to Pittsburgh. Captain Bissell explained that "the frequent Deaths Imigrations Bankrupts" and other reasons for noncollection meant the loss fell upon him "in an Injurious manner." Captain Eaton, one of Wayne's staunchest supporters, also requested leave, saying, "I have a family with whom I connected myself in a critical moment and in a delicate situation." Financial concerns made it mandatory that he be in New England on March 20. Although unable to base his claim on veteran service, he hoped to be detached to duty there and agreed to wait patiently until February 1 for an answer. If he could not be assigned to one of the New England states by that time, Eaton assured Wayne that he would be compelled to resign his commission. Both Bissell and Eaton eventually received positive responses and were posted to New England, and thus two of the legion's best officers would miss the culmination of Wayne's campaign because of the press of personal business.[22]

In addition to the large number of officers seeking furloughs, some left through the normal process of attrition. On November 24, Captain Pratt informed Wayne of his desire to resign his commission and sent along the results of examinations conducted by Surgeon General Richard Allison and Surgeon's Mate Joseph Strong. The latter doctor certified that Pratt had been a patient since leaving Hobson's Choice, his disease being "a remitting fever which passed through a course of the most severe symptoms and terminated in an obstinate and very debilitating intermittent [fever]." Allison concurred, stating that Pratt suffered from "an obstinate and very dangerous fever," was much debilitated, and could perform no duty during the upcoming winter. Wayne approved Pratt's application, and his resignation was accepted on December 5.[23]

Two officers lost their commissions after being found guilty of violating the Articles of War. Lt. Micah McDonough ran afoul of Major Mills for gross misconduct while in command of the guard at Fort Greeneville. McDonough tried to explain to Wayne that his actions resulted after "the extreme acuteness of pain I suffered deprived me of the power of Judging between wright and wrong." He then assured his commander, "I didn't err from wilful neglect but from imbecility of a mind deranged & weakened by severe indisposition." If anything, McDonough argued that he was "much more unfortunate than blame worthy." Wayne did not accept the lieutenant's excuses, and he was dismissed on December 29. Captain Peirce arrested Captain Cummins at Fort Washington for some unknown infraction and, after a general court-martial, that officer was dismissed on February 9, 1794.[24]

A schism had also developed among the officers who remained in the legion, several of whom hinted at the problem in correspondence with General Wayne. In a letter offering his resignation, Lt. Lewis Bond had written, "I am not Disgusted with the Service—nor any individual in it." Captain Bissell's request for leave was not made under "any discording Humour Whatever." Major McMahon assured his commander, "I shall be one of the last that will turn my back upon you." But the strongest warning came from General Posey: "I am aware that you are not without your enemies who will be ready to lay hold of and take advantage of every mishap. Indeed some whom you hold friendly inclined to you, I have some reason to believe may endeavor to insinuate and place many of your operations in such a point of view, as to mislead the populace, and prejudice government. But be that as it may truth will ultimately preponderate." Rumors of trouble between Wayne and Wilkinson had become fact. Officers had begun to align themselves into two factions, although as the above statements indicate, no one appeared to be willing to discuss the situation publicly.[25]

Anthony Wayne was not stupid, and he knew exactly what was happening among the officers of his command. In a private letter written to Secretary of War Knox on November 15, the general named names:

> The same baneful leaven, which has been, & is yet fermenting (in the Atlantic States) against the most Worthy & Emaculate Character of this, or any other age—and against all the confidential Officers of Government has also been fermenting in this Legion, from the moment of my first landing at Hobsons Choice.
>
> The rights of man, has been held up as a Criterian, even of Military Government. Attempts have frequently been made to evade & disobey Orders, under various & unworthy pretexts & idle quibles, unknown at any period before *that time* in the Legion.
>
> The most *visible* & acting person is a Major *Cushing*, who is a very artful, & seditious man there is a Capt Guion, not far behind, but with less art.

Under the influence of these two officers, others were encouraged in the belief that the country owed them the right to come and go as they pleased. When denied furloughs, inexperienced officers were encouraged to submit letters of resignation and depart without waiting for their applications to be approved. Wayne assured Knox, "I am endeavoring to fix upon the principal, when an example shall take place, that will effectually prevent such doctrine or attempts in future."[26]

This blunt talk must have startled Henry Knox, but there were even more accusations. The failure of the contractors had been "highly reprehensible," so much so that Wayne now believed them to be involved in a criminal conspiracy against the legion. In his own words, "I have but too much cause to believe, that the neglect on the part of the Contractors, was occassioned by a many headed monster." Despite repeated verbal and written orders, Elliott and Williams had completely failed to live up to its contract to establish large stockpiles at the advanced garrisons. To Wayne this meant only one thing, that "it most certainly was expected, that I shou'd be compeled to retreat, for want of supplies." As the conspirators had been unable to compel a retreat, Wayne warned Knox, "probably the next attempt will be to default my advance." While the general had yet to determine who was masterminding this conspiracy, information began to point in the right direction. From the dragoon camp at Bellipherontia, Cornet Blue wrote to his commander: "I have had a Conversation with Lieut. Campbell Smith, who I would beg leave to recommend you to be aware of. I know his Sentiments and know they are not favourable, he is attached to General Wilkinson and I am convinced will go to any lengths to serve him." In addition to this, Blue also reported that a merchant had arrived from Philadelphia with the astonishing news that some senators had tried to impeach Wayne "at the Request of Wilkinson on the Charges of Peculation Speculation Fraud &c." In addition to watching out for Indians, Wayne had to henceforth keep members of the James Wilkinson faction under close observation.[27]

CHAPTER 14

Wayne Reclaims
St. Clair's Battlefield

Plagued by worries about the construction of Fort Greeneville, dissent among his officer corps, a contractor that did not ship enough supplies, a War Department that had fled the nation's capital, and even an occasional Indian threat, General Wayne now learned that an epidemic of smallpox had broken out at Fort Washington. Haskell's company had introduced that disease into the Cincinnati area when it reached Hobson's Choice on October 1. Now Captain Peirce reported that some of his men had become infected in "the Natural way" and a few of them had died from "the Most Malignant Kind" of disorder. Finding it impossible to stop the spread of this dreaded disease, Peirce consulted with Surgeons Richard Allison and Joseph Strong, who advised him to inoculate every man who had not already been immunized. The captain found twenty-one soldiers who had not yet contracted smallpox, had them inoculated, and by mid-December they were all "in a fair way of recovery." When two soldiers of the Second Sub-Legion caught the disease at Fort Washington while acting with the escort for General Wilkinson's super convoy, Wayne had them immediately sent back to Fort Jefferson to stop its spread into Fort Greeneville. There Wilkinson had the "pocky soldiers" isolated in one of the blockhouses, with a guard consisting of men who had already survived the contagion.[1]

Wayne clung steadfastly to his belief that "cleanliness & regularity in diet, is ever conducive to health, & on the Contrary—that irregularity & want of that attention are the principle causes of disease in all Armies." To counter the smallpox outbreak, he ordered that soldiers breakfast precisely at eight o'clock and have dinner promptly at one o'clock, meals being prepared in messes. Meat was to be boiled and made into soup, thereby retaining all of its nutrition. Roasting and frying was prohibited since he felt that meat prepared in that manner lost "a great part of its nourishment by drying up & waiting over the coals or before a fire." One officer from each battalion was to visit the men's huts each day at mealtime to ensure that these regulations were being followed. Despite the general's emphasis on keeping clean and eating well, smallpox appeared at

Fort Hamilton, where Major Doyle took it upon himself to inoculate soldiers at that garrison. Wayne was livid, terming Doyle's action "a measure truly reprehensible." The major offered the excuse that since Captain Peirce had inoculated the garrison at Fort Washington, he felt authorized to do so at Fort Hamilton because "infected persons have frequently been about this Garrison in a State of the Disorder most proper for communicating the Contagion." The malady continued unabated for months and was still raging at Fort Washington, and "at every post between this and Greenville," when Ens. Ferdinand Claiborne arrived there on February 27, 1794. In serious danger of becoming infected, Claiborne took the prudent advice of older officers and underwent inoculation.[2]

Smallpox quickly spread to the civilian population north of the Ohio, "a calamity which (as far as human life was concerned) was far more destructive than the Indians had been." Ezra Ferris remembered that the malignant form of smallpox "spread with such rapidity that its progress could not be arrested until it had reached the remotest station." He continued: "All business was suspended, as well as all assembling for public purposes, or military trainings, and the whole attention of the people was directed toward finding out the best and most speedy way of eradicating the disease from the country before spring. Houses most detached, where they could be had, were selected for pest-houses, and all who were willing to risk the process of inoculation were encouraged to resort to them as speedily as possible, where men were prepared to inoculate them without charge." In recalling this epidemic, one early resident of Cincinnati, noting that the outbreak began at Fort Washington, claimed that "nearly one third of the soldiers and citizens were destroyed by it." Among that number was David Strong Jr., seven years of age and son of the lieutenant colonel, who died on the morning of November 29. The only hope among this widespread misery was that somehow Indian raiders would become infected and carry the disease back to their villages.[3]

The house at Columbia belonging to Pastor John Smith, "a very friendly and benevolent man," had been used as a pest house by many of his neighbors and parishioners. After the epidemic began to abate, they returned to assist in "cleaning up," as it was termed. Every part of the home was scoured and scrubbed thoroughly, while each item of clothing and bed linen was carefully washed. Pastor Smith's family spent the night before a roaring fire, dressed in old clothing that would be discarded in the morning, while their belongings aired out in the frosty night air. Next morning when the Smiths went to retrieve their clothes, they discovered that all the garments had been stolen, leaving the family "in rather a bad fix." A few nights later, Indians penetrated into the very heart of the Columbia settlement and stole two horses. The militia turned out and pursued the horse thieves for four days but abandoned the search and headed for home. While on Harmar's Trace, Capt. Ephraim Kibbey and his men spotted two warriors coming toward them. Kibbey's militiamen formed an ambush, killed the Indians, and took their scalps. Upon examining the Indian packs, they found and recognized Pastor Smith's missing clothes. After reaching home with their trophies, the scouts were promised a substantial reward by Smith, although it seems the payment was never made.[4]

James and Ann Wilkinson had been staying at Fort Jefferson while the general recovered from his bout of influenza. When he became convalescent, the Wilkinsons invited the general in chief to join them for Christmas dinner. Their invitation arrived on December 20, just as Wayne himself was suffering from a second attack of influenza. Two days later, he complained, "my Head & breast are greatly effected from the severity of the Cough attendant upon this Caitiff complaint." Wayne proposed as a compromise that the couple come up to Fort Greeneville for "a fine turkey on New Years day," then they would all get together on the twelfth day of Christmas for an old-fashioned celebration. The general's decision to forego Christmas dinner was not based upon his delicate state of health, but rather, in deliberate understatement, upon "other arrangements, for reclaiming some ground & articles that were lost in front, some time since." Wilkinson was invited along, provided he might "conveniently get Clear of Christmas— & not alarm your Anna," something he was unable to do. Wayne had decided to play Santa Claus and give the Washington administration a wonderful Christmas present— the legion would march north and reclaim St. Clair's battlefield.[5]

Major Burbeck assembled a column consisting of the companies of William Peters, Joseph Shaylor, William Lewis, Alexander Gibson, John Jeffers, Russell Bissell, Howell Lewis, and William Eaton, supplemented by an artillery detachment of four howitzers, a total force of about three hundred soldiers. This force tramped north on the morning of December 23 and camped inside a timber breastwork some three miles south of the battlefield. Soldiers were up at dawn on December 24 and marched to the main branch of the Wabash River, where Burbeck decided the best site for a fort was directly on the site of battle. Front, rear, and flank guards were posted in timber redoubts, with patrols scouting well beyond. Four blockhouses, each twenty feet square, were laid out so that howitzers could be fired from embrasures on three sides. According to Wayne's instructions, the blockhouses were built simultaneously so that within two hours, the entire command could take shelter inside them, even if unfinished, should the Indians attack. When the blockhouses had reached a suitable height, they were connected by a palisade of upright pickets. Shutters for the embrasures and doors for the sally ports were constructed of musket-proof timber. Wayne had informed the major before he marched that this advanced post would be called Fort Recovery.[6]

Henry Burbeck had been born in Boston on June 8, 1754. His father, William Burbeck, had studied gunnery and was a civilian employee in the ordnance department of the British Royal Artillery. At the age of twenty, the young man joined Capt. Amos Paddock's famous Provincial Artillery Company, which eventually sent almost thirty officers to the Continental Army, and he served throughout the Revolution as an officer in the Third Regiment, Continental Artillery. On April 5, 1790, Captain Burbeck and his company of regulars built Fort St. Tammany at the mouth of the Saint Marys River in Georgia. The captain remained there until the spring of 1792, when he was promoted major and assigned to command the artillery in Wayne's new army. Burbeck's many years of service had proved that he was more than competent to march a strong detachment into Indian country and construct Fort Recovery on the site of St. Clair's humiliating defeat.[7]

He reported that the battlefield "had a very melancholly appearance—nearly in the space of 350 yards lay 500 skull bones—300 of which we buried while on the ground; from thence for five miles on, and from the roads through the woods, was strewed with skeletons, muskets, &c." When Burbeck's force first reached the site, Captain Butler rode up to Lt. Robert Purdy and Sgt. Maj. Thomas Underwood, to whom he made a highly personal request. Butler asked the two men to search the battlefield for "a large spredding Oak," under which his brother, Gen. Richard Butler, had pitched his marquee. The captain told them how he had "propped him up, set him on his mattrass & left him with a loaded pistol in each hand." He wanted Purdy and Underwood to examine any bones that lay under that conspicuous tree, specifically telling them to scrutinize the femurs, Richard Butler having broken his thigh while a youth. Underwood remembered performing that gruesome task and wrote, "we went to the place directed & found part of his bones, his skul and both thy bones, one we discovered had been broken." When informed of their discovery, Captain Butler arranged for his brother's remains to be decently interred.[8]

Suspecting that the Indians "wou'd more than probably dispute the Occupancy of a *favorite Ground,*" General Wayne had followed Burbeck's command with a detachment of infantry mounted on packhorses. After the major had the blockhouses started and a palisade under construction, Wayne ordered a large hole dug inside the perimeter of Fort Recovery. Enlisted men then commenced the grisly task of collecting the many bones and depositing them in this pit for burial. Sergeant Underwood noticed, "on every skul bone you might see the mark of the skulping knife." Another man recalled that "in many instances thare were perfect Skeletons the bones being yet united by the ligaments or sinews and where white and Indians had fallen together the white skulls could be easily distinguished from those of the Indians as the skulls of the whites were most invariable broken by the tomahawks." Soldiers also began to gather up the hundreds of muskets that littered the ground and found that, in most cases, their locks had been removed, stocks had been broken, and barrels bent by a savage fury directed against anything American. A few items could be salvaged, but most of the debris was worthless junk. After a hard day of labor, Burbeck's men prepared to spend Christmas Eve at their lonely post in the middle of the wilderness. Only one more task awaited them. According to nineteen-year-old George Will Jr., "when we went to lay down in our tents at night, we had to scrape the bones together and carry them out to make our beds."[9]

General Wayne had a two-fold purpose in reclaiming St. Clair's battlefield. By building a fort on that site, he could threaten the Indians by bringing elements of the legion ominously closer to their centers of population and serve notice that this bloody ground no longer belonged to them. Just as importantly, the advance to Fort Recovery would allow his men to recover the artillery that St. Clair had lost and the Indians had been unable to remove. In its flight from the battlefield of November 4, 1791, the American army had abandoned eight artillery pieces—three brass 6-pounders, three brass 3-pounders, and two iron carronades. One of the carronades had been recovered and removed to Fort Jefferson by General Wilkinson's militia party in the winter of 1792. The remaining seven field pieces had been concealed by the Indians, but men who had scouted the battlefield in succeeding months had been able to locate some of them. As soon as Burbeck's working parties had the construction well under way, a few men were sent to search for the cannons. The major was happy to report, "We found in the Creek, which is directly in front of the garrison, two brass cannon a six and three pounder, which was taken and left by the enemy on the 4th of Nov."[10]

After the basic construction of this new fort had been completed, General Wayne assembled his command for a fitting ceremony. Artillerymen fired a salute with the newly recovered 3-pounder and 6-pounder, a solemn observance that was marred by an explosion of some loose powder that seriously burnt Major Burbeck and his servant. Wayne gave command of this new post to Captain Gibson with these words: "I have no difficulty from your well known Character & from a full confidence in your bravery & Judgment to commit the defence of Fort Recovery to your Charge, which you will Maintain at every expence of blood." Gibson's garrison would consist of his own rifle company, Bissell's infantry company, and a detachment of twenty-six artillerymen. Wayne had intended to place one howitzer in each blockhouse, but the 6-pounder and 3-pounder were substituted for two of them, which were returned to Fort Jefferson. Wayne's orders to Gibson were succinct: "You will keep out constant & proper Patroles—& in due season you will send some confidential men to reconnoitre the Indian Villages at Au Glaize & endeavour to determine the course & distance by these parties which you may Occasionally send out, together with the Waters & Nature of the Ground over or thro' which the trace or path passes." Gibson was also to keep his commander advised of the state of his garrison's health, ammunition supply, quartermaster stores, and rations in addition to "any interesting discoveries or intelligence you may make or receive."[11]

Burbeck's command and Wayne's mounted infantry returned to Fort Greeneville on December 28, when Wayne announced the successful completion of their mission in a general order:

> The Commander in Chief returns his most grateful thanks to Major Burbeck, and to every officer, non-commissioned officer and private belonging to the detachment under his command, for their soldierly and exemplary conduct during their late arduous tour of duty, and for the ready cheerfulness with which they faced and surmounted every difficulty at this inclement season, in repossessing the field of battle, and erecting thereon Fort Recovery, a work impervious to savage force, as also for piously and carefully collecting and interring the bones and paying the last respect and military honors to the manes of the those heroes who fell on the 4th of November 1791, by three times three discharges from the same artillery that were lost on that fatal day, but now recovered by this detachment of the Legion.

Wayne ordered the contractors to issue an extra ration and a gill of whiskey to each man in Burbeck's detachment as "a small compensation for the fatigue they endured with so much alacrity & fortitude." In honor of his new citadel, he decided that the parole for that night would be "Fort" and the countersign would be "Recovery." The general summed up his accomplishment in a report to Secretary Knox: "Fort Recovery is now furnished with a sufficient Garrison well provided with Ammunition Artillery & Provision, Commanded by an Officer (Capt. Gibson) who will not betray the trust reposed in him!"[12]

New Year's Day, 1794, was celebrated at Fort Greeneville with a grand review at ten o'clock in the morning. Every man entitled to a new uniform had received one, and the sight of the legion perfectly arrayed in fresh clothes and bright weapons must have been truly impressive, although the only spectators would have been teamsters, packhorse drivers, sutlers, contractor clerks, and other civilian bystanders with ties to the army. Following this review, General Wayne and a cavalcade of officers rode down to Fort Jefferson, where they dined with General and Mrs. Wilkinson. Major Buell was among the party and described the lavish dinner prepared by the Wilkinsons: "Bill of fare: roast venison, roast beef boiled, and roast mutton boiled and roast veal boiled and roast turkey and fowls; raccoons, possums, bear meat, pies made of chickens, mince, apples, tarts, &c., &c. Sweetmeats of every kind, preserves and jellies, floating island and ice cream; plum pudding and plum cake, vegetables of every kind, a plenty of the best wine, at evening we had tea and coffee in high style." Their appetites sated by this fabulous banquet, Wayne and his officers started for Fort Greeneville, arriving well after dark.[13]

At least one group of soldiers did not share in the festivities. Joseph Collins, now an assistant deputy quartermaster but previously one of Wilkinson's confidential agents, had been sent on a scout toward Girty's Town with a sergeant, a corporal, and twelve privates from Eaton's company. He was to determine whether the stream there ran into the Auglaize, the Saint Marys, or the Miami River. When about thirty-five miles from Fort Greeneville, the Americans unexpectedly came upon an Indian camp, and Collins ordered the Vermont soldiers forward, seeing it was "less dangerous to attack, than to attempt a retreat, after being discover'd." A brisk skirmish ensued, the surprised warriors fighting with "savage fury" and the soldiers firing upward of a dozen rounds each. Seeing he was outnumbered, Collins withdrew, and "the Enemy probably *sore* from the encounter did not find it expedient to pursue!" Three Green Mountain boys were left dead on the field, Collins and another Vermonter were wounded, and the remainder had their clothing "perforated by rifle balls." They claimed to have killed seven or eight Indians before they left the field. Survivors of the scout returned to Fort Greeneville on January 3 with their story.[14]

General Wayne immediately sent Captain Eaton and a detachment of eighty men, guided by Collins, to complete the reconnaissance to Girty's Town. After sketching the streams and Indian paths in that region, Eaton was to visit Collins's battleground and bury his dead. Wayne also authorized him "to sacrifice a few of the Savages to their Manes, provided it can be done without risking too much—ever bearing in mind that if you do attack or are attacked that your dependence must be upon the bayonet." Eaton scouted over fifty miles in advance of Fort Greeneville and, upon his return, "routed, plundered and burnt" an Indian camp on the headwaters of the Miami, the residents fleeing before the legionnaires and leaving behind several hundred skins. After burying the Vermont men and counting seven dead Indians, the detachment returned. This would be William Eaton's last service in the field; a week later he set out for Philadel-phia bearing dispatches from Wayne to Secretary Knox.[15]

While Eaton conducted his scout, Wayne ordered Asa Hartshorne to take another detachment and open a road to Girty's Town, where he anticipated erecting a fort. Hartshorne was to start on January 6 along the well-worn Indian path from the north-east redoubt at Fort Greeneville to the Stillwater River and on to Girty's Town, clearing a road "to admit of Waggons passing freely." The lieutenant was furnished a wagon to carry a grindstone and the men's packs, the arms of the road cutters being carried by those standing guard. Like all other detachments, Hartshorne was ordered to camp inside a breastwork each night and to keep small scouting parties hovering around his main body. Wayne estimated that it would take four days to open about thirty miles of road. He also instructed Hartshorne to keep a lookout for a flag of truce and "give the most pointed & positive orders to your people not to fire upon any flag."[16]

Within hours of Captain Eaton's arrival, and while Hartshorne was still in the field, an Indian and a white man approached Fort Greeneville bearing a white flag. The two messengers were taken to headquarters, where they spoke directly with General Wayne. Identifying themselves as George White Eyes and Robert Wilson, the latter an Irish trader and interpreter, the men said they had been sent by the Delaware Nation with peace proposals. They also claimed that their mission had been approved by the Shawnees and other nations of the Indian confederacy. Stunned by this sudden change of events, Wayne told the ambassadors that they would meet in council the following day. The general did not know what to make of "this extraordinary embassy." He did believe, how-ever, that it had been precipitated by the recent construction of Fort Recovery, the scouts by Collins and Eaton, and Hartshorne's new road to Girty's Town. Yet Wayne was not convinced that the Indians sincerely wanted peace, and he suspected they had come for-ward "insidiously to gain time, in order to secure their winter provision, & to withdraw their women & children from pending destruction, as well as to gain an opportunity to reconnoitre our position & to discover our Numbers—which they have never hereto-fore been able to ascertain." Although suspicious of their motives, Wayne was willing to discuss peace with the Indian ambassadors.

Wilson was kept at the fort, while White Eyes and an officer went back into the for-est to bring out two more chiefs who were waiting to see if the original pair of messen-gers had been well received. Next day, a brief council was held. The Indians "declared it to be the sincere wish of their brethren, to live in friendship with their white brothers, and to close the road to the further effusion of blood." White Eyes did most of the speak-ing, one officer noting that "the yellow ambassador speaks very good English." They declared that the Indians "should have made peace with our commissioners the last summer, if Brandt had not talked *double* to them." If General Wayne could agree to another treaty negotiation, these messengers stated, "they would bring in thirty of the chief warriors immediately to treat."

Wayne responded that, after considering prior deceptions, it was impossible to believe the Indian messengers. If they were truly sincere, "they would have no objection to his proceeding, and establishing forts upon the banks of the Lakes, for their security and his own, where whilst drinking the waters, he would be better enabled to meet them in council." He also insisted upon "convincing and unequivocal proofs" of a desire for peace. This could only be accomplished by the Indians "bringing in and delivering up all and every of the Americans or white people, now in your possession, to the officer commanding at Fort Recovery, or on the same ground where the action on the 4th of November, 1791, took place; and that on or before the next full moon, which will be on the 14th of February." The Indian delegation "consented, gave a string of wampum, told him their young warriors should be called in, and would meet him at the time appointed." To show their sincerity, George White Eyes left the son of Buckengales as a hostage. Telling Secretary Knox that "time will soon determine the sincerity or perfidy of their Hearts," Wayne informed his superior that he would suspend his plan to erect a new fort at Girty's Town for a month to avoid antagonizing the enemy. He tentatively planned for a treaty negotiation to commence on May 1, "so as to be in perfect readiness at an early period to operate with effect, shou'd it prove abortive." Wayne had no intention of wasting another campaign season on false promises.[17]

Reaction in the legion was mixed. Major Burbeck questioned how much "these copper coloured fellows" really desired a treaty but noted, "this is the first time the savages have made overtures of peace." As for himself, Burbeck declared, "my voice is decidedly for peace, if done with honor to the United States." Another man assured his friends, "You need not doubt we shall have a peace immediately." One officer saw both aspects of the problem: "They are a cunning subtle people, and should be cautiously guarded against, at the same time our reputation as a free, and liberal nation, might suffer, did we not, even at this period, establish them as our friends and allies." Other officers were not fooled by this apparent Indian trickery. One of them remarked that the current peace overture was nothing more than "a manoeuvre to gain time and avert the impending storm." Another argued that the peace mission resulted because "we beat up their hunting camps, steal away their Squaws from the Villages, and keep the poor devils in constant alarm." A third man suggested, "this is but another piece of Indian war-policy, calculated to suspend the operations of our army against their towns—and it is not improbable that their good friends and neighbors the British have dictated to them that policy." As for their commander, Wayne remained sanguine, although he lamented that a "Golden favorable Opportunity" was slipping away for showing the united Indian nations "the effect of the Bayonet Espontoon & fire of the American Legion."[18]

Indians did not take long to violate the truce, although those responsible probably had not heard of the peace mission. On January 15, three Elliott and Williams wagons loaded with corn were ambushed about two miles south of Fort Hamilton. One of the drivers escaped and brought word of the attack to Major Doyle, who dispatched one sergeant and a dozen men to investigate. This party discovered that two horses from one wagon had been stolen but the oxen pulling the other two wagons had been left alone. The loads were intact, but two drivers were missing, one of whom was discovered scalped near the scene over a month later. Signs about the wagons indicated that only three

Indians had been involved. After recounting the attack, one resident of Cincinnati observed that the Indians had "an odd way of showing their sincerity" for peace and asked, "Are we to be duped one year more by those savages, or will Congress devise some effective measures for the protection of their suffering brethren on the frontiers?" Following this isolated strike, attempts on the convoys ceased, convincing at least one captain that the enemy were "heartily sick of the war, and consequently serious in their intentions for peace."[19]

There was one other menacing incident attributed to Indians, occurring on the evening of January 17. The grass being dry, "some rambling savages set fire to it" twenty miles to the east. Everyone went out in the gathering twilight to watch as "a column of fire, three hundred yards front, which approached the Cantonment at the speed of ten miles an hour, exhibited a spectacle truly grand and sublime." Fortunately, the fire burned out before threatening Fort Greeneville. The expansive prairies were covered with "the most luxuriant growth of grass ever seen" and, in the opinion of an officer stationed there, "would supply the army of *Xerxes* with forage for a century." Although not quite as large as that Persian emperor's army, the Legion of the United States had settled in for the winter. Upon returning from a visit to headquarters, one Cincinnati resident exclaimed, "I had the great pleasure and satisfaction of viewing in a wilderness, 2500 of the most regular, most harmonious, and best disciplined troops I have ever yet beheld, either in the United States, or any other part of the world." He added that General Wayne "merits the highest approbation of the country at large" for his conduct in raising, training, and advancing his command deep into Indian territory. One officer also pointed to Wayne as the reason for the legion's success: "Nothing can equal the attention and industry of the Commander in chief, not the smallest irregularity of the camp escapes his notice; the training of his troops, and the rendering them healthy and comfortable, is his constant care; at the same time he treats his officers and men with the most friendly politeness— he exacts from them the respect due to his elevated rank." While Wayne received his share of praise, one disgruntled officer portrayed affairs differently: "Many officers have been cashiered, and many it is expected will experience the like fate; a few have retired in disgust, and thus matters stand. . . . As to privates, the present army is composed of a set of great vagabonds. I am one among many, whose property has been severely plundered by them. The officers here, themselves say that the service could not suffer by the dismission of three-fourths of the soldiers—'Tis a poor presage." Residents in the Atlantic states must have been confused by these seemingly inconsistent reports from the frontier.[20]

As with most disputes, there was some truth on each side. Depredations by enlisted men were widespread, if not constant. When rumors circulated that grain stockpiles at Fort Jefferson had been broken into, Lieutenant Colonel Hamtramck responded to headquarters, "the corn is under Locks and keys, and the hay under a Stockade, protected by a Guard and Sentinels." Asserting that this was "the truth and the whole truth," he could finally placate his commander, who was willing to believe the worst. Captain Peirce continued to intercept men "who had stroled from the army" and reached Cincinnati, sending them back to Fort Greeneville under guard. Lieutenant Colonel Clark's detachment from the Upper Ohio also had its share of criminals. When his convoy reached Fort Washington, the missing supplies included a keg of spirits, a quantity of civilian shoes, and a number of keys, all items that could not be replaced in Cincinnati.[21]

The problem of criminals in the ranks could be traced to recruiting officers in the Atlantic states, who continued to send forward substandard individuals. The questionable tactics of recruiters became plain when disabled men began to ask for their discharges. Such was the case with John Bacon of the Third Sub-Legion. After serving about eighteen months, Bacon sought a discharge, claiming he was not longer fit for duty since "my Leggs, and Thighs and up to my Joints is all full of Pains." He continued, "I have a kind of Rhumatism, as in Summer and other changable Days a Fever-ague, and of extream Sickness, that sometimes I can scarcely get over with it, and I cannot wrest Nights or can Walk." In his petition to General Wayne, the private explained that he had received a little education from his father, a minister in Ireland. He then came to America and was sold as an indentured servant for a term of four years. Bacon described how, after completing his indenture, Captain Cummins "took the advantage of me that he was drunk and making me drunk likewise giving me the Bounty as he wore military cloths and I though[t] he was an officer I was oblidge to stay with him but being so ignorent that I did not know better and did not know what I was a doing and put me quite distracted and out of my Head." Portraying himself as "a destressed Creature" and "a poor Simple Man," Bacon simply wanted to go home to Ireland.[22]

When officers filled their quotas in taverns, they were bound to enlist a few of the dregs of society along with men who would make good soldiers. After Captain Eaton arrived in Philadelphia on March 7, one of his duties was to investigate all charges against soldiers then in that city's jail. He found some interesting cases. Patrick Lynch had enlisted under Captain Mills and deserted at Reading, Pennsylvania. Under Eaton's questioning, Lynch confessed that he had been locked up on September 6, 1792, escaped two weeks later, and had remained at large until July 1793. He also admitted that he had "been whipped in New York for robbery." Thomas Lee owned up to being a deserter, but Eaton recommended clemency since he was but a "poor simple fellow." Michael Brown (alias Coffee) had enlisted on April 10, 1792, and joined Jeffers's company. That fall, he was convicted of killing a hog at Pittsburgh and was sentenced by a civil court to one year's confinement at hard labor. After serving his sentence, Brown was ignored by the officers then in command at Pittsburgh and eventually ended up in Philadelphia. On December 11, 1793, he was jailed on a charge of stealing property from a Mr. Durant but was acquitted. Authorities arrested Brown again on March 6, 1794, this time "on a charge of assault and battery on his wife," to which was added the charge of desertion. Despite his criminal record, Eaton recommended that Brown be allowed to rejoin the legion.[23]

Among the incorrigibles, none was more notable than Miles Winslow, who deserted from the Springfield rendezvous on February 14, 1794. Twenty years of age and a resident of Brookfield, Massachusetts, Winslow was described in the following manner: "Very dark Indianish complexion, long black hair, grey eyes, remarkable low forehead; had on and carried with him, a round felt hat, bound with black binding, a short cloath coloured Coatee, one pair of Fustian Overalls, London brown Coat, two pairs uniform white Overalls, and a regimental jacket, other cloathing unknown." Bent on mischief, he broke into the printing office of James Hutchins and stole "a number of Bibles," a dozen pocket books, a few dictionaries, and some shoes. Winslow then burglarized the store of Norman Adams, where he made off with some cash and a few hair queues. The blackguard then robbed the bake house of William Eaton (no relation to the captain) of considerable property. In announcing this crime spree to the public, Captain Lyman urged the public to become actively involved in the search for Winslow and offered the standard ten-dollar reward (plus "all necessary charges"). For their part, the three victimized businessmen offered an additional ten dollars "for the apprehension of the Villain" and return of their possessions.[24]

General Wayne continued to be pestered by officers who either sought furloughs or permission to resign. Among the former was Major McMahon, who was surety for a man who had left Virginia, thereby exposing his own property to confiscation to settle the debt. Not wishing to see his family distressed because of another man's obligation, McMahon felt compelled to ask for a leave of absence, though he declared to Wayne, "I had rather go to the Oglaisse than go home at this season." Surgeon Nathan Hayward requested a leave to attend to personal matters, stating in his petition, "I was appointed in the Army in October 1786, and had only four months and ten days furlough since that time." But Wayne took a different view and responded, "You will please to recollect that you have not been more than ten Months with the Legion, immediately after an indulgence of a Four Months furlough." He refused Hayward's appeal with the simple statement, "The present crisis will not admit of the absence of any of the Surgeons." Lt. Jonathan Taylor asked permission to visit an ailing father whom he had not seen in five years, noting hopefully that he "lives within 70 miles of Fort Washington." Wayne disapproved this application in the same blunt manner he had done previously, responding, "The scarcity of Officers—and the situation of the Legion will not admit of a single furlough, upon any pretext whatever."[25]

While most requests for leave were rejected, General Wayne still continued to approve the resignations of officers who no longer wished to serve under him. Lieutenant Bond repeatedly asked permission to accept an inheritance, claiming that his allegiance and service had been given "in Return for a Garanteed Right of Going and Coming when I please." If he could not obtain a leave, he would resign. Bond asked the general, "Why Sir, should I Sacrifice more to my Country than my Country will for me?" More than happy to purge another friend of Major Cushing, Wayne quickly accepted Bond's resignation. Ens. Reasin Beall, who had been threatening to resign seemingly almost every day since receiving his commission, announced on New Year's Day, 1794, that he was "determined not to make the army my Profession." Wayne agreed and approved his resignation two days later; Beall went home to Washington, Pennsylvania, and got married. Surgeon's Mate Thomas Hutchins resigned "from a total disrelish to the line of his profession" on December 14, 1793.[26]

When sentenced to be dismissed by a court-martial, Captain Faulkner expressed his desire to remain in the "Cerves." If that request could not be granted, he asked Wayne to "Exsept of my Regnaishen." When the general did accept his resignation on January 30, 1794, the former captain returned to running his tavern in Washington, Pennsylvania. But Faulkner had grand aspirations of publishing a book. He retained copies of all of Wayne's general orders, including those issued after he left the legion, as well as the decisions of courts-martial and the general's remarks upon them. To these Faulkner was prepared to add his journal for the years 1790–94, including remarks upon the campaigns of Harmar and St. Clair. The author assured prospective readers that his book's value would lie in its "truth, conciseness, and plain narrative." All of Faulkner's material was to be published under the title *Gen. Wayne's Military Guide*, said octavo volume to contain between four hundred and five hundred pages "on good paper." Faulkner, supported by a number of friends, proposed to sell his book by subscription for two dollars, "as soon as it is evinced that a sufficient number of subscribers can be obtained." When there proved to be no demand for such a volume, the project was abandoned. Although the field of American history has arguably suffered by the loss of this work, at least one book editor was mercifully spared a daunting task of rewriting the savage butchery of English grammar and spelling that characterized all of Faulkner's writing.[27]

CHAPTER 15

A Second Winter of Discord

CAPTAIN FAULKNER'S PROPOSED BOOK, concentrating on official records and documents, would have failed to mention one of the most colorful characters in the legion. Although a soldier, Josiah Hunt, who was "a stout, well-formed, heavy-set man," enjoyed hunting. Officers at Fort Greeneville soon recognized his talent and exempted Hunt from all garrison duty in exchange for supplying them with game during the winter. He had authority to enter and leave the post without being challenged by sentinels, a privilege enjoyed by no other enlisted man. While unfettered by military discipline, Hunt's duty was the most dangerous of them all. Indians had been seen climbing trees outside the walls to get a better view of anyone leaving the fort. From their elevated positions, warriors could discern the direction that individuals or small parties would take, making it easier to waylay and scalp unsuspecting victims. Hunt avoided these aerial spies by leaving the post late at night, explaining, "When once I had got into the woods without their knowledge, I had as good a chance as they."

After entering the forest in safety, Hunt would travel a considerable distance toward where he planned to stalk his prey the next morning. To avoid freezing to death in bitter cold, the hunter would take his tomahawk and dig a hole about the size of a large hat. Into this he would place bark from a white oak. Starting this afire with flint and steel, he covered the flames with crisscrossed strips of bark until his unique coal pit was filled. When the fire had begun to burn well, Hunt covered it over with dirt, leaving two air holes on the perimeter of the pit. The white-oak ashes kept heat well and became a wilderness furnace, its temperature regulated by blowing into the air holes. After his fire had been prepared, Hunt spread a layer of brush to keep him off the frozen ground and sat down with this coal pit between his legs. Covering himself with a blanket, he slept by taking short naps in a sitting position, thus keeping warm while avoiding the use of an open flame that would signal his position to Indian scouts.

Every snap of a twig or branch roused him from his catnaps, and Hunt would slowly uncover his head, scanning the darkness for danger while holding his rifle at the ready. One author graphically described the hunter's many solitary nights:

> A lone man in a dreary, interminable forest swarming with enemies, bloodthirsty, crafty and of horrid barbarity, without a friend or human being to afford him the least aid, in the depth of winter, the freezing winds moaning through the bare and leafless branches of the tall trees, while the dismal howling of a pack of wolves—
>
> "Cruel as death, and hungry as the grave;
> Burning for blood, bony, gaunt and grim,"
>
> might be heard in the distance, mingled with the howlings of the wintry winds, were well calculated to create a lonely sensation about the heart and appall any common spirit.

Looking like an old stump as he huddled over his coal pit, Private Hunt was always "calm, ready and prompt to engage in mortal combat," but he chose to avoid his foe rather than confront him.

The hunt began at first light. Gliding noiselessly through the forest, he would simultaneously watch for game and keep a sharp lookout for Indians. Whenever he spotted a deer, Hunt would carefully place a rifle ball into his mouth, "ready for reloading his gun with all possible dispatch." After downing his target, he rapidly loaded his rifle and waited patiently to see if the shot had attracted any attention. When all appeared safe, the hunter dragged his deer to a tree and began skinning it, always with his back to the tree and his rifle within reach. He would skin the carcass for a few minutes, pause and carefully scan the trees, then resume, maintaining that work-and-watch routine until the deer had been dressed and cut into quarters. Hunt formed the skin into a rude knapsack and placed the meat inside, then carried his burden back to Fort Greeneville. His keen senses of sight, hearing, and smell, along with an inordinate amount of caution, allowed the solitary woodsman to survive the winter season and amass the considerable sum of seventy dollars for meat he delivered to headquarters.

Josiah Hunt was not unknown to the Indians who roamed this same trackless forest. Their most bold and crafty warriors had tried to catch him unawares, though without success. They had found remnants of the little coal pits and marveled at his cunning genius. Some got close enough to glimpse Hunt from time to time, and they could even describe his manner of dress and the unique cap he always wore—"a raccoon's skin with the tail hanging down behind, the front turned up and ornamented with three brass rings"—but no Indian got close enough to take a shot. Praise for their quarry was effusive: "Great man, Capt. Hunt—great warrior—good hunting man; Indian no can kill!" One day, three Indians got within gunshot of Hunt, although they were unaware of his presence. He took aim and waited patiently for two of them to align, thinking he could shoot both with one ball and be evenly matched with the remaining warrior. But they never did fall into line, so Hunt, who could have shot any one of them, allowed his pursuers to slip off into the wilderness without knowing how close they had come to being killed.[1]

Others were not as successful in evading the Indians as Hunt had been. One day, the servants of Majs. John H. Buell and Thomas Hughes, soldiers by the names of Mallory and Poor, left Fort Greeneville in search of game. Contrary to orders, the pair did not return by nightfall. Next morning, Poor came back saying that Indians had chased him almost up to the gates and his friend Mallory was dead. Major McMahon was ordered out with a party to pursue the enemy and rescue Mallory, if he were still alive. Poor went along as a guide but was still so frightened that he could not remember where the two men had been ambushed. Unable to find any trace of a struggle, Poor was dismissed as a whimpering coward. A few days later, after Mallory still had not shown up, Capts. Edward Miller and Asa Hartshorne took out another search party. This time Poor was able to locate the right trail, and the soldiers found Mallory, who had been killed and scalped, with a turkey and three squirrels still tied to his back. They buried him where he had fallen and returned to Fort Greeneville convinced that hunting in these woods was not quite as safe as Josiah Hunt had made it appear.[2]

Dangers abounded in the wilderness beyond that posed by roving Indians. There were bears and wolves, countless varieties of disease-carrying insects, venomous snakes, poisonous plants, contaminated water, and more. One snake, termed an "anaconda," killed near Fort Recovery supposedly "measured twenty six feet seven inches and a half, and was thick in proportion." It was covered "with great scales; at the edges of which stuck out large stiff bones, almost as sharp as a needle, the shape of which resembled a fishes fin." When opened up, the stomach was found to contain "a panther, several squirrels of different species, birds, insects, and snakes of inferior kind; all of which had been swallowed whole and not a bone broken." Those who doubted the existence of such a creature were informed that they could see the actual skin of this American anaconda in a Philadelphia museum.[3]

General Wayne had no interest in such forest creatures, though. His focus was on Fort Recovery, and the first priority was to get it into shape to repulse any attack the Indian confederacy might mount to regain the site of their impressive victory. An order to Capt. Richard Greaton at Fort St. Clair hurried forward "all the men capable of marching, belonging to the Companies of Gibson and Bissell" under the command of Sgt. Samuel Dold, who had gone there to bring on his captain's baggage. After the men from Fort St. Clair arrived, Gibson reported on January 12, 1794, that his garrison consisted of but 138 noncommissioned officers and enlisted men, the soldiers being in remarkably good health, with only a handful on the sick list. Concerned about morale in his isolated post, the captain inquired of Wayne whether his troops were to be supplied with whiskey, an article that arrived soon after. From this small command, Gibson was ordered to send out a scouting party, consisting of Dold and four soldiers, toward the towns at the Auglaize. This detachment started out on January 18, having been instructed that the firing of the 6-pounder would be a signal for them to return instantly.[4]

After Wayne had concluded his peace conference with the Delaware chiefs, he dispatched a letter to Gibson, informing him that "any incursion into their neighbourhood at this crisis might be deemed inconsistent" with peace talks. The general therefore enjoined him to "prevent any enterprise taking place against them from your garrison until further orders." As soon as this message reached Fort Recovery, Gibson fired off the 6-pounder to recall his scouts. Fortunately, the wind conditions were favorable and a heavy charge of powder was used so that Dold was able to hear the signal, although he estimated that his party was about thirty miles from the post. The sergeant had accomplished little on his abbreviated reconnaissance except for "marking the south sides of the trees at proper distances" for future reference. Scouting for the next month would be confined to the immediate area around the fort. Despite a limited search, no trace of the missing cannons had been found, although two deserted Indian camps had been located. Signs about them indicated they were not in use when the fort was constructed.[5]

Wayne warned Captain Gibson that he should keep a sharp lookout for flags of truce borne by Indians who should be bringing their prisoners to freedom at his garrison, all of whom were to be fed at public expense. Upon their arrival, both flags and prisoners were to be sent back to Fort Greeneville, escorted by a sergeant, corporal, and twelve men. Although an Indian party might appear peaceful, the captain was to be on his guard at all times because "the most scrupulous precaution & pointed vigilance are necessary to combat the art and treachery of the insidious enemy." Wayne said pointedly, "you will on no pretence admit them within the walls of your Garrison; and all risque & danger must be removed in your intercourse with them." The fort commander was to use his own judgment as to the number of white people he would allow inside his walls, but he was again cautioned "that if treachery is intended, it must not succeed." Upon receipt of these orders, Gibson responded that he was happy to see that Wayne's maneuvers had forced the Indians to seek peace "at so small an expence of Blood." He also assured his commander, "My Character as an Officer, I trust, will be sufficient checks to prevent a relaxation of my Vigilence."[6]

Since its construction, Fort Recovery had been officered by Captains Gibson and Russell Bissell and Lts. James Glenn and Samuel Drake, and Gibson was desperate to augment his leadership staff. There was no ensign assigned to his company, and Ensign Daingerfield of Bissell's company was convalescent in Kentucky. Glenn stayed at the post longer than expected, hoping that when the Indians brought in their prisoners, one of them would be his half-brother. When that failed to happen, Gibson reported that his lieutenant "finally concluded to take farewell of the service" and resigned effective March 3. After a long delay, Wayne approved Bissell's application for leave, and he departed on March 12, leaving Gibson and Lieutenant Drake as the only officers at the legion's most vulnerable post. To alleviate this critical shortage, the captain recommended that Samuel Dold, "a young man of Reputable parentage," be promoted to ensign in his rifle company. He was effusive in his praise of the young sergeant, saying: "His conduct in the army has been uniform throughout, and as far as have come to my Knowledge met with the approbation of all his superiors who knew him. I can Venture to say that he is a young man of Sobriety & good understanding, Void of all those Vices which too often proves destructive to those who practice them." Gibson concluded his recommendation with the observation, "he has never once disobeyed my orders nor incured my displeasure, which is a singular Circumstance." Although trusting Gibson's judgment, Wayne informed him that nothing could be done for Dold since Congress was still in session and the Washington administration preferred to wait to make appointments until an ill-disposed Senate adjourned.[7]

The quest for St. Clair's cannons continued without success, although searchers did start to make some interesting discoveries. A few Indian graves were found, one of which yielded a rifle that the soldiers brought in as a souvenir, along with the "Ear trinkets" of the deceased warrior. Captain Gibson also had his men collect and bury what bones still remained around the garrison, a substantial collection that included an additional one hundred skulls. Spare time was devoted to cutting down underbrush and removing some fallen trees for a distance of about 250 yards around the fort and to building a detached blockhouse on the banks of the stream. Wood was either used for fuel or placed into large piles and burned. So much chopping had been done that the only grindstone available to sharpen hatchets and axes at the garrison had nearly worn out. By the end of February, Gibson could report that the clearing "adds much to the appearance of the place, and prevents the Enemy from the Great advantages of cover which they once had on this ground." Sergeant Dold continued to lead scouting parties, despite high water and freezing temperatures that made "their feet much hurt by breaking through the Ice." At times, it was so bitterly cold that even the express messengers found "their feet was generaly frosted." Dold's scouts eventually began to make sense of the maze of creeks that flowed through the country beyond Fort Recovery, discovering which ones flowed into the Wabash, the Saint Marys, and the Auglaize Rivers. Gibson would occasionally fire his 6-pounder so Dold could keep his bearings on these expeditions, although his supply of cannon powder had become dangerously low by spring.[8]

A rather strange occurrence stunned the occupants of Fort Greeneville on January 23 when the Seneca chief Captain Big Tree (also known as Stiff Knee) committed suicide with his own knife. Wayne convened a court of inquest composed of thirteen officers, Lieutenant Colonel Strong presiding and Ensign Hyde acting as coroner. Their investigation revealed that Big Tree had arrived at Fort Greeneville only a few days before the Delaware peace delegation. He sat in on the council and that night argued with the Delawares. According to the officers' findings, "from that time to the moment of his Death he was melancholy & deranged untill the last moment of his death when stabbing himself with his own knife." Their official ruling was that Big Tree was insane at the time of his death. The chief was buried on January 24, with most of the legion officers attending the funeral, after which they adjourned to General Wayne's new house for a glass of wine in Big Tree's memory. There was a suspicion that perhaps the Delawares "gave him something which put him out of his reason," although there was no evidence of any poisoning. In transmitting the result of this inquest, Wayne reminded the Senecas "that many of your people had died last Summer in consequence of something you had eat, when at the Council with the hostile Indians at the Rapids of the Miami of the

Lake." Noting that the chief New Arrow had died and Captain O'Bale had nearly suc-
cumbed, Wayne insinuated that the hostiles were responsible and called this mode of
war "cowardly & base." As a sign of affection for Big Tree and the Seneca Nation, Wayne
sent clothing to the chief's wife and daughter, mourning clothes and rifles to his brothers,
ordered the commander at Fort Franklin to build a house for the family, and instructed
that officer "to give them plenty of Provisions & everything they may want & to provide
& take care of them."[9]

Two other extraordinary deaths occurred at Fort Greeneville on Washington's Birthday. As part of the celebration, Wayne ordered fifteen rounds be fired from the artillery
in each redoubt "in honor of the day, that gave birth to General George Washington, the
Illustrious President of the United States of America." In order to spread this observance
to the enlisted ranks, he also ordered the issue of a gill of whiskey to each man and
extended a general pardon to all prisoners then in confinement. It was a sad coincidence
that whiskey caused a tragedy on the morning of February 22. Ensign Bradshaw and
Lieutenant Huston had been good friends. On the evening of February 20, Bradshaw sat
drinking in his hut when Huston walked in unannounced to share the bottle. Somewhat
under the influence, Bradshaw shouted, "Damn you, I don't keep tavern, leave my house!"
Huston departed after a second warning and refused to accept Bradshaw's apology the
next morning. Egged on by a few friends, Huston sent a challenge and included a post-
script that if Bradshaw should refuse, he would be announced to the legion as a coward.
Major Buell recalled, "there was the most quarreling, jargon and confusion throughout
the whole legion" as officers took sides in the controversy. Bradshaw had no choice but to
accept the challenge, and the two officers agreed to meet for satisfaction on Washington's
Birthday.[10]

Both men shared an Irish heritage and were thought of as "promising young officers." Huston had been a weaver before joining the army, but Bradshaw had come from
a family of "rank and distinction." The latter was described variously as "bred to the law"
or "bred a physician" and was apparently a man "of great genius and excellent education,"
but he had become too addicted to the bottle. Now the two Irishmen were to meet on
the field of honor. Lts. Bernard Gaines and Samuel Tinsley acted as seconds for Bradshaw and Huston, respectively, and the antagonists agreed to fire pistols with rifled
barrels at ten paces. They met at eight o'clock in the morning, and both men fired almost
simultaneously. Bradshaw was struck in the breast and expired "after a few convulsions."
Huston fell with a wound in the side and, after suffering in great pain, died a few hours
later. The former was a favorite among the officers and was given a ritual Masonic funeral
by them, while Huston was popular among the soldiers, who carried him back to his hut.
Both men were dressed in their best uniforms and buried side by side, although only a
few officers came to Huston's funeral. General Wayne allowed the drums to beat at both
burials but would not allow any firing over their graves. Some of the older officers were
overheard to say that they were glad both men had been killed. The whole affair had
been ridiculous, and now two good officers were dead over "a mere point of etiquette"
resulting from "some trifling misunderstanding, and altercation of words."[11]

Dueling was all too common in America, and affairs of honor in the legion were numerous. Following the deaths of Bradshaw and Huston, Major Buell remarked that this was the fifteenth duel fought within a year, "all by young officers" who had no experience in the Revolution to give them status. Offended pride was the driving force behind the code duello, and most reasons for sending a challenge now seem "ridiculous in both purpose and practice." Some challenges during this period resulted in confrontations that were designed to kill, though, and there are several reports of fights with pistols by civilians seated in chairs across a table from one another. Yet most were not meant to finish off the opponents but simply for the aggrieved parties to receive "satisfaction," which came when weapons were fired and, occasionally, blood was drawn. In the opinion of Surgeon's Mate Joseph Strong, who treated some of the officers wounded in single combat: "Duelling is but a miserable resource for the security of wounded honor. It makes wounds but does not heal them." Capt. Solomon Van Rensselaer observed "that neither the severe penalty of the law, nor regard for a future state, is any restraint on this fashion." He continued that when officers "of fierce courage and of high spirits" seek revenge, the legion rids itself of troublemakers, "but they generally lay aside good characters before they fall." On a practical note, Van Rensselaer saw that the deaths of Bradshaw and Huston "will cause a vacancy for the promotion of my friend Visscher."[12]

One of the first duels that winter at Fort Greeneville resulted from a quarrel between Captain Price of the infantry and Lieutenant Pope of the artillery. Their seconds had determined that Pope should fire first, and he shot Price through the body, although the captain did not fall. The seriously wounded officer, "altho' his adversary's life was then in his power, heroically, and with a composure of mind that will ever do him honor, fired his pistol in the air." Capt. Thomas Lewis, one of Wayne's aides, and Major Cushing, one of Wayne's outspoken critics, also fought a duel. When Lewis fired, his ball hit Cushing dead center in his gold watch, destroying the timepiece but saving its owner's life. One wag who heard the story supposedly remarked, "It must be a good watch to keep time from eternity." According to one tally, by the end of the spring of 1794, duels between legion officers had accounted for the deaths of three men and the wounding of eight others.[13]

Although not involved in the various duels, Capt. John Jeffers, commanding the invalids at Fort St. Clair, finally realized that his hernia would prevent him from taking the field in 1794. After relieving Captain Greaton, the new post commander busied himself with putting the fort in order and completing paperwork. Soldiers burnt about 150 bushels of coal as the smiths repaired axes and other tools, Jeffers vowing to continue "untill every article is put in the most perfect order." As for the paperwork, the garrison records were a mess since "some articles have been made & others been found," and Jeffers advised Wayne that "it will be difficult for the General to compare the returns with my receipt." As for clothing, the captain made no report since the uniforms were "not worth putting into a return." In order to impress any Indians that might bring their prisoners into Fort Recovery, Wayne had ordered the dragoons to return to Fort Greeneville from Bellipherontia. When the horsemen passed by Fort St. Clair, Jeffers composed a letter to Wayne stating that "with the assistance of the Truss if you would add a Horse I would be able to go on," for the truss gave him "considerable relief." When the post surgeon said that active campaigning was out of the question, as "it might prove my ruin," Jeffers pigeonholed his letter. In a later message, the captain assured Wayne that the spirit was willing, even if his body could not stand the strain. Referring to the general as his "military father," he reminded him of the Revolution, saying, "I have followed you to victory & I am willing to follow you again." He continued, "Jeffers is not the man that will leave his Dear General Bleeding on the Field." Despite his willingness to serve, Captain Jeffers was forced to offer his resignation before the legion left Fort Greeneville.[14]

The legion lost another veteran officer on the morning of March 20 when Maj. Ballard Smith of the Fourth Sub-Legion, dissolute and dissipated by a lifetime of whiskey drinking, died at Fort Washington. Speaking of those acquainted with Smith, the editor of the Cincinnati newspaper noted: "They knew his foibles; they knew his virtues. As a soldier, his courage was unquestionable; as a man, his conduct was such (allowing for the frailties of human nature) as placed him on a respectable scale in society." His corpse was followed to the grave by Lieutenant Colonel Strong, Major Cushing, Captains Butler and Peirce, subalterns, and a funeral detachment from the garrison. This coterie of soldiers was joined by a number of civilians, including officers' wives, the territory's acting chief magistrate, and "the most respectable citizens" of Cincinnati. Minute guns were fired from Fort Washington as everyone pretended that the old sot was actually a valued officer. In a bit of irony, the notice of Smith's death in *The Kentucky Gazette* appeared beside a notice by Peyton Short, who announced that he was "authorized to purchase DISTILLED SPIRITS, For the use of the Army."[15]

Major Cushing was on hand to attend Smith's funeral because he was under arrest in Cincinnati. Cushing had kept up his campaign against Edward Butler, Wayne's adjutant general, and even managed to get Lieutenant Colonel Hamtramck involved in the persecution. The problem between Butler and Hamtramck hinged on the latter's order to furnish an ax for a detail and the former's apparent refusal to do so. Hamtramck explained somewhat condescendingly to Wayne that "implicit obedience to Orders is the Vital Spirit of an army and without which we can not exist." Speaking of Butler's important office, he continued, "I hope it will not Screen him from being called to answer on so important a point." Wayne apparently took "great umbrage" at Hamtramck's remarks and advised that officer "to be more circumspect in future." The lieutenant colonel put on a little song and dance, explaining that by his definition, the word "screen" had referred to Butler's office and not to the commander in chief. In his own words, "it could not possibly mean your Excellency, but the office itself." Abandoning his earlier bravado, Hamtramck confessed, "I know not how to treat a Superior with disrespect, particularly one of your dignity and rank."[16]

Butler had offered to resign his appointment and revert to commanding a company, but Wayne would not hear of it and concluded that Cushing had magnified a "personal misunderstanding" into a matter of "private pique." Cushing pushed so hard that Butler preferred charges and placed him under arrest, a situation that Wayne had hoped to avoid since he needed every officer for "duties far paramount to the trifling consideration" of the major's case. When Cushing demanded a general court-martial be immediately impaneled, Wayne responded, "patience sir is a good virtue—a virtue that you must learn to exercise." His immediate concern was the movement of supplies by the super convoys, not "the Mutinous conduct of any individual." His last word on the subject of Cushing's trial left no doubt as to who would make that decision: "You may therefore rest assured that a General court Martial shall be order'd as soon as circumstances will admit, of which I am the proper judge." Cushing's trial was finally convened on December 11, 1793, and concluded on January 8, 1794, the panel of officers deliberating on four separate charges of neglect of duty and disobedience of general orders. After the "fullest investigation of the charges exhibited against Major Cushing, and taking into consideration the general orders and military regulations," the court exonerated him on every charge. Moreover, the court stated that "*all* and every part of the charges are *groundless*," and the major's actions were "actuated by a propensity to promote good order, regularity and military discipline in the Legion." Rebuffed in the malicious prosecution of Cushing, Wayne ordered him liberated and returned to duty. To rub salt into the wounds of the general and his supporters, Captain Guion copied a portion of the trial record and sent it to Cincinnati for publication.[17]

Cleared of all charges against him, Major Cushing remained at Fort Washington until early March, settling his accounts and awaiting orders. He finally prepared to leave for Fort Hamilton with a detachment marching to headquarters under Major Cass, sending his baggage forward on March 8. But before he could depart the following day, the major reported he was "stopped by the Sheriff, at the suit of John Armstrong." In fact, Armstrong had filed two suits, one for sixty dollars and a second for one thousand dollars, the sums, according to Cushing, being "so large, when contrasted with my property, or my credit, as to leave me without the means of obtaining bail." Being thus in the hands of the sheriff in Cincinnati, Cushing wrote to headquarters and advised General Wayne that he was "under the necessity of continuing here for the present." Cushing's arrest was retribution for Armstrong, who had been driven out of the legion by General Wilkinson, the major's mentor in fomenting trouble. Armstrong had hoped that leaving the legion would end his troubles with the Wilkinson clique, but his suits had been filed "for liberties taken with my character." After explaining his action to General Wayne, Armstrong then penned a warning that "there are characters under your command, and I fear one near your person, who are placed as spies on your conduct ready to comunicate in a secret manner to the Supreme Authority, any and every inadvertency which at an unguarded moment might and does happen with all men." He also advised his former commander that "a most scurilous piece was some time since penned in camp & forwarded to the printer, who was wise enough to return it." Inquiry failed to reveal the author of the letter in question other than "by conjecture."[18]

This letter alluded to by Armstrong was but one portion of a campaign to sully Wayne's reputation and downplay his accomplishments with the legion. By April, some "indistinct reports" that the general had borne his authority "with a rigid hand" reached

Philadelphia and had been repeated "in whispers by a few members of Congress." The War Department was afraid that this whispering campaign might be "exaggerated by reverberation." To show the nation that the administration's support for its commanding general remained firm, Secretary of War Knox published the following note: "It is with great pleasure, sir, that I transmit you the approbation of the President of the United States, of your conduct generally since you have had the command, & more particularly for the judicious and military formation and discipline of the troops—the precautions you appear to have taken in your advance, in your fortified camps, and in your arrangements to have full and abundant supplies of provisions on hand. Continue, sir, to proceed in this manner, and your success will be certain." In a confidential letter to Wayne, Knox hoped that this public message would be "a counter-balance for any opinion of the disorganizers be they who they may." His personal belief was that the allegations "died of their own imbecillity," so Knox assured his old friend that "while I have any agency in the public affairs that I shall sincerely endeavor to guard you from all misrepresentations."[19]

General Wayne was aware that "misrepresentations" by a "disappointed & restless faction" emanated from officers of the legion who had opposed his sometimes harsh insistence on subordination and discipline. Yet he assured a Pennsylvania friend that great progress had been made against "the Democratic (I had nearly said—the Demon cratic) phalanx." The twin evils of "insubordination & inebriation" had been indulged by previous commanders, but by now the legion was "tolerably well purged" of inferior officers. But a few "dark Characters behind the Curtain" remained and spread rumors that the many resignations had resulted from a complete disgust with Wayne's style of command. In fact, according to Wayne, the officers in question "were compeled to quit the service from their own bad Conduct." If his management style offended some, he could point to the legion with pride and claim that he had elevated it from "a contempt- able mass of Rabble." The general had hoped to be supported by Congress as well as the Washington administration, but that did not happen. A bill in the House of Represen- tatives to spur recruiting and authorize more supplies had been passed but was quashed in the Senate. When word of this rebuff reached the western forts, about sixty "very fine old soldiers," who had waited to see if they might benefit from provisions of this bill before reenlisting, promptly asked for and received their discharges. Other soldiers con- tinued to do likewise at the rate of about ten a day. Wayne estimated that this failure by Congress would cost his command 350 men by the end of May and double that num- ber by the end of the year.[20]

Wayne's handling of the legion was suddenly called into question by an article enti- tled "Stubborn Facts" that appeared in the *Martinsburg Gazette* on April 16 and was widely copied in the nation's press. According to the editor, these interesting particulars came from "a gentleman from General Wayne's camp, who may be depended upon." Although the officer tried to remain anonymous, word soon reached President Washington that it was actually Lieutenant Glenn, who had just reached his home in Berkeley County, Virginia, after resigning his commission. Beginning with an account of the Delaware peace mission, Wayne was portrayed as appearing sorrowful at the prospect of peace, "being bloated with ideas of his military prowess" and wishing only "to be dealing in blood." After some unflattering references to the general's confusion over how the various streams flowed in advance of Fort Recovery, Glenn really began to vent his spleen. He assured the *Gazette* editor that "the discontent, the drinking, gambling, quarrelling, fighting, and licentiousness of almost all ranks, exceeded all example." These "melancholy truths" resulted directly from the personal conduct of General Wayne, "whose manners are despotic, whose judgment is feeble, infirm and full of prejudice; whose temper is erasible and violent; whose language is indecent and abusive, and whose conduct to his officers is capricious and irregular, being at one time childishly familiar, and at another tyrannical and over-bearing."

Glenn's vituperation did not stop with these charges. He continued that Wayne, "instead of restraining excesses by his authority; instead of reprehending the dissolute, and cultivating the meritorious officer, he makes no distinctions but in favor of his tools, spies and toad eatters." In addition, "acting above all laws divine and human, he assigns the Sabbath for extraordinary fatigue, and overturns, without reason, or suppresses in violation of law, the proceedings of a general court martial." Wayne had also "confounded all ideas of infamy and honor" by allowing an officer to resign with honor after having been convicted of "fraud and forgery" by a court-martial. The lieutenant then inserted his own view of the controversy between Captain Butler and Major Cushing, claiming that the general "has arrested men of rank and worth on vexatious pretences, and has kept them in confinement, and denied a trial for months, whilst at the same time he has screened his pimps and parasites from justice, and has refused them to the law." Glenn concluded his tirade with the simple observation, "That such things should exist is lamentable, but that they do exist is too true to be denied, & it requires no spirit of prophecy to foretell what will be the end of a military corps, thus constructed and thus conducted." After reading this poison from a former officer of the legion, President Washington termed it "very unpleasant" and confessed to being "at a loss to decide what notice ought to be taken of such a publication."[21]

An anonymous friend of General Wayne, styling himself "A Friend to Truth," belatedly responded to Lieutenant Glenn's accusations in the columns of *Dunlap and Claypoole's American Daily Advertiser*. Referring to this "base and cowardly attack upon the character and conduct of General Wayne," he characterized it as "so replete with scurrility as to afford an antidote to its poison, and render a refutation hardly necessary." Although Glenn's identity remained hidden from the general public, Wayne's friend referred to him as a "paltroon" and "a rancorus assassin" whose outrageous claims were "as false as his heart is venomous." In defense of the general, the writer pointed out that Wayne trained and disciplined those brave enough to fight Indians, but "the coward and the worthless he cashiered or drummed out of his camp." These latter officers, "in their vagrant state," or "their hirelings" had conspired to concoct the lies spread through the *Martinsburg Gazette*. Secretary Knox's message to Wayne, dated March 31, was produced, buttressed by a letter written by Gen. Charles Scott, who happened to be in Philadelphia when the controversy erupted. Scott met at least three times with President Washington and also spent much time with Secretary Knox, assuring his friend Wayne that "nothing has given me more pleasure than having it in my power to do you Justice." Admitting that he had found discontent in the legion, the Kentuckian said that there was no single overriding reason for it. As for his own observations, he claimed that Wayne acted "with great sobriety and extreme attention to the duty of the army." While Scott's volunteers were in the field, the commander in chief exhibited "the most unwearied attention to every, the most minute thing possible in person." Army affairs appeared to be conducted "with great propriety," and General Scott asserted, "I believe there is not an officer that served with me under General Wayne's orders but will cheerfully serve under him again." Having concluded his defense of the legion commander, "A Friend to Truth" ended with a cry of defiance: "Read this ye callumniators and blush at your detection."[22]

CHAPTER 16

Elite Units and Intrigue

GENERAL WAYNE HAD SENT HIS dragoon squadron to winter quarters at Bellipherontia so the horses and men would be in perfect shape for campaigning in the spring of 1794. After building their encampment, the horsemen settled down into a quiet routine. When Major Winston finally arrived from Virginia, he inspected the four troops and reported to Wayne, "I found the Squadron, well situated, the men in their Huts, Stables complete except the Racks & Mangers, all of which are now complete, the men healthy except about 20 with the Smallpox." The only major deficiency appeared to be in the number of horses, there being thirty-nine more men than mounts. Winston himself was without a horse and asked Wayne to have the quartermaster buy two for him, "not having it in my power to make the purchase myself." The major assured his commanding general that "every exertion and pains shall be observed in order to have the Cavalry in complete Readiness when ordered to take the field." Wayne warned Winston that certain Frenchmen had allegedly begun recruiting men in Kentucky for an attack upon Spanish posts on the Mississippi. If Kentucky governor Isaac Shelby failed to suppress this expedition in the traditional manner, the dragoons were to "obey his orders with promptitude" and be "in perfect readiness to advance to any quarter at a moments warning."[1]

Officers enjoyed their new quarters near the "people of fashion and hospitality" in Lexington. Although the difficulty of getting large amounts of forage to Fort Greeneville had compelled Wayne to send the dragoons back to Kentucky, they did not remain there long. Either to impress any Indians who might come to make peace in mid-February or to chastise them if they failed to appear with their captives, Wayne ordered the dragoons to return to the head of the line. Winston's squadron arrived on February 19, five days past the deadline imposed on the Delaware chiefs by Wayne. With no Indians to impress, Captain Van Rensselaer said, "It was intended the light troops should make an excursion into the enemies country; destroy their towns and establish garrisons, &c." The legion's horsemen were certainly "prepared to give the tawny sons of the wilderness chace," but inclement weather prevented such an enterprise. Major Winston and his dragoons, after accomplishing nothing of consequence, headed back to Bellipherontia on February 22, acting as an escort to quartermaster and contractor packhorses that had accumulated at Fort Greeneville. Returning to winter quarters on March 1 after a march of 160 miles, Winston was urged to "use every exertion to recruit your horses & to put your arms & Accoutrements in the most perfect order."[2]

Dragoon officers, who had always been favorably treated by Wayne, generally supported their commander, and the four troops were now becoming an important asset to the legion. Capt. Robert MisCampbell articulated their attitude in a letter to Captain Van Rensselaer, commander of the sorrel troop: "Give me health of Body, Peace of Mind, a Pretty Girl, a clean shirt, and a Guinea, and I'm Rich and happy. . . . I am determined to possess a happy mind; that's enough for me or for any soldier." In an effort to keep morale high, MisCampbell was not above giving strict, "fatherly" guidance to Cornet Posey, son of the recently retired general. He admitted, "I love the young man for his amiable Disposition, therefore cannot Refrain from giving my advice." Although he lamented the loss of Major Rudolph as commandant of dragoons, Van Rensselaer could write with pride, "The cavalry is well formed, and is most assuredly a very fine corps." Infantry officers were somewhat jealous of their mounted counterparts, who, after all, had their own special encampment at Bellipherontia. Ens. Nanning Visscher, writing from Cincinnati while on convoy duty, expressed that sentiment in a letter to his friend Van Rensselaer, advising him, "we have taken quarters at Munson's Tavern, where we live in Clover, and even this, I expect is not better living than your Horses have." Visscher closed by urging the captain to bring his "Troop of Snorters" up north to where the action was.[3]

Despite Visscher's plea, it was MisCampbell's troop that left Bellipherontia first. Wayne ordered Major Winston to send forward one troop "with all possible dispatch," following with the remainder of his squadron so that it would reach Fort Greeneville on April 15, "prepared for an Active campaign in a Wilderness" and carrying only "what is indispensibly necessary light & portable." Cornet Blue would remain at Bellipherontia with the invalid men and horses. Blue's was a laughable command. Many of the horses were worthless and had to be turned over to the quartermaster for public sale. As for the troopers, most of them were barefoot since "their boots had been taken away from them and given to other men," those who marched north to the Ohio. Some of the lucky men had "a few old legs" that were fitted to ordinary shoes. As for weapons, the detachment, which would number fifty-five, had only ten sabers and five pistols. MisCampbell's well-equipped advance detachment arrived at Fort Washington on April 10, being held up by three days of continuous rain and the resulting flood waters in Mill Creek. The captain reached Fort Hamilton on April 14 with sixty-three noncommissioned officers and privates. Next morning, a trader by the name of Lyons came into that post and informed General Wilkinson that Indians had stolen six of his horses. Cornet Daniel Torrey and twenty dragoons were sent in pursuit of these raiders. Torrey's party followed the trail of Lyons's stolen horses for nearly twenty miles but abandoned the pursuit when it became clear that the Indians could not be overtaken.[4]

The dragoon squadron, which had been plagued by repeated changes in troop commanders since its inception, would lose two more before Wayne began his campaign. Captain Lee was the first to go, cashiered on February 20 by a court-martial for being drunk and abusive to a sentinel. A petition to reinstate the officer was sent directly to President Washington, who seriously mulled over Lee's former service, together with his "most respectable" family, which had been "made unhappy by his present disgrace." After considering the captain's appeal, Washington decided that this verdict "may be a warning to him in future" and told Secretary Knox to issue him a commission in a new artillery company. Despite this lenient treatment, William Lee never served in that branch of service, and his military career was over. Major Winston lost another troop commander when Capt. Tarleton Fleming died. That Virginian had long been in a "verry great ill state of health, his life has for a long time been despar'd of," yet he was finally able to join his troop in Kentucky. Never well enough to take the field, Fleming died on June 17 at Fort Hamilton. As senior lieutenant, James Taylor assumed command of Lee's troop, while Lt. Leonard Covington would eventually replace Fleming.[5]

Although but nineteen years of age, Captain Van Rensselaer already had a reputation throughout the legion as an outstanding dragoon commander. He had endeared himself to the enlisted men of his troop when a superior officer, contrary to general orders, detached two of the captain's men for use as express riders. Van Rensselaer refused to allow them to perform that hazardous and fatiguing service, even when threatened with arrest for apparent insubordination. But his men applauded him for supporting their rights against those in positions of higher authority, and as a result, he "gained their respect, confidence and good will." That was the last time any officer tried to misuse a dragoon from the sorrel troop.

Captain Van Rensselaer's greatest fame had come the previous fall, when the troop was stationed at Fort Hamilton. General Wilkinson, out to have a little fun with the captain and his dragoons, maneuvered the horsemen about the parade ground until they were facing a stone wall that surrounded his personal garden. Assuming that they would halt upon reaching that obstruction, Wilkinson gave the command, "Charge!" Van Rensselaer spurred his mount to a gallop and jumped him effortlessly over the wall, followed by every member of the sorrel troop. Down went the wall as hooves clipped the stones and, before the general could shout "Halt!" the galloping horses transformed his cherished vegetable patch into a huge tossed salad, inflicting "utter destruction" upon the crops. Mortified by the results of his order, Wilkinson "stifled his feelings" and recalled the troop "with the gravity of a stoic." After a few more maneuvers, Wilkinson carefully aligned the men facing the river. Again he shouted "Charge!" and again Van Rensselaer spurred his horse forward. The dragoons "dashed down the steep bank into the river and plunged headlong in the deep water before they could be countermanded." A cornet was swept from his horse, but the captain quickly plucked him from the reach of his mount's thrashing hooves. The general watched in shock and concern as reckless dragoons struggled with a strong current until "all the gallant fellows ascended the opposite bank in triumph." Wilkinson then "expressed himself quite satisfied with the result, and never afterwards thought it expedient to try any more experiments with that troop, and from that time they were his particular favorites."[6]

The most elite corps in Wayne's command was a small detachment of scouts and spies organized by Capt. William Wells. Heretofore, that duty had fallen to the band of rangers employed by Capt. George Shrim, but now Wells and his small party of intrepid woodsmen took over the role of spies. He gathered together what many would call the riff-raff of the frontier, restless men who were completely at home in the wilderness but could not really find a niche in polite society. Among these frontiersmen were the former packhorse driver Robert McClellan, Wilkinson's secret operative William May, and others such as Dodson Tharp, Paschall Hickman, Joseph Young, Tabor Washburn, William England, David Thomsom, and William Ramsey, the latter of whom Wells apparently stole from Shrim's company. These spies operated on horseback, all splendidly mounted, while other scouts conducted their operations on foot. Wells and McClellan began their spying activities on January 1, 1794, and others joined up as the mood struck them. One extraordinary tale began to circulate about McClellan and May. Out on a reconnaissance during the depth of winter, May discovered that McClellan was nearly frozen. They dismounted, and May tried unsuccessfully to start a fire with flint and steel. By now, McClellan had become "stupid" as the cold sapped his remaining strength. Afraid for his partner's life, May quickly killed his own horse, disemboweled the carcass, and shoved McClellan inside. He finally got a fire started, and the two men were able to survive their incredible ordeal without any permanent injuries.[7]

Wells and his band of spies had an even stranger experience on March 13, while scouting toward the old French settlement at Loramie's store, which had been destroyed over a decade earlier. Wayne had ordered them out to bring in a captive who could be interrogated as to enemy intentions, their reward to be the standard one hundred dollars for the first prisoner and fifty dollars for a second. Encountering a small Indian camp, the spies crept close and discovered two warriors. They killed one and captured the other, taking their horses as well. But the Indian captive proved to be a white man named Miller, who had been captured by a Shawnee war party in 1782. When he reached Fort Greeneville, Wayne found Miller to be "a perfect savage," although he could speak English "tolerably well," and ordered him confined in the guardhouse. He appeared "reserved and sulky," offering no useful information at first. But repeated interviews with the prisoner disclosed that his full name was Christopher Miller and he had been born in Chester County, Pennsylvania, in 1770. His parents moved to a settlement along the Salt River in Kentucky, where he was captured along with his elder brother, Nicholas. After unsuccessfully trying to convince Christopher to escape with him, Nicholas set out alone through the wilderness and reached his home in Kentucky. When news of Miller's recovery reached Kentucky, Nicholas came north to see his brother and hear his story.[8]

Christopher Miller soon confessed that he had left Grand Glaize with five Shawnee warriors about three weeks before his capture, their object being to steal horses. After taking two animals, the party split up. Miller and one Indian started home, while the remainder headed for the fallen timber near Fort St. Clair, where they hoped to ambush some wagons or patrols. But Miller's most important intelligence concerned the Indian response to Wayne's proposals at the peace negotiation with the Delaware chiefs and some British perfidy. The important men of the Miami, Delaware, and Shawnee Nations had met at Grand Glaize and approved giving up their prisoners and making peace. Alerted about this threat to Indian solidarity, Col. Alexander McKee dispatched Simon Girty and Matthew Elliott from Detroit with a request that the Indians not make peace with the Americans "upon any terms whatsoever." Miller also told Wayne that McKee had promised "they shou'd be furnished with Arms Ammunition Clothing & Provision, in abundance by the British at the foot of the rapids—on Condition that they would continue the War." All of these supplies would be available "when the grass was four Inches high." The British also vowed that they "wou'd use every influence" to persuade the Chippewas, Wyandottes, and other Lake Indians to join the Miami, Shawnee, and Delaware warriors at the Auglaize. This combined Indian army would then venture to give battle to Wayne's legion, but in the meantime, warriors should ambush convoys on the military road and send out small parties to steal horses. Miller had been on one of these latter excursions when he was captured.[9]

There was some suspicion as to whether Christopher Miller could be trusted, and for good reason. While living with the Shawnee Nation, he had helped them make war against white settlers. Charles Cist described one such encounter between Miller and sixteen-year-old William Fuller in August 1791: "When he saw him, he attempted to run, fearing that Miller might be an Indian. Miller called out, 'Don't run.' The boy spoke up and said, 'Who are you?' 'My name is Miller.' Young Fuller supposed it to be a Thomas Miller, at North Bend, and stood still, waiting the other's approach. As it was now dark, it was not until Miller had got nearly up to him, that he perceived his mistake, and endeavored to make his escape. Being somewhat lame, he was, however, soon overtaken and captured." Given his willingness to help kill and capture white settlers, it was not until Christopher Miller, along with his brother Nicholas, had joined Captain Wells's spy company and began to kill and capture Indians that he gained the complete confidence of the soldiers.[10]

Miller's news that the British had actively discouraged the peace process came as no surprise to anyone. For over ten years, Britain had ignored the Treaty of Paris and steadfastly refused to give up its military posts on what that country had acknowledged as U.S. soil. Now, unrest in Europe and British impressment of seamen from U.S. vessels had increased resentment and outrage toward King George III and his minions. Captain MisCampbell thought that war between the two countries was "inevitable though not actually declared" and stated that it was about time "to look forward to great and Brilliant actions in the East." Writing from Fort Greeneville to a friend in Cincinnati, another officer observed: "You seem to dread a British war; but I have doubts whether we should not pray for it, I mean the people of the United States. Our country is invulnerable, and we have little to lose; whilst our inveterate and persecuting foe, will hazard her West-India and other American possessions; domestic commotion, and a revolution.

No nation can retard the rising importance of our country, but Britain, and our aggrandizement must keep pace with her depression." He admitted that some individuals would incur loss and misfortune, but that the American values of "economy, industry, union and integrity" would ultimately prevail.[11]

Captain Van Rensselaer asserted that, should Britain eventually drive America to open hostilities, "I do believe our army can reduce all the posts, from Detroit to Quebec." While the captain hoped that U.S. claims against "that haughty and imperious nation" might be settled peacefully, he steadfastly believed that merely satisfying the country's businessmen was not enough and the United States "must not suffer the western posts to remain in the possession of the British." Van Rensselaer also felt that the Indian war "will exhaust millions of money & cut off thousands of lives to no effect & unless we insist on the removal of garrisons which belong to a foreign power from our territory, we may expect no peace." He concluded his denunciation, "We sincerely hope our government will no longer suffer, with impunity, a nation that pretends to be at peace with us to occupy our forts; thro' the means of which they not only distress our trade, but make the merciless savages instrumental in butchering our defenceless men, women, and children."[12]

News that Christopher Miller imparted about British treachery subverting peace negotiations confirmed information that had been gathered a few days earlier. Major McMahon had led a scout toward Grand Glaize and captured two Delaware Indians, a warrior and his squaw. Captain Wells was along on McMahon's scout and interpreted during the interrogation of these prisoners, who confessed that "the Chiefs proposed a compliance with the requisition for a surrender of the prisoners." This was impossible to do on short notice since many of the white captives were "out a hunting with their masters." A council of Indian leaders had agreed that several important dignitaries would visit General Wayne prior to bringing forth their prisoners and the Delaware captives, unaware of British interference, were surprised that such a visit had not already occurred. Since this incident occurred some three weeks beyond the deadline imposed for delivering prisoners at Fort Recovery, Wayne concluded that the Delaware tale was "altogether a fiction," at least until Christopher Miller corroborated it a few days later.[13]

As winter turned to spring, Indian parties again started to harass small convoys on the military road from Fort Washington to Fort Greeneville as well as many settlements north of the Ohio River. On March 4, a small band attacked two wagons about nine miles south of Fort Hamilton, killing two men, burning the wagons and their cargo, and making off with a few cattle. Jacob White was first on the scene and discovered one man lying dead in a small stream, ever after known as Bloody Run. One week later, Indians stole twenty horses from the contractor at Fort Hamilton, pursuers finding only "a Scalping knife, Spoon, and Blanket" dropped by the raiders. One resident wrote that Indians "are generally in Columbia two or three times a week in the night, and frequently steal our horses and scalp our valuable neighbors and citizens." Among those townsmen killed was David Jennings, "a man of excellent character as a citizen and christian," who was ambushed on March 24. By the end of April, Indian encounters had become almost a daily occurrence near Fort Hamilton. On April 22, a man named Moore was waylaid about six miles south of that post but escaped. Two soldiers, leading a few horses about a mile behind Moore, were also fired upon by a party of some fifteen Indians. Abandoning their horses, the men took to their heels and successfully eluded the attackers after a six-mile chase through the woods. Next day, a hunter reported that he had wounded an Indian, and a search party brought in his rifle but could not find a body. On April 24, some packhorse drivers employed by the quartermaster heard firing and found a horse that had been shot. That same day, another hunter saw a pair of Indians about two miles distant, followed by the killing the next morning of two men between Fort Washington and Fort Hamilton.[14]

Despite this increase in Indian activity, by mid-April, General Wayne had concluded that "few if any of the horses lately lost from the vicinity of any of the chain of posts, were taken or stolen by the Savages." He felt that they had been taken instead by "some of the unprincipled part of the discharged soldiery," now little more than bandits, and "many of whom are more to be guarded against than even the Indians." Wayne specifically mentioned two former legionnaires, a Sergeant Kinsey and Private Cooney, who had stolen public horses on March 30. These two criminals confessed their deed to soldiers in Peters's company, which was then on the march to Fort Greeneville. When two horses disappeared from the convoy, that theft was attributed to Kinsey and Cooney since no Indian sign was discovered. Wayne sent notification of these deeds to Major Doyle at Fort Hamilton and Captain Peirce at Fort Washington, ordering the pair of renegades to be placed in irons if caught at either post. Peirce had already been keeping a sharp lookout for deserters headed either into Kentucky or down the Ohio River, so he simply added these two names to the list of desperados. To assist his own patrols, the captain offered a "handsome reward" to a few of the settlers, in essence creating a force of bounty hunters to help rid the country of marauders.[15]

In describing these lawless discharged soldiers, Wayne referred to them as "in contemplation to join the banditti under Mr. G R Clark." This alluded to a scheme concocted by George Rogers Clark, the Revolutionary hero, and his brother-in-law, Dr. James O'Fallon, around Christmas, 1792. Disgusted with the way he had been treated after the war, Clark planned to use his prestige to raise an army in Kentucky, then descend the Ohio and Mississippi Rivers, capturing Spanish garrisons and, eventually, New Orleans itself. This overthrow of the Louisiana territory would be accomplished under the auspices of the French government, most notably Edmund Charles Genet, French minister plenipotentiary to the United States. Although dissipated by intemperance, Clark saw himself as the natural leader for all Kentuckians distrustful of the Washington administration, which had failed to secure open navigation on the Mississippi. His army, while fighting under the French flag, would overthrow the Spanish and allow Kentucky produce to flow unfettered to natural markets. Since the United States was at peace with Spain, an ally of Britain, Clark realized that he must remain circumspect while raising a French army on American soil. In a letter to Genet, Clark confided that he must "guard against doing any thing that would injure the U States or giving offence to their Govt."[16]

By mid-November 1793, rumors circulated that Clark had received a commission as a major general in the French army and an appointment as commander in chief of the French Revolutionary Legion on the Mississippi. Blank commissions had been furnished so that he could appoint his own officers. Boats were under construction, and a French paymaster had supposedly arrived to pay off recruits for Clark's amphibious force. Plunder was to be divided among the troops, and after Louisiana had been conquered, land grants would be awarded according to military rank. Agents for the French legion began to recruit in Kentucky, and by the end of January, it was rumored that over one thousand men had signed on, including Gen. Benjamin Logan, one of the most influential officers in the Kentucky militia. To avoid any apparent conflict with state or federal law, Logan advised Clark, "I have taken my leave of appointments in this state of the united states and do presume I am at liberty to go to any foreign country I pleas and intend so to do." Writing from Clarksville, John Montgomery assured Clark that he could personally raise "Several Hundreds for your Service," including "several old veteran officers" who would be "exceedingly Serviceable in raising and Dessiplening troops."[17]

Gentlemen in the western territory continued to argue in favor of Clark's plan to wrest Louisiana from Spanish control, one of them saying that "it would open the Road for millions of the human race, to emigrate to this favored spot, on which nature has lavished its gifts." He continued, "The road once opened, would be the means of civilizing not only the natives of the soil, but (if I may be allowed the expression) the Spaniards themselves over the gulph of Mexico, whom priestcraft and ignorance has made useless to society." A successful campaign would give Americans "full possession of the navigation of the most noble river within their territory." Much of the preparation in Kentucky had gone on behind the scenes to avoid an international incident, but General Clark went public on January 25, 1794, with an announcement in *The Centinel of the North-Western Territory* of his proposal "for the reduction of Spanish posts on the Mississippi":

> All persons serving the expedition to be entitled to one thousand acres of Land—those that engage for one year, will be entitled to two thousand acres—if they serve two years or during the present war with France, they will have three thousand acres of any unappropriated Land that may be conquered. The officers in proportion pay & as other French troops. All lawful Plunder to be equally divided agreeable to the custom of War. All necessaries will be provided for the enterprise, and every precaution taken to cause the return of those who wish to quit the service, as comfortable as possible, and a reasonable number of days allowed them to return, at the expiration of which time their pay will cease. All persons will be commissioned agreeable to the number of men they bring into the field. Those that serve the expedition will have their choice of receiving their lands or one dollar a day.

One Virginian visiting in Boonesborough, Kentucky, said that Clark's expedition was well supported, and he had "taken a part in this business" and planned to return home "with a canoe load of southern silver." In order to preserve peace between Spain and the United States, members of Clark's command would expatriate themselves and become French citizens before descending the Mississippi.[18]

General Clark issued commissions that proclaimed that recipients were "to serve in an expedition designed against the Spaniards of Louisiana and the Floridas by order of Citizen Genet, Minister Plenipotentiary of the French Republic." As recruiting continued, boats were constructed, one of which was outfitted for artillery. The plan was for "very short brass cannon" to be smuggled in barrels from the Atlantic states to the Falls of the Ohio for use by Clark's legion. Military supplies and food were stockpiled "on the Credit and faith" of Clark and France, but one agent confessed to being leery of such an arrangement, saying, "I am ruened if neglected." Another of Clark's men went to Lexington, where he purchased two more boats, a large quantity of powder, and one ton of cannonballs, all on credit.[19]

Upon prompting from Philadelphia, Gov. Arthur St. Clair issued a proclamation that urged all citizens of the Northwest Territory to avoid Clark's scheme and listed the dangerous consequences that would await them if they ignored his warning. Governor Shelby, sensing that the Louisiana expedition was extremely popular in Kentucky, was more hesitant. General Wayne offered Shelby the use of Major Winston's dragoon squadron in suppressing Clark's French legion, then promised more troops would be sent, if necessary, "notwithstanding our proximity to the combined force of the hostile Indians." The governor waited a month before responding and then assured the general, "there is not the smallest probability that such an enterprise will be attempted." Even if Clark should put his scheme in motion, he advised Wayne, the Kentucky militia "are able and willing to suppress every attempt that can be made here to violate the laws of the Union." Rebuffed by Shelby, all Wayne could do was alert Lieutenant Hunter at Fort Steuben to Clark's proposed campaign, "a business which [the] Government can not suffer to pass unnoticed." Wayne ordered Hunter "to discover the truth of it, & give me the earliest intelligence of the intended time & place, from whence the premeditated expedition (if any) is to set out—together with the force & plan of operation." The lieutenant was also instructed to determine whether some of Clark's recruits had already assembled at the mouth of the Cumberland River, for rumors were circulating that several boats had been seized en route to New Orleans. Wayne also directed Hunter to warn boats passing his garrison toward the Mississippi that they ran the risk of "being seized by those *Marauders*."[20]

Pressure from the Washington administration failed to budge Governor Shelby from his tacit support of General Clark. One historian paraphrased the governor's response thus: "I can find no law which empowers me to stop this expedition. If you wish it stopped legally, pass a national law that will cover the case. Moreover, I decline to call out the state militia to suppress by force an enterprise which may never materialize into action; for premature or ill-advised action will agitate and inflame public sentiment in this state. If you want me to suppress the enterprise by force, command me to do so under the constitution and I will carry out such constitutional command." Now aware that Shelby would not do the federal government's dirty work, President Washington issued his own proclamation on March 24, warning citizens "against enlisting any citizen or citizens of the United States, or levying troops, or assembling any persons within the United States" for Clark's expedition "at their peril." Individuals were admonished to "refrain from enlisting, enrolling or assembling themselves for such unlawful purposes, and from being in any wise concerned, aiding or abetting therein." Washington also charged "all courts, magistrates and other officers" to exert their influence to "prevent and suppress all such unlawful assemblages and proceedings, and to bring to condign punishment those who may have been guilty thereof."[21]

A number of factors doomed Clark's proposed campaign against Spain's Mississippi forts and the city of New Orleans. Quarrelling among factions and between Clark and O'Fallon, the two men who had hatched the original scheme, slowed recruiting. As a result of complaints from Philadelphia and a change in the French government, Minister Genet was recalled, and the plan lost its appearance of legitimacy. Men who had pledged their credit for supplies and boats were never reimbursed and became liable for those bills. Washington's proclamation was the deathblow to Clark's scheme. Kentuckians learned that they would be in violation of federal law and could be prosecuted for enlisting in the French Revolutionary Legion on the Mississippi. This stopped any further recruiting and caused those already enrolled to simply give up and go home. The ignoble end of Clark's dream was characterized as "an elaborate lamp without oil" that had simply flickered out.[22]

To ensure that this and any future attempts against Spanish possessions would be quashed, Secretary of War Knox ordered Wayne to "immediately" build a new post on the site of old Fort Massiac. Originally constructed in 1757, the fort was named after the Marquis de Massiac, French minister of marine, and had stood on the northern bank of the Ohio about eight miles below the mouth of the Tennessee River. After being abandoned in 1764, an apocryphal story grew about a party of Frenchmen who had been massacred on that spot while trying to establish a trading post. By 1794, the location was commonly referred to by Americans as Fort Massac, a corruption of both fact and legend, and it was Secretary Knox's intention to fortify the site with a blockhouse and redoubt. Thinking that Major Doyle was ideally suited to command the new post, General Wayne made him an offer: "How shou'd you like taking post low down the Ohio or wou'd you prefer advancing with the Legion, consider and let me know your wishes." Doyle responded on April 25 that he had been in his country's service almost "from my Childhood to the present day" and had hoped to continue in active service. But his health had taken a downward turn, and he was forced to confess, "I could now render little service in the field and it is with pain that I am obliged to acknowledge that a Garrison is the only place where I could Render the service which my Country now requires."[23]

With Major Cushing under arrest in Cincinnati, Wayne took advantage of this opportunity to rid himself of another nemesis by sending Guion's company to garrison Fort Massac. Guion's men, carrying all their clothing and baggage, left Fort Greeneville on the morning of May 7 for Fort Hamilton, where Major Doyle would join them. Major

Burbeck sent along a detachment of artillerymen to man Doyle's four artillery pieces—one 6-pounder, one 3-pounder, and two howitzers. Massac's garrison would total eighty officers and men. Upon reaching Fort Washington, Guion's company received spades, picks, axes, a grindstone, military stores, food for six months, and everything "indispensibly necessary," including over eighteen thousand rations of whiskey. Since Doyle had been to the site previously, Wayne allowed him to judge the proper location for the post, where he would "erect as good a work as the materials you can command will allow," so long as it conformed to the dimensions outlined by the general. He was furnished with eight oxen that could be hitched to the artillery limbers and used to drag timber to the construction site.[24]

Major Doyle was briefed on the status of George Rogers Clark's expedition and received a copy of President Washington's proclamation of March 24 to guide his actions. This information was augmented by "secret and confidential" instructions penned by Secretary Knox on March 31:

> If this design should be persisted in, or hereafter revived and any such parties should make their appearance in the neighbourhood of your garrison, & you should be well informed that they are armed and equipped for war, and entertain the criminal intention described in the President's proclamation, you are to send to them some persons in whose veracity you could confide; and if such person should be a peace officer he would be the most proper messenger; and warn them of their evil proceedings, and forbid their attempting to pass the fort at peril. But if, notwithstanding every peaceable effort to persuade them to abandon their criminal design, they should still persist in their attempts to pass down the Ohio, you are to use every military means in your power for preventing them, and for which this shall be your sufficient justification, provided you have taken all the pacific steps before directed.

This was an extraordinary message because it gave Major Doyle permission in writing to fire upon U.S. citizens, even though they might be masquerading as French nationals. Happily, Clark's campaign fizzled before Doyle was forced into such a position.[25]

The one-legged major had other troubles to occupy his attention. On May 24, while Doyle's detachment was loading supplies aboard their boats at Cincinnati, Deputy Sheriff Silvanus Reynolds tried to serve a writ on Catherine Beverly. Captain Guion intervened and took the woman, who happened to be his mistress, to a private dwelling. Reynolds sought the assistance of Darius Orcutt, and the two men confronted Guion, who still refused to let them have his woman. When Orcutt replied that they would raise a posse, the captain sent a man to summon his company from the riverbank. Within minutes, almost forty armed soldiers had responded to Guion's summons. He formed his company in front of the house where Beverly was hiding and ordered them, if a posse or militia party should appear, "to blow them to hell." Guion then summoned his mistress and marched her, protected by his soldiers, to a boat on which she remained until Doyle's detachment descended the Ohio. The major thought Beverly unfit society for his own wife, who accompanied the detachment, and positively refused to allow Guion to take her to Fort Massac. When she was discovered onboard near Fort Steuben, Doyle arrested the insolent captain on the evening of June 4 for "disobedience of Orders & Mutinous Conduct."[26]

John Ludlow, sheriff of Hamilton County, lodged a complaint against Guion for his "conduct towards two civil officers of [the] Government of the said County & in violating & preventing the free Operation of Civil Law & justice, by rescuing & causing to be rescued, by *force & arms* a certain Catherine Beverly of Cincinnati when in the Custody of said Officers." When notified of Guion's outrageous conduct and his arrest by Major Doyle, General Wayne ordered him to proceed to Cincinnati, turn himself in to Sheriff Ludlow, and await trial for his offenses. Wayne advised Ludlow that Guion had been ordered to Fort Greeneville for a court-martial and would soon pass through Cincinnati, where he would be within the sheriff's jurisdiction. The message was clear: Wayne wanted the troublemaker arrested according to civil law, "which is paramount to the Military—a principle that shall ever be supported." Although claiming that the original complaint was "a vile falsehood, engendered by jealousy, and founded in malevolence," Guion agreed to submit "silently" and await justice. Wayne must have been ecstatic to be rid of first Major Cushing and then Captain Guion, the two most outspoken members of General Wilkinson's clique, and both now under humiliating civil arrest in Cincinnati.[27]

Aside from the events involving Captain Guion, Doyle's descent to Fort Massac was relatively uneventful. His party consisted of Guion's infantry company, an artillery detachment of one sergeant and six privates, George Wilson and four other employees of Elliott and Williams, and eight Chickasaws on their way home. One boat ran aground at the Falls of the Ohio but was brought through safely after part of its load was removed. Several small boats were torn apart at that point, the lumber being used to reinforce the remaining craft "so that the balls might not pass through in case of an attack." Doyle's convoy, consisting of a dozen boats of various sizes and shapes, left Fort Steuben on June 4 but had gone but a few miles when one of the Chickasaws died. The flotilla put ashore "to bury him with the honors of war." A few days later, Doyle began to stop every day for a few hours to cut pickets for the stronghold they would soon construct. Aware that he would be exposed to attack until some sort of palisade was erected, the major wanted his building materials ready as soon as the boats touched shore. The soldiers encountered several small parties of civilians, some of whom offered to hunt for the garrison and tagged along to make some money with their rifles. Doyle's command reached the site of Fort Massac on the evening of June 12, and his soldiers labored all night building a small circular enclosure inside the ruined French fort. By daylight, they had mounted the artillery, and Doyle's temporary citadel was "in a good posture of defence," offering a place of safety while work commenced on the permanent structures.[28]

CHAPTER 17

Supplying the Legion in the Field

ALTHOUGH DISTRACTED BY EVENTS to the south, General Wayne remained focused on Fort Recovery and kept up a constant communication with Captain Gibson. Captain Bissell left that post for New England on March 6, and although happy to see his friend accommodated, Gibson was disappointed to lose "so Valuable an Officer, and so agreeable a companion." The post commander was pleased to report that Bissell had "paid every attention to the preparedness of the troops & works for protection & defence" as well as being "alert and Vigilant" at all times. Unsure whether any more officers might be forthcoming, Gibson asked that Lt. Jonathan Taylor, who had previously served in his Virginia rifle company as an ensign, be assigned to his command. Wayne was unable to honor the request.[1]

Sergeant Dold continued to reconnoiter toward Grand Glaize, although his scouting was often curtailed by bad weather and high water. But Wayne still needed more information on "the course & Distance & Nature of the Ground" in the direction of the Indian villages and kept pressing Gibson on that subject. He also continued to pester the captain about searching for the remainder of St. Clair's missing cannons. An Indian captured by William Wells's spies confessed that "the Indians hid a six pounder under an old tree about 200 yards over the little Creek which falls into the large Creek" at Fort Recovery. Wayne told Gibson that they "turned up the log scraped a hole in the ground & turned the log back upon its former berth." All of the captured artillery was thus hidden, except for two pieces thrown into the creek and already recovered. Frost now being out of the ground, the general ordered Gibson to begin turning over all the logs about his garrison, probing under them for the missing guns. The captain promptly sent Lieutenant Drake and a small party in search of the 6-pounder. Hard rains curtailed the search, but Drake's men did find eight army pickaxes under one log and some artillery drag ropes under another. Gibson vowed to continue this search "untill all the logs are examined for a reasonable distance round." Although unable to find the missing cannons, work parties continued to discover "articles of publick property" hidden beneath logs, just as the Indian prisoner had claimed.[2]

Those searching for cannons kept on constant alert because Indians seemed to roam the woods around Fort Recovery. Mysterious rifle shots would occasionally be heard when no troops were outside the garrison. One day while out in search of game, Sergeant Burk, who was dressed in hunting clothes, encountered an Indian about ten miles from the post. The Indian could have killed him, but he seemed unsure of Burk's identity because of the sergeant's clothing and cautiously gobbled like a turkey. Burk did likewise. Then the Indian hooted like an owl. Burk threw down the game he was carrying and jumped behind a tree. Unable to get a shot at each other, the stalemate ended when both warriors silently crept away in opposite directions. Sergeant Dold continued to turn up fresh Indian signs within a day's march of the post, on one occasion finding a fishing pole and hearing the report of four rifles along a creek suspected of being the site of Little Turtle's hunting camp. While scouts and hunters continued to encounter small groups of roving Indians, search parties kept turning over logs. At the end of March, they found a blacksmith's anvil and quantities of musket balls. More discoveries could have been made, but Gibson had most of his men at work strengthening the fort. He added a second story to each of the four blockhouses, building them to overhang the first story, "so as to admit of shooting down" upon attackers. This construction project ended on March 31, and the captain marked the fort's completion by hoisting a garrison flag from one of the new blockhouses.[3]

Ensign Daingerfield reached Fort Recovery on April 18, commanding twenty-four soldiers who escorted a small supply of contractor stores, including some whiskey, and ten "Stall fed Cattle." Daingerfield's escort was accompanied by Captain Wells, a few of his spies, and several Chickasaw warriors, who were "going in quest of prisoners scalps & information." Wayne cautioned the ensign that, should the Indians attack, "you are to force your way at the point of the bayonet." The general's letter of introduction to Gibson described Daingerfield as "a Virginian of worth & Education & descended from one of the first families of that State with some of whom you may probably be acquainted." The ensign and his party reached their destination without incident, although one of the cattle broke loose and ran off.[4]

On April 19, Captain Wells and his party, reinforced by Sergeant Dold and four privates, set out for the Saint Marys River, promising to alert Gibson if Indians were discovered. Gibson retained Daingerfield's detachment for a few days and formed fifty of his best soldiers into a strike force to act against the hostiles Wells anticipated finding. The spy captain had indeed encountered an Indian camp of eight to ten warriors, attacked them, and wounded several before they made their escape. Although somewhat at a disadvantage because of the ground, Wells reported that "his men all behaved well." After seizing a pack and a war club abandoned by the fleeing Indians, the scouts returned to Fort Recovery, Dold and Robert McClellan acting as rear guard. This encounter occurred too far from the post for Gibson to sally forth to assist, so he sent the convoy escort back to Fort Greeneville and disbanded the strike force. Lieutenant Drake was dispatched with a small party to investigate firing heard by Dold and McClellan on Beaver Creek, so named for the large numbers of that animal living there, but found no trace of Indians. Gibson asked permission of Wayne to accompany Wells on his next scout, but this request was refused as post commanders were still not allowed to leave their garrisons.[5]

The Chickasaws that reached Fort Recovery were the first from that nation who came north to fight with the legion in 1794. They had arrived at Fort Washington in early March, destitute of arms, ammunition, and clothing (all of which were supplied to them by Captain Peirce), then went forward with Major Cass's detachment. Another group of warriors arrived in mid-May under their chief Coloselege, a relative of Capt. James Underwood who had served with Wayne the previous year. This entire party consisted of Coloselege, Underwood, fifteen warriors, and one James Donaldson, hired as an interpreter. They carried certificates from Gen. James Robertson and Gov. Isaac Shelby attesting to "their friendly Views, and of their wish to act against the hostile Tribes." Encouraged by the treatment he had received during his earlier service, Underwood was nevertheless concerned that the Chickasaws would not be employed in as much scouting as they wished to perform. Chickasaw blood had been spilled by the hostile confederacy, and warriors from that nation were "resolved to have hair." Unable to speak English, and with no one in the legion who could speak the Chickasaw dialect, Underwood asked General Robertson to express their concern over the scouting issue and send along an interpreter to air their views in person.[6]

After they reached Fort Greeneville, Wayne put the Chickasaws to work, sending them on a scout for "hair" and prisoners toward Roche de Bout with Major McMahon and fifty riflemen. Donaldson did not seem to speak much of the Chickasaw language and made a lousy interpreter, so Wayne sent him back home with a message to General Robertson asking for "as many Chickasaw warriors as may incline to join the Legion." Scouts who could not communicate the intelligence they had gathered were of little use, so Wayne urged that further Indian reinforcements be accompanied by "some good interpreter." An additional party of five Chickasaws and seventy Choctaws, accompanied by a "Linguister," arrived in June to take an active part in the war. They brought news that "several hundred more are ready at a Moments Notice to take up the War hatchet on the part of the United States." Leading men from the Choctaw Nation had two requests of General Wayne. They first asked that upon the war's end, each leader might be furnished with "a hatt with feathers in it," an indication that they had won respect while fighting with the legion. Choctaw chiefs also asked that no whiskey be given to their men unless absolutely necessary. Wayne promptly issued an order forbidding any person "from giving or furnishing" friendly Indians "with any kind of Spiritous Liquors whatever."[7]

This last directive expanded a general order of January 24, 1794, that prohibited sutlers from selling whiskey or other liquor without a written permit from an officer. Benjamin Van Cleve was one civilian who ran afoul of Wayne's prohibition against the unauthorized sale of spirits. He had been engaged by his uncle, Robert Benham, to keep a sutler's store at Fort Greeneville and took out six horses loaded with liquor and other supplies. Benham's partner, Alexander Andrews, currently ran the shop but had not yet settled his business affairs, so Van Cleve returned to Cincinnati with his horses and took six more loads out to Greeneville. Upon reaching that post, Van Cleve set out his merchandise in the shop formerly operated by Andrews and took up residence in the hut of a Mr. Morrow, who was principal armorer in the laboratory. Van Cleve's stock of groceries included several horseloads of whiskey, "cherry bounce," and other liquors. Benham instructed his nephew to secretly sell the alcohol, "a notorious practice amongst Sutlers." Van Cleve had dispensed all but a few gallons of brandy when he tried to collect a two-hundred-dollar bill due to Benham by Lt. Aaron Gregg. The indebted officer sought to escape payment and turned Van Cleve in for violating the order against selling alcohol.

On April 4, a sentinel was posted outside the Benham and Andrews store with orders to allow neither persons nor goods in or out. Van Cleve appeared before a court-martial on April 6, charged with "selling bartering or giving spirituous liquor to a soldier, or soldiers of the third sub-legion on the night of the third instant & thereby occasioning intoxication & irregularity among the soldiers of said sub-legion." Facing an array of seven officers, with Captain Ford as president, the young clerk pleaded not guilty. Several enlisted men were examined and implicated Van Cleve in the improper sale of cherry bounce, followed by Lieutenant Gregg's testimony that there was "much irregularity [and] intoxication amongst the soldiers of the company he belonged to." The court found Van Cleve guilty and sentenced him to forfeit all the liquor in his possession, to leave Fort Greeneville, and never to return to the legion in the capacity of sutler. His sentence was made known on April 11, and he left Greeneville five days later, penniless and chagrined by his public reprimand.

Benjamin Van Cleve had more troubles than his court-martial. While away at supper on April 2, some unknown persons broke into his shop and stole his trunk, some books, other personal items, and a sum of money estimated at about fifty dollars. Motivation for the robbery might have been the fifteen hundred dollars that Van Cleve had luckily sent away just a few hours earlier. His pocketbook and trunk were found next morning, but Van Cleve recovered little else other than some business papers and a few items of clothing. On April 8, despite the sentinel's presence outside, Van Cleve found an intruder inside the store and called for help to apprehend him, but the thief managed to escape with a few dollars in cash. A few days later, someone tapped the remaining keg of cherry bounce and siphoned off half of it without being detected. Prior to Van Cleve's arrest, Benham had written to him requesting an estimate of how much stock was still on hand in the store. Van Cleve, thinking this tally would simply be used to replenish goods, provided figures without taking the time to weigh or measure anything. Benham used this careless inventory when he sold out to his partner, Andrews, who, discovering that he had made a bad bargain, accused Van Cleve of embezzling the missing property. In addition to the public humiliation of his sentence and the unfounded charges made by Andrews, Van Cleve never received his wages for work performed as a sutler's clerk.[8]

A list of goods available in sutler stores at the headquarters of the Legion of the

United States was compiled on March 10, showing the following prices (in shillings and pence) then being charged:

Spirits, gallon	50/0	Kentucky brandy, gallon	36/0
Whiskey, gallon	22/6	Cider, gallon	20/0
Common wine, gallon	40/0	Beans, bushel	60/0
Corn, bushel	30/0	Potatoes, bushel	60/
Loaf sugar, pound	5/0	Brown sugar, pound	4/6
Coffee, pound	4/6	Chocolate, pound	5/0
Butter, pound	4/6	Cheese, pound	3/9
Candles, pound	4/0	Soap, pound	3/0
Pepper, pound	15/0	Chewing tobacco, pound	4/6
Apples, dozen	3/9	Eggs, dozen	3/9
Salt, quart	2/6		

It is interesting to compare prices for these items in the Cincinnati market at this same period. Some of the corresponding prices were butter, 1/0; brown sugar, 1/10; whiskey, 5/0; and coffee, 2/6. The tremendous markup reflects the difficulty of transporting goods by packhorse through Indian country and the consequent risk encountered by businessmen in supplying the army with luxuries.[9]

Theft was always a hazard for sutlers doing business with the legion. On May 23, Sgt. Stephen Ogden and Pvt. Jacob Christey, both of the First Sub-Legion, conspired to rob the store run by David Conner, agent for Samuel Creigh of Cincinnati. The pair successfully made off with goods worth about twenty pounds sterling but proceeded to gamble much of their booty away while playing cards. Ogden and Christey were charged with the theft and found guilty, both sentenced to receive one hundred lashes, and the sergeant to be reduced to the rank of private. All stolen goods remaining in their possession were returned to the Creigh firm, both men having half of their pay stopped to reimburse the owner for his loss. William Thomas was accused of being an accessory to the theft but was acquitted for lack of evidence. Another court took up the matter of theft from the business of a trader named Silver in Cincinnati by soldiers from the garrison of Fort Washington. George Gaull pleaded guilty to leaving his post while on guard to commit the crime and was sentenced to receive one hundred lashes. Lorin Jones, charged with being Gaull's accessory, and Cpl. Henry Goodrich, charged with aiding and abetting the robbery by allowing the two soldiers to absent themselves while on duty, were both found not guilty.[10]

General Wayne tried to avoid trouble with his sutlers by curtailing their hours of operation, ordering them to remain closed from retreat in the evening until reveille, but this remedy failed to restrain the traders. When George Ludwell was found to have illegally dispensed whiskey to the soldiers, a court-martial sentenced him to be drummed out of camp after receiving one hundred lashes. Another sutler, Solomon Brewer, was charged with "keeping a disorderly store" by selling whiskey and playing cards with enlisted men. Found guilty only of gambling, Brewer was drummed out of camp "with a Dirty Pack of Cards about his neck." James Robinson was accused of "extortion & Imposition in his dealings with the soldiery" but was acquitted for lack of evidence. One of the most notorious cases involved Pvt. Philip Reily and Samuel Farewell, yet another dishonest sutler, who were charged with "Gambling, Cheating and Defrauding Sergeant Healey out of Ninety five Dollars," an exorbitant sum in Fort Greeneville. Both defendants were found guilty and received one hundred lashes, Farewell's property being seized to reimburse Healey for his losses. The sutler was then drummed out with a pack of cards around his neck and a label on his forehead that read, "The just reward of Cheating and Gambling." As a lesson to Healey, whom he thought "ought to be punished as a Gambler," Wayne deposited the ninety-five dollars with the paymaster until such time as he deemed the sergeant fit to manage his money in a more restrained manner.[11]

While unscrupulous sutlers stole from the soldiers and the soldiers responded in kind, Elliott and Williams appeared immune from theft since the firm dealt strictly in army rations and only occasionally lost some whiskey. The contractors sustained most of their loss from Indian parties that continued to ambush convoys headed north. One such column was attacked on May 13. Major Winston had commanded the escort on its trip back to Fort Washington and had been ordered to bring the convoy safely back to Fort Greeneville. Winston and a detachment of riflemen apparently stayed behind to escort fifty loaded wagons, sending seven hundred packhorses on ahead under the protection of Lieutenant Clark, who complained that "all action & Laborious commands" fell on him. Clark had recently spent three weeks on the Wabash without provisions, telling his brother, "I like to have Starved," and "I had once more to Depend on my Rifle for Subsistants." Now he commanded about sixty infantry and twenty dragoons, the only other officers with his escort being Lt. Edward Turner and Ens. Robert Lee.[12]

About eighteen miles from Fort Washington, at 1:00 P.M., Clark's advance guard—Cpl. James Waters and six privates—was attacked by a party of about sixty Delaware and Shawnee warriors. Waters and his men were quickly overwhelmed, killed, and scalped. The head of the packhorse column was thrown into confusion, drivers running for safety and their horses fleeing into the woods. As soon as they heard the firing ahead, the officers responded. Lieutenant Turner and Ensign Lee charged forward with fifteen dragoons, and Lieutenant Clark raced up from the rear of the column, bringing the remaining infantry with him. Pressed by the dragoons and seeing Clark's reinforcements coming up, the Indians cut loose a large number of packs and saddles, mounted some forty of the horses, and fled after only fifteen minutes of fighting. The attackers left behind one dead warrior, seven rifles that had been dropped when their owners went after scalps, forty blankets, and some food. After examining the ground, Clark suspected that several additional Indians had been shot "as they bled plentifully in Several places." Delaware chiefs took six American scalps to Roche de Bout and gave them to Colonel McKee, who dispersed the "hair" to arouse the various Lake Indians to action.[13]

After driving off the attacking force, Lieutenant Clark found that his losses amounted to eight killed and two wounded. He sent a messenger on to Fort Hamilton,

Lt. William Clark. From Nellie Kingsley, *Four American Explorers*, 1902.

and Lieutenant Colonel Hamtramck relayed the news to General Wayne at Fort Greeneville. Wayne reacted swiftly, sending Howell Lewis and Robert MisCampbell with a
mixed force of light infantry and dragoons to intercept the Indian marauders. The general cautioned Lewis that, if he struck their path, he should "guard a surprise upon your
part, as the savages make a practice of forming an ambush upon their own trail." Lewis
was also instructed to leave a corporal and six men in camp, who would remain two or
three hours, then follow the legionnaires to discover if the Indians were actually pursuing them. Wayne also dispatched Major Buell with two hundred soldiers to meet the
convoy and reinforce the battered escort. Although he saw many signs of Indians, Buell

was not molested, and he met the packhorses and wagons between Forts Hamilton and St. Clair, escorting the provisions and clothing safely on to Greeneville.[14]

General Wayne had high praise for Lieutenant Turner and Ensign Lee, "who charged & defeated three times their number of savages" who had chosen the ground and were "flushed with temporary advantage" by their defeat of Corporal Waters's advance guard. To honor the pair, Wayne ordered that on the night of May 17, the camp guards should use "Turner" as their parole and "Lee" as the countersign. Almost as an afterthought, Wayne noticed the escort commander, saying that he was "much obliged to Lieut. Clarke [*sic*] of the 4th Sub Legion, and the troops under his command for the rapidity of their march to support the van guard." The conduct of these three officers, along with their men, had reinforced the general's belief that Indians "cannot sustain a determined charge." Clark was bitter over the minimal recognition he received, saying that no credit had been given for the way he arranged his troops, "only for my supporting the front." He continued, "An officer under my rank, a passenger who attempted to Charge but found the Indians to numours retreated & Received the Lorels of that day." Clark concluded his observations with the bitter note, "Kissing goes by faver."[15]

There was some criticism of Major Winston, who had apparently stopped at Griffin's Station on Mill Creek when Clark's advance was attacked. Hamtramck reminded Wayne, "the Major had my Direction in writing to Escort in, and out the Convoy, and I suppose that he must have some very good reason for not Complying." John Johnston, who was with the convoy, was more harsh: "The officer in command was blamed, but not brought to court martial. Had his force been properly distributed in front and rear no attack would have been made." Once again, Winston was late and not where he should have been, two accusations that had continued to haunt his career, but once more he escaped punishment.[16]

Many of the officers had given up hope that the legion would begin a campaign any time soon. One of them admitted, "we have been in a 'moving, halting posture,' since the 1st of December, but it would seem that the longer we continue here, the more firm our attachment to the spot, and at present it is altogether uncertain when we may move, or where." Another officer, writing to an old comrade in Connecticut, assured him that "there never was a more expensive army, in proportion to its numbers, than this." Not only did all provisions have to be carried forward on packhorses or driven on the hoof but also "about one third of the army is constantly employed in escorting the provisions, which is a most fatiguing service." The prolonged waiting and constant shuttling of convoys as soon as the weather improved that spring went hand in hand. Until the stockpile of stores could be increased, the legion did not have enough rations or forage for a campaign, and it could not go into the field while one-third of its numbers were on escort duty. This period of watching and waiting, broken only by a few sallies by select commands, would continue.[17]

While the advent of spring brought high water that sometimes curtailed the legion's scouting activities, it also brought increased Indian activity. Richard Miller, a dragoon carrying express dispatches to headquarters, left Fort Hamilton at 6:00 P.M. on April 30. He had been gone but ten minutes and had just crossed the Miami River when three shots rang out. One of the sentries saw Miller fall from his horse, which galloped back to the garrison. The post commander sent out a sergeant and twenty men, who found Miller dead and scalped. The soldiers pursued for a short distance, following the trail of blood left by a badly wounded Indian who had been shot by a Mr. Moon of nearby Bruce's Station. Moon just happened to be nearby when Miller was killed. He dodged behind a tree, took careful aim, and shot an Indian about fifty yards away. Others in the attacking party picked up their wounded comrade and fled, carrying off only Miller's saber. On May 1, an express rider from Fort Washington was fired on about five miles south of Fort Hamilton by a party of Indians who chased him to within two miles of the latter post.[18]

Later that month, Captain Slough was sent back to Fort Hamilton from Fort Greeneville to bring forward flour with a convoy of seven hundred packhorses and an escort of 120 infantrymen and thirty dragoons. Slough was concerned for the convoy's safety, writing on May 28, "I am very certain I shall be attacked on my way out, as the Indians are very thick round us, and my spies have discovered a very large trail between this and Fort St. Clair." A small quartermaster train had been attacked the day before about seven miles south of Fort Hamilton. The men managed to escape unhurt but abandoned their packhorses and a large load of empty bags. An express rider galloping by later saw the bags still laying in the road but did not stop since he was fired upon. A detachment sent from the fort to recover the bags found that they had been taken away by a party of about fifty Indians. That same day, Sergeant Reynolds led a few mounted men on a scout from Fort Hamilton toward Cincinnati and bumped into about one hundred hostiles, who chased them for nearly four miles. Slough felt that his only hope of getting through to Fort Greeneville was if the Indians concentrated their strength on a convoy under Lieutenant Colonel Strong, which had recently left Fort Washington. While Slough's convoy carried only flour, Strong's had supplies "of more consequence to the enemy." Even if he should be attacked by an overwhelming force, Slough vowed, "If I am unfortunate I will be brave, and meet my fate like a soldier."[19]

Strong's command left Fort Greeneville on May 21 and encountered no difficulty on the return to Fort Washington or on the trip back north until near the fallen timber. After leaving camp just north of the fallen timber and progressing about a mile, soldiers guarding the right flank of the column were driven in by a large party of Indians, estimated to number at least two hundred, although only about fifty had actually been seen. Some of the Indians came within a few hundred yards of the convoy, but they did not press the attack. Strong sent Lieutenant Tilton with a detachment on foot and Lieutenant Covington with some dragoons to investigate. Signs found by these two parties led them to estimate the enemy's numbers at closer to three hundred, a force that could have done considerable damage had they not been discovered by Strong's alert flankers. Despite rainy weather, General Wilkinson took another pack train south from Fort Greeneville and passed Strong's command at Fort St. Clair. Having seen no Indian signs, Wilkinson, although feeling "some solicitude for his safety," ordered Strong to continue north. As for his own march, Wilkinson found "the men and officers much exhausted by the depths of the Road, & the darkness of the Night, the thick folliage of these woods being impenetrable to the rays of the Moon." Lieutenant John Reed and several men became exhausted and, being no longer able to keep up, "were necessarily left behind." The demand for supplies was so great that it was common for convoys to continue after dark and for men to be left to their peril if unable to keep pace.[20]

Convoys marching north from Fort Washington carried more than food and forage. Sub-legion quartermasters had been ordered to outfit the troops with new summer uniforms, each officer and soldier to receive two pairs of linen overalls, two shirts, and two pairs of shoes. General Wayne was especially concerned about replacing the inferior shoes that had recently been issued. The last bunch had been of the moccasin type, and he had found that two pairs of that style were "not equal to one pair of the common shoes that we had last year." In fact, Wayne noticed, "they go to pieces in the course of one escort to Fort Washington & back again." If proper footwear could not be obtained, the general asserted, "the Legion will most certainly be barefoot before the middle of June." Wayne recommended several alterations in the uniform to Secretary of War Knox, including brown or blue overalls instead of white and "a strong Military Cocked Hat in place of flimsy round ones." He also suggested continued issue of the long uniform coat, which would be "warm & comfortable during the Winter" but could be cut down to a short coat in spring, the excess material to be used "for repairing or mending them."[21]

Wayne was particularly irritated with the legion hats, "which with the least wet dropt over the ears and eyes of the men & entirely looses their form." To remedy "the heterogeneous forms, and the very inferior quality of the hats," he ordered Major Belli to immediately purchase 3,800 yards of narrow white binding in addition to sixty-five yards of white, sixty-five yards of red, seventy-five yards of yellow, and eighty yards of green rattinet, a thin woolen fabric, for use as plumes. Belli was also to procure one hundred bearskins "of the best & blackest hair," one thousand needles, and fifty pounds of thread. Patterns for hats and caps were distributed to the various companies, and the above supplies issued proportionally so the soldiers could begin modifying their headgear. The infantry companies were to wear hats with their crowns covered by bearskin, while the rifle and light infantry companies were to sport caps with plumes, all accessories matching the colors of the sub-legion to which the troops belonged. To ensure implementation of his hat order, Wayne held a review and inspection to enjoy the "military & Martial appearance" of the legion. In order to keep the uniforms and newly decorated hats neat and clean, the general ordered that any officer "who shall see or discover any soldier or soldiers carrying any kind of Meat upon their shoulders or heads to the abuse or injury of their Clothing" should immediately punish the offender with twenty lashes. To complete the legion's image, Wayne ordered his troops to appear "fresh shaved" and with their hair "well Powdered." It would not be long before the legion began its long-delayed campaign, and Anthony Wayne wanted his soldiers to look their best while killing Indians.[22]

Unfortunately, some of the new uniforms were ruined by the excessive fatigue work conducted when weather permitted. As at Fort Recovery, all of the blockhouses at Fort

Greeneville were raised another story. The four artillery bastions were enclosed, loop-holes cut, and firing steps constructed. On May 27, "every Non Commission'd Officer & Soldier not actually upon Guard or other Duty" was placed into one of three detach-ments, either wielding an ax, a spade, or a pickax. Construction work began on "the line of Defence around the Citadel" at 5:00 A.M. and continued each day until 2:00 P.M., with a one-hour break for breakfast. The only incentive was a gill of whiskey every day while the work was in progress. Fifty volunteers, "all good scythe Men accustomed to Mowing with the English scythe," and fifty "good Hay Makers" began work in the prairies on June 7, their heavy labor being rewarded with a gill of whiskey and an extra half ration. These haymakers were protected by the companies of Edward Butler and Howell Lewis, the fatigue party also carrying their arms and ammunition to and from the prairies. If this were not hard work enough, Wayne had soldiers cut planks and build a "Battery," or three-sided court, so the officers could play "fives," an early form of handball. The general wanted his officers to have regular exercise, so many of them, especially the younger ones, gathered about the "five ally" when off duty. Building a handball court was the last straw for William Sullivan, an Irishman who deserted after having served about a year in the legion. When taken to the Auglaize by Indians, Sul-livan confessed, "the duty is extremely hard and the men are punished severely for slight offences." He furnished his captors with additional information of some impor-tance, including the fact that Chickasaws had joined the Americans; the spies under Wells and May, who "dress and paint themselves like Indians," were given rewards for scalps; and "one thousand Dollars are offered for the scalp of Simon Girty." Omi-nously, Sullivan also reported that "greater secrecy than was usual is now observed, among all the officers of the Army."[23]

Private Sullivan's information, although generally accurate and helpful to the British, was misleading in one respect—the spies under Captain Wells were given rewards for *prisoners*, not scalps. But those rewards were available too. On May 17, *The Centinel of the North-Western Territory* published a remarkable notice. The prominent citizens of Cincinnati and Columbia, hoping "to prevent savages from committing depredations on defenceless citizens," had signed an agreement to offer rewards for Indian scalps. Bounty hunters would be paid for scalps taken between April 18 and December 25, 1794, under the following conditions:

> That for every scalp having the right ear appendant, for the first ten Indians who shall be killed within the time and limits aforesaid, by those who are sub-scribers to the said articles, shall, whenever collected, be paid the sum of $136; and for every scalp of the like number of Indians, having the right ear appendant, who shall be killed within the time and limits aforesaid by those who are not subscribers, the Federal troops excepted, shall, whenever collected, be paid the sum of $100; and for every scalp having the right ear appendant of the second ten Indians who shall be killed within the time and limits aforesaid, by those who are subscribers to the said articles, shall, whenever collected as aforesaid, be paid the sum of $117; and for every scalp having the right ear appendant of the second ten Indians who shall

be killed within the time and limits aforesaid by those who are not subscribers to the said articles shall, whenever collected, be paid the sum of $95.

To limit the extent of their liability for this unique offer, subscribers limited the killing zone to an area ten miles above the mouth of the Little Miami and ten miles below the mouth of the Big Miami, bounded on south and north by the Ohio River and an imaginary line drawn twenty-five miles from the river. Of course, hunters could simply kill Indians outside this designated area and swear they were shot down inside the established boundaries so they could collect the reward. To further their war of extermination, these upper-class members of Cincinnati and Columbia society made no distinction between warriors, wives, elderly, invalids, or children. The genocidal message was clear: Indians must be exterminated in the Northwest Territory, period, no argument. The reason was also clear: Settlers craved the fertile prairies along the rivers and did not want to wait any longer for the legion to drive off the Indians.[24]

Residents of Columbia did more than just pay for scalps. While in that village on business for the quartermaster, Samuel Henley met Captain Kibbey, who had received public praise for recently following some Indian raiders and killing two of them. Kibbey advised Henley of his desire to raise a company of fifty men to serve as scouts under General Wayne, so long as they would receive the same pay as Kentucky volunteers and he could command the unit. Henley passed this information on to Wayne for his consideration. Kibbey then contacted Col. Oliver Spencer and pressed that gentleman to write Wayne and recommend him. Spencer complied, telling the general, "We have no men really to spare from the Settlement, but I find there are a Number who wish to engage for this Campaign on the Same footing with the Kentucky Militia either as Spies, or Join the Militia from Kentucky when they Shall march." Spencer said that all Kibbey needed to know was when his company would be needed and "whether it will make any difference in their pay whether they are Mounted, or not." John Armstrong also wrote from Columbia and recommended Kibbey as "a Man of considerable enterprise" who would "willingly join the Army this Campaign with a party of Active Militia on foot, should he meet incouragement." Kibbey's lobbying efforts were successful, and on June 29 Wayne authorized him to raise a company of spies such as James Flinn had led the previous year. The new captain was to rendezvous his company at Fort Washington on July 5, then attach his volunteers to the next convoy marching to headquarters.[25]

Kibbey, described as "a man of Herculean strength and undaunted courage," was popular in the Columbia settlement. One story circulated that he was once challenged to a duel by a British officer, who asked him to name the time and place for their mortal combat. He supposedly responded, "Here is the place, now is the time," and handed one of a brace of pistols across a table to the astonished Englishman, who promptly changed his mind. James B. Finley remembered that Kibbey was "a true Jersey blue, fully adequate to any emergency growing out of his highly responsible position." The brothers John and Thomas McDonald thought him to be "a bold and intrepid soldier" and quickly joined his company to fight Indians. Although volunteers generally came forward a little slower than Kibbey had predicted, seventy-five men had signed on to follow him by July 18. His second in command was Lt. William Brown, originally of Stamford, Connecticut, who had received the first Badge of Military Merit, presented personally by General Washington on May 3, 1783, for singular service at Yorktown. This badge, "the figure of a heart in purple cloth or silk," was the first ever presented in the American army and would later be revived as the Purple Heart decoration. Kibbey's muster roll included many names that indicate relatives signed up together, either brothers like the McDonalds, father and son like William Williams and William Williams Jr., as cousins or as uncles and nephews. For residents of Columbia, fighting Indians was a family affair.[26]

CHAPTER 18

The Indian Army Gathers

THE U.S. SENATE HAD BELATEDLY acted upon promotions and appointments in the legion, sending on to President Washington an approved list of officers, some of them taking their rank from as far back as February and March 1793. This complete enumeration was published in general orders on June 8 and, in most cases, merely confirmed officers at the rank they had already been filling for many months. By way of illustration, these promotions affected all of the officers at Fort Recovery except Captain Gibson. Samuel Drake had been acting as a lieutenant and was referred to as such in official communications since February 28, 1793, when Lt. John Bird was promoted captain. Now he was officially recognized at that rank. The same held true for William Daingerfield, who was hereafter acknowledged as an ensign, although he had been acting in that capacity since May 1, 1793. General Wayne also had kept his promise to Captain Gibson, and the list of newly commissioned ensigns contained the name of Sergeant Dold, making him now the fourth officer at Fort Recovery.[1]

This list of appointments brought one interesting ensign into the legion, a nineteen-year-old named Peter Frothingham who resided in the Northwest Territory. Details of his earlier years are no longer known, but Frothingham was a full-fledged hypochondriac who apparently enjoyed diagnosing and treating his personal diseases. He had tried to cure a case of "the itch" a year or two earlier by rubbing mercury ointment on the affected areas, which resulted in eruptions on his arms and legs. When Surgeon's Mate Joseph Andrews tried to prescribe a treatment for this problem, he discovered that the ensign had "a quantity of medicines, lotions & unguents almost equal to the contents of my Chest, like a person who has dabbled sufficiently in medicine to render it a dangerous tool." He further stated that Frothingham "seemed determined to try a little of each of his articles, expecting that in so large a number, he could not fail in finding the proper remedy for his complaint, without considering the ill effects that would result from the variety." Thin and with a "melancholic temperament," the ensign had apparently medicated

himself into an outbreak of dropsy by the use of drugs such as cathartic salts and flowers of sulfur. Andrews described the young man as "temperate to a criminal excess,"
despite regularly consuming a quart of wine each day. Although a Methodist, when he
died at the age of twenty, Ensign Frothingham did not exhibit "that christian fortitude,
that his affectation of religion" had led brother officers to expect.[2]

Promotions and appointments from Philadelphia, in addition to bringing forward
some interesting characters, also provoked controversy among officers of the legion. In
his general order announcing the changes, Wayne included the statement, "The President has not thought proper to appoint a Brigadier General, in the room of Brigadier
General Posey, resigned—The incomplete state of the Legion at present does not admit
of that measure." This remark galled Lieutenant Colonel Hamtramck, who as senior
field officer should have succeeded Posey. Expressing his "Mortification of seeing myself
unnoticed," Hamtramck lashed out at Wayne on June 9, telling him that "the Calculated expectation every officer has in entering in the Army is to fill the Vacancies by seniority; this expectation is the vital Spirit that gives Comfort under the hardships which
are Concomitent with the profession of arms, and without which, a Gentleman never can
have any inducement to come into, or Continue in the Army." He reminded General
Wayne, "my Command is one wing of the Army, and the other Commanded by a
Brigadier General," and asked, "Can Eighteen years devoted to the Service of my Country, and that with irreproachable Conduct have any Claim?" After suggesting that a
brevet to the rank of brigadier would allow him to save face and "Continue to enjoy the
Confidence of my Country," Hamtramck assured Wayne that without such recognition,
"I would not wish to continue a moment in the Service." Although he would remain in
the army until his death nine years later, no elevation to the rank of brigadier, either full
rank or brevet, was ever forthcoming for John Francis Hamtramck.[3]

General Wayne received more than one letter expressing disapproval with this latest round of promotions. Maxwell Bines wrote to state his outrage at "the injury done
me in my rank" when he learned his promotion was effective as of February 10, 1794. He
explained the particulars of his case: "In the General Orders of the 22d of August last,
by the power vested in you, I was promoted to the rank of Captain, vice Carbury
resigned; to take the rank from the 20th of April 1793, & was to be respected & obeyed
accordingly—but the General order of yesterday recognising the promotions & appointments in the Legion, made by the President of the United States, by & with the advice
of the Senate, speaks a very different language & deprives me of nearly ten months rank,
by which means ten Captains are brought over my head, all of whom I conceive myself
justly entitled to rank." Believing that he had been unjustly slighted, Bines asked Wayne
to correct the mistake and guarantee that he would rank from April 20, 1793, assuring the
general that his continued service rested upon resolving that point of honor. Wayne obviously had no power to overrule the wishes of President Washington and could do nothing to give Bines the satisfaction he deserved.[4]

Ensign Lee, who had just recently been recognized for his intrepid conduct while
with Lieutenant Clark's escort, wrote to complain that Jesse Lukens, who had joined the

legion almost one year later, stood higher on the list of lieutenants than did he. Noting that Lukens's promotion was dated only a few months after "his primitive acceptance," Lee did not want to serve in the same sub-legion with an officer he considered his junior. His solution was simple. Lee asked Wayne if he could merely continue as an ensign until a vacancy occurred in a different sub-legion; the general ignored this strange request. Amid the outpouring of pique and outraged honor, Wayne did receive one message that certainly must have made him smile. Lieutenant Colonel John Clark, commanding the Fourth Sub-Legion, requested permission to resign because ill health compromised his ability "to undergoe the hardships of a Campaign & the toils incident to the present service." Clark expressed a hope that his departure would "bring into command an Officer who will perhaps be able to render more service to his Country than I could possibly do." Having previously expressed an opinion that Clark knew less about military affairs than some sergeants, Wayne was delighted to accommodate him and even allowed a few days for Clark to arrange his affairs before accepting the resignation.[5]

Despite repeated pleas to the War Department asking officials to recruit the legion to full strength, the only significant addition to military strength in 1794 did General Wayne no good. On May 9, Congress approved what it styled a "Corps of Artillerists and Engineers," authorizing twelve new companies of artillery that the general did not want and could not use on the frontier. This corps would consist of four battalions of four companies each, the artillery already in service to constitute one battalion. Instead of assigning veteran artillerymen, who could not be spared by Wayne, to recruit the additional companies, the War Department appointed a slew of new officers. Some were veterans of the Revolution, but many had never before served as either artillerists or engineers. One provision of the act allowed President Washington to "cause such proportion of the said corps to serve in the field, on the frontiers, or in the fortifications on the seacoast, as he shall deem consistent with the public service." It was obvious that these new companies were destined for seacoast duty as a response to the threat of war with Britain. An estimate of expenditures for the War Department in 1794 included money for 134 iron cannon to be used in fortifications, forty mortars, and fifty brass field pieces, the latter to be cast out of old mortars. Other expenditures seemed to be more than excessive, given that the legion's current strength combined with the newly authorized artillery companies would not total over five thousand soldiers. These included cleaning and repairing twenty-six thousand muskets, the purchase of one thousand rifles, the construction of carriages for 230 brass field cannon, and large quantities of ordnance stores and military supplies. As with many of the bills approved by Congress, none of these items addressed the legion's most pressing need—manpower.[6]

Out at Fort Recovery, Captain Gibson did not need congressional appropriations to strengthen his garrison; he simply went out and found what he needed. After a long period of diligent searching, Gibson was able to report on May 11 that he had found two of St. Clair's missing cannons, a brass 3-pounder and an iron carronade, which he mistakenly referred to as a howitzer. Both had been uncovered between the fort's palisade and the rear redoubt, the 3-pounder "buried in the bed of an old log that had mouldered away and the Howitz about five yards from it, under a log but so small that it had never been suspected." Wayne was delighted at Gibson's find and replied, "I think it is not impossible that an other Six pounder & two threes [actually two 6-pounders and one 3-pounder] are not far off—probably the Six pounder may be within the area & directly under the surface of Fort Recovery or below." He also advised that the missing guns might still be in the creek, covered over by earth from banks that had fallen in during spring floods. Wayne hastened forward some round shot for the newly discovered guns, along with small-arms ammunition, thirty head of cattle, and thirty-five horseloads of flour.[7]

Gibson encouraged Wayne to again interrogate the Indian prisoner who had claimed to know the whereabouts of one of the missing 6-pounders. This interview did not prove productive. But on June 22, Ens. Samuel Dold captured two Shawnee warriors who conveyed extremely valuable information. These captives were taken on the Maumee River about twenty miles above Grand Glaize, along with five horses and a quantity of deer and bear skins. After intense questioning, the Indians pointed out a spot where one of the 6-pounders had been buried, under a log as Christopher Miller had related and about one-half mile from the garrison. This cannon, along with the two located a month earlier, were mounted on carriages in the blockhouses, significantly increasing the firepower at Fort Recovery. The last two missing pieces were not located during Wayne's campaign. Apparently, Ensign Dold located the 3-pounder in late November 1794, but the last 6-pounder remained buried until 1832, when it was uncovered by a farmer plowing a field. As finally constituted, the ordnance at Fort Recovery consisted of two brass 6-pounders, two brass 3-pounders, two brass howitzers, and one iron carronade, making that post a virtually impregnable fortress in the wilderness.[8]

The two Shawnee warriors captured by Ensign Dold were escorted back to Fort Greeneville and examined in front of General Wayne. They claimed to be from a party of about twenty who had spent the spring and summer hunting opposite the mouth of the Kentucky River. Their group had stolen about fifty horses from settlements along the Salt River, had killed one man, but had taken no prisoners. Shortly after starting home, these two warriors met three Delawares and a Potawatomi on their way to steal horses around Big Bone Lick. These newcomers told the Shawnees that a council of chiefs had been held at Grand Glaize, where the assembled leaders agreed that the British "were always setting the Indians on like dogs after game pressing them to go to war & kill the Americans but did not keep them." The council had determined on peace unless the British came through with military assistance, announcing "that they wou'd not be any longer amused by promises only." In the opinion of the chiefs, "War or peace depended upon the Conduct of the British." Of course, General Wayne already knew that Alexander McKee had disrupted these peace talks, but this information again showed him how close he had come to a peaceful settlement of the Indian war.

The Shawnees also revealed that a British force had advanced into U.S. territory and constructed a fort at Roche de Bout. Blue Jacket, principal warrior of the Shawnee Nation, had been sent by the British to encourage the Chippewas and other Lake Indians to assemble at this new fort, where they could join the redcoats and other Indian nations in a war with Wayne's legion. Dold's captives then gave the general some firsthand information about the strength and leadership of his Indian opponents. Their nation had perhaps 380 warriors at Grand Glaize but could typically bring only 300 of them into action under their great warriors Blue Jacket and Captain Johnny. About 480 Delaware warriors lived at the Glaize, and the vaunted Miamis, many of whom had moved west toward Vincennes and the Mississippi, could now only muster 100 fighters. The Wyandottes could be counted on to furnish 150 fighting men, their typical contribution. These informants did not know how many men other nations might send to fight with the Indian army, but they were positive that the Chippewas would be the most numerous. Wayne was delighted to obtain this much intelligence, even though much of it was secondhand. News of the British fort confirmed rumors of its construction and worried the general, who now had to make plans to contend with "a Heterogeneous Army composed of British troops the Militia of Detroit, & all the Hostile Indians NW of the Ohio."[9]

The treaty ending the Revolution had contained a provision that creditors on both sides would have free access to collect their debts, but when individual states passed laws curtailing British rights to collect lawful bills, the new U.S. government had no power to stop them. Britain used this situation as a pretext for refusing to evacuate forts located on what was now U.S. soil, another provision of this treaty. The real reason was that Britain had no intention of giving up its lucrative fur trade centered around the Great Lakes. By encouraging Indian nations to continue their warfare against the United States, British officials hoped to promote an unstable situation on the frontier, with the Indians forming a buffer between the United States and Canada. Wayne's advance to Fort Greeneville, and then to Fort Recovery, concerned both military and political leaders in Canada, who felt his ultimate goal was Detroit. Heeding a plea from Lt. Col. Richard England, commander of the Detroit garrison, Gov. Gen. Lord Dorchester ordered Col. John Simcoe, lieutenant governor of Upper Canada, to reoccupy an outpost abandoned by the British in 1783. This site was on U.S. soil, about eleven miles up the Maumee River from its mouth at Lake Erie, and within two miles of Colonel McKee's trading post near Roche de Bout.

Governor Simcoe had commanded the Queen's Rangers during the Revolution and was familiar with General Wayne and his capabilities, having fought against him several times. The British minister at Philadelphia, George Hammond, offered his opinion of the officer who had been selected to avenge St. Clair's defeat: "General Wayne is unquestionably the most active, vigilant, and enterprising Officer in the American Service, and will be tempted to use every exertion to justify the expectations of his countrymen & to efface the Stain which the late defeat has cast upon the American Arms." It soon became clear that Lord Dorchester, fearful of Wayne and the American legion, had exceeded his authority when he received a pointed letter from George Hammond, who offered his opinion on the subject of erecting new posts along the Maumee: "I am afraid that they cannot be considered to be within the Limits of the Post at Detroit, the *immediate* protection of which, as well as the other Posts in our possession, on the American side of the Treaty Line, is the only object to be attended to." Simcoe assured Hammond that the site of the old fort, originally built in 1781, had always been considered a dependency of Detroit, even if it had been abandoned "in some respect" after the war's end. Colonel McKee weighed in with his observation that this had never been American territory since "the British flag has been flying every year since that period, during the Summer Months while I was waiting the arrival of the different Nations of Indians, to deliver to them the presents directed by His Majesty." After these assurances, no more was said about the legality of Fort Miamis, which was constructed under the supervision of Lt. Robert Pilkington, Royal Engineers, and garrisoned by detachments from the Twenty-Fourth Infantry and Royal Artillery. Despite these lame protests from Simcoe and McKee, the construction of Fort Miamis was a clear violation of international law and an invasion of U.S. territory by British military forces.[10]

To assist Wayne in his advance, the War Department authorized him on March 31 to again call out as many mounted volunteers from Kentucky "as he should judge necessary" for a term of four months. Secretary Knox explained the need for Kentuckians in a letter of instruction to Charles Scott: "Much dependence is placed upon this Species of Troops for the rapidity of their movements and their Knowledge of Indian Warfare—a Glorious opportunity is now present to them of distinguishing and perpetuating their fame and of preventing their Country perhaps forever from being subjected to the depredations of Savage barbarity." Knox estimated that two thousand men would be needed, all of whom would receive a small advance payment, part of what he felt was "ample compensation" and "perhaps the highest given upon the face of the Globe for Military Service." Scott would again command the Kentuckians, with the rank of major general, and his companies would rendezvous at Georgetown. Wayne was still not comfortable about using volunteers and complained to Knox, "Wou'd to God that early & proper means had been adopted by Congress for the Completion of the Legion I wou'd not at this late hour have to call for Militia Auxiliaries from Kentucky who may not have a relish to meet this Hydra now preparing to attack us." The general considered Simcoe's new fort outright "aggression," which would "give confidence to the Savages & Stimulate them to continue the War at all events." Wayne assured Knox that, although the Indians might outnumber the legion and the Kentucky Volunteers, they could not excel the American troops, "even if they shou'd be reenforced by the Governor of Canada with all his red Myrimidons."[11]

Many residents of Kentucky still harbored a resentment against the Washington administration for quashing the expedition of George Rogers Clark. Wayne thought there was "a pervading spirit of Opposition to the measures of the General Government, in the State of Kentucky," citing a report from Major Belli to illustrate "the present temper of the people." Belli related that, while in Lexington on May 24, a noted orator, "after an elaborate speech of two hours, concluded with this declaration, 'I wou'd not be displeased to see the *British* in possession of the N.W. banks of the Ohio as our Neighbours.'" The contractors, who were already out of favor with Wayne, had more bad news when their purchasing agents informed Robert Elliott that Kentuckians "peremptorily refused to receive Bank notes in payment for any kind of supplies, nor wou'd they deliver any unless first paid for in *specie*." Given the public sentiment, Wayne expected many of the volunteers to simply take their pay advances and never turn out to serve with the legion. Writing from Frankfort, where he had gone in search of reasonably priced horses for the dragoons, Capt. Thomas Lewis saw that many officers who had served in 1793 took "great umbrage" when Governor Shelby did not reappoint them for the current campaign. Shelby intended to make new appointments from the Kentucky militia, but this plan offended the populace, who claimed that these captains would never be able to fill their companies.[12]

Luckily for Wayne, turmoil in Kentucky did not impede the legion's campaign. His left flank along the Lower Ohio and Wabash Rivers remained secure, guarded by garrisons at Fort Steuben, Fort Massac, and Fort Knox. Following General Putnam's peace treaty with the Wabash and Illinois Nations, Fort Knox, the oldest of the three posts, had become a relatively quiet and boring place, now commanded by Captain Pasteur. His only problems seemed to be with the ne'er-do-wells of his command, who, like soldiers at Fort Greeneville, slept on guard, insulted superiors, got drunk, went into the village of Vincennes without permission, forged passes, and stole from comrades. All things considered, punishment at Fort Knox was more lenient than that imposed under General Wayne, the maximum sentence being seventy-five lashes for the most serious of offenses. Hoping to gain intelligence from that area, Wayne wrote to Maj. Francis Vigo, the most prominent civilian in the Vincennes area. Referring to Vigo as "a Gentleman of integrity and influence," the general promptly asked him if he could do something very ungentlemanly: "Wou'd it be practicable to bribe or purchase the Spanish express from St. Louis to Detroit to deliver his dispatches to Capt. Pasteur." Realizing that this was "delecate business," Wayne also inquired if Vigo could send an agent, either an Indian or Frenchman, to Roche de Bout, "in order to discover the Number & designs of the Enemy." To facilitate such a transaction, Wayne sent Captain Pasteur $120 to cover any initial expenses.[13]

General Wayne's right flank on the Upper Ohio and Allegheny Rivers was in a somewhat more tenuous condition. Two attacks on boats in the Allegheny and one of its tributaries occurred on May 30. In the morning, a canoe was fired on; one man was killed and two wounded. In the evening, a boat that had just started for Kentucky was attacked near Chambers' Station by about a dozen warriors who fired from shore, following the boat as it drifted downstream. Of the males on board, two were killed, one was mortally wounded, and another escaped, while the craft gently floated down to Pittsburgh, where the women and children were brought safely ashore. About this same time, the settlement at Pine Run was evacuated when some twenty Indians were discovered in the area, causing a "very general alarm" on that frontier. There was fear that some of these raids on the Allegheny had been committed by warriors from the heretofore peaceful Six Nations. To ensure their loyalty, Pennsylvania raised four companies of state troops to be used for building and garrisoning a post at Presque Isle on Lake Erie, which would interrupt communications between the Six Nations, "who had become wavering and suspicious," and the hostiles opposing the legion.[14]

This Pennsylvania detachment marched north and reached Fort Franklin in mid-June, finding that post "in a wretched state of defense," according to Capt. Ebenezer Denny. Lt. John Polhemus commanded a garrison of less than two dozen invalids who were incapable of repairing the defenses, though "under great apprehension of an attack." The fort was "worse than any frontier station you ever saw." One officer observed that "the pickets might do to enclose a garden, and do look more like a fence than any thing else," being surrounded outside by a ditch in which "500 Indians might lay secure." Before the Pennsylvanians arrived, Polhemus kept the place locked shut "day and night" as if under siege by the supposedly friendly Indians who surrounded the fort and acted "exceedingly insolent," treating the American soldiers "with the utmost contempt." The lieutenant had sent repeated reports on the condition of his post to Secretary Knox, all of which were ignored, leading Polhemus to conclude that the War Department intended the place "shall go to wreck." Pennsylvanians could not march away and leave Fort Franklin in such a pitiable shape, so they immediately went to work. Captain Denny reported, "A new set of pickets was brought from the woods, and in four days an entire new work erected round the block-house, which we left in tolerable defensible order."[15]

General Wayne was hopeful that his contentious relationship with Elliott and Williams had finally produced some beneficial results. He advised Secretary Knox that, although the contractors remained "defective" after being "too much countenanced by certain ambitious factious restless Characters," they had finally been forced "to make more efficient Arrangements." Wayne's peremptory order for Quartermaster General O'Hara to take charge of the contractor's operation and make the required deliveries at the expense of Elliott and Williams had caught that firm's attention. By the end of May, the general could report that he had "obliged the Contractors to come forward with supplies." Referring to the "nefarious faction" in Congress that had opposed formation and completion of the legion, Wayne could proudly boast that, in his command, "the neck of that faction is in a great Measure broke." He had even confronted James Wilkinson, his second in command, whom he suspected of being "the cause of the defaults of the Contractors." Although many of the officers had apparently taken sides in the dispute between these two generals, there being oft-heard expressions throughout the legion that "such an Officer is in favor of Wayne—such a one in favor of Wilkinson," the commander in chief now realized that he could no longer trust his most senior subordinate. With some of Wilkinson's secret dealings finally out in the open and his firmest adherents, Thomas Cushing and Isaac Guion, in jail, General Wayne must have felt more confident as his legion prepared to advance.[16]

That confidence was not shared by all members of the officer corps. Noting that "our enemies have increased in all quarters," one officer wrote, "We are now preparing for an active Campaign; How it will turn out God only knows." Doubting whether the legion could subsist both itself and the Kentucky Volunteers, he thought that British activity kept the entire frontier in a state of flux. A couple of Potawatomi captives, taken by one of Captain Gibson's scouting parties on June 5, had become talkative after being thrown into irons and boasted that the British "have come forward, and told them they were going to War with America and assist them in every thing necessary to support their Cause." They said that the British had built a new fort at McKee's trading post and were rumored to have fifteen hundred troops within thirty miles of the legion. Governor Simcoe had promised the Potawatomis "arms, ammunition, provision, and clothing, and everything they wanted, on condition they would join him." The two captives told how all of Simcoe's speeches were "as red as blood; all the wampum and feathers were painted red; the war pipes and hatchets were red, and even the tobacco was painted red."[17]

Writing to a friend still at Bellipherontia, one unidentified officer said that Colonel Simcoe had three regiments at Roche de Bout, but he confessed to not knowing whether they would simply support the Indian army or if "they intend to meet us in the woods and give us battle." A second officer offered his observation on the British: "That imperious and haughty nation can never forgive us for compelling them to acknowledge us independent, and whenever an opportunity hath offered, have not failed to treat with the utmost indignation the American flag." He also asserted that "the time is not very far distant" when the European invaders would receive "that punishment which they so deservedly merit." Estimates of the number of troops the legion could carry into action varied from fourteen hundred to seventeen hundred, while the opposing army was said to number "2000 red savages and 1500 white ones." One observer summed up the tense state of affairs when he admitted, "much bloodshed is pretty certain."[18]

On June 28, General Wayne advised Captain Gibson that a pack train of over three hundred horses would leave Fort Greeneville at reveille the next morning bound for Fort Recovery. Gibson was to expect at least twelve hundred kegs of flour, plus a few additional supplies, that he was to place under temporary cover along one of the inside walls of the stockade. Wayne informed him that three parties of friendly Indians, one of Chickasaws and two of Choctaws, were scouting toward the Auglaize and the headwaters of White River. In order to avoid a potentially embarrassing mistake, the general alerted the captain to the fact that each of these Indian scouts wore "a bunch of Yellow ribbon tied to their top knot" and told him to pass that information on to everyone at his post. The topknot was simply a tuft of hair left uncut on the crown of the warrior's head "by way of Ornament or to serve as a trophy of war for a successful enemy."[19]

William Wilson, an agent for the firm of Elliott and Williams, had charge of the contractor's stores and employees, while Major McMahon commanded the convoy's escort. His detachment included ninety riflemen from the companies of Asa Hartshorne, Thomas Lewis (under Lt. Robert Craig), and Joseph Shaylor (under Lt. John Michael). Lts. Hastings Marks and Andrew Shanklin accompanied the riflemen. A small detachment from Fort Recovery, then at Fort Greeneville under Ensign Daingerfield, would reinforce the escort and return to its station. McMahon's party also included fifty dragoons led by Capt. James Taylor, Lts. Leonard Covington and George Dunn, and Cornet Torrey. Before this convoy left Fort Greeneville, Wayne warned McMahon that his friendly Chickasaw and Choctaw scouts could be distinguished by their yellow ribbons. The major reached Fort Recovery on the evening of June 29 "without seeing any Indians or signs," saw his cargo safely stowed inside the stockade, and made camp outside the walls about one hundred yards to the rear.[20]

While soldiers from McMahon's escort and the garrison of Fort Recovery slept that night, an Indian army larger than the one that had vanquished General St. Clair lay encamped within a few miles of that post. This army had formed at Grand Glaize in mid-June and was joined on June 14 by a party of fourteen British officers, servants, and enlisted men. Several hundred Ottawas and Chippewas reached the Glaize on June 15, their arrival being saluted by six hundred warriors, who formed into one line and fired their rifles and muskets to welcome their northern comrades. A grand council was held the next day, and its members agreed that "every white man either English or French residing among or getting their livelihood by the Indian Trade or otherwise now within the limits of their Country shall immediately join the Indian Army to defend the territory in which their mutual interest is so greatly concerned." The assembled warriors, having been constantly encouraged by the British to defend their territory, were happy to see Captain Elliott's party of officers. The council resolved that these officers should accompany an advance against General Wayne's army and presented Elliott with strings of black wampum to signify their determination to conduct war. The officers and their entourage saw that this invitation "permitted of no alternative," so all but the senior officers changed from their red coats into frontier garb "for fear of mistakes in Action."[21]

General Wayne's army was said to be "rich with horses, blankets and clothing," so the Indians, based upon their previous success over Generals Harmar and St. Clair, would move to attack sincerely believing that "it was going to be an easy victory, and of but short duration." Jonathan Alder, a native of New Jersey, went along with the Indian army. Born on September 17, 1773, he had been captured in March 1782 by warriors from the Mingo Nation who killed and scalped his brother. Alder was taken to a village on Mad River, where he was adopted by an old man and woman, who also had three daughters. He had fond memories of his adoptive parents: "They could not have used their own son better, for which they shall always be held in most grateful remembrance by me." Mary, one of his new Indian sisters, did not take kindly to young Alder, treating him like a slave and calling him an "onorary lousy prisoner." Homesick and captive in a strange world where he could not understand the language or stomach the food, Alder would often retire to a favorite walnut tree and cry for hours over his fate. He felt more at home when he began to learn the Mingo dialect, and after a few years, he was given an old musket with instructions to start hunting. Alder was among those who assembled at the Glaize, but the Indians did not force him to take up arms against the legion—he chose to go along voluntarily.[22]

There were too many Indian mouths and not enough provisions at the Grand Glaize, so food began to run short. Most of the pork and flour had been consumed before the arrival of Captain Elliott's party, so they were reduced to what the French called *Gross sacre Gieux*, or boiled Indian corn. As for quantity, the British mess was "a mere *scramble*, that is to say him who can eat the fastest reaps the best share." On June 18, the army was augmented by 127 Mackinac and Saginaw warriors, who not only added to overcrowding at the Glaize but also reportedly had "committed depredations and ravished the women" in villages of other nations whose men had left to go to war. Hoping to avoid any further outrages, Capt. Blue Jacket ordered future reinforcements be directed along another route, away from defenseless old men, women, and children. The Indian army, estimated at close to fifteen hundred by one of Elliott's men, began to move south in two divisions. The first and largest, about one thousand warriors, was composed of Wyandottes, Mingos, Shawnees, Ottawas, Chippewas, and Miamis. The second group, mostly Delawares under Buckengales, with some Potawatomis and stragglers from other nations, apparently lingered behind to enjoy a shipment of rum, while other nations accused them of "not being hearty in the war."[23]

The Indian advance was slow, for the army had to hunt for food along the route. John Norton described how the column deployed hunters: "When a number hunt together they sometimes extend the line for several miles, leaving a space from a hundred to two hundred paces between each man, the two flanks generally projecting a little in advance. They start and partly envelope all the game contained in the extent they pass over, and overwhelm them with their bullets. This method of hunting is called waeneaghrontye, and is practiced by War parties, and villages when the inhabitants hunt in a body, to procure meat for a feast." One of the British officers, who, because of his "confined Latitude"—that is, being on American soil—only signed his daily journal "J.C.," said that the main column stopped every afternoon at 1:00 or 2:00 P.M. to allow the hunters time to kill enough game for the evening meal. Little Otter's detachment of Ottawas, on its march from Roche de Bout to the fallen timber south of the Glaize, had by itself killed five bears and forty deer.[24]

On June 25, the main Indian column was joined by fifty Saginaws. Buckengales sent word that he and the Delawares were finally en route, the rum obviously having been consumed. These reinforcements overshadowed the fact that a small group of warriors, who lived at the mouth of the Detroit River, got discouraged and went home. The main army continued south by southwest "in open Files leaving an interval of about ten rod between each," while hunters killed game to the front and its flanks. On June 26, some scouts saw an American detachment "*dress'd like Indians*," obviously one of the Chickasaw or Choctaw parties then in the field. Next day, when within thirty miles of Fort Greeneville, the Bear Chief, an Ottawa who had titular command of the army, sent some Mingos and Wyandottes to reconnoiter toward that post, then dispatched a small party of Ottawas and Chippewas in the direction of Fort Recovery. While the Indian leadership was looking for information about Wayne's intentions, the general had his Chickasaws and Choctaws out looking for the enemy. One party composed of forty-five Choctaws and ten white rangers headed in the direction of Roche de Bout. Four of these Choctaws were surprised near Girty's Town by the Ottawa and Chippewa detachment, which killed Capt. Bobb Sallad and drove off the others. This party of Choctaws reached Fort Greeneville on June 28 with news that the enemy was "in great force and advancing," and "there were a great number of white men with the Indians."[25]

Various bands continued to join the main Indian army until it numbered almost 1,250 men, although about 100 had no firearms. The Delaware column still had not appeared, and Bear Chief's warriors began to complain about this shabby reinforcement. To spur along those lagging behind, a runner headed back toward Grand Glaize with Bobb Sallad's fresh scalp. Emboldened by their initial encounter with the Choctaws, the Ottawas and Chippewas "seemed to be seized with a strong inclination" to attack Fort Recovery, the closest legion post. Leaders of other nations protested in council, pleading for the Indian army to continue south and confront Wayne's main force. British officers urged their allies to cut off the isolated forts from their main base of supply on the Ohio by interdicting the convoys, leaving them to wither as a flower does after its stem has been cut. But the Lake Indians had become fixated and could not be swayed, eventually persuading the entire confederacy to move against Captain Gibson and his small command in their forlorn wilderness outpost. This massive Indian army advanced in at least a dozen columns, hunters acting as before and killing as many as two hundred deer and a like number of turkeys each day in order to feed the ravenous multitude. Captain Elliott's party was concerned that their approach, noisy as it must have been, would be discovered and the garrison alerted. Fortunately, such was not the case, and the huge Indian army settled into large camps a few miles from their objective on the night of June 29. Spies came in with news that hundreds of packhorses were even then tied up outside the walls, easy pickings for those always on the lookout for plunder. Indian leaders must have smiled at this news, for they were already planning to take Fort Recovery and again possess St. Clair's old battlefield, soon to be stained with the blood of Major McMahon's unsuspecting troops.[26]

CHAPTER 19

Battle at Fort Recovery

SOLDIERS INSIDE FORT RECOVERY heard the firing of several rifles to the north and east on the evening of June 29 but paid little attention. So many sightings of small Indian scouting parties had occurred over the past few months that the troops had been lulled into a false sense of security. About 5:00 A.M., a mixed company of Chickasaws and Choctaws, identified by their prominent yellow ribbons, appeared at the fort gates. Not a single member of the scouting party could speak English, but Capt. James Underwood, who was known to the officers, tried to convey important intelligence by means of rudimentary signs. Underwood, who appeared "much agitated and fatigued," could not seem to get his message across the language barrier. Captain Gibson remembered, "all we could understand from him was that he had Seen a great many Tracks & heard much fireing." Alerted to the possibility of a more substantial enemy presence, Gibson prudently dispatched a patrol of four men to reconnoiter about the post before he would allow the convoy and its escort to return to Fort Greeneville. When the patrol returned and reported no Indian signs had been discovered, the captain assumed that all was safe. Normal military duty began for the day. A seven-man detachment went out to the cattle pens and released the animals to graze. When the animals did not seem interested in eating, the men returned to the fort for breakfast, intending to corral them later.[1]

William Wilson had the packhorse drivers up early, and by seven o'clock, they had eaten, adjusted all the empty pack saddles on their strings of animals, and turned them out to graze along the road back to Fort Greeneville. Major McMahon and his officers were still at breakfast in the fort while the pack animals moved out of the cleared ground and into the woods. By now, the advance of the Indian army had arrived, and small parties began to take up positions around the fort, although most of them concentrated along the road. Suddenly, a few shots rang out and the forest echoed with yells as warriors dashed forward, some on foot and others on horseback, upon the unwary packhorse drivers. Jonathan Alder, the white captive with the Mingo detachment, arrived just as the fighting began, and he recalled, "the first exciting thing I heard was the whites hollering, 'Indians, Indians!'" Leaving his hat behind, Major McMahon rushed outside, mounted his horse, shouted to Captain Hartshorne to send the riflemen to his flanks, and waved for the dragoons to follow him. McMahon and his mounted men, expecting to meet little opposition, charged forward through a confused mass of stampeded horses, drivers running for their lives to the fort, and Indians in close pursuit. The dragoons had gone perhaps two hundred yards into the woods when they were ambushed by a large group of warriors who rose up out of small creek bed and fired almost point blank into the riders. Many of the dragoons and horses fell, and as he reined in and started to give orders, Major McMahon was killed, "the ball entering the fore part of his neck, and passing nearly central to the back part." Cornet Torrey fell dead, and Captain Taylor, finding himself suddenly surrounded, spurred his horse to the rear. A ball slammed into his back, fracturing a lumbar vertebrae, but Taylor kept his saddle and sped to safety. Lieutenant Covington's horse was killed, throwing the young officer to the ground. Leaderless and greatly outnumbered, the surviving dragoons, whether mounted or on foot, raced for the safety of Fort Recovery.[2]

Pressing their advantage, the Indians advanced "with impetuosity" upon Captain Hartshorne, who had posted his riflemen at a strong position on a small hill inside the woods, with other hostile parties moving against his exposed flanks. While still an ensign, Hartshorne had "providentially" survived Harmar's fight by "faltering over a log in his retreat," but Providence now turned a blind eye. Indian fire "increased to a prodigious weight," but the captain attempted to stem the retreat by sending Lieutenants Michael and Marks with small detachments to his flanks. But nothing could stop the overwhelming force arrayed against the outnumbered band of riflemen. Hartshorne went down with a wound in the leg, some said in the thigh while others said in the knee, and Lieutenant Craig was killed, prompting the collapse of this hastily improvised defensive line. A couple of soldiers tried to carry Hartshorne to the rear, but the Indians were already between them and the fort. The captain, saying that "he was a dead man," ordered a faithful sergeant to leave him behind and told them, "Boys save yourselves." As his would-be rescuers hurried off, Capt. Thomas McKee rode up and assured Hartshorne that "if he would surrender he should be well treated." Having previously resolved to never fall into the hands of the Indians, he swung his espontoon and knocked McKee from his horse. Balancing on one leg, Hartshorne continued to defend himself, swinging his espontoon at McKee's black servant and an Indian companion. Kept at bay by this stout defense, the Indian fired an arrow into his chest, and the servant sprang forward to kill Hartshorne with his tomahawk.[3]

Thus far, Captain Gibson and his troops had heard the firing and screams of battle but had not seen any of the action since it had taken place outside the cleared area around the stockade. Now, panic-stricken and wounded dragoons and riflemen began to fall back into the open, it becoming obvious to all spectators that they were witnessing a disaster. Lieutenant Marks, "a very active strong young man," had been slightly wounded and was alone, fighting with his espontoon until it broke into pieces. Several warriors rushed forward to capture him, one actually having the officer in his clutches, but he wrenched free, knocked his would-be captor down with a fist, and escaped. Marks raced for the fort gate at the same time Lieutenant Michael came running in from the opposite direction under a heavy fire. He had lost every man of his small detachment but three. Realizing that the escort was being slaughtered, Gibson dispatched Lieutenant Drake, Ensign Dold, and twenty men, "all the men who could be spared from the garrison," to their assistance. Drake's small reinforcement reached the forest's edge just as "the Escort & Savages met them, much intermixed." They slowed the Indian pursuit for a few minutes, at one point "beating the enemy back at the point of the bayonet," allowing many to escape who otherwise would have been killed. Despite this bold advance, the unstoppable warriors came on from every direction and forced Drake's men to retreat toward the fort.[4]

The lieutenant had once been greatly insulted by another officer, yet chose not to accept a challenge, an action that prompted some talk of cowardice. William Henry Harrison explained how Drake declining to fight a duel had no relevance to that officer's courage: "Throughout the whole affair, Drake's activity, skill, and extraordinary self-possession, were most conspicuous. The enemy observed it as well as his friends. The numerous shots directed at him, however, were turned aside by providential interference, until he had accomplished all that he had been sent to perform. He then received a ball through his body and fell; a faithful corporal came to his assistance, and with his aid he reached the fort; and those two were the last of the retreating party that entered it—Drake making it a point of honor that it should be so." One of the last soldiers to enter the fort was a Sergeant McAnnally, who had been shot in the breast and lagged behind the others because of his wound. An Indian chased him up to the gate, near which stood a couple of trees about two feet apart that gave shade for men on guard. McAnnally's pursuer "jumped from one tree to the other to escape being shot as he was in range with the block houses." Finally, a Choctaw inside the fort fired and killed him as he passed between the trees.[5]

After their initial repulse, the dragoons attempted to rally at the creek upstream from the post but were scattered by heavy fire. The remaining riders galloped to a detached blockhouse at the watering place below the fort but were again dispersed, "which forced the few remaining to take shelter in the Garrison." Jonathan Alder remembered, "the Indians run the whites so close that some of them swung off their horses and got into the fort as best they could." Animals mad with fear galloped wildly in every direction through the cleared space around the fort and among the trees. Alder noticed that the dragoon horses "were finely equipped with saddles and bridles and horse pistols." Thinking to himself, "here was my chance to get a horse already equipped, if I could only catch one," Alder took position behind a tree. Several mounts came close by, almost near enough for him to reach the bridles, but they all ran off when he tried to capture them. He saw many companions intent on catching horses, some running crouched over to within fifty yards of the fort, before circling back to cover.[6]

As the big gate slammed shut behind Lieutenant Drake, Indian attackers "surrounded the Garrison & fired from every Direction, and advanced as far as They could find Stumps & Trees To cover Them," some taking shelter within seventy yards of the walls. Still unable to catch a horse, Alder hid behind his tree and watched the chaos. An Indian nearby, who was shooting as fast as he could load, asked why he did not fire his rifle. Alder first responded that he saw nothing to shoot at, then confessed, "I didn't want to shoot." His comrade suggested a withdrawal if he had no intention of fighting, noting that soldiers were nonetheless firing at him by pointing out where one ball had struck the bark just over Alder's head. This battlefield was no place for a pacifist, so the Indian shouted, "If you ain't going to shoot, you had better fall back out of reach before you are shot." The danger became evident a few moments later when his friend stuck his head out from behind a tree to fire again. Alder watched the warrior "clap his hands to his chin and then stoop and pick up his gun and then start and run, half bent, as far as I could see him," in search of medical attention for a flesh wound in the face.[7]

Isaac Paxton, one of Captain Gibson's riflemen, kept firing from a blockhouse as the enemy "assailed the fort with great fury, rushing up to within less than fifty yards of it, some of them carrying axes and hatchets for the purpose of cutting down the pickets." They were met by "a galling fire" that forced them to retreat to the woods "at a most respectful distance," where they commenced a largely ineffectual fire against the fort. Paxton recalled, "The balls were heard continually striking against the pickets and logs of the blockhouses, and whizzing over the heads of those in the garrison." The stockade and blockhouses were literally "everywhere perforated with bullets." Large numbers of ounce balls, "fired at such a distance as not to have momentum sufficient to penetrate the logs," littered the ground, mute testimony to Colonel McKee's supplying the hostiles with British muskets and rifles from the stores of the Indian Department. Amazingly, there were no soldiers killed within the fort, even though balls would occasionally pass through small gaps between timbers of the stockade and fly into embrasures in the blockhouses. Paxton had a narrow escape when one ball struck a log in the blockhouse and "glanced off, passing through his clothes without doing him any bodily harm."[8]

Elliott's party of British officers were disgusted with how events had progressed. After a stunningly complete victory over McMahon's escort and a major blow to Wayne's supply line by the capture of several hundred horses, the Indians "were so animated" that they "foolishly kept up a continual fire for a whole day upon the Fort," with no result other than to run up their own casualties. John Norton called it an "ill concerted attack, the stockades being too high to climb over, and being unprovided with scaling ladders, they could only fire in at the loop holes on the enemy, whilst they were fully exposed to their aim from the Fort, and considerably annoyed by a blockhouse." The Indians made several attempts to capture the isolated blockhouse across the stream, where the dragoons had tried to rally, the strongpoint being manned by Corporal White and six privates. Captain Gibson had prudently stockpiled there a keg of cartridges and some sixty spare muskets, which White's men used liberally, giving the enemy "a warm reception" and maintaining their post against tremendous odds. It was later thought that "this small party destroyed more of the enemy than were killed from the fort."[9]

After the attackers had been beaten back by the fort's vigorous defense, Captain Gibson ordered his troops "to fire Deliberately least they should exaust their amunition in Vain." Restrained by no controlling authority, the warriors continued to fire at anything that moved, including all of the horses that remained tied close to the walls. Having blunted this initial attack with small-arms fire alone, Gibson now ran out his cannons and proceeded to fire solid shot, canister, and shells into the forest, though he admitted that it "seemed to take Little effect." While the artillery fire may not have inflicted many casualties, it had a tremendous psychological effect. Alder was still hiding behind his tree when he heard what he naively thought was the sound of artillery fire far behind him. He admitted, "I now began to feel pretty scared, as I thought we were surrounded." Then a cannon fired from the fort, followed by an explosion overhead and the screaming of shell fragments that struck all around him. Although willing to endure the musketry and rifle fire, Alder could not stand artillery rounds and fled back to the road. Had it not been for General Wayne's insistence that Gibson locate St. Clair's missing cannon, Alder might have witnessed an artillery duel at Fort Recovery. According to information later disclosed to Lieutenant Harrison by British officers, when the Indian army left Roche de Bout, it was accompanied by a sergeant, six artillerymen, and a number of horses loaded with fixed ammunition matching the caliber of those cannon previously hidden under logs and in the creek. During the battle, Indians turned over large numbers of logs as they unsuccessfully searched for the weapons they had left behind. General Wayne reported, "I therefore have reason to believe that the British and Indians depended much upon this artillery to assist in the reduction of that post; fortunately, they served in its defence."[10]

Defenders of the fort could see "a person of distinction" moving among the warriors at the wood's edge but out of normal rifle range. Several soldiers nevertheless fired without effect at this man, who was outfitted in "a three-cornered hat and plume and gay apparel." Finally, a Chickasaw shot at him with a double charge of powder, and the mysterious stranger disappeared, leaving behind his distinctive hat and plume. This gentleman appears to have been a Captain Beaubien, who was shot "thro' the body very near the Heart." A prisoner captured later asserted that one British officer had been wounded and was "carried on a bier several miles, but died of his wound." This would account for a discovery by American scouts of several biers discarded at Beaver Creek, one of which was "verry Elegantly made." Chickasaw and Choctaw scouts had seen "three British officers, who were dressed in scarlet, and appeared to be men of great distinction, from being surrounded by a large body of white men and Indians, who were very attentive to them." Among this crowd at "headquarters" was the notorious Simon Girty, whom James Neill, a captured packhorse driver, observed was "dressed and painted like other savages."[11]

One other singular event occurred during the day's fighting. An unknown number of Chickasaws and Choctaws somehow got into the rear of the Indians besieging the fort, either by sneaking out of a sally port or by having shadowed the enemy on their advance. These friendly Indians took advantage of the Chippewas and Ottawas by shooting into their backs while they fired at the blockhouses. These men of the Lake Nations promptly accused their allies, the Shawnees and the mysteriously delayed Delawares, of killing and scalping their warriors, arguing it was "impossible for so few men as was at the garrison, should kill so many of them." This was in addition to a statement by one mortally wounded chief who "declared with his dying breath, that he got his wound from a red man." An Indian prisoner taken after the battle believed that the various nations had "quarrelled much, and fired upon each other." Small parties of Wayne's Indian scouts hovered about the hostile Indian army, skirmishing whenever they sensed an advantage and creating confusion in the enemy ranks.[12]

After it became apparent that their onslaught had failed, Indian leaders held a council and decided to try a surprise attack later that night. Most of the army moved back about a mile and camped. After they had withdrawn and left only a few warriors to watch the fort, three soldiers brazenly ran out and scalped a dead warrior who had been killed by Dold about seventy yards from the post. While wandering about to locate his friends, Jonathan Alder caught one of the packhorses still running loose and, happy with his share of the plunder, lay down to sleep in one circular camp of about five hundred Indians. About midnight, Alder was startled awake by the crash of rifle fire as a second attack commenced, this one lasting about two hours. As with the previous assault, he learned that this one "hadn't accomplished anything, but had got a great many killed and wounded." Captain Gibson was writing a report of the day's battle to General Wayne when the midnight attack began and, after relating the defeat of McMahon's escort, advised him, "They are still round the Garrison giving & receiving shots & yells." Gibson confessed to having no idea of the enemy strength, although both Lieutenant Drake and Ensign Dold said there could not possibly be less than five hundred. After firing from the last sortie died down, the captain gave his written report of the affair to Corporal Thompson and Private Hunter, who had both volunteered to carry it through Indian lines and on another twenty-four miles to General Wayne at Fort Greeneville, the closest U.S. post. The pair departed on their dangerous journey under a heavy covering fire from the blockhouses. These intrepid messengers reached headquarters and delivered Gibson's dispatch on the afternoon of July 1, relaying the first concrete news of the Indian attack. Major Buell said that officers at Fort Greeneville had "heard the firing but did not know what it was" until the arrival of Thompson and Hunter, "a Circumstance which ought to signalize their Names," according to another member of the legion.[13]

The Indians spent that night, which was pitch black and foggy, using torches to scour the battlefield for dead and wounded, which occasionally prompted a shot from the garrison if the searchers happened to venture too close. All but ten bodies had been removed by dawn the next morning. The old chief who headed the Mingo camp announced that one warrior, who had shared their circle, was lying wounded under the walls of the fort. This injured companion must be brought off, "for it would be an everlasting shame and disgrace to the nation to let that man lie there and be massacred by the whites." A warrior named Big Turtle volunteered to lead a rescue party since he knew where the man could be found. The chief selected three others, including Alder, to assist, telling them: "Nary a one of you was out last night and have run no risk. Now go and fetch that man away." Big Turtle's party discovered their man lying in open ground within sixty yards of the fort and under the rifles of alert soldiers. The situation did not appear encouraging, but these four young men raced for their fallen comrade, dodging right and left to avoid the balls that seemed to "fly like hail." Reaching their goal, the rescuers stopped momentarily and grabbed either an arm or leg and sprinted swiftly back toward the trees, ignoring complaints from their writhing burden. Alder recalled, "As we moved on there was a perfect storm of bullets following us, whining by on the right and the left, cutting up the dirt on both sides of us." Big Turtle's thigh was grazed by a ball, the only wound among the party, although the men all had holes shot through their clothing. Their heroics were in vain, however, for Alder noticed the man's wound was in the intestines and had already started to turn green with mortification. He thought to himself, "we are four live men, risking our lives for one dead man."[14]

A few scattered warriors opened fire on the blockhouses on the morning of July 1, but there was no enthusiasm in their attack, and they faded back into the woods after Captain Gibson fired a few artillery rounds at them. At 8:00 A.M., he sent out a small party "to discover whether the Savages had Gone Off, or was waiting for an advantage." Isaac Paxton was with this scout that advanced into the woods in search of the enemy. He spotted several and had just raised his rifle to fire when he heard some of the fort's cannons fire off a few rounds. Assuming the post was again under attack, Paxton ran back to find that Gibson had recalled his search detail after spotting large formations recrossing the creek above and below his fort, firing a few shells to hurry them along. Three hours later, Gibson himself emerged from the gate with "as many men as the Garrison Could afford," sending out patrols to scout the area. By one o'clock, the captain had cautiously concluded that the enemy had retreated, carrying their dead on captured packhorses, and his soldiers began to collect the bodies of legion comrades and the scalps from dead Indians, "but with much Caution."[15]

After talking the matter over, the Lake Indians concluded that any commitment to the confederacy had been fulfilled and they could now freely return home with their scalps, prisoners, and horses. As strangers in this country south of their homeland, they could count on no provisions at Fort Recovery or at Grand Glaize on the return but must still rely on hunting for their food. Just as the army began to break up, word came that the Delawares were only a few miles off and would arrive within a couple of hours. The Lake Indians could not be stopped, but the remainder of the confederacy waited for the dilatory Delawares before deciding upon a course of future action. A council was held with the new arrivals, but with the combined army reduced to but five hundred warriors, nothing more could be done at Fort Recovery. Buckengales and his Delawares would watch Wayne's legion, with their scouts probing for weaknesses in his arrangements, but the remainder of the Indians would simply go home. When informed of the decision, Jonathan Alder went back to retrieve his captured packhorse, to which he had strapped all his possessions—a blanket and a brass kettle. But someone had allowed the animal to stray off in the woods, and there was no time to look for it, so Alder marched north, as if a metaphor for the entire Indian army, with only his rifle and the clothes on his back. Provisions remained scarce since the army's hunters had been very thorough in massacring game on the march south, so many Indians "killed and ate a number of pack horses in their encampment, the evening after the assault; also, at their next encampment, on their retreat, which was but seven miles from Fort Recovery." Evidence of these meals was discovered by Wayne's scouts.[16]

The Indians took along James Neill and two other contractor employees captured in the first few minutes of the fighting. Neill, a native of Nelson County, Kentucky, had been stripped of all his clothes and tied to a stump about a half mile from the fort. While thus confined, he watched as Simon Girty became enraged with another of the prisoners, an Irishman, whom he declared ought to be hanged for having worked for the Americans. Girty also boasted to Neill that he had personally scalped Captain Gibson, who was, however, still very much alive; Girty's actual victim was undoubtedly either Major McMahon or Captain Hartshorne. On the march north from Fort Recovery, Neill was twice prepared to be burnt alive, but for some unknown reason, the Indians changed their minds. After a tedious three-week journey, Neill and his captors reached Michilimackinac, where he was ransomed by Capt. William Doyle of the Twenty-Fourth Regiment, commandant of that post. Doyle gave him some food and a pass to Detroit, where Lieutenant Colonel England sent him on to Niagara. Lieutenant Governor Simcoe issued Neill another pass to proceed into U.S. territory and return home, presenting the astonished Kentuckian with eleven dollars to pay for expenses.[17]

After the Indians had moved out of sight and made no more demonstrations against his post, Alexander Gibson continued the gruesome task of recovering the legion dead and verifying the number of Indians killed. After completing a search of the battlefield for bodies, he was able to make a complete report of the casualties sustained in the attack on the convoy and the subsequent defense of Fort Recovery. Major McMahon, commanding the escort, was killed. In the dragoons, Cornet Torrey and eight privates were slain, while Captain Taylor, three noncommissioned officers, two musicians, and six privates were wounded. Casualties among the dragoon mounts were thirteen killed, thirteen wounded, and seventeen missing. In the ranks of the riflemen, Captain Hartshorne, Lieutenant Craig, one sergeant, and six privates were killed, while one noncommissioned officer and five privates were wounded. The garrison of Fort Recovery lost one private killed and Lieutenant Drake, three noncommissioned officers, and seven privates wounded. Of the contractor's employees, two were dead, one wounded, and three missing. Elliott and Williams lost heavily in horses, 46 being killed, 9 wounded, and 204 taken by the Indians. All thirty head of cattle taken out to graze had vanished.[18]

Before they departed, warriors of the Indian army had heard "a great groaning" from the wounded inside the fort. Surgeon's Mate Joseph Andrews certainly had his hands full, with thirty patients suffering from a variety of injuries. These included, among others, Captain Taylor's fractured vertebrae, Lieutenant Drake's wound in the groin, Pvt. William Gorman's gunshot wound through his left elbow, and Pvt. Samuel Neely's upper

thigh, shot through by a ball that just missed the bone. There were so many injured soldiers that Dr. Andrews felt compelled to ask for additional hospital stores. By July 2, the
burial details had found and interred seventeen soldiers, all that could be located on this
battlefield atop a battlefield. These men had made a chilling discovery when they came
to the remains of Captain Hartshorne. His body had been mutilated in the typical way,
but his killers "had put two leathern hearts into an incision they made in his breast, as
testimony that he had courage enough for two men." Hartshorne's sword was recovered
and presented to Captain Miller, a friend of the family from Middletown, Connecticut,
who wore it on one side and his own sword on the other throughout the ensuing campaign. Miller also carried two of Hartshorne's personal salt cellars in his saddlebags until
his return home, when he presented them, along with the sword, as mementos to the
grieving family.[19]

A few Indians fired upon the burial squads, prompting Captain Gibson to lead a
strong party into the forest's edge, where his soldiers spent a few minutes yelling and
waving, no doubt with many obscene words and gestures, urging the Indians to come out
and fight. The warriors, concealed in thick brush and timber, yelled back, but kept their
distance. Gibson's detachment held its ground while the dead were buried and the horse
carcasses dragged out into the woods. A few shells thrown at the enemy convinced them
that silence was more prudent than taunting the troops, and they remained quiet thereafter. At reveille that day, General Wayne dispatched Captain Brock with two companies and a party of Choctaws to carry forward much needed ammunition, artillery
rounds, cattle, hospital stores, and medicine to Fort Recovery. Brock's orders stated the
now "indispensible Necessity of being well guarded against surprise" and commanded his
detachment, if attacked, "to force their way at the point of the bayonet & by the superior force of their fire." It was Wayne's intention to "endow that Garrison with Ammunition & stores" before the enemy, "sore from the late action," could regroup and attack
again. Brock was not to reinforce the garrison but would return to Fort Greeneville after
delivering his shipment of supplies. Christopher Miller galloped forward with dispatches
so that he could join with Ensign Dold in following the Indian trails, which Wayne
hoped might "point out the best route to Auglaize."[20]

Indian losses out of the approximately fifteen hundred warriors in the battle at Fort
Recovery are hard to determine. One of the officers with Captain Elliott's party wrote
in his diary that three had been killed in the initial attack, while seventeen had been
killed besieging the fort, "and as many wounded." On July 5, Alexander McKee advised
officials in Detroit that the Indian army lost "16 or 17 men, besides a good many
wounded." Thomas Duggan of the British Indian Department had access to both written
reports and interviews with Indians heading home and declared that seventeen had been
killed "by the Garrison in attempting to Rush into the Fort after the pursued." Duggan
mistakenly passed along news that the Chickasaw chief Mountain Leader had been
killed, when it was actually Capt. Bobb Sallad, Piomingo being in Philadelphia at the
time. The Indians also claimed to have killed William Wells and William May, in addition to Captain Gibson and two other officers. Both Wells and May were still alive and

kicking, while the attackers had wrongly assumed that Major McMahon was Gibson. When the Chippewas returned to Michilimackinac, they told Captain Doyle that the Indian army had lost "twenty-five persons Among all The Nations who numbered fifteen Hundred." They confirmed that three-fourths of that total arrived after McMahon's escort had been repulsed and only participated in attacking the fort.[21]

David Zeisberger ran a mission on the Thames River east of Detroit and conversed with many of the Lake Indians as they returned home. An express passed through his settlement on July 9 with news of the battle, that "some twenty Indians perished, and one Frenchman also." Three days later, a band of Chippewas arrived and confirmed the earlier report but related that "thirty Indians had fallen, instead of twenty; how many whites, they knew not, except one." Another Chippewa war party came through on July 16 and informed Zeisberger that "forty Indians had died." On July 25, more warriors stopped, this party claiming "One hundred and thirty were killed in the battle, and many who were wounded have since died." By July 29, those straggling home said simply that "the Indians have lost many men." A Potawatomi warrior captured less than a month after the fight confessed that "the Indians carried off all their dead, except a few that lay too near the fort, in the course of the night after the Assault." He also claimed that the Chippewas and Ottawas, as well as the other nations, hid their dead after removal, "nor do they like to talk of them, nor let one nation know how many another had lost." These circumstances made an accurate count of Indian casualties virtually impossible. The Potawatomi captive, however, reckoned the death toll at nine Shawnees, six Potawatomis, ten Chippewas, two Wyandottes, and sixteen Ottawas, a total of forty-three warriors. Over the years, including time spent as an Indian agent, Williams Wells was told repeatedly that the Indian army had lost "between forty and fifty killed, and upwards of one hundred wounded, a number of whom died." In his opinion, "This was the severest blow I ever knew the Indians to receive from the whites." A British officer complained of the bungled attack, "I must observe with grief that the Indians had never it in their power to do more—and have done so little."[22]

Proud of the way his greatly outnumbered command had defended Fort Recovery and beaten off a determined foe, Captain Gibson issued the following garrison order:

> The commanding officer, feels happy in having the opportunity thus publicly to express his most grateful and sincere thanks to every non-commissioned officer and soldier of this garrison, and must do them the justice to say that they merit the highest applause for their attention to orders, their firmness and bravery on the 30th ult. by which he and his brother officers have acquired the highest approbation and most grateful thanks of the commander in chief.
>
> He wishes in a more particular manner, to return his thanks to the detachment under the command of Lieut. Drake, who sallied out of the garrison as volunteers, and so nobly sustained the charge of so powerful a body of savages, and when elated with every appearance of success, to the last extremity, covered and defended the retreating escort, by which means some officers and many brother soldiers were saved.

General Wayne sent Gibson a letter on July 3 that lamented the loss sustained on June 30, then continued:

> Permit me to communicate through you my most grateful thanks and highest approbation of the conduct of the escort and garrison at Fort Recovery; for their gallant defence of that important post, and compelling from one thousand to fifteen hundred ferocious savages, to retreat with slaughter and disgrace, from the same field, where they were proudly victorious on the 4th of November, 1791.
>
> Present my best compliments to those intrepid wounded officers, Captain Taylor of the dragoons, and Lieut. Drake of the infantry, and assure them of my anxious wishes for their safe and speedy recovery.
>
> You will also please to accept my best thanks for, and highest approbation of your own good and officer like conduct upon that trying occasion.

In his report of the affair to Secretary Knox, Wayne hailed Gibson as "the gallant defender of fort Recovery," but his greatest praise was reserved for the enlisted men. Joseph Fitzgerald, one Gibson's Virginia riflemen, was there when Wayne visited the fort a month after the battle. In a story that was passed down through his family for generations, Fitzgerald related how the general "rubbed the shoulders of every man, saying they were the 'bravest boys in the world.'"[23]

CHAPTER 20

Wayne Prepares to Advance North

NEWS OF THE ATTACK ON FORT RECOVERY spread quickly through the Ohio River settlements. A Fourth of July celebration at Cincinnati included a public toast, "The memory of Major McMahon and his gallant brethren in arms, who fell on the 30th ultimo, overpowered by an host of savages, and may the names of Hartshorn, Craig, and of Torry, never be forgotten." Notwithstanding this pall thrown over their observance, the country's birthday was celebrated "with becoming glee, by a joyous band of free hearts and willing spirits from the Army and the City." Captain Peirce's artillerists fired a salute at noon, and four hours later the officers and civilian dignitaries sat down to "a handsome and plentiful dinner" that featured "the juicy high flavored venison of the forest, and the delicious turtle of the Ohio." Participants called it a night at 8:00 P.M., following a series of fifteen toasts that were each accompanied by the booming of a cannon from the fort. In addition to the toast already noted, offerings included obligatory compliments to President Washington, Congress, cabinet officers and foreign ministers, and American women. Other messages with a military slant included tributes to General Wayne and his legion, the heads of the various staff departments—"may they feed well, physick well, pay well, cloath well and carry well"—and the Kentucky Volunteers. Another urged, "War with Britain, or speedy concessions," and the final sentiment, greeted with shouts and applause, suggested, "A mixture of Lake water with Kentucky whiskey, for the use of the Legion."[1]

The Fourth of July was ushered in at Fort Greeneville with a national salute of fifteen rounds fired from the artillery park. The entire legion assembled on its parade ground for an inspection and review by General Wayne, who appeared pleased and paid his troops "some very handsome compliments." To preserve order on this special holiday, the general had commanded that every sutler store and shop be closed for the day so that no alcohol would be sold in any form. Instead, he ordered the customary extra gill of whiskey be issued by the contractors "to every Non Commission'd Officer and Soldier upon the Occasion." That evening, Lt. Joseph Elliott put on a much anticipated pyrotechnic display of "sky rocketts, Cracker Serpants etc." This fireworks performance took on an unexpected dimension when one of the rockets set the laboratory on fire, threatening to blow up the legion's stockpile of artillery shells. Soldiers quickly started throwing buckets of water on the burning building, but several boxes filled with shells caught fire before the conflagration could be contained. Artillery officers, at "great risk" to their personal safety, raced inside the flaming laboratory, brought out the burning boxes, and removed the fuses, thereby averting potential disaster.[2]

Shortly after Lieutenant Elliott's impromptu fireworks display, that officer fell in a duel, being shot in the right side by a ball that passed through his body and lodged near the spine. Surgeon's Mate Charles Brown extracted the projectile, but Elliott complained that he still had "a great deal of pain." Surgeon John Scott probed the wound and discovered a piece of clothing that had been driven into Elliott's body by the bullet. After removing this source of infection, the lieutenant began to mend. In another affair of honor, Ens. Francis Johnston shot Lieutenant Purdy in the hip. These were not the first duels of 1794. That honor had gone to Lt. Hamilton Armstrong and Lieutenant Diven, who shot the former officer through the left side of the head, inflicting what was thought to be a mortal wound. Surgeon's Mate Joseph Strong described Armstrong's injury, saying, "The ball entered the cheek near the nose, passed out behind the ear." Strong was fed up with dueling, which he considered "but a miserable resource for the security of wounded honor. It makes wounds but does not heal them."[3]

The last duel at Fort Greeneville occurred between two dragoon officers and came about because of the fight at Fort Recovery. Lieutenant Dunn had his personal mount killed there by Indians, so after returning to Fort Greeneville, he selected as a replacement a public horse that had been ridden by the servant of Cornet Blue. Upset by Dunn's selection, on July 13, Blue requested him to give back the horse. Dunn politely remarked, "Mr. Blue if you had been so unfortunate as to lose your horse and my servant had a horse which suited you to ride you certainly should have him." Blue responded, "In this way you always take the advantage of rank and were I to take such satisfaction as I want you would arrest me." To this Dunn replied, "I will not, take what satisfaction you please." Blue immediately left and sent off a challenge to the lieutenant, who accepted. Dunn and Blue met on the morning of July 14, Lieutenant Covington being a second to the former and Cornet Posey to the latter. Dunn fell mortally wounded at the first fire and was carried back to his hut. As he lay on his deathbed, Dunn sent for his killer and, after gazing upon him for a few minutes, said weakly: "Mr. Blue, you see the distressed situation into which you have brought me, you have without foundation thought me to be your enemy. I now declare to you I was always your friend. You are a passionate young man, Mr. Blue, look on me and let it be a warning for you to govern your passion in future and I forgive you and wish that you may prosper hereafter." All of the officers attended Dunn's funeral, his death being "much lamented," and some even spoke openly of prosecuting Blue, who remained incommunicado in his hut. Major Buell wrote that for once, a duel had not been "in consequence of liquor," although the alleged slight to Cornet Blue "was a very trifling business."[4]

Unfortunately for the legion, disaffection among officers extended to the very highest ranks. On May 16 and 20, General Wilkinson dispatched complaints to Secretary Knox about the way Wayne had allegedly mistreated him. After showing these grievances to President Washington, Knox replied, "the circumstances of the difference of opinion and coolness between you and General Wayne causes great pain both to the breast of the President and mine." Both men were apprehensive "lest a dissension which appears from representations from the army to be by no means Secret should cause some violent injury to the Service." Relying upon Wilkinson's "patriotism," Knox explained that he could not go public with the general's grievances until they were "supported by well authenticated evidences" but vowed not to "shield any officer of whatever rank from any charge for military crimes." Wilkinson's letters no longer exist, so there is no way of knowing what military crimes he alleged Wayne had committed. At this point, Knox admitted, "All that I can do is to regret the disagreement which exists between two officers high in rank, and of whose experience and talents a favorable opinion is entertained."[5]

The rift between Wayne and Wilkinson was now common knowledge. After conversing with Charles Scott, Winthrop Sargent explained the embarrassing situation to Knox on July 23, just days before the campaign would finally begin: "I am very unhappy to find it generally known in this country that there is a Want of Harmony with Genl Wayne & Wilkinson—Scott spoke of it and lamented the same in a manner that evinced it no Secret." While in Cincinnati, Wilkinson called on Sargent, "spoke like a man very much disgusted with Service," and mentioned that he had asked for a court of inquiry into his conduct. While Wilkinson only hated Wayne, he despised General Scott, whom he portrayed as "a habitual Drunkard" and refused to even talk with his fellow Kentuckian. Sargent agreed that Scott "too often drinks to Excess," basing his conclusion on "Information of very respectable persons at the different Settlements upon the Ohio." But in justice to Scott, he informed Knox that during their last meeting, the general "was perfectly sober and collected." Given the rancor between Wilkinson and the two friends, Wayne and Scott, it was little wonder that an officer could cautiously predict "Success and good Fortune, provided no Discord should intervene to prevent it amongst Officers."[6]

As if to compound Wilkinson's discontent, two of his servants, Michael Moore and Joseph McCourtney, both soldiers in their mid-twenties from the First Sub-Legion, deserted from Fort Washington on the night of July 8. Moore had formerly worked for the late Maj. Ballard Smith before joining Wilkinson's "family." He was described as "a handsome, slim, genteel made fellow," somewhat of a dandy, and "an excellent barber and hair dresser." Moore liked to wear a beaver hat and could be identified by a bright red silk handkerchief that he often wore around his neck. McCourtney was tall, "rudely round shouldered," and frequently had sore eyes. Both men took rifles and were supposed to have descended the Ohio River toward Louisville. The worth of the pair to

Brig. Gen. James Wilkinson. From
Robert R. Jones, *Fort Washington at
Cincinnati*, 1902.

Wilkinson was evident in the rewards posted for their capture, forty dollars for the talented Moore and a standard ten dollars for McCourtney.[7]

General Wilkinson's misfortunes paled in comparison to those of Jonathan Cass. The major was a veteran of the Revolution who had enlisted the day after the Battle of Lexington and fought in nearly every major action in New York and New Jersey. Cass was described as "a fair representative of the substantial yeomanry of New England, who, struggling with the disadvantages of straitened circumstances, and of a very limited education, by the power of intellect and force of character, added to virtuous principles, attain for themselves, by unceasing exertion, an honorable position in life, and only rest from their work until they rest in the grave." Cass had a commanding appearance, being six feet tall, "of perfect form, without superfluous flesh, black hair and piercing black eyes, and commanding brow." Shortly after reaching the frontier, while out reconnoitering, "his horse, in jumping over the trunk of a prostrate tree, fell, and in coming down fell upon and broke one of Major Cass's legs below the knee." Dr. Strong had the major under his "constant attention for three months in order to prevent mortification" and considered his patient to be "the most troublesome case I ever took unto my care." But

Cass's injured leg, because of "bad surgery," never healed properly and "required daily dressing for about thirty-five years, and was painful all that period."[8]

Aware of the fragility of human life, many soldiers made out their wills while they waited for the campaign to begin, often naming comrades as beneficiaries for their meager estates. Cpl. James Devine made out his will at Fort Washington, naming Sgt. Samuel Perkins as sole heir. Sgt. Tunis Voorhees listed two heirs, Surgeon's Mate Strong and Pvt. William Higginson of MisCampbell's troop. When MisCampbell made out his own will, he included the following bequest: "My Silver Hilted Sword I give to my beloved friend Capt. Soln. Van Rensselaer in confidence that he will never disgrace it." General Wayne also composed a will, his witnesses being Quartermaster General O'Hara and two aides-de-camp, Thomas Lewis and Henry DeButts. His stated reason for so doing was "the certainty of death and the probability that that event is not far distant, from the awful and solem interview now on the point of taking place between this Army and the Hostile Savages of the West." His property was listed as the landed estate of Waynesborough, a lot in Harrisburg, a lot and house in Philadelphia, fifteen hundred acres of land in western Pennsylvania, another fifteen hundred acres in Georgia, and a large landed estate in Nova Scotia. Upon his death, Wayne's property was to pass to his son, Isaac, and daughter, Margaretta.[9]

Following a general review of the legion on July 13, Wayne called all of his officers together and advised them to make ready for a campaign "at a moment's warning." He said that they might "go to-morrow or next day or perhaps it may be a week, but at any rate we shall go on a campaign soon." There was much to do. The quartermaster passed out ten axes to each company for use in road cutting and fort building. Tents were issued in the proportion of two for the line officers and one for every eight enlisted men, three horses being furnished to transport each company's load. All "heavy and Useless Baggage" was deposited in the citadel, soldiers taking only "what is indispensibly Necessary such as their Uniforms and summer clothing, Blankets, Knapsacks, which must be compressed into the smallest Compass Possible for the ease of the Men in Marching thro' the Woods & Brush." Officers were to outfit themselves as nearly as possible "in the same Uniform, Hats and Caps with the soldiers belonging to their respective Corps." All officers in command of rifle, infantry, and light infantry companies were to carry espontoons instead of firearms because Wayne felt "that an Officer who attempts to fire at an Enemy in time of Action, can not perform his Duty, or Pay proper attention to his Command." Women would be allowed to accompany the legion, but those with children were "positively forbidden from advancing." Detailed instructions for marching, signaling, camping, and forming for battle were published. To assist with staff work, Wayne appointed Capt. Thomas Lewis an extra aide-de-camp and Lt. Campbell Smith the permanent judge advocate general of the legion.[10]

Officers and soldiers of the legion were anxious for the campaign to begin. William Wells, Ensign Dold, and Christopher Miller had reconnoitered the Indian trails leading north from Fort Recovery and determined that the best route to Beaver Creek was "the trail made by the Savages on their retreat." The tone of affairs at Fort Greeneville was captured in a hurried letter written on July 14: "The General's dispatches just going off, I have only to acquaint you with our vigorous measures for a campaign, which, we fondly flatter ourselves, will be conducted to the fullest satisfaction of the Union; at least I will dare to pronounce this much, no officers have ever exerted themselves with more assiduity and pains, from our faithful commander down to the lowest grade, with very few exceptions. Should we be victorious, I promise myself the felicity of being with you and our mutual friends on or about Christmas." Daniel Bradley wrote in his journal, "time only will determine our fate." His main concern was that the Kentucky Volunteers would not come forward in large numbers for the campaign, making him "fear the consequences." In his opinion, should the understrength legion advance with only minimal assistance from the Kentuckians, following any subsequent failure, "the blood will rest at the doors of Congress."[11]

Captain Bradley need not have worried. Gen. Charles Scott's Kentuckians were coming back for another attempt at the Indians. Scott had been appointed a major general of the Kentucky Volunteers by the War Department on May 14, 1794. Three days later, Secretary Knox ordered him to raise two thousand mounted volunteers, organized into six battalions of four companies each, privates to be paid $1.00 per day and captains to receive $1.835 per day, with other ranks in due proportion. Each battalion would be commanded by a major, making him subordinate to commandants of the four sublegions. As in 1793, Scott's force would be divided into two brigades, Gen. Robert Todd commanding the battalions raised on the north side of the Kentucky River, and Gen. Thomas Barbee those from south of that river.[12]

Many of the volunteers who had served in 1793 were back for revenge on Indians who had claimed the lives of close family members over the years. Maj. William Russell of Todd's brigade was one such man, his brother Henry having been killed in 1773. Born on March 6, 1758, in Culpeper County, Virginia, Russell was pursuing Indian raiders with Daniel Boone at such a young age that comrades had to carry his share of the provisions and baggage. Although but a youth, he served as a lieutenant during the Revolution, leading a mounted company at King's Mountain and fighting at Whitsell's Mills and Guilford Court House. Following the war, Russell moved to Fayette County, Kentucky, where he had received one thousand acres from his father, who had inherited the military tract from one of William's uncles. Situated about six miles from Lexington along the Elkhorn River, Russell's land contained a cave from which flowed a large spring. He built a large house, which had "a picturesque and rather romantic view," on an elevation near this spot and called his home Mount Brilliant, a "most attractive place" that was "famous in those days for its generous and elegant hospitality." William Russell married Nancy Price on Christmas Day, 1786, and the couple would eventually have sixteen children. He served in both the Virginia and Kentucky legislatures and accompanied Scott and Wilkinson on their mounted raids against the Eel River Nation, becoming the type of officer that Kentuckians liked to follow.[13]

Maj. Aquilla Whitaker, one of General Barbee's battalion commanders, was born in Baltimore County, Maryland, in 1755 and first visited Kentucky twenty years later. He brought his family to Sullivan's Station, near the Falls of the Ohio, in 1779 but moved to Shelby County in 1783. A brother, John Whitaker, was killed by Indians while clearing ground for his home near the county seat. Aquilla took advantage of every attempt to avenge John's death by joining a number of expeditions against marauding Indians, including one in 1781 that almost resulted in his own death. A party of warriors had invaded Jefferson County, and Whitaker raised a company of fifteen men to pursue them. The whites followed their quarry to the Falls of the Ohio but were surprised by the Indians as they crossed the river. A furious fight, "one of the most desperate conflicts fought in the early days of the State," ensued, and the Indians retreated after losing over twenty of their number. Nine of the fifteen men in the pursuing party had been killed or wounded in the bloody encounter. Whitaker was described as "a man of medium stature; possessed great strength and energy; was a bold and daring leader; possessed a high degree of military skill; was characterized for sound judgment and great integrity; was fond of adventure and solitude." He was twice married and fathered a total of eighteen children.[14]

Among Whitaker's captains was Bland Ballard, who was born on October 16, 1761, near Fredericksburg, Virginia. He came to Shelby County, Kentucky, in 1779 and joined many of the raids against Indian towns, being severely wounded during George Rogers Clark's attack on the Piqua towns in 1780. On March 31, 1788, a party of almost two dozen Delawares attacked the Ballard family cabin at Tick Creek. His sixteen-year-old brother, John, was the first to fall, being killed about daybreak near the woodpile. Bland came running with his rifle from nearby Tyler's Station and "treed in such a position so as to guard the front door of his father's house." While some Indians began firing at Bland, others went around behind the house, knocked out the chinking between the logs, and fired at those inside. They shot Mr. Ballard, who killed at least one attacker before dying. Mrs. Ballard, Bland's stepmother, ran from the cabin as the Delawares burst through the back door. She was overtaken and tomahawked in the yard. Elizabeth, aged one, was killed inside the cabin, and her sister, Thersia, aged two, was struck down and thrown into a puddle outside. Warriors dragged the wounded fourteen-year-old Benjamin about seventy yards, with the apparent intention of taking him captive, but his struggles prompted the Indians to kill him as well. As his family was tomahawked and scalped one by one, Bland Ballard continued to load and fire, killing or mortally wounding six of the attackers before they fled, a number that was later confirmed by two white prisoners. Miraculously, little Thersia still had signs of life; Bland "stitched up her wounds on the head and face," and the girl survived her brush with death. Ever after, Ballard considered Indians to be "a faithless treacherous race and the enemy of his own" and felt no sympathy over their extinction. When asked how many Indians he had killed in any one day during his illustrious career, Ballard would always refer to this episode and remark, "I killed six one morning before breakfast, & not a very good morning for the business."[15]

Simon Kenton, one of Kentucky's most famous Indian fighters, did not join this latest expedition, although he had received a captain's commission. When Joshua Baker was appointed his lieutenant, Kenton refused to serve with the man and simply decided to stay home. Baker was elevated to captain and William Sudduth appointed lieutenant, with Michael Cassidy as ensign of the company. Like so many other Kentuckians, Sudduth had lost a relative to marauding Indians, a brother, Ezekiel, who had been murdered at Hood's Station. William had been born on November 25, 1765, in Fauquier County, Virginia, the son of John and Anne Sudduth, whom he remembered as "reputable, but not wealthy." The Revolution interrupted his schooling, which during his first eighteen years consisted of but ten months of formal education and "ten days to learn Surveying." Sudduth reached Kentucky in 1785 and quickly became a great hunter, later recalling that within nine months of his arrival, he "had killed Sixty Buffaloe beside deer, bear, elk & turkees." When General Scott called for volunteers in 1794, Sudduth quickly raised an independent company but was informed that only authorized units would be accepted for service. After discharging his recruits, Sudduth received a lieutenant's commission and raised most of Baker's company.[16]

Michael Cassidy, Captain Baker's ensign, was born in Dublin, Ireland, on October 22, 1755, but left for America in 1767 after a dispute with his family over money. He worked as a cabin boy on the *Maryland Merchant*, and the captain apprenticed him to a merchant in Baltimore. Cassidy fought in the Revolution, then migrated to Mason County, Kentucky, where he established a station bearing his name. His personal appearance was described as "peculiar," for he was "very low of stature, measuring only five feet three inches, and yet heavy enough to weigh one hundred and seventy pounds." This unusual body shape may have saved his life on one occasion. In October 1785, Cassidy and two companions camped along Plum Lick Creek while en route to the Blue Licks. They were surprised by Indians, who quickly killed the other two, saving the pint-sized Cassidy, whom they took to be a boy, for the smallest warrior to butcher. But the peculiarly shaped Irishman "did not propose to be led like a lamb to the slaughter" and fought back vigorously until clubbed to the ground by other Indians. When his hand happened to clutch onto a knife, he sprang up and brandished it so wickedly that his attackers backed off momentarily. Cassidy instantly "darted like a deer into the deep woods and made his escape," carrying scars from this encounter to his grave. He also carried emotional scars from the killing of a man named Stuart. Hearing a gunshot one evening outside his settlement, Cassidy grabbed his rifle and raced toward the sound. Stuart, who was dressed like an Indian and had fired at an owl, saw Cassidy coming and hid behind a tree. When Stuart raised his head to identify himself, Cassidy shot him through the forehead and forever considered that to be "the most regretful act of his life."[17]

Volunteers, including such old hands as Zachariah Holliday and Garret Burns, began to come forward during the first days of July, and companies and battalions hurried to Georgetown, Kentucky, where they were mustered into federal service by Captain Butler, Lt. Isaac Younghusband, and Ens. Richard Chandler. Each man was supposed to receive fifteen dollars as an advance payment, although Butler had nothing but large-denomination bank bills to offer them, causing "a great deal of firing and disorder." Many men refused to sign up unless Butler promised that, upon their return, at least a portion of the pay should be in specie. As soon as they had been mustered and paid, units were sent north to the Ohio River, where boats waited to ferry horses and men across to Cincinnati. This mustering process concluded on July 15, when General Scott confessed that he had once again fallen short of his recruiting goal. Instead of two thousand mounted volunteers, he would be joining the legion with but sixteen hundred, the short-fall being blamed on the demand for farm laborers and a general unwillingness to accept U.S. currency. Nevertheless, Scott bragged about his new command, claiming that "there was Never Seen so fine a Set of Men together well armd & well Equiped in every point of view." The first volunteers were scheduled to reach Fort Washington on July 17, and the rear three days later, many officers wagering whether General Scott could actually have one thousand men across the river on the latter date. William Price's battalion was the first to arrive and started north on July 18 as an escort to a convoy of packhorses and a herd of cattle. Wayne ordered General Todd to follow with the remainder of his brigade, accompanying stores and rations that the quartermaster and contractor had stockpiled at Fort Washington and "taking every possible precaution to guard against accident or surprise." Although the Indians were still "sore from their late defeat" at Fort Recovery and would probably not molest a well-guarded convoy, Wayne still feared that "they possibly may make some attempt upon our escorts if they should find them neg-ligent or off their Guard."[18]

Major Russell's battalion camped temporarily at Mill Creek, and when Maj. Not-ley Conn's companies arrived, he was told to find a campsite within four or five miles of Cincinnati and to let General Todd know "where to find you in case I shall want to give any instructions." On July 20, enough men from Barbee's brigade had crossed the Ohio River to allow those who had wagered one thousand men would be across by that evening to collect their winnings. Except for Conn's battalion, all of the Kentuckians remaining in the Cincinnati vicinity marched for Fort Greeneville on the afternoon on July 21. In response to a summons from Wayne, General Scott galloped ahead to a conference at headquarters, accompanied by the companies of Capts. Daniel Barbee and John Arnold. Before he left, General Scott conferred with Sargent and bragged that he had assembled eighteen hundred troops who were all "damn'd fighting Fellows" and without doubt "the best Party that ever came out of Kentucky." Sargent's personal observation seemed to discount Scott's contentions. He saw "not quite 1700" volunteers, "the greater Part well armed and mounted" but thought there were "too many old men and Boys and too great a proportion of meager Garrans [broken down horses] for long march & arduous Enter-prise." Besides their questionable appearance, discipline was lacking, and Sargent reported that for several days, "they have rioted in this Town." Whether they were "damn'd fighting Fellows" or "old men and Boys," each of these Kentucky men had some personal reason to fight Indians. For Nathaniel Hart, aide to General Barbee, it was a dis-turbing memory of his youth. Hart's father had been killed by Indians in 1782, so he accompanied his mother in January 1783 when she went to Logan's Station to authenti-cate her husband's will. There he found that "Twenty-three (23) widows were in atten-dance upon the court—to obtain letters of administration on the estates of their husbands, who had been killed during the past year." This number did not include many more men from that particular county who had been killed "leaving no estate which required administration."[19]

General Todd's brigade reached Fort Greeneville on July 25 and camped in the prairie, Barbee's brigade remaining at Fort Hamilton to escort another large convoy of stores. Orders stated that brush was to be cleared about the volunteer camp for a space of "at least 20 feet," horses were to be tied up at night to stakes driven into the ground, and all bells to be stopped. No guns were to be fired in or near the campground unless at an Indian, "under pain of Receiving ten lashes without the priviledg of a Cort marshall." General Scott ordered Major Price to assemble a select corps of guides and spies, subject only to the orders of himself or General Wayne, the major selecting the companies of Joshua Baker and John Arnold for that duty. Although only two battalions and two companies of volunteers had reached Fort Greeneville, the Kentuckians prepared to march in eight columns, separate from the legion, with orders given by bugle calls. As for the legion, the infantry would march in a series of parallel columns, protecting the wagons, supplies, packhorses, and artillery, the main body being screened by successive circles of dragoons, light infantry, and riflemen.[20]

Wayne had selected Major Buell to be commandant of Fort Greeneville and oversee affairs at Fort Jefferson. Buell's garrison consisted of Capt. John Sullivan and Lts. William Diven, Peter Shoemaker, and John Michael, along with Capt. James Taylor, who was still suffering from the wound inflicted at Fort Recovery. The major also had under his charge 520 legion troops, twelve Kentuckians too sick to march, seventy-three women, twenty-three children, thirty Choctaws, and seven Indian prisoners. Buell's orders for the security of Fort Greeneville were very specific. There would be guards constantly in the four bastions and the four blockhouses of the citadel. Small guard details were also to watch over the ovens and stockpiled hay, both outside the stockade. The main gates were to be kept "bolted & locked, from Sun set at night until sun rising in the morning," opening in daytime only for the entrance or exit of convoys and escorts. Normal in-and-out traffic was to use the sally port next to the stream. At night, sentinels were instructed "to cry out with an Audible *All's Well* in order to keep them from sleeping & to make them vigilant." Above all else, General Wayne warned Buell that he was to defend Fort Greeneville "to the last extremity at every expence of blood & as long as you have one man capable of discharging a Musket or Gun."[21]

As the legion engaged in the hustle and bustle of packing and drawing provisions for its long-delayed campaign, Eaton's Vermont company received a new commander. Capt. Maxwell Bines, a Pennsylvania veteran of St. Clair's campaign, was ordered on July 24 to turn over Fort Jefferson to his successor and take command of the Green Mountain Boys. Much had changed since the company had left its rendezvous at Bennington. Lieutenant Underhill and Ensign Hyde were still with the legion at Fort Greeneville, but the latter had finally lost the judge advocate general post to Lieutenant Smith. A few of the enlisted men had died, several had been killed and wounded in the skirmish near Fort Recovery, and some had deserted, but the bulk of the company remained. News from their home state must have made them eager for a fight with the

British and their Indian allies. In mid-June, a British deserter had crossed into Vermont and began work for a farmer at Hungerford. A sergeant and a squad of redcoats, all under arms, came in pursuit of the deserter, took him into custody, and attempted to return to Canada. They were overtaken by the farmer and his neighbors, who said the man could not be taken by force. Encouraged by this show of support, the deserter broke free and ran off. The soldiers "levelled their pieces at him; but being threatened with instant death if they broke the peace by persisting, they declined firing." A peace officer placed the British soldiers under arrest "for breach of peace," and they were taken to Burlington for trial. There was much discussion over whether the soldiers should be tried by a civilian or military court, but the dispute ended when these invaders of Vermont's sovereign territory jumped bail and disappeared north of the border. Vermonters sang about their single-handed victory over the British army:

> Sing Yankee doodle, 'twill go on,
> 　　Green Mountain boys are handy;
> Blood and wounds—the war's begun,
> 　　Sing Yankee doodle dandy.

It was reported that the British then turned to Indian bounty hunters, who were promised the equivalent of ten dollars for every deserter from their army who could be recaptured.[22]

A gentleman in Burlington pointed out that Green Mountain residents cared little for the "arrogance, haughtiness and impudence" of their northern neighbors and boasted that "no men ever would enter into a war with more cheerfulness and spirit than the Vermonters would against them, if the policy of the Union would admit of it and a call was given." It was common knowledge that the British encouraged and equipped the Indians against the legion "as far as they can possibly go without making it so notorious as to be accountable." Officers openly boasted in Montreal coffeehouses that the commandant at Detroit had often paid the royal bounty for American scalps. It was enough for one writer to "damn the whole British government." Amid all this tumult, William Eaton, who had raised Vermont's only company in the legion, now commanded the recruiting depot at Springfield, Massachusetts, where he advertised for "young men accustomed to the use of fire arms." As part of his plea for volunteers, Eaton urged them to "put on the arms and uniform of the Federal Legion; drive out or reduce to peace those blood crested agents and allies of British barbarity," and "possess the country for an everlasting inheritance." In a prelude to the manifest destiny that would sweep the country half a century later, Eaton concluded his appeal: "Be strong and of good courage; fear not nor be afraid of them; and the Lord your God will drive them far out of your sight—from the wilderness, and this DETROIT, even unto the great river, the river MISSISSIPPI—and unto the great sea, towards the going down of the sun, it shall be your coast."[23]

CHAPTER 21

The Campaign Begins

SOMETIME BETWEEN SEVEN AND EIGHT o'clock in the morning of July 28, a single cannon fired from the east bastion of Fort Greeneville, announcing the commencement of General Wayne's campaign to determine the destiny of the Northwest Territory. His troops had already been waiting an hour for the signal gun, which prompted "the Drums, Trumpets, Fifes, &c. strike up the forward Move." After describing the moment, one soldier wrote: "Greenville adieu! Many anxious and tedious Hours shall pass e'er I visit you again." Wayne's force consisted of approximately two thousand soldiers of the legion and 720 mounted volunteers, at least eight hundred Kentuckians having been left behind to escort convoys. Brigadier General Wilkinson led the legion's right wing, the First and Third Sub-Legions, and Lieutenant Colonel Hamtramck commanded the left wing, the Second and Fourth Sub-Legions.[1]

The first two or three miles of the route was "choked up with Bushes" and "closely timbered covered with undergrowth." As the march continued, the soil turned "deep and swampy," with men trudging through mud up to their ankles. Lt. John Bowyer noticed that the weather was "extremely warm" and water in the small creeks tasted "very bad." The movement was a shambles from the beginning. Dragoons, outfitted in "boots, spurs, and Sabres," led their horses, which were heavily laden with six days' rations of corn, through "prickly-ash thicketts, fern bottoms, and deep swamps." As the dragoons from the right struggled to keep up, Lt. John Webb noticed that Captain Springer's light infantrymen had fallen even farther behind. General Wayne, who marched in a road, "cleared and free from all impediments," saw no reason to adjust the pace, except for a few short halts. After having gone eight miles, the column stopped for an hour at noon, then went another three miles and crossed Stillwater Creek, "a small muddy Creek" some forty feet in width, and finally halted at 2:00 P.M. Troops were spread out over a mile to the rear and straggled into camp during the next hour, but the baggage did not arrive until about six o'clock. Two companies from the left wing had become lost for several hours before regaining their bearings. This first day's march was a fiasco. Captain Mis-Campbell complained that "a Board of the ablest officers in Europe or in the world, were they employed for the purpose, could not have designated an order of March more absurd feeble and defenceless." Wilkinson said disgustedly, "1000 Indians might have approached our right flank, within half a mile, undiscovered." According to Wayne's orders, the legion fortified its Stillwater camp with a log breastwork "abt. 600 yards Square," the volunteers setting up their own camp. Cattle were penned inside with the troops, an arrangement, which in case of attack, would undoubtedly "create much confusion."[2]

On the morning of July 29, reveille sounded an hour before daylight, the breastworks were manned, and soldiers stayed under arms until there was light enough for roll call. When the camp first began to stir, dragoons, packhorse drivers, and wagoners fed, watered, saddled, and harnessed their animals. Immediately thereafter, thirty minutes was allowed for striking, packing, and loading the tents and other baggage. The legion resumed its march at 5:00 A.M., hurrying forward as if in pursuit of a routed enemy through another "bright and hot" day with only one twenty-minute halt. Lieutenant Clark saw that for a second day, "the Dragoons & Light Troops Sust'd considerable fatigue & Injury from the thickness of the Woods, and Brush thro which they passed on the Flanks." The baggage again lagged miles behind the main column, and seemingly everyone complained of the rapid pace set by General Wayne. Quartermaster James O'Hara observed that "the transport of his department would be destroyed by the pre-cipitancy of the March," and indeed, several horses did die on the road. General Scott thought "it would never do to march in such order," while Major Hughes, commanding the First Sub-Legion, reported his men were so fatigued that he encountered "great dif-ficulty to prevent their falling out of the line." Even Captain Wells found fault with the march, saying that, if it were not modified, "we shall be most undoubtedly whipped." To all this criticism, some to his face and some behind his back, Wayne only laughed and bragged that "it was the shortest march he had ever made."[3]

Wayne's force reached Fort Recovery that afternoon after covering about thirteen miles, and Captain Gibson greeted the general with a salute of fifteen rounds from can-nons in the south and east blockhouses. The legion crossed the Wabash River and camped less than a mile beyond the post on ground occupied by the Indians during the battle. Finally reaching the site where St. Clair's army had fallen as "an unhappy Sacri-fice to Savage Fury," one soldier confessed, "it animates us with additional Desires of being revenged" and "leaves no Doubt of Victory whenever the Enemy will give us an Opportunity of trying the Issue." Gibson's rifle company and Bissell's infantry company, now under Ensign Daingerfield, which had together successfully defended Fort Recovery, were now ordered to join their proper battalions for the march north. Lieutenant Drake, although still suffering from his wound in the groin, was appointed commandant of the post, Lieutenant Visscher being second in command. The new garrison would consist of two sergeants, two corporals, and thirty-two privates, one-half to be furnished from each wing of the legion. After lauding "the prudent & gallant conduct" of Gibson, Wayne gave Drake his instructions: "The utmost vigilance & precaution will be necessary for the safety & good government of this Fort; and discipline & cleanliness absolutely essential to the good order & health of the troops now committed to your charge."[4]

About two in the morning, sentinels in the volunteer camp claimed to have fired at and been fired upon by skulking Indians, alarms that caused the legion and Kentuckians to man their breastworks most of the night, thus leaving little time for sleep since the march resumed at 5:00 A.M. on July 30. As Wayne's force left Fort Recovery behind and started into the wilderness, one enlisted man sent up a silent prayer, "May an all-wise Director inspire this Legion with Strength and Power, to do Justice to themselves, their Country and their deceased Friends, a Recollection of whose dying Groans calls on and bids us be steady, brave and undaunted." Lieutenant Clark remembered, "We proceeded with usial Velocity Through Thickets almost impervious thro Marassies, Defiles & beads of Netles more than waist high & miles in length & on the left flank crossed the water course on Which F. Recovery Stands, more than one dozen times." The weather was still hot, and Lieutenant Bowyer noticed there was "no water except in ponds, which nothing but excessive thirst would induce us to drink." There was no running water to be found, but the wet soil had been the breeding ground for huge mosquitoes, which now attacked every square inch of exposed skin. Pioneers, two soldiers detached from each battalion company and overseen by Ens. Thomas Swaine, had to cut the road beyond Fort Recovery, so this march was consequently slower and much more orderly, with frequent halts when the columns would catch up to the ax men. General Wayne was often with the advance parties, either encouraging the pioneers in their labor or imprudently riding ahead of the advance guard with his staff to reconnoiter. After a march of eleven miles, the legion reached Beaver Creek about 3:00 P.M. The stream seemed to have no current and "was full of grass and mud, the banks being so swampy that the pack horses and wagons could not pass," so Wayne decided to bridge the creek the following day. As the legion settled into its nightly camp, scouts brought an unwelcome report that there was no potable water for at least the next twelve miles.[5]

July 31 was spent in "building a bridge over the Bog." A fatigue party of two officers and fifty-two enlisted men began work at daylight under the immediate supervision of Quartermaster O'Hara. Taking advantage of the delay, Wayne sent Lt. Samuel Vance with one hundred ax men, guarded by 120 Kentuckians, across Beaver Creek to begin clearing a road toward the Saint Marys River. There they were to await the arrival of the legion surveyors, Daniel Cooper and Robert Newman. The hope was that O'Hara's bridge would be completed in about three hours, so the main force could catch up to Vance's pioneers that afternoon, but that estimate proved overly optimistic. The reality was that the bridge proved to be "a Difficulty almost insurmountable, as the Creek is a wide and deep Water, the Bottom of which is a perfect Mud." When completed, the bridge over Beaver Creek measured fourteen feet wide and three hundred feet long, the construction of which took ten hours. Through an oversight, Captain Miller's guard detachment had not been sent forward to reinforce Vance, so the pioneers, Kentuckians, and a party of Captain Kibbey's scouts, isolated miles in advance of the legion, constructed a small breastwork to protect themselves overnight. Wayne's orders explicitly stated that this advance detachment was to defend its encampment while there remained "one man capable of receiving an enemy upon the point of his bayonet or discharging his piece."[6]

The legion marched across the new bridge at 5:00 A.M. on August 1, "with Lettle confusion," and covered about nine miles through "low flat Grounds, thick woods & Much underBrush." Once again, there was only foul-tasting surface water to drink. Unknown to Wayne and his soldiers, they had entered a region that would later be designated the Black Swamp, an area that encompassed the Maumee River basin. This gloomy, silent region was so heavily forested that its dense foliage completely blocked the sun's rays for miles at a time. The topsoil was about one foot thick and "composed of a black, decayed vegetable matter" that was extremely fertile. But because of this rotting vegetation, the water contained sulfur compounds that made it taste terrible (although later settlers found it to be an excellent laxative). One of the first surveyors in the Black Swamp made the following observations: "*Water!—water!—water!—tall timber!—deep water!—not a blade of grass growing, nor a bird to be seen.*" Early residents of the Black Swamp liked to brag that they could grow two crops on their land each year. When incredulous newcomers asked how that could be possible, they responded with a laugh, "One of ice, and the other of *frogs!*"[7]

After a march of about nine miles, with no real impediment except for "two or three small Swamps," the legion caught up with Lieutenant Vance's pioneers, who had stopped at an "excellent spring" on the edge of a large open prairie. General Wayne called a halt so that everyone could enjoy some water that was actually fit to drink. About half past twelve, the legion re-formed and marched out from the never-ending canopy of leaves into bright sunlight. Lieutenant Clark tried to capture the moment, writing, "we immurged Suddenly, into an open extensive and bountiful Plaine or Pararie which affords an ellegent Seenery, handsomly intersperced with Small Copse of Trees & abounding in every Species of the Greatest Variety of Herbage." The generals rode into the prairie and watched the men march through this luxuriant "Garden-Spot," which was about two miles wide and stretched an estimated eighteen miles east and west. Lieutenant Bowyer called it "the largest and most beautiful prairie I ever beheld," and Francis Jones, General Scott's aide, described the tract as "well cloathed with Grass and interspersd with delightfull Clumps of Trees much superior to anything of the Kind I ever seen before." The joy of again marching in sunlight was tempered by "the entence heat of the Sun," which made the passage "not a little fatiguing." In the middle of this opening, the legion crossed the track made by General Harmar's army in 1790 when on its way to the Miami villages, an ominous reminder of hard work yet to come.[8]

Just beyond this marvelous prairie was the Saint Marys River, "In General a small muddy stream, but at this Place it is near ninety Feet wide." The legion crossed to the north bank, erected a breastwork "in an almost impervious thickett of Brambles, shrubs and small growth," and set up camp while the Kentuckians encamped on the south bank. General Wayne had determined to build a small fort at this point, so he, Lieutenant Colonel Hamtramck, and Captain MisCampbell began to scout about for the best location. Deciding that this new post should be constructed on the south bank of the river, Wayne ordered General Scott to shift his Kentuckians about a half mile downstream. At 4:00 P.M., after the camp had been fortified, Wayne had the legion pack up, recross the Saint Marys, and due to the lateness of the hour, bivouac in two lines parallel with the river. Light infantry and rifle companies established their camps as a screen to protect the main body. Despite this unexpected move, there was still light enough for some men to bathe and catch a few fish before going to sleep. Francis Jones spent the last few hours of daylight examining the remains of an old Indian town that stood near the Kentucky camp. Although the cabins were but mere ruins, there were still large fields of corn. But based on the size of the undergrowth, Jones estimated that the region had not been inhabited for ten to fifteen years.[9]

On this afternoon, General Wilkinson took offense when Wayne issued some orders to his sub-legionary quartermasters rather than give them to the wing commander as he technically should have done. Wilkinson considered the result to be such a confusion "as was never before experienced by military men," obviously an exaggerated overstatement considering the long history of military campaigns. Acknowledging his *"personal dislike"* of Wayne, Wilkinson felt that the legion commander consequently suspected him "of entertaining a disposition & wishes adverse to all his actions." Given the many negative comments in Wilkinson's journal, Wayne's assessment of his subordinate now seems to have been quite correct. Jacob Burnet, a civilian who was on cordial terms with both generals, remarked that Wilkinson's state of mind "predisposed him to pursue an unfriendly course towards General Wayne, and to avail himself of every opportunity to diminish the respect and confidence in him, which military officers ought always to feel towards their Commander-in-chief." Burnet portrayed Wilkinson as having a public deportment that was "easy and graceful," while he "manifested great suavity of manners." Wayne, however, "though an accomplished, well educated gentleman, possessed a firmness, decision, and bluntness of character, which, at times, had the appearance of roughness, if not rudeness, and occasionally gave offence." The two were completely incompatible. Wilkinson's polished nature could not hide his treachery from Wayne, who treated his rival as the scoundrel he truly was. This contentious situation was perhaps best described by Lt. Hugh Brady: "Wilkinson was jealous of W. could not be second and was worth nothing when he got to be first."[10]

As the feud between Wayne and Wilkinson simmered, disaster struck. Robert Newman, one of the surveyors hired by General O'Hara to mark the legion's route, disappeared under mysterious circumstances. After surveying a portion of the road cut by Lieutenant Vance's pioneers, Newman left camp after supper, claiming to be under orders given by O'Hara. When he could not be located on the morning of August 1, O'Hara said that he had issued no such orders to Newman. Daniel Cooper, the other principal surveyor, asked Captain Wells what he thought had become of the missing man. The spy captain said that "he must be either lost or fallen in the hands of the Indians." Scouts soon discovered signs that showed "four of the enemy had retreated precipitately with a horse," supposing this was evidence of an Indian party that had taken Newman. When news of this incident spread, Lieutenant Bowyer wrote, "It is hoped he will not give accurate information of our strength." Officers quickly assumed the worst. Wayne soon denounced Newman as a "villain" who "deserted from the army near the St. Mary's" and gave the Indians "every information in his power, as to our force, the object of our destination, state of provision, number and size of the artillery, &c. &c. circumstances and facts that he had but too good an opportunity of knowing, from acting as a field quartermaster on the march." One of Wayne's officers agreed, saying that Newman had "deserted to the enemy (and if we are to judge from circumstances, he was employed by the British for this purpose) and gave the enemy the first information of the approach of our army."[11]

While American officers had divided opinions on Newman and his strange disappearance, British officials were undeceived. Newman and his Indian companions reached Grand Glaize on August 2, and an express was sent on to Colonel McKee, advising him that "a deserter came in this morning, but from his dress he does not appear to be a common person." McKee thought this intelligence so important that he wrote a report of the circumstances just before midnight and immediately dispatched his message to Detroit. When Newman reached McKee's store on August 4, the colonel conducted an interview, then sent the deserter himself to Detroit so that Lieutenant Governor Simcoe "should be possessed as soon as possible of the information of this man." McKee, possibly on the alert because of Wilkinson's previous operatives who had infiltrated British and Indian confidences, did not credit all of Newman's story and advised Lieutenant Colonel England that the deserter might be trying "to deceive us." But after examining Newman himself, England found him to be "a smart sensible young man, and acquainted with the opinions of the people he quitted." The interviewer tried to win Newman's confidence by giving him new clothes and tasty food, apparently with good results. When England passed the talkative deserter on to Simcoe, he advised the lieutenant governor that "all the information Newman has hitherto given proves correct."[12]

Robert Newman gave three accounts of his actions, each one different from the others. Born in Culpeper County, Virginia, he had resided in Jefferson County, Kentucky, near the Falls of the Ohio for two years. Newman had no regular occupation, his last civilian job being that of a schoolteacher. When interviewed by Colonel McKee, he claimed to have joined the legion on July 23 with the advance of General Scott's Kentuckians. The surveyor also admitted that, after marking the road from Fort Recovery to the Saint Marys River, "he left the Army in hope of getting to Detroit where, as he had been informed by another prisoner who escaped, his brother now lived." After giving an estimate of the American force and its ordnance, Newman advised McKee that it was Wayne's intention to advance first to Grand Glaize, then to Roche de Bout, and "his operations against Detroit will commence from hence in the Spring." By his calculations, the legion would reach Roche de Bout on or about August 17.[13]

After returning to American soil, Newman drafted a letter that first appeared in the *Catskill Packet* but was soon widely copied in the nation's press. In this version of his story, he claimed, "I was captured returning from the river St. Mary's to Beaver creek, about 11 miles in advance of Fort Recovery, the first day of August." There was no mention of trying to contact his brother in Detroit. He supposedly avoided injury or death when taken "by exercising a little art, and telling a story, to mitigate the barbarity, and avert the cruelty which prisoners generally experience when taken by the savages." Newman curiously gave no details of his capture, stating those were things "which only concern me and the Indians." Although his captors asked "a number of questions," they supposedly "made but very little enquiry concerning Gen. Wayne's army, or his intentions." There were a few more questions at the Delaware town, where men from that nation believed Newman "to be their friend." Colonel McKee's questioning was more intense, there being many inquiries about his personal life. It was Newman's impression that McKee "doubted my friendship to the Indians, and suspected me as a spy." When McKee pumped the deserter for information about the legion's strength and Wayne's plans, he confessed that he had been "very liberal in gratifying him in his desires." Newman seemed adept at telling the British exactly what they wanted to hear. At Detroit, Lieutenant Colonel England asked pointedly whether General Wayne intended to attack Fort Miamis. Newman replied that, in his opinion, if "there should be a British post in his road, no doubt he would treat it as he would an Indian village." In his interviews with England and Lieutenant Governor Simcoe, Newman made no mention of any attempt to attack Detroit, confessing, "I knew nothing of Gen. Wayne's orders, or what Congress had directed him to do."[14]

From New York, Newman made his way to Philadelphia, where he boldly walked into the War Department and proclaimed himself a former captive of the Indians, "alledging that he had been captured by three Indians on the first day of August as he was returning from an advanced party of the Army." Since he was a civilian employee of the quartermaster, no one suspected him of desertion, let alone having betrayed his government. Secretary Knox was absent in New England, but his staff kindly furnished Newman with twenty dollars, and he left Philadelphia by stage for Carlisle on the first leg of his long journey back home to Kentucky. A few days after his departure, Wayne's dispatch of August 14, accusing him of being a villain and deserter, reached the War Department. Chief Clerk John Stagg immediately sent a confidential message to Major Craig at Pittsburgh, urging that officer to keep a sharp lookout and to arrest Newman if he should pass through that town. So as not to alert the traitor, all mention of him was omitted from Wayne's dispatch when it was released to the public prints. Major Craig located Newman on board a Kentucky boat and "had him immediately secured & Confined in Fort Fayette" until he could be sent on for trial. The prisoner assured Craig that he was not a deserter but admitted being "apprehensive he will not be able to prove his Inocence." Taken by a sergeant and three men to Fort Washington, Newman waited there "in close Confinement & in Irons" until Wayne was ready to interview him.[15]

Upon being brought before the general, Newman was subjected to an intense interrogation that disclosed the real facts behind his strange disappearance. A number of years previously, he had met a shady character named James Hawkins, who in 1794 prevailed upon him to join a conspiracy by carrying a letter addressed to Colonel McKee at Roche de Bout. This letter was mysteriously given to him by "a tall good looking man, dressed in Soldiers Cloathing" near headquarters on the night before the legion left Fort Greeneville. The stranger advised Newman, "Your safety alone depends on the security of that Letter." The messenger deserted on August 1 and met up with a small party of Indians, who took him to McKee. While at Grand Glaize, Newman became acquainted with Capt. Matthew Elliott, whom he discovered was the brother of Robert Elliott, contractor of supplies to the legion. Captain Elliott's conversation indicated that a series of letters had passed between him, his brother, and General Wilkinson, although Newman could not learn the nature of this clandestine correspondence. Wilkinson also passed along several letters to British officers, who, although they looked forward to the information contained therein, at times seemed a little uncomfortable with the arrangement. When first approached by Hawkins, Newman assumed "there was a scheim planed for Keeping up the Army, on the Western frontieers of the United States and Continuing the Same by defecits, or other means, for the purpose of enriching some individuals." He had no idea there was a more sinister plot afoot.

While most of the men and officers Newman conversed with were guarded in their answers and observations, one George James, a native of Culpeper County, Virginia, who seemed to be implicated in this strange business, was more talkative. Newman reported, "By the Genl drift of His Conversation I Believed the Command of this Army was expected by him to be given, to Genl Wilkinson or some man who would answer Their ends better than the present Commander." Although one other officer had apparently rebuffed James's offer of a bribe, it appeared as though Wilkinson had already accepted money or had signaled his intention of doing so; his motivation may have been to raise money to pay gambling debts. (One of the early residents of Cincinnati remembered that the general had "run in debt, and gambled with every body who would play with him.") Conversation with Maj. E. B. Littlehales disclosed that "he expected The Command of the army wou'd be given to General Wilkinson, and if not to him, to some man, who is Capable of Seduction." But the most stunning part of Newman's discoveries was that this conspiracy, in which he had been a willing pawn, was involved in far more than "filling the Coffers of a few individuals." British officials, in league with Wilkinson and an unknown band of civilians, had made overtures for nothing less than "The Union of Canady, and the Country Northwest of the Alleghany Mountains and to form a Seperate empire distined from the United States!" They would use the Indians "as mere tools or Creatures to trouble the fronteers in order to prevent a Dissolution" of the legion, which under General Wilkinson, could be used to enforce and protect a union between Kentucky and Canada. This "Happy event," as Littlehales and Elliott called it, would allow Kentuckians "to have the advantages of the Lakes and the Number of Blessings which would follow," a much brighter future than if they were to "Continue united to the Atlantic States, whose interest was in direct opposition to theirs." Unfortunately, Wilkinson's involvement in this scheme of international intrigue came to light only after the campaign had ended.[16]

While still on the march north, and fearful that Newman had betrayed the legion, Wayne seemed determined to root out any additional traitors. He singled out Daniel

Cooper, who had confessed to writing an incriminating letter found laying on the road-way by Capt. Richard Taylor of the volunteers, then recanted his confession when hauled before General Wayne. He told the general, "It appears Mr. Numan has turned Traitor to his Cuntry, but I dont know why that should be any reason that I shoud." Although he pleaded to be returned to his position as surveyor, Cooper was placed under arrest and confined until Wayne could sort out the treachery. Somehow, the firm of Robertson and Mackay in Cincinnati was suspected of being involved in the plot, rumors circulating that the partners "were guilty of Carrying on a Criminal Correspondence with the Enemy." When Surgeon General Richard Allison repeated that charge in a letter that became public, the two partners wrote to Wayne and protested their characterization as traitors. They vowed to "sacrifice every shilling we are possessed off" to protect their good names and refute gossip that they were "Spies & Criminals."[17]

While his involvement on the periphery of the grand plot to unite Canada and Kentucky was criminal enough, Newman's desertion placed the legion immediately at risk. Although the column had been shadowed by Indian scouts, they assumed that Wayne was headed for the Miami villages, the goal of both Harmar and St. Clair. Newman brought the first intelligence that Wayne's immediate plan was strike Grand Glaize. This fact was corroborated by Abraham Williams, a spokesman for the Wyandotte Nation, who stated categorically, "Newman most Certainly was not captured by the Indians—but came in Voluntarily to give them notice of the Advance of the Army." He also stated that "the Indians wou'd have been completely surprised at Grand Glaize but for the arrival & information given them by this man." The Indians always remembered the debt they owed to Robert Newman. Long after Wayne's campaign had ended, Te-ta-boksh-ke, king of the Delawares, said to the general: "You have in your prison a man (Newman) who came in to us a year ago, and proved the preservation of many of our women and children, by the information he gave us; for this we cannot help feeling grateful. Now, your children, the Delawares, all beg of you to spare the life of this man as he has been instrumental in saving many of us from destruction."[18]

Unaware of the havoc Newman had caused, on August 2, Wayne ordered fatigue parties from the legion to begin constructing a small stockade and two blockhouses on the south bank of the Saint Marys River. Although the location now seemed high and dry, Captain Wells declared that he had seen flood waters up to his knees on the site of the new post. Wayne ordered Wells and a few spies to reconnoiter the route to the Auglaize River, while Captain Kibbey and his "Columbian Scouters" operated in a more westerly direction. The general wanted prisoners, but Wells objected to the size of his detachment, saying that if he took along two hundred Kentuckians, he could bring in several captives. Wayne "paid no attention to this proposition." Men not at work on the fortification formed themselves into fishing parties, which used the following method: "Eight or ten soldiers sewing their Blankets together, enter the Water, and moving with the Stream for twenty or thirty Yards, make the shore; at some Times catching from eight to ten Fish of an excellent Size and Quality, such as Pike, Pickeron, Pearch, Salmon, Trout, &c." General Scott's Kentuckians had no work to do on the fort and so spent most of the day dragging brush nets through the river. When several legion officers came to call, Scott's mess served up "a Salmon and pike." There were so many successful fishermen that "the greater Part of the Army" was supplied with fish for supper, a welcome respite from army rations. But the relaxing pleasure of fishing was lost on Capts. Edward Miller and Edward Turner, both of the Second Sub-Legion, who had words that resulted in a challenge being issued. Their friends, with the memory of Lieutenant Dunn's recent death still fresh, persuaded the pair of antagonists to make peace, and according to Miller, "the affair was settled."[19]

August 3 dawned "very hot and dry, without any appearance of rain," although there was a small shower in the afternoon. One enlisted man stated that work on the fort was "going on with Spirit," while Lieutenant Clark noticed that it continued with "Wonderous Slowness." A small group of Kentucky officers rode down the stream in search of another campground since General Barbee was momentarily expected with the mounted volunteers from south of the Kentucky River. They discovered more deserted Indian villages on the edge of the prairie, the scene disclosing "here a beautifull Cops of Trees and there an extensive natural Meadow weaveing with Grass and Flowers." Soldiers from the legion also did some exploring and, on the north side of the stream, found a spot where the Indians had camped after the fight at Fort Recovery. Rummaging over the ground, one of them found "a bag with a quantity of paint and such trifles," not much of a souvenir, but one that was the center of much conversation. To escape the afternoon heat, General Wayne lay down on a cot in his marquee, which had been pitched among the trees.[20]

About three o'clock, the legion camp plunged into chaos when a large beech tree toppled over onto the tents of General Wayne and his aide-de-camp, Henry DeButts. Officers and men came running to help rescue the two officers while word spread rapidly that the general had been killed, creating great confusion and panic in camp. Fortunately, the rumor proved false. Both officers had been in their beds when the tree came down, smashing the cot of DeButts and coming within six inches of crushing the general to death. Wayne was dragged from his tent, seriously injured in his left leg and ankle and apparently without a pulse. Volatile drops, a form of smelling salts, were administered by a surgeon, and the general quickly revived, "more Sceared then hurt." Investigation revealed that an old stump had absorbed most of the force from the falling tree. Wayne wrote that this "accidental circumstance" was all that "prevented the body of the tree from crushing me to atoms." Wilkinson said that the general's escape was simply "miraculous," and he had missed "being mashed to Death" by mere inches. Lieutenant Clark attributed the accident to one of Fortune's "unaccountable pranks," which could have proven deadly had the tree fallen "a few feet more to the right or left." Upon examining the fallen beech, it was determined that "a fire had been kindled and carelessly left burning" until the tree had partially burned through and toppled over. This startling accident left General Wayne "much bruised" and in "great bodily pain," although he insisted upon mounting his horse for a ride around camp to reassure his soldiers.[21]

Work ceased on the fort during this crisis, and many thought the legion would "be detained here some time in consequence of it." Wayne would have none of that talk. He

sent his adjutant to Wilkinson and Hamtramck with instructions "to turn out every officer off Duty, to proceed to the Fort now erecting and lend every assistance to forward
the Works." The fatigue parties labored long after dark, one of the enlisted men remarking, "all is Hurry," and Lieutenant Clark observing that "time Waited not for us, & night
came on e're the work was yet done." Such was the haste that the original fatigue party
had worked the entire day and into the night with nothing to eat after breakfast and but
precious few rest breaks. General Barbee's brigade of mounted volunteers joined Wayne's
force that night, bringing along large quantities of food and supplies. One of the Kentuckians also brought a letter written by Lieutenant Visscher, stationed at Fort Recovery,
to Solomon Van Rensselaer. Visscher wished to know whether the dragoons "have yet
had an opportunity for slashing with temporary advantages." If not, he sent his wishes
that such an opportunity might soon present itself and that Van Rensselaer might "be
honorably killed!!" He jokingly assured his friend, "To hear of your death wou'd be a
good story for me to carry home, and wou'd so well please all your friends!" Although the
fort had not yet been completed, Wayne could wait no longer, and the legion would
march on the morning of August 4, taking Captain Van Rensselaer to his rendezvous
with an Indian bullet.[22]

Wayne appointed Lieutenant Underhill, who was somewhat indisposed, to command this new post at the Saint Marys, which he named Fort Randolph in honor of
Edmund Randolph, who had recently succeeded Thomas Jefferson as secretary of state.
Alerting Underhill to "the honor attending a prudent & successful government of an
advanced Post in an enemys Country" as well as "the ignominy & public injury consequent upon misconduct or want of vigilance in a commanding officer," Wayne had but
few orders. His primary directive was to the point: "You will without intermission compleat the works now committed to your charge—you will with unwearied watchfulness
guard your Post & command from surprise or accident from the Enemy and if attacked
you will defend yourself whilst you have a man left capable of wielding an arm." Underhill's garrison consisted of fifty noncommissioned officers and privates, all invalids and
cripples except perhaps twenty "able to Work." Lieutenant Clark could not help but
notice this pathetic command, writing, "thus was he left to finish and Defend this miserable Hold, in the midst of the Enemys Country without the smallest provability of being
reinforsed or aided in the Completion of the Works." A few Kentuckians, "very Sickly"
and unable to continue, also were left at Fort Randolph, including Ens. George Price of
Taylor's company, who died on August 5.[23]

General Wilkinson also expressed sympathy for Lieutenant Underhill and his unen-
viable assignment. The stockade was only half complete, the only suitable timber being
across the river and "at a considerable distance," especially since it would have to be hauled
by hand. The walls of both blockhouses had been raised, but they had no roofs, had not
yet been chinked, and needed to have doors cut in them. No provision had been made to
leave ammunition for the garrison, but Major Burbeck took it upon himself to make sure
Underhill had a good supply of cartridges. The lieutenant was not unaware of his plight,
expressing his despair to Burbeck and Surgeon John Carmichael by wishing "the Indians

would immediately come and tomahawk himself and his detachment, to prevent him from cutting his own throat."[24]

Although he and his men worked until dark for two successive days, Underhill could not accomplish more than completing the palisade, which still had no gate to block the fort's entrance. There were so few men able to work and the invalids were so sick that the lieutenant reported he would be "very fortunate if Some of them are not obliged to Leave working at the Garrison to dig Graves." The contractor had left supplies but no weights to be used for measuring rations. With all of his men engaged in construction work, the seven cattle at the post were put under care of contractor employees, who promptly allowed them to wander off. When Underhill attempted to report deficiencies to General Wayne, he discovered that he had no stationery and could only dispatch a letter after one of his men offered a few sheets of paper. It was not until August 15 that the lieutenant had his fort "in Tolerable Order for defence" and had started to clear away brush and logs that could be used for shelter by attacking Indians. Mindful of the successful defense of the detached blockhouse by Corporal White during the attack on Fort Recovery, Underhill recommended that a similar strongpoint be built opposite the stream from the fort. Fortunately for this isolated and virtually helpless garrison, the Indians did not make an attempt on the post, which could have been taken with a minimum of effort. Curiously, Underhill's post was given a new name. Someone must have noted that, while forts had been named for President Washington and members of his cabinet (Jefferson, Hamilton, Knox, and Randolph), the territorial governor (St. Clair), and heroes of the Revolution ([La]Fayette, Steuben, and Greeneville), the vice president of the United States, John Adams, had not been so recognized. To rectify that oversight, the name of Lieutenant Underhill's garrison, a squalid, puny, insignificant, second-rate post, was changed to Fort Adams so as to recognize the importance of the vice president.[25]

CHAPTER 22

Americans Occupy Grand Glaize

THE LEGION CROSSED THE SAINT MARYS River at 5:00 A.M. on August 4 and again headed north, those soldiers to the right and left of the newly cut road passing "through intolerable thick woods & the earth covered with Snagley underwoods & almost impassable Defiles." The route passed through one small prairie and touched the northwest edge of another, but for most of the day, the soldiers moved through a landscape that appeared to be "wet and swampy at any other Season" but was now virtually destitute of water. Capt. John Cooke remarked that drinking water was "scarce," while the Kentuckians found "little or no water & that very bad." The day was sultry, and there were "many short halts," during which soldiers were "obliged to dig holes in boggy places and let it settle" in order to find even bad-tasting water. After making about ten miles, Wayne halted his command in late afternoon at a small creek that paralleled and eventually emptied into the Auglaize River. Lieutenant Clark called the stream "a Small durty water," and Captain Cooke said it was "a small muddy run," while an enlisted man referred to it as "a small Pond." All agreed, though, that the water was "foul and disagreable to the taste," as was the liquid in several nearby stagnant pools.[1]

A body of Kentucky troops was to have preceded the road cutters, but they did not march until the legion had left camp. To remedy this oversight, henceforth guards in the volunteer camp would move in advance of the line of march at 5:00 A.M. each morning, preceded only by Maj. William Price's battalion of scouts. This arrangement was put into practice on August 5, when the legion marched another twelve miles through country similar to that encountered the previous day. The shortage of drinking water was eased by a small shower of rain and a spring-fed creek, about fifteen feet wide, whose contents were judged "stagnant and muddy" but an improvement over that available during the previous three days. Wilkinson brought it to Wayne's attention that General Scott's command, which generally stopped to the legion's rear, had yet to sleep in a fortified camp. Wayne promised to take care of the matter.[2]

Wayne's army left camp at the usual hour on August 6 and made about twelve miles before halting that afternoon. The road was cut through "thick swampy country" and required frequent halts, making it an easy march for the foot soldiers until the legion finally stopped fifty-six miles beyond Fort Recovery. William Wells advanced with his spies in the morning and discovered an Indian village some six miles distant. The general selected Major Price's battalion of scouts and Kibbey's Columbian Scouts to make an attack, guided to the spot by Wells. They returned about sundown with news that their target had long been abandoned and no Indians were seen, although scouts did discover the fresh tracks of about eighteen warriors heading toward Grand Glaize. One of the most important events of August 6 came when Generals Wayne, Wilkinson, Scott, and Todd met that night to discuss Major Price's raid on the abandoned village. It was here that Wilkinson actually spoke to Scott for the first time since the campaign began, urging that the Kentuckians be used as a body, instead of in small detachments, at critical times. Scott, who reciprocated Wilkinson's hatred, reluctantly responded that "it was the wish of his heart" to do so. The fresh tracks found by Major Price were assumed to have been made by the small party that had attacked Fort Recovery on the morning of August 4. Lieutenant Drake reported that this attack began with an ambush of a four-man fatigue detail at work between the detached blockhouse and the spring. Apparently, an inattentive guard had allowed the Indians to creep to within ten yards of the workmen. When the warriors opened fire, workmen and guards all sprinted for either the blockhouse or the fort gate. Soldiers stationed in the blockhouse opened a heavy fusillade on the attackers, driving them back to cover in the nearest trees, from where they concentrated their fire on the southeast blockhouse of the fort but did no damage and inflicted no casualties. When the Indians appeared to draw off, Drake rolled out his cannons, which fired solid shot and grape, and howitzers, which lobbed shells filled with rifle and musket balls. The only losses were four horses owned by invalid Kentuckians and a like number belonging to the quartermaster.[3]

The federal army started off at the regular hour on August 7, following the same small stream for about four hours until it emptied into the Auglaize River, here about one hundred yards wide and flowing through a delightful valley full of fertile soil and pleasant views. Wilkinson's right wing crossed the river, finding "the water deep and a flat smooth Rock at bottom," then headed downstream. This disposition seemed unwise, for Wilkinson's half of the legion was often out of touch with the main body, struggling around river bends and over elevations and ravines, separated "more than a mile on the opposite Banks of a river in many places unfordable." The legion passed by the old Indian town that Wells had reconnoitered, finding less than a dozen cabins and some untended cornfields. Lieutenant Bowyer, tired of army rations, hoped they would soon find occupied towns in which, he had been told, there would be "all sorts of vegetables, which will be very acceptable to the troops." When the army encamped, Bowyer's wish was realized as the men found "plenty of roasting ears, beans, potatoes, etc." in old fields. The right wing marched through a rich bottomland containing many walnut and sugar maple trees, where Indians in previous years had established sugar camps, but saw no hostiles before building its own breastwork camp. Soldiers from Wilkinson's wing had, however, seen "many old Indian settlements now grown up in weeds briars & shrubs almost impervious." Just before dark, a party of Kentuckians out grazing their horses on the south bank fired at and wounded an Indian, who slipped away in the darkness. These shots started an alarm that caused soldiers to run to their breastworks, but no other warriors appeared, despite numerous signs that pointed to Wayne's force being in close proximity to the foe.[4]

During the day, Wayne had consulted with Wilkinson, informing him "that he intended to march forward to the first evacuated town, there to fortify, deposit his waggons and heavy baggage under a guard of 250 Men and proceed rapidly to Grand Glaize." This effectively put an end to Wilkinson's repeated suggestions that the Kentuckians be sent ahead as a sort of strike force, hitting the Indians before they could prepare a defense for their villages. Many months before, Wayne had decided to build a fort at Grand Glaize, now only a few miles distant, so this information was but a screen to stop Wilkinson's interference with strategic planning. As might be expected, Wilkinson did not take the rebuff well and complained, "the Old man unfortunately cannot consent to divide the smallest portion of reputation with any officer; he is therefore unwilling to make respectable detachments or to suffer any officer of Rank to precede him at any point of his march." He continued his invective, claiming that Wayne had "to be first every where, even at an Indian Cabbin, Corn-Crib or Vine-patch" and considered "every mite of reputation acquired by a subordinate as so much ravished from his rightful pretensions."[5]

The morning of August 8 was blustery, overcast, and stormy, heavy rains falling most of the day, the first real rainfall, other than a couple of short showers, the Americans had seen since leaving Fort Greeneville. Wayne ordered General Todd's brigade across the river to reinforce Wilkinson's right wing, the mounted men covering his right flank, and the soldiers slogged through mud en route to the Maumee River. Both wings passed deserted Indian towns and luxuriant fields of corn and vegetables in a downpour that lasted until noon. As the army approached the confluence of the Auglaize and Maumee Rivers, soldiers marveled at the scene. Lieutenant Bowyer recorded his impressions, writing: "This place far excels in beauty any in the western country, and believed equalled by none in the Atlantic States. Here are vegetables of every kind in abundance, and we have marched four or five miles in cornfields down the Oglaize, and there is not less than one thousand acres of corn round the town." Taking a moment to speculate on the future, Bowyer continued, "This country appears well adapted for the enjoyment of industrious people, who cannot avoid living in as great luxury as in any other place throughout the states, nature having lent a most bountiful hand in the arrangement of the position, that a man can send the produce to market in his own boat." Another soldier agreed with Bowyer's assessment, writing, "The flourishing State of the Productions of this Country convinces me of the Fertility of its Soil, and its Pleasantness is most unsurpassingly beautiful."[6]

Captain Cooke observed that some towns gave evidence that the Indians had "recently evacuated this place and in great hurry and confusion," a number of cabins and stores having been set on fire by soldiers despite the relentless rain. Lieutenant Clark

agreed that the residents seemed to have fled "with precipation and the greatest con-
sternation." One soldier wrote, "Numbers of Brass Kettles are found in the Weeds, and
every Thing so situated as to wear the Appearance of a sudden Departure of the Savages;
Chisels, Hammers, Augers, &c. are likewise found, which induces me to believe white
Men have resided here—The many Barrels, Kegs, &c. to be seen strengthens this Belief."
Soldiers began to disperse in search of plunder, some of them quickly locating the home
of Blue Jacket, the famous Shawnee warrior, which was destroyed in retribution for his
role in St. Clair's defeat. James Morrow, one of the artificers, made the best find, a trunk
containing $859 in bank notes. Most of the men were less fortunate and contented them-
selves with gathering vegetables for supper, including corn, beans, cucumbers, peas,
potatoes, squash, pumpkins, and melons. These well-tended gardens extended out of
sight in every direction, making the green river valleys seem like a Garden of Eden.[7]

That afternoon, Wayne sent Christopher Miller to guide Wilkinson's force across the
Auglaize River at a ford the scouts had discovered. The reunited legion established its
camp in the angle formed by the Auglaize and Maumee, while the Kentuckians settled
into tents on the opposite bank of the Maumee. General Wayne officially congratulated
the legion and their Kentucky auxiliaries "upon taking possession of the grand Empo-
rium of the Hostile Indians of the West." He continued, "The extensive & highly cultivated fields & Gardens on the margins of those beautiful Rivers, show us that they
were the Work of many hands & affords a pleasing prospect of bountiful supplies of
Grain &c. as the troops progress toward the Lake." The occasion was worthy of a celebration, so Wayne directed the quartermaster to issue a gill of whiskey to each man. On
a more practical note, the rain had played havoc with the weapons. Every firearm from
which the ball could not be extracted was ordered discharged at precisely five o'clock,
immediately following the firing of a cannon from the artillery park. Thereafter, anyone
firing a weapon without authorization within hearing of the camp would be punished
for giving a false alarm. This order was to be read to every soldier at retreat that night,
"to the end that no persons whether belonging to the Legion, to the Mounted Volunteers—or followers of the Army—may plead ignorance thereof." Since Indians would
surely hover about the region in hopes of finding stragglers, all men were confined to their
camps unless in the company of an officer or assigned to a fatigue, guard, or scouting
party.[8]

Unknown to the American soldiers, most of the Indians had fled Grand Glaize
when Robert Newman brought the news of Wayne's advance. The captive Jonathan
Alder recalled, "We now packed up everything, and started for the old English fort at
the Maumee rapids." Some families, however, had remained until the last minute. Joseph
Kelly had been captured by the Shawnees on April 7, 1791, while working the fields with
his father at Belleville. The warriors tried to take Joseph's father prisoner, but he
"defended himself so stoutly with his hoe, having no other weapon, that the Indians were
obliged to shoot him." Although an older brother escaped to the nearby garrison, seven-
year-old Joseph was carried off to a town near Sandusky, where he was adopted by an
elderly couple who had lost five sons in conflicts with the white men. Here was a lesson

for those civilized Christian settlers who fought the supposedly savage Indians: "After losing five sons, these untutored natives of the forest adopted the child of their mortal enemies, and treated him as their own!" Young Joseph was with the women, children, and old men in one of the Grand Glaize villages when Wayne's vanguard approached. So rapid was the Americans' march that residents "had no time to take any provisions, and only a few kettles and blankets, but hurrying into their canoes pushed off down the Maumee into the vicinity of Detroit." Joseph always remembered "with what regret they left their fine fields of corn, which he had assisted to cultivate, already fit for roasting ears, the beans, and the squashes, with large patches of water-melons." When the Indian families left their villages at the mouth of the Auglaize, they were "surrounded by plenty," but one day later, "the American army destroyed all their crops; cutting down and wasting the corn, and burning the dwellings where their forefathers had lived for many, many years."9

John Brickell was another white captive who barely escaped from Wayne's fast-advancing force. He had been taken prisoner on February 9, 1791, at a small settlement two miles north of Pittsburgh along the Allegheny River. Upon reaching a town on the Auglaize, Brickell was adopted by a Delaware warrior named Whingwy Pooshies, or Big Cat. He remembered that his Indian family "treated me very kindly and in every way as one of themselves" and that "honesty, bravery and hospitality are cardinal virtues with them." Brickell said of the Delawares, "as a nation they may be considered fit examples for many of us Christians to follow" since they "follow what they are taught to believe right more closely, and I might say more honestly, in general, than we Christians do the divine precepts of our Redeemer."

One sacred belief of Delaware life was "an eye for an eye, a tooth for a tooth, and blood for blood," warfare being an important part of that nation's creed. Big Cat had fought against St. Clair, and Brickell described the outcome: "We then found ourselves a rich people. Whingwy Pooshies' share of the spoils of the army was two fine horses, four tents, one of which was a noble markee, which made us a fine house in which we lived the remainder of my captivity. He had also clothing in abundance and of all descriptions. I wore a soldier's coat. He had also axes, guns, and every thing necessary to make an Indian rich. There was much joy amongst them." In June 1794, Brickell, along with two warriors and a boy, started on a hunting expedition along Blanchard's Fork of the Auglaize River. They had been gone for about two months and chanced to return the night before the legion reached Grand Glaize. The four hunters found the towns "entirely evacuated" but assumed that residents had gone to Roche de Bout to receive their annual presents from the British Indian Department. After camping overnight in a cornfield on an island, they were startled next morning by another Indian giving an "alarm whoop, which is a kind of yell they use for no other purpose." The newcomer shouted that white men were closing in and they must run for their lives. Brickell remarked on their response: "We scattered like a flock of partridges, and leaving our breakfast cooking on the fire. The Kentucky riflemen saw our smoke, and came to it, and just missed me as I passed them in my flight through the corn. They took the whole of our two months' work, breakfast, *jirk,* skins and all."10

Content with their plunder and an unlimited supply of fresh vegetables, General Scott's Kentuckians did little more on August 9 than "lay in Camp all Day." Some of the more ambitious volunteers scoured the various villages for shelled corn, which they sold to Quartermaster O'Hara for three dollars per bushel. At the other extreme, 160 noncommissioned officers and privates from the legion reported for fatigue duty and were given axes "for the Purpose of Cutting Logs for the Block Houses and Picquets" for a new post to be built at the confluence of the Auglaize and Maumee Rivers. The individual logs, or pickets, intended for use in the walls were to be fifteen feet in length and a minimum of one foot in diameter "at the smallest end." An additional work party of soldiers erected the pickets. While construction began, pioneer detachments began to work on grading the river banks at the ford. Despite these labor-intensive projects, Lieutenant Bowyer thought that, because of this current halt, "the troops will be much refreshed, as well as the horses and cattle, the latter being much wearied." Some officers thought the location of this new post to be poorly chosen. According to Captain Cooke: "My principal objection is, that the ground on the north side of the Miami [Maumee] commands it. The Fort as it stands is in my opinion so near the banks of both rivers, that in the course of three years at most the banks with a part of the Fort must inevitably wash away." Wayne dismissed such concerns by declaring, "this route would never be used but once, for the purpose of bringing up a supply of provision."[11]

Sometimes the soldiers would simply stop and gaze about them in wonderment. Lieutenant Clark was amazed by the scene that presented itself from the site of this new garrison, "commanding a handsome View up & down the Rivers, the Margins of which as far as the Eye can see are covered with the most luxurient groths of Corn, interspurced with Small Log Cabbins arround all of which you observe theire well cultivated gardens." This pause at the Grand Glaize allowed the men to catch up on the news from elsewhere. Intelligence from Fort Greeneville disclosed that the Indians had been relatively quiet in that quarter. Major Buell could report, "I have now got my garrison in order and every officer knows his command and their different duties are pointed out to them and the staff officers are appointed." Capt. James Taylor had recovered sufficiently to assume command of the dragoons assigned to one of the bastions, while Captain Sullivan had charge of troops from the First and Fourth Sub-Legions and Lieutenant Shoemaker led soldiers of the Second and Third Sub-Legions. Pickets around the citadel had been erected, stumps were being removed, and Buell had "got locks on all the gates." The only casualty among members of the garrison was a soldier named Cotton, Buell's servant, who had been killed and scalped after leaving the protection of a convoy headed for Fort Washington. The legion lost another soldier when John Frank, a veteran of the Revolution and of St. Clair's army, chose not to reenlist, received his honorable discharge at Fort Greeneville, and started for his home in New York. But after only a scant two hours of civilian life, Frank "was captured by the Miami nation of Indians, and . . . was detained in bondage, suffering extreme hardships and cruelties, nearly three years, before he made his escape!"[12]

Rev. David Jones, successor to Chaplain John Hurt, had at last reached Fort Washington on July 31 en route to minister to the men of Wayne's legion. Jones was a Baptist clergyman who had served as a missionary to the Indians of the Northwest Territory during 1772–73. Driven out of his pastorate by Tory neighbors during the Revolution, he became pastor of the Valley Baptist Church in Chester County, Pennsylvania, then began service as an army chaplain in 1777. Most of his army service had been spent with General Wayne, whose friendship resulted in Jones being appointed legion chaplain on May 13, 1794. His arrival at Cincinnati prompted Winthrop Sargent to announce that fact to Henry Knox and to warn the secretary of war that Parson Jones might bear watching. Reminding Knox that he had always considered Jones "a man of Sedition," Sargent recounted how, while at a Pittsburgh tavern, he had personally witnessed the minister censure President Washington and his administration's policies. He continued, "In this Country and upon the river he has been very imprudently expressing himself upon the Excise Law and to appearance encouraging by his Conversation an opposition thereto." Sargent cautioned, "Men of his Zeal you know have great Influence over common minds," telling Knox that "a Line of private admonition" might be needed to restrain this outspoken pastor. He even confessed that if Jones "was not a public servant and soon going out to the Army," he should, as a magistrate of the Northwest Territory, "obtain some kind of Security" so the new chaplain "would not contaminate the minds of *this people*."[13]

Chaplain Jones announced his arrival to General Wayne, expressing not only his disappointment that the legion had already left Fort Greeneville but also his determination to follow as soon as he could do so "with any Degree of Safety." Jones explained that his tardiness had been caused by being detained at Fort Fayette by the "Tumult" created by enforcement of the Excise Law of 1791. While there had always been opposition to this tax on whiskey, a near rebellion had broken loose in western Pennsylvania. When David Lenox was appointed U.S. marshal for Allegheny and Washington Counties, he began a strict policy of enforcing writs against men delinquent in paying the whiskey tax. According to David Jones, "a general Dis-Satisfaction Prevailed." On July 15, irate residents fired two guns at Marshal Lenox and John Neville, excise officer for the Western District of Pennsylvania. These were not meant to injure or kill the two men but merely to frighten Lenox into giving up his writs and Neville into resigning his commission. When this warning had no effect, a crowd of about 150 armed and angry men surrounded Neville's home in Pittsburgh. When the crowd fired a few shots into the house to emphasize its demands, Neville shot back and wounded six of the mob. Caught off guard by Neville's defiance, the disorganized group dispersed. Neville sent to Fort Fayette for assistance in defending his family and home, and Lt. Col. Thomas Butler sent a sergeant and twelve men "until such time as the storm would blow over."

Abraham Kirkpatrick, a friend of John Neville, joined those defending the house, a pitiful guard considering the large numbers of rioters who would surely reappear the next morning. Neville was urged to escape while he could, Kirkpatrick agreeing to remain with the soldiers and protect his property. When the insurgents began to arrive, Neville crept out a back window and hid in a thicket before they could completely surround the building. After a series of demands were rejected by Kirkpatrick, the rioters, now numbering over seven hundred, ordered all armed men inside Neville's house to march out and surrender their weapons. When this too was rejected, a "brisk fire" commenced and lasted perhaps an hour, during which time three defenders were wounded; the attackers lost one man killed and several wounded. Rioters set fire to the barn, stables, kitchen, and granary, everything being consumed, including several horses and a large amount of grain. Kirkpatrick's defenders, minus two privates who were "supposed to have gone off with the insurgents as they were not men of good character," kept the rebels at bay until the house itself was in flames, then surrendered. Neville escaped to Fort Fayette, where he was joined by Lenox. The two men, guarded by Capt. John Crawford, a sergeant, and six men, made their way to Wheeling and on to the Muskingum River, whence they took horses for Philadelphia by way of Clarksburg.[14]

Emboldened by their success, the mob called for all those opposed to the Excise Law to meet at Braddock's Field, where a crowd of between four thousand and five thousand men assembled with their weapons. When the leaders decided to march to Pittsburgh, they wisely sent a delegation to Lieutenant Colonel Butler, informing him that "they had no hostile intentions respecting the garrison or the public stores." Butler responded that "if they meant to keep out of danger, they must not come within reach of his cannon." The mob prudently bypassed Fort Fayette and, after marching through the streets of Pittsburgh, quietly dispersed. As might be expected in such a singular crisis, rumors abounded. One correspondent wrote: "We are all in confusion at present, owing to the late contest with general Neville. The wild Irish have assumed the reigns, and have threatened to shoot every man who may not choose to oppose the old, in hopes to establish a new government." One report circulated that Lieutenant Governor Simcoe had promised to supply arms and ammunition to the insurgents, and some men even talked about seeking shelter in Canada. While the mob celebrated its victory, President Washington issued a proclamation denouncing armed opposition to lawfully appointed officers conducting the nation's business, then called for thirteen thousand militia to be raised in the states of New Jersey, Pennsylvania, Maryland, and Virginia. No matter what the cost, Washington would put down this whiskey rebellion, "causing the laws of the United States to be duly observed in the western parts of the State of Pennsylvania."[15]

Although obviously concerned by these reports of rebellion in Pennsylvania, General Wayne remained focused on the task at hand. Work continued on the new fort, but when progress did not meet his expectations, the general displayed his "apparent wrath" and "scolded and swore hard" at officers and men alike. Wilkinson became so offended by his commander's "indelicacy" that he determined to avoid Wayne on all occasions, "except on points of duty." Until August 10, General Scott's command had chosen not to fortify its encampment, but on that day 140 axes were distributed to the Kentuckians for use in constructing breastworks. Despite their seemingly autonomous relation to the legion, Wayne was now determined to have his entire force under cover at every halt. He also published some general orders to clamp down on the independence exhibited by his Kentucky auxiliaries, including a prohibition on swimming in the river or crossing it to forage in the cornfield opposite the new post. Foraging parties were to consist of at least ten men, carrying their arms, and they were positively forbidden to burn any of the remaining Indian cabins or huts. A court-martial was impaneled to investigate the conduct of unruly volunteers, who had never been seriously interested in conforming to military discipline.[16]

Among those hauled before Major Whitaker's court were Andrew Morrow and Simon Brown. Morrow, a private in Capt. Joseph Colvill's company, was confined by order of General Scott after using "abusive language" toward his commanding general. (Considering Scott's legendary virtuosity with the cussing vocabulary, one can only shudder at the invective that would offend his own ears.) The private pled guilty but offered the excuse that "intoxication Deprived him So far of his senus that he did not know Mjr Genl Scott from any other person." The court sentenced Morrow to receive twenty-five lashes. Simon Brown, a private from Bartlett's company, was arrested by his sergeant when he refused to stand guard, although he had been warned it was his turn to do so. Brown also was sentenced to receive twenty-five lashes. The court did find that Jacob Allison of Francisco's company was innocent of being asleep at his post. When General Wayne reviewed the sentences, he confessed to being "extreamly distressed to See a Volenteer Receive Corporal Punishment." He pardoned both Morrow and Brown, deeming that act "a Sufficient Warning not only to them but to the whole Corps as they May rest assurd that no indulgence of this Kind neede be Expected in future."[17]

While General Wayne attended to details, Captain Wells and a party of spies—Robert McClellan, Paschall Hickman, William May, and the Miller brothers, Christopher and Nicholas—had been to Roche de Bout, "almost in reach of the fire from the British Garrison." John McDonald explained the tactics employed to obtain information:

> On the west bank of the Maumee was an Indian village. Wells and his party rode into the village, as if they had just come from the British fort. Being dressed and painted in complete Indian style, they rode through the village, occasionally stopping and talking to the Indians in their own language. No suspicion of who they were was excited, the enemy believing them to be Indians from a distance, coming to take a part in the battle which they all knew was shortly to be fought. After they had passed the village some distance, they fell in with an Indian man and woman on horseback, who were returning to the town from hunting. This man and woman were made captives without resistance.

The spies set out for Grand Glaize with their prisoners, but shortly after dark they came upon a small Indian camp, this one consisting of a large marquee and a smaller tent. McClellan cockily said to Wells, "Let's pay these fellows a visit." Wells demurred, saying the camp appeared too large for their small group. His lieutenant responded with a hint of reproach, "If we pass them by unvisited, it will be the first time we have ever thus acted." Stung by this apparent rebuke, Wells decided to drop in for a visit. McClellan, seeing that his little joke had gotten out of hand, had no choice but to go along.[18]

Capt. William Wells. Courtesy the Indiana State Library, Indiana Division, Picture Collection.

The spies bound and gagged their prisoners, leaving one of their number as a guard. Captain Wells and the other four men boldly rode up to the Indian camp and casually inquired if there was any food to share. Expecting to find only seven or eight warriors, the spies suddenly found themselves almost face to face with about fifteen Delawares gathered around a campfire. Wells began to carry on a conversation with several of the Indians as they cautiously walked their horses into the light cast by the fire, carefully keeping their rifles ready for action. While Wells spoke, an old Indian kept eyeing McClellan, who concluded that this warrior had not been fooled. Suddenly there was a shouted warning. Rifles flashed as the outnumbered spies got off the first shots, then spurred their horses to escape. Indians lunged for their rifles and fired at the fleeing strangers as they disappeared into the night. Wells was struck by a ball that fractured some bones in his wrist, causing the spy captain to drop his rifle, while McClellan was hit by a ball that shattered his shoulder blade. The men claimed to have killed three warriors and wounded another, but the Indian account forwarded to Detroit remarked simply, "They killed a Delaware woman." After making their escape, the spies bandaged up their wounded officers, then headed toward Grand Glaize. John McDonald was effusive in hailing this encounter: "They had come off unscathed in so many desperate conflicts, that their souls were callous to danger! As they had no rivals in the army, they aimed to outdo their former exploits. To ride in to the enemy's camp, and enter into conversation with them, without betraying the least appearance of trepidation or confusion, proves how well their souls were steeled." But McDonald was dead wrong. McClellan's innocent dare had turned into a stupid and foolhardy act of bravado. Now two of the legion's best spies had been lost at a most critical time. Captain Cooke understood that loss when he wrote, "The wounds of McClellan and Wills will prevent them going with us, which will be some disadvantage to the operations of the army, particularly in the loss of Wills who is a valuable man."[19]

General Wayne had ordered two hundred volunteers to descend the Maumee River and lay out a camp at Snake Town on the morning of August 12, and this party encountered Wells's spy detachment on its way back to camp. The Kentuckians continued on their way and found some of the finest vegetables that Francis Jones had ever seen, though there were rattlesnakes among the corn and bean plants. By the time this detachment returned to Grand Glaize, the spies had come in, the wounded had been tended by surgeons, and Wells's adventure had become the subject of much talk and rumor. The two Shawnee captives responded to questions, confirming that Robert Newman "came of his own accord" from the legion and provided important information to the Indians regarding Wayne's strength and intentions. Captain Cooke reported that Newman also counseled them to avoid attacking the American encampments "but when marching, and not to endeavor to out-flank us but to attack in a body." He also told his Indian friends "how to distinguish the officers from the soldiers." The Shawnee couple also informed Wayne that there were some two hundred British soldiers in Fort Miamis, seven hundred warriors camped in that vicinity, and another five hundred Indian fighting men supposed to be on the way. Captain Elliott, Captain McKee, and Robert Newman had gone to

Detroit to bring out a large force of militia. The Shawnee warrior also said that "the Indians talked of stepping on one side and letting the army go on to the British or that if the British did not now come forward to assist them they would join the Americans." He also said that the councils had discussed sending a flag of truce to the legion but were afraid that the bearer would be killed.[20]

Wayne had been confined to his bed with an attack of gout in one of his feet since August 10, lying in bed and generally looking ill. Several days later, the attack had also afflicted his knee, Surgeon General Richard Allison finding the general "in agony" and unable to move without severe pain. Despite his poor health, Wayne interviewed the prisoners and thought their answers required the dispatch of one more peace overture. With Captain Wells wounded, the only man fluent in the Indian language and familiar with their customs was Christopher Miller, the former captive and current spy. Wayne discussed the situation with Miller and assured him confidentially "that if he would undertake the task, and should succeed in the undertaking, he should receive from his Government an independent fortune." Wilkinson did not agree with Wayne's selection of Miller as a messenger to his former captors, doubting that his attachment to the American cause was very strong. He concluded that, "should Miller prove treacherous he will give information that we have no cannon with us and may expose us in other respects—we dread the consequences." But Wilkinson objected not only to Miller but also to the plan in general, stating that sending off a flag of truce "will carry with it an aspect of diffidence on our part and will be mischievously interpreted by the British."[21]

As a sign of good faith, General Wayne released the Shawnee warrior captured by Wells at Roche de Bout and sent him along with Miller. The general advised Secretary Knox that he had decided "to offer the enemy a last overture of peace" now that the legion's advance had placed "every thing that is dear and interesting [to them] now at stake." If the Indians should refuse this final offer and choose war, the bloody consequences would "be upon their own heads." On the afternoon of August 13, Miller and the unidentified Shawnee warrior—one, a former captive of the Shawnees; the other, a recent prisoner of the Americans—set out on horseback for Roche de Bout, carrying the following message:

> To the Delawares, Shawanese, Miamies, and Wyandots, and to each an every of them, and to all nations of Indians, northwest of the Ohio, whom it may concern:
>
> I, Anthony Wayne, Major-General and Commander-in-chief of the Federal army now at Grand Glaize, and commissioner plenipotentiary of the United States of America, for settling the terms upon which a permanent and lasting peace shall be made with each and every of the hostile tribes, or nations of Indians northwest of the Ohio, and of the said United States, actuated by the purest principles of humanity, and urged by pity for the errors into which bad and designing men have led you, from the head of my army, now in possession of your abandoned villages and settlements, do hereby once more extend the friendly hand of peace towards you, and invite each and every of the hostile tribes of Indians to

appoint deputies to meet me and my army, without delay, between this place and Roche de Bout, in order to settle the preliminaries of a lasting peace, which may eventually and soon restore to you the Delawares, Miamies, Shawanese, and all other tribes and nations lately settled at this place, and on the margins of the Miami and au Glaize rivers, your late grounds and possessions, and to preserve you and your distressed and hapless women and children from danger and famine, during the present fall and ensuing winter.

The arm of the United States is strong and powerful, but they love mercy and kindness more than war and desolation.

And, to remove any doubts or apprehensions of danger to the persons of the deputies whom you may appoint to meet this army, I hereby pledge my sacred honor for their safety and return, and send Christopher Miller, an adopted Shawnee, and a Shawnee warrior, whom I took prisoner two days ago, as a flag, who will advance in their front to meet me.

Mr. Miller was taken prisoner by a party of my warriors, six moons since, and can testify to you the kindness which I have shown to your people, my prisoners, that is, five warriors and two women, who are now all safe and well at Greenville.

But, should this invitation be disregarded, and my flag, Mr. Miller, be detained, or injured, I will immediately order all those prisoners to be put to death, without distinction, and some of them are known to belong to the first families of your nations.

BROTHERS: Be no longer deceived or led astray by the false promises and language of the bad white men at the foot of the rapids; they have neither the power nor inclination to protect you. No longer shut your eyes to your true interest and happiness, nor your ears to this last overture of peace. But, in pity to your innocent women and children, come and prevent the further effusion of your blood; let them experience the kindness and friendship of the United States of America, and the invaluable blessings of peace and tranquility.

ANTHONY WAYNE

GRAND GLAIZE, 13th August, 1794.[22]

CHAPTER 23

March Up the Maumee

GENERAL WAYNE HAD NO INTENTION OF waiting for a reply to his message of peace. The fort was nearing completion, and the legion would soon be free to resume operations. After examining the unnamed post, General Scott supposedly remarked, "I defy the English, Indians & all the devils in hell to take it"; Wayne promptly christened it Fort Defiance. Four blockhouses projected outward at each corner from the line of pickets that connected them so that artillery could be fired at attackers through embrasures on three sides of each structure, the same type of plan used earlier at Fort Recovery. Smaller buildings inside the stockade were used as officer quarters and storehouses. There were two gates, one facing the confluence of the two rivers and the second directly opposite, the former being used by watering parties who could descend in relative safety to a small sandbar under cover of fire from two blockhouses. Major Hunt would assume command of the post. Born in Boston in 1755, Hunt was a minuteman in Craft's company during the fighting at Lexington and Concord, being wounded shortly thereafter during the Battle at Bunker Hill. He participated in Wayne's storming of Stony Point, where "having cut down some picketing, and putting forward with his leg through an aperture, Hunt was run through the calf of his right leg with a British bayonet, when his assailant was in turn bayonetted by a Sergeant next to him." Wounded a third time at Yorktown, Hunt served until the end of the Revolution, then returned to the army as a captain under General St. Clair. Those left behind at Fort Defiance under Hunt's command would include Major Hughes, Capt. Robert Thomson, Lts. Isaac Younghusband and Charles Hyde, Surgeon's Mate Joseph Andrews, "all of the Sick and Lame of the Regular Troops," and thirty ailing Kentuckians. About seventy Chickasaws and Choctaws, despite their previous vows of fidelity, suddenly turned hesitant and, in the words of Captain Miller, "would not go on with us." Most of the wagons and heavy baggage were also left inside the fort "so that the Army may move as light as possible."[1]

Wayne had expected to leave Fort Defiance on August 14, but a heavy rain that lasted most of the day and his recurring battle with gout postponed the departure until the next day. Pioneers turned out and began clearing a road toward Snake Town, the road cutters being protected by Ephraim Kibbey's scouts. Mindful that there was but one set of muster rolls for the mounted volunteers, "which possibly may be lost" over the next few days, Wayne ordered the company officers to make out two duplicate rolls to ensure that records for his high-priced auxiliaries might be scrupulously maintained. Although the legion had yet to leave the Grand Glaize, a rumor had gained credence in the Atlantic states that the campaign had already reached a satisfactory conclusion. Two men from Canada claimed that Wayne had dispatched all of his mounted men under General Scott to take Fort Miamis. According to their report, Scott ordered the British commander to surrender his post and remove his garrison from U.S. territory. When that summons was denied, Scott reportedly said, "If the fort was not instantly evacuated, they would attack it sword in hand, & put every man to death." Intimidated by the close approach of the mounted Kentuckians, the garrison supposedly marched out and grounded their arms without a fight. Scott then gave the British soldiers a day's provisions and sent them packing, enjoining them "*never to let him catch them again within the territory of the United States.*" Startled by this British action, combined with their recent defeat at Fort Recovery, leaders of the Indian confederacy allegedly "sent a hatchet and string of wampum to Simcoe, saying that the hatchet was too blunt." This account of Scott's fictitious capture of Fort Miamis was eagerly read by eastern readers starved for news from the frontier, but not a word of it was true.[2]

The legion marched for Snake Town at 5:00 A.M. on August 15, the movement being captured in the glowing prose of an enlisted man: "In anxious Expectation we wait the Signal for a Move; at length the sprightly Drums bids the hardy Soldiery resume their Duty, the Lines are formed, the March begins, and the lovely Music of the Legion adds additional Life to the steady, firm and undaunted Steps of its Veterans. With Chearfulness and Life the March is continued nine miles down the Miami of the Lakes to Sneakes-Town, where as usual we halt and encamp." Reality differed somewhat from this enthusiastic depiction. The entire legion, except for the riflemen and light infantry of the right wing and one brigade of mounted volunteers, waded across the Maumee to its north shore in "the Greatest confusion & disorder." Lieutenant Clark watched as if "every man seemed to be for himself and I at once saw Dragoons sev'l pices of Artillery Infantry & Riflemen with several waggons nos. of pack horses all huddled together in the river." General Wilkinson estimated that one thousand Indians could have defeated Wayne's entire force in a matter of minutes had they attacked during this disjointed crossing. Affairs did not improve as the legion's center constantly crowded Wilkinson's infantry marching along the riverbank, the two commands becoming "frequently intermixed." Wilkinson also feared for the safety of his riflemen and light infantry on the south bank should Indians attack, declaring that the volunteers "would make little resistance, and that his light troops in that quarter would be sacrificed."[3]

Wayne's attack of gout had worsened, but he insisted on leading his troops on horse-back, though he could not mount without assistance. Wilkinson thought he seemed "deranged and incoherent" on the march, and "the state of his health exasperates his naturally bad temper." Musing on what might happen, Wilkinson assumed that "the debility and irritability of the C in C would in case of attack distract him or perhaps produce a fit—happy situation this for the army!" While in a critical mood, Wilkinson also lashed out at an old foe, Edward Butler, now of the Fourth Sub-Legion but formerly Wayne's indispensable assistant. After the desertion of Newman and the arrest of Cooper, Butler took up the compass and acted as surveyor for the road. Dismissing him as a fool for giving up "an active and honorable station to succeed a traitor," the general noted that Butler, "in laying out our incampment has made an Error of 150 yds in each side." Misery loves company, so after his troops had marched from the Grand Glaize gardens, Wayne directed that the flour ration be cut in half to conserve the limited supply on hand with the pack train. One enlisted man added that "the beef rations [were] not equal to half a ration in quality."[4]

All troops south of the Maumee River crossed to the north bank on the morning of August 16, concentrating Wayne's entire force in anticipation of imminent action. Scott's main body of volunteers marched on the legion's left, but sizeable mounted parties were detached to both front and rear. This day's route was over rough, brushy country, criss-crossed by ravines, gullies, and "short steep hills," which caused many brief halts pleasing to those marching on foot. The luxuriant cornfields had been left behind, only a single patch being visible on the south bank. One soldier sought to supplement his half ration of flour and, disobeying orders, crossed the river to pick corn, but he did not return and was presumed taken by the Indians. General Wilkinson took this occasion to complain about the situation into which Wayne had taken the legion, writing, "it is a singular spectacle to see an army 100 miles removed from its magazines and near 300 from any auxiliary force, advancing at half allowance of provision upon an enemy whom they have not yet seen." It was singular indeed.[5]

General Wayne's state of health seemed better that morning, although Wilkinson thought him "still feeble and indisposed." The constant jostling of his painful leg resulted in a halt being called at about noon, "the Indisposition of the Commander in Chief rendering it necessary for him to be refreshed with a few Hours Rest and Concealment from the Sun, which now shone forth extremely hot." While enjoying this midday pause, Christopher Miller suddenly appeared with a response to Wayne's final peace proposal:

> The Warriors of all our Nations were here on our feet to meet you when we heard you were coming against us—then we received your Speech by a Man who had been with us before & a Shawenoe man you had taken prisoner a few days ago—Brothers you can't imagine how glad we were to find you had still some pity for our Women & Children—Brothers don't be in too great a hurry—You know very well we are not like you white people who do not consult in the manner we do—You have only to write & your Business is done, but we Indians must do all our Business with every Nation of the Confederacy which takes up a great deal

of time—Brothers if you are sincere in your hearts you will set down still where you are & not build Forts in our Village—And in the Space of ten days you shall see us coming with the Flag before us as you have mentioned.

The Flag which is now sent to you in return—it is the Wish of the Warriors that there shall be a continual communication of our Speeches to each other— And when you have read our Speech which is greatly moved by sincere tokens of Your Friendship & your Pity to our Women & Children then we further expect that we shall have likewise an Answer to our Speeches. We will also sit down again here with our Warriors till that time.

Miller told various officers that the letter had been written by Young White Eyes and that the majority of Indians were in favor of war. But Abraham Williams, a half-blood Wyandotte who spoke good English, confirmed that many Indians were ready to accept Wayne's offer. According to Williams, the great Indian leader Little Turtle, whom historians have portrayed as leader of those seeking peace with Wayne, was actually aligned with the war faction. It was Little Turtle who suggested, "We will stop our Brother for ten days, we shall then have all our force collected and will go up and fight him." At the insistence of Little Turtle, Capt. Joseph Bunbury of the Fifth Regiment wrote the Indian response. Colonel McKee confirmed the significance of this message, saying, "It is entirely caculated to gain a few days time in hopes that the Poutewatomis and Indians about Detroit may increase their strength."[6]

Miller had reached the Foot of the Rapids on the morning of August 14. Amid all the commotion caused by his arrival, Colonel McKee heard Miller tell the Indians that "the designs of the Army were against the English." After McKee confronted him about this statement, Miller agreed to take the following oath, sworn to before Captain Elliott and representatives of the various Indian nations: "I, Christopher Miller, sent to this place as a Flag from General Wayne Commander-in-Chief of the American Army, to the hostile indians do make oath & swear that the said General desired me to inform the indians, if they would withdraw themselves, or come and make peace with him, his designs were not to be directed against them, but to drive away the English from the Country." Up at Detroit, Lieutenant Colonel England still felt that "Wayne's Instructions do not authorize him to attack the British Posts notwithstanding his Gasconade to Miller." Even when combined with Robert Newman's claim that Wayne intended to build a fort at the Foot of the Rapids, England still thought it to be "very vague Information" that left "room for much Conjecture."[7]

But Lieutenant Colonel England was taking no chances. In early August, the leading Wyandotte chiefs had come to him, bringing the hatchet that Lt. Gov. Henry Hamilton had given that nation during the Revolution. They demanded that England scrape off the rust and sharpen the hatchet, symbolically demanding British assistance against Wayne's invasion of their homeland. If that help did not materialize, the Wyandottes warned him that they would stand aside so that Wayne would "take you by the hand and sling you across the River." Realizing that the Indian confederacy might prove to be a weak link in his defense of Detroit, on August 9, England bolstered the detachment already at Fort Miamis by sending a new commanding officer, Maj. William Campbell of the Twenty-Fourth Regiment, fifty soldiers from that regiment, a squad from the Royal Artillery, a detachment of the Queen's Rangers, and two small howitzers. Francis Baby led about one hundred unarmed Canadian workmen to the Maumee, where they assisted in completing the post. Lt. Col. William Caldwell took Capt. Daniel McKillip's militia company to reinforce the fort or "to be employed as Major Campbell may direct." Information from Detroit indicated that "all was in great confusion and alarm" over Wayne's approach, one observer noting, "The shops are closed, the merchants have gone to the Miami against the foe, and all the militia and men in the country must go thither." Lieutenant Colonel England advised Lieutenant Governor Simcoe, "I have ordered the Militia Commanders to have their Regiments ready to move at the shortest notice, whether in the whole or by detachments as may be considered expedient."[8]

Officers in the legion seemed united in their opinion that the Indian's pacific response was but a ploy to gain time. General Wilkinson dismissed Christopher Miller's return message as written "in terms equivocal, & I think sarcastic." Lieutenant Clark said it "was generally understood as a Challenge," while Captain Miller said he expected "an Action in the Course of 24 Hours." Another soldier observed, "Thus much says British Policy thro' the Medium of the artful Elliot, M'Kee and the just spoken of White-Eyes; but discerning WAYNE is too well guarded against their Wiles, and like a discreet and politic General he is moving his Army on." And so he was, marching a few more miles before settling into his fortified camp.[9]

The legion was up and on the move at the usual hour on the morning of August 17, both officers and men being "thoughtlessly in high spirits." General Wilkinson listened to soldiers say "the enemy are to vanish on our approach," then called them "sanguine and ignorant" for repeating such nonsense. Lieutenant Clark, who marched with Hamtramck's left wing, bemoaned the "thickness of the woods" they had to pass through. He also wrote enviously of those who traveled through more open country: "The right wing of the army expereanced no inconveneance, but on the contrary enjoyed many pleasing Seans & Prospects afforded from the banks of the River and could but behold with pleasure the gentle gliding of the waters over the Broad Rocky Bead [Bed]." The main body marched about fourteen miles that day, but the left wing became lost at one point and went an additional two miles out of its way before getting back on track. Sometime that day, one of the legion captains and an artificer got into a violent argument, the officer striking at his adversary with his sword. The artificer avoided the stroke, disarmed his attacker, and threatened his life by placing a knife to his chest. Bystanders separated the antagonists, but the unidentified officer placed the artificer under arrest. General Wayne, who was still unable to mount his horse and even had trouble standing unaided, released the artificer and declared that "he ought to have put the Officer to death." There was no further inquiry into the altercation, but other quartermaster employees heckled the unidentified officer without mercy.[10]

Wayne's army halted for the evening at the Head of the Rapids of the Maumee River. Francis Jones noticed that the river was about six hundred yards wide at this point and resembled a flooded meadow. One area resident explained that the term "rapids" referred to "shallow water, strong currents and a rocky bottom, which cause the whole surface of the water to appear foaming and white, like breakers at sea." The Kentuckians camped opposite three small islands and discovered that the riverbed was formed of "shelly Rock," which allowed the horsemen to easily cross to the opposite bank. Signs of Indians became more common, trails being discovered and sentinels occasionally firing at furtive shadows. A detachment of mounted scouts hunting for the enemy encountered an Indian scouting party; both groups fired at one another and retreated, the only American casualty being a wounded horse. One soldier described the tension that gripped them all: "We suppose ourselves now within seventeen Miles of Roch De Boo, at which Place, as has been before observed, the whole Force of the Savages lie encamped; therefore to-morrow will in all Probability produce a Victory or a Defeat—the latter we fear not, the former we flatter ourselves we are assured of; and now it is that the Hearts of American Veterans beat high with that Courage, which will no Doubt shortly gain them immortal Honor." He concluded with the bold assertion, "Be this as it may, resolved we are on *Victory* or *Death*."[11]

Due to the enemy's proximity, General Wayne delayed his advance on August 18 for a few hours while the country ahead was thoroughly scouted. Interesting discoveries were made when the march commenced, as one soldier reported: "In our Rout we pass several small Vilages, among the common Cabins of which there were large and convenient Store-Houses, in which many Books of Accounts were found of thirty Years standing, likewise Silversmith's Tools and many other Articles, which proves that extensive Connections have been kept up in this Quarter between the Whites of Detroit and the Savages." Soldiers examined the remains of six or eight stores that had supposedly been kept by French traders for well over one hundred years. The river meandered in a northeasterly direction, the north bank being level, thinly timbered, dotted here and there with orchards, and covered with grass and peavine, which the horses found to their liking. Here at Roche de Bout, the end of the upper rapids, the river began to broaden and the current became more sluggish and choked with weeds, again giving an illusion of being a flooded meadow. Captain Miller thought the scene had a "very eligent and Romantic Appeerence," and William Clark said it appeared to be "one of the most beautiful Landskapes ever painted."[12]

Roche de Bout was reached after a march of only nine or ten miles. Lieutenant Clark described the impressive natural landmark as "a small Island of Creggy Rocks of Considerable hight, the top of it is only accessable by one Small point, its Summit is covered with Small groths of Cedar." This rock towered about thirty feet above the surface and looked like a circular house plopped into the river, the cedars increasing its apparent height and seeming to form a roof. Canadians had given it the French name for standing rock. As yet unknown to the white men, there was a legend associated with Roche de Bout that involved the Ottawa Nation:

> One of the young [boys of the] tribe, engaged in playing on Roche de Boeuf (Rock in the River), fell over the precipice and was instantly killed. The dusky husband,

on his return from the council fires, on being informed of the fate of his prospective successor, at once sent the mother in search of her papoose, by pushing her
over the rocky sides into the shallow waters of the Maumee. Her next-of-kin,
according to Indian law, executed the murdering husband, and was in turn executed in the same manner, until the frantic passions were checked by the arrival
of the principal chiefs of the tribe. This sudden outburst cost the tribe nearly
two-thirds of its members, whose bodies were taken from the river and buried
with full Indian honors the next day.

Although the riverbed was formed of black stone, inland the soil was obviously fertile and
had been cultivated by the natives.[13]

   With Wells and McClellan incapacitated, Wayne turned to George Shrim, ordering
that officer to take out a mounted party of five scouts and search for signs of the Indian
army. After penetrating far enough to glimpse the first Indian villages, Shrim's detachment was ambushed by a large party of warriors on horseback and chased away. The celebrated scoundrel and daredevil William May was taken prisoner by a Delaware after his
horse fell on the smooth black rocks in the river. When May did not return to camp,
Lieutenant Bowyer concluded, "What his fate may be must be left to future success."
According to a second-hand story, May, who was at first rumored among the Indians to
be the elusive Captain Wells, saw there was no escape and sought to do as much damage
to his captors as possible. He confessed to them that General Wayne only had an army
of about five hundred soldiers and that he did not expect to be attacked. Inspired by this
apparent superiority in numbers, the Indians, who now recognized their prisoner from
his earlier stint working undercover for Wilkinson, decided to kill him. The white captive John Brickell explained how May's luck finally ran out: "They told him, 'We know
you—you speak Indian language—you not content to live with us; to-morrow we take
you to that tree, (pointing to a very large burr-oak at the edge of the clearing which was
near the British Fort), we will tie you up and make a mark on your breast, and we will try
what Indian can shoot nearest it.' It so turned out. The next day, the very day before the
battle, they tied him up, made a mark on his breast, and riddled his body with bullets,
shooting at least fifty into him." Thus ended the life of the celebrated William May—
criminal, villain, rogue, secret agent, and scout—the quintessential frontiersman who
seemed to delight in the deadly cat-and-mouse life of stalking and fighting Indians.[14]

   Wayne's gout seemed to be easing somewhat, and he began to stand unaided,
although he still could not mount or dismount his horse without the help of two men.
This constant pain had begun to wear on him, a fact that became obvious during a con-
sultation with Wilkinson, Hamtramck, and Scott on the afternoon of August 18. Wayne
informed them that, based upon information brought back by Shrim, he planned to build
a fortification at that spot in which he would deposit all the provisions and impedimenta.
At the suggestion of Wilkinson, soldiers were ordered to sleep with their weapons and
wearing their accouterments. Wayne proposed to send about five hundred Kentuckians,
supported by a like number, to reconnoiter, but General Scott said that he feared bringing
on a general engagement. Wayne responded with "an heavy Oath," declaring that "he

wanted to know the nature of the intermediate ground and the position of the enemy."
After this meeting concluded, Hamtramck swore "*the Old man was mad!*" Meanwhile,
Major Price had been downriver toward Fort Miamis with his battalion of scouts. He
reported finding one spot where, judging from the ground and the extent of displaced
foliage, a large body of Indians had apparently laid an ambush for the legion.[15]

All indications pointed to the Indian confederacy having assembled a sizeable army
to oppose Wayne. Previous successes against Harmar and St. Clair had emboldened the
warriors beyond reason, and their leaders "again determined to commit the fate of themselves and their country to the issue of a general battle." According to Lt. William Henry
Harrison, "This was all that was wanted by the American commander." No longer would
the Americans be seeking small raiding parties, whose ambushes and hit-and-run tactics gave them every advantage. An Indian army would be unwieldy, with no tactics other
than surprise, so the advantage in a large-scale fight would have to go to the side with
mobility and firepower. Harrison later explained: "The tactics which had been adopted
for the American Legion, had been devised with a reference to all the subtilties, which
those of the Indians were well known to possess. It united with the apparently opposite
qualities of compactness and flexibility, and a facility of expansion under any circumstances, and in any situation, which rendered utterly abortive the peculiar tact of the
Indians in assailing the flanks of their adversaries."[16]

Everyone slept soundly that night since there were no alarms to disturb the slum-
bers of tired men. Legionnaires were up before sunrise on August 19, and everyone not
on guard pitched in at seven o'clock to work on a formidable breastwork, forty-one miles
in advance of Fort Defiance, that would hold all the supplies the men could not carry on
their persons. At this point, Wayne wanted information more than anything else.
Kibbey's Columbian Scouts went out to screen the construction project, while Captain
Shrim led a mounted party of spies back toward the Indian villages they had seen the day
before, returning in a few hours after one of them had been wounded in a skirmish. The
Kentuckians had expected to resume the march but soon learned that Wayne had other
plans. Major Price's battalion was again sent to reconnoiter the enemy, supported by
General Todd's entire brigade of volunteers, Francis Jones later writing that "a Genl &
severe action was expected to take place every Mile we advancd from this place."[17]

Price divided his men into equal detachments, each commanded by one officer, that
marched about one hundred yards apart on a wide front so that the entire force could not
be ambushed. Some of these scouts came upon a party of mounted Indians, whom they
drove back toward Fort Miamis in a bloodless chase, during which Zachariah Holliday
said there was "not a gun fired." About this time, Major Price discovered an apparent
ambush in his front and started to withdraw. Seeing this first detachment retreat, others also began to fall back until Price's entire battalion had reached General Todd's
brigade, about one mile to their rear. Todd ordered his force back to safety, where Price
informed Wayne that large numbers of Indians had evacuated their camps southwest of
the British post. The storehouses of McKee and other traders seemed to have been abandoned, but a bend in the river prevented any direct observation of Fort Miamis itself.

That afternoon, Wayne summoned Price and ordered him to take his two companies, about 150 men, on a wide circuit around the Indian forces until he struck the Maumee River below the British fort. He would then advance up the river, surprising the Indians by suddenly appearing in their rear. Price protested, saying that his tired horses could not make the required twenty-mile trek. Wayne relented and sent the Kentuckians back to camp. On their way, Lt. William Sudduth caught a loose horse that was "verry bluddy," indicating that its rider had been seriously wounded in one of the recent skirmishes.[18]

Lieutenant Bowyer saw the wisdom in constructing a fortified cache, explaining that thus "the men may be light for action" should the enemy "favor us with an interview, which if they should think proper to do, the troops are in such high spirits that we will make an easy victory of them." Captain Pike was placed in command of the logically named Fort Deposit, which would stockpile the knapsacks, baggage, provisions, cattle, and horses of the quartermaster and contractor until a battle could resolve the campaign. The captain received one special order in regard to provisions, Wayne writing, "The articles of whiskey being nearly exhausted, you will prevent a drop of it from being consumed until further orders." Pike's command would consist of six men from each battalion company, and all of the sub-legionary paymasters and quartermasters would remain behind with their invaluable statements, vouchers, and rosters. General Scott detailed one captain, two subalterns, and ninety-six enlisted men to assist in the defense of Fort Deposit, "Whilst the army is in advance." He commanded his Kentuckians to obey the orders of Captain Pike "upon all occasions," but the personal baggage of the volunteers was to be kept under the alert guard of a sergeant and twelve men at all times. Although but three sides of the fort had been completed by nightfall, everything was hustled inside "without regularity, but in vast disorder." When completed the following morning, according to Garret Burns, Fort Deposit consisted of "ditches, two feet deep, upon the earth thrown out of which, timber had been carried, and the loose brush from the inside thrown upon the outside."[19]

That afternoon, spy Paschall Hickman returned from a visit to the neighborhood of Fort Miamis and reported that the "British Union-flag is flying" from the ramparts. He had examined the fort and, though not able to estimate the size and number of its ordnance, did confirm that it was of regular construction, with barrack walls forming part of the exterior wall. Wayne issued an order that the troops should be ready to move at 2:00 A.M. on August 20, modifying the regular order of march by having the formations march two men deep and in closer order than previously. The center column would consist solely of the howitzers and their ammunition. At halts, troops were to form in two lines to receive the enemy should he appear. Both officers and men were instructed to "dress in their proper uniforms," a habit Wayne had emphasized since the legion's original formation at Pittsburgh over two years earlier. To remind his soldiers of what would be expected of them, the parole and countersign for that night were given as "Bayonet" and "Sword." Despite conducting offensive operations into Indian country, Wayne expected the enemy to strike first, forcing him to fight defensively. Yet if an attack should become necessary, the order to do so would come only from General Wayne and "shall not be attempted but by his positive order." Officers became excited about the order to advance shortly after midnight, believing that a night attack would "Supprise the Enemy in theire Camp." Some argued strongly in favor of the proposal, while nearly everyone else thought it at least worthy of discussion. This whole plan was negated by a later order postponing any advance until 5:00 A.M. the following morning. There were several alarms that night, a dozen of General Scott's sentinels firing at what they assumed to be Indians scouting their camp. The only known casualty was a soldier from the legion who happened to be wandering about in the wrong place and was wounded by one of the trigger-happy Kentuckians.[20]

Warriors from the Indian confederacy had been waiting for Wayne to advance. They had gotten their women and children out from between the invaders and Fort Miamis by placing them in camps along the Maumee River, stretching from the fort, to Swan Creek, and to the shores of Lake Erie itself. This massive influx of refugees from Grand Glaize had brought several thousand dependents to the area, which combined with the arrival of hundreds of Lake Indian warriors, placed a major strain on available food supplies. British provisions eased the crunch, but pressure had mounted on Indian leaders to drive Wayne from their lands, for to accept his peace demands would be tantamount to cowardice. On August 18, all available warriors moved about two miles south of Fort Miamis and formed a line in the trees on the north edge of a small prairie, planning to ambush the legion as it passed through this open ground. When the Americans failed to appear, the Indians returned to camp, thus allowing Major Price to safely reconnoiter the site of their now-abandoned trap. While Fort Deposit was under construction on August 19, the Indians, still "in good spirits," arranged a line from the river bluffs into the timber and waited for what they expected to be "another St. Clair victory." They had been ready for battle early that morning and, alerted by the advance of Price's mounted scouts, stayed in position until nightfall. These two days had placed a strain on the Indian ranks, which "suffered much from thirst and hunger." In typical fashion when battle was imminent, most of the Indians had eaten only an evening meal on August 17, 18, and 19, believing that "if a man is wounded in the bowels when he is empty that his entrails are not so likely to be cut as when they are full." But there were many complaints from the warriors that they could not continue on but one meal a day, and that undoubtedly a meager one because of over-crowding in the immediate vicinity. At a council held on the night of August 19, Indian leaders admitted that Wayne might wait several days before attacking and gave their fighters permission to eat breakfast the following morning.[21]

August 20 dawned rainy and wet. Tired warriors, mindful of the Americans' previous inactivity, loitered in their camps before preparing the first breakfast they had tasted in three days. Only the Wyandottes, about 150 strong, promptly headed for their place in some timber blown down years before by a tornado. Captain McKillip's militia company from Essex County in Canada joined them on the right flank of the Indian position. Near the Foot of the Rapids, Abraham Williams watched various detachments straggle up to join the Wyandottes, aligning toward the river in the following order: Mingo, Delaware, Shawnee, Potawatomi, Ottawa, and Chippewa. A few Miamis, remnants of

that once-dreaded nation, fell in with the others, and a party of Mohawks from the supposedly peaceful Six Nations added their firepower to the Indian army. The warriors
formed a ragged line "about Six deep, scattered as the trees," on a diagonal from the river,
the right considerably in advance of the left, which rested on bluffs overlooking the
Maumee River. A broad floodplain, choked with rank vegetation, was left unoccupied.
The left was formed in an open wood, mostly oak trees with little underbrush. As the
line wound toward the right, the woods became thicker, this natural cover being augmented by the fallen trees on the Wyandotte front.

Abraham Williams and his brother Isaac estimated that the Indians numbered
between eleven hundred and twelve hundred warriors, including about one hundred ado-
lescents. About one hundred fighters had no guns, being armed only with tomahawks.
There was considerable difficulty in determining the actual numbers involved since so
many warriors acted on their own. Captain Tommy, a mixed-blood Shawnee, was one
such individual. He had stayed north of Fort Miamis the previous night, then rowed a
canoe upriver with his squaw, son, and infant daughter to join the fight and get his share
of plunder. Some of Captain Tommy's fellow warriors had assumed their places, others
were casually on their way, still more were cooking breakfast, and a tardy few were still
sleeping. Just as the Indians lazily prepared for battle, alert scouts brought the long-
awaited news: the Legion of the United States was on the move.[22]

CHAPTER 24

Battle of Fallen Timbers

AFTER AN EARLY MORNING THUNDERSTORM drenched everyone at Fort Deposit, the federal troops divested themselves of every type of baggage, including knapsacks, and "carried nothing but a blanket and two days provisions per man." The legion formed in columns, General Wilkinson's right wing next to the river; headquarters, packhorses loaded with the reserve ammunition, and artillery train in the center; and Lieutenant Colonel Hamtramck's wing on the left. The command was surrounded by its typical screen of light troops. General Todd's brigade of mounted volunteers marched to the left and slightly to the rear of Hamtramck, while General Barbee's brigade of Kentuckians rode in the rear. Major Price's battalion of two companies, which had been over the ground toward Fort Miamis the two preceding days, led the advance of Wayne's force as a "Corps of observation." Captain Kibbey's Columbian Scouts had forded the river to the south bank the night before, with instructions "to scour the woods, and rouse the Indians, who were supposed to be concealed on that side, and likely to endanger the rear of the American troops, as they could easily have crossed by wading the ripple above the rapids." Following a careful reconnaissance, Kibbey could report that there were no Indians to be found on the south shore that morning.[1]

Wayne got his troops moving between seven and eight o'clock, the sky gradually clearing and the weather turning hot and humid. As he rode along at the head of his troops, General Wilkinson took note of the landscape. The Maumee River seemed to be "bubbling over a Rocky sheet" in its bed, being bordered on the north by "a luxuriant prairie" from one-quarter to one-half mile in width. Beyond the floodplain, bluffs covered with small timber and brush rose to a height of nearly one hundred feet. Atop these bluffs, the ground leveled off. Timber thickened to the north, where the land became increasingly "swampy and in some places almost impervious from the underwood and small growth." Wilkinson found that his wing encountered many troublesome "deep, steep and short ravines, runing nearly at right angles to the general course" of the bluffs.

Lieutenant Clark, marching through the tangle of underbrush on the left, "found the way extremely bad," the forward movement being "much embarrassed by the thickness of the woods."[2]

Major Price's battalion of scouts moved forward at a brisk clip, causing the front guard of the legion, seventy-four soldiers commanded by Captain Cooke, to hurry in order to keep up. Wayne had ordered Price "to keep sufficiently advanced, so as to give timely notice for the troops to form in case of action." When he had gotten to within a half mile of where Indians had been encountered on August 19, the major ordered a halt, and the Kentuckians refreshed themselves by drinking some water and removing all their excess clothing. Price's scouts generally advanced behind two vedettes, who moved about one hundred yards in advance of the main body "to guard against surprise." These men were always "called out in rotation as they stood on the list" so that everyone could share in this hazardous duty. Due to the danger that lurked just ahead, Lieutenant Sudduth asked for volunteers from Baker's company on this particular morning and was gratified when almost half of his men stepped forward. Thomas Moore, from Woodford County, and William Steele, of Fayette County, were selected to lead the advance.[3]

Moore and Steele stripped for action, mounted their horses, and headed for Fort Miamis, warily eyeing every thicket and tree. They had not proceeded more than one hundred yards before Indians, concealed by trees and tall grass, opened fire. Both men fell from their horses as the company galloped forward to within twenty yards of the concealed foe. Steele was already dead, but some Kentuckians jumped down and rescued the mortally wounded Moore. Enemy fire intensified, so Major Price shouted for his men to retreat, the route of which took them along the diagonal Indian line. Lieutenant Sudduth remembered that, as warriors jumped from cover to shoot at the scouts, they fired "with a tremendious roar at a verry short distance." Another party of Indians, led by several on horseback, advanced toward Price's command and began shooting. A ragged volley from the Kentuckians slowed their attack. Sudduth, Luke Hood, and Harry Martin aimed at one of the opposing horsemen, but the lieutenant was just a few seconds faster than his companions and shot the Indian from his mount. Those warriors advancing on foot now began to draw near and opened a "verry heavy fire" that elicited another order from Price to retreat. Among those wounded was John Montgomery of Arnold's company, who was struck by a ball that entered his left elbow and passed out his forearm, inflicting an injury that would prevent him from extending or contracting the fingers of his hand.

The scouts had gotten about seventy yards ahead of their pursuers when someone called out that a wounded man had been left behind. Sudduth glanced back and saw one of his scouts running at top speed to avoid being taken by the Indians, who were now only about forty yards behind him. The lieutenant turned back with five of his men to effect a rescue. When they reached their comrade, the warriors, then only about thirty yards distant, dropped into the weeds and opened fire. After the wounded man had tried unsuccessfully to climb up on Sudduth's horse three times, William Richie and Harvey Martin "lit from their horses & lifted the man up." The lieutenant seemed to look right into the muzzles of the enemy's rifles, and he noticed that "the bark of the trees flew into our faces" as balls struck nearby. Just after the wounded man got up behind him, Sudduth's horse was shot and became unmanageable. As his comrades galloped off and the Indians advanced with raised tomahawks, the wounded animal reared up several times and refused to budge. Just when the enemy began to close in, the horse started for the rear. The rider remembered: "I gave him the spur & pushed him on the blood gushing out of the wound, his mouth & nose verry fast. He ran about one hundred and fifty yards & stoped. I leaped off him & left the man, who informed me afterwards that the horse fell immediately after I left him. We had got far enough in advance of the Indians for the wounded man to save himself." Sudduth ran after his men and got up behind one of them just as the advance guard of the legion came up. When the scouts stopped for a moment, Cpl. Thomas White gave up his horse to the lieutenant, who quickly loaded his rifle and began to re-form the company.[4]

Some time before Privates Moore and Steele rode into the enemy ambush, General Wilkinson had spurred his horse to the edge of the bluffs, hoping to catch a glimpse of Alexander McKee's complex of buildings on the opposite shore and Fort Miamis a couple of miles to the north. He then rode over to report what he had seen to General Wayne, but the commander was more intent on coordinating his advance and, according to a story told by General Scott, "cursed him, and told him to go to his post." This anecdote came by way of Capt. Marcus Richardson, who admitted, "Wilkinson I always regarded as a slippery fellow." Wilkinson returned to the bluffs with Robert Elliott, the contractor; Surgeon Nathan Hayward; and Wayne's aide Henry DeButts, whom the general had undoubtedly sent along to make his own observations and, perhaps, keep an eye on his "slippery" subordinate. Just after reaching this high ground in advance of the right wing, Hayward called everyone's attention to some galloping horsemen. These stragglers were dismissed as more volunteers "in quest of plunder," a common sight recently, until gunshots were heard to the front. About fifty volunteers burst into view, retiring "in great confusion and before a faint fire of the enemy." DeButts galloped off to headquarters, and Wilkinson described the moment as "critical" since no orders had yet been given to form the legion for battle. While one of Wilkinson's aides carried his order for the First Sub-Legion to form into line, the general halted some disorganized Kentuckians and gave them a short inspirational speech about "name fame and Country," convincing at least a few to turn about and fight the Indians, who were now but 150 yards distant. When Wilkinson rode off to supervise the formation of the right wing, "the moment his back was turned they broke and resumed their flight thro' the 1st Sub Legion."[5]

Following the retreat of Major Price's scouts, Indian fire concentrated on the front guard of the legion, under command of Captain Cooke and Lt. John Steele, who led the right and left detachments, respectively. Cooke's guard was about four hundred yards behind Price's scouts when the attack began, and the captain watched helplessly as the horsemen, "without returning the fire fled until they came in front of the guards about 80 yards." Acting according to Wayne's order of August 25, 1793, Cooke ordered his men to fire on the retreating Kentuckians, stopping them in their tracks and diverting them

toward the river. If these were the men encountered by Wilkinson, their rough treatment by Cooke's detachment may have dissuaded them from rendering the legion any
more assistance. Some Indians left their cover to pursue the scouts and encountered the
right wing of the guards, who immediately opened fire "in very good order." A few men
on Cooke's right thought the Indians had slipped into their rear and "got into confusion
and began to fly." Of the thirty-seven men in his wing, the captain could only rally about
one-third, whom he led back to join Steele's half of the guards. Warriors now started "a
heavy fire" on the remaining guards, who stood their ground long enough to respond
with "three well-directed fires." Cooke remembered that the Indians then "pressed so
hard upon the guard, that we were obliged to retreat and fire for about one hundred
yards, by which time they came on so close and in such numbers, that I was obliged to
direct the guards to make the best of their way to their respective companies." As John
O'Brien ran to the rear, he received a rather singular wound, being "shot in the low part
of his back, the ball passed through the bottom of his Belly & lodged in a certain part
in front, in his Penis." If O'Brien survived this potentially fatal injury, his extraordinary
wound must have been the butt of men's jokes for months.[6]

By the time Captain Cooke's guard detachment collapsed, General Wayne had
deployed two light infantry companies across the front of Wilkinson's wing and two
more in advance of Hamtramck's left wing. From the river, the companies of light
infantrymen stretched inland in the following order: Lieutenant Gaines, First Sub-
Legion; Capt. Howell Lewis, Third; Captain Brock, Fourth; and Haskell's company,
Second. The various sub-legions formed behind this screen of skirmishers in the same
order. Just by chance, the companies of Captain Cooke and Lieutenant Steele stood next
to one another in the battle line, the former on the right of the Fourth Sub-Legion and
the latter on the left of the Third. Cooke remembered, "we accidentally met them on
our flight, at which time they were advancing in good order," and he immediately
replaced Ens. Thomas Swaine at the head of his infantry company. Wilkinson had meanwhile ridden toward the left, where he found the Third Sub-Legion formed "much to
close," and he hastily arranged them properly. While there, he observed that Howell
Lewis's light infantrymen had been pushed back and become intermingled with some
troops of Hamtramck's wing. When the general saw Captain MisCampbell, senior officer in the dragoons, riding by with his black-horse troop under a scattered fire from Indians about one hundred yards distant, he asked, "What was the matter in front?" Mis-
Campbell answered, "Every thing is confusion," and asked what he should do. Wilkinson
said that the captain's troop was not under his command but recommended he fall back
and form in the rear.[7]

As senior captain, Jacob Kingsbury, the hero of Dunlap's Station, commanded the
Third Sub-Legion that day because Lt. Col. Henry Gaither and one of the majors were
then serving in Georgia, while the other two majors were incapacitated. But the captain
was well qualified for his command, for in the words of Lieutenant Harrison, "Sparta nor
Rome never produced a better soldier." To Kingsbury's right, Gaines's light infantry had
been pressed backward, although still "firing as warmly as the smallness of their number

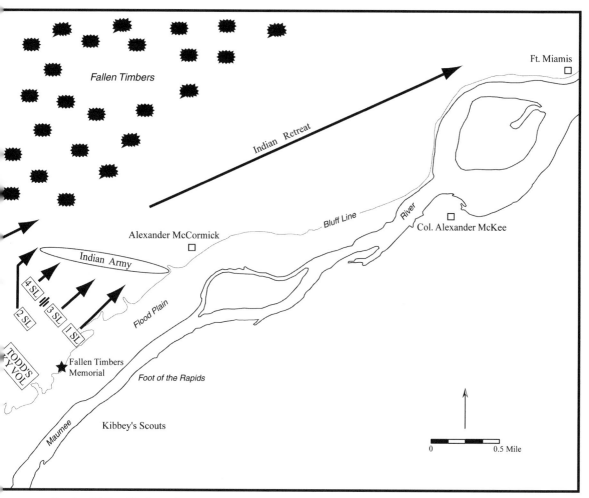

Battle of Fallen Timbers, August 20, 1794

would permit," so that the enemy had advanced to within about eighty yards of Kingsbury's command. Just ahead, fugitives from Captain Cooke's front guard had thrown
part of Howell Lewis's light infantry into disorder. Lewis commanded the left of his line
to retire about forty yards, "where he formed them and joined the right, which had stood
their ground." Enemy fire intensified, and Reuben Thacker, formerly a blacksmith from
Fluvanna County, Virginia, before enlisting in Lewis's company, was struck by two balls,
one in his lower abdomen and a second that entered near his spine and fractured his
clavicle and humerus, leaving his right arm virtually useless. At this point, Kingsbury
noticed that Wilkinson "appeared cool, and self-possessed; and, I thought, exposed himself more than necessary." The captain asked permission to charge, but since Wilkinson
had received no orders from Wayne to counterattack, his request was denied. The general then sent a sergeant to order Captain Springer to advance along the bluffs with a portion of the Third Sub-Legion rifle battalion and get behind the Indian line. But Springer
mistakenly descended into the floodplain, where there were no Indians and his company

could hardly force its way through the rank vegetation; Wilkinson quickly ordered him back up to the high ground. After Lieutenant Schaumburgh delivered an order on this flank, he charged into a thicket and actually drove one warrior "upon the bayonets" of the light infantry.[8]

Everyone seemed to concentrate on fighting those warriors closest to the river, probably because the soldiers could see much better on that part of the field. General Wayne sent Captain MisCampbell to turn the Indian flank along the bluffs, explaining that area "afforded a favorable field for that corps to act in." Wayne may have expected the captain to attack with his entire squadron, but he did so only with the black-horse troop, crossing a deep ravine and then riding through the Third Sub-Legion and into a group of warriors. MisCampbell's charge recoiled when the captain received a mortal wound in the chest. Although Wilkinson could do nothing to save the ill-fated MisCampbell, he did form Lieutenant Webb's gray-horse troop behind the right of his line, with orders to follow at 150 yards distance until such time as the horsemen could deliver an effective blow. Even Lieutenant Sudduth headed for the open ground near the bluffs. Having collected about three dozen scouts from both companies of Price's battalion, he galloped toward the right "in front of the Indian line & passed between them & our Army, as they approached each other." Several times the scouts halted to fire on the foe but continued on, always within gunshot, until they finally rounded the Indian flank, which prompted the warriors there to raise "a schrill hallow" of alarm.[9]

Advancing with the middle column, General Wayne had first been advised of the Indian attack by Lieutenant Schaumburgh, Wilkinson's aide, who immediately rode to the commander upon hearing the first gunshots. Wayne told him that he too had heard six or eight shots. Schaumburgh replied excitedly, "I have heard at least 150 shot." Just then, a portion of Major Price's scouts could be seen galloping back from the Indian ambush, so someone asked what should be done. After a brief pause, Wayne ordered, "Prepare to receive the Enemy in front in two Lines." Wilkinson stated this was the only order his wing received during the entire action, and Hamtramck confirmed that he had received no other orders on the left wing. Yet Wayne, who kept the dragoons, light infantry, and some riflemen purposely under his direction, did give orders. In his report of the battle, he specifically mentions that his three aides—Henry DeButts, Thomas Lewis, and William Henry Harrison—and Adj. John Mills "rendered the most essential service by communicating my orders in every direction." The general was compelled to use his staff to carry even the most trivial instructions because the rainstorm had soaked the drums, which rendered them worthless in transmitting orders. Afraid that Wayne's impetuosity might carry him into harm's way, Lieutenant Harrison spoke up: "General Wayne, I am afraid you will go into the fight yourself and forget to give me the necessary field orders." "Perhaps I may," replied Wayne, "and if I do, recollect that the standing order for the day is, 'Charge the damned rascals with the bayonet.'" Schaumburgh singled out young Harrison for lavish praise. He said of his fellow lieutenant: "Harrison was in the foremost front of the hottest battle—his person was exposed from the commencement to the close of the action. Wherever duty called, he hastened, regardless of danger, and by his efforts and example contributed as much to secure the fortune of the day, as any other officer subordinate to the commander-in-chief."[10]

As soon as the legion began to form for action, Wayne sent for his artillery. Lieutenant Pope, commanding Peirce's company, and Captain Ford brought forward their teams of horses and, within a few minutes, had unloaded their howitzers, sixteen of which comprised the legion artillery, according to Abraham Glassmire. Sgt. Maj. Thomas Underwood said that Pope took the honor of firing the first shell, but after firing only a few rounds, the lieutenant ordered his gunners to switch to grape and canister as the Indians exploited their advantage over Captain Cooke's front guard. The ground was obviously unsuited for artillery because of the timber, but Pope's men kept up their fire anyway. Over in the Indian ranks, Captain Tommy would always remember how the howitzers continued to fire with a loud "waugh! waugh," pelting the warriors with iron fragments and splinters from the trees. Underwood was so close to the fallen timber that he could see the Indians "load & fire then fall down & load, then rise and fire again." After the battle, General Wayne confronted Ford, "whose men warm with fatigue & nearly exhausted had pulled off their Coats." In the course of an enraged outburst, the general exploded at one enlisted man, "I have fought under the hotest and the coldest suns and such a thing never was permitted nor shall it now be done—it is damned cowardly."[11]

While General Wilkinson almost immediately formed his right wing into a single line when confronted by the enemy, possibly because the relatively open ground allowed him to assess the situation better, Lieutenant Colonel Hamtramck obeyed Wayne's order to form in two lines. The Fourth Sub-Legion came into line first, with the Second Sub-Legion initially formed in reserve, but as the Indians appeared to be farther into the woods, Hamtramck sent the Second to prolong the left of the Fourth. Captain Price said that it took the Fourth Sub-Legion "less than five minutes" to form its line, a timeframe quite possible given the small number of men in the battalion companies. Alexander Gibson and Edward Butler had marched their rifle companies on the inland flank of the Fourth that morning, the soldiers "in single file, with a space of six feet between each two, consequently the two companies formed quite a long line." Isaac Paxton, one of the defenders of Fort Recovery, chanced to be at the very rear of the riflemen when the firing began. He and his comrades found themselves "a considerable distance" from the line being formed by Maj. Jonathan Haskell and, after being briefly thrown into confusion by the wrong commands of a platoon leader, "had to run or move very rapidly to gain their position in front." The riflemen were desperately needed with the advance, where Captain Brock's light infantry, along with Howell Lewis's men to the right, "had to sustain an unequal fire for some time, which they supported with fortitude." Among Brock's casualties were two men shot dead, Pvt. William Merrill and Lieutenant Towles. The latter's father, Col. Oliver Towles, had loved to read Shakespeare, so the young lieutenant must have been familiar with a line from Titus Andronicus that may have flashed through his mind in those last moments, "Sleep in peace, slain in your country's wars!"[12]

Pressure on the Fourth Sub-Legion increased. Q.M. Sgt. Eli Edmondson, a veteran of St. Clair's battle and formerly a sergeant in Brock's company before being elevated to staff duty, joined his old comrades and soon fell mortally wounded. Slough's company was temporarily thrown into disorder when that officer fell, struck by a ball that entered just below his stomach and injured the liver, diaphragm, and one lung. Just before Slough was hit, it seemed that the Wyandottes and Captain McKillip's Canadian militiamen might outflank Major Haskell's command. The left of his line was held by Bines's company, the Green Mountain Boys originally enlisted by William Eaton. Men in Wilkinson's wing could plainly hear the loud roar of musketry as the Vermonters held back the determined enemy. At least six of them were killed and another mortally wounded while repulsing this attack, one of them, Levi P. Senter, falling dead next to Captain Slough and "within reach of his espontoon." On the opposing side of this fierce contest, about a half-dozen Canadians were killed, including Captain McKillip, along with a number of prominent Wyandotte chiefs.[13]

As the roar of battle continued toward the left flank of Major Haskell's Fourth Sub-Legion, General Wayne took several steps to reinforce those troops. He first ordered Hamtramck to advance Lieutenant Colonel Strong's Second Sub-Legion obliquely to the left of Haskell. This movement was led by Captain Miller's battalion of infantry, which encountered "a very heavy fire" but arrived in time to halt the Indian advance. Wayne also directed General Scott "to gain and turn the right flank of the savages, with the whole of the mounted volunteers, by a circuitous route." Scott ordered General Todd's brigade, marching to the legion's left and rear, to dismount and "move forwards in a lo swampy ground with a great dale of fallen Timber and thick brush." Francis Jones said the underbrush "rendred the place difficult to see a Man 10 yds." General Barbee's brigade, marching in the rear, was also sent for, but the fighting was over by the time these troops reached the battlefield. Despite the unfavorable terrain on his left, Wayne sent forward Captain Van Rensselaer and his sorrel troop. The captain ordered a charge and, "while in the act of cutting down an Indian who was aiming at the troop from behind a tree, he was shot through the lungs, being struck in the center of the breast-bone by a rifle bullet which passed out transversely near the right shoulder." Van Rensselaer, who had just celebrated his twentieth birthday on August 6, "with the blood rushing from his breast, mouth and nose, maugre [despite] the dangerous wound, refused to be dismounted from his charger, but maintained his seat in his saddle until the enemy were effectually routed, when, and not till then, would he consent to be lifted off." Among those following Van Rensselaer into the timber were two brothers, Sgt. John and Pvt. Edward Wingate, natives of New York who had signed up to avenge the defeat of St. Clair. Edward was killed as he rode at his brother's side.[14]

Major Conn's battalion of the mounted volunteers dismounted and plunged into the wilderness on the left of the legion. They entered an area that was defended by the Wyandottes, who raised their peculiar war cry, "a low guttural sound" that was mistaken by novices for the sound of bells. When new men asked what that noise was, veterans replied calmly, "You'll soon find out." As Rawlings's company moved toward the sound of tinkling bells, Garret Burns noticed a man lying dead and, supposing him a Kentuckian, remarked, "There lies one of our brave fellows." Someone else replied, "Look at his face." Burns turned the body over and, discovering that the face was painted all over, realized he had mistaken the Wyandotte for one of his comrades. Before they had left Kentucky, Burns and his friend, John Hinkston, had made a pact that "we would bring back a scalp or lose our own." Now they had an opportunity to make good on that promise.

Of all the participants in this engagement, Garret Burns, left the most detailed account. He remembered: "The Indians then fired, and we returned the fire, rushing on them as they treed to re-load. I singled out one Indian, and leveling my rifle, fired. I was behind a tree, as he was, and struck him before he had the same chance at me. He ran off, although wounded, and I saw him no more. I re-loaded, and, rushing on again, I discovered an Indian in a sink-hole, his body, from the hips up, being exposed to view. He had fired, and while he was loading his gun, I drew up against a hickory sapling, exclaiming, 'Your life, or mine!' and blazed away." By now, the individual gunshots had merged into a roar that echoed through the forest, and although Burns could not hear his own rifle, he knew it had fired from the blaze and smoke that came from the muzzle. He continued his narrative: "I saw the Indian fall, and rushing on, seized him by the hair to take his scalp, but finding that I had lost my hunting-knife, I snatched his from his belt. His was a bran new scalping-knife, red handled, and the blade was as bright as when it came into his hands. He caught the knife by the blade, but I wrenched it from him, cutting off three of his fingers as he let it go. I then put my foot on him to pin him down, and took the scalp off. He gave but one quiver, and the breath left his body. I took his gun, a beautiful rifle, and broke the stock of it across a log. I then took up my own rifle, and re-loaded as quickly as possible." Garret Burns had a scalp, but his friend Hinkston had been wounded and could be forgiven for not living up to their pact. Burns had now fired but twice. When a third target appeared, he just barely avoided shooting Frank Smith when that man suddenly raised up between him and the Indian. Moments later, Burns was alongside of two Bourbon County neighbors, John Jackson and Jonathan Carmack, when the former received a mortal wound. He recalled, "I left him to the care of Carmack, and pursued the flying enemy."[15]

After the Second Sub-Legion had prolonged the American left so that it stretched almost two and one-half miles from the river, General Wayne reported, "I ordered the front line to advance and charge with trailed arms, and rouse the Indians from their coverts at the point of the bayonet, and when up, to deliver a close and well directed fire on their backs, followed by a brisk charge, so as not to give them time to load again." His dispassionate words seem to misrepresent the excitement that gripped the general on the field of battle. One enduring story tells of how, once he saw the legion go forward with bayonets, Wayne "became so excited that he was about to dash personally into the conflict." Staff officers, "seeing a strange fire in his countenance, and that he reined up his horse for a dash," ordered two men to grab his reins at the bridle and restrain the mount. Now in a rage at being kept behind the lines, Wayne supposedly shouted: "Let me go, damn them; let me go! Give it to them, boys!" Some officers never received the order to advance but did so on their own initiative. On the left, Captain Miller ordered his battalion of the Second Sub-Legion to charge, though he noted, "The whole line Charged nearly at the same time." Cooke's company went forward moments after the captain returned from his post with the front guard. Lieutenant Clark wrote that after Hamtramck stopped the Indian attack in the thickets, "the charge both on the Right & left both became Genl. & the Enemy was repulsed with precipation." Major Haskell, commanding the Fourth Sub-Legion, said: "The troops charged upon them with the bayonet, and drove them two miles, through a thicket of woods, fallen timber, and under-brush, when the cavalry fell upon and entirely routed them." Benjamin Price, one of Haskell's company commanders, received an order to charge, "which was pursued with a great deal of velocity, and without the smallest halt for three fourths of an hour; after which time there was not an enemy to be found."[16]

Indians began to give way before the legion advance. Many acted individually, like Captain Tommy, who "would fire, retreat, tree, re-load, & fire & retreat again." The Indians "reluctantly left the ground, stained with the blood of their friends & relations." Determined groups of warriors sustained one another as they withdrew: "The party who had fired retreated and passing the other party, stopped in the rear to load, the other awaited the approach of the enemy, fired, retreated, and waited in the rear, to support their friends in the same manner, until they had got at a sufficient distance when they all retired, carrying off their wounded." One soldier had just rushed into the fallen timber and was about to spring over a downed tree when an Indian raised up and fired in haste, missing his mark. Although unharmed, the soldier called it "a close shave, for the bullet whizzed through the lock of his right temple, causing that ear to ring for an hour after." The unlucky warrior, whose body was naked above the waist and painted with a vertical red stripe on his back, jumped up and began to run zigzag through the maze on the forest floor. The soldier, Josiah Hunt, the famous hunter of Fort Greeneville, calmly aimed at the prominent red stripe and shot his attacker dead. One story circulated that three Indians attempted to escape by crossing the river but were killed one after another by a runaway black man who had accompanied Captain Kibbey's scouts on their recon-naissance of the far bank. One young soldier, who received his discharge shortly after the battle, returned to Pittsburgh and gave the following succinct account: "The Indians possessed an advantageous ground of wood, rising and hollow grounds—they fired upon the army and yelled. Out-fired and out-yelled by the army; in 15 minutes the Indians gave way, and were then pursued and cut down by the horse."[17]

Tom Lyons, a member of the Delaware Nation who had been born in New Jersey, followed Captain Pipe into the fight against the Americans and was perhaps the ugliest man on the battlefield that day. One settler described him as "about six feet high, quite lean—very like a mummy in the consistence and color of his skin, with a long protrud-ing chin, some missing teeth, short upper lip, a low forehead, a protruding crown, jet eyes, very fierce and piercing, and wore a dress, never very tidy nor clean." Lyons detailed the battle against General Wayne from the perspective of a Delaware warrior: "Me hear his dinner horn—way over there go toot, toot; then way over here it go toot, toot—then way over other side, go toot, toot. Then his soldiers run forward—shoot, shoot; then run among logs and brush. Indians have got to get out and run. Then come Long Knives with pistols and shoot, shoot. Indians run, no stop. Old Tom see too much fight to be trap— he run into woods—he run like devil—he keep run till he clear out of danger." Lyons declared of Wayne, "He be one devil to fight," and whenever he recalled the battle, "Old Tom" would gesture wildly and grimace as he acted out the fighting, convincing spectators that the Indians had been terrified by the legion's attack.[18]

Since he was not a chief, the Shawnee warrior Tecumseh did not play a prominent leadership role in the engagement, but he did lead a band of followers, including two of his brothers, into the battle. Tecumseh's small party was among those Indians who began the attack on Major Price's mounted scouts. After firing off a few rounds, he made the mistake of inserting a ball down the barrel of his rifle before putting in the powder, thereby disabling his weapon. When pressed by the infantry, Tecumseh's men began to fall back, but he rallied them and boasted that he would show them how to fight if someone gave him a gun. He was handed a fowling piece, and the Shawnees attempted another stand, but they again retreated from the legion's bayonets and stopped in the shelter offered by a thicket. After soldiers fired into their hiding place, the Shawnees let loose their own ragged volley and took to their heels, leaving behind the body of Sauwaseekau, one of Tecumseh's brothers, who had been killed by the Americans.[19]

General Wilkinson had ordered the First Sub-Legion to advance in support of the ill-fated charge of MisCampbell's black-horse troop, but resistance on that front, next to the river, had been remarkably light, the enemy falling back "from ravine to ravine loading & firing at a considerable distance" as the troops advanced. The wing commander thought that this light resistance might be an attempt to lure the legion into an ambush, so he rode directly to Wayne to advise that a halt be made so the lines could be re-formed. Wayne agreed but almost immediately ordered the advance along the bluffs resumed when the Indians and Canadians attacked the Fourth Sub-Legion. Wilkinson's men surged forward again, though "much disordered," and left the artillery, light infantry, and riflemen well to the rear. Lt. Campbell Smith, the general's aide, rode off to deliver a message to General Wayne but was shot in the right breast as he returned, just as the Indian fire on the right started to die down.[20]

While Hamtramck's soldiers began to push back the enemy and catch up with the right wing, Wilkinson saw Lieutenant Covington charging from left to right with a squad of dragoons from the bay-horse troop. Upon reaching the bluffs, Covington turned and started to the front against some Indians retreating in the distance. Wilkinson sent Lieutenant Schaumburgh to bring up Lieutenant Webb's gray-horse troop from the rear and shouted for Covington to halt. Sensing that this dragoon officer was racing to his death as had MisCampbell earlier, Wilkinson personally spurred his horse and galloped off to recall the bold Covington. He reached the dragoons "close upon the rear of the Enemy," so close in fact that the general passed within a few paces of one Indian who unaccountably held his fire, although another warrior, about sixty yards off, wounded Wilkinson's servant in the shoulder. Covington saw the danger and "charged this son of the woods, sword in hand and killed him on the spot." By this time, Webb had arrived with his troop, and the combined force of dragoons continued to harass the warriors, who were now more interested in flight than fight. Within a few minutes, Covington had personally killed two Indians and Webb another. One of the Canadian militia had been chopped up so badly by the dragoons that a rumor circulated that he had been captured, "then quartered alive." Infantrymen trying to keep pace with the dragoons discovered the bodies of "Indians cut and hacked in a horrid manner."[21]

Bugles and drums sounded the retreat, and the Americans stopped wherever they happened to be, except for the dragoons under Covington and Webb, who continued to slash at fleeing Indians. Wayne reported that nine hundred of his troops, all that had actually gotten into action, had defeated an Indian army of about two thousand, driving the enemy almost two miles through the wilderness. He wrote to Secretary of War Knox, with obvious pride, "This horde of savages, with their allies, abandoned themselves to flight, and dispersed with terror and dismay, leaving our victorious army in full and quiet possession of the field of battle." General Wilkinson disagreed and wrote that "this looks more like unto a drawn battle than a victory," but he soon reconsidered and remarked that "this affair does not deserve the name of a Battle." In the overall scheme of military history, Wilkinson was certainly right. Fallen Timbers was more of a skirmish than a major battle. Casualties had been light, and the fighting had lasted somewhere between sixty-five and eighty minutes, depending on which participant furnishes the estimate. But Wilkinson may have dismissed the fight's significance after being piqued by Wayne's conferring the most honor upon Hamtramck's Fourth Sub-Legion, the general in chief exclaiming that "he had seen in front of the 4th S Legn at one view, 400 Savages as naked by the eternal God! As they came out of their mothers Wombs!"[22]

The legion remained on its newly won ground for about four hours. A quick search was made for the wounded, who were turned over to the surgeons. Men took advantage of this halt to cool down, enjoy some water and a bite to eat, and then celebrate their victory with a small issue of whiskey, although none of the latter was given to the Kentuckians. Wayne rode along the line, telling the troops, "He always floged Indians & British where ever he went." After searching for their fallen friends, Scott's mounted volunteers halted near the legion, saw that wounds were dressed, and constructed litters for hauling the more seriously wounded. Sentinels were placed to guard against surprise by the Indians, who were still thought capable of renewing the fight. Garret Burns happened to be on guard when two men came out of the woods, driving before them a Frenchman disguised as an Indian. Burns halted the captive, who started "bowing repeatedly" and begging the guard not to shoot as he was a prisoner. The two captors damned Burns for not killing him. The man was immediately recognized by Lieutenant Colonel Hamtramck as a Canadian trader from the Wabash River named Antoine Lasselle, who was immediately "loaded with irons." He had been found hiding near the riverbank, "painted and dressed as a Savage," carrying "a double barrelled fusee." An examination of Lasselle's captors revealed that he "was actually taken in arms and made resistance when he was taken." Lasselle was lucky to be alive, being the only prisoner taken by either side in the battle. This had been a fight to the death, a fact emphasized by one story showing the combativeness of both sides. A soldier detached from his company chanced upon a solitary Indian in the timber, the two attacking one another with bayonet and tomahawk. The tale concludes, "Two days after they were found dead, the soldier with his bayonet in the body of the Indian—the Indian with his tomahawk in the head of the soldier." Whether true or not, the story is a perfect metaphor of the hostility displayed in Anthony Wayne's fight at the Foot of the Rapids of the Maumee River.[23]

CHAPTER 25

Confrontation at Fort Miamis

AFTER THE BATTLE, CAPTAIN VAN Rensselaer was discovered sitting with his back against a tree, "smiling with complacency while the blood was oozing from his lungs." The dragoon officer was taken to General Wayne's own tent, where he fainted from loss of blood while being tended by Lieutenant Harrison. Surgeons John M. Scott, Nathan Hayward, and John F. Carmichael examined Van Rensselaer, then turned their attention to other injured men, one of the doctors remarking, "This poor fellow is too far gone, no use attending to him." But their probing had revived the patient, who startled them by yelling, "Damn you, dress me!" The surgeons immediately decided that anyone having that much energy and pluck deserved to be saved, so they returned and tended his wound. Two litters were built to carry Captains MisCampbell and Van Rensselaer, both suffering from similar wounds, back to Fort Deposit. Robert MisCampbell was placed in one, but Van Rensselaer refused to leave the battlefield in a litter. General Wayne witnessed this and remarked, "You young dog! how then are you going?" As befitted a descendant of one of the original Dutch patroons, the captain replied proudly, "I am an officer of the cavalry, and shall go on horseback." The general responded, "You will drop by the way." Van Rensselaer answered simply, "If I do, just cover me up and let me lie there."

The young officer was lifted onto his sorrel horse and, supported on each side by one of his dragoons, rode back to Fort Deposit, while the other wounded officers were carried in litters, the whole being guarded by a detachment of mounted volunteers. Van Rensselaer was thought to be dying, and the surgeons were surprised that he eventually recovered, saying but one in a one thousand ever survived such a wound. They credited the captain's remarkable recuperation to his determination to ride back to Fort Deposit, this "gentle movement" keeping the blood from congealing in his lungs and allowing him to cough up accumulated clots and pus. Put simply, the constant motion, combined with his upright posture, kept the wound clean. Van Rensselaer's friend

Captain MisCampbell, who was carried in a litter, was not so lucky. His lungs became congested, and he died of suffocation on the route. Two days after reaching Fort Deposit, Van Rensselaer felt well enough to write to Lieutenant Visscher at Fort Recovery: "I *have* been at a place where I might have slashed with temporary advantages, had not a Rifle Ball from an Indian of the 'Charley's' slashed through my lungs on the 20th Inst. The wound is considered very dangerous by the Surgeons, but has not taken away appetite or Spirits, nor shall it till the last moment. If you write home don't make my friends at all uneasy by letting them know that I am in danger until there is a certainty of its proving my dissolution; and even then I do hope they will not repine at my lot, as I will die in the arms of victory and in a glorious cause." After telling of MisCampbell's death, the proud dragoon captain concluded: "My aged Parents will grieve. Adieu, Adieu my dear Visscher, may you be well and happy is the wish (and perhaps the last one) of your sincere friend." Despite his gloomy prognosis, Van Rensselaer's healthy constitution led to a recovery from his wound, although it would be two years before he could return to active service.[1]

Captain Van Rensselaer shared a hospital tent with Jacob Slough, aged twenty-nine and formerly a resident of Lancaster, Pennsylvania. The rifle ball that passed through Slough's body was extracted on the afternoon of the battle by Surgeon Carmichael, who discovered that the projectile had lodged two inches below the scapula and near the spine. As with Van Rensselaer, the surgeons were stunned by Slough's seemingly miraculous recovery. Within a week of being shot, the captain felt well enough to request a leave of absence so that he could recuperate at the home of his father, Matthias Slough, where he would be tended by Gen. Edward Hand, an old friend of the family. The young officer received his leave and returned east with Van Rensselaer, but by the time he had reached Winchester, Virginia, exactly two months after his injury, the local newspaper reported, "the wound is now perfectly healed." Still, a number of internal ailments resulting from this rifle ball tearing through his body eventually forced Slough to relinquish his commission in 1796.[2]

Although Captain Prior of the First Sub-Legion was listed as wounded in Wayne's report, his injury must have been minor since General Wilkinson failed to mention it in his two surviving accounts of the fight. But the general had much to say about the wound incurred by his aide-de-camp, Lt. Campbell Smith, who was struck in the right breast by a ball that passed through his body and exited under the left shoulder. Wilkinson complained loudly of the manner in which Smith was treated by General Wayne, who was initially under the misapprehension the lieutenant had been shot while off chasing Indians with Leonard Covington's dragoons and complained "he had got his wound out of the line of his duty." When he finally stopped by to see Smith two days later, Wayne apologized by saying that "his feelings would not permit him to see him while his life was despaired of," a sentiment Wilkinson termed hypocrisy. Like Van Rensselaer and Slough, the aide was young and strong, so Lieutenant Webb could write within a few weeks, "Our friend Lieut Smith mends very fast & is now in Camp."[3]

Capt. Solomon Van Rensselaer. From Catherine Bonney, *A Legacy of Historical Gleanings*, 1875.

When Garret Burns's tour of guard duty was over, he started for his company's bivouac but happened to see Captain Rawlings lying on a blanket. Rawlings had been hit by two rifle balls, the most serious wound in the lower abdomen. Burns remembered, "He grasped my hand and begged me not to forsake him in case of a fresh attack, but to put him on a horse." Of course, he promised to do so. As Burns talked with Rawlings, General Wayne passed by and, noticing the captain's sword, asked, "What officer is that?" When told it was Captain Rawlings of the mounted volunteers, the general dismounted and examined the wounds himself, telling the patient that "he was a live man yet, as the bullets, although they had shattered the hip and back-bone, had missed the vitals." Wayne ordered him to be carried to Fort Deposit, along with Van Rensselaer and Slough. The general, who undoubtedly had seen many such wounds during the Revolution, was correct in his diagnosis, for Rawlings did recover after a long convalescence. Casualties among General Scott's Kentuckians totaled twenty officers and men either killed or wounded.[4]

The legion had lost 26 killed and 87 wounded, an aggregate of 113 casualties. This loss fell primarily upon the Fourth and Third Sub-Legions, which lost 41 and 39 men killed and wounded, respectively, although the former had a much greater proportion killed. The First Sub-Legion, which had fought in the more-open ground near the river, lost 12 men and the Second, which was last to be engaged, had only 8 casualties. MisCampbell's dragoon squadron had a dozen men shot, and Indian sharpshooters managed to wound a single artilleryman. It is impossible to present a complete list of names of those killed and wounded in the legion, and a partial roster would seem to give preference to some over others. The names of most of those killed or those who died from their injuries have been preserved, either on the battle monument or on crumbling old muster rolls, but the names of those merely wounded have long since been lost to history. The suffering of these anonymous soldiers can only be imagined by noting that twenty-five of the eighty-three enlisted men wounded in the battle were still hospitalized at Fort Defiance on January 1, 1795, almost five months after being shot.[5]

Of those killed, Robert MisCampbell received the most attention. His fall was mentioned by just about every participant in the battle, the best eulogy perhaps coming from the pen of one of his troopers:

> Among the Killed was that *good, brave, gallant* and *intrepid* Captain Robert Mis Campbell, of the Second Troops Light Dragoons, and then commanding Officer of the Cavalry, who fell in a charge on the Enemy in an early Part of the Action; by which the Legion was deprived of one of its bravest Officers, before he had an Opportunity of rendering his Country those Services which were to be expected from his Bravery. It would be vain for Abilities like mine to attempt to describe the deceased Captain Cambell's Virtues; but to do Justice to his Memory I cannot avoid observing, he was possessed of every Qualification which constitutes the *Gentleman*, the *Officer* and a *good* Man: and as he was when living generally loved, now that he is dead I believe he is as generally lamented.

Captain MisCampbell was as much beloved as his name was misspelled. Nearly everyone assumed that the "Mis" was a middle name rather than what it actually was—a variation of the more typical "Mc" and "Mac" prefixes on Scotch and Irish surnames.[6]

The captain's odd name led to one bizarre story that gained credence among gullible readers. A rumor circulated after the battle that a Lieutenant Miss Campbell had fallen in Wayne's battle and that officer "was previously known to be a woman." Andrew Coffinberry, in his poetic tale *The Forest Rangers*, admitted that "no such incident ever occurred," but the story was too good to ignore, so he added a few additional details anyway:

"Oh, help! here, help!" a soldier cries,
"Our brave lieutenant Campbell dies!"
Then on him many a gaze was turned;
His vengeance now no longer burned;
For grappling with the tyrant death,
His bosom heaved—he gasped for breath;
And tears distilled from many an eye,
That saw the beardless hero die.
Wrenching apart the bloody vest,
Lo! They exposed a maiden's breast.

The author did add a note to his account that related a discussion with Abraham Glass-mire, who claimed no knowledge of a "Lieutenant" Campbell but said that Captain Mis-Campbell "was reputed a man, and had every visible appearance of such—that he had often shaved him during his life, and that his beard was similar to that of a man." There is no credible evidence whatsoever that the dragoon captain killed at Fallen Timbers was anyone other than *a man* named Robert MisCampbell.[7]

Although the Kentuckians had taken it upon themselves to hunt for their fallen comrades, there was no systematic search of the battlefield for casualties. General Wayne was more interested in reconnoitering the ground between the battlefield and Fort Miamis, keeping his troops in the ranks and ready for an advance rather than allowing them to roam through the timber. Although he had received no orders to do so, Wilkinson, and undoubtedly Hamtramck on the other wing, sent back "a small detachment" to look for casualties. Several wounded men were overlooked in this hasty search. Sergeant Edmondson of the Fourth Sub-Legion died where he fell after two days of suffering. Another soldier from the First Sub-Legion was found clinging to life on August 21 but expired a few hours after being brought to the surgeons. Wilkinson berated Wayne's conduct in ignoring his wounded, writing that, "for a single Man sacrificed by such cruel negligance, a Genl deserves to be hanged." If Wayne escaped being hanged, God would ensure that "damned he certainly will be." Lieutenant Clark pitied the soldiers in their distressed plight, saying that "no set of men in the like disabled Situation ever expereanced much more want of Conveniancies &c." The wounded were conveyed back to Fort Deposit on the morning of August 22. Except for Captain MisCampbell and Lieutenant Towles, who had been interred immediately after their deaths, in the summer heat, the bodies of dead soldiers "were left to ferment upon the surface," where they quickly became "the prey of Vultures" until their burial.[8]

When his scouts returned with word that the Indians had vanished, Wayne ordered the march resumed, leaving his wounded and surgeons behind under a small guard. After a short march, the legion halted within a mile of Fort Miamis and "in full view of the British Garrison." General Wilkinson thought the panorama quite beautiful, "the River meandering in various directions thro a natural meadow in high cultivation & of great extent, this meadow bounded by noble eminences, crowned with lofty timber on either side." The river here ran north and south, the eastern bank being scattered with Indian villages, and the western bank being guarded by the fort, which flew the British flag. In the middle of the river was a large island, "well Cultivated with Corn & beans and a number of Stacks of Hay," which was visited by the mounted volunteers "in one hour after the army got to the ground." The legion and General Scott's Kentuckians fortified their camps in the usual manner, creating a base of operations for the next two days. The Americans were so close to the British post that John Cooke "could discern the officers and soldiers walking around the garrison and a flag flying." For their part, British officers "heard a host of axes & Saw fires & Tents." General Wayne had defeated the Indian army, but any confrontation with the British inside Fort Miamis must wait for the morrow. Wilkinson recalled that, content with their success that day, "we beat our Drums Blowed our trumpets & went to Bed."[9]

Not everyone went to sleep. John Johnson, formerly a member of the Queen's Rangers during the Revolution, deserted and joined the British inside their fort. He gave Major Campbell extremely valuable information regarding Wayne's army, telling him that half of his force, some sixteen hundred to seventeen hundred men, was composed of mounted volunteers, who would return home on October 10. Soldiers had been on half rations of flour, a deficiency that was filled by the Indian corn and vegetables, and although the legion remained healthy, the Kentuckians "were beginning to be sickly." The deserter could not give much information about the battle but did confirm that Antoine Lasselle had been captured. Johnson also claimed that "it was a conversation among the men that they were coming against this Fort."[10]

While the enemy now had an accurate assessment of his force, General Wayne obtained equally vital intelligence about the fort's defenses from a British deserter. John Bevan, a drummer in the Twenty-Fourth Regiment, walked down to the river to wash his shirts about eight o'clock on the morning after the battle, then slipped through the abatis and crept away to the Americans. He told Wayne that there were four companies from his regiment in the fort, each averaging about fifty officers and men, which had been joined by a detachment of Butler's rangers and some sixty Canadians. Bevan stated that the total number of defenders was somewhat over 400 men, although disease had actually reduced the garrison to the point that it numbered but 160 effectives, supplemented by Capt. Alexander Harrow with a half-dozen sailors and a couple dozen Canadian militia. The fort contained four 9-pounders, six 6-pounders, two large howitzers, and two small swivel guns, all well supplied with ammunition. Bevan reported that Robert Newman, whom he characterized as "a deserter," had informed Major Campbell "the object of the American war was to take that post and garrison; that General Wayne told the troops not to be uneasy about provisions, that there were plenty in the British garrison." In response to Newman's information, an express had been sent to Lieutenant Governor Simcoe, who was momentarily expected to arrive with reinforcements. Regarding the battle, Bevan could give but little news, although he did say that "the retiring Indians appeared much dejected and much altered to what they were in the morning before the action." The deserter claimed to have overheard a conversation between Colonel McKee, Captain Elliott, and Major Campbell, during which it was stated that the Indian and

Canadian force amounted to about two thousand men. One company of Canadian militia, under Lieutenant Colonel Caldwell and Captain McKillip, "all white men and armed with British muskets and bayonets," had fought against Wayne. This last statement was evidence that the British had done more than simply supply the Indians with arms and food. To the American commander, this looked like war.[11]

Wayne assembled a court of officers "to enquire and determine whether Anthony Lasselle comes under the Character of a Spie, having been discovered secreted & Painted within the Lines, two hours after the Defeat of the Savages in the Action of Yesterday." Hamtramck, who had first recognized Lasselle, acted as president of the inquiry. Before the court convened, Wayne complained that the prisoner had been allowed to wash his face, grumbling, "If the Court had seen him while he was painted they would have had no doubt of his being a Spy." Shortly afterward, the general went to see the prisoner, drew his sword, and calling him a "damned infernal Villain," threatened, "I'll cut off your head." During the court's inquiry, Lasselle, whose remarks were interpreted by Hamtramck, claimed that only nine hundred Indians and one company of militia had opposed the American army. One of his comments proved that Wayne's tactics had been perfectly executed. When asked why the Indians did not fight better, Lasselle replied that the soldiers "would give them no time to load their pieces, but kept them constantly on the run." The accused was formally charged, convicted by a court-martial, and sentenced to death before Hamtramck could successfully beg for clemency. John Johnston, a friend of Lasselle in later life, remembered that the Canadian trader, although he did not speak English, understood his situation perfectly: "He was a man of wit and drollery, and would often clasp his neck with both hands, to show how near he had been to hanging by order of mad Anthony."[12]

The legion remained in camp all day on August 21, Lieutenant Clark reporting that everyone was "all full with expectation & anxiety, of storming of the British Garrison," the only task remaining since "the Savage[s] were no more to be found." Wayne ordered Major Price to bypass Fort Miamis and reconnoiter downstream toward Lake Erie. This detachment found no Indians but saw many places where the enemy "had tread down the weeds like a log had been roled over it." Then the general took a party of Kentuckians up to personally examine the fort that boldly flew a British flag in American territory. Accompanied by Generals Scott, Todd, and Barbee and attended by a large cavalcade of officers, Wayne spent about thirty minutes inspecting the fort with a spyglass. The general and his entourage found that this new post was "built of white oak logs very high & thick and fill'd in with Clay, with large Deep Ditch at the outside except so far as protected by a high & deep bluff rising from the River Bank." The walls had embrasures for cannon that would fire grape shot at any attackers. After concluding his observations, Wayne collected the mounted volunteers, who had virtually surrounded the fort, and started back to camp.[13]

Herman Bowmar, brigade major in General Todd's command, was at the rear of the column and just opposite the fort gate at a distance of about two hundred yards when "an Elegant cloth'd officer apeard out of the Gate with a white Flag hoisted about the size of an umbrella or long parisoll." The generals were all some three hundred yards in advance, so Bowmar, indulging his curiosity, galloped up to the officer and inquired if there were anyone he wished to see. Captain Spears, accompanied by a small detachment including some musicians, replied coldly, "I want to see the General, Sir." Bowmar, ever the loyal Kentuckian, responded, "Which Genl, Wayne, or Scott did he wish to see?" Spears, undoubtedly miffed by this bumpkin posing as a soldier, said, "The Commander in Chief, Sir," and kept riding. Bowmar shouted that he could see General Wayne at his marquee, then continued on to General Todd's headquarters. But Spears stopped at one of the outposts, where he turned over a letter written by Major Campbell and addressed to General Wayne.

> An Army of the United States of America said to be under your Command, having taken Post on the banks of the Miamis, for upwards of the last twenty four hours, almost within reach of the Guns of this Post, being a Post belonging to His Majesty, the King of Great Britain, occupied by His Majesty's Troops, and which I have the honor to Command, it becomes my duty to inform myself as speedily as possible in what light I am to view your making such near approachs to this Garrison.
>
> I have no hesitation on my part to say, that I know of no War existing between Great Britain and America.

Captain Spears did not wait for a reply, having been told that "the Woods were full of Rifle Men, and they were Affraid of his Safety, from Accident."[14]

Indeed, the countryside around Fort Miamis was full of Kentucky troops, who seemed to be enjoying the fruits of their victory. Major Campbell called his situation "a very extraordinary one," with mounted men "skirting the Wood all around us." As he wrote to inform Lieutenant Colonel England of his letter to Wayne, Campbell noted, "A number of the Officers are looking at us from the Point of Colonel McKee's Island." Zachariah Holliday listed some of the items appropriated by the mounted volunteers, saying, "Wayne's men took every thing in the shape of fine garden vegetibles around the fort—a hundred acres of corn in prime roasting ear, as well as a large quantity of cut stacked hay—*all* taken." Francis Jones wrote that the Kentucky campground was directly opposite McKee's compound, "which we had the pleasure of seeing reduced to Ashes." William Sudduth remarked that "the men destroyed the corn that stood near the garrison, burnt their hay, & gardens, & every out house." Campbell's garrison could do nothing but helplessly watch the conflagration that surrounded them.[15]

While General Scott's men wreaked havoc on storehouses of the British Indian Department and the carefully tended Indian fields, General Wayne composed a reply to Major Campbell's inquiry. Captain DeButts, accompanied by a sergeant, a trumpeter, and six dragoons, delivered this response to the gates of Fort Miamis:

> Without questioning the Authority or the propriety Sir, of your interrogatory, I think I may without breach of decorum observe to you, that were you intitled to an Answer, the most full and satisfactory one was announced to you, from the

Muzzels of my small Arms yesterday morning in the Action against the hoard of Savages in the vicinity of your Post, which terminated Gloriously to the American Arms—but had it continued until the Indians &c were drove under the influence of the Post and Guns you mention—they would not have much impeded the progress of the Victorious Army under my command, as no such Post was Established at the Commencement of the present War, between the Indians and the United States.

After dispatching this reply, Wayne ordered two days of rations brought forward from Fort Deposit. His first impression had been that Fort Miamis was "too strong to be stormed," and the army did not have enough provisions to carry out a prolonged siege. The pompous attitude of Major Campbell had convinced him to take a closer look.[16]

During their many trips to McKee's Island and the eastern bank of the Maumee River, both soldiers and volunteers discovered a curious natural phenomenon. Francis Jones explained, "the River is very wide here and from every observation of the officers a regular Tide flows here to the hight of 18 inches." Lieutenant Gaines wrote to his father, "I observed a regular tide to rise about three feet every day; which has caused much speculation amongst us—from what cause it originates, or whether it be temporary." Most men seemed to think the mysterious tide was a temporary aberration, but Gaines did not agree. Recalling the tides near his Virginia home, the lieutenant asserted that the "ebb & flood" of the Maumee River "were as regular, to the time, as I ever saw them on James river; and cannot be occasioned by wind, as many assert." This tide had to be taken into consideration by foragers, since the Maumee could only be forded in the morning and evening hours.[17]

There was little rest that night because of an alarm at 2:00 A.M., resulting from sentinels firing at two deserters. Soldiers raced to man the breastwork in anticipation of a night attack but were soon relieved and sent back to sleep. The morning of August 22 was "very cool," a welcome relief from the oppressive August heat. At 9:00 A.M., General Wayne took four companies of light infantry, four troops of dragoons, some riflemen, and a detachment of mounted volunteers back to have a closer look at Fort Miamis. The troops formed in the thick woods that surrounded the post "in silent Order" while their general began his inspection. Wayne studied the post "closely and on every point," discovering that it was weaker than he had first thought and susceptible to being taken by siege operations. He inquired of Quartermaster O'Hara how many entrenching tools were on hand. When O'Hara responded three hundred, the commander in chief "appeared sanguine and determined." When Wilkinson asked how he could contain the British cannon fire, Wayne said bluntly that "his Rifle men would kill every bugger of them who shewed his face" at an embrasure.[18]

Despite flirting with the idea of taking Fort Miamis, either by assault, siege, or a combination of both, there were several drawbacks to such an attempt. Of utmost concern was the critical state of provisions. Although the Indian corn was still supplementing half rations of flour, other deficiencies must soon develop in the daily issue. After making several objections on technical grounds, Wilkinson pointed out "the fatal consequences which must ensue if he should have 3 or 400 men wounded," an argument Wayne found convincing. Lieutenant Harrison recalled that this close examination "showed but too clearly that our small howitzers, which had been transported on the backs of horses, our only artillery, could make no impression upon its massive earthen parapet, while the deep fosse and frasing by which it was surrounded afforded no prospect of the success of an escalade, but at an expense of valuable lives, which the occasion did not seem to call for." In hopes of provoking Major Campbell, Wayne and his attendants rode to "within pistol shot of the garrison." Lieutenant Bowyer claimed this was done "in hopes of bringing a shot from our inveterate but silent enemies," but the British proved "too cowardly to come up to our expectations." A story made the rounds that General Wayne ordered one of his soldiers to climb down the riverbank immediately next to the fort and bring up a pail filled with water. The man replied, "Why, General, were I to do so, they would shoot me from the Fort." Wayne responded, "That's the very thing I want them to do, John, let them kill you, and we'll massacre every soul of 'em." When the British failed to fire upon the insolent Americans, the general recalled the troops and returned to camp.[19]

Seething with resentment at Wayne's arrogance, Major Campbell dispatched another note to the legion commander:

> I have forborne for these two days past to resent those Insults you have offered to the British Flag flying at this Fort, by approaching it within pistol shot of my Works, not only single, but in numbers with Arms in their hands.
>
> Neither is it my wish to wage War with Individuals, but should you after this continue to approach my post, in the threatening manner you are at this moment doing, my indispensable Duty to my King and Country, and the honor of my profession will Oblige me to have recourse to those Measures, which thousands of either Nation may hereafter have Cause to regret, and which I solemnly appeal to God, I have used my utmost endeavours to avert.

This nicely worded threat to fire upon any Americans thereafter drawing too close to Fort Miamis was never enforced, and the Kentuckians continued their campaign of confiscation and destruction.[20]

Major Campbell's terse threat did not sit well with General Wayne, who upped the ante in this international game of bluff poker with a note of his own:

> In your letter of the 21 instant you declare "I have no hesitation on my part to say, that I know of no War Existing between Great Britain & America."
>
> I, on my part, declare the same, and that the only cause I have to entertain a contrary idea at present, is the hostile Act that you are now in commission of, i.e. by recently taking post far within the well known and acknowledged limits of the United States, and erecting a Fortification in the Heart of the settlements of the Indian Tribes, now at war with the United States.
>
> This, Sir, appears to be an Act of the highest aggression, and destructive to the peace and interest of the Union:—hence it becomes my duty to desire, and I do hereby desire and demand in the name of the President of the United States that you immediately desist from any further Act of Hostility or aggression:—by

forbearing to fortify and withdrawing your troops, Artillery and Stores under your orders and directions forthwith, and removing to the nearest post occupied by his Britannick Majesty's Troops at the peace of 1783:—and which you will be permitted to do, unmolested by the troops under my command.

Campbell was not about to abandon his post upon the mere summons by a bullying American officer, even if he happened to be the famous Mad Anthony Wayne, and sent yet another letter to the general's headquarters:

> I have this moment the honor to acknowledge the receipt of your letter of this date—In answer to which I have only to say, that being placed here in the Command of a British Post, and acting in a Military Capacity only, I cannot enter into any discussion either on the right, or impropriety, of my occupying my present position, these are matters that I conceive will be best left to the Ambassadors of Our different Nations.
>
> Having said this much, Sir, permit me to inform you, that I certainly will not abandon this Post, at the Summons of Any power whatever, until I receive Orders to that purpose from those I have the honor to serve under—
>
> I must still adhere to the purport of my letter this morning, to desire that your Army or Individuals belonging to it, will not approach within reach of my Cannon, without expecting the Consequences attending it.
>
> Although I have said in the former part of my letter that my situation here is totally Military, yet, let me add, Sir, that I am much deceived if His Majesty the King of Great Britain had not a post upon this River, and prior, to the period you mention.

In response to this last message, Lieutenant Clark said the soldiers "for spite Burnt all the Indian Hutts throughout the vicinity of the Garrison and put the finishing stroke to the Distruction of the Cornfields, Gardens, Hay Stacks &c &c." Major Haskell summed up the inferno that had swirled about Fort Miamis for two days, boasting, "we burnt their out-houses, destroyed all their gardens, cornfields, and grass, within musket shot of the place, and all below for eight or nine miles, without any opposition."[21]

On the morning of August 23, General Wayne formally congratulated his army on its "brilliant success in the Action of the 20th Instant, against the whole combined force of the Hostile savages aided by a body of the Militia of Detroit, & countenanced by the British post & Garrison close in their rear." He noted that the Indian army had "fled with disorder precipitative & dismay leaving their packs provisions & plunder" because "the British have neither the power or inclination to afford them that protection which they had been taught to expect." As for that vaunted European power, Wayne boasted that "a numberous Garrison well supplied with Artillery have been compeled to remain tacit Spectators of the General conflagration around them & their flag displayed at the Post, insulted with impunity, to the disgrace of the British, & to the honor of the American army."[22]

Since Major Campbell had declined to surrender his post and the legion did not have enough provisions or heavy artillery for a siege, there was nothing for Wayne to do but retrace his steps back to Fort Deposit. First, however, there had to be a military ceremony for those who had fallen. The commander in chief ordered the legion and mounted volunteers drawn up in line under arms and ready to march at noon on August 23, when the artillery fired three rounds of shells from each of their howitzers, followed by the musicians playing "The Dead March." Lieutenant Bowyer said that "the ceremony was performed with the greatest solemnity," but General Wilkinson, by now finding fault with virtually everything that Wayne did, carped that it was "a pageant so truly ridiculous as to excite the derision of every person of observation or candor." In a letter to a friend, Wilkinson explained that they had "made a rediculous gasconade, by firing our little Pop Guns Howizer." Wayne's soldiers formed a line so that each company could sweep over the battlefield upon ground where it had fought. Since the area had been thoroughly scoured "many times by light parties," this last search was to locate axes, blankets, and other equipment dropped as men lightened their loads before entering the fight. Most of the equipment was gone, either found by stealthy warriors shadowing the victorious legion or, most likely, stolen by the Kentuckians. Lieutenant Webb, an officer with the dragoons, confessed, "Out of 14 swords of the Kill'd & wounded only one can be found & a quantity of other Equipments gone, no one knows how."[23]

Soldiers wondered aloud what had become of the Indians as they marched back to Fort Deposit. Although they had no way of knowing, the vaunted Indian army had collapsed and could no longer offer any organized resistance. Having lost many of their leaders, and while being pursued by the dragoons, frightened Indians headed for the refuge offered by Fort Miamis. But Major Campbell "shut the fort gates against both British whites & Indians" as if they were enemies. When Lieutenant Colonel Caldwell brought the remnants of Captain McKillip's company back to the fort and found the gates locked, he told the men to simply go home. According to Jonathan Alder, "This one thing did more towards making peace betwixt the Indians and the Americans than any one thing, because for weeks before this fight had taken place the Indians had been promised aid and protection by the British." When the warriors demanded that long-promised assistance, their British "allies" refused all help. Alder remembered, "It was an act the Indians never forgot." John Norton agreed with Alder, saying, "The conduct of the British Fort dispirited the Confederates much more than the issue of the battle, which they had fought with very inferior number, and in a disadvantageous position, without considerable loss; this they considered as a misfortune that might be repaired with glory,—another time; but the former, they did not know how to remedy."[24]

John Brickell said that many of the Delawares were killed, including the man who had captured William May, an important loss since he happened to be that nation's only gunsmith. Delaware warriors who reached David Zeisberger's mission deplored the lack of Indian unity and howled about British treachery, swearing that they would abandon their land and move southwest to territory under Spanish control. Zeisberger translated a blistering message that was sent to British officials: "Look at the graves on the Miami, look farther on, where the bones of the young folk lie, on whom the beasts have fed. Thou art the cause of their death. Thou hast always preached to us and said: 'Behold, the

States are taking away your land. Be brave, act like men. Let not your land be taken from you. Fight for your land.' But now we have got at the truth. The States have struck thee to the ground and overcome thee. Therefore hast thou given them our land in order to have peace from them, but thou tellest us to fight for it, so that we may all be blotted out. See, this is the truth." Captain Tommy had stayed in the fight long enough to see "how the cavalry cut and slashed with their long swords, mercilessly cutting off Indians arms and heads." Feeling his cause was hopeless, he, along with hundreds of others, headed for the fort. Those closed gates "caused an indignation & hatred in his bosom ever after against what [he] never failed to describe as the 'damn British.'" Captain Tommy loaded his family back into their canoe, set off downstream, and never stopped until they reached Canada.[25]

For their part, the British were completely disgusted with the feeble effort shown by the Indians. Lieutenant Colonel England complained that they had "forfeited every pretension to a Warlike or Gallant Character. They behaved excessively ill in the Action at the Falls and afterwards fled in every direction," many not stopping until they had reached Lake Erie some eighteen miles downstream. Panic was so widespread that "the appearance of fifty Americans would have totally routed them." Major Campbell was at a loss to understand what had happened. All he knew was that firing had broken out upstream from his garrison, then after a short while, the officers saw "a number of Indians coming down upon us in the open, but by far the greatest number of them had been noticed under cover of the wood." Campbell had his men stand to arms, closed the gates, and filled in gaps in the abatis, effectively isolating Fort Miamis from the flood of humanity that would soon engulf it. Writing on the night of the battle, Campbell said: "It has been a great relief to my mind that the Battle did not happen so near to this Fort, so as to commit me. You may imagine that we shall not sleep very soundly to-night."[26]

The major claimed, perhaps somewhat naively, that he did not know "what Mr. Wayne's people mean by burning all the Indian hutts in the neighbourhood, and all the Hay on Colonel McKee's Island." Campbell did issue strict orders for his officers and men "to remain silent, notwithstanding any insults that were offered to them, and not to attempt to fire, unless indeed an actual attack were made on the place." These orders proved to be necessary since, during Wayne's two inspections of the fort, some of the Americans used "the most gross and illiberal language to the British soldiers on duty." But even Campbell's patience finally wore thin. After two days of watching the Americans ride about at their leisure and burn everything combustible, the major assured Captain Bunbury that, should Wayne persist in reconnoitering under the British guns, "I shall certainly fire upon him." Indeed, after he had forbidden any further approach to his garrison, a troop of cavalry "came so near as to occasion the Major to order a cannon to be pointed at them and the ball to be lighted." The lieutenant prudently withdrew his dragoons, but for a few tense moments, the British commander of Fort Miamis and an unknown lieutenant of the American legion brought their two countries perilously close to the brink of war.[27]

Major Campbell may have been an unwilling spectator to the battle, but Alexander McKee of the Indian Department was an eager participant. Abraham Williams said that on August 20, the Indians "went to the fight with great reluctance and only from the persuasion of McKee." The colonel tried to mask the embarrassing truth by reporting, "there were never more than 400 Indians engaged during the whole day and these stood the Shock of a great part of their Army for upwards of two hours and lost in the whole but 19 men." Every part of McKee's statement was an outright lie. Americans found between thirty and forty Indians "who had been shot or bayoneted as they attempted to run from one tree to another." It was suspected that many more had been killed, but this could never be ascertained because "a profound silence was observed on the subject by the Indians." When the Indians began to retire, McKee managed to rally many of them behind the fort, but after a few minutes they broke again. The colonel galloped ahead of the fugitives, and his entreaties caused them to rally a second time about a mile below the fort. But again they broke and fled toward where their families huddled near Swan Creek. By now, the warriors "absolutely refused to fight again." A week after the battle, McKee spread a story, possibly true, about the Americans, who "besides scalping and mutilating the Indians who were killed in Action, . . . have opened the Peaceful Graves in different parts of the Country, Exposed the Bones of the consumed & consuming Bodies, and horrid to relate have with unparralelled barbarity driven stakes through them and left them objects calling for more than human Vanegeance." Not even such a horrific tale could stimulate Indian rage against the Americans. Broken British promises had broken the spirit of the confederacy.[28]

CHAPTER 26

Regrouping at Fort Defiance

GENERAL WAYNE RODE WITH LIEUTENANT Colonel Hamtramck's left wing on the march back to Fort Deposit. Undertaking to direct the course himself, that wing wandered too far to the west and got lost for about two hours. In order to correct his mistake, Wayne angled back toward the river and eventually bumped into the rear of General Wilkinson's right wing. Although he had difficulty navigating in the woods, the commander had made an important discovery, at least in his own mind. He had personally seen ten dead Indians, one of whom "was one of the finest figures and most superlative looking fellows he had ever beheld." After riding over the battlefield, the commander in chief concluded that the American legion had been opposed by "2000 Indians and the whole Detroit militia," this combined enemy force losing four hundred dead in the engagement. When informed of these inflated numbers, Wilkinson rightly called Wayne's pronouncement "an idle Gasconade."[1]

Having regained their equipment and received rations, the Americans left Fort Deposit on August 24 and began to retrace their steps to Fort Defiance. Believing that the rear of the army might be vulnerable to enemy attack, General Wayne rode with Major Price's battalion of scouts, which acted as rear guard. Ahead of the scouts marched a detachment of light infantry, which followed Lieutenant Covington's troop of dragoons. Shortly after commencing the day's advance, Wayne, who had gotten the entire left wing of the legion lost the day before, called up to Covington that "the Dragoons were mad" and "were entirely out of place." Covington replied that he marched where his orders indicated. The general then told his lieutenant, "You shall take no orders from the adjt Genl, you are to take orders from me only," and his orders were "to dress by the Light Infantry." Thoroughly confused, Covington responded, "Why Sir they are in my rear and I cannot see them without looking behind me." Wayne, or "Caesar," as Wilkinson sarcastically called him, put an end to the conversation by saying, "No matter, you are to dress by them & are to take no orders from any person but myself." Not surprisingly, Wilkinson observed, "the order of March was this day loose and negligent."[2]

Indians had been spotted rummaging about Fort Deposit after the army had left, so Wayne assumed this would occur at every campsite. On the morning of August 25, Major Price took a select squad of his scouts and set an ambush after the army marched. He went forward a couple of miles, then filed off, circled around, and came up behind the old camp. Lieutenant Clark called it "a trifling stratigim," but sure enough, eight Indians appeared and began poking through what the soldiers had left behind. Scouts rushed forward and wounded three, all the warriors managing to flee but one. Price, who was "a large, heavy, resolute man," seeing that the Indian left behind was still alive, "clubbed his gun" and beat the wounded man to death, the blows being so forceful that he broke his rifle in two at the breech. The major calmly exchanged his now worthless rifle for the Indian's weapon, mounted his horse, and rode off amid accolades from his comrades.[3]

The march that day was haphazard, with first one column, then another, moving ahead, depending upon the terrain. In his haste to regain Fort Defiance, Wayne passed by a previously fortified camp in order to cover more ground, but soon "the clouds thickened, the rain poured, the roads became almost impassable," and the army was forced to halt after only a few additional miles. The wounded men and pack train had advanced about three miles farther than the main body and were forced to turn about and retrace the route back to camp, not arriving until after dark. One wagon, carrying four men whose bones had been broken by enemy rifle balls, "jolted, jostled, and overset." General Wilkinson said sympathetically that "these poor wretches have great cause to lament the day on which they engaged to serve their country." Lieutenant Clark's company manned one of the outposts surrounding the legion encampment that night, and he admitted, "The Savage was round my redoubt, late at night, making most Dreadfull yells Howling like wolves, & crying like owls, which kept me up all night & my Men under arms, expecting hourly a charge from the Enemey, as I was 300 yds. From Camp." Since all Indian resistance had crumbled, the sounds that kept Clark on alert really were wolves, owls, and other night creatures rather than warriors mimicking their cries. The night was also filled with noise from the volunteers, who had been "fireing off their Guns & Hollowing unnecessarily" most of the day. That racket had become so annoying that Wayne sent a general order to the Kentuckians' camp reminding officers of their duty in controlling their men.[4]

Due to the late hour of their halt and the necessity of constructing a breastwork, troops spent the morning of August 26 drawing provisions, and the legion made a very late start. This day, the Americans marched to Girty's Town, where soldiers destroyed "the whole of their Corn and Vegitables," then on to Snake Town, where they halted in one of their old breastworks. At the suggestion of Surgeon General Richard Allison, all of the wounded, who had been "neglected, unnecessarily harrassed and put to great torture" on the march, were sent ahead to Fort Defiance in litters, on horseback, or in wagons. All agreed this was the most humane course of action, although Surgeon John Carmichael inadvertently had wounded men from the artillery and cavalry placed in wagons filled with axes and entrenching tools. In addition to the "frequent shocks of a wagon on the worst of roads," tools constantly flying about in these springless wagons left the injured "lying in extreme pain." By the next day, Lieutenant Bowyer could report that all the wounded had reached Fort Defiance and "were happily fixed in the garrison, and the doctors say there is no great danger of any of them dying."[5]

The army moved out early on August 27 on "a very fatigueing March" due to the mud caused by an almost constant rain that had fallen since leaving Fort Deposit. Upon approaching Fort Defiance, General Wayne sent Captain DeButts ahead so that he and the men could be properly welcomed by a salute of fifteen rounds from the howitzers of that post. After a long delay, the legion moved about a mile up the west bank of the Maumee and fortified a camp on ground "high & dry, but cut with ravines" in midafternoon. General Scott's command established its camp about two miles up the Auglaize River, while the riflemen of the right wing settled in on the east bank of the Auglaize about one and one-half miles from the legion. General Wilkinson complained of this disposition, explaining that the camp was "badly fortified," with less than seven hundred infantry, in addition to artillery and dragoons, to man breastworks that extended almost one thousand yards. This camp was protected mainly by the outposts, manned by light infantry, "who in general trust to their Serjeants" instead of their officers. In fact, men of this light corps, much coddled by Wayne, thought themselves "independent of the officer of the day."[6]

Although the Choctaws had not participated in the Battle of Fallen Timbers, the victory there meant they could start home with honor. Major Buell's garrison at Fort Greeneville had been "impatient to hear from the army," but when some of the Choctaws arrived there on August 29 with tidings of a great battle, Buell admitted, "they cannot talk English and we have no interpreter," so the suspense continued. Just at nightfall, another group of Choctaws, one of whom could speak some English, came with news that General Wayne had beaten the Indian army and driven it past the British fort. Captain Butler's wife asked in desperation whether there were any tidings of her husband and whether he had fallen. One of the Indians said that he had seen the captain since the battle and calmed her fears by describing his appearance. Overjoyed that her husband had survived, Mrs. Butler passed out enough liquor to make the entire Choctaw party drunk, and they started a fight that the soldiers managed to break up before anyone could be killed. After the Indians sobered up, Buell sent them on their way.[7]

When one party of Choctaws reached Cincinnati, a rumor quickly swirled around town that they had brought along a white female child, "naked bound, and suffering." Winthrop Sargent, still acting governor of the Northwest Territory, reported this story "was most industriously circulated, and so dressed up, as to interest, in a very extraordinary manner, the Feelings and Passions of the people generally." He investigated but "could find no sufficient Grounds to believe the Tale founded in fact." Whipped into a frenzy by vicious gossip and some free-flowing liquor, men of the village armed themselves with clubs and rocks and attacked the friendly Choctaws, seriously injuring a number of them. The mob withdrew but returned a few hours later, this time "armed and accoutered as for War," and surrounded the camp. Seeking the captive that never existed, drunken white men, who made no distinction between friendly and hostile Indians, rummaged through the Choctaw camp, "putting them in great Terror." Alarmed by these outrageous breaches of the peace, Sargent, fearful "for the Lives, not only of the said Indians but of some of the Inhabitants," empowered Justice of the Peace William McMillan to call out a posse and disperse the marauders.

The acting governor also ordered Maj. John Ganoe to form twenty militiamen and a couple of noncommissioned officers at the churchyard and use them in a way "as shall seem best calculated to establish and preserve Order at Cincinnati, and afford Protections to the Chactaw Indians." Sargent then wrote to Captain Peirce at Fort Washington, explaining, "although I have ordered out a militia Guard and shall make every possible Exertion to prevent mischief, it appears to me that it cannot be done unless you take the Indians into the Fort—and immediately." Peirce declined to take the Choctaws into his stockade but did send a detachment of regular troops to guard their camp overnight. Sargent repeatedly ordered the rioters to disperse, but they continued to roam the streets of Cincinnati "in hostile Array—committing unlawful Acts to the Disturbance of the peace and Terror of the good people thereof," even firing twice into the governor's own home. Before they crossed the Ohio River on September 9, Sargent met with the victims of this brutal treatment and assured them of the "sincere Friendship of the united States to the Chactaw and Chikasaw Nations," words that must have proven as insulting as the wounds inflicted by the mob of Indian-hating whites.

Sargent had promised the Choctaw warriors that "prompt effectual Measures" would be used to identify and punish those criminals responsible for the outrage. When justice did not seem timely, he wrote to one of the territorial judges:

> The hostile Disposition of the old Frontier Settlers to all red people without Distinction—and which it must be confessed has but too often led them to Acts of very great Injustice—is fast gaining Ground in this Country, and if not speedily checked must have the Tendency to continue the United States involved in War with the Indians whilst any of those people exist within their Territories—
>
> I know it to be a favourite Doctrine with some that they should be all exterminated, but at this Idea Humanity revolts and it is our Duty to do Justice to all men.

The entire affair was presented to a grand jury, which was obviously opposed to giving satisfaction "to the red people," the proceedings being arranged so that only two men were indicted on a charge of assault and battery. One was tried "in the Absence of the principal Witness" and found not guilty. A delay in trying the second man allowed him time to arrange an escape from that jurisdiction. In reporting this apparent corruption of justice to the secretary of state, Sargent was forced to admit that "the present Administration of the civil Authority in Hamilton County is inadequate to afford protection to the Indians in Amity with the United States."[8]

Shortly after reaching Fort Defiance, General Todd was to convene a court of inquiry to investigate charges that Lt. Benjamin Ray of Capt. Charles Hazelrigg's company had "behaved unbecoming an Officer and Soldier on the 20th Inst by leaving his Command on the commencement of Action." After examining Hazelrigg, Sgt. Richard Jenkins, and others from the company, the court, presided over by Capt. William Lewis, recommended that Ray be brought to trial for "Shamefully abandoning his post" on the day of battle. After a number of postponements, a court-martial found the lieutenant "guilty of the Charge Exhibited against him and Sentence him to be Cashiered & Dismissed [from] the Service of the United States that his Crime and place of abode, & punishment be Published in the Western Centinell at Cincinnati and Lexington Gazette after which it Shall be deemed Scandalous for any officer to associate with Him." A similar charge was lodged against Ens. William Morrow, and Capt. Joseph Colvill presided over a court that inquired into Morrow's actions. Hazelrigg said that the ensign was "a good soldier." Jenkins and Sgt. John Hickman testified that Morrow "never left his place" beside the captain but endeavored "to keep the Men in order." Sgt. James Thomas saw Morrow throughout the fight and observed "nothing amiss," while Joseph Bradburn said that the accused "behaved himself manly and much like a Soldier." Based upon this testimony, Morrow was acquitted of all charges. Two privates from Capt. Henry Lindsey's company were also tried for leaving their posts after the battle on August 20. John Brown was found guilty of leaving his guard duty without permission and sentenced to receive five lashes. Reuben Searce was found guilty of going back to Fort Deposit and staying for two days without leave, his sentence being a public reprimand by Major Russell, his battalion commander.[9]

One of the first things soldiers did upon arriving at Fort Defiance was to let friends and family members know they were still alive and what they had accomplished over the last month, most boasting of the devastation they had visited upon the Indian country. One officer wrote, "These people appear to live in the greatest plenty; the vast quantity of corn and vegetables you can form no idea of; but I think they must be greatly distressed the ensuing Winter, as we are burning and destroying every thing before us." General Wilkinson agreed, writing that Wayne's army had "destroyed prodijeous quantities of Corn." Major Haskell reported that the legion and the Kentuckians had "marched through the Indian settlements and villages for about sixty miles, destroyed *several thousand acres of corn*, beans, and all kinds of vegetables, burned their houses, with furniture, tools, &c." Another officer boasted: "For forty miles below us, we have destroyed innumerable acres of corn; and gardens finely cultivated have afforded us vegetables in abundance. Upon the smallest calculation we must have destroyed between three and four hundred thousand bushels of grain." It was speculated that, given the loss of their food supplies, the Indians could not survive the winter, "unless their friends the British are remarkably kind to them," but there were grave doubts whether the latter had enough rations to go around. Wayne had been completely successful in his effort to shift the burden of war to the Indians, despoiling their country in a most terrible fashion. The total ruin inflicted upon residents of the Auglaize and Maumee River basins would not again be duplicated on American soil until William Tecumseh Sherman marched through the Confederacy in 1864–65.[10]

After reaching Fort Defiance, one officer said that he hoped to be home "before the budding of the leaves again," but he confessed, "I have been so long immured in these wilds that my first entrance into a civilized country would I believe, bring ridicule upon me." Isolation on the frontier magnified even the tiniest of pleasures. Francis Jones could hardly wait to supplement his army rations by fish from the Auglaize River. The same day he reached Fort Defiance, Jones and his friend Nathaniel Hart made torches of hickory bark and went night fishing, catching a salmon, a pike, and several of the smaller species. When the two anglers attempted to try their luck the next night, General Scott forbade them since riflemen had spotted a small party of Indians that day. An appeal was only partially successful, for Scott ordered them to "fish along the shore close by the Camp." For Edward Miller, the highlight of August 28 was taking three glasses of wine with General Wilkinson. But Captain Miller seemed to enjoy an alcoholic beverage now and then. Before he left Fort Defiance, the captain would receive five gallons of whiskey from Major Buell and over three gallons from Lieutenant Colonel Strong.[11]

"As a small Compensation for the fatigues they have for several Days experienced," Wayne ordered the quartermaster to issue a gill of whiskey "to every Man belonging to the Federal Army." He also announced that his army would "probably remain on this Ground for some Days," so latrines were to be dug and "every precaution taken to preserve the Encampment clean and healthy." The general also declared that a review would be held on August 30, so the men set to work cleaning and burnishing their arms, then washed and mended their tattered uniforms "so as to appear in the most Military Condition possible." Officers were cautioned "not to permit too many Men at one time to take their locks off or to be engaged in Washing" in case the Indians suddenly make an attack on the camp.[12]

A convoy of all the horses and wagons belonging to the contractor and quartermaster left for Fort Recovery on August 29, the escort consisting of General Todd's entire brigade of mounted volunteers. Quartermaster O'Hara and Robert Elliott, the contractor, personally accompanied this convoy so they could speed the delivery of rations and supplies, all of which were running critically low. Troops had been on half allowance of flour for two weeks, and even the vast Indian gardens were beginning to fail, foragers having to roam farther and farther in search of vegetables. Lieutenant Webb wrote, "The poor pittance of Provision Drawn at present would not keep body & soul together, was it not for the Vegitables, that we obtain when Foraging." General Wilkinson noticed that the dragoon horses, now on short rations of corn, "are declining fast and in ten days more we shall not have a particle for them except the grass and herbage of the woods and prairies." In the opinion of Lieutenant Clark, "the exastance of this army depended on the safe and speedy return of this escort." Webb agreed, saying, "It will be serious & alarming times, with us shou'd Gen. Todd's Escort fail." The convoy also took back Major Hughes, Captain Slough, Captain Van Rensselaer, and Lieutenant Younghusband, who had all received furloughs "to go home to repair their healths." Lieutenant Bowyer said of the four officers, "I believe the two first and the last mentioned, if they never return will not be lamented by the majority of the army." Wilkinson was incensed that Wayne should furlough Younghusband, "worn down with liquor & debauch," calling it "extraordinary" and "injurious to the service and a wrong done to the meritorious officer."[13]

While the troops anxiously waited for rations to be forwarded from Fort Recovery, on August 31, Wayne instituted a few guidelines regulating those searching through Indian gardens. Individual soldiers were no longer allowed to forage for vegetables. At 9:00 A.M. every morning, one man from each mess formed into detachments under the various sub-legion quartermasters, then these organized parties went off several miles in search of foodstuffs. Thereafter, any enlisted man found more than a half mile beyond the sentinels without a written pass would be considered a deserter. This last order was in response to a sudden and dramatic increase in desertion, which no doubt resurfaced after the Indian threat virtually disappeared and runaways could keep their bearings in the wilderness by following Wayne's military road back to Fort Miamis.[14]

While he waited for the return of Todd's convoy, General Wayne began to strengthen Fort Defiance, planning to put it "in such a state of defence as to repel the efforts of British force, should it happen that a war with Great Britain takes place." Three hundred men with axes, picks, and shovels assembled on the morning of September 1 and began work under the supervision of Major Burbeck. The blockhouses, each containing one howitzer, were to be strengthened to withstand artillery fire. Burbeck's detachment also began digging a ditch eight feet deep and twelve feet wide around the fort, except on the side facing the Auglaize River. Dirt from the ditch was thrown in toward the pickets, forming a wall of dirt eight feet thick that was kept in place by logs. The outside wall of this defensive ditch was held up by installing fascines, or bundles of sticks tied together, that were placed so as to prevent cave-ins. Sharpened pickets jutted out from the log wall of the ditch to slow down any assault. A narrow bridge of earth crossed the ditch in front of the gate facing the confluence, where the garrison obtained drinking water. On the opposite side of the fort, access was gained by "a falling gate or drawbridge which was raised and lowered by pullies, across the ditch." Although Lieutenant Clark complained that "the work goes on at the Fort Sloly," Lieutenant Bowyer thought it began "to put on the appearance of strength, and will in a few days be able to stand the shock of heavy cannon."[15]

While work details from the legion toiled on various construction projects, the mounted volunteers did little more than consume provisions. The monthly return dated August 31 shows that 1,611 Kentuckians were serving in some capacity. Those not on escort duty began to chafe at military subordination. They refused to turn out when the trumpets called them into line every morning "or at any other time." When Capt. Jesse Richardson's company was ordered out for duty, he responded by ignoring those instructions and went off foraging with some of his men. On August 31, General Wayne was forced to remind officers of some basic tenets of discipline, such as keeping their "full Number of Sentinels Day & night & Stop every person going out of Camp," and "no Sentry is to be Sufferd to Set down on his post upon any Pretence what ever." Despite stringent instructions from the commander in chief, disobedient Kentuckians continued

Fort Defiance. From Charles Slocum, *History of the Maumee River Basin*, 1905.

to sleep while on guard, leave their posts, ignore orders, and fire off their rifles "in & near Camp." This last bit of rowdy behavior was starting to irritate the legionnaires, who were often called into line to repel the Indians only to learn that the "attack" had been volunteers having fun.[16]

The independent attitude of General Scott's men probably resulted from boredom, for there was little to do besides forage for food. Maj. John Caldwell led a scouting detachment up the Auglaize River on September 1 but found no recent trace of Indians. All the corn had been destroyed previously, but Caldwell's men did burn sixteen houses that remained standing and ruined the Indian gardens, the major ordering "the bean Vines pulld up and pumpkins cut to pieces." That same day the volunteers moved about a mile up the Maumee to a location Francis Jones called "the most Beautifull Camp we have had, since we set out." The land was high and level, covered with oak trees, and contained "watter Clear [with] a rapid current." Wayne ordered the breastworks built to a height of five feet, not so much for defense as to keep the volunteers busy. All the brush inside the camp was either burnt or thrown outside, and latrines were dug so that the entire area could be kept "Sweet and Clean." When not involved in one of these activities, men could attend public sales, where the effects of deceased soldiers were auctioned off. Obviously, the highest-priced possession of every dead man was his horse, but many men did not have the means to purchase one. General Scott's two aides, Samuel Postlethwait and Francis Jones, pooled thirty-five dollars to bid on a bay horse that had belonged to a volunteer killed on August 20, the money to be delivered to Major Price no later than January 1, 1795.[17]

When Wayne dispatched General Todd to Fort Recovery, he told that officer to wait for the arrival of a herd of cattle from Fort Greeneville, then return as quickly as possible with the beeves and loaded packhorses. After advising the Kentuckian to keep small parties several miles in front and rear of his main body, Wayne told him, "Your own reputation as an officer and the benefit of the Servus require that you take every possible precaution to Guard against Surprise and if attacked to repulse and defeat the enemy at all events." Upon reaching Fort Adams, formerly Fort Randolph, on September 1, Major Russell wrote to his brother and explained what might be expected of the Kentuckians: "Todd's brigade is here, this far on their way to Ft. Recovery, as an escort to provisions for the army. They expect to return and join the main army by the 15th inst. It is hard to tell what our road will be from there, though I incline to believe Barbie's brigade will then return in for another escort, and at the same time the army will proceed up to the old village [Kekionga] where we shall probably be met by Barbie's brigade on their return. Then I think we shall return to Kentucky. These are my ideas just as they occur, and do not undertake to say that this will certainly be the case." When Todd reached Fort Recovery, he received a message from Elliott and Williams that the firm had forwarded 250 head of cattle and fifty head of sheep, along with a dozen axes to be used for "making Strong Pens" for the livestock every night. The contractors also sent some hay to be used as new padding in the packsaddles, repairs that were considered "absolutely necessary" to keeping the horses fit, even though it would delay Todd an additional day. The contractors also begged him not to move the loaded horses more than fifteen miles a day, which was about as far as the tired animals could go without undue stress.[18]

While quartermaster and contractor employees readied the cargo, Todd sorted through his men and culled out those too sick to march or still suffering from wounds received on August 20. The latter would return to Fort Greeneville with the first detachment heading south, while the former would be left at Fort Recovery and join that garrison when they had recovered their health. Those fit for duty were warned to be ready to march promptly at 7:00 A.M. on September 5, each man being issued six pounds of flour the night before since there would no time for distributing rations that morning.[19]

Just after sunrise on September 5, General Wayne dispatched Major Price and his two companies of scouts to reinforce General Todd's command. But when an express arrived two days later from Todd that the packhorses had started to give out and the convoy would be unavoidably detained, Wayne sent an express rider back to him with orders for Price to press forward with the cattle. If any more packhorses should fail, Todd was to encourage his men to haul the loads on their own horses, for which they would be compensated. This news from the convoy "Could not but create a few unpleasant Sensations on the minds of the Soldiery as both the meat & Bread was now Exhorsted," as Lieutenant Clark phrased it. He also complained that, "as for Liquers, we have been long sence been compel'd to do without." General Wilkinson reported that on September 7, "the whole stock of the Contractors stores are 900 lbs flour— 2000 lbs beef, 9 Kegs of salt & 10 Boxes Soap." He summed up the state of affairs by remarking, "Critical indeed is our situation, embosomed in a wilderness impracticable to land transport in the Winter and 170 or 80 miles distant from the source of supplies." Wilkinson's assessment of the supply problem was certainly correct. In fact, if not for the unexpected volume of Indian corn and vegetables found along the rivers, the legion would have starved in a manner that would have made the suffering at Valley Forge look like a spring picnic.[20]

Hard work on the fort, a constant diet of vegetables, and frequent rainstorms were blamed for a dramatic increase in sickness. On September 1, Lieutenant Bowyer, who was ill himself, wrote that "the soldiery gets sick very fast with the fever and ague," and the next day confessed, "I believe the longer we continue in this place the worse it will be." Throughout the right wing, General Wilkinson saw that "the men are becoming very sickly owing to the too free use of unripe vegetab[l]es & great fatigues." As for diagnosing the various complaints, he wrote that "debility seems to be the general predisposing cause—agues, fevers & fluxes, the prevailing disorders." Disability caused by these diseases, combined with large detachments for fatigue work and foraging, meant that the legion probably could not even defend its fortified camp if it happened to be attacked. On September 2, according to Wilkinson, "the right wing had not 120 Combatants left to defend their lines more than 600 yards in extent."[21]

Wayne was intent upon completing additions to Fort Defiance before General Todd's convoy returned. When Capt. Daniel Tilton had an argument with one of the artificers and had him confined for "insolent behaviour," the general rode directly to that officer's tent and "in a violent rage in presence of the soldiery reprimanded and abused him in gross terms." Even Wilkinson admitted that Wayne had displayed "great industry" during the construction, being ably seconded by Captain Butler, "a man of Herculean limbs and inured to manual labor from his youth," who proved to be "adroit with the ax, the spade or the pick." It was Wayne's plan to strengthen Fort Defiance so it would "defy all the artillery of Canada," making it secure against 12-pounder solid shot and ten-inch shells. As his modifications approached completion, Wayne viewed the fort with its commander, Major Hunt, and told him, "If the British came to see him he would only have to turn up his breech [buttocks] to them." When Hunt asked what he should do then, Wayne responded with a laugh, "Why tell them to kiss your arse."[22]

While the commander in chief retained a positive outlook, morale was on the decline in his elite dragoon squadron. With Major Winston indisposed by illness and all four troop commanders either dead or wounded, the remaining officers seemed to lack their previous cocky attitude. Lieutenant Webb expressed the sentiment felt by anyone who has in vain anticipated approval from a superior, writing, "we must wait the call of imperious Commanders & when we Do our Duty well, if they but smile, we must think ourselves overpaid altho: they found their fame upon *our* Merits." Even though times had been hard on both men and mounts, the dragoons at least had hopes of returning to Kentucky for the winter. There would first be an advance to build another fort at the Miami villages, but then Lieutenant Webb was sure the mounted arm would again be sent south, where the young officers would "cut some *foolish Capers.*" In a letter to Captain Van Rensselaer, who was still hospitalized at Fort Greeneville, Webb wrote: "If we reach Kentucky once more, you shall hear of some rare Doings, Courting, Gallanting, Balls & Assemblies. You will wish to be with us." Cornet Blue agreed that there would be fun times again, boasting, "Silver lace for a Coat would be a good thing to wear in Lexington amongst the Ladys."[23]

While dragoons daydreamed about dancing with pretty girls in Kentucky, the scouts and spies were occasionally sent out to look for Indians, who were thought to be either assembling for another battle or organizing raids against the convoys. Kibbey's Columbian Scouts had bivouacked at the confluence of the Maumee River and Bean Creek, a small stream that empties into the river opposite the volunteer camp, where, at least for several days, their most important duty was to keep the horses at headquarters supplied with corn. Captain Shrim's spies were sent on a mission south and east of the Auglaize River and returned a day later, having made no discoveries other than the trail of a solitary Indian and the sound of a single gunshot. Wilkinson did not seem surprised by Shrim's inability to find the enemy, for he considered that officer "a poltroon and no woodsman." Upon Shrim's return, Captain Kibbey was dispatched up Bean Creek and then off to the east, but he too failed to find any Indians.[24]

The scouts and spies had been looking in the wrong direction, for a small group of Indians had ambushed a group of six officers' servants and one woman on September 10. Captain Price's waiter escaped and carried the news to Major Buell that their party, en route to Fort Greeneville for supplies, had started early, against orders, and had been attacked just a mile north of that garrison. Buell immediately dispatched Captain Sullivan with a mixed party of legionnaires and volunteers to investigate. Sullivan soon returned with the bodies of three soldiers who, according to Buell, had been "killed and scalped and tomahawked more than I have ever seen any before." The dead men were interred that night, "with the honors of war" and a salute "fired over their graves." In case the missing men and woman had gotten lost in the woods, Buell ordered a cannon to be fired every fifteen minutes all night so they might find their way, but the three had vanished. Two days later, an express from Fort Jefferson brought word that Indians had been seen near that post and Lieutenant Marschalk had been wounded. Marschalk somehow acquired an old "blunderbuss" and probably loaded it with too much gunpowder. When he fired the antique piece, its recoil kicked the wooden stock into his face, inflicting a nasty injury and knocking out two teeth. Buell sent Surgeon's Mate David Davis to patch up the lieutenant, the doctor returning later with news that "the Lieut. will recover."[25]

By September 10, foragers were going as far as twelve to fifteen miles in search of vegetables to feed the hungry soldiers. Joy spread throughout the camps that day when, just shortly before noon, Major Price arrived with the cattle herd, followed about four hours later by General Todd with the packhorses and sheep. William Clark could not contain his glee and wrote with enthusiasm, "Rost Beef was here again." Lieutenant Bowyer was not so elated as his brother officer, for he groused, "We received no liquor by this command, and I fancy we shall not receive any until we get into winter quarters, which will make the fatigues of the campaign appear double, as I am persuaded the troops would much rather live on half rations of beef and bread, provided they could obtain their full rations of whisky." Despite the arrival of provisions, supplies were still so short that, instead of the full daily ration, only half rations of flour were issued. This was due to a number of factors, including the almost impossible task of supplying the army by packhorse trains, the fact that over a ton of flour had been left at various locations when packhorses had given out, and the arrival of reinforcements—Captain Preston; Ensigns Henry Bowyer, Thomas Lewis, and George Strother; and sixty soldiers—which meant more men to feed.[26]

General Wayne sent a scathing letter to Elliott and Williams just after the arrival of Major Price and the cattle herd. He pointed out that for four days, "the troops have been totally destitute of beef or flour—& only subsist upon green corn & pumpkins," after having lived on a half allowance of flour for thirty days. The cattle could supply rations for two weeks, while the flour brought by General Todd was only enough for eleven days. Wayne pointed out bluntly, "famine with all its concomitant horrors threatens us on one Quarter whilst a fierce & savage enemy are waiting with impatience in the rear, to take advantage of our wretched situation." He continued, "The question then is, shall the interest & Dignity of the Nation, & this small but Gallant Army be sacrificed, on account of the Neglect or imbecility of the Contractors?" The answer to this rather undiplomatic inquiry was of course not. Quartermaster O'Hara was again ordered to supplement the inept contractors, but now Wayne went one step further. He informed the firm that henceforth, mounted volunteers would be paid three dollars for every one hundred pounds of flour they carried forward from stockpiles at Forts Recovery and Greeneville. This additional expense would be deducted from payments to the contractors in a manner to be settled "at a future date." For now, the general just wanted rations and forage moved as quickly as possible because he planned to advance up the Maumee River on September 14.[27]

Two more officers joined the legion on September 11, having pushed ahead from Fort Washington with an escort of just eight men. They proved to be Major Cushing, recently released from custody by the sheriff of Hamilton County, and Chaplain David Jones. Neither received an enthusiastic welcome. Lieutenant Webb referred with contempt to "poor Jones, L.L.D. whose wounded mind, or entrails Laudanum alone can heal. He has been several times Distracted, See the Effect of Hard Drink." As for Cushing, that officer received "an uncivil & ungenteel reception" when he presented himself to General Wayne, who "neither rose to salute or asked him to sit down." Wayne undoubtedly would rather Cushing had remained under arrest, but since he had reported for duty, some place must be found for him. As ranking officer present, Cushing would command the First Sub-Legion during the subsequent campaign, an assignment Wayne could not tolerate. To remove Cushing from a position of trust and responsibility, the general sent him the following order: "You are to repair to Fort Defiance immediately, & put yourself under the Command, & receive & obey the Orders of Major Thos Hunt, the Commandant of that Important post." Wayne closed with what might seem like an innocuous expression but, in this situation, actually dripped with sarcasm, saying, "Wishing you a pleasant tour of duty." Lieutenant Clark, a firm supporter of Wilkinson and Cushing, called this embarrassing treatment of the latter a "low condesention & resentment" by Wayne.[28]

On September 11, one day after General Todd's arrival, General Barbee's brigade was sent back to Fort Recovery for the twelve hundred kegs of flour remaining there. Todd's experience on the road had proven that no reliance could be placed on livestock worn out by convoy duty, exhausted horses either giving out completely or, perhaps worse yet, slowing the entire resupply process. Wayne needed fresh animals, so he had Barbee's men take all the ropes they could find to use in lashing kegs of flour to their own horses, although many objected because the loads would injure their mounts without the use of pack saddles. The general figured that each horse could carry two kegs with ease and even suggested that this method of transport would allow Barbee's brigade to defend itself better since the loads could be used as temporary breastworks during an attack. The horsemen would be "liberally rewarded" with six dollars for the trip, in addition to the lucrative wages they already enjoyed. To sweeten the offer, Wayne agreed that, if the volunteers brought forward the flour, they would be discharged on October 10, about one month early. General Scott appealed to his men not to lose the honor they had gained on August 20 and hoped there would "not be a Single Man whose horse is fit for Service, that will refuse coming into this Measure." Although unsure as to how many of the men could be talked into hauling flour, Barbee's brigade headed for Fort Recovery at sunrise on September 11, with orders to meet Wayne's army at the Miami villages at Three Rivers.[29]

CHAPTER 27

A Fort at Three Rivers

IN PREPARATION FOR AN ADVANCE into the heart of Indian country, General Wayne ordered Surgeon General Richard Allison to minutely examine all sick and wounded with the legion, and those unable to march were added to the garrison at Fort Defiance. After the addition of these injured and invalids, Major Hunt's command consisted of almost two hundred men, the officers including Major Cushing, Capts. Robert Thomson and Daniel Britt, Lieutenants Pope and Lee, Ensign Strother, and Surgeon's Mate Joseph Andrews. Leaving so many officers to oversee so few enlisted men seemed "Extreodinary" and "totally inixplicable" to Lieutenant Clark, particularly when officers were already scarce. At least in the cases of Cushing and Pope, the post was a good place to tuck away those potential troublemakers. The remaining line officers were probably left because of indisposition, a practice that Wayne had followed all that year. Hunt was ordered to form his command into two battalions and defend his post "to the last extremity." Recent additions to the fort's defenses made it impregnable to every type of attack but a prolonged siege carried out "by regular Approaches aided by very heavy artillery." Such an extended contest would buy time for the legion to return to Hunt's relief and drive off the enemy, who must, of course, be British, for the Indians lacked artillery and the capability to carry out siege operations. The major was to keep a sharp lookout for Indians coming to his post with a flag of truce. If such a party did appear, Hunt was to "receive & treat them with kindness" but take care to "never admit more than one or two Indians within the Gates" on any occasion.[1]

The Indian woman captured by William Wells and his spies before the battle was given a good horse and sent off to find her people, escorted for the first few miles by a detachment of Major Price's scouts. She carried "a long & handsome talk" to the sachems and warriors of the hostile nations as well as a letter from Antoine Lasselle to his brother, "respecting the necessary Steps for obtaining his Liberty." Wayne's message reminded the Indians that it had been "one moon" since he sent his last peace proposal from Fort

Defiance, inviting all the hostiles to join in discussions "for settling a permanent fair &
honorable peace with all & every tribe or Nation of Indians North of the Ohio." After
recounting his previous invitation to talk, the general continued:

> But you were deaf to this request & to the voice of peace—you again took the
> advice of those bad white men & in place of meeting me as friends, you prefer'd
> war, & instead of the Calumet of peace you suddenly presented from your secret
> coverts the scalping knife & tomahawk—but in return for the few drops of blood
> we lost upon that Occasion we caused rivers of yours to flow.
>
> I told you "that the army of the United States was strong," you only felt the
> weight of its little finger; I informed you "that the British had neither the power
> or inclination to protect you"—you have severely experienced the truth of that
> assertion—be there fore no longer blind to your own true Interest & happiness,
> but listen to the Voice of peace & permit me now to draw a veil over the late trans-
> actions & to bury in deep Oblivion & to obliterate from the mind all remembrance
> of past Injuries.

Having explained how the Indian nations had made the wrong choices in their war with
the United States, General Wayne now told them what they must do to achieve peace:

> If you now wish for peace & to be restored to the possession of your culti-
> vated lands & hunting ground come forward with all the American prisoners now
> in your hands—& in exchange you shall receive all such prisoners as I have
> belonging to your Nations.
>
> Appoint a number of your Sachems & Chief Warriors to attend them, bring
> with you some of your most confidential Interpreters—& I hereby pledge my
> sacred Honor for your safe Return & for your kind treatment whilst with me.
> Open your minds freely to me, & let us try to agree upon such fair & equitable
> terms of peace, as shall be for the true interest & Happiness of both the white &
> red people & that you may in future plant your Corn & Hunt in peace & safety—
> & that by an interchange of kindness & good offices towards each other we may
> cement that brotherly love & affection which shall endure to the end of time.

If the Indian nations should decide to pursue the path of peace, Wayne assured them
that Major Hunt would receive their emissaries with kindness and send an officer to
conduct them to legion headquarters.[2]

General Wayne had no intention of waiting for a reply to this latest proposal and
announced that the army would march precisely at 7:00 A.M. on September 14. A road
would be opened by the pioneer detachment, composed of the legion's best ax men and
guarded by Ephraim Kibbey's scouts. Major Price's battalion would again form the
vanguard, one battalion of General Todd's brigade would bring up the rear, and his other
two battalions would march on the legion's right flank, its left resting upon the Maumee
River. Wayne had to be especially careful with the disposition of his forces, for his army
had been woefully reduced by battle casualties, disease, desertion, and garrisons left at
Forts Adams and Defiance. After General Barbee's brigade had departed for Fort

Recovery, Francis Jones asserted "there cannot more than half the number of men march from this place that marched from Greenville."[3]

When two men from the artillery deserted on September 10, General Wilkinson thought that "from them the enemy will certainly learn our situation." Indeed they did. Edward Tonor and William Carleton, both natives of Ireland, stole horses and rode to Fort Miamis, where they met with Major Campbell and gave not only the current news but also what Wayne intended to do for the next few weeks. According to them, the Americans would march on September 13, "leaving a garrison of about two hundred men, with intention of advancing to the Forks of the Miamis River, called as the Informants learn, St. Joseph and St. Mary's to erect another fortification there and after leaving a garrison they believe the main body of the Army rendezvous at Fort Greenville." Other than missing the date of departure by a day, this information proved completely accurate. Deserters who left over the next several days, despite a twenty-dollar reward for their return either "dead or alive," informed Campbell of the exact state of affairs in Wayne's command, including the size of his force, the use of volunteers to carry flour since the packhorses were "entirely unserviceable," the shortage of provisions, the prevalence and types of disease, the invalid garrison at Fort Defiance, and the appointment of Lieutenant Colonel Hamtramck to command the new fort. Deserters traveled both ways on Wayne's military road, so the American deserters told Campbell of four British deserters that had reached Fort Defiance before their own departure. Informants also stated that Drummer John Bevan, who had run away from Fort Miamis after the battle, had been given a horse and fifty dollars by General Wayne, then sent back to safety in Kentucky. In words that must have brought a chill to the hearts of Colonel McKee and others in the British Indian Department, the two American deserters claimed that Wayne intended "to bring about a Peace with the Indians, in hopes of obtaining the entire Indian trade."[4]

After a stay of about three weeks at Fort Defiance, Wayne's army left camp on the morning of September 14 and, with but a single stop, marched eight hours in the rain before halting. The command encamped in "a very rich bottom" along the Maumee over eleven miles from the Auglaize. Next morning, in order to avoid a number of large ravines and the meandering of the river, the road was laid out a considerable distance into the woods. This region was swampy, being thick with timber and underbrush, and Lieutenant Clark said, "the whole country has the appearance of being under Water during the winter season." Captain Preston, commanding the rear guard, became confused by keeping too near the river and got lost when he was unable to hear the signals in heavy undergrowth. After marching another eleven miles that day, Wayne's army built breastworks along a small creek about two miles from the river. When Preston's command, including a number of surgeons who were riding with him, did not appear, signal guns were fired all night. Many of the missing soldiers followed the sound of the guns and reached camp by tattoo, but some men spent that night in the woods. Preston came up with much of the baggage on the morning of September 16. That day, the army marched about twelve miles, camping at the Thirty-Four Mile Tree (the distance measured by

road from Fort Defiance), Wayne's route having inclined back to the left and again parallel to the river. This day, the road was very rough and the woods choked with brush,
although the trees were "very lofty" and the soil "generally rich and well watered." Kentuckians from Todd's brigade caused several alarms by firing at game, but the only sign
of Indians was discovered by Robert McClellan, who saw two warriors spying on the
army's movements.[5]

The army moved at 6:00 A.M. on September 17, fording several small streams with difficulty due to their being "extreemley Mirery," the mud causing a number of packhorses
to give out and several wagons to break down. Soldiers passed through several small villages, one of which was said to have been home to James Girty, that had been burned by
General Harmar in 1790. After making about fourteen miles, the legion halted directly
opposite the confluence of the Saint Joseph and Saint Marys Rivers late in the afternoon,
waited until the area had been thoroughly scouted, then waded across the river and
bivouacked so late that not all of the tents could be pitched. There appeared to be some
five hundred acres of cleared land visible, both rivers being navigable for small craft, and
the region gave indications of having once been "one of the largest settlements made by
the Indians in this country." Even though villages at this location had previously been
outposts of civilizations, now most everything was "grown up with Thorn Crabb & Plumb
Trees." The site seemed to never have been reoccupied following its destruction by Harmar. For those poking about in the underbrush on the old battlefield, bones could still be
found, including "skulls which had marks of the tomahawk and scalping knife."[6]

On the morning of September 18, while the legionnaires and mounted volunteers
fortified their camps with earthen breastworks, timber being scarce along the rivers, General Wayne reconnoitered and decided where to locate his new fort. Cornet Posey said
of the site, "Nature never formed a more Beautiful Spot for the purpose, a high & commanding situation on the south side of the Miami and immediately at the Confluence
of the Rivers St. Marie & St. Joseph which form the Miami." Lieutenant Clark noticed
that the place was "tolerably elevated & has a ready command of the mouth of the two
rivers." This day was also marked by the arrival of the four British deserters forwarded
to headquarters from Fort Defiance for interrogation. Wayne interviewed a private
named Simcox, who admitted that he and three comrades from the Twenty-Fourth Regiment had left Fort Miamis on September 14. Simcox, a soldier in the Fifth Regiment,
had been part of a detachment from that command, along with a squad from the Queen's
Rangers, sent forward from Niagara to reinforce the fort. This force had gotten to within
a few miles of the post on August 21 but returned to Lake Erie since the Kentucky Volunteers virtually surrounded Major Campbell's garrison. Simcox also asserted that 1,600
warriors still remained in camps along Swan Creek, some eleven miles below Fort
Miamis. This last statement was erroneous, for by now the Indian Department was issu-
ing provisions to 2,500 Indians, only 860 of whom were fighters. The redcoats also said
that about twenty-five American deserters had reached Fort Miamis, but the Indians
refused to sell six other white captives to the British, had already scalped one, and "had
the rest ready painted & their heads shaved for burning."[7]

There was rain off and on all night, and a downpour continued most of the day on September 19, Lieutenant Bowyer thinking, "the clouds have the appearance of emptying large quantities on this western world." Although work details had been curtailed by the weather, soldiers began to construct a fish dam across the Maumee, the waters of which were then rising, in order to have something to eat since the beef was almost gone and supplies of flour had been exhausted. After another storm overnight, General Barbee's brigade arrived with the flour from Fort Recovery early on the morning of September 20, an event that one enlisted man called "a pleasing Circumstance." Cornet Posey wrote that the newly arrived shipment of flour "enabled the *Poor Hungary* Solider once more to Draw his whole Ration." Despite delivering 553 kegs of flour, Barbee brought no other provisions, and one officer wrote, "the absilute want of Salt becomes now a Serious matter." The entire stock of rations available to the army consisted of this convoy of flour and forty-four cattle. Several sutlers had brought forward some cattle, sheep, and other supplies with Barbee's convoy, but there was little money with which to make purchases. Their prices per pound were: beef and mutton, twenty-five cents; bacon, seventy-five cents; coffee, sugar, and chocolate, one dollar; butter, seventy-five cents; cheese, one dollar; and whiskey, eight dollars per gallon. The merchants also had some raisins, tobacco, and other delicacies, but prices for these items were not recorded. Capt. John Francisco had returned from carrying dispatches to Fort Washington and accompanied Barbee's convoy, bringing along some luxuries for General Scott's mess and a few current newspapers.[8]

General Wayne took advantage of this lull in operations to inform Secretary of War Knox of what had been accomplished recently and what he planned to do in the coming days. The general explained how he had strengthened Fort Defiance and then marched to his present location, cutting a wagon road forty-eight miles through the wilderness "without seeing an Enemy or meeting with any interuption from them." Wayne then explained that Barbee had brought flour, but he only had five days of beef on hand, and the army was "without a particle of salt or a single drop of any kind of spirits." Although he did not mention the fact to Knox, this supply problem was compounded by the resignation of Maj. John Belli, whose operations had been a critical component in the supply of Wayne's army. Although his resignation would not be effective until November 8, Quartermaster O'Hara immediately appointed Samuel Henley to succeed him. Wayne hoped that the legion could "maintain the Ground we have acquired," but he told Knox that "two powerful obsticles" stood in the way. First was the inability of the contractors to forward enough rations and forage, a problem that had haunted western armies for years. Second was the expiration of the terms of service for many men in the First and Second Sub-Legions. In fact, the general pointed out that, in the course of six weeks, these two units would not number more than two companies each. That was not all, for as Knox was well aware, by the beginning of summer, the whole legion would be "nearly Annihilated" by the expiration of enlistments. In the general's opinion, "all we now possess in the Western Country must inevitably be abandoned unless some effectual & immediate Measures are adopted by Congress to raise troops to Garrison them."[9]

As for the fort he had started to lay out, Wayne said he would commence construction "as soon as the Equinoctial storm is over," which was then continually drenching the camps, a further discomfort when added to short rations and worn-out uniforms. He also advised Secretary Knox that he felt constrained to reduce the size of the post from the dimensions originally specified in 1792, "both for want of time as well as for want of force to Garrison it." He would soon be without his mounted arm, for the Kentuckians were becoming restless and homesick, while the horses of the dragoons had become so worn down by hunger and hard work that it was necessary to dispense with patrols. The general planned to begin building his new fort on Monday, so he ordered the artificers, pioneers, and a fatigue party of one hundred soldiers, the whole totaling between two hundred and three hundred men, to assemble at 7:00 A.M. on September 22 and begin cutting timber under the supervision of Major Burbeck.[10]

Sunday was marked by several significant events. Early that morning, General Todd's brigade started for Fort Greeneville with all the quartermaster and contractor horses judged able to complete a march of that length. As he had done with Barbee's brigade, Wayne promised Todd's men three dollars for each keg of flour they would transport back to the army. Major Price marched with Todd's command, having special orders to drive back a herd of cattle "with all possible dispatch." The second noteworthy incident came shortly after Todd's departure, when Chaplain David Jones held church service and based his sermon upon a text from the Book of Romans: "But what shall we say to these things, if God is with us who can be against us." Captain Cooke remarked on this special occasion, "This was the first time the army had been called together for the purpose of attending Divine service since I joined it." The riflemen being on guard duty, Lieutenant Clark said they were "Deprived of the Blessing of a Short Sermon." Later in the day, Cornet Blue returned to camp after pursuing some deserters with a squad of twenty dragoons, the detachment having seen none of the runaways or Indians. Blue's party did not even see four men who deserted that very day and made off with three horses owned by officers.[11]

Major Burbeck's working parties began to prepare timber promptly on September 22, although that officer and General Wayne made numerous alterations to the plans for the fort. The reason for these changes were obvious. Although Fort Defiance had been modified to a state-of-the-art fortified post from the more typical blockhouse-and-stockade variety, it would conform to the most modern principles of military engineering from the very beginning. Pioneers had started to clear the ground on September 19, but actual construction did not commence until six days later, when men began to erect barracks and bastions. The entire project would last almost a month. Two additional ax men from each company were detailed on September 24 to assist the artificers in cutting and trimming timber, this duty being rewarded by an extra half ration, not much incentive when all that meant was "very pore beef & musty flour." Fatigue parties were increased soon after by "every Officer and Soldier not actually on Guard or other Duty." When it became obvious the horses were "so weak that they could not bring the timber half as fast as they could put it up," artificers removed wheel assemblies from the wagons and used them to haul logs, officers driving "teams" of from fifteen to thirty soldiers.[12]

Kentuckians felt Wayne's wrath when he discovered that they had chopped down trees for firewood that had been marked for constructing the fort. He thought better of Scott's men when they volunteered for fatigue duty, digging the ditch and building the earthen wall around the walls and bastions. They soon tired of this hard labor but agreed to work on a detached blockhouse to guard the watering place and a ravelin, or breast-work, on the east side of the post. The Kentuckians soon abandoned that assignment as well. Garret Burns wrote the only known contemporary description of Wayne's new fort, which he said "was built of the largest kind of oak logs." Burns explained, "The walls of the fort were double, the space being filled up with earth, afforded by a ditch dug out-side, which was fourteen feet deep and as much wide." Basic timber construction was completed on October 12, leaving earth to be moved and roofing and finishing work to be done on all interior buildings. Fatigue parties were finally discontinued on October 21, and Wayne had himself a formidable post, built according to the most modern engi-neering principles, that could withstand any artillery the British might bring to bear should hostilities commence.[13]

After Barbee's convoy returned with flour, his men were disappointed when only half rations were issued. Majs. John Caldwell, Nathan Huston, and Aquilla Whitaker, commanding the battalions in Barbee's brigade, explained their concern in a letter to their commander:

> The Captains in behalf of their respective Companies have represented to us that they have for a considerable time lived on half Rations of Flour without com-plaining as they supposed the good of the Service required it, but expected after using their exertions to bring forward a quantity of flour by packing their Horses and becoming pack horsemen themselves (which they were not induced to do from the consideration of three Dollars pr hund weight but to promote the good of the service) that they would certainly receive their full Rations; but they find themselves herein disappointed, and as they do not see the necessity of making any further sacrifices to self Deniel, and in fact are not able to subsist on it, are sorry to say they cannot submit to such treatment any longer; at the same time they declare their Willingness to do their duty and demean themselves as good Soldiers provided they can get their full Rations of Flour, Beef and Salt.

All three majors added that these concerns were "justly founded" and requested General Barbee, as their superior officer, to use his influence "to have those complaints removed." Barbee could do little more than forward this startling letter on to General Scott so that he would know his troops were mighty close to mutiny. This bit of blackmail by the Ken-tuckians worked, for that same day, Wayne ordered the contractors to "Issue full Allowance of Flour & Beef to all the Army in future & also the other component parts of the Ration." Because of his complete reliance on the Kentuckians for escort duty as well as packing pro-visions, the general had no choice but to give in to their demands.[14]

Salt had given out on September 19, and everyone sorely missed that part of the ration. Lieutenant Bowyer wrote, "we have not one quart of salt on this ground, which occasions bad and disagreeable living." Among the volunteers, the men were all "distressd for want of salt," while Lieutenant Clark claimed that "the increasing sickness of the Army" was due to "the long want of Salt." When someone displayed a mere pint for sale, the first offer of three dollars was instantly refused, and it eventually sold for double that price. Clark wrote with despair, "God only Knows what would be the consequence, if this Escort falls a sacrifice" to the Indian army, then confessed, "I can see no end to our fatigue & Sufferings on there Safe returns." The situation was bad indeed, for on Sunday, September 28, Captain Cooke would write, "Contractors out of beef and bread and not a grain of salt to be had." Luckily for the army, Major Price arrived that afternoon with 150 cattle, some of which were slaughtered, issued, and wolfed down, even without salt. Benjamin Van Cleve, the sutler's clerk who had been thrown out of Fort Greeneville for selling liquor, returned to the legion with Price's command as one of the cattle guards. He remembered that the army ate "10 beeves per day issued regularly in rations & the Kentucky militia destroyed at some times about as many more."[15]

Liquor brought out by sutlers who accompanied Barbee's escort did not last long. Within a few days, Captain Miller was forced to borrow some from Lieutenant Elliott of the artillery and pay two dollars for an additional quart of whiskey. There was no discount for buying in bulk, and John Bowyer remembered that a ten-gallon keg of whiskey was sold on September 24 for eighty dollars. General Todd's brigade arrived in the evening on September 30 and brought flour, cattle, salt, *and* whiskey. Francis Jones remarked that "the Salt was most acceptable," but the liquor had more of an effect because soldiers stole a large quantity from the quartermaster and became intoxicated. Sutlers again sent wagons and packhorses loaded with goods for the army, and Lieutenant Clark took note of the current prices: brown sugar and chocolate, one dollar a pound; butter, seventy-five cents; mutton and flour, twenty-five cents; salt, one dollar per quart; tobacco, one dollar a pound; and whiskey, from six to eight dollars a gallon. Miller received a shipment from Abijah Hunt that totaled five pounds sterling for twenty pounds of raw sugar and one pound of pepper. The bill for sundries sent forward to the captain by the trader Levi Munsell amounted to more than twice that total. For those unable or unwilling to pay these exorbitant prices, migratory birds offered a culinary diversion from beef and flour. Some of General Scott's mess dined one night on a wild goose that had the misfortune to land in one of the camps.[16]

To continue the shuttling of convoys, General Barbee's brigade was told on October 1 to prepare for another trip, this time to Fort Greeneville. This order caused "discontent and murmuring among the Officers & Men," the latter of whom marched through their camp chanting, "Home! Home!" Lieutenant Bowyer noted that "the volunteers appear to be uneasy, and have refused to do duty," claiming that General Wayne had promised they would be discharged on October 10 if they agreed to pack flour from Fort Recovery. Already on the verge of mutiny, the Kentuckians were apparently stirred to a fever pitch by Major Caldwell, who urged them to refuse to comply with these new marching orders.

This mutinous remark prompted General Scott's adjutant general to prefer charges against the major for "mutinous and Seditious Conduct" and "Unofficer like and un Gentleman like Behaviour." Scott assembled his officers and explained that the legion was "too weak" to both build the new garrison and escort supplies. He then reminded them that their term of service had not yet expired and asked "whether they intended to goe or not." The general concluded by saying, "if they made the smallest delay they should lose all their pay and be reported to the war office as revolters." General Wayne visited Barbee's camp, told the mutineers what they might expect should they disobey his order, promised that they should be discharged immediately upon their return from Fort Greeneville, and issued each man four days rations of whiskey to win them over. But the generals had not been very persuasive. Only a few officers and men followed Barbee when he started south that afternoon about five o'clock.[17]

Those who remained continued to grumble until about 8:00 P.M., when "a great nois and Quarreling" broke out among the intoxicated and disaffected soldiers in Barbee's section of the camp. Samuel Postlethwait, Scott's aide, walked into this maelstrom and began writing down the names of officers and men who had refused to march, an action that seemed to alarm the rowdy volunteers. Many seemed to think "there was some trick in it" and refused to give Postlethwait their names, declaring that their officers had given them permission to stay behind for a variety of inventive reasons. Employing every weapon at his disposal, Wayne turned to rudimentary psychology when he gave out the parole and countersign that night, the former being "Barbee" and the latter "Gone." Next morning at daylight, after sleeping off their drunk, everyone from Barbee's brigade, except the sick excused by a surgeon, started after their general and caught up with his command about five miles to the south.[18]

It had been assumed that a chaplain would be able to moderate the rough lifestyle of a soldier, but David Jones proved unable to provide much spiritual leadership. The legion was given a half day off of fatigue on Sunday, September 28, but there was no church service. Instead, Jones went to deliver a sermon to the volunteers, most of whom were out grazing their horses, so the event was postponed until Monday. When the minister showed up to conduct his service, he found that General Scott had forgotten to issue the necessary order, and Jones was forced to put off his sermon until Tuesday. Scott instructed his men to graze their animals early that day, then prepare a small arbor for the divine service, which would be held at noon. The third time was a charm, and Reverend Jones preached what was deemed "an excellent sermon" from the Book of Isaiah on the topic, "There shall be no destruction on the Mountain of the Lord." Any long-term benefit from this discourse was probably wiped out by the arrival of Major Price's cattle herd a few hours later. The second time Dr. Jones preached to the legion was at ten o'clock on October 19, when the troops marched by platoons and formed on the ground between the fort and the blockhouse in response to church call. That day, Jones spoke on a topic from the Book of Romans, but William Clark was not impressed, saying, "The Sublimety of his reasoning did not penetrate verry deep into the minds of our troops as it wanted Some connection." Besides, it was hot.[19]

While soldiers from the legion were no saints, many of their Kentucky counterparts had turned into very active cattle rustlers. There had always been plundering of the contractor's stores, but hungry volunteers now elevated that crime to an art form. Richard Sloane, one of the firm's agents, reported on depredations that occurred during the first few days of October. On the second of that month, a cattle driver discovered several of the volunteers dividing up meat from a slaughtered cow. That same day, Robert Scott and Sgt. William Owens, two responsible soldiers from Major Conn's battalion, reported finding the head and hide of another cow that had been butchered. On the morning of October 3, these two men found another animal that had been killed and divided up near the volunteer camp. That afternoon, Captain Kibbey and a small party went after five cattle that had mysteriously disappeared but could only find the remains of one. On October 4, a contractor employee rescued a cow from five men who were driving it off into the woods, the would-be thieves cursing the rescuer. That evening, the drivers noticed a number of volunteers "conceil'd in the Thickets" and later came upon another slaughtered beef, while other animals had simply disappeared. In a complaint lodged with General Wayne, Sloane alleged that seventeen cattle had disappeared that night, the loss to Elliott and Williams amounting to almost three hundred pounds sterling.[20]

Thefts such as these, along with many others unrecorded, compelled General Wayne to order an end to such heinous behavior in the legion on October 25, after the volunteers had left for home. His general order read:

> The alarming and Villainous excess to which Marauding, Plundering and Stealing have been recently carried on, by the unprincipled part of the Soldiery belonging to the Legion, is such as to require the most exemplary Punishment.
>
> The Commander in chief therefore offers a Reward of Twenty five Dollars to any Person or Persons who will discover the Principal or Principals concerned in killing any of the Cattle or Sheep belonging to the Publick, or to the Contractors (without proper Authority).

Guards who allowed such thefts on their watch would be considered as responsible as the actual criminals. This order was read to the soldiers of every sub-legion that evening at retreat. To reinforce his point, the parole that night was "Marauding" and the countersign was "Death."[21]

To show their contempt for General Wayne's order, several guards from the First Sub-Legion stole a bullock from Dodson Tharp, chief artificer, butchered the animal, and hung the horns on Wayne's own tent. The general was not amused. An intensive investigation soon revealed that the culprits were Cpl. James Reading and Pvts. John Frymiller, John Hassell, Elwine Crowell, and David Johnson. Wayne convened a court-martial, with Captain Bradley as president, and within a matter of hours, that panel had returned its guilty verdicts. Corporal Reading was sentenced "to be hanged by the Neck, until he is Dead," while Frymiller, Hassell, and Crowell were to receive one hundred lashes. Johnson was found to be less complicit and was sentenced to receive seventy-five lashes. All five were to have $4.98 withheld from their pay to reimburse Tharp for his loss. Although he pardoned Crowell, General Wayne approved the remaining sentences, thereby curtailing theft and practical jokes for the remainder of the campaign.[22]

While justice was swift for Corporal Reading and cohorts, poor Antoine Lasselle remained in confinement. Even though William Wells had assured General Wayne that Lasselle was "a good man" and had helped ransom American captives from the Indians, the general said he was "a damned rascal" and kept him locked in irons without his clothes. He remained a captive until mid-October, when Ensign Strother arrived from Fort Defiance with Tappan Lasselle, who had come to trade three former captives of the Indians, whom he had ransomed, for the life of his brother. One of the prisoners was a thirteen-year-old girl named Nancy Chapman, who had been captured on May 11, 1790, near the Muskingum River. John Glass, her brother-in-law, happened to be a private in Bartlett's company of mounted volunteers and he came forward, identified Nancy, and took her home after giving Wayne a receipt for the youngster. The other two captives were soldiers who had been taken prisoner during the attack on Lieutenant Lowry's convoy the previous year. After completing this prisoner exchange, the Lasselle brothers started back for Fort Defiance after promising to furnish that garrison "with stores at a moderate price." For one, Captain Miller was afraid that the two Frenchmen had seen too much during their visit to the Americans and that information regarding the legion's weakness, gained from "unrestrained observations and the Information of the Soldiery," might be communicated to the British. The brothers headed for Detroit but stopped over at Fort Miamis, where the officers listened sympathetically to Antoine's tales of woe and gave him a coat. He confessed to having brought with him a copy of his court-martial, along with a few newspapers and a letter from General Wilkinson to Lieutenant Colonel England. Wilkinson's chatty note apparently expressed a wish to obtain a buffalo blanket, but England carefully forwarded this inappropriate letter on to Lieutenant Governor Simcoe, lest he be "suspected of having an improper correspondence" with an American officer.[23]

On October 12, General Wayne decided to inspect the eight-mile portage between his fort and the headwaters of the Wabash River. Accompanied by Generals Scott and Todd, aides, staff members, and a large retinue of officers, Wayne set off at about 9:00 A.M., the whole entourage guarded by the rifle companies of Howell Lewis and Thomas Lewis and a detachment of mounted volunteers. Moving on a southwest course, Francis Jones noted that they rode through "a tillable beautifull Country a little waveing and well timbered with young tall straight White Oak with some Hickory & Beach." Prior to the destruction of the Miami villages in 1790, French traders had obviously carried on a lively trade between Detroit and Vincennes over this route. There were tracks of wagons and carts visible in what was still a very good road. This portage crossed a number of smaller streams, some of which had been spanned by now-rotted bridges, while a few causeways crossed swampy areas. The Wabash River was "very narow and Deep about 5 feet at the Landing place," where old camping grounds could still be seen. General Wayne examined the area and, according to Captain Miller, "found a place formed by Nature for the Erection of a Garrison and marked a tree for that purpose." The general did not discuss any future plans regarding a fort at this end of the portage, so Miller assumed that "what this portends is still in the womb of fate."[24]

Wayne was now seriously considering the use of water transport to supply his advanced posts in order to trim a dependence on packhorses and wagons. To test the possibility of supplying Fort Defiance from his new post, head artificer Dodson Tharp built a flat-bottomed boat, christened *Adventure*, that was capable of carrying twenty-five barrels of flour. She was launched on October 7 and, after being loaded with whiskey, salt, and hospital stores, set out on her maiden voyage the following afternoon, manned by a crew of eight. Before *Adventure* had gone a mile downstream, she struck a rock and capsized, losing much of her cargo in the accident. Crewmen scrambled to retrieve the supplies, probably devoting more attention to the whiskey than the other items, then repacked the stores and again set off for Fort Defiance. *Adventure* finally reached her destination, and by the end of the month, even British officers had learned of the successful trip. Encouraged by the somewhat modest success of Tharp's craft, Wayne directed him to build another, this one patterned after Kentucky boats used on the Ohio River. This new vessel was more substantial than the first, the latest measuring forty feet long and twelve feet wide, a sizeable boat to be plying the inland waters following its launch on October 17. By that time, there were not enough supplies to spare, and the water was "by far too low to take her Down."[25]

General Wayne wrote to Secretary Knox and informed him of the decision to establish a waterborne supply route. His reason for doing so was obvious. The general explained that, from his base at Fort Washington, the overland route stretched 175 miles to Fort Defiance and then another 150 miles to the post then under construction at the headwaters of the Maumee River. In spring and fall, cargo could be shipped by water for all but 35 miles, a distance that could be reduced to 20 miles during periods of high water in the smaller streams. Considering Wayne's problems with supplying an army by packhorses alone, this water route, in his opinion, would be "the most economical & surest mode of transport in time of War & decidedly so in time of peace." It would lead up the Big Miami River to Piqua Town, thence up Loramie Creek, and across the portage to the headwaters of the Saint Marys River. This route would supply the new post, while a second small portage from the Saint Marys to the Auglaize River could carry supplies directly to Fort Defiance. It was Wayne's intention to build three new forts at critical points on the new route, then abandon Forts St. Clair, Jefferson, Greeneville, and Recovery. With the construction of a blockhouse along the Wabash River at the western end of the portage from the Miami villages, Wayne would control "all the portages between the heads of the Navigable waters of the Gulfs of Mexico & St Laurence & serve as a barrier between the different tribes of Indians settled along the margins of the Rivers emptying into each." In simple terms, General Wayne and the Legion of the United States, with important assistance from General Scott's Kentucky Mounted Volunteers, had won control of the transportation network in the Northwest Territory.[26]

CHAPTER 28

End of a Successful Campaign

FOLLOWING THE VICTORY AT FALLEN TIMBERS, encounters between Indians and soldiers almost ceased, but the dreary duty at isolated frontier forts that guarded the legion's lines of communications continued without interruption. Often the garrisons were so small that post commanders had but few men from whom to select noncommissioned officers. Such was the case at Fort Knox, where Captain Pasteur reduced Cpl. Benjamin Palmer to private on August 16 after being found guilty of drunkenness while on guard duty, pointing out Palmer's "Shameful and unsoldeiry conduct in this Instance of his neglecting the Safety of the Garrison, when he had the honour of the charge of it." But having no one else available as a suitable replacement, Pasteur restored Palmer to the rank of corporal ten days later. As for assisting General Wayne in his campaign, all the captain could do was forward intelligence gleaned from friendly Indians, who told him, "the hostile Indians are crossing the Mississippi [westward] every day," saying, "there is no withstanding the Americans." Pasteur continued, "Several of the chiefs of the Wabash have been to see me; they say the Indians above are crying, and they believe what I had told them before was very true, for the British would soon cry as well as the bad Indians; but they hoped their father would have a little pity for their bad brothers."[1]

At Fort Massac, Major Doyle had so many of his garrison sick that he claimed, "the mere defence of my garrison, from the number of my men, is all that Government will expect from me." When a new detachment of troops arrived, Doyle could finally obey his standing orders and send two parties of five men to watch the mouths of the Cumberland and Tennessee Rivers, supplying each group with a canoe so they could immediately report any unusual activity. Major Cass had not wanted to leave the field, but his fractured leg and a dangerously ill wife forced him to relinquish his post with Wayne's column. Assigned to Fort Washington, he confessed, "I felt a greater anxiety at not being able to Join my Corps this active Campaign than I did on account of my leg," even though he nearly lost the limb. The major wrote to Wayne on October 2 and reported that his leg had healed quicker than expected, despite one doctor removing a section of bone that now "must be supplyd by nature." Garrison duty had no appeal for Cass, who told Wayne the moment he was cured, "I will Join the Legion with one leg an inch shorter than the other" and "much crookeder." Extended duty on the frontier led to long separations from wives, who occasionally strayed, leading to situations like one described by Pvt. John Bell in a legal notice: "Whereas my wife *Rachel Bell*, (during my service in the United States Army) hath without any just cause absconded herself from my bed and board; these are therefore to forewarn all persons from crediting her on my account, as I am determined not to pay any debt of her contracting."[2]

Although much closer to the concentration of Indians at Swan Creek, soldiers at Fort Defiance saw virtually none of the enemy. Warriors, however, continued to lurk about in the woods, their presence indicated by notices posted on trees around the garrison:

> Wanted, for his Majesty's 1st American regiment, or Queen's rangers, of which his Excellency Lieutenant Governor Simcoe is colonel commandant, fifty active young men.
>
> Gentleman volunteers shall receive ten guineas bounty money each, on their approval, at the headquarters of the regiment, enter into free quarters, be clothed, accoutred, victualled, and paid agreeably to his Majesty's regulations. None need apply to <BLANK>, but which as are perfectly fit for the most active service, at least five feet four and a half inches high, healthy and stout.

Referring to this notice and its source at Fort Miamis, one American officer pointed out "the lengths they [the British] pursue to destroy the confidence of our soldiery, and prolong a war, which might have happily terminated, but for the establishment they have unjustly made in our country."[3]

The depression that afflicted many soldiers and led large numbers into drinking and gambling is evident in a letter from Lieutenant Visscher to his friend Captain Van Rensselaer, finally in New York recovering from his wound. Visscher thought of how the two of them must spend the winter—the captain, a bona fide war hero, at home among family, friends, and female companions, while he, "without ever having heard the noise of guns," remained at that lonely outpost, Fort Recovery. Visscher continued: "But alas! it appears that I must content myself with the little limits of a Garrison, secluded from the society I will ever hold dear. How oft, in the dear and heartful enjoyments of my Melancholy walks, have yon Romantic groves witnessed my narrative of love; and when the drear night appears, I retire to my Room, where in a state of chaos, the thoughts of home, and a thousand other things rush on my mind like a torrent. I generally take up Thompson's description of a Winter Season or some other book, on which I muse till sleep overcomes me." His thoughts often turned to an aged father, bothered by "imbecility of body, and the troubles of his mind." Visscher confided, "oft in some of my melancholy moments, do the thoughts of him steal from me unobserved a pathetic tear, and when I draw a similitude between his present and his former situation, I am like Niobe all tears."[4]

Lieutenant Visscher also alluded to officers who had recently died. Among those were Lt. William S. Grayson, who had originally been commissioned an ensign in the Fourth Sub-Legion but had recently been promoted into the newly expanded artillery and engineer establishment. Aged twenty-two years and educated at Columbia College, Grayson died on October 1 in Norfolk, Virginia, and the local press, citing the "esteem of his acquaintances, and admiration of his friends," lamented the death of one who "bid fair to be an ornament to his profession." Capt. Nicholas Hannah expired in Alexandria, Virginia, on October 11. His remains were interred in the Presbyterian cemetery after a Masonic ritual, his funeral service being witnessed by "a numerous collection of his fellow citizens, who will long regret the early fate of a brother and a friend." Lieutenant Younghusband, who had recently been furloughed, got no farther than Fort Jefferson, dying there on the morning of October 16. Although he had expressed a wish to have his body cremated, Younghusband was taken to Fort Greeneville and buried with military honors that same night. His funeral was attended by Major Buell and all the officers and gentlemen at that post. William Maxwell, editor of the Cincinnati newspaper, had but a short acquaintance with the deceased officer but could testify to his "*extreme honest candour*" and "*many virtues*." Maxwell concluded his notice of Younghusband's death with the observation, "If he possess foibles, spare them ye creticks, he lies in a wilderness where few but the real soldier will find it convenient to visit his grave."[5]

The most important individual to die during Wayne's campaign was Robert Elliott, a native of Franklin County, Pennsylvania, and then a resident of Hagerstown, Maryland, one of the partners in the contracting firm of Elliott and Williams. He had returned to Fort Washington to hurry forward supplies to Wayne's starving army, starting north on October 6 with a convoy consisting of two hundred packhorses, three hundred cattle, three hundred sheep, and twenty-five wagons. Elliott had written to Captain Peirce at Fort Washington and asked for a suitable escort, but that officer could only furnish one sergeant, one corporal, and twelve privates for that portion of the route between his post and Fort Hamilton. Peirce added, "Could I furnish one hundred I would do it with pleasure." While scouting ahead of the vulnerable convoy with his servant, Elliott was ambushed and killed by two Indians concealed along the road about four miles south of Fort Hamilton. His servant escaped by spurring his mount to the nearby garrison, but Elliott's body was left lying beside the road, ignored by the convoy as it hurried forward to safety. The contractor was described as "an uncommonly large man, being both tall and heavy, and weighed nearly three hundred pounds." Elliott also wore a wig, which came off easily when one of the killers attempted to scalp the victim, causing him to exclaim, "Damned lie!"

The body was recovered and placed in a wooden coffin by a detail of soldiers sent from Fort Hamilton. On the morning of October 7, his faithful servant, mounted upon the contractor's own horse, a magnificent animal worth $120, started for Cincinnati with a wagon bearing the corpse and a small escort. When nearly to the fatal spot where Elliott had been shot, the same pair of Indians fired upon his funeral party, killing the servant and scaring off everyone else. The Indians sprinted forward and broke open the box in hopes of finding valuables but found only the corpse, minus the wig, and removed it to search unsuccessfully for treasure hidden underneath. Captain Miller was puzzled by the removal of Elliott's body, which was left lying in the mud along a small creek, "as it's a given opinion that the Indians after taking the scalp have gained the utmost of their wishes in War fair." Frustrated by their bad luck, the warriors took the horses and Elliott's business papers from the wagon and started for the camps on Swan Creek. Word of these attacks had reached Cincinnati, and a party of militia and a few volunteers came out, retrieved both bodies, and buried them in the cemetery at that village.[6]

Reaction to Robert Elliott's murder was immediate and emotional. William Maxwell wrote in the columns of *The Centinel of the North-Western Territory:* "In him an affectionate widow, a numerous and lovely offspring, *have to lament the loss*, of a generous and tender husband, a fond and affectionate parent. The individual, a kind and liberal benefactor—and the public, a zealous active and faithful agent." Maxwell concluded his eulogy with the observation, "An honest man is the noblest work of God." Elliott's hometown newspaper, *The Washington Spy*, said: "Thus died, in the prime of life, a useful, active, and ornamental member of society, a man of the strictest virtue and honor, of generosity unbounded, and of benevolence universal—whose fate will long, long be deplored by all those who ever had the pleasure of his acquaintance. He has left an affectionate and amiable wife and children to mourn, more especially, so tender an husband, so kind a father—a loss irreparable indeed!!!" Ann Elliott, his widow, eventually filed a claim against the United States over her husband's death on behalf of herself and ten children. Her assertion was the contract with Elliott and Williams had stipulated that the army would provide proper guards and escorts for all convoys. Congress appropriated two thousand dollars in 1804 to settle Ann's claims, and that same year, Pres. Thomas Jefferson appointed two of the Elliotts' sons as midshipmen in the U.S. Navy.[7]

Elliott's death had far-reaching implications for the legion. General Wayne declared that "this Crisis will render more defective & greatly derange that department already but too defective & deranged, so much so as to hold up nothing but famine to this army & the western posts." The general dispatched Quartermaster General James O'Hara to Fort Washington, ordering him to stop at every other post along the way and make a complete inventory of both stores and transport belonging to Elliott and Williams. O'Hara was to use "all possible dispatch" in sending forward supplies, using horses and wagons belonging to his own department as well as those owned by the contractors. Although he would consult with agents of the firm, henceforth all procurement and shipment of supplies would be O'Hara's responsibility. The quartermaster was to immediately fill any deficiencies by purchase and keep "fair & particular accounts" so that the contract could be "settled at the treasury at a future day." He had inherited a prodigious task, for Wayne expected him to deliver at least 550,000 complete rations by the end of March 1795. Although this critical turn of affairs occupied his immediate attention, Wayne's problems with the firm of Elliott and Williams were about over. On October 10, Tench Coxe, commissioner of revenue for the Department of the Treasury, signed a new contract for furnishing rations to the legion in 1795 with another firm, the partners being Alexander Scott and Matthew Ernest.[8]

General Barbee's brigade of ill-tempered volunteers returned from Fort Greeneville on October 12 with ninety-six horseloads of flour, about enough for a three-day supply. By now, it had become painfully obvious that the volunteers "were Heartily tired of the Campaigning." Wayne summoned General Scott to headquarters on October 13 and told him that he was sending them home. The Kentuckians were to draw provisions for the first leg of their journey, which was to begin that afternoon, but General Scott spent too much time at headquarters going over details, and their departure was postponed until the morning of October 14. Wayne's order dismissing these troops concluded with a note to Scott that read: "Permit me now sir thro' you to return my most grateful thanks to Brigaiders General Todd & Barbee, to the Field & other Officers, & to the Non Commissioned Officers & privates in general of the Mounted Volunteers of Kentucky for their good & Soldierly Conduct, during the time for which they have been in service." Wayne also wrote a note for Scott to deliver to Governor Shelby, in which he again thanked the executive for all his efforts in raising troops and assured him that they had "render'd very essential service to the Union & enabled me to carry into effect the object of the Campaign." In a letter to Secretary of War Knox, the general admitted that, despite being homesick, "The conduct of both Officers & men of this Corps in General has been better than any Militia I have heretofore seen in the field for so great a length of time." These effusive comments may have been motivated more by politics than military performance. After all, on September 10, when informed that a Kentuckian had accidentally shot a legion soldier, Wayne had declared to Major Price "that he had rather six of the militia had been shot." Cornet Posey shared Wayne's dislike of the volunteers, informing a fellow officer, "a number of them died at Green Ville Prior to their being discharged who had (from, I believe a Cowardly disposition) been left at that Place, and not accustomed to the many Hardships & fatigues of a Soldier's life took sick and died for Spite."[9]

General Scott's men were up and in the saddle by 7:30 A.M. on October 14. The command was led by one of Major Price's companies of scouts, followed in turn by General Todd's brigade, the baggage and men without horses who carried a few sick men in litters, General Barbee's brigade, and Price's other company. The two brigades and two select companies alternated their place in the column from day to day. Captain Butler and Ensign Chandler had preceded the Kentuckians to Fort Washington, where they were to conduct "a critical Muster of his Corps with the utmost dispatch," verifying the reason for every absence, "whether occasioned by sickness, death, wounds or other disability received since the corps left Kentucky." Particular attention was to be paid to men who mustered with their own horses. If the animals had been killed, captured, or died in the service, their owners would be entitled to compensation for their loss. Since many of the volunteers had sold their mounts, captains would have to furnish affidavits confirming that the horses had been lost while on duty in order to avoid fraudulent claims. Scott's homesick Kentuckians made good time, covering the 150 miles to Fort

Washington in seven days. At Fort Recovery, Lieutenant Drake greeted them with seven rounds of cannon fire and military music. Scott's mess "Dined Drank and enjoied ourselves perfectly" at Drake's table. Upon reaching Fort Greeneville, Major Buell gave the volunteers a fifteen-gun salute. After eating another good meal with Paymaster Caleb Swan, Scott and his staff rode ahead to Fort Jefferson, where Lieutenant Marschalk, although still suffering from his encounter with the blunderbuss, gave them a warm reception. Capt. George Ingersoll, however, treated the Kentucky officers "with indifference" at Fort Hamilton, but they were happy to dine on venison and fish fresh from the Big Miami River.[10]

The main column reached Fort Washington on October 20, and Captain Butler began to muster out the companies one by one over the next few days. Francis Jones left Cincinnati and crossed the Ohio River at dark on October 22. He was in the saddle by sunup, made good time over good roads, and traveled forty-two miles that day. Next morning, Jones got another early start, reaching Georgetown just before sunset in a light rain. His journal ended on October 25, with the entry, "Cloudy got to Lexington to Breakfast." Lieutenant Sudduth described the end of his military service: "After I was mustered I procured boats & by night crossed my men & horses over the Ohio & went about two miles to Banklick & encamped. We started next morning before day, persued our journey, camped in the woods that night. The next day we arrived in Paris and were the first troops that reached there and the next day got home which was the 26th of October. I left home on the 16th of July, being absent 108 days, & slept but three nights in a house. So ended my Indian warfare." And so ended the service of the Kentucky Mounted Volunteers. One can only concur with a soldier from the legion who said that Maj. Gen. Charles Scott's troops had "rendered their Country more Services than any Volunteers have before done."[11]

Having decided to send the Kentuckians home, General Wayne had no choice but to use soldiers from the legion to guard his supply convoys. On October 10, he dispatched Alexander Gibson and his rifle company, with forty dragoons under Lts. Leonard Covington and Abraham Jones and Cornet Posey, to Fort Greeneville, where he would meet the convoy that Robert Elliott had brought forward until his untimely death. Gibson safely escorted it into camp on October 16, bringing thirty thousand rations of flour, 150 cattle, three hundred sheep, and salt. This delivery was not without a price, Covington having lost fourteen horses on the trip. A corporal sent back to Fort Greeneville by Lieutenant Clark brought that officer some bacon and sugar to vary the tiresome issue of beef and flour. Captains Springer and Brock left camp with their companies on October 18, bound for Fort Greeneville on escort duty with the recently arrived packhorses, accompanied on this trip by Lieutenants Webb and Jones and Ens. William Blue, who had charge of about ninety invalid dragoon mounts that needed more to eat than the sparse grass that remained; about two dozen of the dragoons were to be permanently dismounted. Springer's escort returned on October 26 with six hundred kegs of flour and a quantity of salt, all of which was immediately deposited with the new garrison. By this time, the legion had again been on half rations for several days. Although not privy to records relating to rations, Captain Miller had concluded, "should the whole of the Army Continue at this post the probability is that we shall consume the Rations full as fast as they can be Brought on." In addition to provisions, Springer also brought along two representatives each from the Wyandotte, Delaware, and Ottawa Nations who wanted to discuss peace. It was well that the Indians were so inclined, for Wayne could now only spare one or two rifle companies and a few dragoons with broken-down horses for each escort. His convoys were again as vulnerable as they had been in October 1793, when Lieutenant Lowry's command had been overwhelmed near Fort St. Clair.[12]

Considering Wayne's long stay at the headwaters of the Maumee, the constant shortage of rations, and presumably some short tempers that resulted, it seems remarkable that only three quarrels involving officers resulted in charges being filed. Shortly after reaching this site, Ens. Francis Johnston, commanding Slough's company, caused Cornet Blue to be arrested after that dragoon officer had abused Johnston's orderly sergeant. Additional charges were brought against Blue, but according to John Bowyer, "a number of their friends interfering the dispute was settled" after Blue asked Johnston's pardon. Almost simultaneously, Captain Brock preferred charges against James Morrow, the legion's master armorer, for hitting and abusing Sergeant Porter of his company, for the use of "insulting and abusing Language" against an officer, and most importantly, for "presenting a Rifle at Captain Brock, when in the Execution of his Duty." Wayne released Morrow after promising Brock that he should be tried before the court-martial then impaneled to hear Cornet Blue's case. After hearing testimony, the court found Morrow guilty on all charges and sentenced him to receive fifty lashes and to ask the pardon of both Brock and Porter. General Wayne disapproved the corporal punishment, deeming it "Rong to punish by whipping a Warent Officer," but did make Morrow go through the humiliating procedure of apologizing in front of the legion.[13]

The last incident requiring a trial began on October 8, when Major Hughes arrested Lieutenant Hyde, followed by the arrest of Hughes by Lieutenant Colonel Hamtramck. On October 20, a court tried Hyde on a charge of "Unofficerly, and Ungentlemanly behavior" toward Hughes, with the following specifications:

1. For writing things tending to his Prejudice, as a Gentleman & his superior Officer.
2. For Mutinous Conduct in engaging in a Party against him and endeavoring to compel him to resign, and leave the service, and threatening that if he did not, he should probably be broke, and in presuming to dictate to him to resign, to prevent being broke.
3. For Declaring in the Presence of Officers, that as long as he the Major should be in the Army, he should not be long out of an Arrest.

Deliberations concluded swiftly, and Hyde was found not guilty, a sentence that was just as quickly approved by Wayne. Hughes was supposed to be the next defendant to appear before the court, but after seeing how the Hyde trial had ended, he wrote a letter asking permission to resign rather than face the embarrassment of being found guilty by a court.

Wayne accepted his resignation, allowing Hughes pay and emoluments until January 1, 1795, providing him time to reach his home in Rhode Island, covering twenty miles per day, "the rate at which the Members of Congress are allowed for traveling."[14]

There had been several bad storms during the stay at the Miami villages. The first had occurred on September 27 after a morning marked by wind and thunder. That afternoon, the camps were swept by "a most violent storm of Thunder wind Lightening and Hail of a very large size." One officer said the shower of hail lasted fully ten minutes and the hailstones were "very large." Two days later, another storm struck and was described thus in Captain Cooke's journal: "A very heavy rain at 4 P.M., with loud and sharp claps of thunder accompanied with a whirlwind, which blew down the top of a very large tree within a few steps of Gen. Wayne's markee." The fall of this tree so close to Wayne's tent reminded everyone of the accident that had nearly killed the general while camped along the Saint Marys River early in the campaign. As the season progressed, nights grew colder and frost appeared in the morning. On October 3, a small shower of rain suddenly turned to snow, a harbinger of the winter now not far off. Next morning, Lieutenant Bowyer awoke to a frost normally seen in December, noting that "it was like a small snow; there was ice in our camp-kettles 3/4 of an inch thick." Severe frosts blanketed the camps for two days, then on October 8 came a combination of snow, hail, and rain. As the month continued, Captain Miller said the weather was "very fine for the season but Cold Nights with considerable frosts." A break in the wintry blasts lasted for a number of days, a condition of bright skies and moderating temperatures that the Indians called "a latter summer," but was soon followed by stronger winds and rain, coupled with more frost and a little snow. The legion would soon have to move into winter quarters.[15]

On October 21, General Wayne announced that Lieutenant Colonel Hamtramck would command the newly completed post, his garrison to consist of about three hundred soldiers from the companies of Captain Porter, artillery; Captain Kingsbury, First Sub-Legion; Captain Greaton, Second Sub-Legion; Captains Sparks and Reed, Third Sub-Legion; and Captain Preston, Fourth Sub-Legion. Other officers assigned to the post were Lts. Charles Wright, Hugh Brady, and Ebenezer Massey, Ens. Elijah Strong, Thomas Bodley, and Joseph Campbell, and Lt. John Wade as fort major. Surgeon John Elliott and Surgeon's Mate David Davis would attend to the sick. The garrison marched up to the fort's gates, where they formed and listened to a fifteen-gun salute. Then Hamtramck, having requested permission to name the new post, issued his first garrison order, which christened the site Fort Wayne in honor of the general who had led them to victory. After the men gave three cheers for their leader, Hamtramck marched his men inside and dismissed them to settle into their new home.[16]

Signs immediately began to point toward a march back to Fort Greeneville. Lieutenant Colonel Strong was appointed to command the left wing in place of Hamtramck. Officers were to send in requisitions for shoes, which were needed by almost everyone, the men "being nearly Barfooted," according to William Clark. There being only a few pairs of shoes on hand, it was decided that only "those that are Actually barefoot" could be supplied. Wayne postponed his march until early on Monday, October 27, waiting for

Captain Springer to reach Fort Wayne with his convoy of flour. The movement was delayed a few more hours that morning so that troops could witness the hanging of Cpl. James Reading and the flogging of those found guilty of placing bull's horns on the general's tent. Reading was the second soldier hanged during the campaign, a deserter having suffered the same fate after being retaken by a patrol sent out by Major Hunt. This latter occurrence had curtailed desertion from Fort Defiance, but a simple order issued by Wayne had the same effect. The commander in chief had instructed Robert McClellan to hunt down deserters with his spy company, and he actually killed one. This extreme measure was confirmed by an Irishman named Grant, who deserted from the cattle guard with a friend and reached the Indian camp at Swan Creek, where he stated they "were followed & his comrade killed." After news of McClellan bringing back deserters dead or alive spread through the command, Captain Cooke thought it "somewhat extraordinary" when a man ran away from Thomson's company.[17]

It was still cold and somewhat frosty when the legion began to march shortly before noon, following the trace of Harmar's army over eight miles, then stopping for the night at one of the camps made by that general four years earlier. October 28 dawned cold and clear, the legion marching shortly after sunrise and halting at another of Harmar's campsites along a small stream after covering about fifteen miles. It was raining slightly when Captain Miller commanded Captain Andrews to have his company complete its portion of the breastworks. Andrews responded that "if he had time after his men had mad[e] their fires, and pitched their tents he would," but "if he had not time he should not." Andrews made no attempt to comply with Miller's order, and no additional work was done on the breastworks, leaving that portion of the line in "a very defenceless situation." Wayne had his troops on the road by eight o'clock on the morning of October 29, and they marched about twelve miles before reaching the Saint Marys River, which they forded and again stopped in one of Harmar's camps. Here a court-martial was held for two enlisted men from Slough's company who had managed to steal all of the salt held by the contractor, obviously not too great a quantity if two infantrymen could conceal the entire amount. Soldiers exploring the area found a litter and an Indian grave, supposedly holding a casualty from the fight at Fort Recovery on June 30.

The legion took up its march at sunrise on October 30, following Harmar's trail about a mile and a half through heavy timber, until the column reached a large prairie judged to be some four miles by five miles in extent. At the edge of this clearing, the column came upon Wayne's road from Fort Recovery to Fort Adams and followed it for a few miles before again turning onto the road cut in 1790. This track was used all the way to Girty's Town at the Saint Marys River, where the troops camped on a high bank near an "Excellent spring of water" after marching about eighteen miles. This day, Wayne was informed that a large convoy of packhorses and cattle under Captain Sullivan had started toward Fort Wayne, but the captain had changed his route after learning the legion had started its return march. Wayne kept his men in camp on October 31 and ordered them to fortify while they waited for Sullivan's command. Upon its arrival, a portion of the convoy was sent on to Fort Wayne, with rations for the use of that post and Fort Defiance, while the remainder of the packhorses and cattle was consolidated with the legion's baggage train. As the troops waited at this camp, Captain Kibbey, who had been ordered to scout the Saint Marys with a small detachment in a canoe, came in and reported to General Wayne that the stream was impracticable for small craft bearing heavy cargoes. On November 1, the men marched before sunrise and passed through a number of small Indian villages, halting after a trek of twenty-one miles.[18]

The next day was Sunday, November 2, and being only sixteen miles from Fort Greeneville, John Cooke recorded that they marched "early and rapidly." Lieutenant Harrison rode ahead to inform Major Buell "that the army was nigh." Buell quickly assembled his entire garrison on the parade ground and had artillerymen move two 6-pounders outside the gates. When General Wayne and his staff got to within a half mile of the fort at about 3:00 P.M., the gunners "commenced firing with both cannon and continued until he got within the fort." Out in the column, one soldier recalled how much he was delighted when "once more with pleasure we view the American Flag displayed in Greenville Citadel." He remembered their reception: "On our Appearance at No. 4 Pickett, we were saluted with 15 Guns from the Citadel, and 15 Platoon-Guns were discharged on our entering the Fortifications, accompanied with three Cheers from the Garrison Troops." The legion responded with its own fifteen-gun salute and three cheers for their mates who had held Fort Greeneville. Officers then marched the companies to their respective parade grounds, where the men were dismissed and sent back to their huts, which some found "very much out of repair." In honor of the legion's return, everyone was issued a gill of whiskey. Buell invited Generals Wayne and Wilkinson, their aides, all of the field officers, the adjutant general, the surgeon general, and the "full surgeons" to the best meal circumstances would allow. Afterward, there were several hours of conversation and a ball that lasted until midnight. Major Buell caught the spirit of the day when he wrote that "joy sparkled in the countenance of every one." An enlisted man was swept up by the enthusiasm and recorded in his journal a bold prophesy that would ring true in coming generations: "AMERICA! what glorious Days mayest thou soon hope for, when thy Armies shall excel the Veterans of Alexander—thy Fleets command the Ocean, and give Laws to the World."[19]

Wayne's Peace

ALMOST AS SOON AS THE LEGION REACHED Fort Greeneville, General Wayne began to receive requests for furloughs from officers who had been long separated from family, friends, and business interests. He granted as many as possible, then turned his attention to discharging the scouts and spies, who were now an expensive luxury since the troops were in winter quarters. First to go was Ephraim Kibbey's company of scouts, which was sent home to Columbia and mustered out effective November 9, 1794. Wayne praised Kibbey for his "Officerlike Conduct," then asked that officer to pass along his "highest approbation of their cheerful obedience of Orders upon all Occasions." George Shrim's company of spies remained until the end of November, when all were released from service except for Amos Derbin, who had enlisted in the Fourth Sub-Legion. The spies of William Wells's company were mustered out in two stages. Those who had joined during August left on November 10, while the original core (Wells, Robert McClellan, Paschall Hickman, Christopher and Nicholas Miller, Dodson Tharp, William Ramsey, and Tabor Washburn) were kept on until December 6. As a result of the wound received in his attack on the Indian camp in August, Wells lost the use of his arm, received a pension, and was appointed Indian agent at Fort Wayne for several years. He was killed by Indians during the evacuation of Fort Dearborn at Chicago on July 15, 1812. Warriors cut off his head and removed his heart, cooking the latter and dividing it into small portions so that each man could acquire his courage.[1]

When the scouts returned home, they were hailed as conquering heroes. News of Wayne's victory at Fallen Timbers had spread "almost with the rapidity of lightning," and Ezra Ferris recalled that "the people were almost frantic with joy." He also noted, "On their return, every portion of the army, and every individual who had belonged to it, was cheered in the most enthusiastic manner by the citizens, and to have belonged to Wayne's army was enough to elevate any individual (in the estimation of the people) almost to the pinnacle of fame." Writing almost sixty years after the battle, Ferris confessed that he felt as though he should still "throw my hat in the air and raise a hurrah in honor of Wayne and his victorious army."[2]

On December 17, 1794, a small party of French Canadians and Indians, led by Antoine Lasselle, came to Fort Wayne and began a dialogue aimed at commencing the peace process. Within two weeks, delegations from the Potawatomi, Chippewa, Wyandotte, and Ottawa Nations had arrived and promised to "bury the hatchet, and live on terms of amity and friendship with the United States." One officer in the garrison observed, "The clouds which have so long obscured the rising prospects of this western hemisphere, began to be dispelled by a dawn of reason, which has beamed upon the bewildered minds of the deluded savages, and British influence, and British gold, are losing their efficacy." By mid-January 1795, most of the Miami had arrived at Fort Wayne, although the Delawares and Shawnees, "immediately under the influence of McKee, and so adjacent to the British posts, that their intentions have been frustrated," hung back. Embassies from the Indian nations confessed that the Great Spirit had finally opened their eyes and directed them to make peace with the United States, but one skeptical officer believed, "it was the glare of our bayonets on the 20th August, last, that has thus illuminated their minds." General Wayne agreed with that officer, admitting, "the bayonet is the most proper instrument, for removing the Film from the Eyes—& for opening the Ears of the Savages, that has ever been discover'd." As winter dragged on, all of the nations of the former Indian confederacy sought peace, save the reluctant Delawares and Shawnees, actuated by the fact that they were "in a state of starvation, having no bread for more than four months." Even proud warriors confessed to being "reduced to the greatest want and distress."[3]

On February 7, 1795, General Wayne was pleased to finally receive a delegation of Delawares and Shawnees led by the war chief Blue Jacket. That distinguished leader admitted that they had made a mistake "in placing any confidence in the British, having been deceived by them with respect to the forces which general Wayne could bring against the Indians." The great chiefs of the Shawnee and Delaware Nations now spoke in favor of peace, signed a preliminary treaty that established a truce on the frontier, and as the other nations before them had done, agreed to meet at Fort Greeneville on June 15 to conclude a grand treaty between the Americans and all Indians north of the Ohio River. Following this meeting with Blue Jacket, Wayne could assure Secretary Knox, "The whole of the late Hostile tribes have now come forward with overtures of peace, 'their eyes & ears are no longer closed, & the darkness with which they were so long surrounded has disappeared.'" Impressed by the force of the legion and the ability of its commander, the Miami Nation, "one of the most obstinate of the belligerent tribes," had expressed a wish to return to Fort Wayne and rebuild the village destroyed in 1790, where they could raise their corn crop. Other nations came forward to Forts Wayne, Defiance, and Greeneville when spring returned, determined to live and hunt near those garrisons "in the utmost security."[4]

No better illustration of the change in Indian attitude toward the British can be offered than a letter written by an officer at Fort Greeneville on May 16, 1795:

A few days since I was on command at Fort Defiance; and during my stay I had the pleasure of seeing the whole Delaware tribe come up the river, with their squaws and children, in a very submissive manner, to settle upon their old farms. There was a trader with them, a Mr. Wilson, who had with him a large store of goods to open at Fort Defiance. The commanding officer at the British fort, Miami, ordered that Wilson and his goods should not pass. Bocongahelas, the war chief of the Delawares, insisted that he should—a contest ensued—at length the British commander sent out a subaltern with some soldiers in a canoe, to prevent Wilson's passing. The canoe ran along side the foremast of the perogues of merchandize, and the officer grappled it with his hand. Bocongahelas finding the matter to be serious, entered a canoe with a few warriors, dashed in between the perogue and British canoe, ran against the officer's arm and almost broke it—telling him if the British wanted fighting he would give them enough of it—but they are cowards, continued he, or else they would not have let Gen. Wayne's army come here and piss in their spring, without fighting. Wilson and his goods passed.

Clearly, the duplicity by British authorities of promising aid and support to the Indians, then closing the gates and huddling inside Fort Miamis during the crisis of battle, had led to deep-seated bitterness between the former allies.[5]

Although all organized resistance to the Americans had collapsed, the war chiefs admitted that it was impossible to contact all of their hunting parties and tell them of the cessation of hostilities. Roving warriors had continued to attack individuals or small detachments all through the autumn, winter, and spring. Lieutenant Drake lost two soldiers from his garrison at Fort Recovery when they were ambushed less than a mile from the post. Lieutenant Underhill reported in late November 1794 that two express riders had been attacked, one being killed and the other shot through the chest. Two men long overdue from a hunt near the mouth of the Scioto River prompted a search that disclosed one of them "cut to pieces in an inhuman manner" and the other carried into captivity. On February 17, 1795, while some of the Indian peace delegates were still at Fort Greeneville, one band of warriors attacked a small convoy with stores headed to that place, killing three and wounding four others, then that same evening stealing about twenty horses from Fort Hamilton. In early May, the mail boat was fired on by Indians concealed on shore between Limestone and Gallipolis, one man being killed and two badly wounded. These isolated incidents kept nerves on edge, but when Captain Ingersoll returned to Boston, he assured people that "travelling was safe" on the frontier, except when encountering those few banditti "who had not heard of the armistice."[6]

General Wayne had expected to begin treaty negotiations at Fort Greeneville on June 15, but the tardy arrival of some nations postponed the opening ceremonies for a month. After several weeks of sitting in council, Wayne signed what would thereafter be referred to as the Treaty of Greeneville with the nations of the Wyandotte, Delaware, Shawnee, Ottawa, Chippewa, Potawatomi, Miami, Eel River Miami, Wea, Kickapoo, Piankashaw, and Kaskaskia. The first article declared, "Henceforth all hostilities shall cease; peace is hereby established, & shall be perpetual, and a friendly intercourse shall take place, between the said United States and Indian tribes." Other articles of the treaty addressed a prisoner exchange; the ceding of title to approximately two-thirds of the present state of Ohio, plus sixteen parcels of land surrounding U.S. military posts and strategic points still on Indian land; and a one-time grant of $20,000 of goods, followed by a distribution of $9,500 annually. The remainder of the ten articles addressed hunting rights, trade, the relinquishment of land, and establishing a system to mediate complaints. Wayne's Greeneville accords were signed by American officers, Indian chiefs, interpreters, and witnesses on August 3 and sent to Philadelphia, where it was ratified by the U.S. Senate and signed by President Washington on December 22, 1795.[7]

Of all the provisions of this treaty, the exchange of prisoners produced the most emotional results. An officer at Fort Greeneville described the scenes that came under his observation when the Indians brought in some of their captives:

> I have been a witness to parents receiving their children, who have been absent 15 or 16 years, and had grown to an adult state, but could not speak one word of English—likewise some of the Indians who had been with our people, and totally lost their mother tongue. Husbands meeting their wives, and wives their husbands, on both sides. The other day a beautiful girl came in, who was married to an Indian; her father was here in quest of her—she had been gone about 12 years, and was seven years old when she was taken—her father despairs of having her restored to him again, she appears quite afraid of him.
>
> One respectable old man from Kentucky had two sons, whom he met here, the oldest could speak a little English, and remembered the time of his capture. The father took them both home; they stayed with him but a few days, then stole two of his best horses and left him.

This officer concluded his letter with the observation, "I believe white savages are harder to be civilized than Indians."[8]

Scores of civilians, looking for long-lost sons, daughters, mothers, or fathers, made the arduous journey to Fort Greeneville. Many others sent descriptions of loved ones, and Wayne found himself deluged by list upon list of settlers, as well as a few soldiers, who had been carried off from the frontiers of Pennsylvania, Virginia, Kentucky, and the Northwest Territory. Stephen Ashby's family had been ambushed by a band of Potawatomis in 1789 while descending the Ohio River. The Indians had captured their boat and then killed his oldest son when he refused to surrender, after which one of the attackers "opened him, took out his heart, broiled it on the coals of the fire, and ate it in the presence of his afflicted parents." Upon being warned that his captors intended to burn him alive, Ashby and one son escaped, leaving his wife, four sons, and two daughters to their fate. He spent the next six years seeking information about his family and, "being a man of remarkable firmness, perseverance and bravery," sold his farm to fund his search. Ashby served on expeditions under John Hamtramck and Charles Scott and was wounded while a soldier under Arthur St. Clair in 1791. He became a constant visitor to legion headquarters at Fort Greeneville, where his devoted quest won the admiration of

General Wayne and his officers. Ashby was there during the treaty negotiations and, when the Indian prisoners were released, recognized the man who had desecrated his oldest boy's body but could not avenge his death because of the circumstances. That fall, Ashby journeyed to Fort Wayne, where he welcomed the return of his wife and children from captivity at the Illinois River and the village of Elkhart along the Saint Joseph.[9]

John Brickell had been freed shortly before the treaty talks. About the beginning of June 1795, the Delaware chief Whingwy Pooshies told his adopted son that they must go to Fort Defiance. There the Indian father, his white son, and the fort's officers sat in council. Whingwy Pooshies told Brickell to stand up, then addressed him: "My son, there are men the same color with yourself. There may be some of your kin there, or your kin may be a great way off from you. You have lived a long time with us. I call on you to say if I have not been a father to you? if I have not used you as a father would use a son?" Brickell admitted that he had always been treated as if his own son. Whingwy Pooshies continued: "I am glad you say so. You have lived long with me; you have hunted for me; but our treaty says you must be free. If you choose to go with the people of your own color, I have no right to say a word, but if you chose to stay with me your people have no right to speak. Now reflect on it and take your choice, and tell us as soon as you make up your mind." Brickell thought hard for a few moments, then said softly, "I will go with my kin." The old warrior responded: "I have raised you—I have learned you to hunt. You are a good hunter—you have been better to me than my own sons. I am now getting old and cannot hunt. I thought you would be a support to my age. I leaned on you as on a staff. Now it is broken—you are going to leave me and I have no right to say a word, but I am ruined." After concluding his remarks, Whingwy Pooshies sat in his seat with the tears streaming down his face, John Brickell matching him teardrop for teardrop. Father and son then parted, never to see or hear from one another again.[10]

Maj. Gen. Anthony Wayne did not live long enough to enjoy the full fruits of his victory over the Indian confederacy. A resolution by Congress thanking the men of the legion and Scott's Kentucky Volunteers failed to recognize Wayne personally, for leaders of the Antifederalist Party thought such credit would be a dangerous precedent since the general had simply been doing the job he had been paid to do. Despite the official stance of Congress, Wayne was celebrated as a hero when he returned to Philadelphia in February 1796, although that summer he was back on the frontier to supervise the surrender of British posts south of the Great Lakes to the American army. The general was returning to Philadelphia when he suffered an attack of gout on November 17 at Presque Isle (now Erie), Pennsylvania. Captain DeButts said that the disease "by turns affected his feet, knees and hands, with considerable inflammation and a great deal of pain" that lasted until November 30. After a few days of relief, he was "violently attacked with the gout in his stomach & Bowels," which prompted one attendant to remark that "his sufferings for several days past have indeed been extreme." DeButts reported on the morning of December 3, "it appeared that the gout had taken possession of his stomach, where it remained with unconquerable obstinacy and extreme torture" until Wayne's death on December 15, 1796, between the hours of two and three o'clock in the morning. His remains were interred the following day with military honors. By then, Wayne's legion had already disappeared. On November 1, the Legion of the United States had been disbanded and its various sub-legions renamed the First, Second, Third, and Fourth Regiments of Infantry.[11]

In 1809, Isaac Wayne journeyed to Erie, Pennsylvania, had his father's remains disinterred, and brought the bones back to St. David's Church in Radnor Township, Delaware County, for reburial. Old soldiers have always boasted of having been with great commanders on important battlefields—with Napoleon at Austerlitz, with Wellington at Waterloo, with Grant in the Wilderness, with Patton at the Bulge—but these boasts had nothing at all to do with being physically present on those days. It meant being a part of something bigger than themselves, something that was so important that it would transcend time itself, a pride in sharing a victory with one of the great commanders of history. Anthony Wayne's troops felt that way about him and, as old men, would boast of being with Wayne at Stony Point, with Wayne at Monmouth Court House, or with Wayne at Fallen Timbers. Their respect for him never died. On the day of the general's funeral, Samuel Smiley, a sergeant of the Fifth Regiment of the Pennsylvania Line who personified every soldier who had ever served under Wayne, refused all offers of a carriage ride and, though seventy years of age, proudly walked the entire distance from Waynesborough to the cemetery at St. David's Church "to show the affection with which he cherished the memory of his beloved commander." Even as an old man, Smiley still considered himself one of Anthony Wayne's soldiers.[12]

During the last two years of Wayne's life, he was witness to an immense tide of migration from the Atlantic states to Kentucky and the Northwest Territory. By the fall of 1794, one Pennsylvania resident could write, "There is no bounds to Interior Settlements, population is so rapid," advising his correspondent, "the road through Bedford to Pittsburgh which in your time was a wilderness is now as thickly settled as between Lancaster and Philadelphia." At Pittsburgh, the gateway to the Ohio valley, land prices had exploded, and the local editor observed that "the banks of the Monongahela, from M'Kee's Port to Red Stone, are lined with people intending for the settlements on the Ohio, and Kentucky." Residents out west wrote to their friends back east and urged them to come on, specifying that tradesmen, especially carpenters, weavers, tanners, shoemakers, wheelwrights, and blacksmiths, could find "work plenty, and good wages." Emigrants were advised to purchase good boats, travel in small groups, bring money, and employ "stocks of care and patience for the journey." In late 1795, one gentleman who floated down the Ohio River, on which once even military convoys could not travel in safety, saw at least four hundred boats on his twelve-day trip. He estimated that these craft carried at least six thousand passengers, not counting the thousands of other families going downriver ahead of and behind him. Following the Treaty of Greeneville, the Ohio became America's major east-west artery, funneling settlers into the continent's heartland, where they could claim and clear land in safety. In the winter of 1795–96, the white population of the Northwest Territory was estimated to be about fifteen thousand persons. Less than five years later, the 1800 census counted over forty-five thousand residents, with the population of Kentucky rising in proportion. Cincinnati quickly earned its nickname as "Queen City of the West," the number of professional men and mechanics there rising almost threefold between 1795 and 1810. This explosive growth in population north of the Ohio River resulted in the State of Ohio being admitted to the Union in 1803.[13]

There are monuments to Anthony Wayne in numerous places in the United States, including fine equestrian statues of him a few miles from Waynesborough—which is still preserved as a historic site—at Valley Forge and in downtown Fort Wayne, Indiana. A marker on the Fallen Timbers battlefield commemorates his victory on August 20, 1794. Eleven counties in states east of the Mississippi River bear his name. Hundreds, if not thousands, of businesses, parks, and schools have been named in his honor. Although he has been dead now for over two hundred years, Anthony Wayne has had a number of biographers, and writers continue to discuss various aspects of his career, all with varying degrees of accuracy. If American historians were called upon to decide Wayne's legacy, there would surely be wide disagreement as to just which one of his many accomplishments was the most important. Perhaps his greatest legacy—a generation of peace and security on the frontier—was enjoyed by those who had never even heard his name.

As a man, Anthony Wayne was at times capricious, petty, spiteful, bull-headed, and unforgiving. In the tradition of most surviving Revolutionary War generals, he was also overweight and drank too much, both weaknesses contributing to occasional severe attacks of gout. This disease, combined with recurrent spells of malaria, often left him more irritable than normal. He was not an easy man to like. As a general, and contrary to his nickname "Mad Anthony," he was patient, thoughtful, prudent, and decisive in judgment. As with the greatest commanders in history, he not only mastered battlefield tactics but also recognized the importance of logistics in keeping his men fed, clothed, armed, and reinforced in a timely manner. Wayne remained focused on his goals, rewarding his supporters with promotion and recognition but banishing those who opposed him. He ruled with an iron discipline tempered by leniency. Considering the appalling condition in which he found the army in 1792 and all that he had accomplished by the time of his death in 1796, Anthony Wayne must rank with the most successful army commanders in American history.

Indian opponents acknowledged Wayne's battlefield prowess by calling him "Blacksnake" in recognition of his resemblance to the most cunning reptile of the region's swamplands. After Blacksnake's victory at Fallen Timbers, there was widespread misery and suffering among the Indian nations due to the dramatic shift in the balance of power in the Northwest Territory. Emboldened to apparent invincibility by success over the armies of Josiah Harmar and Arthur St. Clair, coupled with lavish promises from the British, Indian leaders had remained adamant that all Americans must abandon their settlements northwest of the Ohio River. Yet Indian hegemony was a chimera. Native Americans had adopted the technology of war—muskets, rifles, and gunpowder—but their tactics remained rooted in ancient lessons learned while hunting animals of the forest. Offensive goals could only be attained by ambush and surprise, while a good Indian defense consisted of avoiding the same. If unsuccessful in the first strike against a bushwhacked opponent, there was never a viable second option, as proven in the ill-advised attack on Fort Recovery. Furthermore, and probably most importantly, Indian social structure could not hope to support a sizeable multinational coalition for any length of time against a well-organized invader.

For Americans, the best defense was a good offense, pushing an army farther and farther into Indian lands, thereby forcing the elusive enemy to assemble and defend threatened families and homeland. After being forced to congregate, the Indian army, stripped of its ability to ambush a vigilant foe, became an easy target for the Americans. General Wayne realized that the key to success on any battlefield was twofold, mobility and firepower, and had trained his legion to employ both. Once he successfully deployed his forces along the banks of the Maumee River, his opponents had no real chance.

Unable to effectively counter this method of warfare, the Indian nations found themselves incapable of protecting their own homes. Their villages and crops left a smoking rubble, starving Indians turned first to the British for provisions, then to the Americans. Fortifications sprang up at strategic sites to solidify the American presence, although they were more governmental centers and Indian agencies than military posts. Following Wayne's successful campaign, white settlers swarmed into the pacified Ohio country. Unable to contain these intruders without British assistance, the Indians could do little more than watch helplessly as their ancestral forests were transformed into cornfields. Relations between Indians and Americans soon settled into a deplorable cycle of treaty signing, encroachment by whites on Indian land, and calls for removal of the natives. So many settlers continued to pour into the Northwest Territory, the first steps of what would later be termed America's "Manifest Destiny," that subsequent Indian uprisings under Tecumseh in 1811 and Black Hawk in 1832 would be foredoomed to failure. Before whites arrived, Indian nations had shared the bounty of boundless forests and waterways. Following the Treaty of Greeneville, they grudgingly admitted that the land northwest of the Ohio River now belonged to the Americans—Maj. Gen. Anthony Wayne and his Legion of the United States had taken it from them.

NOTES

ABBREVIATIONS

Alder MSS	Jonathan Alder, "Story of the Indian Captivity of Jonathan Alder," typescript, Allen County Public Library, Fort Wayne, Ind.
ASP: Indian Affairs	U.S. Congress, *American State Papers: Documents, Legislative and Executive, of the Congress of the United States,* vol. 1, *Indian Affairs* (Washington, 1934)
Draper MSS	Lyman C. Draper Papers, The State Historical Society of Wisconsin, Madison
Hart Journal	5U93–108, Lyman C. Draper Papers, The State Historical Society of Wisconsin, Madison
Kentucky Orderly Book	16U1–116, Lyman C. Draper Papers, The State Historical Society of Wisconsin, Madison
Kentucky Volunteers MSS	Papers Relating to the Kentucky Volunteers, The Presbyterian Historical Society, Allen County Public Library, Fort Wayne, Ind.
Knox MSS	Henry Knox Papers, The Morgan Library, New York City
M804	Revolutionary War Pension and Bounty-Land-Warrant Application Files, Publication M804, U.S. National Archives, Washington, D.C.
Sargent MSS	Winthrop Sargent Papers, The Massachusetts Historical Society, Boston
Randolph Journal	Richard C. Knopf, ed., *A Precise Journal of General Wayne's Last Campaign* (Worcester, Mass., 1955)
Simcoe Correspondence	E. A. Cruikshank, ed., *The Correspondence of Lieut. Governor John Graves Simcoe, with Allied Documents Relating to His Administration of the Government of Upper Canada,* vols. (Toronto, 1923–31)
Wayne MSS, HSP	Anthony Wayne Papers, The Historical Society of Pennsylvania, Philadelphia
Wayne MSS, WLCL	Anthony Wayne Papers, William L. Clements Library, University of Michigan, Ann Arbor
Wilkinson Journal	Dwight L. Smith, ed., *From Greene Ville to Fallen Timbers* (Indianapolis, 1952)

PROLOGUE

1. Smith, *St. Clair Papers,* 2:262–63; Denny, *Military Journal,* 163–65; St. Clair, *Narrative,* 214–18; Morning Report for Nov. 4, 1791, dated Nov. 17, 1791, Sargent MSS.

2. Cist, *Sketches,* 113; *St. Clair's Defeat,* 27–28; Reynolds, *Pioneer History of Illinois,* 180.

3. *St. Clair's Defeat,* 28–30.

4. *Columbian Centinel,* Dec. 28, 1791; *Maryland Gazette,* Jan. 5, 1792; *Connecticut Courant,* Dec. 19, 1791; Roosevelt, *Winning of the West,* 4: 350; *Carlisle (Pa.) Gazette and the Western Repository of Knowledge,* Feb. 29, 1792; Sargent, "Diary," 256, 259.

5. Sargent, "Diary," 260, 268; *Baltimore Daily Repository,* Dec. 28, 1791; *Carlisle (Pa.) Gazette and the Western Repository of Knowledge,* Feb. 29, 1792; Roosevelt, *Winning of the West,* 4:355; *Columbian Centinel,* Jan. 7, 1792.

6. Roosevelt, *Winning of the West,* 4:350–51; *Connecticut Courant,* Dec. 19, 1791; Van Cleve, "Memoirs," 26; Sargent, "Diary," 268–69.

7. Sargent, "Diary," 261; Roosevelt, *Winning of the West,* 4: 351; *St. Clair's Defeat,* 30.

8. *Baltimore Daily Repository,* Dec. 28, 1791; Roosevelt, *Winning of the West,* 4: 354; Sargent, "Diary," 266.

9. Denny, *Military Journal,* 167; *Carlisle (Pa.) Gazette and the Western Repository of Knowledge,* Feb. 29, 1792; *Columbian Centinel,* Jan. 7, 1792.

10. Sargent, "Diary," 261–62, 265–66.

11. Van Cleve, "Memoirs," 26–27; Sargent, "Diary," 262; *Columbian Centinel,* Jan. 7, 1792; *Carlisle (Pa.) Gazette and the Western Repository of Knowledge,* Feb. 29, 1792.

12. Howe, *Historical Collections of the Great West,* 1:108; Littell, "Memoir of Captain Eliakim Littell," 83–104; Littell, *Family Records or Genealogies of the First Settlers of Passaic Valley; Records of Officers and Men of New Jersey,* 7; Dillon, *History of Indiana,* 284; Drake, *Biography and History of the Indians,* 570; McDonough to brother, Nov. 10, 1791, Michael McDonough Papers, The William L. Clements Library, University of Michigan, Ann Arbor; *Impartial Intelligencer,* Feb. 12, 1792; *Washington Spy,* Mar. 21, 1792; Hutton, "William Wells," 183–84. The quotation is from Howe, *Historical Collections of Ohio,* 2:231.

CHAPTER 1

1. Smith, *St. Clair Papers,* 2, 265–66; Casualty List, Nov. 17, 1791, Sargent MSS; *Carlisle (Pa.) Gazette and the Western Repository of Knowledge,* Feb. 29, 1792.

2. *Connecticut Courant,* Dec. 19, 1791; Ordnance Lost, Nov. 17, 1791, Sargent MSS; Wells, "Indian History," 203.

3. *General Advertiser,* Mar. 13, 1792; Mansfield, *Life and Services of Daniel Drake,* 384.

4. *Pennsylvania Archives,* 4:674–78, 689–90.

5. Ibid., 721, 724–26.

6. *Calendar of Virginia State Papers and Other Manuscripts,* 5:483, 488, 489–90, 548, 569; *Dunlap's American Daily Advertiser,* June 22, 1792.

7. *Maryland Gazette,* Mar. 8, 1792; *Brunswick (N.J.) Gazette,* Apr. 10, 1792; Cist, *Cincinnati Miscellany,* 2:31.

8. *Maryland Gazette,* Apr. 5, 1792; Cist, *Cincinnati Miscellany,* 2:31; Dillon, *History of Indiana,* 284–85; *Brunswick (N.J.) Gazette,* Apr. 3, 1792; Sargent to St. Clair, Feb. 5, 1792, Sargent MSS.

9. *Brunswick (N.J.) Gazette,* Apr. 3, 1792; Atwood, "Major Shaylor," 410–12; Burton, "Wayne's Orderly Book," 348–49; *Connecticut Courant,* July 2, 1792; Heitman, *Historical Register,* 1:719.

10. Wilkinson to Sargent, Mar. 19, 1792, Sargent MSS; Wilkinson to Knox, July 6, 1792, Wayne MSS, HSP.

11. Cist, *Sketches,* 133–34; Carter, *Territorial Papers,* 3:365; Wilkinson to Knox, Feb. 14, 1792, Knox MSS.

12. Garrison Order, May 11, 1792; Garrison Order, May 14, 1792; and Wilkinson to Sargent, June 2, 1792, Sargent MSS.

13. Wilkinson to Sargent, June 2, 1792, Sargent MSS; Carter, *Territorial Papers,* 3:376–78.

14. *ASP: Indian Affairs,* 227, 229–30; Burnet, *Notes,* 129–30; Sanders, "Colonel John Hardin and His Letters to His Wife," 10–11.

15. *Dunlap's American Daily Advertiser,* Aug. 21, 1792; Spencer, *Indian Captivity,* 6–7, 34–40, 151, 153; Knox to Sargent, Aug. 8, 1792, Knox MSS; Roosevelt, *Winning of the West,* 1:81.

16. Strong to Wilkinson, June 25, 1792, Wayne MSS, HSP; Buell, *Memoirs of Rufus Putnam,* 273–74.

17. *Kentucky Gazette,* July 21, 1792; Buell, *Memoirs of Rufus Putnam,* 295–96; "John Heckewelder's Journey," 45–46; Schaffer Deposition, July 23, 1792, Wayne MSS, HSP; *Record of the Court at Upland,* 463.

18. Howe to Wilkinson, Aug. 23, 1792, Wayne MSS, HSP.

19. Lowry to Wayne, Nov. 6, 1792, Wayne MSS, HSP.

20. "John Heckewelder's Journey," 46.

21. Edmunds, "Wea Participation," 247–50; Buell, *Memoirs of Rufus Putnam,* 327; Hutton, "William Wells," 189–90; Volney, *View of the Soil and Climate of the United States,* 374.

22. "John Heckewelder's Journey," 45, 49; Buell, *Memoirs of Rufus Putnam,* 296, 297; Edmunds, "Wea Participation," 250.

23. *Dunlap's American Daily Advertiser,* Nov. 8, 1792; "John Heckewelder's Journey," 167; *The Providence Gazette and Country Herald,* Mar. 30, 1793, p. 3; Carter, *Territorial Papers,* 3:385–86.

24. Carter, *Territorial Papers,* 3:386–87; "John Heckewelder's Journey," 178.

25. "John Heckewelder's Journey," 179; Wilkinson to Knox, Nov. 1, 1792, Knox MSS.

26. Knopf, *Anthony Wayne,* 147; *Pittsburgh Gazette,* Feb. 2, 1793.

CHAPTER 2

1. Fitzpatrick, *Writings of George Washington*, 31:509–13, 515; Cullen, *Papers of Thomas Jefferson*, 23:242.

2. Cullen, *Papers of Thomas Jefferson*, 23:242.

3. Ibid., 401; Wayne to Knox, Apr. 1, 1792, Knox MSS.

4. Cullen, *Papers of Thomas Jefferson*, 23:400, 401; Knox to Wayne, Apr. 12, 1792; and Wayne to Knox, Apr. 13, 1792, Wayne MSS, HSP; Moore, *Life and Services of General Anthony Wayne*, 168.

5. Nelson, Anthony Wayne, 5–7; Wayne, "Biographical Memoir," 193–94; Brice, *Fort Wayne*, viii–ix; Bicknell, "Major General Anthony Wayne," 278–79; Eberlein and Lippincott, *Colonial Homes*, 170–72.

6. Wayne, "Biographical Memoir," 193–94; Brice, *Fort Wayne*, ix.

7. Nelson, *Anthony Wayne*, 9–16; Bicknell, "Major General Anthony Wayne," 279–80.

8. Heitman, *Historical Register*, 1:1010; Billias, *George Washington's Generals*, 260, 287; Nelson, *Anthony Wayne*, 15; Tucker, *Mad Anthony Wayne*, 17; Wayne to Stockton, Jan. 3, 1777; and Wayne to Washington, Sept. 2, 1777, Wayne MSS, HSP; Phillips, *Roots of Strategy*, 202; Stille, *Wayne and the Pennsylvania Line*, 357.

9. Nelson, *Anthony Wayne*, 22–26, 31–41; Wayne to Moore, Jan. 2, 1777, Wayne MSS, HSP; "Original Letters from Gen. Wayne," 58.

10. Heitman, *Historical Register*, 1:1010; Nelson, *Anthony Wayne*, 51–64; Eberlein and Lippincott, *Colonial Homes*, 171; Wayne to Wayne, Oct. 6, 1777; and Wayne to Peters, May 13, 1778, Wayne MSS, HSP; Wayne to Wharton, Apr. 12, 1778, Wayne MSS, WLCL.

11. Phillips, *Roots of Strategy*, 201–2, 245, 246; "Orderly Book of the Second Pennsylvania Continental Line," 39, 54, 246.

12. Nelson, *Anthony Wayne*, 78–82; Tucker, *Mad Anthony Wayne*, 135–42.

13. Nelson, *Anthony Wayne*, 97–101; Brice, *Fort Wayne*, viii, xii; Tucker, *Mad Anthony Wayne*, 155–61.

14. Stille, *Wayne and the Pennsylvania Line*, 361, 363–65; *Army and Navy Chronicle*, Apr. 27, 1837.

15. "Itinerary of the Pennsylvania Line," 273–74; Nelson, *Anthony Wayne*, 132–44, 203–4.

16. Jones, *History of Georgia*, 505–11.

17. Ibid., 512–14.

18. Ibid., 518–21; Nelson, *Anthony Wayne*, 170, 177–85; Wayne to Morris, Sept. 2, 1782, Wayne MSS, HSP; Heitman, *Historical Register*, 1:1010.

19. Nelson, *Anthony Wayne*, 188; "Letters of Gen. Wayne to Gen. Irvine," 340–41. This last source mistakenly identifies the letter's date as May 18, 1781.

20. Nelson, "Anthony Wayne," 476–77; *Biographical Congressional Dictionary*, 870; Knopf, "Anthony Wayne," 36.

21. *Maryland Gazette*, May 3, 24, 1792; Stone, *Life of Joseph Brant*, 2:316; Brooks to Knox, Apr. 24, 1792; Knox to Williams, May 3, 1792; Williams to Knox, May 6, 1792; and Hull to Knox, May 27, 1792, Knox MSS.

22. Fitzpatrick, *Writings of George Washington*, 31:510, 32:105; Hall, *Romance of Western History*, 330; Knox to Wilkinson, July 17, 1792; and Knox to Wayne, July 20, 1792, Knox MSS.

23. Waddell, *Annals of Augusta County*, 347; Burnet, *Notes*, 36–37.

24 War Department, Unfinished Letter, Mar. 2, 1792, Knox MSS; Heitman, *Historical Register*, 1:1068.

25. Burnham to Knox, Dec. 24, 1791, Knox MSS; *Middlesex (Conn.) Gazette*, Jan. 21, 1792; *American Mercury*, Feb. 13, 1792; Wilkinson to Wadsworth, Sept. 18, 1792, James Wilkinson Papers, Library of Congress, Washington, D.C.

26. Knox to Wilkinson, July 17, 1792, Wayne MSS, HSP; War Department, Unfinished Letter, Mar. 2, 1792, Knox MSS; Heitman, *Historical Register*, 1:173, 203, 900, 932; *Maryland Gazette*, May 3, 1792.

27. *Maryland Gazette*, Mar. 29, May 3, 1792.

28. Ibid., Mar. 29, May 24, 1792; Jackson to Knox, Feb. 12, 1792, Knox MSS.

29. *Maryland Gazette*, Mar. 29, May 24, 1792.

CHAPTER 3

1. Undated Recruiting Instructions, Wayne MSS, HSP; Recruiting Instructions, Box 45, No. 12, Torrence Papers, Cincinnati Museum Center, Cincinnati, Ohio.

2. Knox to Wayne, June 22, 1792, Wayne MSS, HSP.

3. Shaw, *Narrative*, 156–57.

4. Whittlesey, *Ancestry and the Descendants of John Pratt*, 46; *Middlesex (Conn.) Gazette*, Apr. 7, 1792; *Connecticut Courant*, Apr. 9, 1792; *American Mercury*, Apr. 16, 1792; Harold W. Ryan, "Daniel Bissell—His Story" (undated article in author's possession); Heitman, *Historical Register*, 1:221, 804.

5. *Ancestry of John Hutchinson Buell*, 4–8; *Connecticut Courant*, Apr. 16, Oct. 29, 1792; *The Phenix*, Apr. 21, 1792; *American Mercury*, June 18, 1792.

6. Heitman, *Historical Register*, 1:472, 648, 974; Conrad, "Edward D. Turner," 1; *Columbian Centinel*, Feb. 15, 1792; *Impartial Intelligencer*, Mar. 14, 1792.

7. *Western Star*, May 1, Oct. 2, 1792.

8. *Columbian Centinel*, Apr. 18, 25, 1792; *Western Star*, Apr. 24, 1792.

9. *Brunswick (N.J.) Gazette*, Apr. 3, May 8, July 17, 1792.

10. Backus, "Cornelius Sedam and His Friends," 29–34; *Brunswick (N.J.) Gazette*, July 17, Aug. 7, 1792.

11. Heitman, *Historical Register*, 1:1017; *New Jersey Journal*, June 27, 1792.

12. *New Jersey Journal*, June 27, 1792; *Baltimore Daily Repository*, July 31, 1792.

13. *Maryland Gazette*, Aug. 23, 1792.

14. Heitman, *Historical Register*, 1:806; Dorman, *The Prestons*, 52–54, 57–59; Johnston, *The Johnstons*, 193.

15. *Virginia Gazette and General Advertiser*, Oct. 17, 1792.

16. Copies of Winston to Knox and Knox to Winston, Nov. 25, 1793, Wayne MSS, HSP.

17. Heitman, *Historical Register*, 1:920; Aler, *History of Martinsburg and Berkeley County*, 127.

18. *Baltimore Daily Repository*, Aug. 4, 1792.

19. Stephenson to Wayne, Nov. 27, 1792, Wayne MSS, HSP.

20. Howe, *Major Bezaleel Howe*, 2–19.

21. Bonney, *Legacy*, 1:91; Van Rensselaer to Wayne, Dec. 18, 1793, Wayne MSS, WLCL.

22. Bonney, *Legacy*, 1:92–94; Heitman, Historical Register, 1:356; Davidson to Clark, Apr. 13, 1792; Clark Account, Aug. 10, 1792; Clark to Knox, Aug. 13, 1792; and Davidson to Wayne, Sept. 18, 1792; Wayne MSS, HSP; Knopf, *Anthony Wayne*, 105–6.

23. *Life of the Late Gen. William Eaton*, 51.

24. Heitman, *Historical Register*, 1:631; Williams, *History of Washington County*, 112, 175; *Washington Spy*, Jan. 4, Apr. 4, 11, 1792.

25. Williams, *History of Frederick County*, 1:90–91, 139; Heitman, *Historical Register*, 1:281; *Baltimore Daily Repository*, Mar. 7, 1792; Carbery to Wayne, Nov. 7, 1792, Wayne MSS, HSP.

26. *Washington Spy*, July 11, 1792.

27. *Baltimore Daily Repository*, July 20, 1792; *Maryland Journal and Baltimore Advertiser*, June 5, 1792.

28. Tousey, *Carlisle and Carlisle Barracks*, 163–64.

29. *Impartial Intelligencer*, May 16, 1792; Murray, "The Butlers," 9–13.

30. *Carlisle (Pa.) Gazette and the Western Repository of Knowledge*, July 4, 11, Aug. 8, 1792; Knox to Wayne, June 22, 1772, Wayne MSS, HSP.

31. Heitman, *Historical Register*, 1:904, 913; Lewis, *Third Biennial Report*, 59; Burton, "Wayne's Orderly Book," 355; Wayne to Springer, Aug. 2, 1792; Springer to Wayne, Oct. 11, 1792; and Springer to Wayne, Dec. 10, 1792, Wayne MSS, HSP; Knox to Springer, June 15, 1792, Wayne MSS, WLCL.

32. *Vermont Gazette*, May 4, 18, 1792; *Herald of Vermont*, June 25, 1792.

33. *Vermont Gazette*, May 25, 1792; *Life of the Late Gen. William Eaton*, 10–14, 429, 445, 446.

34. *Vermont Gazette*, June 1, 8, 1792.

35. *Brunswick (N.J.) Gazette*, Aug. 7, 1792.

36. *Vermont Gazette*, Aug. 10, 1792; *Greenfield (Vt.) Gazette*, Sept. 6, 1792.

37. *Vermont Gazette*, Aug. 31, Sept. 21, 1792.

38. Ibid., Sept. 21, Oct. 12, 1792; *Gazette of the United States*, Sept. 12, 1792; *Brunswick (N.J.) Gazette*, Sept. 11, 1792; *Baltimore Daily Repository*, Oct. 3, 1792.

39. *Vermont Gazette*, Nov. 30, 1792, Mar. 22, 1793; Knopf, *Anthony Wayne*, 122.

40. *Vermont Gazette*, Nov. 30, 1792.

41. *Impartial Intelligencer*, July 4, 1792; Clothing Receipt, Aug. 4, 1792, Wayne MSS, HSP; Underwood, *Journal*, 2.

42. Knox to Sargent, Apr. 4, 1792, Knox MSS; Knopf, *Anthony Wayne*, 21.

43. Knopf, *Anthony Wayne*, 26, 27, 32, 69–70; Fitzpatrick, *Writings of George Washington*, 32:113, 127.

CHAPTER 4

1. Moore, *Life and Services of General Anthony Wayne*, 170; Wayne to Delaney, June 8, 1792; and Wayne to Knox, June 15, 1792, Wayne MSS, WLCL.

2. *Carlisle (Pa.) Gazette and the Western Repository of Knowledge*, May 23, 1792.

3. Ibid.; Wayne to Page, June 29, 1792, Wayne MSS, HSP; *Maryland Herald and Eastern Shore Intelligencer*, July 24, Aug. 21, 1792.

4. Craig, *Life and Service*s, 1, 8–10, 14–19, 27, 50–56; "Major Isaac Craig, Extracts from His Letter Books," pt. 2, 123.

5. Evans and Stivers, *History of Adams County*, 2:522–24; "Re-Interment of Major John Belli," 178–81.

6. Darlington, *Fort Pitt*, 200–203.

7. "Major Isaac Craig, Extracts from His Letter Books," pt. 2, 28, 35, 121–29.

8. Wayne to Wilkinson, June 16, 1792, Wayne MSS, HSP.

9. Burton, "Wayne's Orderly Book," 350; Knopf, *Anthony Wayne*, 58.

10. Burton, "Wayne's Orderly Book," 352, 355–56; *Maryland Gazette*, Aug. 30, 1792.

11. Burton, "Wayne's Orderly Book," 351–52.

12. Knopf, *Anthony Wayne*, 28–29; Fitzpatrick, *Writings of George Washington*, 32:134–35.

13. Knopf, *Anthony Wayne*, 49–50.

14. Ibid., 64, 67; Wayne to Taylor, Aug. 8, 1792, Wayne MSS, HSP; Burton, "Wayne's Orderly Book," 358.

15. Knopf, *Anthony Wayne*, 64–65; Burton, "Wayne's Orderly Book," 358–60.

16. Knopf, *Anthony Wayne*, 96; Fitzpatrick, *Writings of George Washington*, 32:135; Burton, "Wayne's Orderly Book," 371, 381.

17. Knopf, *Anthony Wayne*, 89; Lambing, *Historical Researches in Western Pennsylvania*, 32–35.

18. Knopf, *Anthony Wayne*, 65, 67, 89; Burton, "Wayne's Orderly Book," 365.

19. Knopf, *Anthony Wayne*, 67–68; *Baltimore Daily Repository*, Sept. 7, 1792; Burton, "Wayne's Orderly Book," 364.

20. Burton, "Wayne's Orderly Book," 362, 363, 367, 368; Knopf, *Anthony Wayne*, 99.

21. Knopf, *Anthony Wayne,* 93, 94, 105; Burton, "Wayne's Orderly Book," 378; *Baltimore Daily Repository*, Sept. 25, 1792.

22. Burton, "Wayne's Orderly Book," 372–76, 382–83.

23. Knopf, *Anthony Wayne*, 93, 104; Burton, "Wayne's Orderly Book," 385.

24. Knopf, *Anthony Wayne*, 107, 166; *Augusta Chronicle and Gazette of the State*, Oct. 6, 1792; Heitman, *Historical Register*, 1:173, 203–4.

25. Burton, "Wayne's Orderly Book," 389, 393, 396–97.

26. Knopf, *Anthony Wayne*, 88, 106, 110; Adams, *Dictionary of American History*, 2:418; Heitman, *Historical Register*, 1:270, 389, 579.

27. 1X12, Draper MSS; "Biographical Memoirs of Major Gen. William Henry Harrison," 71–72.

28. *Baltimore Daily Repository*, Sept. 25, 1792; Knopf, *Anthony Wayne*, 92–93.

29. Burton, "Wayne's Orderly Book," 388; Reward Poster, Sept. 26, 1792; Jones to Wayne, Oct. 1, 1792; Lewis to Wayne, Oct. 1, 1792; DeButts to Rudolph, Oct. 12, 1792; Rudolph to Lewis, Oct. 12, 1792; and Lewis to Wayne, Oct. 22, 1792, Wayne MSS, HSP.

CHAPTER 5

1. *ASP: Indian Affairs*, 318.

2. Fitzpatrick, *Writings of George Washingto*n, 32:126, 167–68.

3. Commager, *Documents of American History*, 119; Abbott, *History of the State of Ohio*, 372–73; Knopf, *Anthony Wayne*, 72.

4. Knopf, *Anthony Wayne*, 73–76, 78.

5. McCully to Wayne, June 29, 1792, Wayne MSS, HSP; *The Phenix*, Mar. 17, 1792; *Maryland Herald and Eastern Shore Intelligencer*, May 1, 1792.

6. *Webster's American Military Biographies*, 40; Drake, *Book of the Indians*, bk. 5, p. 60; Stone, *Life of Joseph Brant*, 2:313.

7. *Report of the Commission to Locate the Site of the Frontier Forts of Pennsylvania*, 2:594–96; Heitman, *Historical Register*, 1:571; Wayne to Jeffers, June 25, 1792, Wayne MSS, HSP; Knopf, *Anthony Wayne*, 68; *Historical Records of the Town of Cornwall*, 214–15.

8. Wayne to Steele, July 30, 1792; Cass to Wayne, Aug. 23, 1792; Wayne to Cass, Aug. 30, 1792; Wayne to Hughes, Sept. 20, 1792; and Eaton to Wayne, Nov. 13, 1792, Wayne MSS, HSP; Knopf, *Anthony Wayne*, 108, 118.

9. Burton, "Wayne's Orderly Book," 361, 363, 385, 390.

10. *Impartial Intelligencer*, June 13, 1792; *Baltimore Daily Repository*, Aug. 31, 1792; *Oracle of Dauphin and Harrisburg (Pa.) Advertiser*, Sept. 9, 1793.

11. *Baltimore Daily Intelligencer*, Aug. 4, 1794; *Washington Spy*, Aug. 15, 1792.

12. *Baltimore Daily Intelligencer*, July 7, 1794.

13. *Carlisle (Pa.) Gazette and the Western Repository of Knowledge*, Sept. 12, 1792; *Baltimore Daily Intelligencer*, July 7, 1794.

14. *Dunlap's American Daily Advertiser*, Apr. 30, 1792.

15. Knopf, *Anthony Wayne*, 121; *History of Beaver County*, 599–601.

16. Wayne to Eaton and Faulkner, Nov. 8, 1792, Wayne MSS, HSP; Burton, "Wayne's Orderly Book," 400; Knopf, *Anthony Wayne*, 129; Fitzpatrick, *Writings of George Washington*, 32:235.

17. Burton, "Wayne's Orderly Book," 404–5; Underwood, *Journal*, 2.

18. Eaton to Wayne, Nov. 13, 1792, Wayne MSS, HSP.

19. Knopf, *Anthony Wayne*, 182; Bratten to Wayne, Oct. 10, 1792; Powers to Wayne, Sept. 10, 1792, Wayne MSS, HSP; Burton, "Wayne's Orderly Book," 381.

20. "Major Isaac Craig, Extracts from His Letter Books," pt. 2, 129; Map of Legionville, in Strong to Cogswell, Feb. 26, 1793, M. F. Cogswell Papers, Beinecke Rare Book and Manuscript Library, Yale University, New Haven; Knopf, *Anthony Wayne*, 147–48.

21. Nevill to Wayne, Dec. 17, 1792, Wayne MSS, HSP; *History of Beaver County*, 603.

22. Addison et al. to Wayne, Dec. 6, 1792, Wayne MSS, HSP.

23. Burton, "Wayne's Orderly Book," 405; Heitman, *Historical Register*, 1:777; Bond to Wayne, Dec. 16, 1792, Wayne MSS, HSP.

24. Burton, "Wayne's Orderly Book," 379; Huston to Wayne, Dec. 26, 1792, Wayne MSS, HSP; Hill, *Johnston and the Indians*, 168.

25. Knopf, *Anthony Wayne*, 152.

26. McMahon to Wayne, Dec. 9, 1792; and McMahon to Wayne, Dec. 12, 1792, Wayne MSS, HSP.

27. Wayne to Delaney, Sept. 28, 1792; and Wayne to Hayman, Dec. 28, 1792, Wayne MSS, HSP; Wayne to Delaney, Dec. 25, 1792, Wayne MSS, WLCL.

28. Linn, *Annals of Buffalo Valley*, 219–22.

29. Wilkinson to Wayne, Nov. 18, 1792, Wayne MSS, HSP; *ASP: Indian Affairs*, 224–25.

30. *ASP: Indian Affairs*, 225–26.

31. Wilkinson to Knox, Nov. 3, 1792; Wilkinson to Wayne, Nov. 13, 1792; and Wilkinson to Wayne, Nov. 18, 1792, Wayne MSS, HSP; *Simcoe Correspondence*, 1:330.

CHAPTER 6

1. *Carlisle (Pa.) Gazette and the Western Repository of Knowledge*, Nov. 28, 1792.

2. Smith to Wilkinson, Oct. 28, 1792, Wayne MSS, WLCL.

3. Bradley to Wilkinson, Oct. 23, 1792; and Wilkinson to Bradley, Oct. 25, 1792, Wayne MSS, WLCL.

4. Wilkinson to Knox, Nov. 3, 1792; and Wilkinson to Knox, Nov. 6, 1792, Wayne MSS, HSP.

5. *Biographical Sketch of General John Adair*, 3–9.

6. Young, *Little Turtle*, 33–34, 125.

7. Ibid., 35, 157–58; Wells, "Indian History," 202–3.

8. Wells, "Indian History," 203; *ASP: Indian Affairs*, 335; *Biographical Sketch of General John Adair*, 11; Howe, *Historical Collections of Ohio*, 2:452–53; *Baltimore Daily Repository*, Feb. 9, 1793.

9. *ASP: Indian Affairs*, 335; *Biographical Sketch of General John Adair*, 11; "Extracts from the Orderly Book of the Garrison of Fort Washington," Wayne MSS, HSP.

10. *New Jersey Journal*, Dec. 26, 1792; *ASP: Indian Affairs*, 335; *Baltimore Daily Repository*, Feb. 9, 1793.

11. Howe, *Historical Collections of Ohio*, 2:453.

12. 1A249–50, Draper MSS.

13. Wilkinson to Wayne, Sept. 23, 1792, Wayne MSS, HSP; Chalkley, *Chronicles of the Scotch-Irish Settlement*, 1:247, 2:271; *1787 Census of Virginia*, 1:110; Peyton, *History of Augusta County*, 340–41; *Sketches and Recollections of Lynchburg*, 317–18.

14. Rudolph to Wayne, Jan. 14, 1793, Wayne MSS, HSP; Howe, *Historical Collections of Ohio*, 1:343; Simmons, "Orderly Book," 134.

15. Simmons, "Orderly Book," 135; Howe, *Historical Collections of Ohio*, 1:343.

16. *Kentucky Gazette*, June 23, 1792, Dec. 8, 1793; Belli to Knox, Aug. 10, 1792; Wilkinson to Belli, Nov. 9, 1792; and Rudolph to Wayne, Jan. 14, 1793, Wayne MSS, HSP.

17. Wilkinson to Knox, July 6, 1792; and Wilkinson to Wayne, Nov. 13, 1792, Wayne MSS, HSP; Wilkinson to Wayne, July 12, 1792, Wayne MSS, WLCL.

18. Wilkinson to Wayne, Nov. 13, 1792, Wayne MSS, HSP.

19. Hunter to Wayne, Sept. 1, 1792; and Hunter to Wayne, Sept. 12, 1792, Wayne MSS, HSP.

20. Wayne to Guion, Dec. 12, 1792; and Guion to Wayne, Jan. 1, 1793, Wayne MSS, HSP.

21. Wilkinson to Wayne, Nov. 13, 1792; and Wilkinson to Wayne, Dec. 29, 1792, Wayne MSS, HSP; Sargent to Knox, Nov. 10, 1792, Knox MSS.

22. *Kentucky Gazette*, Dec. 1, 22, 1792.

23. Haskell to Wayne, July 26, 1792, Wayne MSS, HSP; Hildreth, *Biographical and Historical Memoirs*, 345–46; Barker, *Recollections of the First Settlement of Ohio*, 75; *Dunlap's American Daily Advertiser*, Oct. 10, 1792.

24. Simmons, "Orderly Book," 127, 129; Fort Washington Orderly Book, Wayne MSS, HSP.

25. Simmons, "Orderly Book," 127, 131, 133; Fort Washington Orderly Book, Wayne MSS, HSP.

26. Knopf, *Anthony Wayne*, 214; *Gazette of the United States*, Mar. 27, 1793; Wilkinson to Wayne, Apr. 10, 1793, Wayne MSS, HSP.

27. *Western Christian Advocate*, Nov. 20, 1835, May 3, 1839; E1128, Draper MSS.

28. Collins, *History of Kentucky*, 553; *Western Christian Advocate*, Nov. 20, 1835.

29. Collins, *History of Kentucky*, 553; *History of Clermont County*, 178–79; E1127, Draper MSS.

30. *Western Christian Advocate*, Nov. 20, 1835.

31. E1126–28, Draper MSS.

CHAPTER 7

1. Collins Deposition, Feb. 16, 1793, Wayne MSS, HSP.

2. *Pittsburgh Gazette*, Apr. 27, 1793.

3. Ibid.; General Order, Mar. 4, 1793, Wayne MSS, HSP; *Vermont Gazette*, May 17, 1793.

4. *Pittsburgh Gazette*, Mar. 9, 1793.

5. Underwood, *Journal*, 3; "Letters from Dr. Joseph Strong to Captain John Pratt," 238.

6. *Life of the Late Gen. William Eaton*, 15–17.

7. *Maryland Journal and Baltimore Advertiser*, Apr. 18, 1793; Pope and Towles to Wayne, Mar. 29, 1793, Wayne MSS, HSP.

8. Wayne to Jenifer, Mar. 28, 1793; Pope and Towles to Wayne, Mar. 29, 1793; Jenifer to Wayne, Mar. 29, 1793; and Jenifer to Wayne, Mar. 30, 1793, Wayne MSS, HSP.

9. Gassaway to Wayne, Apr. 12, 1793; and Gassaway to Wayne, Apr. 19, 1793, Wayne MSS, HSP; Knopf, *Anthony Wayne*, 224, 232–33.

10. Addison to Wayne, Mar. 6, 1793, Wayne MSS, HSP.

11. Knopf, *Anthony Wayne*, 169–71; Wayne to Knox, Mar. 22, 1793, Knox MSS.

12. Knopf, *Anthony Wayne*, 177, 210–11; Wayne to Knox, Mar. 22, 1793, Knox MSS.

13. Underwood, *Journal*, 1; Wood to Wayne, undated; Dabney to Wayne, Feb. 15, 1793; and Burbeck et al, Mar. 18, 1793, Wayne MSS, HSP; Heitman, *Historical Register*, 1:978.

14. 13CC19–20, Draper MSS; Jacob Slough Pension File, M804; Heitman, *Historical Register*, 1:892, 904, 932; Williams to Knox, Feb. 4, 1794, Otho Holland Williams Papers, The Maryland Historical Society Library, Baltimore; *American Military Biographies*, 323.

15. Wayne to Knox, Mar. 22, 1793, Knox MSS; Knopf, *Anthony Wayne*, 210.

16. Knopf, *Anthony Wayne*, 208–9.

17. Tinsley to Wayne, Apr. 22, 1793; Wayne to Tinsley, Apr. 23, 1793; and Tinsley to Wayne, May 2, 1793, Wayne MSS, HSP.

18. Buell, *Memoirs of Rufus Putnam*, 370, 376, 381.

19. Knopf, *Anthony Wayne*, 176, 198; *Pittsburgh Gazette*, Apr. 27, 1793.

20. *Pittsburgh Gazette*, Jan. 26, 1793; Wayne to O'Hara, Feb. 18, 1793, Wayne MSS, HSP.

21. Burton, "Wayne's Orderly Book," 407–9.

22. *Pittsburgh Gazette*, Jan. 19, 1793; Andrews to Wayne, Mar. 11, 1793; and Wallace to Wayne, Mar. 11, 1793, Wayne MSS, HSP.

23. Carmichael to Wayne, Jan. 5, 1793; and Invoice of Hospital Stores, Jan. 16, 1793, Wayne MSS, HSP; 4CC173–74, Draper MSS.

24. Nelson, *Anthony Wayne*, 238–39; Knopf, *Anthony Wayne*, 232.

25. Knopf, *Anthony Wayne*, 184–85, 191–92.

26. Ibid., 222–23.

CHAPTER 8

1. Knopf, *Anthony Wayne*, 232; Wayne to Cummins, Apr. 23, 1793; and Wayne to Toomy, Apr. 25, 1793, Wayne MSS, HSP; Mead, *History and Genealogy*, 39–40; Burton, "Wayne's Orderly Book," 410–11; *Vermont Gazette*, May 17, 1793.

2. *Pittsburgh Gazette*, May 4, 1793.

3. 30J56, Draper MSS; "Major Isaac Craig, Extracts from His Letter Books," pt. 2, 133–34; *Pittsburgh Gazette*, May 4, 1793.

4. General Order, Apr. 28, 1793, Wayne MSS, HSP; Burton, "Wayne's Orderly Book," 411–12.

5. *Life of the Late Gen. William Eaton*, 18–19.

6. "Distance from Philadelphia to Fort Washington upon the Ohio," Sargent MSS; Elliot, *Sketches*, 132–35.

7. Howe, *Historical Collections of Ohio*, 2:608–10.

8. Ferris, *Early Settlement*, 326; *Celebration of the Forty-Fifth Anniversary of the First Settlement of Cincinnati*, 24; Bonney, *Legacy*, 1:132; Knopf, *Anthony Wayne*, 217–18; *Oxford English Dictionary*, 13 vols. (Oxford: Clarendon, 1961), s.v. "choice," 2c.

9. Ferris, *Early Settlement*, 326–28; Underwood, *Journal*, 4; Brackenridge, *Recollections of Persons and Places*, 19.

10. Cist, *Sketches*, 143–44; Harrison, *Discourse on the Aborigines*, 12.

11. Moore, *Life and Services of General Anthony Wayne*, 176–77.

12. Knopf, *Anthony Wayne*, 234; Burton, "Wayne's Orderly Book," 415, 431, 433–35.

13. Burton, "Wayne's Orderly Book," 429, 435, 443.

14. Wilkinson to Wayne, May 8, 1793, Wayne MSS, HSP; Knopf, *Anthony Wayne*, 242.

15. Wayne to Strong, May 29, 1793, Wayne MSS, HSP; *Western Star*, Sept. 10, 1793.

16. Clark to Wayne, May 15, 1793; Wayne to Hunter, May 25, 1793; and Pasteur to Wayne, June 23, 1793, Wayne MSS, HSP; Knopf, *Anthony Wayne*, 242.

17. DeButts to Doyle, May 30, 1793; Clark to Wayne, June 22, 1793; and Receipt for Indian Stores, July 11, 1793, Wayne MSS, HSP; Knopf, *Anthony Wayne*, 242, 246–47.

18. "Major Isaac Craig, Extracts from His Letter Books," pt. 2, 134–35; Knopf, *Anthony Wayne*, 242; Wilkinson to Wayne, May 15, 1793, Wayne MSS, HSP.

19. Wilkinson to Wayne, May 15, 1793, Wayne MSS, HSP; "Major Isaac Craig, Extracts from His Letter Books," pt. 2, 161–62; Underwood, *Journal*, 1; Gunderson, "William Henry Harrison," 12–13.

20. *Maryland Gazette*, Mar. 21, 1793; Woollen, *Biographical and Historical Sketches*, 21–23; Knox to Wilkinson, May 17, 1793, Knox MSS.

21. *Middlesex (Conn.) Gazette*, June 15, 1792; Pratt to Wayne, Sept. 11, 1793, Wayne MSS, HSP; *Short Sketch of the Life of Mr. Lent Munson*, 1, 5.

22. Detachment Orders, June 28, 1793, Wayne MSS, HSP.

23. *Middlesex (Conn.) Gazette*, Aug. 31, 1792; Detachment Orders, Aug. 19, 1793; and Pratt to Wayne, Sept. 11, 1793, Wayne MSS, HSP.

24. *Dunlap's American Daily Advertiser*, June 17, 1793; Denny, *Military Journal*, 174–75; *Columbian Centinel*, Nov. 2, 1793.

25. Wilkinson to Wayne, May 15, 1793, Wayne MSS, HSP; Knopf, *Anthony Wayne*, 235.

26. Wilkinson to Wayne, May 15, 1793, Wayne MSS, HSP; Carter, *Territorial Papers*, 3:390–91.

Chapter 9

1. Swan to Wayne, May 23, 1793; and Hayward et al. to [?], Aug. 19, 1793, Wayne MSS, HSP.

2. *Dunlap's American Daily Advertiser*, June 19, 1793; *American Herald of Liberty*, July 23, 1793.

3. Smith to Wayne, May 7, 1793; Wayne to Smith, May 7, 1793; and Wayne to Smith, May 8, 1793, Wayne MSS, HSP.

4. Burton, "Wayne's Orderly Book," 422–23; Wayne to Hamtramck, May 25, 1793; Smith to Wayne, June 4, 1793; Wayne to Smith, June 7, 1793; and Smith to Wayne, July 2, 1793, Wayne MSS, HSP.

5. 2W432, Draper MSS.

6. Burton, "Wayne's Orderly Book," 413–14, 421, 457–58; Springer to Wayne, May 14, 1793, Wayne MSS, HSP.

7. Underwood, *Journal*, 5; Burton, "Wayne's Orderly Book," 432–33.

8. Burton, "Wayne's Orderly Book," 439–42, 451–52.

9. Ibid., 430, passim.

10. Cist, *Cincinnati Miscellany*, 2:233; "Dr. Daniel Drake's Memoir," 116; Ramage, *John Wesley Hunt*, 22–27; McBride, *Pioneer Biography*, 2:206.

11. Cist, *Cincinnati Miscellany*, 2:233.

12. Burnet, *Notes*, 53; Ferris, *Early Settlement*, 345–46; *Kentucky Gazette*, Aug. 17, 1793.

13. *History of Warren County*, 358; Cooley, "Benham Brothers," 69–71; Van Cleve, "Memoirs," 26.

14. McBride, *Pioneer Biography*, 2:8, 18; General Order, June 17, 1793, Wayne MSS, HSP.

15. McBride, *Pioneer Biography*, 2:7–9, 17–18, 253–56.

16. Ibid., 199–205.

17. Van Cleve, "Memoirs," 42.

18. Cist, *Cincinnati Miscellany*, 2:234.

19. Strong to Wayne, May 25, 1793; Bradley to Wayne, May 31, 1793; Bradley to Wayne, June 17, 1793; and Taylor to Wayne, Aug. 3, 1793, Wayne MSS, HSP.

20. Wilkinson to Wayne, July 22, 1793; and Wilkinson to Wayne, Aug. 16, 1793, Wayne MSS, HSP.

21. Shaylor to Wayne, May 30, 1793; and Gibson to Wilkinson, Aug. 26, 1793, Wayne MSS, HSP.

22. Lewis to Wayne, July 3, 1793; and Wilkinson to Wayne, Aug. 16, 1793, Wayne MSS, HSP.

23. Knopf, *Anthony Wayne*, 256–57; Wilkinson to Wayne, July 20, 1793, Wayne MSS, HSP.

24. Knopf, *Anthony Wayne*, 262–65.

25. Hurt to Wayne, May 15, 1793; and Putnam to Wayne, June 4, 1793, Wayne MSS, WLCL; Wayne to Hurt, July 12, 1793, Wayne MSS, HSP; Underwood, *Journal*, 6.

26. MisCampbell et al., Aug. 20, 1793; and General Order, Aug. 22, 1793, Wayne MSS, HSP.

27. Richard Brooke Roberts Pension File, M804; Heitman, *Historical Register*, 1:836.

28. General Order, Aug. 22, 1793, Wayne MSS, HSP; Thomas H. Cushing Pension File, M804; Hildreth, *Biographical and Historical Memoirs*, 345; Heitman, *Historical Register*, 1:348.

29. Slough to Wayne, July 3, 1793; and Kingsbury to Wayne, July 19, 1793, Wayne MSS, HSP; Burton, "Wayne's Orderly Book," 471, 472, 473, 477.

CHAPTER 10

1. *Dunlap's American Daily Advertiser*, May 22, 1793.

2. *Virginia Herald and Fredericksburg Advertiser*, Aug. 29, 1793; *Middlesex (Conn.) Gazette*, Aug. 17, 1793.

3. *Providence Gazette and Country Herald*, Oct. 26, 1793; *Columbian Centinel*, Oct. 30, 1793; Burton, "Wayne's Orderly Book," 474.

4. Burton, "Wayne's Orderly Book," 475–76; Heitman, *Historical Register*, 1:571.

5. Brock et al., recommendation, Sept. 13, 1793; and Jenifer to Wayne, Sept., 1793, Wayne MSS, HSP.

6. Smith to Wayne, Sept. 13, 1793, Wayne MSS, HSP.

7. Hyde to Wayne, Sept. 13, 1793, Wayne MSS, HSP; Burton, "Wayne's Orderly Book," 486.

8. Hall, *Romance of Western History*, 330, 331.

9. *Army and Navy Chronicle*, Aug. 2, 1838.

10. "Catholic Officers in the Revolutionary Army," 313–17.

11. Cornelius Sullivan Pension File, M804.

12. Joseph Fitzgerald, Samuel Neely, Reuben Thacker, and James Christy Pension Files, M804; Wilkinson to Wayne, Aug. 28, 1793, Wayne MSS, HSP.

13. Cope to Wayne, Mar. 23, 1793, Wayne MSS, WLCL.

14. Eaton to Wayne, June 16, 1793, Wayne MSS, HSP.

15. Strong et al. to Posey, Sept. 3, 1793; Chandler to Wayne, Sept. 12, 1793; and Taylor et al., undated recommendation, Wayne MSS, HSP.

16. Knopf, *Anthony Wayne*, 235, 263–64.

17. Swan to Butler, Aug. 17, 1793; and Butler to Wayne, Aug. 18, 1793, Wayne MSS, HSP.

18. Wayne to Glenn, Jan. 13, 1793; Glenn to Wayne, Feb. 4, 1793; Glenn to Wayne, Apr. 1, 1793; and Glenn to Wayne, Aug. 5, 1793, Wayne MSS, HSP; *Pittsburgh Gazette*, July 20, 1793.

19. *Greenfield (Vt.) Gazette*, Aug. 1, 1793; *Columbian Centinel*, Mar. 2, 1793.

20. *Greenfield (Vt.) Gazette*, Aug. 1, 1793; Elliot, *Sketches*, 112–17.

21. Bissell Report, Sept. 28, 1793, Knox MSS; McLean to Wayne, July 28, 1793, Wayne MSS, HSP; *Oracle of Dauphin and Harrisburg (Pa.) Advertiser*, June 17, 1793; *Virginia Gazette and Richmond and Manchester Advertiser*, June 27, 1793; Waddell, *Annals of Augusta County*, 359–61.

22. *American Herald of Liberty*, Aug. 13, Oct. 22, 1793.

23. *Baltimore Daily Repository*, June 11, 1793; *Philadelphia Gazette*, July 6, 1793; *Baltimore Daily Intelligencer*, Nov. 2, 1793.

24. Clark to Wayne, July 17, 1793; Cummins to Wayne, Aug. 23, 1793; and Haskell to Wayne, Aug. 27, 1793, Wayne MSS, HSP; Knopf, *Anthony Wayne*, 275–76.

25. Clark to Wayne, Sept. 1, 1793, Wayne MSS, HSP; Knopf, *Anthony Wayne*, 274; *Columbian Centinel*, Oct. 30, 1793.

CHAPTER 11

1. Burton, "Wayne's Orderly Book," 428, 454, 467–70.

2. Ibid., 469–70, 488.

3. General Order, Sept. 1, 1793; and General Order, Sept. 4, 1793, Wayne MSS, HSP.

4. Estimate of Horses Required, June 22, 1793, Wayne MSS, HSP.

5. Phillips Report, June 28, 1793; MisCampbell Report, July 12, 1793; and Strong to Wayne, July 23, 1793, Wayne MSS, HSP.

6. Wilson, *Journal of Captain Daniel Bradley*, 52–54; Wilkinson to Wayne, Sept. 27, 1793, Wayne MSS, HSP.

7. Cushing to Wayne, May 17, 1793; and Wilkinson to Wayne, July 20, 1793, Wayne MSS, HSP.

8. Posey to Guion, July 5, 1793; Guion to Wayne, July 6, 1793; Wayne to Guion, July 7, 1793; and Guion to Wayne, July 11, 1793, Wayne MSS, HSP.

9. *Carlisle (Pa.) Gazette and the Western Repository of Knowledge*, Feb. 29, 1792.

10. Ibid., Mar. 14, Apr. 18, 1792.

11. *Providence Gazette and Country Herald*, Oct. 26, 1793.

12. Hennon to Wayne, Sept. 10, 1793, Wayne MSS, HSP.

13. Knopf, *Anthony Wayne*, 272; Lincoln et al. to Wayne, Aug. 23, 1793, Wayne MSS, HSP.

14. Hamtramck to Wilkinson, Sept. 11, 1793; and Hamtramck to Wayne, Sept. 12, 1793, Wayne MSS, HSP.

15. Wells Interview, Sept. 16, 1793, Wayne MSS, HSP; Knopf, *Anthony Wayne*, 272; *The Phenix*, Oct. 19, 1793.

16. Knopf, *Anthony Wayne*, 273–77.

17. Gibson to Wilkinson, Sept. 17, 1793; idem, Sept. 19, 1793; and Wilkinson to Wayne, Sept. 25, 1793, Wayne MSS, HSP.

18. General Order, Sept. 22, 1793; Wayne to Smith, Sept. 21, 1793; Smith to Wayne, Sept. 25, 1793; and Wilkinson to Wayne, Sept. 27, 1793, Wayne MSS, HSP.

19. Knopf, *Anthony Wayne*, 239.

20. "Notes and Queries," 329; "Major Isaac Craig, Extracts from His Letter Books," pt. 2, 178.

21. Knopf, *Anthony Wayne*, 244; Shelby to Wayne, June 24, 1793, Wayne MSS, HSP.

22. Harrison, *Kentucky's Governors*, 14–15; 10C46–48, Draper MSS.

23. Harrison, *Kentucky's Governors*, 15, 17; Ward, Charles Scott, 96–97, 105; 13CC173, Draper MSS.

24. List of Appointments, July 1793; Scott to Wayne, July 17, 1793; and Adair to Wayne, July 20, 1793, Wayne MSS, HSP.

25. Wayne to Scott, Sept. 12, 1793, Wayne MSS, HSP; *Kentucky Gazette*, Sept. 28, 1793.

26. *Kentucky Gazette*, Oct. 5, 1793; Presley Gray Pension File, M804; Scott to Wayne, Sept. 30, 1793, Wayne MSS, HSP.

27. *Vermont Gazette*, Nov. 15, 1793; *Virginia Herald and Fredericksburg Advertiser*, Oct. 24, 1793; *Carlisle (Pa.) Gazette and the Western Repository of Knowledge*, Oct. 2, 1793.

28. Dawson, *Civil and Military Services of Major-General William H. Harrison*, 292; 2W433–34, Draper MSS.

CHAPTER 12

1. General Order, Oct. 6, 1793, Wayne MSS, HSP.

2. Ibid.; Ferris, *Early Settlement*, 263, 275, 293; Jones, *Reminiscences of the Early Days*, 16; Compiled Service Records of Volunteer Soldiers.

3. Cist, *Cincinnati Miscellany*, 2:55; Wilson, *Journal of Captain Daniel Bradley*, 54.

4. *American Pioneer* 2 (1843): 291–92; Burton, "Wayne's Orderly Book," 491.

5. Millett, "Caesar and the Conquest of the Northwest Territory," 2–21; Judson, *Caesar's Army*, 71–86.

6. Burton, "Wayne's Orderly Book," 491–92; Cist, *Cincinnati Miscellany*, 2:55.

7. McMahon to Wilkinson, Oct. 9, 1793; Melcher to Wilkinson, Oct. 9, 1793; Melcher to Wilkinson, Oct. 10, 1793; Melcher to Wayne, Dec. 11, 1793; and General Order, Dec. 13, 1793, Wayne MSS, HSP.

8. Cist, *Cincinnati Miscellany*, 2:55; *Ancestry of John Hutchinson Buell*, 10–11.

9. Cist, *Cincinnati Miscellany*, 2:55; Elliot, *Sketches*, 138–39, 168–69.

10. General Order, Oct. 14, 1793; Cushing to Wayne, Oct. 13, 1793; and DeButts to Butler, Oct. 15, 1793, Wayne MSS, HSP.

11. Cist, *Cincinnati Miscellany*, 2:55; *Ancestry of John Hutchinson Buell*, 11; Underwood, *Journal*, 8.

12. Burton, "Wayne's Orderly Book," 493, 494; Underwood, *Journal*, 8; *Ancestry of John Hutchinson Buell*, 12; General Order, Oct. 16, 1793, Wayne MSS, HSP.

13. "Historical Anecdotes," 15; Cist, *Cincinnati Miscellany*, 2:55; *Kentucky Gazette*, Nov. 2, 1793; 1O113, Draper MSS; Howe, *Historical Collections of Ohio*, 2:453; *Washington Spy*, Jan. 3, 1794; *Short Sketch of the Life of Mr. Lent Munson*, 2.

14. Underwood, *Journal*, 7; Hamtramck to Wayne, Oct. 17, 1793; and Hamtramck to Wayne, Oct. 19, 1793, Wayne MSS, HSP; Cist, *Cincinnati Miscellany*, 2:55; *Kentucky Gazette*, Nov. 2, 1793.

15. Hamtramck to Wayne, Oct. 19, 1793, Wayne MSS, HSP; *Washington Spy*, Jan. 3, 1794.

16. *Short Sketch of the Life of Mr. Lent Munson,* 2–3; *Simcoe Correspondence,* 2:126–28.

17. Wilson, *Journal of Captain Daniel Bradley,* 55; St. Clair to Wayne, Oct. 21, 1793; Wayne to Edwards, Oct. 22, 1793; and Wayne to Knox, Oct. 23, 1793, Wayne MSS, HSP; Elliott to Williams, Apr. 13, 1794, Otho Holland Williams Papers, The Maryland Historical Society Library, Baltimore.

18. *Centinel of the North-Western Territory,* Nov. 9, 1793; Teetor, *Mill Creek Valley,* 34–37.

19. Teetor, *Mill Creek Valley,* 37–39; Miller to Wayne, Oct. 25, 1793, Wayne MSS, HSP.

20. Peirce to Wayne, Oct. 21, 1793, Wayne MSS, HSP; Carter, *Territorial Papers,* 3:416–17.

21. Knopf, "Two Journals," 250–51; Clark to Wilkinson, Oct. 9, 1793, Wayne MSS, HSP. Textual evidence has allowed this author to conclude that the writer of the "Two Journals" was actually Francis Jones, an aide-de-camp to Maj. Gen. Charles Scott.

22. Knopf, "Two Journals," 253; C1038–39, Draper MSS; Oct. 28, 1793; General Order, Nov. 1, 1793, Wayne MSS, HSP.

23. 27C14, Draper MSS; English, *Conquest of the Country Northwest of the River Ohio,* 2:947–51.

24. 37J95–98, Draper MSS.

25. 9J206–13, Draper MSS; Cist, *Sketches,* 103–15.

26. Hill, *History of Coshocton County,* 246–50.

CHAPTER 13

1. Knopf, "Two Journals," 252–54.

2. Ibid., 254; *Kentucky Gazette,* Dec. 14, 1793.

3. Knopf, "Two Journals," 254; McDonald, *Biographical Sketches,* 261–63.

4. 10C38–39, Draper MSS.

5. Knopf, "Two Journals," 254–55; 14CC269, Draper MSS; Return, Oct. 16, 1793, Post–Revolutionary War Manuscripts, Publication M904, U.S. National Archives, Washington, D.C.

6. Minutes of Council of War, Oct. 31, 1793; Posey to Wayne, Nov. 2, 1793; Scott to Wayne, Nov. 1, 1793; and Barbee to Wayne, Nov. 1, 1793, Wayne MSS, HSP.

7. Knopf, *Anthony Wayne,* 281–82.

8. Knopf, "Two Journals," 255; Wayne to Wells, Oct. 22, 1793; and General Return, Nov. 5, 1793; Wayne MSS, HSP.

9. Knopf, "Two Journals," 255–57; Cist, *Sketches,* 116–17; Scott to Wayne, Nov. 9, 1793, Wayne MSS, HSP; Smith to Williams, Nov. 16, 1793, Otho Holland Williams Papers, The Maryland Historical Society Library, Baltimore.

10. Burton, "Wayne's Orderly Book," 496–501; General Order, Nov. 21, 1793; and DeButts to Hughes, Nov. 30, 1793, Wayne MSS, HSP; Underwood, *Journal,* 7; Wilson, *Journal of Captain Daniel Bradley,* 57; *Ancestry of John Hutchinson Buell,* 13; Knopf, *Anthony Wayne,* 283.

11. O'Hara to Wayne, Nov. 11, 1793; and Wayne to MisCampbell, Nov. 16, 1793, Wayne MSS, HSP.

12. MisCampbell to Wayne, Dec. 2, 1793; and MisCampbell to Wayne, Dec. 17, 1793, Wayne MSS, HSP; *Kentucky Gazette,* Nov. 30, 1793.

13. Knopf, *Anthony Wayne,* 283; Wayne to Flinn, Nov. 14, 1793; and Wayne to Wilkinson, Nov. 18, 1793, Wayne MSS, HSP.

14. Wayne to Strong, Nov. 1, 1793, Wayne MSS, HSP.

15. Burton, "Wayne's Orderly Book," 499–500; *Ancestry of John Hutchinson Buell,* 12–13.

16. Peirce to Wayne, Nov. 15, 1793, Wayne MSS, HSP; *Centinel of the North-Western Territory,* Nov. 16, 1793.

17. Belli to Wayne, Dec. 15, 1793, Wayne MSS, HSP.

18. Hamtramck to Wayne, Nov. 30, 1793; Wayne to Hamtramck and Elliot, Dec. 4, 1793; and Wayne to Wilkinson, Dec. 8, 1793, Wayne MSS, HSP; Woollen, *Biographical and Historical Sketches,* 24.

19. General Order, Dec. 2, 1793, Wayne MSS, HSP; *Ancestry of John Hutchinson Buell,* 13–14.

20. Hunter to Wayne, Nov. 9, 1793; and Hunter to Wayne, Dec. 6, 1793, Wayne MSS, HSP.

21. Lee to Wayne, Nov. 11, 1793; Ford to Wayne, Nov. 12, 1793; Doyle to Wayne, Nov. 27, 1793; Wayne to Doyle, Nov. 28, 1793; Ford to Wayne, Dec. 2, 1793; and Faulkner to Wayne, Dec. 13, 1793, Wayne MSS, HSP.

22. Eaton to Wayne, Nov. 17, 1793; and Bissell to Wayne, Dec. 4, 1793, Wayne MSS, HSP.

23. Strong to Wayne, Nov. 23, 1793; Allison to Wayne, Nov. 23, 1793; and Pratt to Wayne, Nov. 24, 1793, Wayne MSS, HSP; Heitman, *Historical Register*, 2:804.

24. Peirce to Wayne, Nov. 24, 1793; and McDonough to Wayne, Dec. 11, 1793, Wayne MSS, HSP; Heitman, *Historical Register*, 2:334, 663.

25. Bond to Wayne, Nov. 12, 1793; Bissell to Wayne, Dec. 4, 1793; Posey to Wayne, Dec. 8, 1793; and McMahon to Wayne, Jan. 16, 1794, Wayne MSS, HSP.

26. Wayne to Knox, Nov. 15, 1793, Knox MSS.

27. Ibid.; Wayne to Elliott and Williams, Dec. 3, 1793; and Blue to Wayne, Jan. 11, 1794, Wayne MSS, HSP.

CHAPTER 14

1. Knopf, *Anthony Wayne*, 275; Wilkinson to Wayne, Dec. 8, 1793; and Peirce to Wayne, Dec. 14, 1793, Wayne MSS, HSP.

2. General Order, Dec. 1, 1793; Wayne to Doyle, Jan. 23, 1794; Doyle to Wayne, Jan. 27, 1794; and Claiborne to Wayne, Feb. 27, 1794, Wayne MSS, HSP.

3. Ferris, *Early Settlement*, 338–39; 1O52, Draper MSS; *Centinel of the North-Western Territory*, Nov. 30, 1793.

4. Ferris, *Early Settlement*, 340–41.

5. Wayne to Wilkinson, Dec. 22, 1793, Wayne MSS, HSP.

6. Wayne to Burbeck, Dec. 22, 1793, Wayne MSS, HSP.

7. Gardner, "Henry Burbeck," 251–56.

8. *Columbian Centinel*, Mar. 26, 1794; Underwood, *Journal*, 9–10.

9. Knopf, *Anthony Wayne*, 297–98; *Columbian Centinel*, Mar. 24, 1794; Underwood, *Journal*, 10; 1O91, Draper MSS; Johnson, "George Will and George Will, Jr.," 618; *American Pioneer* 1 (1842): 294.

10. General Order, Dec. 22, 1793, Wayne MSS, HSP; *Columbian Centinel*, Mar. 26, 1794.

11. Underwood, *Journal*, 10; Wayne to Gibson, Dec. 26, 1793, Wayne MSS, HSP.

12. General Order, Dec. 28, 1793, Wayne MSS, HSP; *Pittsburgh Gazette*, Mar. 15, 1794; Knopf, *Anthony Wayne*, 298.

13. General Order, Dec. 28, 1793, Wayne MSS, HSP; *Ancestry of John Hutchinson Buell*, 14.

14. Wayne to Collins, Dec. 30, 1793, Wayne MSS, HSP; *Vermont Gazette*, Apr. 25, 1794; *Centinel of the North-Western Territory*, Jan. 11, 1794; Knopf, *Anthony Wayne*, 298.

15. Wayne to Eaton, Jan. 3, 1794, Wayne MSS, HSP; *Baltimore Daily Intelligencer*, Mar. 10, 1794; *Centinel of the North-Western Territory*, Jan. 18, 1794; *Columbian Centinel*, Mar. 1, 1794.

16. Wayne to Hartshorne, Jan. 5, 1794, Wayne MSS, HSP.

17. Knopf, *Anthony Wayne*, 299–301; *Virginia Gazette and Richmond and Manchester Advertiser*, Feb. 27, Mar. 20, 1794; *Columbian Centinel*, Mar. 1, 26, 1794; *Providence Gazette and Country Herald*, Apr. 5, 1794; *Columbian Gazette*, Mar. 6, 1794; *Baltimore Daily Intelligencer*, Mar. 10, 1794; *Kentucky Gazette*, Feb. 22, 1794; *Middlesex (Conn.) Gazette*, Feb. 22, 1794.

18. *Columbian Centinel*, Mar. 1, 26, 1794; *Columbian Gazette*, Mar. 6, 1794; *Virginia Gazette and Richmond and Manchester Advertiser*, Feb. 27, 1794; *American Herald of Liberty*, Apr. 1, 1794; *Baltimore Daily Intelligencer*, Mar. 10, 1794; Knopf, *Anthony Wayne*, 299.

19. Doyle to Wayne, Jan. 16, 1794; and Doyle to Wayne, Feb. 26, 1794, Wayne MSS, HSP; *Virginia Gazette and Richmond and Manchester Advertiser*, Feb. 27, 1794; *Providence Gazette and Country Herald*, Apr. 5, 1794.

20. *American Herald of Liberty*, Apr. 1, 1794; *Baltimore Daily Intelligencer*, Mar. 1, 1794; *Pennsylvania Gazette*, Feb. 19, 1794; *Columbian Gazette*, Apr. 14, 1794.

21. Hamtramck to Wayne, Oct. 20, 1793; Turner to Clark, Jan. 20, 1794; and Peirce to Wayne, Jan. 27, 1794, Wayne MSS, HSP.

22. Bacon to Wayne, Dec. 5, 1793, Wayne MSS, WLCL.

23. Eaton to Knox, Mar. 15, 1794; and Eaton to Wayne, Mar. 27, 1794, Wayne MSS, HSP.

24. *Federal Spy*, Feb. 25, 1794.

25. McMahon to Wayne, Jan. 14, 1794; Hayward to Wayne, Jan. 26, 1794; Taylor to Wayne, Jan. 27, 1794; and Wayne to Taylor, Jan. 27, 1794, Wayne MSS, HSP.

26. Bond to Wayne, Nov. 10, 1793; Bond to Wayne, Nov. 12, 1793; Beall to Wayne, Jan. 1, 1794; and List of Vacancies, Jan. 8, 1794, Wayne MSS, HSP; Heitman, *Historical Register*, 1:202, 229; Hill, *History of Ashland County*, 142.

27. Faulkner to Wayne, Jan. 21, 1794, Wayne MSS, HSP; Heitman, *Historical Register*, 1:415; 4E3, 4E7, Draper MSS.

CHAPTER 15

1. Howe, *Historical Collections of Ohio*, 1:698–700.

2. *Ancestry of John Hutchinson Buell*, 17–18.

3. *Oracle of Dauphin and Harrisburg (Pa.) Advertiser*, Apr. 13, 1795.

4. DeButts to Greaton, Jan. 1, 1794; Gibson to Wayne, Jan. 12, 1794; and Gibson to Wayne, Jan. 24, 1794, Wayne MSS, HSP.

5. Gibson to Wayne, Jan. 24, 1794, Wayne MSS, HSP.

6. Wayne to Gibson, Jan. 17, 1794; Gibson to Wayne, Jan. 24, 1794; and Wayne to Gibson, Jan. 29, 1794, Wayne MSS, HSP.

7. Gibson to Wayne, Jan. 31, 1794; Gibson to Wayne, Feb. 28, 1794; and Wayne to Bissell, Mar. 12, 1794, Wayne MSS, HSP; *Ancestry of John Hutchinson Buell*, 16.

8. Gibson to Wayne, Jan. 31, 1794; Gibson to Wayne, Feb. 12, 1794; Gibson to Wayne, Feb. 24, 1794; and Gibson to Wayne, Feb. 28, 1794, Wayne MSS, HSP.

9. General Order, Jan. 23, 1794, Wayne MSS, HSP; *Ancestry of John Hutchinson Buell*, 15; *Simcoe Correspondence*, 2:195–96.

10. General Order, Feb. 22, 1794, Wayne MSS, HSP; *Ancestry of John Hutchinson Buell*, 16.

11. *Ancestry of John Hutchinson Buell*, 15–16; Cist, *Cincinnati Miscellany*, 2:38; *Baltimore Daily Intelligencer*, Apr. 12, 1794.

12. *Ancestry of John Hutchinson Buell*, 16; Coleman, "Code Duello in Ante-Bellum Kentucky," 125–26; Cist, *Cincinnati Miscellany*, 2:38–39; *History of Warren County*, 946; Barr, *Strong's Letters*, 239; *Baltimore Daily Intelligencer*, May 6, 1794.

13. *Virginia Gazette and Richmond Chronicle*, Jan. 28, 1794; *Ancestry of John Hutchinson Buell*, 17; Barr, *Strong's Letters*, 239; Cist, *Cincinnati Miscellany*, 2:38; Sabine, *Notes on Duels*, 137; *Greenfield (Vt.) Gazette*, July 31, 1794.

14. Jeffers to Wayne, Mar. 1, 1794; and Jeffers to Wayne, Apr. 15, 1794, Wayne MSS, HSP.

15. *Centinel of the North-Western Territory*, Mar. 22, 1794; *Kentucky Gazette*, Mar. 29, 1794.

16. Hamtramck to Wayne, Nov. 22, 1793; Wayne to Hamtramck, Nov. 23, 1793; and Hamtramck to Wayne, Nov. 23, 1793, Wayne MSS, HSP.

17. DeButts to Cushing, Nov. 9, 1793; Butler to Wayne, Nov. 17, 1793; and Wayne to Cushing, Nov. 27, 1793, Wayne MSS, HSP; *Centinel of the North-Western Territory*, Jan. 25, 1794.

18. Cushing to Wayne, Mar. 8, 1794; and Armstrong to Wayne, Apr. 13, 1794, Wayne MSS, HSP.

19. Knox to Wayne, Apr. 3, 1794, Wayne MSS, HSP; *Dunlap and Claypoole's American Daily Advertiser*, July 16, 1794.

20. Wayne to Hartley, Mar. 30, 1794, Wayne MSS, HSP.

21. *Virginia Gazette and Richmond and Manchester Advertiser*, June 26, 1794; Fitzpatrick, *Writings of George Washington*, 33:411.

22. *Dunlap and Claypoole's American Daily Advertiser*, July 16, 1794; Scott to Wayne, Apr. 20, 1794, Wayne MSS, HSP.

CHAPTER 16

1. Winston to Wayne, Jan. 4, 1794; and Wayne to Winston, Jan. 6, 1794, Wayne MSS, HSP.

2. *Baltimore Daily Intelligencer*, May 6, 1794; Wayne to Winston, Feb. 21, 1794, Wayne MSS, HSP.

3. Bonney, *Legacy*, 1:96, 99; *Baltimore Daily Intelligencer*, May 6, 1794.

4. Wayne to Winston, Mar. 24, 1794; MisCampbell to Wayne, Apr. 11, 1794; Wilkinson to Wayne, Apr. 14, 1794; MisCampbell to Doyle, Apr. 15, 1794; and Blue to Wayne, June 20, 1794, Wayne MSS, HSP.

5. Fitzpatrick, *Writings of George Washington*, 33:431; *Centinel of the North-Western Territory*, June 21, 1794; Heitman, *Historical Register*, 1:330, 626, 424, 947.

6. Bonney, *Legacy*, 1:99–100.

7. Return, July 1, 1794, Post–Revolutionary War Manuscripts, Publication M904, U.S. National Archives, Washington, D.C.; 11E74, Draper MSS.

8. Wayne to Wilkinson, Mar. 14, 1794; and Miller Deposition, Dec., 1794, Wayne MSS, HSP; Return, Nov. 18, 1794, Post–Revolutionary War Manuscripts; McDonald, *Biographical Sketches*, 184–88. McDonald's account of the capture of Christopher Miller has been accepted since its first publication in 1838. Yet there are several important errors that cast his narrative into question. The event actually occurred on March 13, yet McDonald has it "in the month of June." He refers to Christopher's brother as Henry, while his real name was Nicholas. The author further says that the spies encountered Miller and two Indians, while Miller's own story says he was with only one Indian. Finally, Nicholas did not join Wells's spy detachment until April 10, 1794, almost one month after the incident in which he supposedly participated. For these reasons, McDonald's account of the capture, although vivid and apparently precise, has not been used in this work except for those portions of which he could have had personal knowledge.

9. Miller Deposition, Dec., 1794, Wayne MSS, HSP.

10. Cist, *Sketches*, 66–67; McDonald, *Biographical Sketches*, 188–89.

11. Bonney, *Legacy*, 1:96; *Centinel of the North-Western Territory*, May 10, 1794.

12. *Baltimore Daily Intelligencer*, May 6, 1794.

13. Bradley to Wayne, Mar. 10, 1794, Wayne MSS, HSP.

14. Bradley to Wayne, Mar. 4, 1794; Doyle to Wayne, Apr. 25, 1794; and Doyle to Wayne, Apr. 26, 1794, Wayne MSS, HSP; Cist, *Sketches*, 87; *Western Star*, June 3, 1794.

15. Peirce to Wayne, Jan. 20, 1794; Peirce to Wayne, Feb. 2, 1794; Wayne to Peirce, Apr. 12, 1794; and Wayne to Doyle, Apr. 14, 1794, Wayne MSS, HSP.

16. Wayne to Doyle, Apr. 14, 1794, Wayne MSS, HSP; Turner, "Origin of Genet's Projected Attack," 650–54; Hall, "Genet's Western Intrigue," 359–61; *Annual Report of the American Historical Association for the Year 1896*, 1008.

17. *Baltimore Daily Intelligencer*, Jan. 3, 1794; *Pittsburgh Gazette*, Dec. 28, 1793; *Columbian Gazette*, Mar. 6, 1794; and Scott to Wayne, Jan. 25, 1794, Wayne MSS, HSP; *Annual Report of the American Historical Association for the Year 1896*, 1018, 1026.

18. *Middlesex (Conn.) Gazette*, Feb. 15, 1794; *Centinel of the North-Western Territory*, Jan. 25, 1794; *Columbian Gazette*, Mar. 17, 1794; Hall, *Genet's Intrigue*, 370.

19. Clift, *"Cornstalk" Militia of Kentucky*, 25; *Annual Report of the American Historical Association for the Year 1896*, 1030–31, 1033–34; *Washington Spy*, June 18, 1794.

20. Wayne to Winston, Jan. 6, 1794; and Wayne to Hunter, Feb. 10, 1794, Wayne MSS, HSP; Butler, *Commonwealth of Kentucky*, app., 524.

21. Henderson, *Isaac Shelby*, 464–65; *Western Star*, Apr. 22, 1794.

22. Hall, *Genet's Intrigue*, 379.

23. Historical Information Relating to Military Forts and Other Installations, Publication M661, U.S. National Archives; Adams, *Dictionary of American History*, 3:354; Dillon, *History of Indiana*, 343; Wayne to Doyle, Apr. 24, 1794; and Doyle to Wayne, Apr. 25, 1794, Wayne MSS, HSP.

24. Burton, "Wayne's Orderly Book," 506; Wayne to Doyle, May 7, 1794; and Wayne to Doyle, May 9, 1794, Wayne MSS, HSP.

25. *Kline's Carlisle (Pa.) Weekly Gazette*, June 25, 1794.

26. Orcutt Affidavit, May 24, 1794; and Wayne to Guion, July 10, 1794, Wayne MSS, WLCL; Doyle to Wayne, June 4, 1794, Wayne MSS, HSP; Van Cleve, "Memoirs," 46.

27. Wayne to Ludlow, July 10, 1794; and Guion to Wayne, Sept. 18, 1794, Wayne MSS, WLCL.

28. Van Cleve, "Memoirs," 45–47.

CHAPTER 17

1. Gibson to Wayne, Mar. 5, 1794; Gibson to Wayne, Mar. 16, 1794; and Gibson to Wayne, Mar. 23, 1794, Wayne MSS, HSP.

2. Gibson to Wayne, Mar. 16, 1794; Wayne to Gibson, Mar. 19, 1794; and Gibson to Wayne, Mar. 23, 1794, Wayne MSS, HSP.

3 Gibson to Wayne, Mar. 16, 1794; Gibson to Wayne, Mar. 20, 1794; Wayne to Gibson, Mar. 26, 1794; Gibson to Wayne, Mar. 31, 1794; and Gibson to Wayne, Apr. 23, 1794, Wayne MSS, HSP.

4. Wayne to Daingerfield, Apr. 17, 1794, Wayne MSS, HSP.

5. Gibson to Wayne, Apr. 23, 1794; Gibson to Wayne, Apr. 24, 1794; and Doyle to Wayne, May 1, 1794, Wayne MSS, HSP.

6. Peirce to Wayne, Mar. 8, 1794; Robertson to Wayne, Apr. 26, 1794; and Peirce to Wayne, May 17, 1794, Wayne MSS, HSP.

7. Wayne to Robertson, June 2, 1794; Peirce to Wayne, June 9, 1794; and General Order, June 16, 1794, Wayne MSS, HSP.

8. Van Cleve, "Memoirs," 42–45.

9. *Pittsburgh Gazette*, Apr. 19, 1794; Van Cleve, "Memoirs," 44.

10. Burton, "Wayne's Orderly Book," 510, 519–20.

11. Ibid., 521, 535–36.

12. Hamtramck to Wayne, May 13, 1794, Wayne MSS, HSP; 2L33, Draper MSS.

13. *Kentucky Gazette,* May 31, 1794; 2L33, Draper MSS; Hamtramck to Wayne, May 13, 1794; and Wayne to Wilkinson, May 15, 1794, Wayne MSS, HSP; *Simcoe Correspondence*, 2:249–50, 252.

14. Wayne to Lewis, May 14, 1794, Wayne MSS, HSP; *Ancestry of John Hutchinson Buell*, 18.

15. *Kentucky Gazette*, May 31, 1794; General Order, May 17, 1794, Wayne MSS, HSP; 2L33, Draper MSS.

16. Hamtramck to Wayne, May 13, 1794, Wayne MSS, HSP; Cist, *Cincinnati Miscellany*, 2:234.

17. *Pittsburgh Gazette*, June 14, 1794; *American Mercury*, July 14, 1794.

18. Doyle to Wayne, May 1, 1794; and Doyle to Wayne, May 2, 1794, Wayne MSS, HSP.

19. *Baltimore Daily Intelligencer*, June 27, 1794; Slough to Wayne, May 28, 1794, Wayne MSS, HSP.

20. Strong to Wayne, June 2, 1794; and Wilkinson to Wayne, June 4, 1794, Wayne MSS, HSP; *Ancestry of John Hutchinson Buell*, 19.

21. Wayne to Knox, Mar. 10, 1794; and Wayne to Turner et al., Apr. 11, 1794, Wayne MSS, HSP.

22. Wayne to Belli, Feb. 7, 1794; General Order, Feb. 24, 1794; and Wayne to Knox, Mar. 10, 1794, Wayne MSS, HSP; Burton, "Wayne's Orderly Book," 524–25.

23. Burton, "Wayne's Orderly Book," 506, 511–13; Underwood, *Journal*, 12; *Simcoe Correspondence*, 2:257–58.

24. *Centinel of the North-Western Territory*, Apr. 5, 1794.

25. Henley to Wayne, June 14, 1794; Spencer to Wayne, June 15, 1794; Armstrong to Wayne, June 18, 1794; and Wayne to Peirce, June 29, 1794, Wayne MSS, HSP.

26. *History of Warren County*, 946; Finley, *Autobiography*, 127–28; McDonald, *Biographical Sketches*, 183; Dickore, "Some Notable Pioneers," 102; Flexner, *Washington in the American Revolution*, 483.

CHAPTER 18

1. Burton, "Wayne's Orderly Book," 513–17; Heitman, *Historical Register,* 1:219, 382.

2. Burton, "Wayne's Orderly Book," 517; Knopf, *Surgeon's Mate*, 81–83.

3. Burton, "Wayne's Orderly Book," 517; Hamtramck to Wayne, June 9, 1794, Wayne MSS, HSP; Heitman, *Historical Register*, 1:496.

4. Bines to Wayne, June 9, 1794, Wayne MSS, HSP; Heitman, *Historical Register*, 1:218, 281.

5. Lee to Wayne, June 9, 1794; and Clark to Wayne, June 9, Wayne MSS, HSP; Heitman, *Historical Register*, 1:304, 625, 627.

6. *Baltimore Daily Intelligencer*, May 20, 1794; *Middlesex (Conn.) Gazette*, Feb. 8, 1794.

7. Gibson to Wayne, May 11, 1794; and Wayne to Gibson, May 12, 1794, Wayne MSS, HSP.

8. Gibson to Wayne, May 14, 1794; Gibson to Wayne, May 17, 1794; Gibson to Wayne, June 24, 1794; and Return of Ordnance, Mar. 31, 1795, Wayne MSS, HSP; Cooke, "Journal," 345; Cist, *Cincinnati Miscellany*, 2:31. Frazer Wilson, in *History of Darke County*, Ohio (1:308), states that the last cannon recovered was "about a four pounder," found by some boys named McDowell while playing along the stream near the fort

site. There was no 4-pounder cannon with St. Clair's army. Judge John Matson's account in the *Cincinnati Miscellany* was written on June 16, 1845, much closer to events relating to the cannon's discovery, and is accepted.

9. Wayne to Knox, May 30, 1794; and Examination of Prisoners, June 26, 1794, Wayne MSS, HSP.

10. Bald, "Fort Miamis," 75–86; *Simcoe Correspondence*, 1:131, 2:324, 344–45; "Canadian Archives," 680.

11. Knox to Scott, May 17, 1794; and Wayne to Knox, May 30, 1794, Wayne MSS, HSP.

12. Wayne to Knox, June 11, 1794, Knox MSS; Lewis to Wayne, June 16, 1794, Wayne MSS, HSP.

13. Quaife, "Fort Knox Orderly Book," 145–49; Wayne to Vigo, May 27, 1794; and Wayne to Pasteur, May 27, 1794, Wayne MSS, HSP.

14. *Middlesex (Conn.) Gazette*, June 21, 1794; *Record of the Court at Upland*, 383.

15. *Columbian Centinel*, July 5, 1794; *Record of the Court at Upland*, 387.

16. Wayne to Knox, May 30, 1794, Wayne MSS, HSP; Carter, *Territorial Papers*, 2:487; Knopf, *Surgeon's Mate*, 75–76.

17. *American Mercury*, Aug. 25, 1794; *ASP: Indian Affairs*, 489.

18. *Kentucky Gazette*, June 7, 1794; *Pittsburgh Gazette*, July 26, 1794; *Virginia Herald and Fredericksburg Advertiser*, July 24, 1794.

19. Wayne to Gibson, June 28, 1794, Wayne MSS, HSP.

20. General Order, June 28, 1794, Wayne MSS, HSP; *Ancestry of John Hutchinson Buell*, 19; *ASP: Indian Affairs*, 489; *Randolph Journal*, 30. Wayne's report lists the officers present at Fort Recovery and in McMahon's escort but for some reason omits Lt. Hastings Marks, who was also there. See Underwood, *Journal*, 13; and Drake, *Aboriginal Races*, 689. Surgeon's Mate Joseph Andrews was also in the garrison, but he was left off Wayne's list since he was not a line officer.

21. *Simcoe Correspondence*, 5:90–91; Drake, *Book of the Indians*, bk. 5, p. 75.

22. Howe, *Historical Collections of Ohio*, 2:169–70; Alder MSS.

23. *Simcoe Correspondence*, 5:91–92; Klinck and Talman, *Journal of Major John Norton*, 182.

24. Klinck and Talman, *Journal of Major John Norton*, 182; *Simcoe Correspondence*, 5:91–92.

25. *Simcoe Correspondence*, 5:92; Klinck and Talman, *Journal of Major John Norton*, 182; *ASP: Indian Affairs*, 488; Wells, "Indian History," 203. William Wells is the authority for Bear Chief leading this Indian army, possibly a compromise leader to placate the many Lake Indians who had come south to fight.

26. *Simcoe Correspondence*, 5:92; Klinck and Talman, *Journal of Major John Norton*, 182.

CHAPTER 19

1. Gibson to Wayne, June 30, 1794, Wayne MSS, HSP; McBride, *Pioneer Biography*, 2:121.

2. Gibson to Wayne, June 30, 1794, Wayne MSS, HSP; *Ancestry of John Hutchinson Buell*, 19–20; Klinck and Talman, *Journal of Major John Norton*, 183; Alder MSS; James Taylor Pension File, M804; Wailes, *Memoir of Leonard Covington*, 10.

3. *Baltimore Daily Intelligencer*, Sept. 4, 1794; Metcalf, *Collection*, 107; Underwood, *Journal*, 13; *Ancestry of John Hutchinson Buell*, 20; "Historical Anecdotes," 15; Bachus to Hartshorne, Dec. 26, 1794, Jacob Kingsbury Papers, Library of Congress, Washington, D.C.

4. Underwood, *Journal*, 13; "Historical Anecdotes," 15; *Baltimore Daily Intelligencer*, Sept. 4, 1794; Gibson to Wayne, June 30, 1794, Wayne MSS, HSP.

5. Drake, *Aboriginal Races*, 688; 1091, Draper MSS.

6. Gibson to Wayne, June 30, 1794, Wayne MSS, HSP; Alder MSS.

7. Gibson to Wayne, June 30, 1794, Wayne MSS, HSP; Alder MSS.

8. McBride, *Pioneer Biography*, 2:121–22, 124.

9. *Simcoe Correspondence*, 5:93; Klinck and Talman, *Journal of Major John Norton*, 183; "Historical Anecdotes," 15–16.

10. Gibson to Wayne, June 30, 1794, Wayne MSS, HSP; Alder MSS; Howe, *Historical Collections of Ohio*, 2:140; *ASP: Indian Affairs*, 488.

11. McBride, *Pioneer Biography*, 2:122; *Simcoe Correspondence*, 5:93; *Kentucky Gazette*, Aug. 2, 1794; Gibson to Wayne, July 10, 1794, Wayne MSS, HSP; *ASP: Indian Affairs*, 488; *General Advertiser*, Sept. 24, 1794.

12. Darlington, *Fort Pitt,* 265; *Kentucky Gazette,* Aug. 2, 1794; *Providence Gazette and Country Herald,* Sept. 6, 1794; *Simcoe Correspondence,* 5:93–94.

13. Alder MSS; Gibson to Wayne, June 30, 1794; and Gibson to Wayne, July 1, 1794, Wayne MSS, HSP; *Randolph Journal,* 31; *Ancestry of John Hutchinson Buell,* 20.

14. *ASP: Indian Affairs,* 487; Alder MSS.

15. Gibson to Wayne, July 1, 1794, Wayne MSS, HSP; McBride, *Pioneer Biography,* 2:123; *ASP: Indian Affairs,* 488.

16. *Simcoe Correspondence,* 2:306, 310, 5:94; Alder MSS; *ASP: Indian Affairs,* 488.

17. Howe, *Historical Collections of Ohio,* 2:233–34; *Dunlap and Claypoole's American Daily Advertiser,* Sept. 24, 1794; *General Advertiser,* Sept. 24, 1794.

18. *ASP: Indian Affairs,* 488; *Ancestry of John Hutchinson Buell,* 20.

19. *Simcoe Correspondence,* 5:94; James Taylor Pension File, M804; Samuel Neely Pension File, M804; Gibson to Wayne, July 1, 1794, Wayne MSS, HSP; Bachus to Hartshorne, Dec. 26, 1794, Kingsbury Papers; 2O115, Draper MSS.

20. Gibson to Wayne, July 2, 1794; Wayne to Gibson, July 2, 1794; and Wayne to Brock, July 2, 1794, Wayne MSS, HSP.

21. *Simcoe Correspondence,* 2:306, 317, 5:93; "1794: The Mackinac Indians Oppose Wayne," 444.

22. Bliss, *Diary of David Zeisberger,* 2:363–66; Darlington, *Fort Pitt,* 265; Wells, "Indian History," 203–4; *Simcoe Correspondence,* 5:94.

23. *Gazette of the United States and Daily Evening Advertiser,* Oct. 25, 1794; Joseph Fitzgerald Pension File, M804.

Chapter 20

1. *Centinel of the North-Western Territory,* July 12, 1794.

2. Burton, "Wayne's Orderly Book," 525–26; Underwood, *Journal,* 14.

3. Underwood mistakenly identified Elliott's opponent in this duel as "Lieutenant Wm. Scott," although that officer did not enter the legion—as an ensign—until 1795, and his promotion to lieutenant did not occur until 1799. Elliott was a captain by 1796. Although other elements of his recollections are out of proper chronology, it appears likely that the duel occurred at this time and Underwood incorrectly remembered Scott as the other duelist. Underwood, *Journal,* 14–15; Heitman, *Historical Register,* 1:402, 870; *Ancestry of John Hutchinson Buell,* 17; and "Letters from Dr. Joseph Strong to Captain John Pratt," 239.

4. *Ancestry of John Hutchinson Buell,* 22.

5. Knox to Wilkinson, July 12, 1794, Knox MSS.

6. Sargent to Knox, July 23, 1794; and Sargent to Knox, July 31, 1794, Knox MSS.

7. *Kentucky Gazette,* Sept. 20, 1794.

8. *History and Biographical Cyclopaedia of Butler County,* 1:284; Smith, *Life and Times of Lewis Cass,* 14–15; "Letters from Dr. Joseph Strong to Captain John Pratt," 239–40.

9. Cummins, "Background of a Gavel," 344; Bonney, *Legacy,* 1:102; Wayne's Will, July 14, 1794, Wayne MSS, HSP.

10. *Ancestry of John Hutchinson Buell,* 22; Burton, "Wayne's Orderly Book," 529, 535.

11. Gibson to Wayne, July 10, 1794; and Gibson to Wayne, July 18, 1794, Wayne MSS, HSP; *American Mercury,* Aug. 25, 1794; *Dunlap and Claypoole's American Daily Advertiser,* Aug. 18, 1794; Wilson, *Journal of Captain Daniel Bradley,* 63.

12. May 17, June 13, 1794, Kentucky Volunteers MSS; C1038, Draper MSS.

13. *Biographical Encyclopaedia of Kentucky,* 138; des Cognets, *William Russell,* 45–47.

14. *Biographical Encyclopaedia of Kentucky,* 669–70.

15. Ibid., 48; *Genealogies of Kentucky Families,* 58–61; 16E11, Draper MSS.

16. Kenton, *Simon Kenton,* 231–32; "Sketch of the Early Adventures of William Sudduth," 47, 52, 62.

17. "Sketch of the Early Adventures of William Sudduth," 47; *Biographical Cyclopedia of the Commonwealth of Kentucky,* 623–24.

18. July 11, 15, 16, 1794, Kentucky Volunteers MSS; 5U93; Kentucky Orderly Book.

19. Kentucky Orderly Book; Knopf, "Two Journals," 259; July 21, 1794, Kentucky Volunteers MSS; Sargent to Knox, July 23, 1794, Knox MSS; Collins, *History of Kentucky*, 474.

20. Kentucky Orderly Book; Burton, "Wayne's Orderly Book," 530–31.

21. *Ancestry of John Hutchinson Buell*, 23–24; General Order, July 26, 1794, Wayne MSS, HSP.

22. Wayne to Bines, July 24, 1794, Wayne MSS, HSP; *General Advertiser*, July 16, 1794.

23. *General Advertiser*, Sept. 4, 1794; *Federal Spy*, Sept. 16, 1794.

CHAPTER 21

1. General Order, July 27, 1794, Wayne MSS, HSP; *Randolph Journal*, 9; *Wilkinson Journal*, 249. Although Dwight L. Smith does not identify the writer of the journal in *From Greene Ville to Fallen Timbers*, in the opinion of this author, it was either written by Brig. Gen. James Wilkinson or dictated to a clerk, and it is therefore attributed to him herein since all evidence points to his authorship.

2. *Randolph Journal*, 9; *Wilkinson Journal*, 249–51; Bowyer, "Daily Journal," 315; Clark, "Journal," 419.

3. General Order, July 27, 1794, Wayne MSS, HSP; Clark, "Journal," 419–20; *Wilkinson Journal*, 251–53.

4. Cooke, "Journal," 312; Clark, "Journal," 419–20; *Randolph Journal*, 10; General Order, July 29, 1794, Wayne MSS, HSP.

5. Clark, "Journal," 420; Smith, *With Captain Edward Miller*, 1; Bowyer, "Daily Journal," 315; *Randolph Journal*, 10; *Wilkinson Journal*, 253–254; Knopf, "Two Journals," 29–30.

6. Burton, "Wayne's Orderly Book," 540; *Wilkinson Journal*, 255; Bowyer, "Daily Journal," 315; *Randolph Journal*, 11; Clark, "Journal," 421; Wayne to Miller, July 31, 1794, Wayne MSS, HSP.

7. Clark, "Journal," 421; Howe, *Historical Collections of Ohio*, 1:903–4, 2:379.

8. Knopf, "Two Journals," 261; Smith, *With Captain Edward Miller*, 2; Cooke, "Journal," 313; *Wilkinson Journal*, 257; Bowyer, "Daily Journal," 315.

9. *Randolph Journal*, 11–12; *Wilkinson Journal*, 257–59; Knopf, "Two Journals," 261; Bowyer, "Daily Journal," 315.

10. *Wilkinson Journal*, 257, 259; Burnet, *Notes*, 276–78; 5U136, Draper MSS.

11. Cooper to Wayne, Aug. 15, 1794, Wayne MSS, HSP; Bowyer, "Daily Journal," 316; *ASP: Indian Affairs*, 490; *Virginia Gazette and Richmond and Manchester Advertiser*, Oct. 23, 1794; *Wilkinson Journal*, 260–61; Clark, "Journal," 422; Underwood, *Journal*, 16.

12. *Simcoe Correspondence*, 2:349, 351, 387.

13. Ibid., 351–52.

14. *Columbian Mirror*, Oct. 28, 1794; *Simcoe Correspondence*, 3:113–14.

15. Stagg to Wayne, Oct. 4, 1794; Craig to Wayne, Oct. 17, 1794; and Peirce to Wayne, Nov. 9, 1794, Wayne MSS, HSP.

16. Newman Deposition, Dec. 1, 1794, Wayne MSS, HSP; 2O120, Draper MSS; Rusche, "Treachery within the United States Army," 486. Rusche has erroneously concluded that Newman was actually working for General Wayne, basing his theory on the fact that a deserter would not have returned to a possible sentence of death. But Newman was a civilian employee of the Quartermaster Department and not a soldier and, therefore, not subject to military sentence. Technically, Newman did not desert, but no other term denotes his actions better than that one.

17. Cooper to Wayne, Aug. 15, 1794; Cooper to Wayne, Sept. 3, 1794; and Robertson and Mackay to Wayne, Sept. 8, 1794, Wayne MSS, HSP.

18. Confidential Intelligence, Nov. 10, 1794, Wayne MSS, HSP; *History of Shelby County*, 69.

19. *Wilkinson Journal*, 261; Cooke, "Journal," 313; Clark, "Journal," 421–22; *Randolph Journal*, 12; Knopf, "Two Journals," 262; Smith, *With Captain Edward Miller*, 2.

20. Bowyer, "Daily Journal," 316; Knopf, "Two Journals," 262; Cooke, "Journal," 313.

21. *Wilkinson Journal*, 262; *Randolph Journal*, 12; Clark, "Journal," 422; Wayne to Wayne, Sept. 10, 1794, Wayne MSS, HSP; Bowyer, "Daily Journal," 316; *Columbian Centinel*, Nov. 22, 1794. Too many historians have added this accident to the Wayne-Wilkinson feud and concluded that the falling tree was actually an assassination attempt. In a force of a few thousand men, all armed with muskets, rifles, pistols, knives, and tomahawks, it is ludicrous to presume that anyone would choose to kill Wayne by felling a tree on him in the middle of the legion camp as he took an afternoon nap. A similar accident had occurred on Sept. 15, 1791,

after a detachment of troops under Capt. Samuel Newman marched from Fort Washington to join St. Clair's main army. Newman related, "abt. 12 O Clock at night a very large Tree fell upon two of Capt. Phelon's Men, one of whom died in abt. Three hours after, the other badly wounded but not dangerous." Quaife, "Picture of the First United States Army," 61. Newspapers from this period occasionally contain accounts of men being killed by falling trees, such as Hezekiah Logan in Poultney, Vermont, on June 14, 1792, and Samuel Minor, of Bennington, Vermont, on April 25, 1793. *Herald of Vermont*, June 25, 1792; *American Mercury*, May 13, 1793. But this author has been unable to find a single reference in the contemporary literature that refers to a tree being used as a deadly weapon.

22. Bowyer, "Daily Journal," 316; *Wilkinson Journal*, 262–63; *Randolph Journal*, 12; Clark, "Journal," 422; Smith, *With Captain Edward Miller*, 2; Hart Journal; Bonney, *Legacy*, 1:101.

23. Wayne to Underhill, Aug. 4, 1794; and Underhill to Wayne, Aug. 5, 1794, Wayne MSS, HSP; Clark, "Journal," 423; Clark, *American Militia*, 66.

24. *Wilkinson Journal*, 264–65.

25. Underhill to Wayne, Aug. 15, 1794, Wayne MSS, HSP.

CHAPTER 22

1. Clark, "Journal," 422; Randolph Journal, 13; Cooke, "Journal," 313; Knopf, "Two Journals," 262; *Wilkinson Journal*, 263.

2. *Wilkinson Journal*, 263–64, 265–66; Aug. 4, 1794, Kentucky Volunteers MSS; Clark, "Journal," 423; Bowyer, "Daily Journal," 316.

3. *Wilkinson Journal*, 267–69; Drake to Wayne, Aug. 5, 1794, Wayne MSS, HSP; Smith, *With Captain Edward Miller*, 3.

4. *Randolph Journal*, 14; *Wilkinson Journal*, 269–71; Bowyer, "Daily Journal," 316; Knopf, "Two Journals," 263; Cooke, "Journal," 313; Hart Journal.

5. *Wilkinson Journal*, 269–70.

6. Bowyer, "Daily Journal," 316–17; *Randolph Journal*, 15.

7. Cooke, "Journal," 314; Clark, "Journal," 424; Randolph Journal, 15; Knopf, "Two Journals," 263; Smith, *With Captain Edward Miller*, 4; Hart Journal.

8. *Wilkinson Journal*, 273; Knopf, "Two Journals," 263; Hart Journal; General Order, Aug. 8, 1794, Wayne MSS, HSP.

9. Alder MSS; Hildreth, *Contributions to the Early History of the North-West*, 65–66.

10. "Narrative of John Brickell's Captivity," 43–52.

11. Knopf, "Two Journals," 263; Clark, "Journal," 424; Burton, "Wayne's Orderly Book," 543–44; Bowyer, "Daily Journal," 317; Cooke, "Journal," 314; *Wilkinson Journal*, 274.

12. Clark, "Journal," 424; *Ancestry of John Hutchinson Buell*, 24–25; *American State Papers*, vol. 1, *Claims*, 208.

13. Jones to Wayne, Aug. 11, 1794, Wayne MSS, WLCL; "Extracts from a Manuscript Journal," 392–93; Heitman, *Historical Register*, 1:580; Sargent to Knox, Aug. 1, 1794, Knox MSS.

14. Jones to Wayne, Aug. 11, 1794, Wayne MSS, WLCL; *Pennsylvania Archives*, 4:73–75, 101–2.

15. *Dunlap and Claypoole's American Daily Advertiser*, Aug. 14, 1794; *Baltimore Daily Intelligencer*, Aug. 16, 1794; *Virginia Gazette and Richmond and Manchester Advertiser*, Sept. 18, 1794; *Pennsylvania Archives*, 4:122–24.

16. *Wilkinson Journal*, 274–75; Aug. 10, 12, 1794, Kentucky Volunteers MSS.

17. Aug. 12, 1794, Kentucky Volunteers MSS; Kentucky Orderly Book.

18. 10E103, Draper MSS; McDonald, *Biographical Sketches*, 192.

19. McDonald, *Biographical Sketches*, 193–94; 10C38–39, 10E103–4, Draper MSS; Smith, *With Captain Edward Miller*, 4; Cooke, "Journal," 314; *Simcoe Correspondence*, 2:371.

20. Knopf, "Two Journals," 263–64; Hart Journal; *Simcoe Correspondence*, 2:366–67; *Wilkinson Journal*, 276–78; Cooke, "Journal," 314–15.

21. *Wilkinson Journal*, 277–78; *American State Papers*, vol. 1, *Claims*, 415, 689–90; *Simcoe Correspondence*, 2:372–73.

22. *ASP: Indian Affairs*, 490.

CHAPTER 23

1. Nelson, "General Charles Scott," 246; *American Pioneer* 2 (1843): 387; Wright, *Hunt Memoirs*, 1; "Biographical Field Notes of Dr. Lyman C. Draper," 1; Heitman, *Historical Register*, 1:557; Smith, *With Captain Edward Miller*, 6; Burton, "Wayne's Orderly Book," 544.

2. *Wilkinson Journal*, 278; Knopf, "Two Journals," 264; Burton, "Wayne's Orderly Book," 544; Aug. 13, 1794, Kentucky Volunteers MSS; *Farmers' Library; or, Vermont Political and Historical Register*, Oct. 14, 1794.

3. *Randolph Journal*, 17; Knopf, "Two Journals," 264; Clark, "Journal," 426; *Wilkinson Journal*, 279–80.

4. *Wilkinson Journal*, 279–80; *Pittsburgh Gazette*, Oct. 4, 1794.

5. Knopf, "Two Journals," 264; Clark, "Journal," 426; Cooke, "Journal," 315; Smith, *With Captain Edward Miller*, 6; *Wilkinson Journal*, 281–82.

6. *Wilkinson Journal*, 281; *Randolph Journal*, 17; Message to Brothers Big Knives, Aug. 15, 1794, Wayne MSS, HSP; James Wilkinson, Journal, Aug. 21, 1794, Leonard Covington Papers, Burton Historical Collection, Detroit, Mich.; *Simcoe Correspondence*, 2:387.

7. *Simcoe Correspondence*, 2:373, 374, 380.

8. Ibid., 2:357, 374, 387, 3:12; Bliss, *Diary of David Zeisberger*, 370.

9. Quaife, "Wilkinson's Narrative," 83; Clark, "Journal," 426; Smith, *With Captain Edward Miller*, 6; *Randolph Journal*, 18.

10. *Wilkinson Journal*, 283; Clark, "Journal," 427; Smith, *With Captain Edward Miller*, 6.

11. Knopf, "Two Journals," 265; Robertson, *Diary of Mrs. John Graves Simcoe*, 99; Bowyer, "Daily Journal," 317; *Wilkinson Journal*, 283–84; *Randolph Journal*, 18.

12. *Randolph Journal*, 19; Knopf, "Two Journals," 265; Smith, *With Captain Edward Miller*, 7; Clark, "Journal," 427.

13. Clark, "Journal," 427; Hopkins, "Journal," pt. 11, vol. 19, no. 3 (1862): 37; Howe, *Historical Collections of Ohio*, 2:155; Knopf, "Two Journals," 265.

14. *Wilkinson Journal*, 285; Bowyer, "Daily Journal," 318; *Greenfield (Vt.) Gazette*, Oct. 9, 1794; "Narrative of John Brickell's Captivity," 52.

15. *Wilkinson Journal*, 285–86.

16. Harrison, *Discourse on the Aborigines*, 38.

17. Knopf, "Two Journals," 265; *Randolph Journal*, 19–20; Hart Journal; *Wilkinson Journal*, 287.

18. "Sketch of the Early Adventures of William Sudduth," 64; 9J206–13, Draper MSS; *Wilkinson Journal*, 287

19. Bowyer, "Daily Journal," 318; Wayne to Pike, Aug. 19, 1794, Wayne MSS, HSP; Cooke, "Journal," 315; Aug. 19, 1794, Kentucky Volunteers MSS; *Wilkinson Journal*, 287; Cist, *Sketches*, 118.

20. *Wilkinson Journal*, 288–89; General Order, Aug. 19, 1794, Wayne MSS, HSP; Clark, "Journal," 428; Aug. 20, 1794, Kentucky Volunteers MSS.

21. Alder MSS; Klinck and Talman, *Journal of Major John Norton*, 184.

22. *Wilkinson Journal*, Oct. 31, 1794, Covington Papers; Alder MSS; Klinck and Talman, *Journal of Major John Norton*, 184; Cist, *Sketches*, 118; 19S245–46, 255–56, Draper MSS.

CHAPTER 24

1. Cooke, "Journal," 316; *ASP: Indian Affairs*, 491; Knopf, "Two Journals," 265; Cist, *Sketches*, 90; 5U126–50, Draper MSS.

2. *Wilkinson Journal*, 289; Clark, "Journal," 428.

3. "Sketch of the Early Adventures of William Sudduth," 64–65; Cooke, "Journal," 316; *ASP: Indian Affairs*, 491.

4. "Sketch of the Early Adventures of William Sudduth," 65–66; John Montgomery Pension File, M804.

5. *Wilkinson Journal*, 289–90; 12CC156, Draper MSS.

6. Cooke, "Journal," 316; Burton, "Wayne's Orderly Book," 470; Underwood, *Journal*, 18. As Cooke has indicated, the front guard consisted of soldiers detailed for that duty from various companies. His own company of infantry did not constitute the advance guard.

7. Kingsbury, *Genealogy of the Descendants of Henry Kingsbury*, 253; *Wilkinson Journal*, 290–91; Cooke, "Journal," 316.

8. *Wilkinson Journal*, 291–92, 297; Reuben Thacker Pension File, M804; Wilkinson, *Memoirs*, 3:254; Bowyer, "Daily Journal," 318.

9. *ASP: Indian Affairs*, 491; *Wilkinson Journal*, 291–92; "Sketch of the Early Adventures of William Sudduth," 66–67.

10. *Wilkinson Journal*, 294; *ASP: Indian Affairs*, 491; 5U126–50, Draper MSS; *History of Sandusky County*, 648; Todd and Drake, *Sketches of the Civil and Military Services of William Henry Harrison*, 17.

11. Underwood, *Journal*, 18; Coffinberry, *Forest Rangers*, 208; 19S255, Draper MSS; *Wilkinson Journal*, 297.

12. *Wilkinson Journal*, 294; McBride, *Pioneer Biography*, 2:129–30; *ASP: Indian Affairs*, 491; *Sketches and Recollections of Lynchburg*, 314.

13. "Casualties of the Battle of Fallen Timbers," 528–29; *Baltimore Daily Intelligencer*, Sept. 30, 1794; Jacob Slough Pension File, M804; *Vermont Gazette*, Oct. 31, 1794; *Simcoe Correspondence*, 2:396, 414; *ASP: Indian Affairs*, 492; Clark, "Journal," 429; Quaife, "Wilkinson's Narrative," 85; *Wilkinson Journal*, 294. Previous historians of the battle have assumed that the Canadian militia and Wyandottes on the right of the Indian line were arrayed against the Second Sub-Legion. A comparison of the casualties incurred by the Second and Fourth Sub-Legions disclose that the latter lost five times the total number of killed and wounded of the former. It is only logical that the heaviest losses on both sides would have come on the same portion of the battlefield, especially since the Second Sub-Legion was under fire for considerably less time than the Fourth. Testimony from participants bears out this interpretation. General Wilkinson wrote that "the 2d S L. scarcely got into the action and the 4th S L. was at one period nearly out flanked." He also stated that the firing "was briskest about the centre," where the Third and Fourth sustained the greatest loss. Lieutenant Clark agreed with this arrangement, writing that the legion received "a most heavy fire, on the extreem left flank," which killed Lieutenant Towles of the Fourth Sub-Legion.

14. *ASP, Indian Affairs*, 491; Smith, *With Captain Edward Miller*, 8; Knopf, "Two Journals," 266; Bonney, *Legacy*, 1:102; McBride, *Pioneer Biography*, 2:173–74.

15. Cist, *Sketches*, 118–20; *Baltimore Daily Intelligencer*, Sept. 27, 1794.

16. *ASP, Indian Affairs*, 491; *History of Sandusky County*, 648; Smith, *With Captain Edward Miller*, 8; Cooke, "Journal," 316; Clark, "Journal," 429; Hildreth, *Biographical and Historical Memoirs*, 347; *Baltimore Daily Intelligencer*, Sept. 30, 1794.

17. 19S246, Draper MSS; Klinck and Talman, *Journal of Major John Norton*, 185; Howe, *Historical Collections of Ohio*, 1:699; McClung, *Sketches of Western Adventure*, 286; *Pittsburgh Gazette*, Oct. 4, 1794.

18. Hill, *History of Ashland County*, 131–32.

19. Drake, *Life of Tecumseh*, 62–63, 81–82.

20. *Wilkinson Journal*, 292–93.

21. Ibid., 293; Quaife, "Wilkinson's Narrative," 85; *Simcoe Correspondence*, 3:29; *Pittsburgh Gazette*, Oct. 4, 1794.

22. *ASP, Indian Affairs*, 491; *Wilkinson Journal*, 295–96.

23. Quaife, "Wilkinson's Narrative," 84–85; Aug. 20, 1794, Kentucky Volunteers MSS; Cist, *Sketches*, 120; Bowyer, "Daily Journal," 319; *Wilkinson Journal*, 296; *Simcoe Correspondence*, 2:397; *History of Sandusky County*, 648.

CHAPTER 25

1. Bonney, *Legacy*, 1:102–4.

2. Jacob Slough Pension File, M804; Slough to Wayne, Aug. 27, 1794, Wayne MSS, HSP; Bonney, *Legacy*, 1:103; *Virginia Gazette and Richmond and Manchester Advertiser*, Oct. 27, 1794.

3. *ASP, Indian Affairs*, 492; *Wilkinson Journal*, 303–4, 306; Bonney, *Legacy*, 1:105.

4. Cist, *Sketches*, 120–21.

5. *Maryland Gazette*, Oct. 2, 1794; Clark, *American Militia*, 43–53; *ASP, Indian Affairs*, 492; Knopf, *Surgeon's Mate*, 4.

6. *Randolph Journal*, 20; Blakeney, *Blakeneys in America*, 40.

7. Coffinberry, *Forest Rangers*, 194–95, 213–14.

8. *Wilkinson Journal*, 295, 302; Clark, "Journal," 431; Quaife, "Wilkinson's Narrative," 86–87.

9. Quaife, "Wilkinson's Narrative," 87; Knopf, "Two Journals," 266; *Pittsburgh Gazette*, Oct. 4, 1794; Cooke, "Journal," 318; Alexander Harrow, *Diary, Burton Historical Collection*, Detroit, Mich.

10. *Simcoe Correspondence*, 1:397.

11. Ibid., 2:398–99; *Gazette of the United States*, Oct. 2, 1794.

12. Burton, "Wayne's Orderly Book," 546; *Wilkinson Journal*, 299–300, 302; *Baltimore Daily Intelligencer*, Sept. 30, 1794; Hildreth, *Biographical and Historical Memoirs*, 347; Howe, *Historical Collections of Ohio*, 2:145.

13. Clark, "Journal," 430; "Sketch of the Early Adventures of William Sudduth," 67; 10CC38–39, Draper MSS.

14. 10CC38–39, Draper MSS; *Simcoe Correspondence*, 2:398, 405.

15. *Simcoe Correspondence*, 1:398; 9J206–13, Draper MSS; Knopf, "Two Journals," 266; "Sketch of the Early Adventures of William Sudduth," 67.

16. Smith, With Captain Edward Miller, 8; *Simcoe Correspondence*, 1:406; *Wilkinson Journal*, 298.

17. Knopf, "Two Journals," 266; Gaines to Wayne, July 10, 1795, Wayne MSS, HSP; 10CC38–39, Draper MSS.

18. Cooke, "Journal," 339; Smith, *With Captain Edward Miller*, 8; Knopf, "Two Journals," 267; *Randolph Journal*, 21; *Wilkinson Journal*, 300–301.

19. *Wilkinson Journal*, 301; Howe, *Historical Collections of Ohio*, 2:141; Bowyer, "Daily Journal," 319; Hosmer, *Early History of the Maumee Valley*, 12–13.

20. *Simcoe Correspondence*, 2:407; 10CC38–39, Draper MSS.

21. *Simcoe Correspondence*, 2:407–8; Clark, "Journal," 431; Hildreth, *Biographical and Historical Memoirs*, 347.

22. General Order, Aug. 23, 1794, Wayne MSS, HSP.

23. Ibid.; Bowyer, "Daily Journal," 320; *Wilkinson Journal,* 302; Quaife, "Wilkinson's Narrative," 88; *American Herald of Liberty*, Nov. 4, 1794; Bonney, Legacy, 1:106.

24. 17S216, Draper MSS; Stone, *Life of Joseph Brant*, 2:390; Alder MSS; Klinck and Talman, *Journal of Major John Norton*, 186.

25. "Narrative of John Brickell's Captivity," 53; Bliss, *Diary of David Zeisberger*, 2:378–79; 19S246, 255–56, Draper MSS.

26. *Simcoe Correspondence*, 2:395–96, 404, 3:21.

27. Ibid., 2:404, 3:10, 98–99.

28. Abraham Williams, memorandum, Leonard Covington Papers, Burton Historical Collection, Detroit, Mich.; *Simcoe Correspondence*, 3:8, 12.

CHAPTER 26

1. *Wilkinson Journal*, 303; Knopf, "Two Journals," 267.

2. *Wilkinson Journal*, 304–5; Clark, "Journal," 433; *Ancestry of John Hutchinson Buell*, 25.

3. 9J206–13, Draper MSS; Knopf, "Two Journals," 267; Clark, "Journal," 433; *Randolph Journal*, 22; *Wilkinson Journal*, 306.

4. *Wilkinson Journal*, 305–6; Clark, "Journal," 433; Aug. 26, 1794, Kentucky Volunteers MSS.

5. Smith, *With Captain Edward Miller*, 9; *Wilkinson Journal*, 306–7; Bowyer, "Daily Journal," 320.

6. *Wilkinson Journal*, 307–9.

7. *Ancestry of John Hutchinson Buell*, 25.

8. Carter, *Territorial Papers*, 3:421–27.

9. Aug. 28, Sept. 11, 13, 18, 1794, Kentucky Volunteers MSS; Kentucky Orderly Book.

10. *Dunlap and Claypoole's American Daily Advertiser*, Oct. 1, 1794; Quaife, "Wilkinson's Narrative," 89; Hildreth, *Biographical and Historical Memoirs*, 348; *General Advertiser*, Nov. 18, 1794.

11. *General Advertiser*, Nov. 18, 1794; Knopf, "Two Journals," 268; Smith, *With Captain Edward Miller*, 10–11.

12. Burton, "Wayne's Orderly Book," 548–49; Bowyer, "Daily Journal," 321.

13. Clark, "Journal," 434; Bonney, Legacy, 1:105; *Wilkinson Journal*, 310, 311; Bowyer, "Daily Journal," 321.

14. Burton, "Wayne's Orderly Book," 549–51; *Wilkinson Journal*, 313.

15. *Connecticut Courant,* Nov. 24, 1794; Burton, "Wayne's Orderly Book," 550; General Order, Sept. 13, 1794; and Wayne to Hunt, Sept. 13, 1794, Wayne MSS, HSP; *American Pioneer* 2 (1843): 387; Clark, "Journal," 435; Bowyer, "Daily Journal," 351.

16. Aug. 29, 30, 31, Sept. 1, 5, 9, 12, 1794, Kentucky Volunteers MSS; Bowyer, "Daily Journal," 321; Clark, "Journal," 434.

17. General Order, Sept. 1, 1794, Wayne MSS, HSP; Knopf, "Two Journals," 268, 269; Aug. 30, Sept. 4, 7, 1794, Kentucky Volunteers MSS.

18. Although dated September 7, the contents indicate that Russell's letter was written on the way to Fort Recovery and must have been composed on September 1. Kentucky Orderly Book; des Cognets, *William Russell.*

19. Kentucky Orderly Book.

20. Knopf, "Two Journals," 269; Kentucky Orderly Book; Clark, "Journal," 435; *Wilkinson Journal*, 321.

21. Bowyer, "Daily Journal," 351; *Wilkinson Journal*, 315, 318.

22. *Wilkinson Journal*, 313, 314, 317, 322.

23. Bonney, Legacy, 1:105–6.

24. Ibid., 1:105; *Wilkinson Journal*, 316–18.

25. *Ancestry of John Hutchinson Buell*, 25–26.

26. Bonney, *Legacy*, 1:105; Knopf, "Two Journals," 270; Clark, "Journal," 435; Bowyer, "Daily Journal," 352; *Wilkinson Journal*, 323.

27. Wayne to Elliott and Williams, Sept. 10, 1794, Wayne MSS, HSP.

28. *Randolph Journal*, 23; Bonney, *Legacy*, 1:106; *Wilkinson Journal,* 324, 326; Wayne to Cushing, Sept. 13, 1794, Wayne MSS, HSP; Clark, "Journal," 436.

29. Sept. 9, 1794, Kentucky Volunteers MSS; Knopf, "Two Journals," 270.

Chapter 27

1. General Order, Sept. 12, 1794; and Wayne to Hunt, Sept. 13, 1794, Wayne MSS, HSP; Clark, "Journal," 436; *Wilkinson Journal*, 322.

2. *Randolph Journal*, 24; Knopf, "Two Journals," 270; Wayne to Sachems, Sept. 12, 1794, Wayne MSS, HSP

3. General Order, Sept. 12, 1794; and General Order, Sept. 13, 1794, Wayne MSS, HSP; Knopf, "Two Journals," 270.

4. *Simcoe Correspondence*, 3:87–89; Bowyer, "Daily Journal," 352.

5. Clark, "Journal," 437; Cooke, "Journal," 341; *Randolph Journal,* 11–12; Knopf, "Two Journals," 271; Bowyer, "Daily Journal," 352–53.

6. Clark, "Journal," 437; Knopf, "Two Journals," 271; Cooke, "Journal," 341; Bowyer, "Daily Journal," 353; Hopkins, "Journal," pt. 7, vol. 18, no. 51 (1861): 805.

7. Cooke, "Journal," 341; Bowyer, "Daily Journal," 353; Bonney, *Legacy*, 1:111; Simcox Deposition, Sept. 19, 1794, Wayne MSS, HSP; Clark, "Journal," 438; *Simcoe Correspondence*, 5:110; Knopf, "Two Journals," 271.

8. Bowyer, "Daily Journal," 353; Knopf, "Two Journals," 271, 272; *Randolph Journal*, 25; Clark, "Journal," 438; *Centinel of the North-Western Territory*, Oct. 4, 1794.

9. Knopf, *Anthony Wayne*, 355–58; Heitman, *Historical Register*, 1:209; Henley to Wayne, Sept. 17, 1794, Wayne MSS, HSP.

10. Knopf, *Anthony Wayne*, 358; Burton, "Wayne's Orderly Book," 555; Smith, *With Captain Edward Miller*, 12; *Randolph Journal*, 25.

11. Wayne to Todd, Sept. 21, 1794, Wayne MSS, HSP; Cooke, "Journal," 341; Clark, "Journal," 438–39.

12. Cooke, "Journal," 14–15; Clark, "Journal," 438; Burton, "Wayne's Orderly Book," 556, 557; Underwood, *Journal*, 19; Bowyer, "Daily Journal," 355; Cist, *Sketches*, 121. For an excellent account of the construction of Fort Wayne, compiled from the available sources, see Walter Font, "A Garrison at Miami Town," *Old Fort News* 56 (1993): 3–7.

13. Knopf, "Two Journals," 274–75; Cist, *Sketches*, 121; Clark, "Journal," 442; Bowyer, "Daily Journal," 356–57; Burton, "Wayne's Orderly Book," 560.

14. Caldwell et al. to Barbee, Sept. 22, 1794; and Barbee to Scott, Sept. 22, 1794, Wayne MSS, HSP; Burton, "Wayne's Orderly Book," 555.

15. Bowyer, "Daily Journal," 353–54; Cooke, "Journal," 342; Smith, *With Captain Edward Miller*, 13; Knopf, "Two Journals," 273; Clark, "Journal," 440; Van Cleve, "Memoirs," 53.

16. Smith, *With Captain Edward Miller*, 13–14; Bowyer, "Daily Journal," 354; Knopf, "Two Journals," 273, 275–76; Clark, "Journal," 440.

17. Knopf, "Two Journals," 273–74; Bowyer, "Daily Journal," 354, 355; Kentucky Orderly Book; Hart Journal.

18. Knopf, "Two Journals," 274; Kentucky Orderly Book; Hart Journal.

19. Knopf, "Two Journals," 273; Sept. 29, 1794, Kentucky Volunteers MSS; Clark, "Journal," 443; Cooke, "Journal," 343; Smith, *With Captain Edward Miller*, 19.

20. Sloane to Wayne, Oct. 6, 1794, Wayne MSS, HSP.

21. Burton, "Wayne's Orderly Book," 561.

22. Smith, *With Captain Edward Miller*, 21; Burton, "Wayne's Orderly Book," 562–63.

23. *Wilkinson Journal*, 320; Smith, *With Captain Edward Miller*, 14, 16, 18; Underwood, *Journal*, 19; Cooke, "Journal," 343; Clark, "Journal," 442; Glass Receipt, Oct. 13, 1794, Wayne MSS, HSP; Bowyer, "Daily Journal," 356; *Simcoe Correspondence*, 3:167; 5:117.

24. Knopf, "Two Journals," 276; Smith, *With Captain Edward Miller*, 16.

25. Clark, "Journal," 441; Cooke, "Journal," 342, 343; Smith, *With Captain Edward Miller*, 15, 16, 17, 18; Knopf, "Two Journals," 275; *Simcoe Correspondence*, 3:161.

26. Knopf, *Anthony Wayne*, 359–60, 363.

CHAPTER 28

1. Quaife, "Fort Knox Orderly Book," 151; *ASP, Indian Affairs,* 540.

2. *ASP, Indian Affairs,* 540; Cass to Wayne, Oct. 2, 1794, Wayne MSS, HSP; *Kentucky Gazette,* Oct. 18, 1794.

3. *Connecticut Courant,* Feb. 16, 1795; *Upper Canada Gazette,* Aug. 21, 1794; *ASP, Indian Affairs,* 540.

4. Bonney, *Legacy,* 1:109–10.

5. Heitman, *Historical Register,* 1:472; *Dunlap and Claypoole's American Daily Advertiser,* Oct. 14, 1794; *General Advertiser,* Oct. 22, 1794; *Centinel of the North-Western Territory,* Nov. 1, 1794; Smith, *With Captain Edward Miller,* 19. Heitman unaccountably has Grayson's date of death listed as December 1794.

6. *Centinel of the North-Western Territory,* Oct. 11, 1794; Cist, *Cincinnati Miscellany,* 2:173; 1065, Draper MSS; *Simcoe Correspondence,* 3:155; Shepard, "War Casualty," 53; Smith, *With Captain Edward Miller,* 15. Historians have been confused over the details of exactly where and in what direction Elliott was traveling when he was killed. The contemporary newspaper account is used as the basis for this description.

7. *Centinel of the North-Western Territory,* Oct. 11, 1794; *Washington Spy,* Nov. 4, 1794; Shepard, "War Casualty," 52, 54–57; Jarvis, *Biographical Notice of Commodore Jesse D. Elliott,* 12–13.

8. Wayne to O'Hara, Oct. 10, 1794; and Scott and Ernest Contract, Oct. 13, 1794, Wayne MSS, HSP; Knopf, *Anthony Wayne,* 359.

9. Clark, "Journal," 442; Bonney, *Legacy,* 1:111; Wayne to Scott, Oct. 13, 1794, Wayne MSS, HSP; Knopf, *Anthony Wayne,* 360; *Wilkinson Journal,* 322.

10. Wayne to O'Hara, Oct. 13, 1794, Wayne MSS, HSP; Oct. 13, 1794, Kentucky Volunteers MSS; Smith, *With Captain Edward Miller,* 15; Knopf, "Two Journals," 277.

11. Knopf, "Two Journals," 277–78; "Sketch of the Early Adventures of William Sudduth," 69.

12. Smith, *With Captain Edward Miller,* 15, 17, 18, 21; Cooke, "Journal," 343; Clark, "Journal," 443; Bowyer, "Daily Journal," 356, 357.

13. Bowyer, "Daily Journal," 354; Cooke, "Journal," 342; Clark, "Journal," 439; Smith, *With Captain Edward Miller,* 13, 14; Burton, "Wayne's Orderly Book," 556–57.

14. Cooke, "Journal," 343–44; Smith, *With Captain Edward Miller,* 19; Burton, "Wayne's Orderly Book," 560; Buell to Wayne, Oct. 26, 1794, Wayne MSS, HSP.

15. Smith, *With Captain Edward Miller*, 13; Knopf, "Two Journals," 272, 273, 274; Cooke, "Journal," 342; Clark, "Journal," 440; Bowyer, "Daily Journal," 355.

16. Burton, "Wayne's Orderly Book," 560; Smith, *With Captain Edward Miller*, 201; Cooke, "Journal," 344; Hamtramck to Wayne, Oct. 18, 1794, Wayne MSS, HSP.

17. Burton, "Wayne's Orderly Book," 560, 561; Clark, "Journal," 444; Smith, *With Captain Edward Miller*, 17; *Simcoe Correspondence*, 5:113, 114; Cooke, "Journal," 342.

18. Cooke, "Journal," 344; Smith, *With Captain Edward Miller*, 21–23.

19. Cooke, "Journal," 344; *Ancestry of John Hutchinson Buell*, 28–29; *Randolph Journal*, 29.

EPILOGUE

1. Wayne to Kibbey, Nov. 6, 1794, Wayne MSS, HSP; Compiled Service Records of Volunteer Soldiers; 4U145, Draper MSS; Brice, *Fort Wayne*, 172, 207–10.

2. Ferris, *Early Settlement*, 350–53.

3. *Connecticut Courant*, Apr. 13, 27, 4, 1795; *Maryland Gazette*, Mar. 12, 1795; Knopf, *Anthony Wayne*, 385.

4. Knopf, *Anthony Wayne*, 384; *Maryland Gazette*, Apr. 16, 1795; *Connecticut Courant*, Apr. 13, 1795; *Middlesex (Conn.) Gazette*, July 10, 1795.

5. *Middlesex (Conn.) Gazette*, Aug. 21, 1795.

6. *Maryland Gazette*, Apr. 16, 1795; Drake to Wayne, Nov. 2, 1794; and Underhill to Wayne, Nov. 27, 1794, Wayne MSS, HSP; *Kentucky Gazette*, Feb. 28, 1795; *American Herald of Liberty*, June 11, 1795.

7. Carter, *Territorial Papers*, 2:525–34.

8. *The Eagle*, Oct. 26, 1795.

9. Esarey, "Indian Captives in Early Indiana," 109–12.

10. "Narrative of John Brickell's Captivity," 54.

11. Nelson, *Anthony Wayne*, 272, 287–88, 296; *American Mercury*, Jan. 9, 1797; "Letters Relating to the Death of Major-General Anthony Wayne," 114.

12. Stille, *Wayne and the Pennsylvania Line*, 350; Eberlein and Lippincott, *Colonial Homes*, 179–80; Bicknell, "Major General Anthony Wayne," 299; Samuel Smiley Pension File, M804.

13. "Letter of Alexander Fullerton to Baron de Rosenthal," 257; *Kentucky Gazette*, Dec. 12, 1795; *Washington Spy*, June 22, 1796; *The Eagle*, Jan. 4, 1796; Burnet, *Notes*, 33; 1062–63, Draper MSS.

BIBLIOGRAPHY

Manuscripts

Alder, Jonathan. "Story of the Indian Captivity of Jonathan Alder." Typescript. Allen County Public Library, Fort Wayne, Indiana.

Cogswell, M. F. Papers. Beinecke Rare Book and Manuscript Library. Yale University, New Haven, Connecticut.

Compiled Service Records of Volunteer Soldiers Who Served from 1784 to 1811. Publication M905. U.S. National Archives, Washington, D.C.

Covington, Leonard. Papers. Burton Historical Collection. Detroit Public Library, Detroit, Michigan.

Draper, Lyman C. Papers. The State Historical Society of Wisconsin, Madison.

Harrow, Alexander. Diary. Burton Historical Collection. Detroit, Michigan.

Heads of Families at the First Census of the United States, Taken in the Year 1790. U.S. Bureau of the Census, Washington, D.C.

Historical Information Relating to Military Posts and Other Installations. Publication M661. U.S. National Archives, Washington, D.C.

Kingsbury, Jacob. Papers. Library of Congress, Washington, D.C.

Knox, Henry. Papers. The Morgan Library, New York City.

McDonough, Micah. Papers. The William L. Clements Library. University of Michigan, Ann Arbor.

Miscellaneous Numbered Records (The Manuscript File), War Department Collection of Revolutionary War Records, 1775–90s. Publication M859. U.S. National Archives, Washington, D.C.

Papers Relating to the Kentucky Volunteers. The Presbyterian Historical Society. Typescript. Allen County Public Library, Fort Wayne, Indiana.

Post–Revolutionary War Manuscripts. Publication M904. U.S. National Archives, Washington, D.C.

Revolutionary War Pension and Bounty-Land-Warrant Application Files. Publication M804. U.S. National Archives, Washington, D.C.

Sargent, Winthrop. Papers. The Massachusetts Historical Society, Boston.

Special Index to Numbered Records in the War Department Collection of Revolutionary War Records, 1775–83. Publication M847. U.S. National Archives, Washington, D.C.

Torrence Papers. Cincinnati Historical Museum, Cincinnati, Ohio.

Wayne, Anthony. Papers. The Historical Society of Pennsylvania, Philadelphia.

———. The William L. Clements Library. University of Michigan, Ann Arbor.

Wilkinson, James. Papers. Library of Congress, Washington, D.C.

Williams, Otho Holland. Papers. The Maryland Historical Society Library, Baltimore.

Newspapers

American Herald of Liberty

American Mercury

Army and Navy Chronicle

Augusta (Ga.) Chronicle and Gazette of the State

Baltimore Daily Intelligencer

Baltimore Daily Repository

Brunswick (N.J.) Gazette

Carlisle(Pa.) Gazette and the Western Repository of Knowledge

Catskill (N.Y.) Packet

Centinel of the North-Western Territory

Columbian Centinel

Columbian Gazette

Columbian Mirror

Connecticut Courant

Dunlap and Claypoole's American Daily Advertiser

Dunlap's American Daily Advertiser

The Eagle; or, Dartmouth (N.H.) Centinel

Farmers Library; or, Vermont Political and Historical Register

Federal Spy and Springfield (Mass.) Advertiser

Gazette of the United States

Gazette of the United States and Daily Evening Advertiser

General Advertiser

Greenfield (Vt.) Gazette

Herald of Vermont

Herald of Vermont, or Rutland Advertiser

Impartial Intelligencer

The Kentucky Gazette

Kline's Carlisle (Pa.) Weekly Gazette

Knoxville (Tenn.) Gazette

Maryland Gazette

Maryland Herald and Eastern Shore Intelligencer

Maryland Journal and Baltimore Advertiser

Middlesex (Conn.) Gazette

New Jersey Journal

Oracle of Dauphin and Harrisburg (Pa.) Advertiser

Pennsylvania Gazette

The Phenix; or, Windham Herald

Pittsburgh Gazette

Providence Gazette and Country Herald

Rutland (Vt.) Courier

Stewart's Kentucky Herald

Upper Canada Gazette

Vermont Gazette

Virginia Gazette and General Advertiser

Virginia Gazette and Richmond and Manchester Advertiser

Virginia Gazette and Richmond Chronicle

Virginia Herald and Fredericksburg Advertiser

The Washington Spy

Western Christian Advocate

Western Star

BOOKS

Abbott, John S. C. *The History of the State of Ohio*. Detroit: Northwestern, 1875.

Adams, James T. *Dictionary of American History*. 5 vols. New York: Charles Scribner's Sons, 1940.

Aler, F. Vernon. *Aler's History of Martinsburg and Berkeley County, West Virginia*. Hagerstown, Md.: Mail, 1888.

Ancestry of John Hutchinson Buell. New York: n. p., n. d.

Ankenbruck, John. *Five Forts*. Fort Wayne: Lion's Head, 1972.

Annual Report of the American Historical Association for the Year 1896. Washington, D.C.: Government Printing Office, 1897.

Atlas of Mercer County, Ohio. Philadelphia: Griffin, Gordon, 1888.

Barce, Elmore. *The Land of the Miamis*. Fowler, Ind.: Benton Review Shop, 1922.

Barker, Joseph. *Recollections of the First Settlement of Ohio*. Marietta, Ohio: Marietta College, 1958.

Battlefields of the Maumee Valley. Washington, D.C.: Sons of the American Revolution, 1896.

Bennett, John. *Blue Jacket, War Chief of the Shawnees and His Part in Ohio's History*. Chillicothe, Ohio: Ross County Historical Society, 1943.

Billias, George F., ed. *George Washington's Generals*. New York: W. Morrow, 1964.

A Biographical Congressional Dictionary, 1774 to 1903. Washington, D.C.: Government Printing Office, 1903.

Biographical Cyclopaedia of the Commonwealth of Kentucky. Chicago: J. M. Gresham, 1896.

The Biographical Encyclopaedia of Kentucky. Cincinnati: J. M. Armstrong, 1878.

Biographical Sketch of General John Adair. Washington, D.C.: Gales and Seaton, 1830.

Blakeney, John O. *The Blakeneys in America*. Little Rock: n. p., 1928.

Bliss, Eugene F. *Diary of David Zeisberger*. 2 vols. Cincinnati: Robert Clarke, 1885.

Bonney, Catharine V. R. *A Legacy of Historical Gleanings*. 2 vols. Albany, N.Y.: J. Munsell, 1875.

Brackenridge, H. M. *History of the Insurrection in Western Pennsylvania, Commonly Called the Whiskey Insurrection*. Pittsburgh: W. S. Haven, 1859.

Brackenridge, H. M. *Recollections of Persons and Places in the West*. Philadelphia: J. Kay Jr. and Brother, 1834.

Brice, Wallace A. *History of Fort Wayne*. Fort Wayne: D. W. Jones and Son, 1868.

Buell, Rowena. *The Memoirs of Rufus Putnam*. Boston: Houghton, Mifflin, 1903.

Burnet, Jacob. *Notes on the Early Settlement of the Northwestern Territory*. New York: Appleton, 1847.

Butterfield, Consul W. *History of the Girtys*. Cincinnati: Clarke, 1890.

Calendar of Virginia State Papers and Other Manuscripts. 11 vols. Richmond: State of Virginia, 1875–93.

Carpenter, W. H., and T. S. Arthur, eds. *History of Ohio, from Its Earliest Settlement to the Present Time*. Philadelphia: J. B. Lippincott, 1865.

Carter, Clarence E., ed. *The Territorial Papers of the United States*. 26 vols. Washington, D.C.: Government Printing Office, 1934–76.

Celebration of the Forty-fifth Anniversary of the First Settlement of Cincinnati. Cincinnati: n. p., 1834.

Chalkley, Lyman. *Chronicles of the Scotch-Irish Settlement in Virginia*. 3 vols. Baltimore: Genealogical Publishing, 1965.

Cist, Charles. *The Cincinnati Miscellany or Antiquities of the West*. 2 vols. Cincinnati: Robinson and Jones, 1845–46.

————. *Sketches and Statistics of Cincinnati in 1859*. Cincinnati, n. p., 1859.

Clark, Murtie J. *American Militia in the Frontier Wars, 1790–1796*. Baltimore: Genealogical Publishing, 1990.

Coffinberry, Andrew. *The Forest Rangers*. Columbus, Ohio: n. p., 1842.

Coffman, Edward M. *The Old Army*. New York: Oxford University Press, 1986.

Collins, Richard H. *History of Kentucky*. Covington, Ky.: Collins, 1882.

Commager, Henry Steele, ed. *Documents of American History*. New York, Appleton-Century-Crofts, 1958.

Craig, Neville B. *Sketch of the Life and Services of Isaac Craig*. Pittsburgh: J. S. Davison, 1854.

Cruikshank, E. A. *The Correspondence of Lieut. Governor John Graves Simcoe, with Allied Documents Relating to His Administration of the Government of Upper Canada*. 4 vols. Toronto: Ontario Historical Society, 1923–31.

Cullen, Charles T., ed. *The Papers of Thomas Jefferson*. 29 vols. Princeton: Princeton University Press, 1990.

Dandridge, Danske. *Historic Shepherdstown*. Charlottesville, Va.: Michie, 1910.

Darlington, Mary C., ed. *Fort Pitt and Letters from the Frontier*. Pittsburgh: J. R. Weldin, 1892.

Dawson, Moses. *A Historical Narrative of the Civil and Military Services of Major-General William H. Harrison*. Cincinnati: M. Dawson, 1824.

Denny, Ebenezer. *The Military Journal of Major Ebenezer Denny*. Philadelphia: n. p., 1859.

Des Cognets, Anna R. *William Russell and His Descendants*. Princeton: n. p., 1960.

Dillon, John B. *A History of Indiana*. Indianapolis: Bingham and Doughty, 1859.

Dodge, Jacob R. R*ed Men of the Ohio Valley*. Springfield, Ohio: n. p., 1860.

Dorman, John F. *The Prestons of Smithfield and Greenfield in Virginia*. Louisville: Filson Club, 1982.

Downes, Randolph C. *Council Fires on the Upper Ohio: A Narrative of Indian Affairs in the Upper Ohio Valley until 1795*. Pittsburgh: University of Pittsburgh Press, 1940.

————. *Frontier Ohio, 1783–1803*. Columbus: Ohio State Archaeological and Historical Society, 1935.

Drake, Benjamin. *Life of Tecumseh and His Brother, The Prophet*. Cincinnati: E. Morgan, 1841.

Drake, Samuel G. *The Aboriginal Races of North America*. New York: Hurst, 1880.

————. *Biography and History of the Indians of North America*. Boston: Benjamin P. Mussey, 1857.

————. *The Book of the Indians of North America*. Boston: Josiah Drake, 1833.

Early History of Western Pennsylvania. Laughlintown, Penn.: Southwest Pennsylvania Genealogical Services, 1989.

Eberlein, Harold D., and Horace M. Lippincott. *The Colonial Homes of Philadelphia and Its Neighbourhood*. Philadelphia: J. B. Lippincott, 1912.

Eggleston, Edward. *Tecumseh and the Shawnee Prophet*. New York: Dodd, Mead, 1878.

Elliot, James. *Sketches, Political, Geographical, &c.* Greenfield, Mass.: Thomas Dickman, 1798.

English, William H. *Conquest of the Country Northwest of the River Ohio, 1778–1783*. 2 vols. Indianapolis: Bowen-Merrill, 1897.

Evans, Nelson W., and Emmons B. Stivers. *A History of Adams County, Ohio*. 2 vols. West Union, Ohio: E. B. Stivers, 1900.

Ferris, Ezra. *The Early Settlement of the Miami Country*. Indianapolis: Bowen-Merrill, 1897.

Finley, Isaac J., and Rufus Putnam. *Pioneer Record and Reminiscences of the Early Settlers and Settlements of Ross County, Ohio*. Cincinnati: R. Clarke, 1871.

Finley, James B. *Autobiography of Reverend James B. Finley*. Cincinnati: Cranston and Curts, 1853.

Fitzpatrick, John C., ed. *The Writings of George Washington*. 39 vols. Washington, D.C.: Government Printing Office, 1931–44.

Flexner, James. *George Washington in the American Revolution, 1775–1783*. Boston: Little, Brown, 1968.

Font, Walter, ed. *A Garrison at Miami Town*. Fort Wayne: Allen County–Fort Wayne Historical Society, 1994.

Genealogical and Family History of the State of Connecticut. 4 vols. New York: Lewis Historical Publishing, 1911.

Genealogies of Kentucky Families. Baltimore: Genealogical Publishing, 1981.

Goebel, Dorothy B. *William Henry Harrison: A Political Biography*. Indianapolis: Historical Bureau of the Indiana State Library, 1926.

Griswold, Bert J. *The Pictorial History of Fort Wayne, Indiana*. Chicago: Robert O. Law, 1917.

Hall, James. *The Romance of Western History*. Cincinnati: Applegate, 1857.

Harrison, Lowell H., ed. *Kentucky's Governors*. Lexington: University Press of Kentucky, 1985.

Harrison, William Henry. *A Discourse on the Aborigines of the Ohio Valley*. Chicago: Fergus, 1883.

Harvey, Henry. *History of the Shawnee Indians from the Year 1681 to 1854, Inclusive*. Cincinnati: E. Morgan and Sons, 1855.

Hay, Thomas R. *The Admirable Trumpeter: A Biography of General James Wilkinson*. Garden City, N.Y.: Doubleday, Doran, 1941.

Heitman, Francis B. *Historical Register and Dictionary of the United States Army*. 2 vols. Washington, D.C.: Government Printing Office, 1903.

Henderson, Archibald. *Isaac Shelby, Revolutionary Patriot and Border Hero*. Raleigh, N.C.: North Carolina Society, 1918.

Hildreth, Samuel P. *Biographical and Historical Memoirs of the Early Pioneer Settlers of Ohio*. Cincinnati: H. W. Derby, 1852.

———. *Contributions to the Early History of the North-West*. Cincinnati: Hitchcock and Walden, 1864.

———. *Pioneer History: Being an Account of the First Examinations of the Ohio Valley, and the Early Settlement of the Northwest Territory*. Cincinnati: H. W. Derby, 1848.

Hill, George W. *History of Ashland County, Ohio*. Cleveland: Williams, 1880.

Hill, Leonard U. *John Johnston and the Indians*. Piqua, Ohio: Stoneman, 1957.

Hill, N. N. *History of Coshocton County, Ohio*. Newark, Ohio: A. A. Graham, 1881.

Historical Records of the Town of Cornwall, Litchfield County, Connecticut. Hartford, Conn.: Lockwood and Brainard, 1877.

A History and Biographical Cyclopaedia of Butler County, Ohio. 2 vols. Cincinnati: Western Biographical Publishing, 1882.

History of Beaver County, Pennsylvania. Philadelphia: A. Warner, 1888.

History of Clermont County, Ohio. Philadelphia:, L. H. Everts, 1880.

History of Ross and Highland Counties, Ohio. Cleveland: Williams Brothers, 1880.

History of Sandusky County, Ohio. Cleveland: H. Z. Williams and Brother, 1882.

History of Shelby County, Ohio. Philadelphia: Sutton, 1883.

History of Warren County, Ohio. Chicago: W. H. Beers, 1882.

Hosmer, H. L. *Early History of the Maumee Valley*. Toledo: Hosmer and Harris, 1858.

Howe, Henry. *Historical Collections of Ohio*. 2 vols. Cincinnati: C. H. Krehbiel, 1889.

———. *Historical Collections of the Great West*. 2 vols. Cincinnati: H. Howe, 1851.

Howe, Herbert B. *Major Beazaleel Howe, 1750–1825*. N. p., n. p., 1950.

Hulbert, Archer B. *Military Roads of the Mississippi Basin*. Cleveland: Arthur H. Clarke, 1904.

Hurt, R. Douglas. *The Ohio Frontier*. Bloomington: Indiana University Press, 1996.

Jacobs, James R. *The Beginnings of the U.S. Army, 1783–1812*. Princeton: Princeton University Press, 1947.

———. *Tarnished Warrior: Major General James Wilkinson*. New York: Macmillan, 1938.

Jarvis, Russell. *A Biographical Notice of Commodore Jesse D. Elliott*. Philadelphia: n. p., 1835.

Johnston, William P. *The Johnstons of Salisbury*. New Orleans: L. Graham and Son, 1897.

Jones, A. E. *Reminiscences of the Early Days of the Little Miami Valley*. Cincinnati: Times Book and Job Printing, 1878.

Jones, Charles C. *The History of Georgia*. Boston: Houghton, Mifflin, 1883.

Jones, Robert R. *Fort Washington at Cincinnati, Ohio*. Cincinnati: Cincinnati Society of Colonial Wars, 1902.

Judson, Harry P. *Caesar's Army: A Study of the Military Art of the Romans in the Last Days of the Republic*. Boston: Ginn, 1888.

Kenton, Edna. *Simon Kenton: His Life and Period*. New York: Doubleday, Doran, 1930.

Kingsbury, Frederick J. *The Genealogy of the Descendants of Henry Kingsbury of Ipswich and Haverhill, Massachusetts*. Hartford, Conn.: Case, Lockwood, and Brainard, 1905.

Klinck, Carl F., and James J. Talman, eds. *The Journal of Major John Norton, 1816*. Toronto: Champlain Society, 1970.

Knapp, H. S. *History of the Maumee Valley*. Toledo: Blade, 1872.

Knopf, Richard C., ed. *Anthony Wayne: A Name in Arms*. Pittsburgh: University of Pittsburgh Press, 1960.

———. *A Precise Journal of General Wayne's Last Campaign*. Worcester, Mass.: American Antiquarian Society, 1955.

———. *A Surgeon's Mate at Fort Defiance*. Columbus: Ohio Historical Society, 1957.

Kohn, Richard H. *Eagle and Sword: The Federalists and the Creation of the Military Establishment in America, 1783–1802*. New York: Free Press, 1975.

Kreidbert, Marvin A., and Merton G. Henry. *History of Military Mobilization in the United States Army, 1775–1945*. Washington, D.C.: Government Printing Office, 1955.

Lambing, A. A. *Historical Researches in Western Pennsylvania, Principally Catholic*. Pittsburgh: Historical Society of Western Pennsylvania, 1884.

Lee, Henry. *Memoirs of the War in the Southern Department of the United States*. New York: University Publishing, 1869.

Lewis, Virgil A. *Third Biennial Report of the Department of Archives and History of the State of West Virginia*. Charleston, W.Va.: News-Mail, 1911.

The Life of the Late Gen. William Eaton. Brookfield, Mass.: E. Merriam, 1813.

Linn, John B. *Annals of Buffalo Valley, Pennsylvania, 1755–1855*. Harrisburg: L. S. Hart Printer, 1877.

Littell, John. *Family Records or Genealogies of the First Settlers of Passaic Valley (and Vicinity) above Chatham*. Feltville, N.J.: D. Felt, 1851.

Lossing, Benson J. *Pictorial Field-Book of the War of 1812*. New York: Harper and Brothers, 1869.

Mansfield, Edward D. *Memoirs of the Life and Services of Daniel Drake, M.D.* Cincinnati: Applegate, 1855.

McBride, James. *Pioneer Biography, Sketches of the Lives of Some of the Early Settler of Butler County, Ohio*. 2 vols. Cincinnati: R. Clarke, 1871.

McClung, John A. *Sketches of Western Adventure*. Louisville: R. H. Collins, 1879.

McDonald, John. *Biographical Sketches of General Nathaniel Massie, General Duncan McArthur, Captain William Wells, and General Simon Kenton*. Dayton: D. Osborn, 1852.

McHenry, Robert. *Webster's American Military Biographies*. Springfield, Mass.: G. and C. Merriam, 1979.

Mead, Spencer P. *History and Genealogy of the Mead Family*. New York: Knickerbocker, 1901.

Metcalfe, Samuel L. *A Collection of Some of the Most Interesting Narratives of Indian Warfare in the West*. Lexington, Ky.: William G. Hunt, 1821.

Miller, Francis W. *Cincinnati's Beginnings*. Cincinnati: P. G. Thomson, 1880.

Moore, Horatio N. *Life and Services of General Anthony Wayne*. Philadelphia: John B. Perry, 1845.

Nelson, Paul D. *Anthony Wayne*. Bloomington: Indiana University Press, 1985.

Palmer, Dave R. *1794: America, Its Army, and the Birth of the Nation*. Novato, Calif.: Presidio, 1994.

Pennsylvania Archives. 2d ser. 19 vols. Harrisburg: Lane S. Hart, 1874–88.

Perkins, James H. *Annals of the West*. Cincinnati: James R. Albach, 1846.

Perry, Robert E. *Treaty City: A Story of Old Fort Greene Ville*. Bradford, Ohio: R. E. Perry, 1945.

Peyton, J. Lewis. *History of Augusta County, Virginia*. Harrisonburg, Va.: C. J. Carrier, 1972.

Phillips, Thomas R. *Roots of Strategy*. Harrisburg, Penn.: Stackpole, 1985.

Posey, John T. *General Thomas Posey, Son of the Revolution*. East Lansing: Michigan State University Press, 1992.

Preston, John H. *A Gentleman Rebel: The Exploits of Anthony Wayne*. New York: Farrar and Rinehart, 1930.

Prucha, Francis P. *The Sword of the Republic: The United States Army on the Frontier, 1783–1846*. New York: Macmillan, 1969.

Ramage, James A. *John Wesley Hunt*. Lexington: University Press of Kentucky, 1974.

Raymond, Ethel T. *Tecumseh: A Chronicle of the Last Great Leader of His People*. Toronto: Glasgow, Brook, 1920.

Read, D. B. *The Life and Times of General John Graves Simcoe*. Toronto: Virtue, 1901.

The Record of the Court at Upland, in Pennsylvania. Philadelphia: Lippincott, 1860.

Records of Officers and Men of New Jersey in Wars, 1791–1815. Trenton, N.J.: State Gazette Publishing, 1909.

Report of the Commission to Locate the Site of the Frontier Forts of Pennsylvania. 2 vols. Harrisburg, Penn.: W. S. Ray, 1916.

Reynolds, John. *The Pioneer History of Illinois*. Belleville, Ill.: N. A. Randall, 1852.

Robertson, J. Ross, ed. *Diary of Mrs. John Graves Simcoe*. Toronto: William Briggs, 1911.

Robertson, Robert S. *Valley of the Upper Maumee River*. Madison, Wis.: Brant and Fuller, 1889.

Rohr, Martha. *Historical Sketch of Fort Recovery*. Fort Recovery, Ohio: Journal Publishing, 1965.

Roosevelt, Theodore. *The Winning of the West*. 4 vols. Lincoln: University of Nebraska Press, 1995.

Russell, Nelson V. *The British Regime in Michigan and the Old Northwest, 1760–1796*. Northfield, Minn.: Carleton College, 1939.

Sabine, Lorenzo. *Notes on Duels and Duelling*. Boston: Crosby, Nichols, 1885.

St. Clair, Arthur. *A Narrative of the Manner in which the Campaign against the Indians, in the Year One Thousand Seven Hundred and Ninety-one, Was Conducted, under the Command of Major General St. Clair*. Philadelphia: Jame Aitken, 1812.

St. Clair's Defeat. Fort Wayne: Public Library of Fort Wayne and Allen County, 1954.

Scamyhorn, Richard, and John Steinle. *Stockades in the Wilderness*. Dayton: Landfall, 1986.

The 1787 Census of Virginia. Springfield, Va.: Genealogical Books in Print, 1987.

Shaw, John Robert. *A Narrative of the Life & Travels of John Robert Shaw, the Well Digger*. Lexington, Ky.: Daniel Bradford, 1807.

Short Sketch of the Life of Mr. Lent Munson. Litchfield, Conn.: Thomas Collier, 1797.

Sketches and Recollections of Lynchburg. Richmond: C. H. Wynne, 1858.

Slocum, Charles E. *History of the Maumee River Basin*. Indianapolis: Bowen and Slocum, 1905.

————. *The Ohio Country between the Years 1783 and 1815*. New York: G. P. Putnam's Sons, 1910.

Smith, Dwight L., ed. *From Greene Ville to Fallen Timbers*. Indianapolis: Indiana Historical Society, 1952.

————. *With Captain Edward Miller in the Wayne Campaign in 1794*. Ann Arbor, Mich.: William L. Clements Library, 1965.

Smith, W. L. G. *The Life and Times of Lewis Cass*. New York: Derby and Jackson, 1856.

Smith, William H., ed. *The St. Clair Papers: The Life and Public Service of Arthur St. Clair*. Cincinnati: Robert Clarke, 1882.

Spears, John R. *Anthony Wayne, Sometimes Called "Mad Anthony."* New York: D. Appleton, 1903.

Spencer, Oliver M. *Indian Captivity*. Ann Arbor, Mich.: University Microfilms, 1966.

Steuben, Baron de. *Regulations for the Order and Discipline of the Troops of the United States*. Boston: I. Thomas and E. T. Andrews, 1794.

Stille, Charles J. *Major-General Anthony Wayne and the Pennsylvania Line in the Continental Army*. Philadelphia: J. B. Lippincott, 1893.

Stone, William L. *Life of Joseph Brant—Thayendanegea*. 2 vols. Buffalo: Phinney, 1851.

Sword, Wiley. *President Washington's Indian War*. Norman: University of Oklahoma Press, 1985.

Symmes, John C. *The Correspondence of John Cleves Symmes*. New York: Macmillan, 1926.

Teetor, Henry B. *The Past and Present of Mill Creek Valley*. Cincinnati: Cohen, 1882.

Thornbrough, Gayle. *Outpost on the Wabash, 1787–1791*. Indianapolis: Indiana Historical Society, 1957.

Todd, Charles S., and Benjamin Drake. *Sketches of the Civil and Military Services of William Henry Harrison*. Cincinnati: U. P. James, 1840.

Tousey, Thomas G. *Military History of Carlisle and Carlisle Barracks*. Richmond: Dietz, 1939.

Tucker, Glenn. *Mad Anthony Wayne and the New Nation*. Harrisburg, Penn.: Stackpole, 1973.

Underwood, Thomas T. *Journal, Thomas Taylor Underwood, an Old Soldier in Wayne's Army*. Cincinnati: Society of Colonial Wars in the State of Ohio, 1945.

U.S. Congress. *American State Papers: Documents, Legislative and Executive, of the Congress of the United States*. 38 vols. Washington, D.C.: Gales and Seaton, 1832–61.

Volney, C. F. *A View of the Soil and Climate of the United States of America*. New York: Hafner, 1968.

Waddell, Joseph A. *Annals of Augusta County, Virginia, from 1726 to 1871*. Bridgewater, Va., C. J. Carrier, 1958.

Waggoner, Clark. *Relations and Experiences of Whites and Indians on the American Continent*. Antwerp, Ohio: C. Waggoner, 1893.

Wailes, B. L. C. *Memoir of Leonard Covington*. Natchez, Miss.: Natchez Printing and Stationery, 1928.

Ward, Harry M. *Charles Scott and the "Spirit of '76."* Charlottesville: University Press of Virginia, 1988.

———. *The Department of War, 1781–1795*. Pittsburgh: University of Pittsburgh Press, 1962.

Webster's American Military Biographies. Springfield, Mass.: G. and C. Merriam, 1978.

Weiss, Harry B., and Grace M. Ziegler. *Colonel Erkuries Beatty, 1759–1823*. Trenton, N.J.: Past Times, 1958.

Whittelsey, Charles B. *The Ancestry and the Descendants of John Pratt of Hartford, Connecticut*. Hartford: Case, Lockwood, and Brainard, 1900.

Wildes, Harry E. *Anthony Wayne: Troubleshooter of the American Revolution*. New York: Harcourt, Brace, 1941.

Wilkinson, James. *Memoirs of My Own Times*. 3 vols. Philadelphia: Abraham Small, 1816.

Williams, T. J. C. *History of Frederick County, Maryland*. 2 vols. Frederick, Md.: L. R. Titsworth, 1910.

———. *A History of Washington County, Maryland*. 2 vols. Baltimore: Regional Publishing, 1968.

Wilson, Frazer. *Fort Jefferson*. Lancaster, Penn.: n. p., 1950.

———. *History of Darke County, Ohio*. 2 vols. Milford, Ohio: Hobart, 1914.

———. *The Peace of Mad Anthony*. Greenville, Ohio: C. R. Kemble, 1909.

———, ed. *Journal of Captain Daniel Bradley*. Greenville, Ohio: Frazer Wilson, 1935.

Winger, Otho. *Little Turtle the Great Chief of Eel River*. North Manchester, Ind.: News Journal, 1942.

———. *The Potawatomi Indians*. Elgin, Ill.: Elgin Press, 1939.

Woehrmann, Paul. *At the Headwaters of the Maumee*. Indianapolis: Indiana Historical Society, 1971.

Woollen, William W. *Biographical and Historical Sketches of Early Indiana*. Indianapolis: Hammond, 1883.

Wright, Richard J., ed. *The John Hunt Memoirs*. Maumee, Ohio: Maumee Valley Historical Society, 1978.

Young, Calvin M. *Little Turtle: The Great Chief of the Miami Indian Nation*. Greenville, Ohio: Calvin M. Young, 1917.

ARTICLES

"Adair's Expedition." *Western Review and Miscellaneous Magazine* 3 (1820): 61–62.

Atwood, M. Jennie. "Major Shaylor." *American Monthly Magazine* 8 (March 1896): 402–15.

Backus, Emma S. "Cornelius Sedam and His Friends in Washington's Time." *Ohio Archaeological and Historical Quarterly* 41 (January 1932): 28–50.

Bald, F. Clever. "Colonel John Francis Hamtramck." *Indiana Magazine of History* 44 (December 1948): 335–54.

———. "Fort Miamis, Outpost of Empire." *Northwest Ohio Quarterly* 16 (April 1944): 75–116.

Barr, Lockwood, ed. "Letters from Dr. Joseph Strong to Captain John Pratt." *Ohio State Archaeological and Historical Quarterly* 51 (1942): 236–42.

Beatty, Joseph M. "Letters of the Four Beatty Brothers of the Continental Army, 1774–1794." *The Pennsylvania Magazine of History and Biography* 44 (1920): 193–263.

Bicknell, Thomas W. "Major General Anthony Wayne." *Journal of the American Irish Historical Society* 10 (1911): 277–300.

"Biographical Field Notes of Dr. Lyman C. Draper." *Bulletin of the Historical Society of Northwestern Ohio* 5 (October 1933): 1–3.

"Biographical Memoirs of Major Gen. William Henry Harrison." *Niles Weekly Register* (supplement) (1816): 71–73.

Bowyer, John. "Daily Journal of Wayne's Campaign." *American Pioneer* 1 (September 1842): 315–22, 351–57.

Brettschneider, Carl A. "Some Personalities and Problems of Supply Affecting the Indian Campaign, 1792–1794." *Bulletin of the Historical and Philosophical Society of Ohio* 10 (January 1952): 299–318.

Brooke, John. "Anthony Wayne: His Campaign against the Indians of the Northwest." *The Pennsylvania Magazine of History and Biography* 19 (1895): 387–96.

Burton, C. M. "Anthony Wayne and the Battle of Fallen Timbers." *Historical Collections, Michigan Pioneer and Historical Society* 31 (1901): 472–89.

———. "General Wayne's Orderly Book." *Collections and Researches Made by the Michigan Pioneer and Historical Society* 34 (1905): 341–733.

Caldwell, Norman F. "Fort Massac: The American Frontier Post, 1778–1805." *Journal of the Illinois State Historical Society* 43 (winter 1950): 265–81.

"Canadian Archives." *Collections and Researches Made by the Michigan Pioneer and Historical Society* 24 (1895): 629–99.

"Captain Thomas Doyle." *American Catholic Historical Researches*, n.s., 4 (October 1908): 334.

Case, Thomas R. "The Battle of Fallen Timbers." *Northwest Ohio Quarterly* 35 (spring 1963): 54–68.

"Casualties of the Battle of Fallen Timbers." *The Ohio Archaeological and Historical Quarterly* 41 (July 1932): 527–30.

"Catholic Officers in the Revolutionary Army." *American Catholic Historical Researches*, n.s., 4 (1908): 313–17.

Clark, William. "Journal of General Wayne's Campaign against the Shawnee Indians in Ohio, 1794–1795." *The Mississippi Valley Historical Review* 1 (December 1914): 418–44.

Coleman, J. Winston. "The Code Duello in Ante-Bellum Kentucky." *The Filson Club History Quarterly* 30 (April 1956): 125–40.

Conrad, Glenn R. "Edward D. Turner, Soldier, Jurist, Planter, Patriot." *Natchitoches Genealogist* 19 (October 1994): 1–8.

Cooke, John. "Captain John Cooke's Journal." *The American Historical Record* 2 (1873): 311–16, 339–45.

Cooley, Elizabeth M. "The Benham Brothers—Robert, Peter, and Richard." *Bulletin of the Historical and Philosophical Society of Ohio* 10 (January 1952): 69–78.

Cummins, Virginia R. "Background of a Gavel." *Daughters of the American Revolution Magazine* 97 (April 1963): 344–45.

Dickore, Marie. "Some Notable Pioneers." *Bulletin of the Historical and Philosophical Society of Ohio* 6 (July 1948): 101–2.

"Dr. Daniel Drake's Memoir of the Miami Country, 1779–1794." *The Quarterly Publication of the Historical and Philosophical Society of Ohio* 18 (September 1923): 39–117.

Edmunds, R. David. "Wea Participation in the Northwest Indian Wars, 1790–1795." *The Filson Club History Quarterly* 46 (July 1972): 241–53.

Esarey, Logan. "Indian Captives in Early Indiana." *Indiana Magazine of History* 9 (June 1913): 95–112.

"Extracts from a Manuscript Journal." *Report of the Pioneer and Historical Society of the State of Michigan* 8 (1886): 392–95.

Gardner, Asa B. "Henry Burbeck." *The Magazine of American History* 9 (April 1883): 251–56.

Gunderson, Robert G. "William Henry Harrison: Apprentice in Arms." *Northwest Ohio Quarterly* 65 (winter 1993): 3–29.

Hall, F. R. "Genet's Western Intrigue, 1793–1794." *Journal of the Illinois State Historical Society* 21 (July 1928): 359–81.

Hall, Virginius C. "Richard Allison, Surgeon to the Legion." *Bulletin of the Historical and Philosophical Society of Ohio* 9 (October 1951): 283–98.

"Harmer's Expedition." *Western Review and Miscellaneous Magazine* 2 (1820): 179–82.

Hay, Thomas R. "Some Reflections on the Career of General James Wilkinson." *The Mississippi Valley Historical Review* 21 (March 1935): 471–81.

"Historical Anecdotes Relating to the Early Settlement of Kentucky." *Western Review and Miscellaneous Magazine* 3 (1821): 15–17.

Hopkins, Gerard T. "Journal of a Visit to the Western Indians in 1804." 19 parts. *Friends' Intelligencer* 18, no. 44 (1861)–19, no. 12 (1862).

Horsman, Reginald. "The British Indian Department and the Resistance to General Anthony Wayne, 1793–1795." *The Mississippi Valley Historical Review* 49 (September 1962): 269–90.

Hutton, Paul A. "William Wells: Frontier Scout and Agent." *Indiana Magazine of History* 74 (September 1978): 183–222.

"Itinerary of the Pennsylvania Line From Pennsylvania to South Carolina, 1781–1782." *The Pennsylvania Magazine of History and Biography* 36 (1912): 273–92.

James, Peter D. "The British Indian Department in the Ohio Country, 1789–1795." *Northwest Ohio Quarterly* 64 (summer 1992): 78–95.

"John Heckewelder's Journey to the Wabash in 1792." *The Pennsylvania Magazine of History and Biography* 12 (1888): 34–54.

Johnson, Grace R. "George Will and George Will, Jr." *The Ohio Archaeological and Historical Society Publications* 40 (1931): 616–22.

Knopf, Richard C. "Anthony Wayne: The Man and the Myth." *Northwest Ohio Quarterly* 64 (spring 1992): 38–42.

Knopf, Richard C., ed. "Two Journals of the Kentucky Volunteers, 1793 and 1794." *The Filson Club History Quarterly* 27 (July 1953): 247–81.

Kohn, Richard H. "General Wilkinson's Vendetta with General Wayne: Politics and Command in the American Army, 1791–1796." *The Filson Club History Quarterly* 45 (October 1971): 361–72.

"Letter of Alexander Fullerton to Baron de Rosenthal." *The Pennsylvania Magazine of History and Biography* 22 (1898): 257–58.

"Letters of Gen. Wayne to Gen. Irvine, 1778–1784." *Historical Magazine* 6 (November 1862): 336–42.

"Letters of Generals Wayne, O'Hara, and Hodgdon." *The Pennsylvania Magazine of History and Biography* 14 (1890): 327–30.

"Letters Relating to the Death of Major-General Anthony Wayne." *The Pennsylvania Magazine of History and Biography* 15 (1891): 247–48.

Littell, S. "Memoir of Captain Eliakim Littell of Essex County, N. J." *Proceedings of the New Jersey Historical Society*, 2d ser., 7 (1882): 83–104.

Mahon, John K. "Anglo-American Methods of Indian Warfare, 1676–1794." *The Mississippi Valley Historical Review* 45 (September 1958): 254–75.

"Major Isaac Craig, Extracts from His Letter Books while Quartermaster at Fort Pitt, 1791–1804." Parts 1 and 2. *Historical Register: Notes and Queries Historical and Genealogical Relating to Interior Pennsylvania* 1 (1883): 289–304; 2 (1884): 27–37, 120–36, 161–78, 261–69.

McNutt, Randy. "Mad Anthony's Battle." *Ohio Magazine* 17 (August 1994): 39–44.

Miller, W. C. "History of Fort Hamilton." *Ohio Archaeological and Historical Society Publications* 13 (1904): 97–111.

Millett, Allan R. "Caesar and the Conquest of the Northwest Territory." *Timeline* 14 (May 1997): 2–21.

Murray, J. A. "The Butlers of the Cumberland Valley." *Historical Register: Notes and Queries, Biographical and Genealogical* 1 (January 1883): 1–17.

"A Narrative of John Brickell's Captivity among the Delaware Indians." *American Pioneer* 1 (1842): 43–56.

Nelson, Paul D. "Anthony Wayne: Soldier as Politician." *The Pennsylvania Magazine of History and Biography* 106 (October 1982): 463–81.

———. "General Charles Scott, the Kentucky Mounted Volunteers, and the Northwest Indian Wars, 1784–1794." *Journal of the Early Republic* 6 (fall 1986): 219–51.

———. "'Mad' Anthony Wayne and the Kentuckians of the 1790s." *Register of the Kentucky Historical Society* 84 (winter 1986): 1–17.

"Notes and Queries." *The Pennsylvania Magazine of History and Biography* 14 (1890): 329.

Odum, William O. "Destined for Defeat: An Analysis of the St. Clair Expedition of 1791." *Northwest Ohio Quarterly* 65 (spring 1993): 68–93.

"Orderly Book of the Second Pennsylvania Continental Line, Col. Henry Bicker." *The Pennsylvania Magazine of History and Biography* 36 (1912): 30–59.

"Original Letters from Gen. Wayne." *Historical Magazine* 5 (February 1861): 58.

Pratt, G. Michael. "Battle of Fallen Timbers: An Eyewitness Perspective." *Northwest Ohio Quarterly* 67 (winter 1995): 4–34.

Priddy, O. W. "Wayne's Strategic Advance from Fort Greenville to Grand Glaize." *Ohio Archaeological and Historical Society Publications* 39 (1930): 42–76.

Quaife, Milo, ed. "Fort Knox Orderly Book, 1793–1797." *Indiana Magazine of History* 32 (June 1936): 137–67.

———. "General James Wilkinson's Narrative of the Fallen Timbers Campaign." *The Mississippi Valley Historical Review* 16 (June 1929): 81–90.

———. "A Picture of the First United States Army: The Journal of Captain Samuel Newman." *Wisconsin Magazine of History* 2 (September 1918): 40–71.

Randall, E. O. "Fort St. Clair." *Ohio Archaeological and Historical Society Publications* 11 (July 1902): 161–63.

"Re-Interment of Major John Belli." *Old Northwest Genealogical Quarterly* 12 (October 1909): 176–84.

Roosevelt, Theodore. "Mad Anthony Wayne's Victory." *Harper's New Monthly Magazine* 92 (April 1896): 702–16.

"Roster of the Officers of the Legion of the United States Commanded by Major General Anthony Wayne." *The Pennsylvania Magazine of History and Biography* 16 (1892): 423–29.

Rusche, Timothy M. "Treachery within the United States Army." *Pennsylvania History* 65 (autumn 1998): 478–91.

Ruston, Jay C. "Anthony Wayne and the Indian Campaign, 1792–1794." *Indiana Military History Journal* 7 (May 1982): 21–25.

"St. Clair's Campaign. *Western Review and Miscellaneous Magazine* 3 (1820): 58–61.

Sanders, Robert S. "Colonel John Hardin and His Letters to His Wife—1792." *The Filson Club History Quarterly* 39 (January 1965): 5–12.

Sargent, Winthrop. "Winthrop Sargent's Diary while with General Arthur St. Clair's Expedition against the Indians." *Ohio Archaeological and Historical Quarterly* 33 (1924): 257–73.

"1794: The Mackinac Indians Oppose Wayne." *Collections of the State Historical Society of Wisconsin* 18 (1908): 442–44.

Shepard, Lee. "A War Casualty of Long Ago." *Bulletin of the Historical and Philosophical Society of Ohio* 10 (January 1952): 48–60.

Shepherd, William R. "Wilkinson and the Beginnings of the Spanish Conspiracy." *American Historical Review* 9 (April 1904): 490–506.

Simmons, David A. "The Military and Administrative Abilities of James Wilkinson in the Old Northwest, 1792–1793." *The Old Northwest* 3 (September 1977): 233–50.

———. "An Orderly Book from Fort Washington and Fort Hamilton, 1792–1793." *Cincinnati Historical Society Bulletin* 36 (summer 1978): 125–44.

———. "U.S. Military Architecture during the Indian Wars and Historic Archaeology: The Case of Fort Hamilton" *Northwest Ohio Quarterly* 64 (autumn 1992): 115–25.

"A Sketch of the Early Adventures of William Sudduth in Kentucky." *The History Quarterly* 2 (January 1928): 43–76.

Smith, Dwight L., ed. "William Wells and the Indian Council of 1793." *Indiana Magazine of History* 56 (September 1960): 217–26.

Tanner, Helen H. "The Glaize in 1792." *Ethnohistory* 25 (winter 1978): 15–39.

Turner, Frederick J. "The Origin of Genet's Projected Attack on Louisiana and the Floridas." *American Historical Review* 3 (July 1898): 650–71.

Van Cleve, Benjamin. "Memoirs of Benjamin Van Cleve." *Quarterly Publication of the Historical and Philosophical Society of Ohio* 16 (Jan.–March 1921): 7–71.

Wayne, Isaac. "Biographical Memoir of Major General Anthony Wayne." *The Casket: Flowers of Literature, Wit, & Sentiment* 4 (1820): 193–203.

"Wayne's Campaign." *Western Review and Miscellaneous Magazine* 2 (1820): 229–31.

Wells, William. "Indian History." *Western Review and Miscellaneous Magazine* 2 (May 1820): 201–4.

INDEX